NEW ENCYCLOPEDIA OF
GARDENING
TECHNIQUES

Royal
Horticultural
Society

NEW ENCYCLOPEDIA OF
GARDENING
TECHNIQUES

SIMON AKEROYD • PAUL ALEXANDER • JIM ARBURY
GUY BARTER • HELEN BOSTOCK • LENKA COOKE • MARTYN COX • COLIN CROSBIE
ANDREW HALSTEAD • BEATRICE HENRICOT • LEIGH HUNT • DAVID JEWELL
NICK MORGAN • DEAN PECKETT • ROSEMARY WARD

MITCHELL BEAZLEY

First published in Great Britain in 2008 by Mitchell Beazley,
a division of Octopus Publishing Group Limited,
2–4 Heron Quays, London, E14 4JP
www.octopusbooks.co.uk

in association with the Royal Horticultural Society.

ROYAL HORTICULTURAL SOCIETY
PUBLISHER Susannah Charlton
COMMISSIONING EDITOR Rae Spencer-Jones

AUTHORS AND CONTRIBUTORS
CHAPTER 1 Paul Alexander, Guy Barter, Andrew Halstead,
Beatrice Henricot, Leigh Hunt, and Rosemary Ward
CHAPTER 2 Helen Bostock
CHAPTER 3 Simon Akeroyd, Lenka Cooke, Martyn Cox,
Dean Peckett with consultants Colin Crosbie and David Jewell
CHAPTER 4 Guy Barter
CHAPTER 5 Martyn Cox with consultant Jim Arbury
CHAPTER 6 Simon Akeroyd
CHAPTER 7 Martyn Cox
CHAPTER 8 Dean Peckett
CHAPTER 9 Nick Morgan
CHAPTER 10 Rosemary Ward
Information on garden pests is by Andrew Halstead; on garden
diseases by Beatrice Henricot; and garden weeds by Rosemary Ward.

MITCHELL BEAZLEY
COMMISSIONING EDITOR Helen Griffin
ART DIRECTOR Tim Foster
ART EDITOR Victoria Burley
PRODUCTION MANAGER Peter Hunt

Created and produced for Mitchell Beazley by
THE BRIDGEWATER BOOK COMPANY LTD
CREATIVE DIRECTOR Peter Bridgewater
ART DIRECTOR Michael Whitehead
EDITORIAL DIRECTOR Tom Kitch
PROJECT EDITORS Simon Maughan and Claire Saunders
EDITORS Annelise Evans and Candida Frith-Macdonald
ASSISTANT EDITOR Richard Gogarty
DESIGNERS Glyn Bridgewater, Andrew Milne, and Virginia Zeal
PICTURE RESEARCH Liz Eddison
ILLUSTRATION ADMINISTRATORS Lorraine Harrison
and Andrew Popkiewicz
INSTRUCTIONAL ILLUSTRATIONS Peters and Zabransky Ltd, Ivan
Hissey, Richard Peters, and Coral Mula
LINOCUT CHAPTER OPENER ILLUSTRATIONS Jeremy Sancha
DECORATIVE SCRAPER BOARD ILLUSTRATION Jane Smith

CONTENTS

Foreword by Inga Grimsey, 6
Director General of the Royal Horticultural Society

CHAPTER ONE

GARDENING BASICS 8
WEATHER & CLIMATE 12
KNOW YOUR GARDEN 14
GARDENING WITH THE ENVIRONMENT 15
KNOW YOUR SOIL 16
DIGGING TECHNIQUES 18
IMPROVING THE SOIL 20
MULCHING 22
MAKING COMPOST 23
LEAFMOULD 25
PESTS, DISEASES & OTHER PROBLEMS 26
WEED CONTROL 39

CHAPTER TWO

WILDLIFE GARDENING 42
WILDLIFE HABITATS 46
HEDGES 49
WILDLIFE PONDS 50
CREATING A WILDFLOWER AREA 52
CHOOSING PLANTS 54

CHAPTER THREE

ORNAMENTAL GARDENING 56
GARDEN DESIGN BASICS 60
PLACING PLANTS 66
ANNUAL PLANTS 74
HERBACEOUS PERENNIALS 77
BULBOUS PLANTS 83
TREES & SHRUBS 88
HEDGES 113
ROSES 117
CLIMBERS & WALL PLANTS 130

CHAPTER FOUR

GROWING VEGETABLES
& HERBS *138*

PREPARING TO GROW *142*
SOWING & GROWING *146*
SALADS & LEAVES *150*
THE CABBAGE FAMILY *162*
STALKS & SHOOTS *171*
PODS & SEEDS *176*
THE ONION FAMILY *184*
ROOTS & TUBERS *189*
VEGETABLE FRUIT *200*
HERBS *206*
COMMON PROBLEMS *210*

CHAPTER FIVE

GROWING FRUIT *216*

PREPARING TO GROW *220*
SOFT FRUIT *224*
TREE FRUIT *240*
APPLES & PEARS *243*
PLUMS *253*
CHERRIES *256*
FIGS *258*
PEACHES & NECTARINES *261*
APRICOTS *264*
MULBERRIES & QUINCES *265*
COMMON PROBLEMS *266*

CHAPTER SIX

LAWNS *274*

POSITIONING THE LAWN *278*
PREPARING THE SITE *280*
SEED OR TURF? *282*
SOWING A LAWN *283*
LAYING TURF *284*
LAWN MAINTENANCE *286*
COMMON PROBLEMS *294*

CHAPTER SEVEN

WATER GARDENING *302*

SITING & DESIGN *306*
LINERS & CONSTRUCTION
    MATERIALS *309*
PUMPS, FILTERS & HEATERS *310*
LIGHTING *311*
FOUNTAINS *312*
MARKING OUT *313*
INSTALLING A PRE-FORMED POND *314*
LAYING A POND LINER *316*
MAKING A BOG GARDEN *318*
MAKING A WILDLIFE POND *319*
PLANTING WATER PLANTS *320*
POND CARE *332*

CHAPTER EIGHT

CONTAINER
    GARDENING *338*

CHOOSING CONTAINERS *342*
RAISED BEDS *348*
PLANTING CONTAINERS *349*
PLANTING HANGING BASKETS *352*
BEDDING PLANTS *353*
BULBS & CORMS *354*
PERENNIAL PLANTS *355*
TREES, SHRUBS & CLIMBERS *356*
VEGETABLES & HERBS *358*
FRUIT *359*
AFTERCARE & MAINTENANCE *360*

CHAPTER NINE

GARDENING UNDER
    GLASS *364*

GREENHOUSES & EQUIPMENT *368*
HOW TO GROW *375*
PLANT SUPPORTS *377*
USING FRAMES & CLOCHES *378*
THE UNHEATED GLASSHOUSE *379*
THE COOL GLASSHOUSE *382*
THE WARM GLASSHOUSE *385*
HYGIENE & MAINTENANCE *387*
GREENHOUSE PESTS *388*
GREENHOUSE DISEASES *390*

CHAPTER TEN

PLANT PROPAGATION *392*

TOOLS & EQUIPMENT *396*
CONTROLLING THE ENVIRONMENT *398*
CONTAINERS *400*
POTTING COMPOSTS *401*
WATERING *402*
GOOD HYGIENE *403*
METHODS OF PROPAGATION *404*
SOWING SEEDS *405*
ROOTS, BULBS, CORMS & TUBERS *411*
DIVISION *422*
STEMS *425*
LEAVES *439*

Glossary *444*
Index *446*
Acknowledgments *480*

Foreword

The Royal Horticultural Society was established by Sir Joseph Banks and John Wedgwood in 1804 as the Horticultural Society of London. For over 200 years it has fulfilled its aim of collecting information about plants from the world over and encouraging the improvement of horticultural practices. Today, the Society remains true to this original remit and continues to uphold the proud tradition and rich history that makes the RHS respected worldwide. However, as an organization at the forefront of horticulture today, the Society is directing its energy towards redefining gardening as a sustainable practice that must be in tune with the environment and one through which we can enthuse and educate children, the future guardians of our fragile natural world.

Reflecting the heritage of the RHS and our driving goals for the 21st century, the *RHS New Encyclopedia of Gardening Techniques* combines traditional methods of gardening, many of which have been practised and documented by gardeners for generations, with the most up-to-date horticultural techniques. As a result, it embraces modern thinking where gardening with the environment, growing your own vegetables, fruit, and herbs, and gardening with children – at home or at school – is becoming less a fashion and more a mindset essential to the 21st-century gardener.

Learn from the experts

Drawn from the vast knowledge of some of Britain's most experienced horticulturists and scientists at the RHS gardens, this book is the authoritative compendium of horticultural techniques. Novice and experienced gardeners of any age will find accessible information on all disciplines of gardening, from growing and maintaining ornamental plants to methods of controlling garden pests and diseases, plant propagation, and growing plants under glass.

Gardening can often appear mysterious, requiring a certain kind of alchemy to achieve the effects that we admire at gardening shows, in public gardens, and in the media. This book explodes that mystery. Through the clear text and nearly 2,000 delightful but practical artworks, gardeners at all levels will not fail to find all the inspiration and education they need, from growing their own edible produce – whether on the allotment or in containers in a small garden – to establishing an environmentally friendly wildflower or water garden at home or at school, achieving that perfectly manicured lawn, or successfully nurturing a collection of exotic flora in the greenhouse.

This encyclopedia is set to become an icon among gardening books – a trustworthy volume that should have its place on every gardener's bookshelf for generations to come.

Inga Grimsey
Director General, Royal Horticultural Society

CHAPTER ONE

GARDENING BASICS

WEATHER & CLIMATE 12

KNOW YOUR GARDEN 14

GARDENING WITH THE ENVIRONMENT 15

KNOW YOUR SOIL 16

DIGGING TECHNIQUES 18

IMPROVING THE SOIL 20

MULCHING 22

MAKING COMPOST 23

LEAFMOULD 25

PESTS, DISEASES & OTHER PROBLEMS 26

WEED CONTROL 39

ASSESSING YOUR GARDEN AND PLANNING TO MAKE THE best of it can seem daunting, but help is all around. Sometimes research is needed, but often all you need to do is look at the surrounding streets and gardens to see what grows well in the area and form ideas for yourself based on what you see.

There is an exciting sense of exploring unknown territory when you take on a garden, and making discoveries of your own is very rewarding. The interactive nature of gardening, with wildlife and with other people, is especially satisfying – so much of modern life is too complicated to comprehend, but this is certainly not true when you are in the garden.

Before you get started you will need to evaluate the soil. This can be a bit tricky, even for experienced gardeners, but it is crucial to do this if you are to grow plants successfully, as soil is the medium in which all garden plants grow. Fortunately, the simple rules in this chapter provide the basic knowledge, sufficient for practical purposes.

Putting theory into practice

Once you have discovered what kind of soil you are gardening on, the next step is to act. Improving the soil structure is the vital first step in making a successful garden, and the most important soil improver is organic matter. Getting, making, and retaining organic matter should be central to your gardening work. Fertilizers quickly feed plants, but they will not work unless good soil structure allows roots to take up the nutrients.

Unfortunately what is good for garden plants is also good for weeds. Gardeners have to vigorously eradicate unwanted plants – it cannot be helped and is not always a joyous task, but the methods advocated in this chapter will make reasonably light work of an onerous job.

❦ Mastering pests & diseases

Although well-grown plants that have good root systems and sufficient nutrients are much less likely to suffer pest and disease damage than plants that have not, troubles arise in all gardens sooner or later. Some problems are instantly recognizable – if you know the tell-tale signs to look for. The giveaway symptoms and treatments for the main pests and diseases of garden plants are described in this chapter.

Unfortunately, not all problems are straightforward to diagnose. Plants have limited ways of expressing stress. As a result, you may find it hard to track back to the origin of brown or falling leaves, for example, which could be due to a multitude of causes. Gardeners have to be 'plant detectives', and this chapter offers you guidance on what clues to look for and how to interpret them.

Not only are powerful chemical remedies no longer available to gardeners, but many people are uneasy about using them in case harm is done to wildlife or people. Fortunately, prevention is much easier than cure, and if problems do crop up the emphasis in this chapter is on managing rather than eliminating them. Management depends on some understanding of the ways problems and garden plants interact, and the life cycles of pests and diseases. Modern gardeners don't find this understanding irksome at all – not only does it help them garden better, but it is also another facet of the fascinating interaction with nature that gardeners can enjoy. Even slugs and snails can be interesting once you know what makes them tick!

CLIMATE & YOUR GARDEN

Understanding your garden in the context of its environment is the key to successful gardening. A garden's environment directly affects what plants will thrive and when tasks should be carried out, so you need to be familiar with the local climate, prevailing weather conditions, and microclimates within your garden – such as sheltered walls, dry shade under trees, and exposed borders – as well as what type of soil you have. Forearmed with such knowledge you are likely to find gardening a much more rewarding experience as you work with, rather than against, nature's will.

Weather & climate

The 'weather' is what happens day-to-day, while 'climate' refers to the general conditions experienced in an area over a long period. This actually makes life simpler for the gardener. Rather than needing to become an expert at interpreting the weather each day, you only need an understanding of the climate in your garden to get on with many gardening tasks. For example, gardeners who know a little about their local climate will know when the last frost of spring is likely to be, and will plant out frost-tender plants accordingly. With climate change, such predictions will become more difficult; the only advice is to watch the weather and adapt as necessary.

MIXED CLIMATE

In this localized climate, the lake shore ❶ has a mild climate due to the water's influence. Slope ❷, which faces south, gets more sun than north-facing slope ❸. Frost pockets ❹ form as cold air flows downhill and is trapped by the ridge. The hilltop ❺ is cooler due to the effect of altitude and wind. The woodland shelters the field ❻ as it filters the prevailing wind. Similar variables will be at play in your own locality.

Water conservation *see page 15* | Looking after your soil *see page 16* | Wildlife gardening *see page 42*

Day length & sunlight

Before you plant, consider the amount of sunlight different parts of the garden get each day. This is a very important determining factor on the type of plants that will grow there. For many plants, sunshine and the accompanying warm temperatures encourage the maximum amount of fruit, flowering, and growth, but there are a great many other plants that thrive in cooler, more shady conditions.

Day length is also worth considering. Not only can it trigger, among other things, leaf fall in autumn and flowering, but the angle of the sun differs greatly during short winter and long summer days, casting more or less shade. You will need to judge the amount of sunlight different parts of your garden get and plant accordingly.

Frost

Frost can damage plants by freezing the water in the cells, causing them to burst. In the case of plants that are not hardy to frost, such as bedding begonias and petunias, it will cause the leaves to blacken and die.

Altitude affects how cold it is. For every 300m (1,000ft) rise in altitude, average temperatures drop by 0.5°C (1°F). This makes hilltops and mountainous areas naturally colder and more frosts can be expected.

Water & wind

When there is insufficient rain or not enough water provided by the gardener, many plants are unable to keep their cells fully inflated with water and they wilt. Where too much rain causes waterlogging, the roots may rot. Wind can also damage plants, particularly when they are in full growth and the foliage acts like a sail.

WIND FLOW

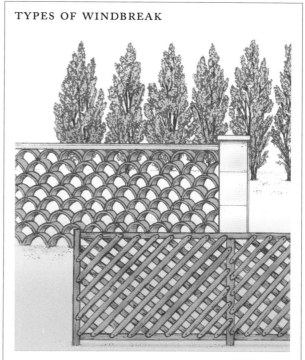

TYPES OF WINDBREAK

The best windbreaks allow some wind to filter through. They can be hedges or natural screens (*top*), or porous walls (*centre*) or fences (*bottom*). Such barriers are also useful at the bottom of slopes as they stop cold air accumulating to form frost pockets.

In each case, you can manipulate the situation to a certain extent – by watering during drought, by improving the drainage of damp soils, or by providing shelter in exposed sites using hedges, trees, or fencing. Alternatively, you can choose plants to suit the conditions.

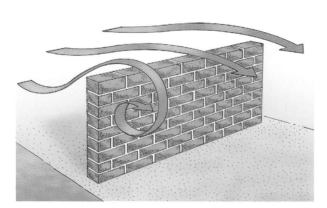

Solid barriers cause turbulence on the lee side. In extreme cases, this can knock plants over and cause walls and fences to collapse.

Porous barriers, like screens of trees and shrubs, are ideal for shelter. They filter the wind, reducing its force and slowing it down.

Know your garden

Once the general climatic conditions are known, you will need to assess what the microclimate is like – the conditions that are unique to your garden. Events such as flooding and hard frosts may only occur every five to ten years, and it is these that will set the limits of what can be regarded as truly hardy plants for your garden. But do look out for what grows locally, as this should provide a good indication of what will thrive.

To begin with, work out the aspect of the garden. South- and west-facing plots are warmer than those that face north or east. Then take into consideration that urban areas often create a 'heat island'. This is where the hard surfaces such as paving and walls collect heat from the sun and release it at night, raising the temperature. This can mean that a city is as much as 4°C (39°F) warmer than the surrounding countryside. Although this sounds good in principle, the high temperatures endured by urban gardens in summer, exacerbated by drought, can make the conditions less than ideal for a number of plants, which may not be tough enough to survive.

Planting microclimates

Careful planting to suit the different microclimates of your garden will ensure you get the most out of the conditions. Typical microclimates in suburban gardens include sheltered areas under trees, shrubs, houses, fences, and walls (which are often very dry as they not only get shelter from the wind but also the rain), cold, shady areas along north- and east-facing walls, and south-facing walls that retain heat in the day and then give it off at night, providing extra protection for tender plants growing against them. Solid fences and walls at the bottom of slopes, dips, and hollows can accumulate cold air in winter, turning them into frost pockets.

MICROCLIMATE

A typical west-facing back garden shows many variations in microclimate that can all be exploited by the gardener. In the example above there are two warm and sunny, sheltered walls: one at the back of the house ❶, which is ideal for tender plants in containers; and another along the side of the garage ❶, which is home to a wall-trained apricot tree. The sunniest spots away from the walls are reserved for the patio, lawn, greenhouse, vegetable patch, and small wildlife pond.

The large tree ❷ at the front of the house casts a lot of early morning shade, while the alleyway ❸ at the side of the house acts as a wind tunnel, affecting the bed on the right of the garden. The fence on this side casts shade most of the day, so the border ❹ is filled with shade-loving plants. The compost heap ❺ occupies a cool, shaded position at the top corner of the garden, away from the house.

FROST PROTECTION

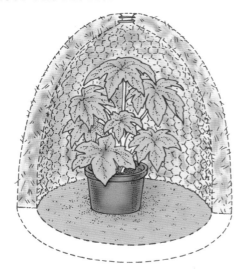

Tender plants need protection from frost to ensure their survival. It is best to lift and store bedding plants in a frost-free greenhouse over winter, but you may need to protect larger specimens outside where they grow, using a thick protective layer of straw, bracken, or horticultural fleece. For tender plants that die back below ground, you should cover the crowns with 15cm (6in) of mulch.

For small trees and shrubs, the protective wadding can be packed around the branches and held in place with hessian sacking and thick string or twine. If this is likely to induce rotting, the packing can be stuffed between 2 pieces of wire netting to make a barrier that can be built around the plant (*shown above*).

For palm trees and tree ferns, gather up the leaves and tie them around the frost-sensitive crown to provide extra insulation.

Looking after your soil *see page 16* | **Wildlife gardening** *see page 42* | **Choice of site** *see page 220*

Gardening with the environment

The aim of any gardener must be to preside over an attractive, healthy, and productive garden that has a minimal impact on the wider environment. This does take more thought, but the result is that resources are saved, and you will have made a positive contribution to the environment. As part of the wider environment, gardens can also be of great benefit to wildlife.

A sustainable approach

To garden in an environmentally sensitive way, you can adopt methods pioneered by organic gardeners. These are all fairly straightforward to put into practice and will minimize your impact on the wider environment, while at the same time promoting all it has to offer.

One of the biggest steps you can take in this direction is to maintain a healthy soil through good cultivation and the regular addition of natural fertilizers, composts, and mulch. Your soil should be teeming with life, which helps aerate the soil so plants can grow strongly, and encourages natural predators that keep pest populations under control.

External inputs to the garden should be naturally derived and, if possible, locally sourced, reclaimed, or recycled. Synthetic pesticides and herbicides should state how best to use them and possible environmental hazards; they are not approved for use in organic systems.

A garden can be built around sustainable principles. Even in this small area, space is found for a bird feeder, a nesting box, a woven fence made from local timber, a compost heap, and a water butt.

WATER CONSERVATION

Efficient use of water is essential if plants are to grow well. Most plants, unless they are a cactus or succulent, need a continuous supply from the soil, which often means that you will need to supplement the water provision – particularly for container plants during summer – when there are long periods between falls of rain. It is important, therefore, to understand how and when to water to get the most efficient results and prevent water being wasted, especially with the threat of longer, hotter summers due to a changing climate.

Apply the water at the base of a plant, rather than over its leaves and branches, and aim to wet the top 30cm (12in) of soil. This moistens the soil around the roots but doesn't provide excessive amounts that simply drain out of reach of the roots. Water is most needed by plants in containers, new plantings, seedlings, leafy salads, and borders next to walls and fences. Established trees, shrubs, lawns, and drought-tolerant plants should not need any extra water, even in the driest of summers. Lawns will look a little the worse for wear after a drought, but they usually green up quickly when the rains return.

Aim to conserve water further by digging organic matter, such as well-rotted garden compost or manure, into the soil. This fibrous matter tends to act like a sponge and hold the water in, rather than letting it drain away. The addition of a thick layer of mulch over the surface of the soil will keep the soil underneath moist by reducing evaporation.

Timer systems (*shown above*) can be connected to irrigation pipes that feed water to sprinklers, seep hoses, or drip-feeders for container plants. Programmable and rain-detecting devices are also available, which makes watering even more efficient.

Store rainwater in water butts, where possible, and use this on the garden rather than turning on the tap. Grey water collected from bathing and showering can be used on all plants except seedlings, fruit, and vegetables.

LOOKING AFTER YOUR SOIL

Healthy soil supplies your garden plants with water, air, and nutrients – essential ingredients for growth. If the soil in your garden is not ideal, there is usually a solution close to hand and most soils can be improved with just a little time and effort. This may mean increasing the water-holding capacity of a light, sandy soil by digging in well-rotted organic matter, or reducing the acidity of a soil by adding a dressing of powdered lime. In this section you will also learn how to make compost and leafmould – both of which are very useful soil additives that you can make at home for free.

Know your soil

There is a complex world below the surface of the garden. The soil has been formed over thousands of years from the breakdown of rocks into mineral particles of sand, silt, and clay. However, this only describes its 'skeleton', usually only making up about half the volume of the soil. The rest is made up of air, water, living creatures, and organic matter (also known as humus), which is derived from plant and animal waste, dead matter, plant roots, soil bacteria, and fungi. The character of the soil is largely determined by the nature of the parent bedrock.

Soil profile
The layered pattern a soil forms on the bedrock is known as the soil profile. The top shallow layer is mostly decaying humus, which helps to retain moisture, improve aeration, and provide nutrients. On cultivated soils humus can decompose quickly, so regular additions of well-rotted organic material are required. Below the humus is the topsoil, ideally 60–90cm (24–36in) in depth, which should be kept well drained, aerated, and fertile – often by regular cultivation. Below the topsoil is the subsoil, containing less organic matter and nutrients.

Types of soil
Garden soils can be defined by the proportion of sand, silt or clay particles they contain and their pH (*see facing page*). It's important to know your garden's soil type as it is one of the determining factors in what plants will grow well.
Clay soils: These tend to be described as 'heavy' and can be sticky when wet, hard when dry and slow to warm up in the spring, but they do contain useful concentrations of nutrients. The addition of organic matter has the effect of improving drainage and increasing the amount of air in the soil. The chemical action of powdered lime can help in the same way if it is added to a clay soil.
Sandy soils: These are easy to cultivate and will warm up quickly in spring, but they dry out quickly and leach nutrients easily. Adding organic matter to sandy soils will improve water and nutrient retention.

A TYPICAL SOIL PROFILE

Key
❶ humus layer
❷ topsoil
❸ subsoil
❹ bedrock fragments
❺ bedrock

SOIL TYPES

Clay soils are made up of very small particles that stick together and make drainage and air penetration slow and cultivation difficult. In your hand, they can be rolled into a sausage.

Sandy soils consist of relatively large particles surrounded by air spaces. Water drains easily and there is plenty of air for plant roots. They feel gritty between thumb and forefinger.

Silty soils contain medium-sized particles that can be sticky and heavy but are also quite nutrient rich. When rubbed between fingers they have a silky feel.

Silty soils: These can be improved by adding organic matter, which helps the texture and workability greatly.

The ideal soil for gardeners is loam, a relatively balanced mixture of clay, sand, silt, and humus. Loam soils are easy to cultivate and retain moisture and nutrients well.

Plant nutrients

A good soil should provide all the nutrients for healthy plant growth. Those required in relatively large quantities are nitrogen, phosphorus, and potassium. Nitrogen stimulates rapid leaf and shoot growth, phosphates stimulate root development, and potassium encourages flowering and fruiting. Other equally important nutrients, such as calcium, sulphur, iron, and boron, are required in lower amounts. The nutrient content of any soil can be boosted by soil additives, particularly fertilizers.

Earthworms, insects, slugs, snails, bacteria, fungi, and many other forms of life all contribute to the nutrient content of the soil and should be encouraged unless their presence is a severe nuisance.

TESTING SOIL PH FOR ITS ACIDITY OR ALKALINITY

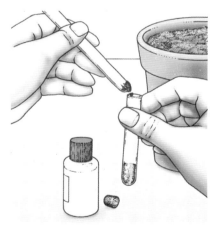

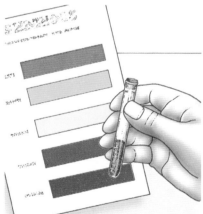

1 **Take small, random samples** of soil from different parts of your garden. Test each one by inserting it into the receptacle provided with a soil-testing kit. Such kits are available in most garden centres.

2 **Shake up the soil samples** in the solution included with the kit. Allow the soil to settle. The solution changes colour depending on the soil pH; this is largely determined by the bedrock and vegetation of your garden.

3 **Soil pH is measured** on a scale of 0 to 14. Most plants suit soils between pH 6.0 and pH 7.5. Higher readings indicate alkaline soil and lower readings acidic soil; always check plants will tolerate your soil pH before you buy.

Digging techniques

The value of physically cultivating the ground is debated, but there are several occasions when it does bring real benefits: it helps control weed growth, is a means of incorporating well-rotted manure, compost, fertilizers, or other additives into the soil, and also relieves compaction and improves soil texture.

Digging the ground is the most effective method of soil cultivation. Generally, you should undertake this in autumn or winter to allow the frost and winter weather to work on the roughly turned soil, and this is of particular value on heavy soils. Ground that is frozen, snow covered, or very wet should never be dug, however, as damage can be done to the soil structure.

To reduce the effort of digging, keep the spade held vertically as it is the most efficient method, and try to lift small manageable amounts of soil each time as it will be quicker and less effort in the long run. Finally, you don't have to dig over the whole plot in one go; it is easier to do a little a day over several days.

Single digging

It is usually sufficient to dig just to the depth of one spade blade. By turning the spade over, you will bury annual weeds and can remove perennial weeds by hand with their roots intact. Organic matter can be mixed in as the soil is turned over. Split the plot down the middle and work down one side and then back the other way.

Double digging

When preparing a new piece of ground or trying to improve drainage by breaking a hard subsoil layer, it is often necessary to double dig. Use the same approach as

SINGLE DIGGING

1 **Dig out a trench** one spade blade deep across one half of the plot to be dug. Pile the soil removed from this trench nearby so that it can eventually be used to fill the final trench. Tip any organic matter that is to be added into the bottom of the trench.

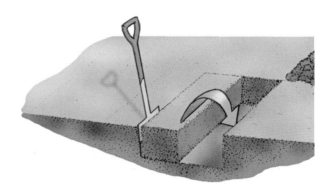

2 **Lift a spadeful of soil** from behind the trench, turning it over into the trench. Work along the trench until another trench has been created. Turn the spade over as you tip off the soil and mix in any organic matter that has been added.

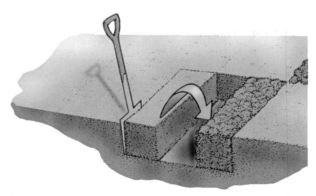

3 **Continue digging further trenches** as in step 2, working backwards and backfilling the previous trench each time, and mixing in any organic matter.

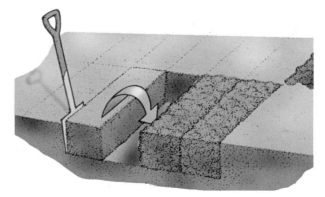

4 **Continue until the end** of the first half of the plot, then turn around and work your way back along the second half. When you come to the final trench, backfill it with the soil removed at the very beginning, which should be right next to where it needs to be.

single digging, but work over the base of the trench to the full depth of a fork, effectively working the soil to the depth of two spade blades. Once the base has been cultivated, you can dig the next trench, putting the soil into the previous trench. Do not allow the subsoil in the base of the trench to mix with the more fertile topsoil, and remember to turn the soil over when backfilling and remove perennial weeds as you go. By forking over the lower layer, keeping it separate from the upper layer, the gardener not only avoids the potential for mixing topsoil and subsoil, but can also fork well-rotted organic material into the subsoil, thereby improving its quality.

Trenching

This technique is very labour intensive, and it is only considered necessary where deep hard subsoil layers are causing drainage problems. Trenching will cultivate the ground to the depth of three spades, and it allows manure

to be deeply incorporated into the subsoil. Remember to turn the soil over when backfilling and remove the deep roots of perennial weeds as you go.

No-dig gardening

Some gardeners believe digging can be harmful to both soil structure and the activity of bacteria and earthworms within the soil. Non-diggers also argue that digging can unearth dormant weed seeds. No-dig gardening simply uses copious amounts of organic material applied to the surface of the ground as thick mulches, and it is left to soil organisms to incorporate the material. Seeds are simply sown into the compost layer on the surface and subsequent mulches are applied around growing plants. There is no doubt this technique works and it also saves labour, but it does require large quantities of well-rotted organic matter. While the soil structure is preserved, the positive effects are seen less immediately.

TRENCHING

1 **Dig a wide trench** one spade blade deep and place the removed soil nearby. Within this trench, excavate a second trench at half the width, so that a step is formed. Make a separate pile for the soil from the second trench. Deeply fork over the base of the second trench.

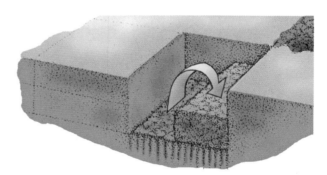

2 **Lift forward the soil** from the other half of the wide trench so that it rests on top of the forked strip. Then deeply fork over the base of the ground just exposed. Well-rotted organic matter can be tipped into the trench at this stage and mixed with the excavated soil.

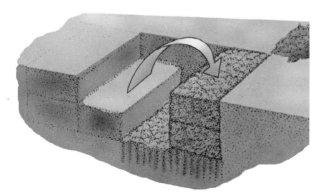

3 **Dig another trench** behind the original trench, to the depth of one spade, turning the soil over so that it sits on top of the soil that was turned over in step 2. Invert the soil as it is moved, so that it is turned upside down, and remove any perennial weeds by hand.

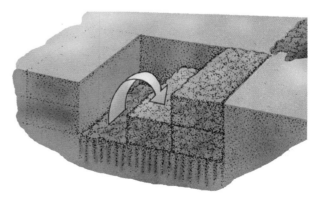

4 **Transfer the layer** of newly exposed soil onto the forked strip in front of it, and cultivate the base of this newly created trench with a fork. Repeat this cycle of cultivation right along the plot until the two piles of soil taken from the first trench are returned to the last trench.

Improving the soil

You can use a wide variety of soil additives to improve the soil, although your choice is often governed by availability and price. Fertilizers come in many forms – both organic and inorganic – while mulches and composts are often added to benefit the soil structure and texture, and minerals are available to manipulate soil pH.

Fertilizers

All fertilizers are labelled to show their nutrient content in terms of nitrogen (N), phosphorus (P), and potassium (K). These are in even quantities for general-purpose fertilizers, such as growmore or blood, fish, and bone; bonemeal and superphosphate is high in phosphorus; tomato feeds and sulphate of potash are high in potassium; and chicken manure and sulphate of ammonia are high in nitrogen. Each has a specific use.

Fertilizers may be applied to the ground a few days before sowing or planting (known as base dressing) or while plants are growing (topdressing). Inorganic fertilizers do not improve soil texture or add to the humus content, but they do act quickly and are richer in nutrients and cheaper than organic fertilizers.

Bulky organic material

Unlike inorganic fertilizers, bulky organic materials improve soil structure and texture. They are also often rich in nutrients, which inorganic fertilizers can lack, and

Inorganic fertilizers are loaded with nutrients and they are easy to handle and apply to the soil. A few, however, can be toxic or caustic, and you should always wear gloves and a mask when handling these.

release their nutrients relatively slowly. It is advisable, however, to compost bulky organic material before use, particularly animal manures, which must never be used fresh as they can scorch young or tender plants due to the

PREPARING ANIMAL MANURE

1 **Mix up animal manure** and find a place where it can be left to rot before use. This will stabilize the nutrients, reduce any toxins it may contain and make it easier to handle.

2 **Stack up the manure** into a heap and water it very well if dry. Firm it down gently in order to get rid of excess air.

3 **Cover the heap** with polythene to keep moisture in and rain out. It should be ready to use within 2–3 months.

MAKING LIQUID FEED

Liquid feeds are fast-acting as they provide nutrients in a form that is readily available to plants. They are easy to come by in the shops but are equally simple to make. Comfrey leaves make a liquid fertilizer high in potash, good for feeding fruiting plants such as tomatoes and peppers. Nettle leaves make a good general fertilizer, as do feeds made from various animal manures. Liquid feeds can be watered onto the soil or directly over the plants and should be applied in dull weather.

1 **Tie the leaves or manure up** in a hessian sack and make a loop in the rope so it can be suspended.

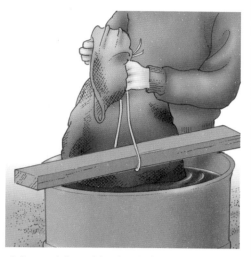

2 **Suspend the sack** in a barrel of water. The water will be ready to use as a feed in a couple of weeks.

freely available nitrogen compounds they contain. Horse manure is the richest, followed by pig, cow, and poultry; dig into the soil in autumn or apply as a mulch in spring.

Garden compost is another useful (and free) source of bulky organic material that is nutrient rich and can be used as a soil conditioner or a mulch. Spent mushroom compost – usually a mixture of manure, loam, and chalk – is a by-product of the mushroom industry and makes an excellent soil conditioner or mulch. It can be used in all soils but avoid using around ericaceous (lime-hating) plants because of the chalk content.

Other valuable materials, beneficial to soil structure but low in nutritional value, include leafmould, cocoa shells, bark chips, and spent hops. Bark chips should be used primarily as a mulch as it can lock-up small amounts of nitrogen from the soil as it decomposes.

Modifying pH

Altering soil pH is a useful way of preparing a soil for plants with specific tolerances. To raise soil pH (reduce the acidity), add ground chalk, limestone, or lime. Chalk is often the cheapest method of raising pH and can be used around plants safely, but it does not always give the quickest results. The packaging should advise on amounts required to raise the pH according to soil type. Lime should be applied in the autumn or winter as it can take some time to take effect, but do not use it with freshly applied manure as it will cause a reaction, thereby reducing its effectiveness. Apply these substances carefully to avoid contact with plants and unprotected skin and eyes.

To reduce soil pH (increase the acidity) sulphur can be applied, as directed on the packaging. Sulphur is broken down by biological factors so takes longer to take effect during winter but is quicker in warmer weather.

CULTIVATING COMFREY

Comfrey plants are easy to propagate by division and can be cut several times during the growing season. The leaves are used as a mulch or to make a liquid feed. 'Bocking 14' is the variety most commonly grown for garden use. Feed the plants annually.

Mulching

A mulch is a loose covering of material on the surface of the soil. Mulches can be either biodegradable – loose organic materials such as compost, manure, leafmould, and bark, all of which will eventually rot down – or non-degradable, such as plastic sheeting, gravel, or glass chippings, which do not add organic matter to the soil.

Most mulches are applied to suppress weeds, but they also help retain moisture in the top layer of soil (beneficial to shallow-rooting plants). Mulches can also help to regulate soil temperature, buffering against extreme highs and lows. Dark mulches absorb sunlight in the day and radiate heat at night, while light-coloured materials will reflect heat rather than store it. The temperature above light mulches can thus be significantly lower at night.

Biodegradable mulches

It is biodegradable mulches that play the most important role in soil management. As they gradually decompose on the soil surface, they are absorbed into the soil by rain and the activities of worms and other soil-borne creatures, and eventually broken down completely. This will improve the soil structure and supply plant nutrients. The quantity and rate at which the nutrients become available depends on the particular mulch.

How to apply a mulch

It is essential that the soil is wet before you apply a mulch, since dry soils are difficult to re-wet once covered with a mulch as it acts as a barrier to rainwater. For the same reason, it is also vital that the soil is warm, since the mulch can act as an insulating barrier. This is particularly the case with light-coloured mulches, so these should never be applied in winter or early spring. Once in place on a warm, moist soil, a mulch helps to keep it warm and moist but prevents it getting too hot or wet. This moderating effect is very good for plant roots and soil life.

Spread the mulch evenly over the soil surface with a garden fork or rake. How thickly you apply it depends on the size of the plants and how much material you have available. Even a 1cm (½in) layer will help to improve the soil structure, but it will take an even layer of mulch 8–10cm (3–4in) thick to control weeds effectively.

In most cases, particularly for trees and shrubs, you should maintain a space between the mulch and the plant stem, as contact can encourage rotting and cause a grafted tree or shrub to shoot from the rootstock. Occasionally, however, mulching up to the stem can be beneficial; for example, tomato and cabbage plants take root into mulch mounded around their stems, helping them grow.

APPLYING A LOOSE MULCH

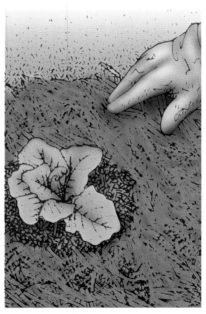

1 **Water the soil well** in advance of mulching if it is dry. This moisture will be locked in by the mulch once it is applied.

2 **Spread the mulch out** by hand around small plants, leaving a space around their stems. Ensure an even coverage.

3 **Keep the mulch clear** of the stems of trees and shrubs. Use a garden fork or rake to spread mulch around large plants.

Making compost

Garden compost is a good source of bulky organic matter that can be made for free from garden and kitchen waste. A good compost heap will readily turn these waste products into a valuable soil conditioner.

Principles of good compost making

To make good, friable compost your heap must be well constructed so that the organic material can decompose rapidly and not turn into a pile of stagnant vegetation. Air, moisture, and nitrogen are all necessary if bacteria and fungi are to break down the raw materials efficiently. Air should be allowed in through the base and the sides of the heap. Water can be applied with a can or hose if the heap shows signs of drying out. Moisture can be retained by lining the heap with sacking, old carpet, or polythene. The nitrogen should be provided in the mix of materials added to the heap (*see following page*). The ideal spot for the heap is in a sheltered, shady place where it is less likely to dry out in the sun and wind.

Well-rotted, friable compost is dark brown in colour and is crumbly in texture. It should be sweet-smelling and is often inhabited by countless soil organisms, such as worms and centipedes. When spread as a mulch or dug in, it makes an excellent soil conditioner.

TYPES OF COMPOST BIN

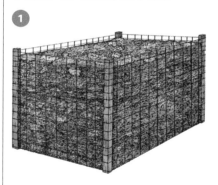

Compost can be rotted down simply by stacking it in a spare corner of the garden. Such heaps, however, may become untidy and the outside of the heap can dry out. Decomposition will take place more rapidly in a home-made or proprietary compost bin that allows air in and retains moisture.

Home-made compost bins vary in design. One of the simplest constructions is a square cage of wire netting ❶, supported by four stout posts driven into the ground. Make sure the front is removable to allow the rotted compost to be easily extracted and turned. For large bins, make a false floor by placing a layer of twiggy branches or brushwood in the base, or support a few short planks on bricks; this will allow air to flow into the heap. Line the inside of the

cage with newspaper to reduce drying out. A piece of sacking, old carpet, or polythene can be placed on top of the heap and weighed down with bricks to help retain moisture and prevent wind-blown seeds getting into the compost.

A more solid structure can be made from angle iron posts and wooden boards ❷, with gaps to allow in air. The internal structure of the heap is the same as with a wire cage. You can use brick or breeze-block structures provided that occasional vertical joints are left unmortared to allow air in. The front of such bays can be equipped with removable wooden slats.

Proprietary compost bins ❸ come in all shapes and sizes. Some have sliding sides to allow the compost to be shovelled out

and lids to keep in moisture. Check that the bin is robust and large enough for the garden's compost needs, bearing in mind the length of time it takes material to decompose. For good results, compost bins should be around 1.2m (4ft) tall. They can be much wider than deep.

A series of two or three compost bins is useful, particularly in large gardens. When one bin is full the compost can be left to decompose and another bin brought into use, keeping a cycle of compost going.

If you do not have room for a compost bin, try worm composting (*see following page*). Alternatively, some local authorities collect green waste for composting, which is eventually resold.

TURNING THE COMPOST HEAP

All plant and animal remains decay naturally without our interference – the composting process is not something that the gardener has invented. The key players are countless micro-organisms, and when suitable materials are worked together in a compost heap, their numbers build up and the rate of decomposition increases. You can help the composting process by turning the heap regularly to allow air to penetrate, giving micro-organisms the oxygen they need.

1 **When adding new material**, break up large clumps with a fork to allow air to penetrate.

2 **Introduce more oxygen** months later by removing the material from the heap and mixing it with a fork.

Compostable materials

All sorts of garden and kitchen waste make good compost if properly mixed. One of the secrets of ensuring rapid and effective decomposition is not to allow large quantities of one particular material to build up in the heap. Try to get a good balance of approximately one third soft and green, sappy (nitrogen-rich) materials to two thirds hard brown (carbon-rich) materials. Nitrogen-rich materials include grass clippings, annual weeds, raw vegetable peelings, tea leaves, animal manure, and hedge clippings. Carbon-rich materials include plant stems, woody twigs, straw, scrunched up newspaper (not glossy magazines), and corrugated cardboard. Do not use any material that has been treated with herbicides (for example lawn clippings) or that is affected by diseases or pests. Shred tough, large or woody prunings to enhance their rate of decomposition.

WORM COMPOSTING

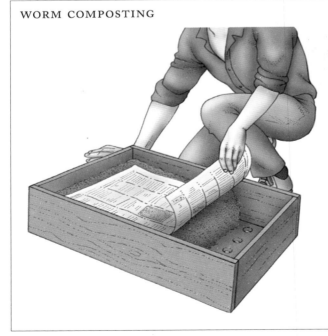

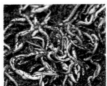

Compost worms are known as 'tiger' or 'brandling' worms because they are striped. They differ from earthworms by living in decaying organic matter. At least 100 worms are needed to start a worm compost bin. You can buy them mail order or gather them from existing compost heaps. The bin can be home-made or bought. It should be rainproof and maintain a damp environment, but be well-drained with a sump or drainage holes so excess moisture can escape. It needs to have a wide surface area and be insulated and portable. The worms are most productive at 18–25°C (64–77°F); try not to let them get too cold over winter or too hot over summer.

A simple wormery can be made from a wooden box with holes in the base. Introduce the worms onto a moist bed of leafmould or compost mixed with shredded paper or cardboard, then begin to add food in small quantities; worms are more likely to be killed by overfeeding than starvation. Cover the contents with wet newspaper or black polythene. If the conditions are right the worms won't try to escape. Worms eat anything that decomposes: annual weeds, tea leaves, vegetable scraps, coffee grounds, food scraps, crushed egg shells, citrus peel (in small quantities), and shredded newspaper are all suitable. Avoid weed seeds, perennial weeds, and diseased material. Cover the bin with a heavy lid to exclude light, flies, and vermin.

Building up the compost heap

Add as much material as possible in any one go, thoroughly mixing the green and brown materials or filling with thin alternating layers. Ensure sufficient moisture is present, but don't allow the heap to become waterlogged.

If you fill the heap in one go with a good balance of materials you may be able to encourage hot composting. Hot heaps compost more quickly, producing useful compost in around six months; they can also kill some weed seeds and diseases. If the heap is filled bit by bit the heap may or may not heat up. Cold composting is slower than hot composting as the compost can take around a year to mature, and weed seeds and diseases often survive. The heap can be turned at intervals to suit you; this can enhance the rate of decomposition and produce a more uniform finished compost.

Once the material has rotted down to form a dark and crumbly texture, the compost should be ready to use as a mulch or soil conditioner. The longer you leave it to decompose, the better the finished compost will be.

Leafmould

Autumn leaves, once rotted down to make leafmould, make one of the best soil improvers. The fallen leaves from any deciduous tree or shrub can be used but it is best to avoid diseased leaves, which can pass on infection (such as rose blackspot or apple scab); leaves with thick veins (such as sycamore leaves) will take longer to rot down. Do not use evergreen or conifer foliage.

Collect the fallen leaves after rain, as it saves watering them later, and pack them into a wire bin or black polythene sacks (with a few air holes punctured in the sides with a garden fork). Leave them to rot down in an out-of-the-way corner. Decomposition is a slow process, taking one to two years, but partially rotted leafmould can be used as a soil conditioner or mulch after a few months.

Leafmould contains few nutrients but is an excellent soil conditioner, improving soil texture and aeration. For a more nutrient-rich leafmould, incorporate chopped comfrey leaves into damp, mature leafmould in thick layers. It is ready to use as soon as the comfrey leaves have disintegrated and the nutrients have been absorbed.

Mature leafmould makes an excellent potting media. It is often used as a peat substitute in potting composts as it has similar characteristics: low pH, good aeration, and excellent water retention. Comfrey leaves can be used to enrich the medium as described above. Potting media intended for long-term container displays will need the addition of one part loam to one part well-rotted manure to every part leafmould.

MAKING LEAFMOULD

1 **Collect leaves after rain** when they are moist. Rake them up, or run a lawnmower over them, which will also shred them and mix them with grass clippings, both of which enhance the rate of decomposition.

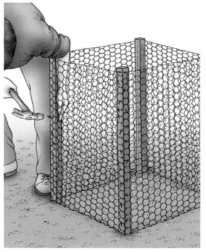

2 **To make a container**, choose a cool, shady place, hammer 4 posts into the ground and staple wire netting to them.

3 **Fill the container** with leaves, pressing them down and watering well if dry. They decay slowly by fungal action over 1–2 years to form a dark, friable material that makes an excellent soil conditioner or mulch.

PESTS, DISEASES & OTHER PROBLEMS

The healthy growth of plants may be disrupted by a pest or disease attack, a nutrient deficiency, or a disorder caused by climatic or environmental conditions. The easiest way of dealing with a problem is to prevent it occurring in the first place, which entails selecting vigorous plants and growing them in the right place, making sure your soil is healthy, and encouraging natural predators. In such conditions the majority of your plants will remain healthy, although it is always worth keeping an eye out so that you can act quickly when the system fails and specific treatment is required.

Know your friends

Although you should encourage a whole range of wildlife into your garden, creatures that are predators of garden pests are particularly welcome. It is useful to recognize these creatures and learn their habits, as this can help you tip the balance between friend and foe in your favour.

Some predators have a limited diet and target specific pests. Hoverfly larvae, for example, feed mainly on aphids. Others, like centipedes and hedgehogs, have a more wide-ranging diet, consisting of what is most available; they will eat more pests during a pest outbreak and thus help to restore the natural balance within a garden.

Sometimes the dividing line between friend and foe is not clear cut. Earwigs, for example, can be pests if you have prize dahlias, but they also prey on aphids and codling moth eggs. The best strategy is to tolerate such creatures and protect vulnerable crops when necessary.

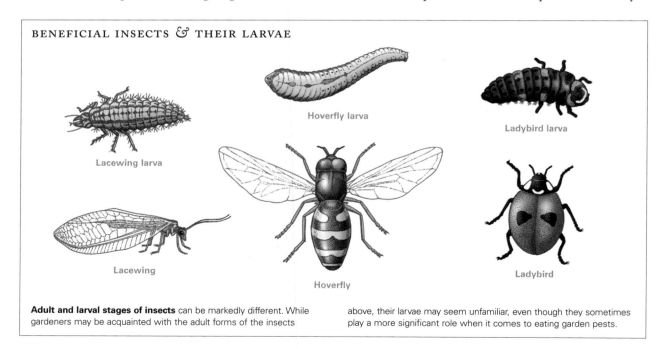

BENEFICIAL INSECTS & THEIR LARVAE

Lacewing larva

Hoverfly larva

Ladybird larva

Lacewing

Hoverfly

Ladybird

Adult and larval stages of insects can be markedly different. While gardeners may be acquainted with the adult forms of the insects above, their larvae may seem unfamiliar, even though they sometimes play a more significant role when it comes to eating garden pests.

KNOW YOUR FRIENDS

Gardening with the environment *see page 15* | **Preventing problems** *see page 28* | **Understanding problems** *see page 29*

PEST PREDATORS

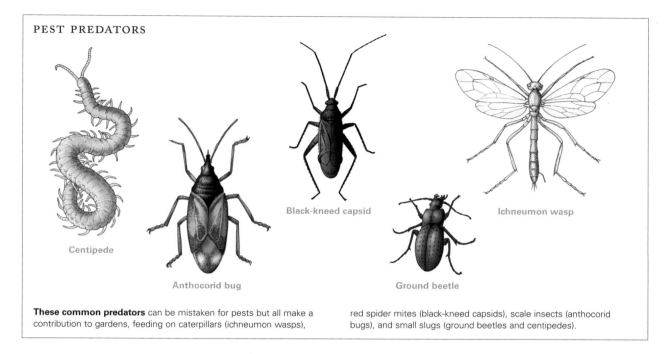

Centipede

Anthocorid bug

Black-kneed capsid

Ground beetle

Ichneumon wasp

These common predators can be mistaken for pests but all make a contribution to gardens, feeding on caterpillars (ichneumon wasps), red spider mites (black-kneed capsids), scale insects (anthocorid bugs), and small slugs (ground beetles and centipedes).

Garden insects, spiders, & centipedes

Most of us are familiar with ladybirds, hoverflies, ground beetles, earwigs, spiders, and centipedes, but there are countless other creatures that go unrecognized. Many of these also have larvae that are completely different from their adult form, which makes identification even harder. The larvae of ladybirds, for example, have tapering bodies that are segmented, greyish-black with orange markings; like the adults, they feed on greenfly, mites, scale insects, mealybugs, and small caterpillars. As a general rule, check when you come across something you do not recognize – beneficial insects can easily be mistaken for pests.

Hoverfly and lacewing larvae are keen predators of aphids, and may also eat other small insects. Ground beetles are seen all year round and are important predators of slugs. They also eat the eggs and larvae of cabbage and carrot root flies and lettuce root aphids. Spiders are found wherever they can build their webs, which catch flies and other small insects.

Garden vertebrates

The more easily identified garden friends must be the vertebrates: hedgehogs, frogs and toads, slowworms, lizards, newts, bats, and birds. Hedgehogs live in rural and suburban areas, hunting mainly at night from mid-spring to mid-autumn, eating a large number of pests such as slugs, millipedes, cockchafers, and caterpillars. Birds are common to all gardens, either as residents or passersby in search of food. They can be a mixed

blessing; song thrushes, for example, like to eat snails, but blackbirds will peck ripe fruit. Small birds such as bluetits, long-tailed tits, and even house sparrows will pick aphids off plants, and starlings on a lawn are probably probing for leatherjackets. Bats are less visible nocturnal garden visitors that should be encouraged as they catch many insects including cockchafers, midges, crane flies, moths, and aphids.

BENEFICIAL AMPHIBIANS

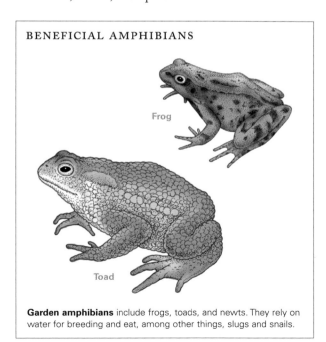

Frog

Toad

Garden amphibians include frogs, toads, and newts. They rely on water for breeding and eat, among other things, slugs and snails.

Preventing problems

Choose plants and varieties that are suited to your garden conditions, give them a good start and they will grow strongly. Plants do, however, vary in their susceptibility to pests and diseases and those that are known to have resistance are a valuable means of preventing a specific, recurring problem, such as blackspot on roses.

Buying healthy plants
Young, vigorous plants will establish more quickly than those that are old and pot-bound. While plants in flower may look more attractive, those not yet in flower are in fact a better buy because the plants will be able to put all their energy into settling in before flowering.

Inspect all new plants for pests and disease, especially those destined for the greenhouse. Bulbs should be firm and show no sign of mould. Always buy certified virus-free seed potatoes and fruit trees and bushes where available. Seeds should be as fresh as possible.

Preventative gardening
With experience, gardeners can learn to incorporate preventative techniques as they cultivate plants in order to avoid problems later. Digging organic matter into the soil will improve its water-holding potential and lessen the effects of drought, which can cause stress to plants. Planting at the correct spacing will encourage good airflow and thwart disease. Sowing times can be adjusted to avoid the periods when certain pests and diseases are most active, while mixed or interplantings can confuse pests, and so reduce large-scale infestations.

THE CABBAGE WHITEFLY CYCLE

Whitefly move on in late spring from overwintered Brussels sprouts, broccoli and other brassicas to newly planted crops ❶. During summer they will move on to other brassica plants ❷. They will spend winter on overwintering brassicas ❸, continuing the cycle of infection. To solve the problem you will need to bury all your over-wintered brassica plants before planting any new crops in spring ❹.

INTERPLANTING VEGETABLE CROPS

Carrot root fly is thought to be deterred by the smell of onions, so a row of carrots is often planted every 4 rows of onions. The effectiveness is questionable, so extra controls may be necessary.

To reduce aphid and root fly damage, alternate rows of cabbages with French beans. Plant out when both types of plant are the same size so that one crop does not dominate the other.

Understanding problems

Despite our best endeavours, plants may suffer from pest damage or diseases. Adverse environmental conditions and shortages of plant foods can also cause unwanted symptoms. Whatever the problem, it is important to identify the cause correctly. Having done so it is useful to know when the problem first appears, when it leaves, how it spreads, the range of plants it will attack, how and where it survives the winter and what level of infestation or infection can be tolerated. This information will help in planning a control strategy.

PESTS

This is the term given to any creature that affects a plant in a way we do not approve. The aim of the gardener is to keep pests at a manageable level.

Many different creatures can act as pests, and they vary considerably. Some, such as slugs and certain aphids, attack a variety of plants; others, such as the lily beetle and potato eelworm, restrict their activities to one or a few plants. Pests may look more or less the same from birth to death, like slugs, or go through several very different stages of growth during their life cycle, like moths. Some creatures are active all year while others may only be active in certain seasons or during the 'pest' stage of their life cycle.

Symptoms & identification

If the pest is visible, identification is relatively easy, although the presence of a creature does not mean that it is the guilty party. Often, symptoms are the only clues the gardener has to go on.

Holes in foliage, stems, or roots, or plants disappearing completely, are caused by pests with biting or rasping mouthparts. Curled leaves and distorted growth are caused by creatures that feed on plant sap, either by piercing the plant tissue or by living within the plant. Be aware that similar symptoms can have different causes. For example, the red blisters that appear on the leaves of red and white currants in early summer are caused by a pest, known as the currant blister aphid. Similar red blisters on peach leaves in the spring, on the other hand, are caused by a disease – peach leaf curl.

KNOWING PESTS FROM DISEASES

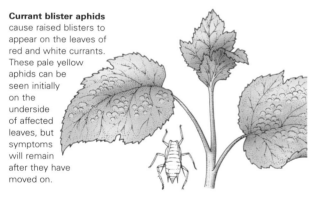

Currant blister aphids cause raised blisters to appear on the leaves of red and white currants. These pale yellow aphids can be seen initially on the underside of affected leaves, but symptoms will remain after they have moved on.

Peach leaf curl symptoms are superficially very similar to the blistering caused by the currant blister aphid. Closer inspection, however, will reveal that no pest is present and the formation of spores on the blisters is a sign of fungal disease.

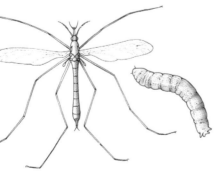

Leatherjackets are a garden pest, feeding on grass roots and causing patches of lawn to turn yellowish-brown during dry spells in summer. Its adult form, the daddy-longlegs or crane fly, however, does not harm plants.

Black bean aphids, or blackfly, are common pests of broad beans. They overwinter as eggs on garden plants such as viburnums and *Philadelphus* when the broad bean food supply is finished.

29

DISEASES

Disease symptoms are caused by fungi, bacteria, and viruses, all of which are mainly too small to be seen. Diseases also tend to be known by the symptoms they produce, such as 'white rot' or 'downy mildew'.

Fungal diseases

The majority of plant diseases are caused by fungi, even though the majority of fungi do not cause diseases. Fungi spread from plant to plant mainly in the form of spores, which are spread by wind, rain, or soil contact. Some disease-causing fungi can live on both dead and living plants, so dead plant material can act as a source of further infection. A few, including rusts and powdery mildews, can survive only in living plants. Some fungi, including club root and onion white rot, produce tough resting bodies, which are difficult to eradicate.

The myriad effects of fungal diseases range from mild to life-threatening. Some affect just a localized area, while others are systemic, meaning they spread throughout the plant. Typical symptoms include death of plant tissue (spots), abnormal increase in tissue (peach leaf curl, club root), change in colour such as silvering or yellowing (silver leaf), wilting (wilts, foot rots), wet rots (damping off), and powdery and fluffy moulds (mildews, grey mould).

Bacterial diseases

These tiny, simple organisms cause few diseases but those they do are difficult to control. Symptoms include soft rots, leaf spots, and cankers. Bacteria are spread in soil water, in and on planting material, and by wind and rain. Their main point of entry is through a wound.

Viral diseases

The majority of viruses are moved from plant to plant by aphids, eelworms, hands, or secateurs. Infected plants may not show obvious symptoms, so it is advisable to buy plants that are certified virus-free.

Symptoms include mottling or mosaic patterns on leaves or flowers, sometimes confused with mineral deficiencies; a virus is initially likely to appear on one or two plants only, whereas a deficiency is more likely to affect a whole row. Once a plant is infected with a virus there is no cure.

IDENTIFYING DISEASES

Viruses on tulips cause the flower colour to break, with the petals having either white streaks or darker streaks than the normal colour. Destroy any plant showing these symptoms unless the plant was bought specifically to exhibit such coloration.

Canker affects apple, pear, ash, beech and *Sorbus* trees. It shows as sunken and discoloured patches on the bark. The branch usually becomes swollen around the canker, which can cause die-back.

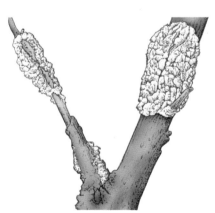

Grey mould causes affected tissues to become covered with a grey fluffy growth of fungus, which should be cut off as soon as it is seen. In severe cases whole plants will need to be destroyed.

Rose blackspot is probably the most common disease of roses. Circular dark brown or black spots develop on the leaves, surrounded by yellowing tissues. As they increase in size, the whole leaf becomes discoloured and falls prematurely.

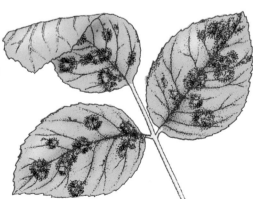

IDENTIFYING DISORDERS

Potassium deficiency causes the scorching of leaves, which may also start to curl, as seen on this bean plant. Such mineral deficiencies are most likely on light, sandy, peaty, or chalky soils on plants that require lots of potassium, such as tomatoes, beans, and fruit.

Oedema is caused by an excess of water in the plant, brought about by a wet soil or overly moist atmosphere. The symptoms are small warty growths on the stems and undersides of leaves, typically seen on eucalyptus, ivy-leaved pelargoniums, peperomias, camellias and vines.

Splitting of fruit, such as tomatoes, and vegetables like carrots and cabbages, as well as the bark of trees, is caused by an irregular supply of water. Heavy rain after drought, for example, will cause very rapid growth, which can lead to splitting.

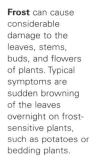

Frost can cause considerable damage to the leaves, stems, buds, and flowers of plants. Typical symptoms are sudden browning of the leaves overnight on frost-sensitive plants, such as potatoes or bedding plants.

Crown rot often occurs where the soil is too wet or waterlogged. Such conditions promote infection by a soil-borne bacteria, which rots the tissue.

DISORDERS

Problems caused by environmental conditions, such as low temperature, day length, or herbicide drift, are known as plant disorders. They can also result from shortages of particular plant foods. Knowing the underlying cause usually makes it easy to correct the problem.

Poor fruit set: Poor pollination will result in a poor crop on vegetable and fruit plants. This may be due to cold, wet, and windy weather preventing the work of pollinating insects, frost killing the flowers or lack of pollen. Providing windbreaks and choosing later-flowering varieties can help to solve the first two problems. Lack of pollen can be due to the absence of flowers of a compatible variety (many fruit trees need a partner nearby). Water shortages and high temperatures can also reduce fruit set, as can poor flowering caused by overfeeding or hard pruning.

Bolting: This is the term used when a plant flowers prematurely, usually a problem with vegetables that are normally picked before they flower. It can be caused by adverse temperatures, day length, root disturbance at transplanting, or shortage of water.

Distorted growth: This can be caused if spray from a weedkiller finds its way onto other plants. Once a plant is damaged in this way there is no cure. Distorted growth may also be the result of frost or pest damage.

Mineral deficiencies: These are caused by shortages of nutrients in the soil, and can be rectified simply by applying the missing mineral to the plant or to the soil. Examples include potassium deficiency (*see above*), lack of iron causing yellowing between the leaf veins, and magnesium deficiency – typically seen on sandy soils.

Taking action

Good cultural practice is not always enough to keep pests at bay. Some, like slugs and snails, are persistent, and defensive action will have to taken if susceptible plants are to survive. The main control measures are chemicals, biological control agents, barriers, traps, and repellents.

Chemical control

Garden chemicals can give rapid and effective control of pests and diseases that would otherwise destroy or badly spoil the appearance of plants. Before their use, make sure that the correct treatment is applied, and follow the manufacturer's instructions carefully. Only apply chemical controls when necessary, and avoid days that are windy, frosty, hot, or wet. In this way, garden chemicals are used efficiently and only as needed.

Wear rubber gloves when handling pesticides. Garden chemicals must be treated with respect at all times, since incorrect use may harm the user or damage plants. After use they must be stored in a locked cupboard where children and pets cannot reach them.

Copper barriers are one of many products available for the exclusion of slugs and snails. It is wise not to rely on just one method of control against these determined pests. Traditional methods, such as baited traps, slug pellets, and hand-picking at night, should not be overlooked.

BIOLOGICAL CONTROLS

Cards bearing whitefly scales killed by *Encarsia* larvae can be hung on greenhouse plants to control whitefly. The larvae develop into small wasps that emerge and lay eggs to parasitize more whitefly. You are unlikely even to notice the tiny wasps themselves.

Aphidoletes pupae help control aphids in greenhouses. Leave them under an upturned pot to hatch, and after a couple of days small flies emerge. The orange larvae are voracious predators of aphids and will kill and eat their prey until fully grown and ready to pupate.

Nematodes (microscopic worms) for controlling vine weevil larvae can be watered onto the soil of individual container plants.

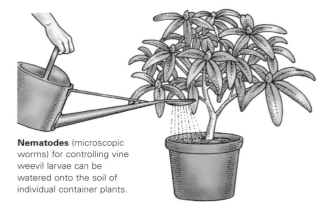

Predatory mites are typically provided in small tubs or tubes. Open and place these on greenhouse plants; the mites soon climb out to search for their prey – red spider mites – which they hunt down and consume in large numbers.

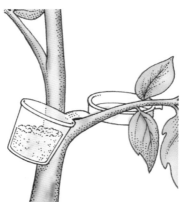

Biological control

This method of control uses natural predators and parasites to keep certain pests in check. Most of these biological control agents are tiny or microscopic and are very specific in their action – the majority of them are only suitable for use in a conservatory or greenhouse as they require warm conditions to be effective. However, some are available for outdoor use, such as the parasitic nematode *Phasmarhabditis hermaphrodita*, which controls slugs. Biological control agents are often supplied by mail order as they have a limited shelf life.

Tips on using biological control

If you plan to use biological control, do not use any persistent pesticides. The aim of biological control is to reduce pest levels and related damage rather than to eliminate pests completely. In some cases this can be achieved with one application, but sometimes you may need a further batch of biological control agents.

There is no advantage in introducing the agent before pests are present. If pest levels are high, try to reduce them using other non-chemical means before using the agent.

Before ordering check that you can meet the required conditions of temperature, humidity, and daylight. Try to use the agents as soon as they arrive, and read the instructions carefully before opening.

Barriers & crop covers

The age-old technique of placing a barrier between a plant and its pest can be highly effective. Tree guards are the classic example, protecting newly planted trees and shrubs from rabbits, deer, and other mammals. Plastic bottles with the base removed can be used to protect seedlings from pests, particularly slugs and snails.

A non-drying glue is available for making sticky barriers on pots and legs of greenhouse staging, which will protect against vine weevil, ants, and woodlice. Wrap a strip of wide sticky tape around first, then smear it liberally with the non-drying glue. The glue can then be removed easily at the end of the growing season by peeling off the tape.

Grease bands can help to protect fruit and ornamental trees from winter moths and ants, which both climb up trunks. Copper bands are available to deter slugs and snails.

BARRIERS

A mini cloche made from the top end of a plastic bottle will protect vulnerable young plants from many pests and the weather. Bell cloches perform a similar function. In both cases, water and air cannot penetrate easily, so they will have to be removed every time the plant needs to be watered, or when there is a risk of overheating.

A grease band applied to a tree trunk will prevent the wingless female winter moths from climbing up to lay eggs on vulnerable trees. If the plant has a stake, either apply the band above the point where the stake is attached or grease band the stake too, as shown.

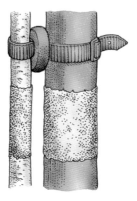

Cabbage root fly mats are made from 15cm (6in) squares of any thick material, such as carpet underlay. Lay the squares flat on the soil around the base of newly planted brassica plants. They form a simple barrier, preventing female cabbage root flies from laying their eggs in the soil near the roots.

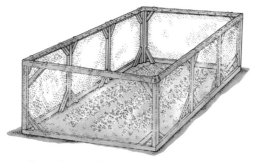

A carrot fly barrier comprises a 75cm (30in) high fine-mesh net erected around a plot of carrots. This gives effective protection as the flies do not fly above this height. The barrier can also be made of clear polythene, but this may get toppled in strong winds.

For food crops, very fine mesh netting is available to protect plants against small pests such as flea beetle, carrot and cabbage root fly, and cabbage caterpillars. These covers are very lightweight and some can be placed directly over a growing crop without the need for any framework for support. They allow air and rain to penetrate.

When using a crop cover it is important to put it in place before the pest is present – usually as soon as the plants are sown. Covers can, if necessary, be left in place for the life of the crop. Be sure to check for weeds and diseases, which can thrive in the sheltered environment.

Keeping out large pests

The only effective control for large pests, such as rabbits or deer, is a wire mesh or electric fence. Plastic netting is usually sufficient to keep out birds and smaller mammals, and for fruit growers, fruit cages are available in many sizes. Deer can be excluded by tall fences.

Grouping soft fruit plants together within a fruit cage is an efficient method of protecting ripening fruit from birds. The netting of these should be removed when fruiting has finished and not replaced until after the blossom has set. This allows access for pest-clearing birds

and pollinating insects and also avoids the danger of snow bringing down the roof. Individual fruit trees can be protected by draping netting over them. This is much simpler where the plants are trained against a wall.

Traps

Traps can be used in the garden to reduce pests in a small area. Pheromone-baited traps and sticky yellow traps are the most commonly used. Traps are also used to monitor the activity of pests so that the timing of an appropriate chemical spray or introduction of a biological control agent can be made accurately.

Some traps use synthetic pheromones (sex hormones) to attract specific moth pests into a trap from which they cannot escape. These traps capture males of codling moth, which affect apples, and plum moth, indicating when it is time to spray against the newly-hatched larvae.

Scaring & repelling devices

Various devices for scaring and repelling cats, deer, rabbits and moles are available. Most are not that effective but may be worth a try if you have a persistent problem and other methods have failed.

COVERING CROPS

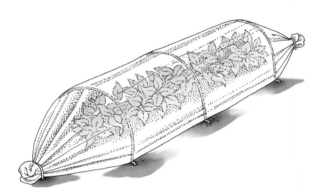

Horticultural fleece is a finely woven material placed directly over a crop and held in place with pegs or stones. It also protects from frost.

TRAPS

A sticky yellow trap is useful for whitefly control in the house and greenhouse. It is a plastic card covered with a non-drying glue, which flying insects adhere to if they settle on it. Several traps may be needed in a greenhouse, and you will need to replace them periodically.

Fine mesh netting is used in the same way as fleece, but does not protect from frost. Hoops are used to support it over the crop.

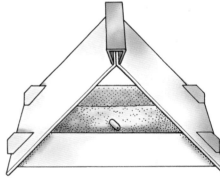

A pheromone-baited trap attracts male codling and plum moths. Hang traps from tree branches when the moths are active in late spring.

Common pests

The range of plants grown by amateur gardeners is extremely wide and, correspondingly, there are many pests that can occur. Listed below are some of the most common, wide-ranging pests. Pests that affect particular plants are listed in the relevant chapters.

Slugs & snails

Seedlings and new shoots on herbaceous plants are particularly vulnerable to slugs and snails. In wet weather they are more active and this increases the damage they cause. Some slug species live in the soil where they damage potato tubers and bulbs.

Slugs and snails cannot be entirely prevented. Concentrate control measures on protecting the more vulnerable plants. Scatter slug pellets containing metaldehyde or ferric phosphate thinly among the plants, or try physical barriers of copper strips, water-absorbent minerals, or repellent gels. Biological control with a nematode, *Phasmarhabditis hermaphrodita*, will control slugs when they seek shelter in the soil but is less effective against the surface-dwelling snails.

Capsid bugs

Capsid bugs are small green or brown insects that suck sap from shoot tips and flower buds. This kills the cells that have been probed in the embryonic leaves, resulting in many small holes in the leaves once they have grown and expanded. Damaged flower buds abort or produce distorted flowers. Many herbaceous plants and shrubs are affected by capsid bugs, including dahlias, geraniums, fuchsias, forsythias, and hydrangeas. Control capsid bugs by spraying with imidacloprid or bifenthrin.

Aphids

Most plants are attacked by these sap-feeding insects, which are commonly known as greenfly or blackfly. Infested plants may suffer distorted growth and become sticky with the honeydew that aphids excrete, which becomes blackened with a sooty mould.

Control aphids before heavy infestations develop. Systemic insecticides, such as imidacloprid and thiacloprid, are absorbed into plant tissues and kill aphids when they feed. Contact insecticides include bifenthrin, pyrethrum, plant oils, and fatty acids. With edible plants, check the manufacturer's instructions to see whether the insecticide is suitable for that specific plant. Biological control with *Aphidoletes* or *Aphidius* can be used against aphids in greenhouses.

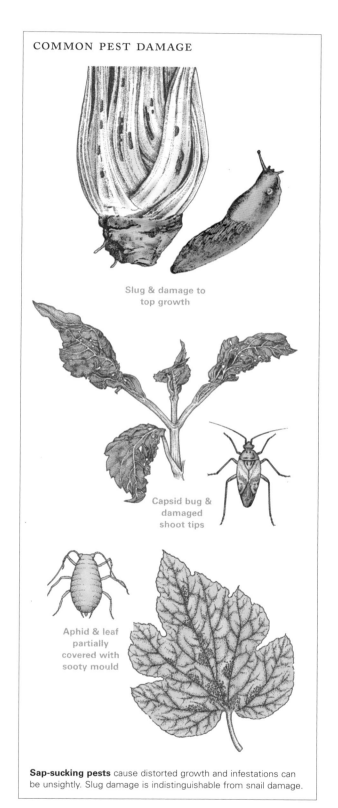

COMMON PEST DAMAGE

Slug & damage to top growth

Capsid bug & damaged shoot tips

Aphid & leaf partially covered with sooty mould

Sap-sucking pests cause distorted growth and infestations can be unsightly. Slug damage is indistinguishable from snail damage.

Rabbits, deer & squirrels

New plants are particularly vulnerable to rabbits and deer, which gnaw bark, especially in winter, causing young trees and shrubs to die. Squirrels eat flower buds and shoot tips, ripening fruits and seeds, and bulbs and corms. They also strip bark from the trunks of trees. Wire netting is an effective barrier; for rabbits, use small mesh netting 1m (3ft) high with another 30cm (12in) below soil level angled outwards to prevent burrowing. Deer need robust fencing, 2m (6ft) tall. Repellent substances and scaring devices are unreliable and at best give only short-term protection. Shooting or trapping must be carried out over a wider area than a single garden if it is to make any difference.

Vine weevil

Both the adult beetles and the grubs damage many plants. The adult weevils are active at night when they crawl up plant stems and eat notches in leaf margins. The larvae are creamy white, legless grubs with brown heads; they feed on roots, especially those growing in containers. Such plants may be killed during autumn to spring.

Search by torchlight for adult weevils on plants showing leaf damage and destroy them. Insecticides are not very effective against adult weevils. Control the larvae by treating pot plants with thiacloprid. Alternatively use biological control with the pathogenic nematode, *Steinernema krauseii*. Treat plants in late summer.

Deer often visit gardens at dusk or early in the morning when there is nobody about. They may jump fences to get in and out, and their grazing can cause serious damage.

Caterpillars

Many caterpillars feed on the foliage and flower buds of garden plants. Damage is often limited to unsightly holes in the leaves but some cause more extensive defoliation. Hand removal is feasible for light infestations. This is more effective if the caterpillars are searched for by torchlight on mild evenings. Heavier infestations may require spraying with bifenthrin or pyrethrum.

MORE COMMON PEST DAMAGE

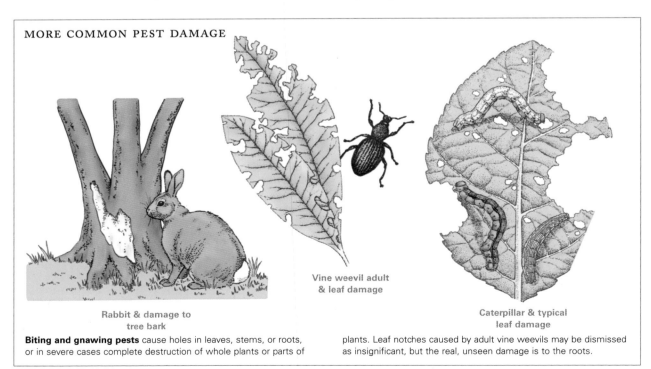

Rabbit & damage to
tree bark

Vine weevil adult
& leaf damage

Caterpillar & typical
leaf damage

Biting and gnawing pests cause holes in leaves, stems, or roots, or in severe cases complete destruction of whole plants or parts of plants. Leaf notches caused by adult vine weevils may be dismissed as insignificant, but the real, unseen damage is to the roots.

Common diseases

As with pests, there are many diseases that can infect plants. Listed below are some of the most common, wide-ranging diseases that you are likely to encounter at one time or another in your own garden. Diseases that affect particular plants are listed in the relevant chapter.

Honey fungus

This fatal disease can affect all woody plants and some herbaceous ones too. Typical symptoms include thinning of the canopy, branch die-back, or the sudden death of a plant. Examination of the stem base or larger roots reveals a white sheet of fungal mycelium growing between the bark and wood, which smells strongly of mushrooms. Sometimes, but not reliably, clumps of honey fungus mushrooms may appear at the base of the trunk or along root runs in mid-autumn. The mushrooms are honey coloured, with white gills and a collar on the stalk.

It is not possible to eradicate an established infection, and ultimately affected plants will die. Honey fungus mainly infects new plants by root contact using rhizomorphs (bootlace-like structures that grow through the soil). You should therefore destroy infected plants, taking care to remove as much of their root system as possible. Severed rhizomorphs in the soil can cause new infections, so leave soil fallow for several months before replanting. Where honey fungus is known to be present it is wise to choose plants that are less susceptible to infection, such as *Acer negundo*, beech, box, ivy, laurel, sweet chestnut, and yew.

Verticillium

This wilt disease affects a broad range of plants, but maples, *Cotinus* and *Catalpa* are most commonly affected. Individual branches wilt and eventually die back, often over successive years. Typically, dark streaking is evident within the vascular tissue of these branches. Sometimes plants may recover.

If the disease is in its early stages, applying an ammonium-based fertilizer to the root zone may encourage the production of a new ring of disease-free vascular tissue. The disease is soil-borne, so badly affected plants and their roots should be removed and replaced with resistant species. You will also need to sterilize tools.

Phytophthora

There are many species of phytophthora (pronounced 'fi-top-thora'), some of which are highly specific (such as holly blight), while others have a wide host range. Infected plants most commonly suffer from a root or stem rot, characterized by an inverted v-shaped lesion

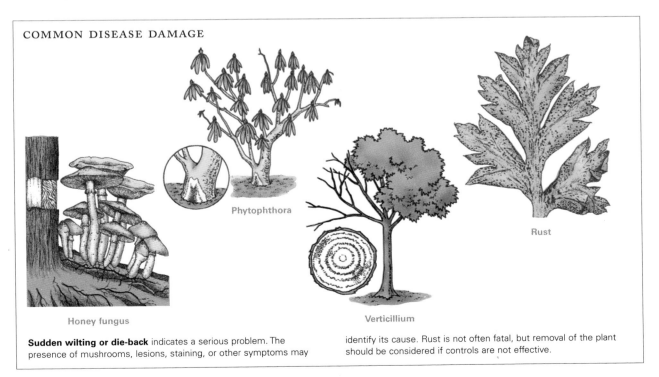

COMMON DISEASE DAMAGE

Phytophthora

Rust

Honey fungus

Verticillium

Sudden wilting or die-back indicates a serious problem. The presence of mushrooms, lesions, staining, or other symptoms may identify its cause. Rust is not often fatal, but removal of the plant should be considered if controls are not effective.

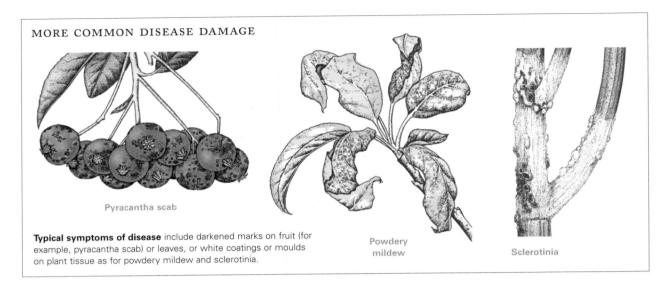

MORE COMMON DISEASE DAMAGE

Pyracantha scab

Powdery mildew

Sclerotinia

Typical symptoms of disease include darkened marks on fruit (for example, pyracantha scab) or leaves, or white coatings or moulds on plant tissue as for powdery mildew and sclerotinia.

beneath the bark at the stem base, together with rotten roots. Die-back of the canopy becomes evident as infection of the root system advances.

Prevention is the only method of control as the disease can remain dormant in the soil for many years in the form of resting spores. On soil that is known to be infected, you should take measures to improve drainage, and it is important to sterilize garden tools and use clean tap water for irrigation to limit the amount of cross infection. Avoid using high-nitrogen fertilizers.

Remove affected plants promptly, including their root system and the soil. If it is possible to identify the type of phytophthora involved, replant with a non-susceptible species. If the type is unknown, it is advised that the affected area be kept free of woody plants for three years.

Rusts

The first sign of infection is the appearance of pustules of powdery orange or brown spores on leaf and stem undersides. Corresponding pale spots on the upper surface of leaves may appear, and the leaves may fall prematurely.

Hygiene is important in controlling an outbreak of rust. Pick off diseased material and destroy it promptly, and at the end of the season, remove dead material. Several fungicides are available to protect against infection or to eradicate existing disease. If rust occurs despite these measures, resistant varieties of plants are often available.

Scabs

Crab apple and pyracantha fruit are susceptible. The fruits develop brown or black scabs, though on pyracanthas they may be reduced to clusters or small,

blackened ruts. Prevent infection of crab apples by destroying severely affected plants and replace with resistant varieties.

Powdery mildews

This large group of related fungi affects a very wide range of plants. Typically, a powdery white coating appears on any part of the plant and infected tissue becomes distorted. The leaves may drop, buds die, or stems die back. Outbreaks are most severe on dry soil. Promptly remove infected tissue to reduce further spread.

If available, grow resistant varieties; improving soil conditions and watering regularly will reduce drought stress. It is equally important to encourage good air circulation around the foliage by proper pruning, and ventilation if in a greenhouse. Spraying infected plants with an appropriate fungicide may also help.

Sclerotinia diseases

These affect many vegetables and ornamentals. Symptoms include sudden wilting, yellowing of basal leaves, and a brown rot of the stem. This is associated with white mould, often containing hard, black structures called sclerotia. These fall into the soil to germinate the following spring to cause new infections. Typically the stem base is attacked, but bulbs, carrots, and parsnips in storage can also be affected.

Destroy infected material before sclerotia can be released into the soil, where they may survive for years. Material should not be composted. The potential host range is very wide, so control weeds that could act as hosts. If infected soil cannot be changed, avoid growing susceptible plants there for up to eight years.

Digging techniques *see page 18* | **Lawn weeds** *see page 294* | **Aquatic weeds** *see page 331*

WEED CONTROL

Successful weeds tend to be fast growing and colonize new ground rapidly. They must not be allowed to invade ornamental or food-growing areas as they out-compete the plants we want to grow by depriving them of water, nutrients, and light. Understanding how weeds grow can help us to control them. Annual weeds survive long term by producing large quantities of seed before dying, while perennial weeds build up food reserves underground; not only do these reserves make perennial weeds harder to pull out, but they allow them to regrow when the top growth is killed. Always aim to remove weeds before they set seed.

Removing weeds

Annual weeds tend to have short, fibrous root systems so are relatively easy to pull up by hand. Their roots rarely survive if the leaves and shoots are killed, so removal with a hoe works well over large areas and between rows of vegetables. Move the blade parallel with the ground, cutting the tops off the weeds just below soil level. It takes immense persistence to control perennial weeds this way.

Digging can be a good way to clear taprooted perennials if you are careful to remove the whole root. Unfortunately, is very difficult to eradicate weeds with creeping underground stems, or storage tubers, by digging alone as any tiny pieces left in the soil will regrow.

Using weedkillers

There are many weedkillers on the market. Before you buy, check that the product is suitable for the type of weeds you want to kill and area you want to treat.

Contact weedkillers: These act quickly to kill the parts of the plant they touch. They are not carried down to the roots so are only effective against annual weeds.

Systemic weedkillers: These tend to act more slowly, but they are carried down to the roots to kill both annual and perennial weeds. Selective weedkillers are effective against many broadleaved weeds, but do not affect grasses, so are ideal for use on lawns.

PERENNIAL WEED ROOT SYSTEMS

Taproots The carrot-like taproots of dandelions, thistles (*shown above*), and docks grow straight down into the soil. They can be removed by deep digging.

Rhizomes Bindweed, ground elder, and couch grass (*shown above*) grow from these underground stems. They break into pieces and can be difficult to dig out.

Tubers The numerous tiny bulbils that develop around the tuberous roots of oxalis (*shown above*) and lesser celandine break off easily and grow into new plants.

39

FORKING OUT WEEDS

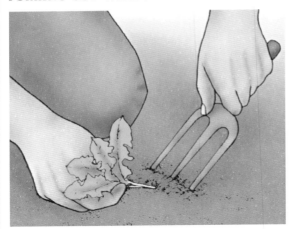

Weeding by hand is effective against most small weeds and many large annuals. If the ground is dry, or the weeds brittle, use a hand fork to help. Hand weeding paths and patios is effective only if weeds are caught while small and easy to pull out.

Residual weedkillers: These remain active in the soil for several months, preventing weeds from regrowing. They are most commonly used on paths and other hard surfaces, but some types can be used with care between established woody plants such as soft fruit. Path weedkillers, used on areas of hard landscaping, usually contain a mix of chemicals to kill existing weeds and prevent regrowth, but they still need to be used several times a year.

Smothering weeds

Mulches and low-growing or spreading ornamental plants are commonly used to provide a cover over the soil to exclude weeds. Loose mulches, such as grass clippings, composted bark, or gravel, will smother small annual weeds and make it easier to pull out any weeds that do emerge, although they will not stop perennials. Bark, cocoa shell, and gravel have the added bonus of looking attractive. Loose mulches work well between established plants, but will need regular topping up. For maximum effectiveness, use a layer at least 8cm (3in) deep.

Sheet mulches, such as black polythene, woven polypropylene, or old carpet, will quickly kill annual weeds. They can also be successful against many perennial weeds, including ground elder, if left in place for two growing seasons. Laid under paths and patios, they will help to prevent perennial weeds from pushing through, and they are a good long-term solution between permanent plants, around trees and for unplanted areas.

Where appearances matter, sheet mulches can be disguised with a thin layer of bark or gravel. The best time to lay sheet mulch is when planting a new bed, so the soil can be well-cultivated, organic matter added and weeds removed before the mulch goes down. Make sure the soil is moist before you lay a sheet mulch, as water will not easily penetrate once the covering is laid. Black polythene is a cheap option for short-term situations,

USING A SHEET MULCH

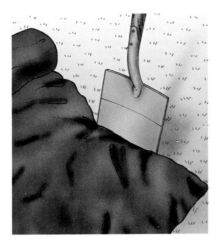

1 Anchor the sheet mulch in position by pushing the edges into the soil or weighting them with bricks. If the mulch is to be planted, then ensure that the ground underneath has been well cultivated and well watered if it is not already moist.

2 Cut a cross in the sheet with sharp scissors or a knife, and using a hand trowel make a small planting hole in the soil beneath to plant in the normal way. Make the cut no larger than it needs to be as weed seeds will settle and germinate on exposed soil.

3 Put the plant through the cut in the sheet mulch and into the planting hole. Firm the soil around it and repeat until all the bed is planted. The sheet mulch can then be covered with a loose mulch of chipped bark, gravel, or pebbles, for example, so it looks attractive.

Giant hogweed is a very tall, invasive weed. Its sap can cause severe skin irritation. Even after removal, seeds remain viable for up to 15 years, so it is difficult to eradicate.

Japanese knotweed is an aggressive weed in Europe and North America. It is very difficult to eradicate as its roots spread widely and up to 3m (10ft) underground.

Himalayan balsam was originally grown for its pretty flowers, but is now a widespread invasive weed. Its curious, explosive seed pods allow it to colonize areas quickly.

such as vegetable plots. Woven polypropylene is much longer lived, and porous to water, so is suited to long-term planting such as shrub beds or paths.

Biodegradable mulches that last only a few months, such as cardboard, newspaper, and straw, can be very useful to help clear weedy ground, such as an overgrown allotment. Cut down all the weeds, spread the mulch over the top and plant through it. Weeds and mulch will rot down together, and the ground will be much more manageable at the end of the season, when it is cleared.

Ground cover

The most satisfying way to discourage weeds is to cover the ground with attractive plants. In ornamental areas you can use groundcover plants that are low-growing and vigorous, spreading out to form a dense carpet that prevents weed seeds from germinating. Sadly, groundcover plants will not prevent perennial roots from regrowing, so it is vital to clear the ground of weeds first. Weeds will also need to be removed until the groundcover plants have knitted together. Alternatively, plant through a suitable sheet mulch. Evergreen shrubs or perennials make the best plants for ground cover.

In the vegetable plot, bare areas can be covered with green manure to exclude weeds. Intercropping, making short-term use of the gaps between widely spaced young plants, also helps deny access to weeds. For example, lettuces can be planted between rows of Brussels sprouts.

Invasive weeds

However bad they are in gardens, most of our weeds are native plants and cause no problems in their natural habitats. Unfortunately, some garden plants have not only become a problem in gardens, but have escaped into the wild. Here they can do real damage by smothering native plants, blocking waterways, and depriving wildlife of its natural food or habitat. Sometimes the damage is obvious, where large areas of Japanese knotweed or *Rhododendron ponticum* prevent anything else from growing. Other times the effect is more subtle, such as the Spanish bluebell cross-breeding with our wild bluebell to create hybrids that could replace the true natives. Many problems with these invasive escapees could be prevented if gardeners simply composted, dried, or burned excess plants, rather than dumping or planting them in the wild.

Legislation

Creeping thistle, spear thistle, curled dock, broadleaved dock, and common ragwort are classified as injurious to agriculture under the Weeds Act 1959. Farmers and landowners are required to control these weeds so that they do not spread, but the law is unlikely to be applied to gardeners. More relevant is the Wildlife and Countryside Act 1981, which makes it an offence to allow specified weeds to escape into the countryside. At present it only applies to giant hogweed and Japanese knotweed.

CHAPTER TWO

WILDLIFE GARDENING

WILDLIFE HABITATS 46

HEDGES 49

WILDLIFE PONDS 50

CREATING A WILDFLOWER AREA 52

CHOOSING PLANTS 54

WILDLIFE GARDENING ALLOWS YOU TO OBSERVE, ENJOY, and encourage nature quite literally on your doorstep. Interest in this topic has never been stronger, as gardens are the place where most people experience their closest and often most memorable encounters with wildlife. As a reason to be active outdoors and a simple source of pleasure, gardening for wildlife can enrich your life and your world.

The role of gardens in wildlife conservation

There are other good reasons for wildlife gardening. Gardens cannot – and, perhaps, should not – seek to replace natural habitats. Yet scientific research clearly shows that gardens are incredibly rich in biodiversity, giving them a key role in easing the negative effect of species and habitat loss. With the decline of ponds and amphibians in the wider countryside, for example, garden ponds have become increasingly important, particularly for some species, such as the common frog. House sparrow numbers have plummeted, but gardeners, by providing supplementary feeding and suitable nest boxes, may help prevent their further decline and eventual disappearance.

Unlike wildlife parks and nature reserves, the role of private gardens in wildlife conservation is often underplayed. In reality, gardens account for a significant proportion of land use, and evidence from individual case studies suggests that the impact of gardening on wildlife is, by and large, a positive one. If this can be assumed to be representative of the nation's gardens, the beneficial effect of gardens on supporting and sustaining wildlife is immense.

Gardens also provide a buffer against negative impacts on biodiversity, such as the loss of green spaces to developers, climate change, and the paving over of gardens for parking. So long as gardens remain connected to each other and to wilder habitats, such as the surrounding countryside, canals, railway embankments, or road verges, they ensure 'green corridors' for wildlife to move freely. In essence, the sum is greater than the parts. Take this away and it is not so much the reduction in plot size as the isolation of gardens that reduces their benefit to wildlife.

How to be wildlife friendly

This chapter focuses on how to maximize the wildlife potential of your garden. The first thing to understand is that all gardens are, to some degree, wildlife gardens. Even the most extreme expressions of gardening, for example a Japanese gravel garden or a velvety lawn, are still likely to harbour some insects, spiders, and soil organisms of many sorts. Once these low-level food chain species are present, higher level species like mice, hedgehogs, and insectivorous birds will be attracted. These then attract other predators, including foxes, sparrowhawks, and owls. Gardens that extend the range of habitats and introduce varied plants as a food source will therefore see biodiversity soar accordingly.

Instead of jumping in, ripping out existing garden features, and replacing them with a 'wildlife garden', it is better to begin wildlife gardening by observing what is already there. The discovery of existing wildlife allows a sensitive approach to managing the garden.

The actions of gardeners have never been more critical. You do not need to have every feature described in this chapter, but if you can increase the diversity of plants and plantings in your garden, you can protect and enjoy the wildlife that they accommodate through the year.

WILDLIFE IN THE GARDEN

To create a suitable environment in your garden for wildlife to thrive, you must take into account two elements: habitat creation and habitat improvement. For the first, consider your garden space as a whole and think about features that will attract insects, birds, and other animals. You might want to create a woodland area, a bog garden, or redesign your garden entirely. For the second, assess your garden or part of it and work on ways to develop existing habitats. For example, you could put up nesting boxes, replace a fence with a hedge, make a lacewing refuge, or add a green roof to a shed.

Wildlife habitats

Gardens are used by wildlife in different ways, and knowing what these are will help you garden for wildlife. Some requirements, such as water, are needed by all creatures. Water is vital for drinking, bathing and, in the case of many aquatic creatures, life and reproduction. Accommodation and food are also needed, but requirements differ greatly between species. Listed here are types of common garden wildlife, with an explanation of how best to attract and provide for them.

Birds

Loved by most gardeners, birds are readily attracted by a year-round supply of clean, ice-free water and food. You should site both in an open area, so the birds are not so vulnerable to predators like cats and sparrowhawks, but with the shelter of shrubs or a hedge nearby.

For water, a shallow bowl or pond edge makes it easy for birds to drink and bathe. For food, put out a variety of bird seed mixes to attract the greatest diversity. Also use a range of feeders: wire-mesh peanut dispensers, seed feeders, bird tables, ground-feeding tables, and fat block holders in winter. Use a mild disinfectant to prevent bird baths and feeding stations from spreading disease.

Natural foods are equally important (*see page 54*). Grow berrying and seed-bearing trees, shrubs, and climbers. Position a blunt stone at the back of the border for thrushes to use as an anvil for smashing open snails. Keep some areas of short grass so that green woodpeckers, thrushes, and blackbirds can probe for ants and worms.

Where safe to do so, leave cavities in trees and walls to allow birds such as tawny owls, starlings, tree creepers, nuthatches, woodpeckers, and house sparrows to nest.

PLANNING A WILDLIFE GARDEN

Key
1. Seat
2. Woodland
3. Mown path
4. Shelter/hide
5. Meadow
6. Rotting logs
7. Mixed hedge
8. Pond visible from all angles
9. Log piles
10. Berrying trees
11. Family terrace
12. Flower border for butterflies
13. Bird table in view of window
14. Shrubs with winter berries

Many wildlife-friendly features can be included in any garden. The gardener's needs must be considered alongside the main wildlife theme so that the garden is also ornamental and practical.

ARTIFICIAL & NATURAL WILDLIFE HABITATS

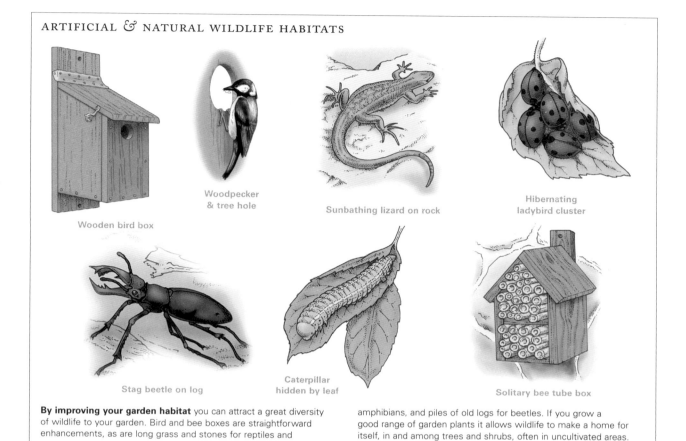

Wooden bird box

Woodpecker & tree hole

Sunbathing lizard on rock

Hibernating ladybird cluster

Stag beetle on log

Caterpillar hidden by leaf

Solitary bee tube box

By improving your garden habitat you can attract a great diversity of wildlife to your garden. Bird and bee boxes are straightforward enhancements, as are long grass and stones for reptiles and amphibians, and piles of old logs for beetles. If you grow a good range of garden plants it allows wildlife to make a home for itself, in and among trees and shrubs, often in uncultivated areas.

Bats

Position bat boxes (*see right*) in trees or on walls, at least 3m (10ft) above ground level. Face them out of the prevailing wind and rain, sited in the shade to reduce temperature fluctuations. Cavities in trees are often used by bats as a cool, humid wintering site, while loft spaces make perfect nursing areas in summer for rearing young.

Grow nectar- and pollen-rich plants, particularly those that attract moths, as these will provide ready meals for bats. Bats and their habitats are protected by law, so check old trees and roof spaces before undertaking any work.

Bees

The lure of pollen and nectar is enough to attract bees to your garden, and as long as there are plants in flower, they will continue to visit. Only apply insecticides early in the morning or late evening and avoid spraying flowers.

Provide nesting sites for solitary bees in the form of open-ended hollow tubes; you can buy them ready-made, or use bundles of drinking straws. Undisturbed hedge bases or sunny banks also make good nesting sites. Bees need a source of shallow water for drinking.

MAKING A BAT BOX

1 **Use 6 pieces** of waste timber to make a simple box, about 20cm (8in) tall and 10cm (4in wide). It needs to be rough-sawn with ridges 1cm (½in) apart on the inside of the back panel, as this helps the bats to cling. Try to use preservative-free wood.

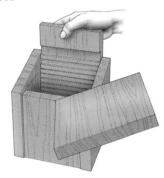

2 **Piece the box** together with screws or nails and make holes in the back panel so the box can be fitted to a wall or tree in the same way. Between the bottom and back panels, leave a gap of about 2cm (¾in) wide so that the bats can gain access.

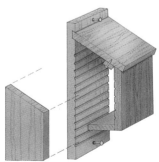

MAKING A LACEWING & LADYBIRD REFUGE

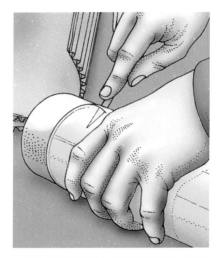

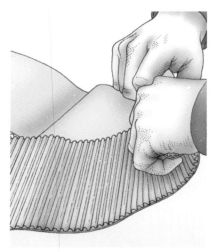

1 **Cut off the bottom** of a 1–2 litre (2–4 pint) plastic drink bottle with a sharp knife. Do not wash it out as any sugary remains are an added attraction. Keep the bottle lid on.

2 **Roll up** a piece of corrugated cardboard. Its width should match the length of the bottle, and the roll should be thick enough so that it fits snugly into the bottle.

3 **Insert the roll** into the bottle and secure it with a piece of string or wire inserted into holes made in the bottle sides. Tie string around the bottle neck and hang it from a tree.

Lacewings, hoverflies & ladybirds

Tolerate some aphids in your garden to ensure sufficient food for these natural predators. Leave stems of herbaceous plants standing through the winter to provide cover and protection for overwintering adults, or make a lacewing and ladybird refuge (*see above*). As with bees, many species of adult hoverfly visit pollen- and nectar-bearing flowers, particularly those with an open centre.

Beetles & centipedes

Rove and ground beetles, identifiable by their black bodies and scurrying habit, are ferocious predators of slugs and other soil pests, as are centipedes. To provide them with cover and good hunting territory, mulch beds with organic matter, grow groundcover plants, leave the soil as undisturbed as possible, and place stones and logs about the garden. Centipedes require a similar habitat.

Butterflies & moths

To enjoy adult butterflies and moths, there must be some tolerance of their caterpillars, which eat plants. It is worth planting swathes of both caterpillar food plants and nectar plants, the latter attracting the largest number of butterflies if planted in full sun. Some butterflies will also feed on fallen fruit, such as apples and pears, if it is left to rot.

Night-flowering plants are needed to attract most moths, although 'sugaring' is also effective. This involves smearing a tree trunk or wooden post with a thick sugary compound such as a black treacle solution.

Hedgehogs

Mulch beds with organic matter to make it easy for hedgehogs to get at their natural foods, including worms, chafer grubs, slugs, and beetles. Provide supplementary feeding with cat food or hedgehog feeds, and put out a bowl of fresh water, but not milk.

Leave some gaps in boundary fencing so hedgehogs can get in and out of your garden. Avoid leaving loose netting or uncovered holes in the garden as these can trap hedgehogs. Steep-sided ponds can cause hedgehogs and other mammals to drown if they fall in; fit ramps covered in chicken wire so they can climb out.

Lizards, slowworms & grass snakes

Lizards and slowworms (legless lizards) can be found in a range of habitats but will be most at home in gardens where there are plenty of rocks and logs for them to hide. Tempt them out by building dry stone walls in a sunny spot. They can sunbathe on the warming stones or hide in the many nooks and crannies.

A corrugated iron sheet makes a great hide-out for grass snakes, and slowworms too. Natural cover can be provided with patches of long, undisturbed grass. Turn compost heaps carefully in case eggs are laid there.

Frogs, toads & newts

A garden pond will act like a magnet to these amphibians, but boggy ground, log piles, and upturned plant pots also attract them and make good hibernation sites.

Hedges

These attractive partitions are very good habitats for garden wildlife. The hedge base becomes a safe highway for reptiles, amphibians, and small mammals, and a dense centre gives birds security for feeding, singing, and nesting. Many hedges bear berries and all support a multitude of spiders and insects that become food for birds, voles, mice, and hedgehogs. As well as providing shelter within, the hedge also acts as a windbreak, creating a warm environment on the lee side that is more likely to attract bumblebees and other pollinating insects.

A mixed hedge selection

Typical native plants for a mixed hedge might include holly, hawthorn, blackthorn, guelder rose, wild privet, spindle, dog rose, dogwood, field maple, and hazel. Non-natives like barberry, pyracantha, and cotoneaster also provide good food resources. Conifers may seem rather barren but they make an excellent wildlife hedge if well maintained; yew has bright red berries loved by blackbirds.

Climbers too can be grown into a hedge. Honeysuckle and ivy are favourites. Make even fuller use of a hedge by allowing some hedgerow trees like crab apple and elder to grow up above the clipped hedge.

Dead hedges

When pruning shrubs, you can use the offcuts to make a 'dead hedge'. First, drive some sturdy stems into the ground to form the uprights. Do this in pairs with a gap down the middle to pack in the prunings horizontally until they reach the top of the uprights. A 'dead hedge' should last for a few years and will be home to many creatures during that time.

HEDGE WILDLIFE

Birds nest in hedges frequently as their dense branches make ideal nesting cradles. Encourage nesting by hanging loose nets of raw materials, like wool, nearby. Avoid trimming hedges during the main nesting season, spring to midsummer.

Wildlife corridors are created by hedges, connecting gardens to each other and to wilder areas, such as neglected land. Unlike a fence or wall, a thick hedge allows animals like foxes and hedgehogs to come and go, while still keeping people out.

Hedge bases are little havens for wild plants and animals. Ivy often grows here, and amid this and collected debris, you will find insects, spiders, and the animals that feed on them. Prune young hedge plants to force low branches to grow (*see page 114*).

A NATIVE SPECIES HEDGE

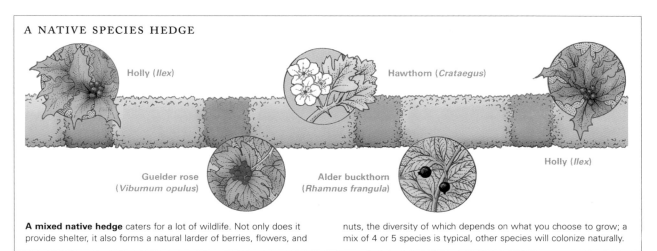

Holly (*Ilex*)

Hawthorn (*Crataegus*)

Holly (*Ilex*)

Guelder rose (*Viburnum opulus*)

Alder buckthorn (*Rhamnus frangula*)

A mixed native hedge caters for a lot of wildlife. Not only does it provide shelter, it also forms a natural larder of berries, flowers, and nuts, the diversity of which depends on what you choose to grow; a mix of 4 or 5 species is typical, other species will colonize naturally.

Wildlife ponds

A good wildlife garden has a variety of water features to provide the greatest range of habitats; these may include a pond, a small cascade with drop pools, a stone trough or barrel, a pebble fountain, or simply a bird bath. Even small balconies can accommodate an old sink filled with rain water, a couple of pond plants, or a dwarf waterlily. With fewer ponds in the countryside than ever before, building a wildlife pond in your garden is extremely worthwhile.

Siting & design

A flexible liner, such as butyl rubber (*see page 309*), gives much more scope to a wildlife-friendly design. Pre-formed and formal ponds often have steep edges, poorly suited to wildlife – they must be fitted with ramps to allow animals that have fallen in to escape.

You will attract the greatest amount of wildlife if at least part of your pond is in sun. A dense marginal planting on at least one side will give young frogs some protection from predators when leaving the pond. A log pile or bog garden (*see page 318*) that adjoins the pond also makes an excellent wildlife shelter and provides a more natural transition between land and water.

Deep-water areas for amphibians to breed and a long, shallow zone or beach are essential. The latter not only provides good access for birds and amphibians but also

Multifaceted, informally designed ponds are the best for wildlife as they include a diversity of niches and habitats. This pond has small waterfalls, dense marginal plantings, lots of hiding places between the rocks, and waterlilies covering part of the water surface.

creates the best habitat for small aquatic creatures that live in the pebbles, mud, and shallow water. The pond edge is also important. Hide the liner by tucking it under turf (*see page 317*). This allows the grass to grow into the pond, making a perfect site for newts to lay their eggs.

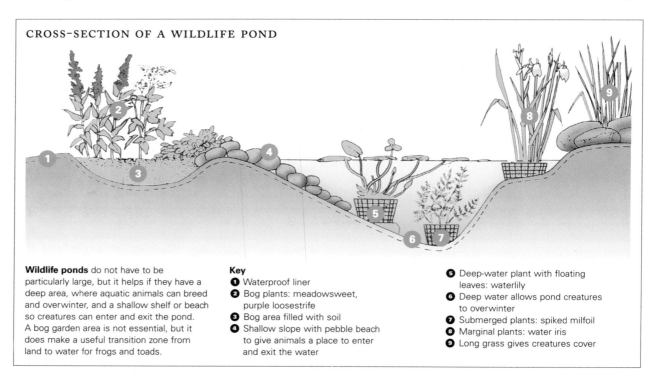

CROSS-SECTION OF A WILDLIFE POND

Wildlife ponds do not have to be particularly large, but it helps if they have a deep area, where aquatic animals can breed and overwinter, and a shallow shelf or beach so creatures can enter and exit the pond. A bog garden area is not essential, but it does make a useful transition zone from land to water for frogs and toads.

Key
1. Waterproof liner
2. Bog plants: meadowsweet, purple loosestrife
3. Bog area filled with soil
4. Shallow slope with pebble beach to give animals a place to enter and exit the water
5. Deep-water plant with floating leaves: waterlily
6. Deep water allows pond creatures to overwinter
7. Submerged plants: spiked milfoil
8. Marginal plants: water iris
9. Long grass gives creatures cover

Large stone slabs or logs also make a good edge, particularly where a few gaps are left to let frogs shelter under the overhang. Lay an old tree branch part in and part out of the water. Dragonflies and damselflies use mossy structures like this for laying their eggs.

Fish & ducks

These animals are not appropriate for a successful wildlife pond, except perhaps for the very largest ponds. Fish are top predators and will make it hard for other aquatic wildlife to compete, especially frogs and newts. Fish and ducks also increase the nutrient content of the water, leading to problems with algae and duckweed.

Children

Gardens where young children play can still be host to a pond; metal grids can be fitted to make them safe (*see page 307*). Alternatively, you could create shallow rills or a bog garden, perhaps by filling in a pre-existing pond with soil. Children should always be supervised around water.

Planting a wildlife pond

This can be left to natural colonization, but most gardeners prefer to plant up directly, as this gives them control over how the pond will look. Choose a range of aquatic plants (*see page 320*). Although it can appear more attractive to leave a big expanse of clear water in the centre of a pond, remember that most aquatic wildlife prefers the security of complex underwater planting.

Introducing plants and animals from other ponds should only be attempted if you are confident that the material is non-invasive and disease free. Never take samples from the wild, or from any pond without the owner's permission. Avoid introducing invasive aquatic weeds (*see page 331*).

Maintaining a wildlife pond

Fill and top up the pond where possible with rain water, but do not be afraid to allow the pond to occasionally dry out, since many invertebrate creatures will survive in the mud at the bottom. Tap water should be used only as a last resort as it can lead to a pH imbalance.

A few leaves falling in the pond is no bad thing, but excessive amounts release toxic compounds into the water as they rot. If netting is used to keep out leaves, ensure it is kept taut to prevent birds or hedgehogs from getting caught. Clear out excessive vegetation and silt in late summer when the water level is at its lowest. Aim to clear only a section or half of the pond in one year to allow re-colonization of wildlife from the undisturbed areas.

ENCOURAGING POND WILDLIFE

Overhanging branches make good perching spots for birds. Larger branches double up as ramps on straight-sided ponds.

Dragonflies and damselflies lay their eggs on moss-covered surfaces, such as half-submerged logs and rocks.

An area of long grass and tall plants at the pond margin is an important haven for young amphibians as they venture out of the pond.

Creating a wildflower area

You can use wildflowers to enrich grassed areas or lawns. The term 'wildflower' usually denotes a native plant, but in a garden setting it is not vital to stick strictly to these; there are many garden variations, as well as non-natives, that have good wildlife interest. Ideally purchase seeds from a local source; never dig up plants from the wild.

Adapting an existing lawn

The simplest way to create a wildflower area is just to let your lawn grow long and let the 'weeds' flower. If the lawn was previously kept free of weeds or a wider range of wildflowers is desired, then you will need to introduce new plants. The most reliable method is to insert plug plants (*see box, facing page, left*) into the grass with the aid of a bulb planter. Bulbs can be introduced in the same way (*see page 84*). Plant in autumn at a density of five to nine per square metre (10 sq ft), having first cut the grass short and removed the clippings.

Excess vigour of grass can be a real problem in a converted lawn. To redress the balance, stop using fertilizers and always remove clippings. In early autumn sow fresh seeds of yellow rattle (*Rhinanthus minor*), a semi-parasitic annual of grass. Rake the grass vigorously prior to sowing to expose some soil, and allow the yellow rattle to seed before mowing.

Spring meadows make use of spring-flowering bulbs and perennials. The area is left uncut until they flower, then left to die down naturally after flowering. The meadow is then kept mown until autumn.

Sowing a meadow

The most satisfactory way to make a meadow is to sow direct onto bare soil in early autumn or spring (*see below*), at a rate of 5g per square metre (¹⁄₄oz per 10 sq ft). For small areas it may be feasible to remove the fertile topsoil and replace it with subsoil. This is not practical for larger

CREATING A WILDFLOWER MEADOW FROM SCRATCH

1 **Remove the topsoil** from the area and fill with less-fertile subsoil 4–6 weeks before sowing. Remove any weeds that appear by hand or with weedkiller, then prepare the ground as for sowing a lawn (*see page 260*).

2 **Bulk up the seed mix** with an equal amount of horticultural sand or barley meal from a pet shop. A typical meadow seed mix consists of 85 percent grass species and 15 percent wildflower species.

3 **Sow the seeds** evenly in early autumn, or spring for heavier soils. Sow half the batch in one direction and half in the opposite direction, before lightly raking in. Water the seeds after sowing and during dry spells.

CONVERTING LAWNS TO MEADOWS

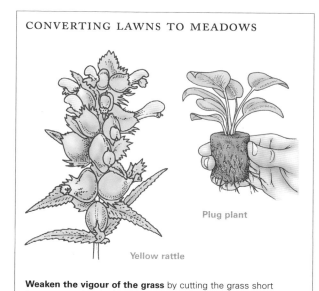

Yellow rattle

Plug plant

Weaken the vigour of the grass by cutting the grass short in autumn and removing the clippings before sowing seeds of yellow rattle. Then insert container-grown wildflower plants into the lawn. Stop using lawn fertilizers.

MOWING A MEADOW

Mow from early autumn to early spring for summer meadows. For spring-flowering meadows, leave them unmown from spring to midsummer, then cut. For an even mix of seasonal flowers, cut just once in early autumn. The height of cut for routine mowing should be no less than 8cm (3in).

When cutting long grass, a hand scythe, power scythe, or strimmer perform well. A rotary mower is suitable for subsequent mowing. Always remove the hay or clippings as this keeps soil fertility low, but hay from the first cut can be left on the surface to dry so that its seeds are dispersed.

areas, although you can still reduce fertility by sowing for a season with oil-seed rape, removing it prior to flowering.

After about 6–8 weeks of growth, cut the meadow to a height of 5–10cm (2–4in), repeating every couple of months throughout the first summer.

Mowing & maintenance

Most meadow mixes contain perennial species that will not flower until their second summer. A meadow tends to be left uncut until its season of interest is over (*see box, above right*). As they can sometimes look untidy in a garden setting, it helps if you define the edges with a closely mown strip and increase interest by mowing a winding path through the centre.

For obvious reasons, selective lawn weedkillers should not be used. Hand weeding may be necessary during establishment of a new meadow to remove undesirable plants like docks, nettles, and thistles. Alternatively, weeds can be spot treated with a glyphosate-based weedkiller.

Cornfield annuals

You can grow cornfield annuals in normal sunny garden borders where soil fertility might be too high for a meadow. Seed mixes are made up of colourful annuals like poppies and cornflowers. Grasses are not usually included, although cereals such as wheat or barley enhance the cornfield effect. Sow fresh seed at 1g (1/30oz) per square metre (10 sq ft) in early autumn for a display lasting from early summer to early autumn, or in spring for a slightly later display.

Summer meadows come into their own towards the end of spring as the grass lengthens. They are mown once the display is over.

WILDLIFE PLANTS

Wildlife is incredibly adaptable to the built environment, but remove plants from the equation and the majority of animals would struggle to survive. From providing organic material for soil organisms to making nesting sites for garden birds, plants perform a myriad of roles. In fact, the act of simply growing plants is probably more important than any other single wildlife gardening activity, and the wider the diversity of plants you grow, the more wildlife you are likely to attract to your garden. Plants are also used to link green areas together, making your garden part of a larger and greater wildlife entity.

Choosing plants

You could say that all gardens are wildlife gardens, but some plants provide more resources for wildlife than others. Before you get bogged down in choosing the 'right' plants, start by deciding on how to use plants to create the most diverse habitats. One way to do this is by varying the heights of planting (*see below*), from low-lying lawns and pond plants, through to long meadow grasses, herbaceous plants, small shrubs, climbers, and finally trees.

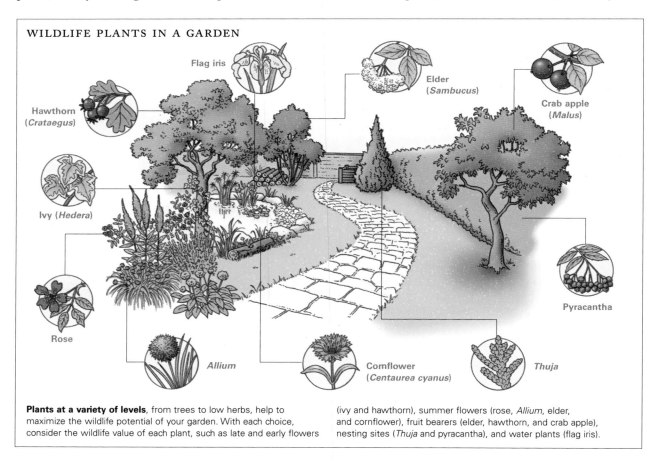

WILDLIFE PLANTS IN A GARDEN

Flag iris
Elder (*Sambucus*)
Crab apple (*Malus*)
Hawthorn (*Crataegus*)
Ivy (*Hedera*)
Rose
Allium
Cornflower (*Centaurea cyanus*)
Thuja
Pyracantha

Plants at a variety of levels, from trees to low herbs, help to maximize the wildlife potential of your garden. With each choice, consider the wildlife value of each plant, such as late and early flowers (ivy and hawthorn), summer flowers (rose, *Allium*, elder, and cornflower), fruit bearers (elder, hawthorn, and crab apple), nesting sites (*Thuja* and pyracantha), and water plants (flag iris).

Purple loosestrife (*Lythrum salicaria*) has late flowers, attractive to bees and butterflies.

Sweet rocket (*Hesperis matronalis*) bears flowers that are very attractive to insects.

Red valerian (*Centranthus ruber*) flowers all summer long, attracting butterflies.

Native verses non-native

You may choose to restrict yourself to growing native plants. However, studies have shown that there are many non-natives that are excellent for wildlife and, unless there is a desire to attract a highly specialized insect or animal, then the need to plant natives at the exclusion of non-natives is hardly justified. The good news is that plants known to be useful to wildlife include a good proportion of ornamentals, which means wildlife gardens can be packed with attractive plants.

The need for trees

Trees, by their very size, are vital to a good wildlife garden. If there are trees in neighbouring gardens and your patch is very small then leave it at that. But if there is a dearth of trees in the area, see if you can make room for one. Whitebeams, rowans, apples, cherries, and hawthorns are all reasonably sized. Consider the impact on your neighbours when planting trees close to boundaries.

Nectar & pollen

Wildlife that visits flowers tends to be adult butterflies and moths, bees, adult hoverflies, and pollen beetles. Choose open, single flowers where the pollen or nectar is readily available, and look for plants with a long flowering season or those that flower particularly early or late in the year when other food sources are scarce.

Berries, fruit & seeds

Relieve some of the time and expense of feeding garden birds with bird food by stocking your garden with plants that offer berries, fruit, and seeds. It is a joy to watch goldfinches eating seeds from your evening primroses,

blackbirds devouring windfallen apples, and fieldfares feasting on holly berries. The principles are very simple; check before you plant to see if a shrub or tree needs separate male and female plants to fruit, and avoid cutting back seed heads until late winter. Other creatures such as mice, voles, and even foxes also enjoy these natural meals.

Larval food plants

It is leaf-eating creatures, especially the larvae of moths, butterflies, and leaf beetles, that are perhaps most fussy about their food plants. If you want to attract a particular butterfly, for instance, it is best to do your homework and find out which plants are needed for the caterpillar stage. Some of these plants may be grasses, so it would make sense to plan a wildflower meadow (*see page 52*) with the desirable grass species in the mix. Plant dense groups of the same plant in large numbers to convince the egg-laying females that your patch will support many hungry mouths. And, of course, be prepared to tolerate some leaf damage.

Planting for small gardens

With gardens getting ever smaller, plants need to be high performers. Those that provide multiple resources – for example by producing not just nectar and pollen, but also seeds, foliage for herbivores, and a dense nesting habitat – are worth including in even the smallest of spaces.

For height, plant a silver birch, holly, hawthorn, or elder, with honeysuckle or ivy grown into the canopy. Lavender and chives are good wildlife plants for pots, while colourful annuals like English marigolds and cornflowers are simple to grow. Red valerian, teasle, sweet rocket, and purple loosestrife will sit happily with other plants in a border.

CHAPTER THREE

GROWING ORNAMENTALS

GARDEN DESIGN BASICS 60

PLACING PLANTS 66

ANNUAL PLANTS 74

HERBACEOUS PERENNIALS 77

BULBOUS PLANTS 83

TREES & SHRUBS 88

HEDGES 113

ROSES 117

CLIMBERS & WALL PLANTS 130

PLANTS GROWN FOR THEIR BEAUTY ARE KNOWN AS ORNAMENTALS. They are planted so that their flowers, scent, foliage, autumn colour, berries, or winter bark can be admired and make our outdoor living spaces beautiful places to be. Creating an ornamental garden is simple if you follow a few basic design rules. Any size of plot, even a balcony, roof space, or tiny courtyard, can accommodate ornamentals.

Types of plants

An understanding of different plant types is required if a design is going to be attractive all year. Some modern designs use planting schemes like single beds of lavender, but gardens are usually more exciting if there is a mix of plants that either complement or contrast in shape, colour, and texture.

Perennials are essentially non-woody plants that live for at least two years. Most die back in winter to ground level and reappear in spring. Annuals grow from seed to flower and then die all in one year, and include many vegetables and some bedding plants, while biennials send out their growth in the first year, flower in the second year, and then die. Bedding plants, usually half-hardy annuals or perennials, are grown for a temporary display and are frequently used in hanging baskets and containers.

Trees and shrubs have a permanent woody structure, may be deciduous or evergreen, and their key features can include flowers, berries, and foliage. Trees usually have one central trunk, while shrubs are usually multi-stemmed and relatively small. A large garden is needed for trees such as oak, beech, or chestnut, but much smaller trees like flowering cherries and Japanese maples can be grown in smaller spaces or even containers.

The key to growing any of these plants successfully is choosing the right plants for the location. Select plants compatible with the soil in your garden; basic soil testing kits can be bought from garden centres. Some plants are sun-lovers while others prefer to dwell in the shade, so check which areas of your garden receive sunlight and at what time of day. Frost hardiness also varies, so overnight temperatures will determine which plants can be grown.

Types of garden

Personal taste will be the main driving force when designing a garden, but it is worth being aware of the different types of gardens and what will suit your needs and plot before starting a design.

A family garden should be as spacious as the plot allows. Lawns provide a soft surface for play, ideally near the house. A patio for dining is useful, as is outdoor storage for toys, bikes, and garden furniture. Avoid poisonous or spiky plants, ponds and water features, and instal secure gates and fences.

Urban gardens and courtyards are usually small spaces, usually surrounded by buildings. The design is often contemporary or formal, with modern hard landscaping material and decking, and low-maintenance architectural plants rather than lawns. Climbers are useful to clothe walls and fences.

Wildlife gardens are increasingly popular. Informal native planting encourages local wildlife: shrubs, hedges, and trees for nesting, meadow grass for a host of insects, and ponds with sloping edges for drinking holes.

Romantic cottage gardens use informal drifts of relaxed planting in wide beds along informal paths, and climbing plants scramble over walls, fences, or rustic pergolas. With the addition of fruit trees against walls, and vegetables and herbs informally mixed into borders, an ornamental garden can be wonderfully varied.

GARDEN DESIGN BASICS

A garden must be functional as well as beautiful to be enjoyed to the full. Early planning is critical in creating a garden that is practical and cohesive. Visit gardens and shows with a notepad to jot down ideas and features that you like, and read magazines for ideas and inspiration. Creating a new garden can be expensive, so you should set a realistic budget from the start when choosing materials to avoid disappointment later on. Buying plants and hard landscaping material, hiring machinery, or paying for the skills of electricians for lighting or water features all adds up financially.

Making a start

From a design point of view, it is easiest to begin with a blank canvas, but most people will be starting with an existing garden and hoping to make changes that will suit their lifestyle and taste.

Deciding what to keep

Begin by making a list of key features in the existing garden that could be tweaked, salvaged, or incorporated into your own plans. There will be no choice but to include some existing features in the design, including trees with preservation orders, surrounding buildings, and dimensions of the plot. Consider how these can be worked into the design of the new garden. Check also that there are no legal covenants that might restrict your plan, such as limits on the height of trees and hedges.

Avoid committing to anything until you have seen the garden in each of its different seasons; gardens look very different in winter and summer. What might appear to be a private and secluded garden in summer might suddenly be overlooked by unsightly buildings in winter when the

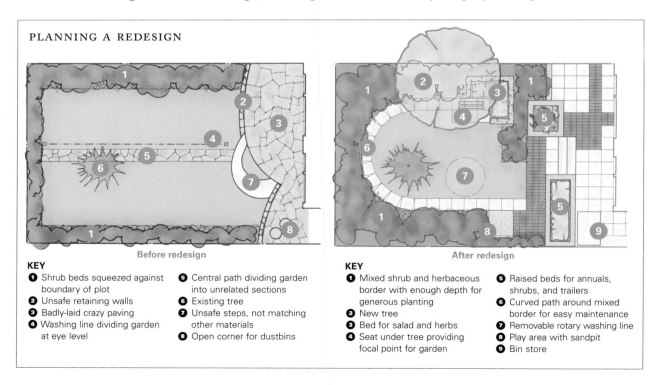

PLANNING A REDESIGN

Before redesign

After redesign

KEY
1. Shrub beds squeezed against boundary of plot
2. Unsafe retaining walls
3. Badly-laid crazy paving
4. Washing line dividing garden at eye level
5. Central path dividing garden into unrelated sections
6. Existing tree
7. Unsafe steps, not matching other materials
8. Open corner for dustbins

KEY
1. Mixed shrub and herbaceous border with enough depth for generous planting
2. New tree
3. Bed for salad and herbs
4. Seat under tree providing focal point for garden
5. Raised beds for annuals, shrubs, and trailers
6. Curved path around mixed border for easy maintenance
7. Removable rotary washing line
8. Play area with sandpit
9. Bin store

LOCATION & DESIGN

Small town gardens can have unappealing views or be overlooked. It may be necessary to enclose the space using fences, walls, or evergreen hedges and trees.

Suburban gardens allow for a broader canvas and may have features in the background that either need screening or – if they are attractive – incorporated into the view.

Rural gardens may back onto fields or other beautiful views. If you are this lucky, keep fences or walls low to incorporate the large sweep of scenery into your garden.

leaves have fallen from the trees. Make a note of all the plants that flowered throughout the year and earmark the ones that you want to save or remove.

Planning your new garden

Consider where the garden is predominantly going to be viewed from. This is usually from one or more of the windows in the house, so study these views before committing a design to reality.

The location of the garden will influence its design. In rural or village locations you may borrow views, while in urban spaces you could need to block them. Gardens near busy roads will need screening from the noise and fences and gates incorporated to keep children and pets safe.

It is important that the style of the garden is in keeping with the design of the house. Contemporary, chic gardens work with a modern house but can look out of place around a rustic old cottage. Use bricks, paving slabs, and other hard landscaping materials that blend in with the architectural features of the surrounding buildings.

Making a sketch

The next stage is to make a simple aerial plan of the garden. Outline the boundaries, the edge of the house, and any features that are definitely staying. Then fill in the additional features that you would like to see in the garden, such as paths, lawns, flower beds, patios, focal points, and utility areas like sheds and compost heaps.

Keep the sketch simple – detailed planting plans can be created of individual features. Add notes about colour, style, and season of interest.

You can use a computer design package, which is easier to manipulate as you develop your plans. Otherwise, draw a sketch of the garden using graph paper for scale and proportion. The plan will be a work in progress and will probably need frequent tweaking when the work starts.

Gardens are viewed from the ground, either from seating outside or from windows. Take your plan and visualize it from these vantage points, perhaps using sketches or drawing on photographs.

Function & practicality

A garden should be not only beautiful, but also practical. Bear in mind the principle that 'form follows function' and create the design around the practical requirements. Otherwise the garden may well become unuseable.

Some basic requirements, such as a shed, a compost area, washing line, or place for the bins, are not very attractive. If a garden is large enough, make one area the 'working' part of the garden. Screen it with trellis or hedging and tuck it out of sight where it does not impinge on the overall design. Avoid placing it at the back of the garden, because it will be a long walk to hang out the washing or put out bins, and try to avoid creating straight, purely functional paths to these utility areas.

Simplicity

Start by concentrating on the composition as a whole before focusing on the smaller design details. A well-designed garden should flow together as a single entity with all the elements in the right place. Simplicity is key to a relaxing and pleasurable space, and is most important in small spaces. Complicated spaces with a plethora of features become disjointed and messy.

Harmony & balance

Objects or plants placed randomly without relation to the style of garden lose their alluring qualities and look cluttered and awkward. In any size of garden, harmony is

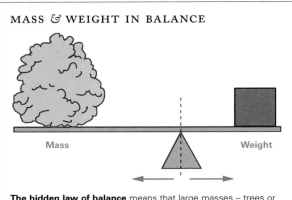

MASS & WEIGHT IN BALANCE

Mass   Weight

The hidden law of balance means that large masses – trees or shrubs – visually balance weightier objects, like walls or buildings. Their size and distance can vary from the centre of balance.

important. A garden without it has a sense of conflict and clashes with the senses. Keep a simple continuous or cohesive theme, such as using the same paving materials for the paths throughout the garden.

Balance is also important (*see below*). Without it, a space feels awkward. A simple example of balance is using two upright trees in containers on either side of an entrance; a tree on just one side would be incongruous. Sometimes balance is more subtle than such mirror symmetry, with the height of a tree one side balanced by the weight of mass planting on the other (*see box, above*).

BALANCE IN PLANTING DESIGN

Sparse planting allows hard landscaping materials and expanses of grass to dominate and draw the eye. It creates a dull, unbalanced space with little foreground interest.

Massed planting balances the tree and large areas of grass, holding attention on the path. The tree now balances the weight of the foreground planting, drawing the eye beyond them.

FOCAL POINTS

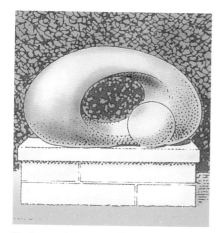

Modern sculptures are often organic shapes that look perfectly at home in a garden.

Gazebos and summerhouses provide a focal point as well as a vantage point.

Individual specimen trees or dramatic foliage plants can be planted as natural focal points.

Focal points & intrigue

Every garden should have focal points to give a sense of purpose to a space and draw you from one area to another. Have only one focal point in any vista, and just one centrally placed focal point in a small courtyard garden. Simple focal points could include a water feature, a statue or sundial, a tree, a view, or even a splash of colour from a strategically placed flower bed. Design the surrounding parts of the garden to blend in and reinforce this focus, with paths, low hedges, and walls leading up towards the focal point.

Remember that if all features of a garden can be seen at once, the space can feel dull. Partially conceal areas of the garden to create a sense of intrigue and excitement.

Garden rooms

Divide large areas, especially long, narrow spaces, into garden 'rooms' to add structure and create different areas of interest. They should never be completely independent but flow from one to another. Create partitions with trellis, arches, or even just a change in planting style. In a small space, low walls divide areas without restriction.

SCREENING

Vertical and horizontal screening can provide both privacy and protection from the elements, whether wind or overhead sun. Here, overhead timbers, fencing, and planting enclose the dining area.

CREATING INTRIGUE

Create a little intrigue by strategically planting trees and shrubs, erecting a screen to hide the end of a path, or creating alcoves or garden rooms using trellis and low walls. A suggestion of a hidden space entices people to explore, and even hiding a functional area behind a screen makes a garden seem more complex and interesting.

Plant qualities

Plants are usually selected for their flower colour, but they can also provide interesting foliage, seedheads, texture, and architectural qualities. When creating a planting list, select a range of plants that provide interest all year.

Shrubs and trees form the framework, usually at the back of a mixed border behind smaller herbaceous plants. Trees also make superb focal points. Choose carefully, because some trees quickly outgrow their allotted space.

Generally, larger herbaceous plants are placed at the back of a border and lower ones in front, using groups of odd numbers (usually three and five). The rules are not rigid; a border is far more interesting if occasional larger plants are closer to the front or partially obscure the view.

Clever colour
Colour planning is essential, because some colours clash, so use a colour wheel to work out which work well together. Colours can create moods and atmospheres. Hot, fiery colours tend to excite emotions, while paler colours appear tranquil or can lighten heavy planting.

Bright, hot colours, such as reds and oranges, tend to seem closer than they really are, while cool, pale colours, such as pastels, blues, or whites seem further away. Pale colours further away from the house can make a garden seem larger, while placing hot colours at the furthest end of a long thin space makes it appear shorter.

Restful green & lawns
Green is a neutral background colour and in foliage or lawns can be used as a foil for many brighter colours. There are many shades of green, and interest can be created with foliage alone.

The soft surface of a lawn is an attractive feature in any garden, and in larger gardens lawns can unify a whole area. Consider interesting shapes, such as circles or ellipses, or even other groundcover materials such as decking, paving, or shingle.

Emphasize long borders and focal points through careful use of colour. Placing warm colours at the front and pale colours further away can seem too simple to work, but the subtle shift lengthens the vista.

A jungle feel in this courtyard garden is created by a range of foliage textures and shades of green. The overall effect is increased by the splash of hot red *Crocosmia* flowers.

PLACING PLANTS

Choosing the right plant for the right place should be the guiding principle when buying any plant for your garden. Plants for a sunny location will have to endure baking hot conditions all day long. Even in temperate climates mini-heatwaves are not unusual, and plants need to tolerate drought if they are to stand any chance of survival. Every garden also has shaded areas, and many gardeners are inclined to see these as problem areas. It is true that profusely flowering annuals will not perform in such conditions, but shade-loving plants range from elegant to dramatic, and a shady spot need never be dull.

Gardens in sun

Plenty of plants revel in hot sun, but some can be frost-tender and may require protection from the elements over winter. Drought-tolerant plants are a good choice but they may struggle with wet autumn and winter weather. Add grit and sand to the soil to alleviate this problem.

Look beyond bright summer flowers

Bright bedding and half-hardy annuals can create a kaleidoscope of colour in sun, and they can be followed with winter bedding, but perennial plants provide more subtle hues. Climbers and shrubs, such as campsis and cistus, also provide impressive floral displays. Try to co-ordinate schemes and avoid clashing colours.

Drifts of colour that extend to both sides of the border are key to prairie-style perennial planting. In all styles, herbaceous plants look most natural planted in odd-numbered groups of 3 or more.

Most fruit plants thrive in sunny locations that help the fruit ripen fully to develop high sugar levels and sweet flavours. Grapevines can be grown over pergolas, while sweet cherries, peaches, and apricots can all be trained as fans on sunny walls. Strawberries are good choices for growing in hanging baskets or containers.

Foliage plants

Many plants that flourish in the hot sun have silvery or velvety foliage to cope with the heat, and most of the herbs with edible or aromatic foliage are sun-lovers. Many ornamental grasses can cope with dry weather and also offer interest through winter months. The same is true of dramatic foliage plants like yuccas, cordylines, agaves, the banana *Musa basjoo*, and palms such as *Trachycarpus fortunei* or *Chamaerops humilis*. Plenty of evergreen shrubs and conifers tolerate drought and give structure and colour during winter.

Style & structure

Look to naturally sunny places for design inspiration. Prairie planting combines ornamental grasses and hot-coloured herbaceous perennials. Mediterranean styles use silvery foliage shrubs and herbs with pergolas, trees, and outdoor dining areas, but these plants need good drainage. Subtropical gardens, with luxuriant growth, foliage, and exotic flowers, are better for heavier, more moist soils.

Create height at the back of borders with shrubs and tall herbaceous perennials like delphiniums or sunflowers. Train climbers like sweet peas, which adore the sun so long as they have nutrient-rich soil, on structures of pea sticks or bamboo canes. Place these taller plants carefully to avoid casting shade on other plantings.

PLANTS FOR SUN

PERENNIALS AND ANNUALS

Achillea **'Moonshine' (shown)** Feathery grey foliage and flat yellow flowerheads.

Calamagrostis x *acutiflora* **'Karl Foerster'** Tall grass for prairie planting with perennials. Summer flowerheads last well in to winter.

Delphinium Traditional back-of-the-border favourite for its blue spires. Needs fertile soil.

Eryngium bourgatii Silver bracts on branching blue stems last well for winter displays. Prefers a poor soil.

Eschscholzia californica Intense orange and yellow annuals for well-drained, poor soil.

Perovskia **'Blue Spire' (shown)** Spires of bright blue flowers and silvery-grey foliage.

Red hot poker (*Kniphofia***)** Leave foliage over winter to protect from cold.

Salvia argentea Rosettes of velvety silver leaves make a perfect foil for bright bedding. Remove flowers for best foliage display.

Sunflower (*Helianthus annuus***)** Wide range of colours and heights to choose from.

Verbena bonariensis Purple flowerheads on wiry stems sway above lower planting. It readily self-seeds.

BULBS

Allium cristophii Globes of purple flowers are held aloft in spring; they dry well.

Crocosmia **'Lucifer' (shown)** Clumps of searing red flowers in summer.

Tulipa **'Queen of Night'** Dark maroon-black blooms; tulips like well-drained sunny sites.

CLIMBERS

Campsis **'Madame Galen'** Grow against a wall for orange, trumpet-like blooms.

Passiflora caerulea Glossy foliage, exotic flowers and occasional inedible yellow fruit.

Rose climbers and ramblers Hundreds to choose from; most perform best in full sun.

Vitis **'Brant'** This grape variety has both fruit and impressive autumnal foliage.

Wisteria **(shown)** Long racemes of purple flowers. Likes a wall with afternoon sun.

TREES & SHRUBS

Abelia x *grandiflora* Fragrant white flowers in summer on arching, semi-evergreen stems.

Artemisia **'Powis Castle' (shown)** Silvery foliage for rock garden or border.

Bottlebrush (*Callistemon***)** Evergreen with striking red flowers and attractive seeds.

Calluna vulgaris Varieties of this popular heather require an acidic soil.

Ceanothus Deciduous or evergreen shrubs with blue flowers, good against sunny walls.

Choisya ternata **Sundance ('Lich')** Scented yellow foliage shrub, intense colour in sun.

Euphorbia characias subsp. *wulfenii* Shrub with lime-green flowers; a foil for perennials.

Helianthemum **'Wisley Primrose'** Low shrub with yellow, saucer-shaped flowers. Suited to dry conditions.

Lavandula angustifolia **'Hidcote'** Scented, bright blue flower spikes and silvery foliage.

Olive (*Olea europaea***)** Attractive silvery foliage and gnarled bark when mature.

Phlomis fruticosa Evergreen shrub with grey-green aromatic foliage and yellow flowers.

Rock rose (*Cistus***)** Drought-tolerant shrub with large, yellow-centred white flowers.

Rosemary (*Rosmarinus***) (shown)** Ideal for dry conditions, with usually blue flowers.

Thyme (*Thymus***)** Low-growing herb for well-drained, low-nutrient soil.

Crocosmia **'Lucifer'** can self-seed, so dig up seedlings, which will be inferior in quality.

Achillea **'Moonshine'** does well in a dry soil, but may only be short-lived.

Artemisia **'Powis Castle'** is a striking foliage plant pruned in spring to keep it compact.

Wisteria sinensis flowers in late spring or early summer. It takes a few years to flower.

Perovskia **'Blue Spire'** prefers a soil that is well-drained but fertile. Prune hard in spring.

Rosemary is a shrubby herb with glossy, aromatic leaves widely used in cooking.

Gardens in shade

An area of shade in a garden should be treated as an asset. There are many plants suited to these conditions, offering a diverse palette of textures and colours. With lower light levels the flower colours are usually softer and more subdued than those of sun-loving plants, creating tranquil havens from the heat of the midday sun.

Types of shade

Light levels range from the dense shade cast by large buildings and evergreen trees to the dappled shade of a deciduous canopy, which can be underplanted with woodland spring bulbs. Canopies can be lightened by thinning tree crowns. Experiment with plants and work with the conditions to create drama and intrigue.

Dry shade is found near buildings or under trees and shrubs that leach moisture from the soil; it creates challenging conditions. Add organic matter to the soil to retain moisture, and water young plants frequently to get them established. For ground cover, try periwinkles (*Vinca*), deadnettles (*Lamium*), epimediums, heucheras, hardy geraniums, and the shrub *Mahonia aquifolium*.

Most woodland bulbs prefer slightly damp or moisture-retentive soil in dappled sunlight, where ligularias and primroses are worth trying. Only moisture plants such as *Trollius europaeus* or *Caltha palustris* enjoy sitting permanently in water in moderate shade.

Large, lush leaves are characteristic of shade-loving plants, so exploit them to make a garden built from texture rather than vibrant colour.

Not many plants flower in deep shade. Evergreen conifer woods are hostile environments where little or nothing can grow, and deciduous woodland plants grow and flower early in the year, before the trees are in full leaf.

Flowers & fruit in shade

Plant bulbs in large clumps, and – for temporary displays – bedding plants like polyanthus primroses, busy Lizzies (*Impatiens*), and begonias. These can also be grown in containers and placed in shade, with new containers replacing them when the display is over.

Cyclamen, winter aconites (*Eranthis*), hellebores, and snowdrops provide a late winter floral display, while mahonia and daphne flowers provide an intoxicating fragrance at the shrub level. The highlight of the year is spring, with shrubs like camellias, rhododendrons, and bluebells (*Hyacinthoides*), and anemones carpeting the ground. Even species daffodils like *Narcissus bulbocodium* work well in light shade. Nothing is more spectacular in a woodland garden than *Cardiocrinum giganteum*, with its display of white summer flowers, and the late-summer flowerheads of *Hydrangea paniculata*.

Even some fruit is suited to shade. Train gooseberries or red currants as fans on shaded walls and let wild strawberries cover the ground under a deciduous canopy.

Foliage interest

The glossy leaves of evergreen shrubs like camellias and rhododendrons provide all-year interest; for a more exotic look try the palm-shaped leaves of *Fatsia japonica*. Distribute evergreens throughout the planting scheme so that shades of green create a backdrop to the flowers. Japanese maples are also wonderful foliage plants for areas in dappled shade.

Hostas and ferns are popular foliage perennials, adding texture and a splash of subtle colour to any planting. *Bergenia cordifolia*, known as elephant ears for the shape of the leaves, is worth trying for dry shade.

Structure & seasonal change

Creating tiers of interest is easier in a shade garden than a sunny garden, because you do not need to worry about taller plants casting shade over smaller ones.

Trees and shrubs like maples or viburnums can provide the backbone to any design. If possible, clothe shade-creating trees or buildings with shade-loving climbers like ivies (*Hedera*), climbing hydrangea, or winter jasmine. Perennials and bulbs create seasonal interest.

GARDENS IN SHADE

Looking after your soil *see page 16* | **Garden design basics** *see page 60* | **Container gardening** *see page 338*

PLANTS FOR SHADE

PERENNIALS & BULBS

Ajuga reptans Glossy, evergreen perennial ground cover with blue spikes of flowers.

Cardiocrinum giganteum Dramatic, 2m (6ft) tall bulbous plant with white trumpet flowers.

Cyclamen coum (shown) Tuberous perennial with white to pink flowers in late winter to spring.

Erythronium 'Pagoda' Slender stems carry pale yellow spring flowers; for moist areas.

Galium odoratum Ground cover perennial with whorls of narrow leaves and small, white starry flowers in summer.

Helleborus niger The Christmas rose is a low-growing perennial that bears large nodding flowers in early spring.

Hosta (shown) Perennial for moist conditions with bold foliage and spires of white or lilac flowers.

Kirengeshoma palmata Large palmate foliage and yellow bell-shaped flowers in late summer.

Lamium maculatum 'White Nancy' Ground cover with silvery leaves and white flowers.

Lily of the valley (*Convallaria majalis*) Scented white flowers; can be invasive.

Pachysandra terminalis Perennial evergreen with dark green leaves and small white spring flowers. Prefers moist soil but tolerates dry.

Solomon's seal (*Polygonatum x hybridum*) White bell-shaped flowers hanging from arching stems in spring.

Trillium (shown) Spring-flowering perennials for slightly acidic, moist but well-drained soil.

Waldsteinia ternata Ground cover for dry sites, with toothed foliage and yellow flowers.

Winter aconite (*Eranthis hyemalis*) An ideal ground cover with golden flowers in winter.

SHRUBS & TREES

Aucuba japonica Tough evergreen shrub with gold-marked foliage that creates a splash of lighter colour in the shade.

Camellia Shrubs with glossy, dark evergreen leaves and white to pink or red flowers.

Cotoneaster horizontalis (shown) Useful for ground cover or trained on a wall.

Crinodendron hookerianum Evergreen shrub with red, hanging flowers.

Dicksonia antarctica Hardy tree fern with attractive fronds and a tall fibrous trunk.

Garrya elliptica Spectacular silver-grey catkins in winter and early spring. Tolerates moderate shade and poor dry soil.

Hydrangea paniculata (shown) Woodland shrub with huge, cone-shaped flowerheads.

Itea ilicifolia Evergreen shrub ideal for planting against shady walls, with holly-like foliage and long catkins.

Ivy (*Hedera*) Train ivies on shady walls or use them as ground cover. Varieties include many variegated forms, such as 'Sulphur Heart'.

Japanese maple (*Acer palmatum*) (shown) Spectacular foliage in autumn.

Rhododendron Woodland shrubs, including azaleas, for dappled shade and acidic soil.

Rubus cockburnianus Ornamental bramble with ghostly white stems, at its best in winter.

Ruscus aculeatus Evergreen subshrub with spine-tipped leaves, suitable for dry shade. Female plants produce small reddish berries.

Sarcococca confusa Evergreen shrub with highly fragrant, white winter flowers.

Vinca minor Ground cover shrub for dry partial shade, with blue flowers over long periods in summer.

Trillium grandiflorum flowers usually open white but fade to pink or lilac.

Japanese maples (*Acer palmatum*) prefer a sheltered spot in dappled shade.

Hydrangea paniculata stems should be cut back to two buds in spring for the best flowers.

Cotoneaster horizontalis bears more flowers and berries in sun but is still useful in shade.

Hosta 'Gold Standard' is typical of a wide range of strongly marked, large-leaved hostas.

Cyclamen coum flowers in varied shades of pink above mottled, heart-shaped leaves.

The spring garden

Bulb-filled borders are almost essential in spring. Planted with perennials to carry on the display, bulbs can die down naturally.

To give structure and good value at other times of the year, choose spring-flowering trees and shrubs that also offer autumn colour, berries, or ornamental bark. For colour, plant bulbs to flower throughout spring. The bulb flowers will show through the bare branches of deciduous shrubs and, later, their dying foliage will be hidden by the shrubs' newly emerging leaves. For frost-prone gardens it is best to avoid slightly tender plants, such as camellias and magnolias; if their buds or flowers are blackened by frost they spoil the garden. Use natural materials like twigs for staking emerging summer perennials.

PLANTS FOR SPRING

PERENNIALS & BULBS

Crocus Low-growing spring or autumn flowers, these can be planted either in containers, at the front of a border, or naturalized in drifts on lawns.

Daffodil (Narcissus) Every garden should make room for this spring favourite. They will tolerate damper conditions than tulips.

Hyacinthus Prized for their spikes of scented tubular flowers, hyacinths need fertile, well-drained soil in full sun or light shade.

Primula Cowslips and other primulas are beautiful naturalized in damp, grassy meadows and banks. There are a range of colours.

Tulipa (shown) Plant these in sunny, well-drained soil; the bright colours of the hybrids will put colour into any border.

TREES & SHRUBS

Amelanchier lamarckii Shrub or small tree with profuse star-shaped white flowers, followed by purple-black berries and vibrant autumn colour.

Camellia Evergreen spring-flowering shrub requiring acid soil and a sheltered spot. It can be trained against a shady wall.

Chaenomeles x superba 'Crimson and Gold' An early-flowering shrub that produces deep red flowers. Suitable for training against walls, ornamental quinces have the added attraction of producing attractive, though unpalatable, fruit in autumn.

Crab apple (Malus) Ornamental apple trees such as 'Golden Hornet' or 'John Downie' are ideal for a small garden, providing masses of blossom in spring and attractive crab apples in autumn.

Flowering currant (Ribes sanguineum) (shown) These ornamental currants produce abundant, deep reddish-pink flowers in pendulous clusters with little maintenance. The strong aroma of the leaves can be too pungent for some.

Forsythia x intermedia Providing a bright splash of gold when its flowers appear in spring on the bare branches, this deciduous shrub can also be used as attractive hedging.

Laburnum x watereri 'Vossii' Deciduous tree that provides a spectacular display of long racemes of bright yellow flowers.

Magnolia stellata (shown) This compact magnolia has white, star-shaped flowers and can be grown on alkaline soil.

Rhododendron Mostly evergreen woodland plants, although deciduous azaleas also belong to this group.

Tulipa 'China Pink' and others are best planted in large groups for maximum impact.

Magnolia stellata makes a wonderful specimen flowering tree.

Ribes sanguineum 'King Edward VII' is compact with dark red flowers and bluish fruit.

The summer garden

Give planting schemes a twist by thinking about shapes, heights, textures, and foliage colours, as well as the flower colour palette.

The vibrant colours and textures of bedding, bulbs, and perennials take centre stage as the garden fills out in summer. Summer bedding is used not just for single beds, but as quick gap fillers, or in hanging baskets and containers. Shrubs and trees become less prominent in summer, with the exception of roses.

Formal rose beds are less common nowadays; instead, you can let ramblers sprawl through cottage-garden plants, and mix soft-coloured old roses with traditional border perennials like catmints (*Nepeta*), penstemons, and delphiniums for a contemporary, vibrant feel.

PLANTS FOR SUMMER

ANNUALS, PERENNIALS & BULBS

***Allium hollandicum* 'Purple Sensation'** This ornamental onion produces large, purple, globe-shaped flowers. Plant them in drifts in sunny borders.

***Astrantia major* 'Claret'** Classic herbaceous perennial producing claret-coloured, pincushion flowers during summer.

Daylily (*Hemerocallis*) The combination of showy red, orange, or yellow flowers and long strap-like foliage make daylilies an outstanding perennial for the front of the border.

***Echinacea purpurea* 'White Swan'** Coneflowers are herbaceous perennials popular for prairie-style planting. This one bears white flowers with deep yellow centres from late summer to autumn.

Echinops ritro A tall architectural, thistle-like plant for the border with metallic-blue, spherical flowerheads in late summer.

***Geranium* (shown)** These hardy herbaceous perennials flower from midsummer to autumn in shades of white, pink, and blue.

Lobelia Popular summer bedding for border edging and containers. Trailing varieties are useful for hanging baskets.

***Miscanthus sinensis* (shown)** The many varieties of this deciduous, perennial grass have impressive green foliage and tassels of flowers in late summer that last well into winter.

***Penstemon* 'Blackbird'** This useful herbaceous perennial produces spires of tubular, deep purple flowers.

Phlox paniculata Popular herbaceous border plant in a wide range of varieties and colours, including blue, pink, and red.

***Salvia x sylvestris* 'Mainacht'** Many tender salvias are used as bedding, but this is a hardy perennial with purple spires of flowers.

TREES & SHRUBS

Calluna vulgaris There are a wide range of heather varieties available, producing spikes of small, bell-shaped flowers from midsummer into autumn.

Fuchsia magellanica This easy, hardy shrub produces abundant red and purple hanging flowers from midsummer to autumn.

***Philadelphus* 'Belle Étoile'** A deciduous shrub, this mock orange produces a mass of white, scented flowers with yellow centres from late spring to early summer.

***Rosa filipes* 'Kiftsgate'** Popular rambling rose producing large clusters of scented cream flowers. Train over a large tree or wall.

Rose varieties come in almost every colour so can be included in most planting schemes.

***Miscanthus sinensis* 'Zebrinus'** has sturdy green foliage banded with yellow stripes.

Geranium 'Johnson's Blue' flowers profusely from midsummer to autumn.

The autumn garden

Late border colour from echinaceas, rudbeckias, and asters is one reason for the popularity of prairie-style planting.

With careful planning you can create a garden where the fiery colour from flowers, berries, and spectacular foliage lasts through the fading light of autumn into winter. For large gardens, *Nyssa sylvatica* or *Liquidambar styraciflua* are ideal trees; for smaller gardens use birches (*Betula*), *Sorbus*, or Japanese maples (*Acer*). Aim for a varied range of berries in the garden, from white to red, perhaps from hedges of evergreens like holly (*Ilex*). In the border, clumps of late-flowering perennials replace the fading flowers of summer, and many will provide structure and texture with seed heads that persist throughout winter.

PLANTS FOR AUTUMN

PERENNIALS & BULBS

***Aster amellus* 'King George' (shown)** This classic border perennial provides purple daisy flowers with yellow centres.
Colchicum autumnale Ideal bulbs for underplanting, called naked ladies because the pale pink flowers appear before the leaves.
***Rudbeckia fulgida* var. *sullivantii* 'Goldsturm'** Flowering well into autumn, the golden flowerheads with black centres are ideal for extending colour in the border.
***Schizostylis coccinea* 'Sunrise'** Perennial with spikes of large salmon-pink flowers in autumn, ideal for the front of the border.
***Sedum spectabile* 'Neon'** This popular perennial produces bright pink flowers above succulent-looking foliage.

TREES & SHRUBS

***Cornus kousa* var. *chinensis* (shown)** Superb tree in all seasons, ideal for the back of a mixed border. In autumn, it produces an impressive display of foliage and fruit.
Crab apple (*Malus*) Fruiting trees with yellow, orange, or red fruit in autumn after spring blossom; ideal for a small garden.
Euonymus alatus The dark green foliage of this deciduous shrub turns bright scarlet in autumn, while red and orange berries split to reveal attractive winged seeds.
Gingko biloba Suitable for a larger garden, the unusually shaped leaves turn an attractive buttery yellow in autumn.
Japanese maple (*Acer palmatum*) Ideal for small gardens with dappled shade. The green leaves of 'Sango-Kaku' turn pale yellow in autumn, others turn purple or red.
***Nyssa sylvatica* 'Wisley Bonfire'** A medium to large deciduous tree providing spectacular autumn leaf colour.
Sumach (*Rhus typhina*) A tall shrub with unusual velvety shoots. It provides fiery autumn colours on the large leaves made up of many leaflets; female plants also bear red fruit.
Viburnum opulus Deciduous shrub equally suited to borders or woodlands, with colourful autumn foliage and glossy red berries.
***Vitis* 'Brant' (shown)** Ornamental grapevine with black, edible grapes and purple autumn foliage. Train it on a pergola in sun.
Yellow birch (*Betula alleghaniensis*) Like many other birches, the leaves turn a mellow, buttery yellow in autumn, lasting well in sheltered sites.

Cornus kousa* var. *chinensis bears unusual strawberry-like fruit and spring flowers.

***Aster amellus* 'King George'** flowers from late summer until mid-autumn.

***Vitis* 'Brant'** provides some of the best autumn foliage of all the grapevines.

Looking after your soil *see page 16* | **Garden design basics** *see page 60* | **Container gardening** *see page 338*

The winter garden

On frosty mornings, grasses like *Miscanthus* are magical, but even without such icy highlights they provide structure and shades of gold.

Winter-flowering plants, evergreen foliage, stems, and berries provide colour in the winter garden, while plant skeletons and catkins provide structural beauty.

Evergreen textures range from fine pine needles to glossy leaves, and may be green, golden, or variegated. Deciduous dogwoods (*Cornus*) or willows (*Salix*) with coloured stems are at their best, while trunks of birches (*Betula*) or gnarled apples (*Malus*) make superb features. Most winter-flowering shrubs produce intoxicating fragrance. Underplant trees and shrubs with snowdrops, winter aconites, early-flowering crocus, and hellebores.

PLANTS FOR WINTER

PERENNIALS & BULBS

***Erica carnea* 'Springwood White'** Lime-tolerant heather that produces white flowers for most of the winter months.
***Helleborus* (shown)** Cup-shaped flowers in late winter make these clump-forming perennials an ideal choice for winter borders.
Snowdrop (*Galanthus*) The delicate white nodding heads of snowdrops appear in late winter and signify the start of another growing season. 'Flore Pleno' has double flowers.

TREES, SHRUBS & CLIMBERS

Black bamboo (*Phyllostachys nigra*) Striking black canes and evergreen foliage make this bamboo perfect for a winter garden.
Christmas box (*Sarcococca confusa*) Like box (*Buxus*), but with small, fragrant flowers. Makes a good low hedge in shade.
***Clematis cirrhosa* var. *purpurascens* 'Freckles'** Climber with bell-shaped cream flowers with red speckles during winter.
***Cornus alba* 'Sibirica'** Deciduous shrub grown for its bright red winter stems. Yellow and orange varieties are available; they make most impact when densely planted in large groups.
***Daphne bholua* 'Jacqueline Postill'** Slow-growing, evergreen shrub unsurpassed for the winter fragrance of its pink flowers.
***Euonymus fortunei* 'Emerald 'n' Gold'** Grown for its bright gold-variegated foliage, which takes on pink hues in winter, this can be grown as a low-growing shrub or trained up walls.
***Mahonia* x *media* 'Charity'** This tough shrub produces yellow flower spikes with a heady scent from late winter onwards. Evergreen foliage is an ideal backdrop for winter-flowering bulbs.
Paper-bark maple (*Acer griseum*) (shown) Several maples have coloured shoots and patterned or flaky bark, continuing to draw attention even after their leaves have fallen.
Silver birch (*Betula utilis* var. *jacquemontii*) Peeling white trunk that may be multi-stemmed or single.
***Viburnum* x *bodnantense* 'Dawn'** A deciduous shrub that produces scented pink flowers on its bare stems all winter.
Wintersweet (*Chimonanthus praecox*) Deciduous shrub known for the delicate perfume of its pale yellow flowers.
Witch hazel (*Hamamelis*) (shown) This deciduous shrub produces scented, yellow to red flowers on its bare branches in winter. 'Pallida' is a popular variety with a strong yellow flowers.

Hellebores flower from winter to spring in many shades, often speckled.

Witch hazels often stand out better if evergreens are planted behind them

Paper-bark maple has cinnamon-coloured, flaky bark, which makes a superb focal point.

ANNUAL PLANTS

Annuals create an almost instant splash of colour in the garden. Whole borders can be grown in a matter of weeks, or individual plants can be used to fill gaps. As their name suggests, annuals are sown and grown, then flower, set seed, and die all in a year. This may make them seem transient, but many annuals will self-seed, some of them abundantly. To fuel their accelerated life cycle, these plants use considerable energy: while many will grow in poor soil, annuals tend to need full sun. Some plants we grow as annuals are truly perennials, either because they are tender or they have a tendency to look messy after their first year.

Growing annuals

There are many advantages to growing annuals from seeds yourself. The cost of a few packets of seeds is far smaller than that of buying in plants. Also, most annuals grow rapidly and quickly transform an area in a few weeks. Annuals bring flexibility to any design, where changes are easy to make and a different choice of flowers can be selected the following year to suit personal taste.

Creating an annual border

To create an entire border of annuals, rather than use them as gap fillers, start by drawing up a planting plan. Ensure that taller plants are towards the back and smaller plants at the front, but occasionally allow taller ones to drift forward. Consider repeating the same plants at intervals to create a sense of unity and balance.

1 **Prepare the ground** by weeding thoroughly, removing all perennial roots. Annuals prefer a light, free-draining soil, so incorporate well-rotted organic matter if the soil is heavy. Rake the soil level, lightly tread it over, and then give it a final rake.

2 **Use sand to outline** where the blocks of different annuals are going to be sown. Use soft contours to shape the planting areas into natural drifts, avoiding straight lines.

3 **Sow in straight drills.** These help to differentiate weeds from sown plants, and so make maintenance easier. Once plants grow, the straight lines will not be distinguishable, but do vary the angles of drills in each section to avoid rigidity.

4 **Once growth is established**, thin out the seedlings according to the instructions on the packet. It is tempting to leave more than specified, but crowded plants will not grow as well and are prone to disease.

Hardy annuals

Commonly grown hardy annuals include poached-egg plant (*Limnanthes*), larkspur (*Consolida ajacis*), sunflowers (*Helianthus*), annual poppies (*Papaver*), love-in-a-mist (*Nigella damascena*), and nasturtiums (*Tropaeolum majus*).

Hardy annuals are sown in spring, often directly into the flowerbeds where they will grow through the year. They can be sown in early spring, as soon as the soil temperature reaches 7°C (45°F).

For an early display in spring, some hardy annuals can be sown in autumn directly into the soil and will successfully overwinter in milder areas. Suitable plants include love-in-a-mist, cornflowers (*Centaurea cyanus*) and honesty (*Lunaria annua*).

Other hardy annuals such as poppies and English marigolds (*Calendula*) are not as hardy and will require some winter protection. Some can be grown directly into the ground and covered with cloches. Others can be grown in pots and kept in a frost-free place such as a greenhouse.

Sowing hardy annuals direct

Sow at the depth recommended on the packet. Rows should be planted about 30cm apart (12in), but check on packets for exact spacings. Pressing a bamboo cane into the soil is the simplest method of creating a shallow drill. Cover the seeds with soil and water using a fine rose. Protect the bed with nets or twiggy sticks to deter birds from removing the seeds. You can leave spaces where half-hardy plants can be slotted into the scheme as plugs once the risk of frosts is over.

Half-hardy annuals

Many popular annuals, including cosmos, petunias, and zinnias, are half hardy. Bedding plants are also often half-hardy annuals, but they can also include other types of plant used for a temporary display.

Half-hardy annuals cannot tolerate frost and should ideally be sown under protection in spring and planted out when the risk of frost is over. It is possible to sow them in autumn, if the young plants can be overwintered in a heated greenhouse. They can also be sown directly into the soil once the risk of frosts is over, but they will flower late in the season.

Sowing half-hardy annuals undercover

Seeds can be sown in most types of containers, from shallow seed trays to plant pots or modules, but the container should be thoroughly washed before use.

SOWING IN POTS

1 **Scatter seeds** on the surface of the compost and sieve a thin layer of compost over them. Lightly firm the compost. Maintain humidity by laying a sheet of glass over the pot or securing a plastic bag over it with a rubber band.

2 **When seedlings emerge**, remove the glass or bag. Once true leaves appear and the seedlings are large enough to be safely handled, transplant them into individual pots. Only ever handle seedlings by the seed leaves.

SOWING USING MODULES

1 **Cells or modules** are ideal for large seeds that are sown individually. Place 1–2 seeds into each cell. Lightly firm the compost. Some small seeds can also be sown as small clumps that are planted out intact into containers or borders.

2 **Push established seedlings** out of the module trays from below with their root systems intact and minimal disturbance. This is not only convenient, but it gets the young plants off to a good start.

GROWING SWEET PEAS

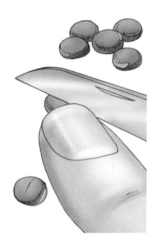

1 **Nick the seeds** with a sharp penknife opposite the eye or scar to let water in and improve germination rates.

2 **Sow into deep pots**, modules, or root-trainers, as sweet peas like a deep root run. Cardboard tubes are also ideal.

3 **Pinch out** the growing tips when the seedlings reach about 8cm (3in). This will encourage a bushier plant.

4 **Train plants** up supports of canes or pea sticks, allowing one plant per support. Tie in stems with twine as they grow.

Fill the container near to the top with seed compost. Tap it to firm the compost and then lightly water and leave for an hour. When sowing, mix fine, dust-like seeds with sand before sprinkling them thinly over the surface. Place pots or trays in trays of water until the compost feels moist. Keep the temperatures between 18–21°C (64–70°F).

Sowing sweet peas

Perfect for the back of borders, sweet peas (*Lathyrus odoratus*) produce a generous display of colour and heady scent. Sow in autumn for early flowering the following spring in warmer regions, but an early spring sowing is best for cooler areas (*see above*).

Seeds should be planted 1cm (½in) deep and about 3cm (1¼in) apart in general-purpose compost. If using cardboard tubes, plant just one seed in each. Water well and keep the seeds at about 15°C (59°F) until the seedlings emerge, then transfer them to a cold frame. Keep the lid of the cold frame open most of the time to harden autumn-sown seedlings, but always close it if frosts are forecast. Give spring-sown plants more protection. When seedlings reach about 4cm (1½in), thin them into individual pots, being careful not to damage the roots. Plants in cardboard tubes can be set out without ever taking them from the tube, avoiding root disturbance.

Sweet peas prefer a deep, rich, and well-drained soil, so add plenty of organic matter before planting. Plant out autumn seedlings in mid-spring, spring-sown plants a couple of weeks later. Leave tendrils on unless growing for exhibition, and pick regularly to prolong flowering.

Maintenance of annual borders

Looking after annuals is fairly simple. Hoe off emerging weeds, but remember some annuals produce seedlings, which can be left in place if wanted for the following year. Some of the taller plants may need staking, and removal of dead flowers encourages plants to continue flowering. When the display is over, the plants can be removed and composted to make way for winter bedding.

WHAT IS A BIENNIAL?

Biennials live for 2 years before dying. They are less popular than annuals, because they do not give the same 'instant' effect. Foxgloves (*Digitalis*) are probably the most widely grown. Some short-lived perennials such as wallflowers (*Erysimum*) are often treated as biennials, sold in the autumn of their first year and discarded after they have flowered in the second year.

HERBACEOUS PERENNIALS

Perennials are to the gardener what paints are to the artist; these are the plants with the largest palette of colours, which can be used to create a horticultural masterpiece. An impressive array of colour is not their only asset. Their size varies from large specimens for maximum impact down to tiny plants that when massed together create a profusion of colour, but most are herbaceous, meaning they are not woody like trees and shrubs, and they generally die back over winter.

Creating a herbaceous border

These plants will remain in the ground for several years, so preparation of the soil is important. Perennials will tolerate either slightly acidic or alkaline soils but ideally they prefer the former. Choose plants suitable for not only the soil but also the level of light.

Planting a border

Clear the ground of surface debris and dig it over, being careful to remove the roots of any perennial weeds. Most perennials prefer soil that is reasonably well drained but with a good moisture content, so incorporate plenty of organic matter and then rake the ground level. Unless the soil is already nutrient-rich, apply an organic fertilizer,

such as blood, fish, and bone, at the rate of 70g (2½oz) per square metre (10 sq ft). Lightly tread over the soil before raking it over again.

Using a planting plan, set out the plants in position before taking them out of their pots. Allow for their size when mature. You need not splash out on the plants in the largest pots, because by the middle of summer those bought in slightly smaller pots reach the same size. Once you are happy with the positioning, they can be planted.

Most herbaceous perennials are sold as container-grown plants. You can buy and plant them at any time of year (*see below*), although they are best planted during spring or autumn as they are more likely to succeed.

PLANTING A PERENNIAL

1 **Water container-grown plants** well and allow them to drain before sliding them out of their containers.

2 **Tease the roots** gently from the sides and bottom. This will encourage quicker root establishment in the ground.

3 **Place the plant** in the hole and adjust the height by adding or removing soil. Firm in using your fingertips, apply a thick layer of organic mulch, and water in well.

Maintenance through the year

There will be plenty of bare soil in the first year of a new perennial border as the plants start to establish, so weeds will readily appear. Reduce these by interplanting with annuals and bedding (*see pages 74–76*), or hoe them off as soon as they appear. The plants will need watering during any dry spells, particularly in the first year.

Mulching & feeding

Mulch beds each year with well-rotted manure or garden compost about 5cm (2in) deep in early spring. Keep the organic matter well away from emerging stems.

Inorganic mulches, such as gravel, add another texture to beds throughout the year and suppress the germination of weed seeds. They are best suited to plants with low-nutrient requirements, such as those in Mediterranean borders, prairie plantings, or dry garden beds.

Borders may need feeding in spring before the mulch is renewed – organic mulches also help to feed the soil. Alternatively, spot-treat any plants looking pale with a liquid feed just before the new growing season starts.

Staking

Staking is an important aspect of flower bed maintenance (*see below*). Without support, many plants would collapse, especially those grown in nutrient-rich soil or top-heavy varieties with large flowers and luxuriant growth. Staking also gives borders a skeletal framework or structure within the planting.

The key to successful staking is to get the support in place early so it will be as effective and as unobtrusive as possible. Put supports in position before the new growth has reached 10–15cm (4–6in) high.

METHODS OF STAKING

Tie plants to stakes with soft twine in a figure of 8. If using bamboo canes for staking, try to ensure that they are well weathered because new canes show up easily. Cane toppers will minimize injury to eyes when working in the border after growth conceals the canes.

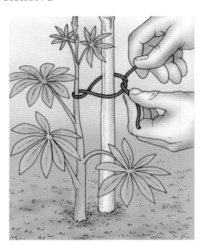

Metal supports last for years, so are good value despite their high initial cost. They are less attractive than supports made of natural materials, although dark green ones are less visible than shiny bare metal. Plant growth usually hides supports by summer.

Natural woven supports are attractive in their own right, and the ideal option where a plant of delicate form may not completely conceal its support. Natural materials will need replacing every year.

Linking stakes are relatively costly if there are many plants to support, but they are sturdy and will last well. They can be put in place around a plant later in the season if you failed to put grow-through supports in place, but they may not be completely concealed.

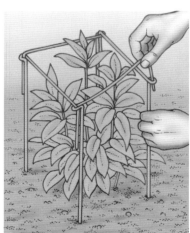

Plants with upright, delicate flower spikes, such as delphiniums, need individual staking with canes. Other plants can grow through larger supports.

If using twiggy branches, push them into the ground around the plant, or group of plants. Bend the top of each branch over to its neighbour and twist them around each other. Create a second tier by twisting the branches around neighbours in the first tier. The most useful twigs for staking are hazel, due to their fan-shaped branches, followed by birch, which should be cut in winter before the twigs have had a chance to break into bud.

An alternative is 10cm (4in) pea netting, ideally black, stretched over frameworks of stout wooden stakes painted black, leaving gaps to allow access. The stems of the plants will thread through the support, disguising the netting.

Division

After a few years, perennials often become congested and lose vigour. Sometimes the plant dies in the centre, or it outgrows its space and invades that of its neighbours.

The best method of renovation is to dig the plants up, and divide them up into chunks with a sharp spade, knife, or saw (*see box, above*). The traditional method of pulling them apart with two forks placed back to back is awkward. Replant divisions elsewhere or compost them. Autumn is the usual time for dividing perennials, but early spring is best in cold, wet areas because plants have a better chance of recovering. Agapanthus, asters, and kniphofias prefer to be divided in spring.

Deadheading

Check the borders regularly, removing faded flowerheads or stems and tidying the plants by removing tired foliage. Deadheading (*see right*) prevents plants from wasting energy on seed production, encouraging prolonged flowering and clean, fresh growth instead. Plants may need extra feeding and watering to encourage a second flush of flowers. Deadheading also prevents a prolific crop of seedlings from plants such as alliums.

Do not deadhead plants that produce attractive fruit or seeds, such as *Iris foetidissima*. It is also not worth deadheading those that have a profusion of tiny flowers. Plants such as *Astrantia* and some geraniums can be cut to ground level to encourage more flowers.

Stopping and thinning

Stopping is a technique used to create a lower, slightly more study plant, less prone to collapse without support. It works particularly well on tall plants, such as heleniums, *Veronicastrum*, and *Eupatorium*, as well as sedums.

DIVISION TO REINVIGORATE

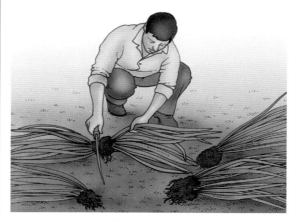

Dividing plants is sometimes a delicate job and at other times a tough one. Fibrous roots can be teased apart, while harder, woody roots need to be cut with a spade or even a saw.

DEADHEADING

Cut entire flowering stems of plants such as delphiniums down to ground level to encourage a smaller second flush of flowers. Apply a general-purpose fertilizer at the same time. Cut other plants, such as phlox, back to a lower set of clean leaves.

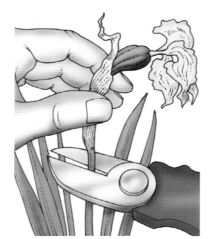

Remove the flowers of bulbs, complete with any swelling seed pod. Large daffodils are best deadheaded to avoid energy being wasted on seed production, but allow short-lived species to set seed and naturalize.

THINNING

Pinch out shoots of multi-stemmed perennials, such as phlox and heleniums, at the base. Thinning the new growth will produce larger flowers on a stronger and healthier plant, because fewer stems are sharing nutrients from the roots.

STOPPING

The traditional way of stopping plants is to individually pinch out the growing tips when they are one-third of their final height. This is often done on asters and helps to produce a denser plant. Plants may be sheared instead.

Cut back early luxuriant growth by one third with shears or secateurs when in active growth in late spring. In deep borders, chopping just the front part will enable the back plants to be seen and increase the depth of field.

Thinning to improve the flowering display is carried out on multi-stemmed plants, and involves removing about one in three stems at ground level when they are about 10–15cm (4–6in) high.

Clearing away old growth

Cutting back herbaceous perennials should take place from autumn onwards. If you leave it until late winter, much of the dead foliage will be well rotted, so there will be less to remove than if the borders are cut back in autumn. The foliage can simply be raked up using a spring-tined rake and added to the compost heap.

Waiting until spring is ideal for slightly tender plants, such as agapanthus and kniphofias, because their old foliage protects the crown over winter. It also suits plants that have attractive seed heads or architectural form, such as sedums or eryngiums, and woody-based plants, such as asters and penstemons. If you intend to renovate a border in spring, old foliage will help to identify the position of the dormant plants. Cut deciduous grasses, such as *Miscanthus*, to ground level in spring, and rake out dead foliage from evergreen grasses, like pampas grass (*Cortaderia*).

CUTTING BACK IN AUTUMN

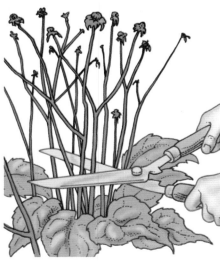

Dead foliage can provide winter shelter for pests and diseases and is not needed by fully hardy plants. Cut back the old growth of perennials such as hostas (*far left*) in autumn or early winter.

Not all stems last well through winter to provide striking skeletal forms. Those of rudbeckias (*left*) and other multi-stemmed plants can become a dark tangle, so cut back to ground level or just above basal leaves.

Pests & diseases of herbaceous perennials

The usual range of garden pests (*see pages 35–36*), such as aphids, slugs and snails, caterpillars, capsid bugs, rabbits, deer, and vine weevil attack perennials, but there are also some pests that feed on very specific plant types.

Earwigs

Active from spring to autumn, earwigs feed on young leaves and petals at night, hiding during the day. Place pots stuffed with dry grass among the plants: the earwigs will creep into them by dawn and can be picked out. For heavy infestations, spray at dusk with bifenthrin.

Leaf & bud eelworm

Microscopic nematodes feed inside the leaves of many plants, including chrysanthemums and penstemons. Infested leaf parts, separated from uninfested parts by the larger leaf veins, turn brown or black, forming discoloured islands in the leaves. Symptoms are mainly seen in late summer to autumn. There are no effective pesticides available for garden use: tolerate the damage or remove the plants. For eelworm-free chrysanthemum cuttings, immerse dormant stools for five minutes in water at 46°C (115°F) to kill eelworms without damaging plants.

Michaelmas daisy mite

The microscopic mites suck sap in the shoot tips and flower buds, scarring the stems and turning flower buds into rosettes of green leaves. There are no effective insecticides for garden use. *Aster novi-belgii* is susceptible to this pest, *A. novae-angliae* or *A. amellus* much less so.

Sawflies

Aquilegias, *Aruncus*, Solomon's seal (*Polygonatum*), and geums can be defoliated by caterpillar-like, pale green or greyish white sawfly larvae. They feed before pupating in the soil, and there may be more than one generation in a growing season. Check vulnerable plants regularly and deal with the larvae promptly. Either remove by hand or spray with thiacloprid, bifenthrin, or pyrethrum.

Hemerocallis gall midge

This tiny fly lays eggs in the developing flower buds of daylilies (*Hemerocallis*) in late spring to early summer. Infested buds contain many white maggots, are swollen, and fail to open. Buds that form after midsummer are rarely damaged, because by then the egg-laying period is over. Pick off damaged buds and destroy them, and choose late-flowering varieties to reduce problems.

PESTS & DAMAGE OF HERBACEOUS PLANTS

Earwig & damage to clematis flower

Eelworm damage

Michaelmas daisy mite damage

Solomon's seal sawfly larva & damage

Bud infested by hemerocallis gall midge

Regularly check plants for signs of infestation. Without effective pesticides, catching problems early is vital to minimize damage.

Chrysanthemum white rust

This fungal disease causes warty, cream or buff pustules on leaf undersides, with yellow pits on the upper surface. Pustules age to tan brown, and leaves may be distorted or killed. Affected plants should be immediately destroyed and neighbouring chrysanthemums sprayed with a fungicide labelled for control of rusts on ornamentals.

Lupin anthracnose

This serious fungal disease of lupins causes large lesions on the stem or leaves and can lead to rapid collapse. Sometimes pink spores are visible in the diseased tissue. No fungicide is currently available to control this disease. Remove affected plants – the fungus can be seed-borne.

Peony wilt

In spring or early summer, shoots wilt and die. They have a brown area at the base, sometimes covered in grey fluffy mould. Brown blotches appear on leaves, mainly at the tips. The fungus spreads by airborne spores and sclerotia in the soil. Promptly cut back affected tissue, if necessary to below soil level, and do not compost. Ideally, carefully replace the soil around the plant crown. This common fungal disease thrives in humid air, so do not let clumps become too dense. No fungicides are currently available.

Hellebore black death & leaf spot

Black death is a viral disease, causing streaked, then blackened and distorted hellebore leaves and flowers. There is no remedy: destroy affected plants, and spray neighbours with an aphicide to reduce spread by aphids.

Leaf spot is a fungal disease causing large brown spots on leaves, which eventually become silvery and may die, weakening the plant. Infection can be very rapid in damp conditions. Remove old foliage before flowers emerge, and destroy obviously affected material promptly.

Aster wilts

Shoots in a clump wilt, often withering from the base up, and over years the whole clump may die. Inspect new plants to avoid introducing diseased material. The fungus spreads via soil and air, so remove infected stems promptly and dig up badly affected clumps. Try resistant varieties.

Delphinium black blotch

A bacterial disease starting on leaves, but spreading to stems and flowers. Bacteria are splashed from the soil and infect through the stomata to cause large black blotches. There are no chemicals available for bacterial diseases on ornamentals, so remove and destroy badly affected plants.

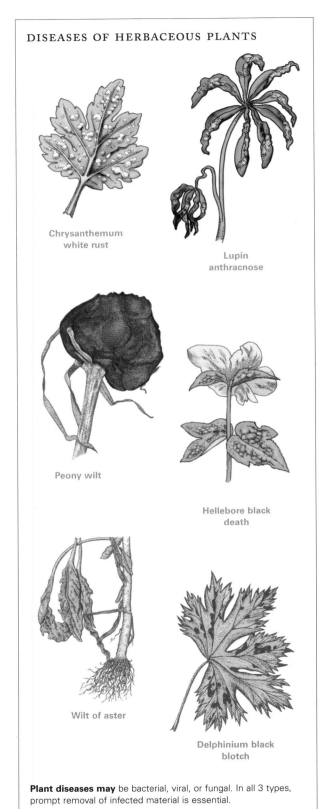

DISEASES OF HERBACEOUS PLANTS

Chrysanthemum white rust

Lupin anthracnose

Peony wilt

Hellebore black death

Wilt of aster

Delphinium black blotch

Plant diseases may be bacterial, viral, or fungal. In all 3 types, prompt removal of infected material is essential.

BULBOUS PLANTS

Bulbous plants are some of the best-known flowers in the garden. Many are spring-flowering, including tulips, cyclamen, daffodils, crocus, snowdrops, bluebells, and alliums. There are also many summer-flowering bulbs like lilies and crocosmias, and late-performing dahlias, to name a few. This chapter includes not only true bulbs, but also tubers, corms, and rhizomes. Essentially, these all have a swollen or fleshy underground storage organ, which enables them to survive periods of dormancy.

Planting bulbous plants

Bulbs generally have only one season of interest. While in flower they provide a glorious display, from large flower spikes to drifts of smaller flowers, and their blooms are sometimes also fragrant. Once flowering is over, however, their foliage fades away and they retire below ground until their season comes again.

How to plant

As a rule of thumb, plant spring-flowering bulbs such as daffodils and tulips in early autumn, summer-flowering bulbs in spring, and autumn-flowering bulbs in late summer. There are exceptions to these guidelines: spring-flowering snowdrops establish most successfully if lifted 'in the green' while in leaf just after flowering, and are transplanted promptly. Pot-grown bulbs can be planted at any time, but they cost a lot more than dry bulbs.

PLANTING BULBS INDIVIDUALLY

Plant each bulb in a hole of the appropriate depth. This is usually 2–3 times the height of the bulb, although a few larger, less hardy bulbs prefer to be close to the surface for maximum heat.

PLANTING GROUPS OF BULBS

1 Prepare the ground well and dig a large hole. Place the bulbs randomly, at least twice their own width deep and apart.

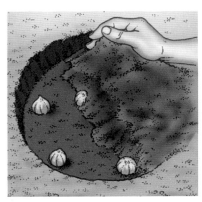

2 Draw the soil back over the bulbs. Do this gently, with your hand rather than a spade, to ensure that the bulbs are not dislodged.

3 Firm the soil by tamping it gently with the back of a rake. Do not tread on the soil, as your weight may damage the bulb tips.

PLANTING BULBS IN GRASS

1 To create drifts of large bulbs like daffodils in rough grass, start by scattering the bulbs randomly over the planting area. Adjust those that are less than their own width apart, leaving the rest where they fall for a natural look.

2 Dig a hole with a trowel where the bulb fell. If you are planting a lot of bulbs, buy a bulb planter. This cuts out a core of turf faster and with far less effort than a trowel. Short-handled types and models with a long shaft that are pushed in with the foot, like a spade, are both available.

3 Remove the core and check the hole is the correct depth for your bulb, crumbling some soil back into the hole if it is not. Scatter a little balanced fertilizer into the hole if the soil is poor.

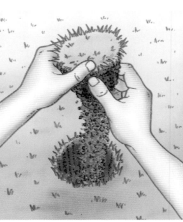

4 Place the bulb into the hole and crumble some soil from the end of the core over the bulb so that it is completely covered with loose soil. Replace the plug of turf over it and firm in gently. Fill any gaps around the plug with loose soil.

The simplest method of naturalizing small bulbs, such as crocus, in a lawn is to make holes with the prongs of a fork and insert the corms into them, back-filling with soil. Alternatively, cut away a section of turf with a spade or a half moon edger and peel it back gently to reveal the bare soil. Lightly dig over the soil with a hand fork and press the corms into it, then replace the turf and firm it in by tamping it down with the back of a rake. Large bulbs can be planted with a bulb planter (*see above*).

Where to plant

There are bulbs for every situation from sun to shade, and for soils from poor to rich, dry to damp. Most prefer well-drained conditions; such bulbs may rot in damp soil.

Bulbs can be planted in mixed borders or in pots that are moved into prominent positions while they flower, and then taken away once the display is over. Use low-growing, early-spring-flowering bulbs at the front of borders, giving them an opportunity to shine before the herbaceous perennials and shrubs take centre stage.

Tulips are frequently used in formal flowerbeds, bedding, containers, and mixed borders. Hybrids are ideal for quick colour but most will rarely flower well for a second year. Robust species types, which require a free-draining soil, are suitable for more subtle planting schemes and can usually remain in the soil for years.

Later-flowering bulbous plants, such as gladioli and dahlias, add vibrancy to late summer and can be used for cut flowers. *Fritillaria imperialis* and *Crinum × powellii* 'Album' add architectural interest, while late-flowering *Eucomis* bring a touch of the exotic to the border.

Bulbs in drifts give large shady areas a natural, long-established feeling. Most woodland bulbs, such as trilliums, snowdrops (*Galanthus*), winter aconites (*Eranthis hyemalis*), and wood anemones (*Anemone nemorosa*) prefer moist but well-drained soil. Fork the soil over lightly and add leaf mould prior to planting. If you have no woodland but only a specimen tree, naturalizing winter- and early spring-flowering bulbs at the base will create seasonal interest while the tree remains bare and dormant.

Crocuses are commonly naturalized on lawns; daffodils are also popular, but when choosing a location remember that you cannot cut the grass until after the foliage of the bulbs has died back. Meadows are another area ideal for naturalizing bulbs (*see pages 52–53*). Among the most popular plants are the snake-head fritillaries (*Fritillaria meleagris*), which thrive in damp conditions, and cowslips or primroses (*Primula*).

Looking after bulbous plants

Permanently planted bulbs generally need little care. Removing dead flowers can increase vigour in the following year, and staking may be necessary for tall or lush plants such as gladioli and dahlias. Leave foliage to die back before tidying the plants up. If flowering diminishes, it is likely that the clumps have become congested; simply lift them when dormant, remove some of the bulbs, and replant.

Storing bulbous plants

Not all bulbous plants can be left in the ground permanently. Hybrid tulips require lifting and storing until autumn once the foliage has died down, and may take two years to reach flowering size again; often they are lifted and discarded at the end of the season.

Most of the bulbous plants used in our gardens are hardy, but there are tender types that may need to be lifted. For example, dahlias and cannas will survive over winter in the soil in milder areas, but not in colder districts. Wherever frost threatens, lift the roots out of the soil and store them somewhere dry and frost-free for the winter. They will also need to be lifted in milder areas if the soil is wet and heavy, to prevent them from rotting during wet winter weather. Some bulbs, such as tender cyclamen or nerines, are best grown in pots and brought under cover in cold winters.

LIFTING & STORING DAHLIAS

1 **When the first frost** blackens the leaves of the plants, cut down the stems to about 15cm (6in) above ground level. Loosen the soil carefully and ease the tubers out.

2 **Remove loose soil** and stand the roots upside down to ensure that any remaining moisture drains from the stems and top of the crown. Keep the roots in a frost-free place for about 3 weeks.

3 **Place the tubers** right-way up in a wooden box and cover them with coir, vermiculite, or similar medium to prevent them from drying out completely. Keep cool but frost free. Inspect regularly and remove any tuber that shows signs of rot.

4 **Encourage new growth** by placing the box in a sunny spot in spring, and watering lightly. In late winter, you can force tubers into early growth by planting them in compost and placing them in a greenhouse. Plant out once all risk of frost has passed.

Pests & diseases of bulbs

While bulbs are in growth, check them for any symptoms of pests and diseases. When lifting them, seasonally or to divide clumps, inspect the bulbs themselves and destroy any showing signs of infection or infestation.

Lily beetle

This native of Asia and mainland Europe continues to spread. Adult beetles are 6mm (¹/₄in) long and bright red with black legs and head; they eat the foliage of lilies (*Lilium*) and fritillaries (*Fritillaria*) from spring to autumn. The reddish brown grubs, which are covered in black excrement, feed from late spring to late summer. Damage reduces the bulb size and may prevent flowering next year. Remove the beetles and larvae by hand, or spray plants with thiacloprid or imidacloprid.

Gladiolus thrips

Thrips are narrow-bodied, sap-feeding insects up to 2mm (¹/₁₆in) long. The adults are blackish brown and the immature nymphs pale yellow. They cause pale mottling of foliage and feed inside the developing flower buds. In heavy infestations the flower buds fail to open. Watch for the early signs of feeding damage on the foliage before flowering starts. If you find thrips, spray with thiacloprid or imidacloprid. Burn or otherwise destroy the foliage and stems in the autumn to kill overwintering thrips.

Narcissus eelworm

Microscopic nematodes within bulbs and foliage stunt and distort growth before killing bulbs. Bulbs cut across show concentric brown rings. There are no pesticide treatments for garden use. Purchase firm, good-quality bulbs, and remove bulbs showing symptoms and any others growing within 1m (3ft) of infested plants.

Narcissus bulb flies

Large bulb flies resemble small bumblebees and attack narcissus bulbs, *Cyrtanthus*, *Hippeastrum*, and snowdrops (*Galanthus*), from late spring to midsummer when the foliage is dying down. Infested bulbs are often killed or produce just a few thin leaves, and contain a plump grub up to 16mm (³/₄in) long. This eats the centre of the bulb, filling it with muddy excrement. Small bulb flies produce many maggots up to 8mm (³/₈in) long, but only attack bulbs already damaged by other pests or diseases. There are no effective pesticides for garden use. Cover valuable bulbs with horticultural fleece when flies are active. Bulbs in sunny positions are most vulnerable.

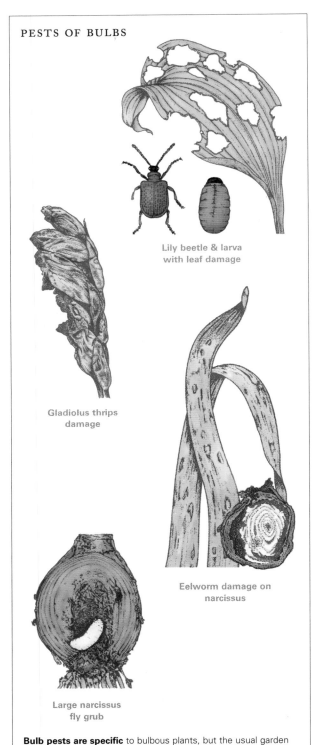

PESTS OF BULBS

Lily beetle & larva
with leaf damage

Gladiolus thrips
damage

Eelworm damage on
narcissus

Large narcissus
fly grub

Bulb pests are specific to bulbous plants, but the usual garden pests, such as aphids, slugs and snails, vine weevil grubs, rabbits, deer and squirrels, may also attack (*see pages 35–36*).

Tulip fire

Brown scorching deforms shoots, and sunken yellow spots with green edges appear on neighbouring tulips. Affected tissue may have a grey mould. Inspect bulbs for lesions with small black bodies before planting. Spread is rapid: destroy affected plants and avoid tulips for three years.

Iris leaf spot

This fungal leaf spot also affects plants such as gladioli and daylilies (*Hemerocallis*), causing elliptical, yellow-margined brown spots or grey spots. Entire leaves may die, usually after flowering. Outbreaks are worst in wet conditions. Remove diseased leaves promptly and clear dead leaves in autumn. Keep plants vigorous; moderate liming of soil and fungicide sprays may help.

Lily disease

This fungal disease causes elliptical, water-soaked spots on the leaves, and may rot the entire leaf and spread to the stem or flowers. No fungicides are available. Remove and burn affected growth and ensure good air circulation.

Snowdrop grey mould

Usually worst in mild winters. Growth is stunted and the leaves and stalk rot, sometimes with grey, velvety mould. Small black bodies may develop on rotting bulbs and survive in the soil to infect others, so check bulbs before planting. Destroy infected clumps, and do not replant.

Basal rot

Affects daffodils and crocus when dying back, mostly in hot summers. The basal plate softens and red rot spreads inside, sometimes with pink mould. Bulbs in the soil rot and the disease spreads. Lift bulbs in early summer, store in a cool, airy place, inspect, and remove soft bulbs. Triandrus, jonquil, and tazetta daffodils are resistant.

Narcissus leaf scorch

Leaf tips show a reddish brown scorch, which may spread, and leaves yellow and shrivel. Flowers may show brown blotches. Remove affected tissue. Avoid chilling bulbs or planting late. Poeticus, polyanthus, tazetta, and poetaz daffodils are vulnerable, but it is not limited to daffodils.

Viruses

A variety of viruses cause concentric rings, pale streaking or blotches on leaves, streaking in flowers, or distortion. Viruses can spread by vegetative propagation, but are carried mainly by insects, such as aphids or thrips, so pest control is important. Destroy infected plants promptly.

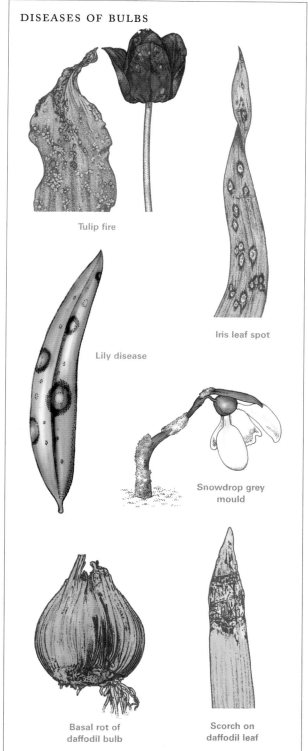

DISEASES OF BULBS

Tulip fire

Iris leaf spot

Lily disease

Snowdrop grey mould

Basal rot of daffodil bulb

Scorch on daffodil leaf

Diseases of bulbous plants may appear above ground, but often fungal infections spread through soil. Prompt removal is vital, and it is best to replace with a different plant type for some years.

TREES & SHRUBS

It is hard to imagine a garden without trees and shrubs. They comprise a huge group of small to very large, evergreen and deciduous plants that can be planted on their own – to be enjoyed as a stand-alone specimen – or in groups, if you have the space. The size and structure of many trees and shrubs make them an essential feature in most gardens as they are a counterpoint to walls, buildings, and other hard landscaping, giving balance to a garden's design. As hedges, trees also provide screening, boundaries, and filters to noise. Low-growing shrubs can be used to cover ground in an ornamental way.

Buying trees & shrubs

Many garden centres and nurseries sell container-grown trees and shrubs through the year; some will also have bare-root and rootballed plants from late autumn to early spring for planting at that time of year. Container-grown trees and shrubs are best planted during this period as well, but they can be planted all year round.

Planting in autumn allows the plant to benefit from warm, moist soil, ensuring it establishes before winter. Container-grown trees and shrubs will require a lot of watering if planted in spring or summer, making them vulnerable to dry weather. Avoid planting during drought conditions or if the ground is frozen or waterlogged.

Selecting a healthy plant

If you want your plants to get off to a flying start, then choose healthy plants. Avoid any that show signs of pests and diseases, or those that have badly damaged branches.

Generally, if you are buying a shrub, make sure it has a good network of evenly spaced branches, and if you are buying a tree, check it has a straight, clear stem with a good head of branches.

When buying container plants, slide off the pot and check the roots. Reject any plant where the roots are spiralling or noticeably pot-bound. The roots of bare-root plants should be damp and show no signs of damage.

THE THREE WAYS TO BUY TREES & SHRUBS

Bare-root plants are available only during the dormant season, usually for fruit, hedging, or rose plants. Plant them immediately.

Rootballed plants come with a ball of moist soil attached to the roots. Check that the wrapping is firmly in place before buying.

Container-grown plants are freely available. Ensure plants are container grown rather than recently potted by the firmness of the rootball.

Planting trees & shrubs

Before planting, remove any weeds from the site, either by hand or with a fork; if the site is covered with deep-rooted perennial weeds, treat with a weedkiller (*see page 39*).

For bare-root plants, look for the flare of the trunk – the area where the upper roots grow from the base of the trunk – and plant just above this level. Do the same for container-grown plants by scraping off the surface of the compost, as some may have been planted too deeply in their pot. A tree or shrub that is planted too deeply may rot at the base of the trunk. As a general rule, however, you should plant container-grown trees and shrubs at the same level as they were in their container.

The depth of the planting hole for trees and shrubs should be the same as the rootball. For most trees, you will only need a hole that is the depth of a spade's blade, but be guided by the rootball and dig the hole accordingly.

In the past, it was recommended that well-rotted manure or garden compost should be placed into the bottom of the hole. However, you should avoid doing this, as trees planted on top of a layer of organic matter can sink into the ground as this material starts to decay.

You should also avoid adding fertilizer when planting as this can harm and burn freshly forming roots. The addition of mycorrhizal fungi (available as sachets in

PLANTING A SHRUB

1 **Dig a round hole** about twice the diameter of the root system, and to the same depth.

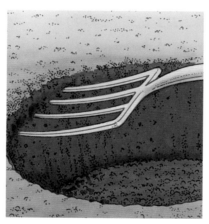

2 **Pierce the sides** of the hole with a fork. You can mix the dug soil with well-rotted organic matter, so long as this soil is only used to fill in around the roots, not below them.

3 **Tease out roots** that have grown around the rootball on container-grown plants. This encourages them to grow outwards, rather than in a circle.

4 **Position the shrub** in the planting hole, making sure that it is at the right level.

5 **Backfill the planting hole** with the excavated soil. Firm it around the roots with your fingers so no air pockets remain.

6 **Soak the soil** around the base of the shrub, mulch thickly, and water regularly through the first growing season.

PLANTING A TREE

1 **Prepare a hole** as for a shrub (*see previous page*). Pierce the bottom with a fork – do not dig it over as the tree will sink after planting.

2 **Place the tree** into the hole, checking that the flare of the trunk is just below the level of the ground. Tease out the roots and backfill the hole with the excavated soil, firming gently.

3 **Drive in a wooden stake** at an angle for container-grown or rootballed trees, pointed into the direction of the prevailing wind. Use a vertical stake for bare-root trees.

4 **Tie the tree** to the stake using a tree tie, about one third of the way up the trunk. Leave a space between the stake and trunk.

5 **Soak the soil** around the base of the tree. Repeat regularly during the first year. Use a tree guard if necessary (*see page 92*).

6 **Mulch thickly** over the roots to hold moisture into the soil. Keep the mulch clear of the trunk to prevent rotting.

garden centres) to the soil, however, can be beneficial, as it can help trees to establish. Mix in the mycorrhizal fungi granules with the soil before it is returned to the hole.

How to plant

Trees and shrubs are planted in much the same way (*see above and previous page*), except that trees need staking and the bottom of their planting hole needs to be pierced with a fork to encourage deeper rooting.

Tease out the roots of container-grown plants before planting to boost speedy anchoring in the soil. If roots are very pot-bound, slice the roots several times with a spade to help them emerge upon planting. Failure to do this leads to spiralling roots and the tree will not establish.

Staking a tree

If at all possible, choose small trees about 1m (3ft) tall, which do not need staking. Apart from saving you time when planting, smaller trees also establish more quickly.

Larger trees will need a stake, the function of which is to help anchor the roots. Stakes are not there to prevent the stem from moving; in fact, stem movement in a breeze is good for the plant as it helps to make the trunk stronger. Put in a stake at 45 degrees for container-grown or rootballed trees (*see facing page*) and a short vertical stake for bare-root plants.

You often see trees that have been staked for many years. This is unnecessary, and if it is needed, then there is probably something wrong with the tree or in the way

STAKING A TREE

Diagonal stakes at 45 degrees are used for container or rootballed trees since the stake will not damage the root system when it is put in place. Round or square stakes can be used.

Sturdy H-stakes are not often seen except in public spaces, where trees may be prone to vandalism. Like diagonal stakes, they avoid damage to the root system.

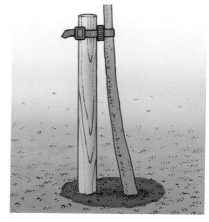

Vertical stakes are unsuitable for container or rootballed plants as it is not possible to get the stake close enough to the tree, leading to the trunk bending. Use for bare-root trees only.

it was originally planted. As a rule, leave stakes in the ground for 18 months after planting, and then remove them carefully so as not to disturb the roots.

To tie the tree to its stake, use a rubber tube or belt for small trees, and a plastic buckle tie for larger trees. Ties should not be so tight as to restrict the growth of stems, or too loose, which can cause the stem to rub against the tie or stake. From time to time, relax ties so they do not restrict growth, and tighten any that have come loose.

The life of a transplant

We often expect newly planted trees to romp away after planting, but newly planted bare-root transplants will take at least three years to grow vigorously (*see below*).

When trees are lifted from the nursery field, they can lose up to 90 percent of their original root system, so in the first year of planting, do not expect too much of the tree, when shoots are likely to be shorter and leaves smaller than normal.

THREE YEARS IN THE LIFE OF A TRANSPLANT

FIRST YEAR
Roots gradually take hold, but as leaves and shoots are smaller and shorter in the first year, energy for root growth will be limited.

SECOND YEAR
Roots spread over a greater distance, so they will be able to take up more water and nutrients, promoting more topgrowth.

THIRD & SUBSEQUENT YEARS
Vigorous growth results now that the root system is fully recovered from transplanting and the roots are well established.

Tree & shrub aftercare

Immediately after you buy a tree or shrub, you need to follow a care programme to ensure that it thrives. If you cannot plant it right away, container-grown specimens can be kept in their pots for a few weeks out of direct sun, and bare-root or rootballed trees can be heeled in (*see below*).

After planting, water thoroughly, then add a tree guard (*see right*) if it is necessary to protect a tree from large mammals like rabbits or deer. Next, cover the ground under the plant with a layer of mulch (*see page 22*), no deeper than 8cm (3in), leaving a gap around the base of the tree so that the mulch does not come into contact with the bark; this can lead to rotting at the base of the trunk.

Water trees and shrubs attentively while they establish (*see below, right*), especially during periods of drought or if it has been planted on well-drained soil. Apply generous amounts of water every fortnight, rather than a sprinkling every few days, to encourage deep rooting.

Feeding & weeding

It is not necessary to feed trees or shrubs after planting. In subsequent years, a slow-release general fertilizer can help to boost the growth of trees growing in poor or very well-drained soil – apply this over the root area, which is roughly determined by the spread of the canopy.

You should keep the root area under the tree free of weeds. A thick mulch should help with this, and it should be topped up as it rots away. If necessary, weed on a regular basis, rather than allowing a carpet of weeds to develop.

Protect the trunk of a young tree from mammals like rabbits, mice, or deer. They can strip the bark and easily kill the tree. Many types of tree guard are available; simple wrap-around guards made from plastic or wire mesh are usually sufficient and can be attached to the stake.

Heavy duty tree guards are made from wire mesh, like chicken wire, or tough plastic. They give extra protection from large mammals. The guard should be supported independently of the tree stake, on 3 or 4 stakes of its own, forming a cage around the trunk.

HEELING IN

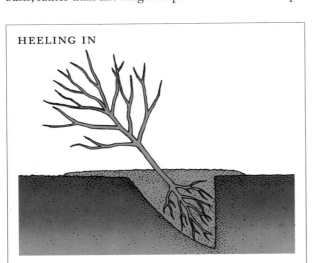

Bare-root or rootballed trees and shrubs must be heeled in if they cannot be planted right away. To do this, dig a hole – or trench, if more than one plant – to the depth of the root system and plant at the same depth as in the nursery (*see page 89*).

WATERING A TREE

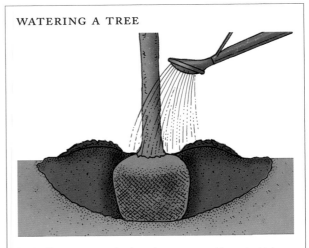

In the first year, watering is perhaps your most important job. To direct water over the roots, a good tip is to create a shallow dip around the trunk, to act as a reservoir, or lay a seep hose over the root area and cover with mulch.

Moving trees & shrubs

Whether you are moving to a new home and want to take a certain tree or shrub with you, or you are planning on implementing a new planting scheme or simply think that a shrub has been planted in the wrong place, you can move a plant to a new position with a little effort.

When to move plants

Ideally, move deciduous trees and shrubs in winter while they are dormant. Evergreens are best moved in early spring, because at this time the plant will be entering its growing season and the roots will be able to soak up water and nutrients from the warming soil, helping it to establish quickly. In winter, an evergreen plant can still lose water from its leaves, even though it is dormant, so if it is moved at this time it will dry out as the disturbed roots cannot not replace lost water fast enough.

Preparing the plant

Dig a trench around the root area and undercut the roots (*see below*), with the aim of creating a large rootball with lots of roots. This will help the plant to re-establish itself quickly. Severing roots is unavoidable when you do this, but if done properly, the plant will recover on replanting.

Moving the plant

You must keep the rootball damp and replant as soon as possible after lifting. Wrap the rootball tightly in wet hessian sacking or an old blanket so it does not dry out.

While small shrubs are easily removed by one pair of hands, if you have a large plant, you will end up with quite a sizeable rootball. Not only will this be heavy to move, but the digging will be hard work. This is a job best done by two people.

MOVING A TREE FOR REPLANTING

1 **Dig a trench** 30cm (12in) wide and 60cm (24in) deep around the root area, which is measured by the spread of the canopy.

2 **Undercut the roots** with a spade and trim back any untidy roots with secateurs. Prepare the new hole ready for replanting.

3 **Lift the tree** carefully, tilting it on its rootball so that an old blanket or hessian sacking can be slipped underneath.

4 **Wrap up** the rootball tightly and tie in place. Spray it with water to keep it damp before replanting as soon as possible.

Pruning & training

The purpose of pruning and training is to influence the way a tree or shrub grows. By doing so, you can create some wonderful effects in the garden.

Some plants need very little pruning other than the removal of dead flowerheads, or the removal of crossing branches or those that spoil the shape. Other plants may be overgrown and need more work to restore them to their former glory. Some need annual pruning to ensure a good display of flowers, fruit, or ornamental stems, while formal hedges or topiary need pruning to maintain a crisp shape. Trees in particular need early training in their formative years (*see below*) to produce a strong framework and an attractive shape.

Whatever your reason for pruning, your trees and shrubs are unlikely to grow, flower, and fruit in the way that you want without any pruning at all. This section shows you how to do it successfully. Do not worry if your plants look different to the illustrations – the basic principles and techniques can still be applied.

What happens when you prune

In general terms, if you remove part of a tree or shrub, you will encourage it to grow. At the end of each shoot is a terminal bud, which is dominant over the buds that grow to form side branches. If the terminal bud is cut off, it results in the growth of side branches below – hard pruning results in more vigorous growth than cutting back lightly. If you cut vigorous growth back hard, this may result in more vigorous growth, so as a rule of thumb, weak growth should be pruned hard, while vigorous growth should be pruned more lightly (*see box, facing page*).

Pruning tools

It is important to buy good-quality tools for pruning. A pair of secateurs is essential for cutting branches of pencil thickness, while a hand-held pruning saw will speedily cut through branches that are more than finger-thick. Fixed-blade models are available, but folding saws are handier as they can be stored in your pocket when not in use. If you have lots of tall trees in your garden, it may be worth buying pruning tools that can be mounted on a telescopic handle, which is safer than climbing a ladder.

For a small run of hedge you should not need anything more than a pair of hand-held shears. An electric hedge trimmer is ideal for more substantial hedges.

Make sure your tools are sharp and clean, as rough cuts or torn branches can result in disease. Cut just above a strong bud, or pair of buds (*see box, above*).

HOW TO MAKE A PRUNING CUT

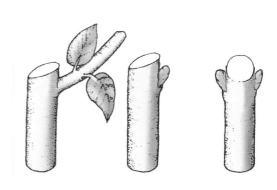

Prune back to just above a strong bud or pair of buds, or a healthy sideshoot, as shown above. The cut should slope away from the bud or shoot. Pruning too close to the bud or shoot will cause it damage; pruning too far away will result in dieback.

EARLY TRAINING

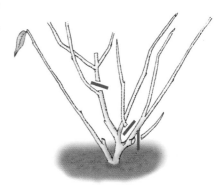

1 **Remove branches** that are crossing or crowded during the first few years after planting as these will spoil the symmetry of the plant. This is especially important for shrubs or trees that cannot be hard pruned when they are older, such as witch hazels, magnolias, or rhododendrons.

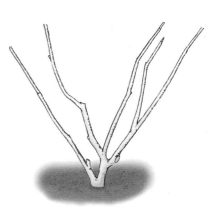

2 **After training** you are left with evenly spaced branches and a balanced, open habit. This forms the permanent woody framework from which the rest of the plant will develop; aim to maintain this open habit on new growth as the plant grows.

Formative pruning

Some trees and shrubs develop a well-shaped branch structure quite naturally, but many benefit from a little help in the early years (*see facing page*), particularly if they can only undergo minimal pruning when mature (*see page 104*).

If you intend to grow trees or shrubs as a restricted form, such as a wall-trained cordon or espalier, then you will need to prune them quite carefully in the first few years to form the shape that you need.

Formative pruning is less vital for shrubs that are pruned hard or for renewal (*see pages 100–103*), but it still helps to create a balanced shape with evenly spaced branches.

Pruning for shape

After initial pruning and training, many trees and shrubs can be left to their own devices, with minimal pruning to remove dead, diseased, or damaged branches. By paying attention to detail, you can maintain an attractive shape through well-judged pruning.

Sometimes, however, branches develop that spoil the shape and symmetry of the plant, and these can be cut out. If one side of your tree has developed more vigorously than the other, giving a lop-sided look, you can lightly prune the stronger shoots and hard prune the weaker ones to restore the balance (*see box, below*).

PRUNING TO MAINTAIN A BALANCED SHAPE

Correct method
Before

Correct method
After

Incorrect method
Before

Incorrect method
After

Some shrubs grow unevenly and present a lop-sided aspect. This can be remedied if strong shoots are lightly pruned – resulting in moderate growth – and the weak shoots cut back hard to stimulate

vigorous regrowth (*shown top*). It is tempting to do the opposite so that on pruning the shape is restored. But when the plant regrows, the imbalance will be even greater than before (*shown bottom*).

WATER SHOOTS

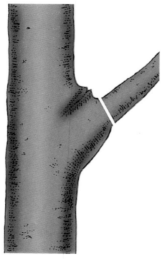

Clusters of shoots can arise on tree trunks and main branches, often around an old wound. They should be cut out each year, in winter, back to the base, as they may weaken other growth.

Pruning to prevent disease

You will want your trees and shrubs to remain healthy, so always prune to remove dead, diseased, and damaged wood. These should be removed as soon as they are spotted to prevent any potential problems from spreading into other parts of the plant. Either cut out the affected branch completely or cut back into healthy wood. If the material is diseased, burn it if possible.

If dead or damaged wood is present, this can act as an easy entry point for disease, and a plant that is in poor health is much more susceptible to infection by further diseases or attack by pests.

You should always be on the look out for dead, diseased, and damaged material. At the same time, you can also give the plant's health a boost by snipping out any very thin or crossing shoots from the centre of the plant. These develop due to lack of light, and removing them will open the plant up and allow air to flow more efficiently through the crown.

Pruning to encourage flowers

Many shrubs are pruned for a better display of flowers. For this to be successful, the timing of pruning is essential and you need to know if the plant flowers on old wood or on shoots that are produced in spring of the same year.

For example, the many varieties of *Buddleja davidii* flower on new wood, and the best floral spectacle comes as a result of hard pruning the shrub in early spring to encourage lots of new branches, which will bear the

PRUNING A LARGE BRANCH

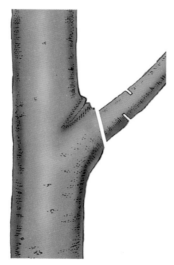

Remove in stages to reduce damage. Finish by sawing straight through the branch, outside the bark ridge and the branch collar.

WHERE TO CUT ON DIFFERENT TYPES OF BRANCHES

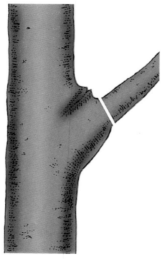

A swollen branch collar and raised bark ridge, above the branch, should be pruned outside the collar and ridge.

If there is no obvious bark collar, imagine an angled line starting from the outer edge of the bark ridge, running away from the trunk.

Hedges *see page 113* | Roses *see page 117* | Growing fruit *see page 216*

flowering wood. Closely related *Buddleja alternifolia*, however, flowers on one- and two-year-old wood, so if it was pruned heavily in the spring, there would be no floral show at all that year.

Any good nursery or garden centre will be able to supply you with this information when you buy a shrub. Established plants are less easy to ascertain; start by identifying the plant and go from there. Flowering trees, such as horse chestnuts or laburnums, tend to be left to their own devices.

Pruning for foliage

With flowering shrubs, it helps to understand what a plant is and how it grows before you start to prune. Golden-leaved elders, purple hazels, and Indian bean trees can all be cut back hard for maximum foliage effect (*see page 103*), whereas Japanese maples need only minimal work (*see page 104*). Where shrubs are grown for their flowers as well as their foliage, as with variegated-leaved *Philadelphus*, practise renewal or minimal pruning.

Other reasons to prune

Further pruning that may be necessary includes removing large tree branches (*see below*), dealing with suckering and water shoots (*see boxes, facing page and right*), or to cut out any reverted shoots – seen on shrubs with variegated leaves, where shoots develop with pure green leaves. These should be cut back to the base, as they are more vigorous and will eventually dominate.

SUCKERING SHOOTS

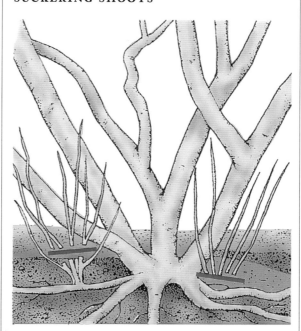

Shoots that arise directly from the roots of a woody plant are known as suckers. These can be a nuisance on trees like sumach (*Rhus*), as they spoil the look of the plant. Suckers that arise on trees and shrubs that are grafted onto rootstocks (*see page 243*), such as roses, are more of a problem – they do not share the same ornamental qualities as the grafted plant, and if left will gradually take over. Pull off each sucker at its point of origin so that the dormant buds are removed at the same time (*right*). If suckers are simply cut off at ground level (*left*), further suckers will result.

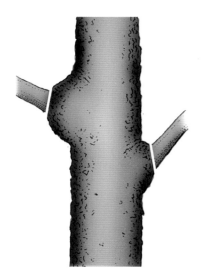

Obvious ridges and collars make branch removal straightforward. Cut just beyond the bark ridge and the swollen branch collar.

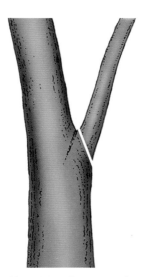

V-shaped branch junctions are weak and should be removed. Cut from the bottom of the branch to avoid damaging the trunk.

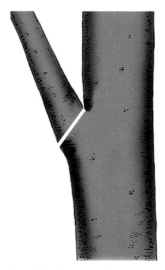

Steep branches may also need to cut from below. Judge the cut carefully so that you do not cut, or remove any material from, the trunk.

Pruning evergreen shrubs

Assuming that they are grown in the right place with plenty of space to develop, and that they have been pruned formatively to create a balanced framework (*see page 94–95*), most evergreen shrubs will grow happily with the minimum of pruning. You will only need to remove the dead heads of fading flowers (*see box, right*) and dead or diseased branches as they are seen.

If there are any wayward shoots, winter-damaged branches, or badly placed growths that spoil the shape of the shrub, these are best removed in spring. This gives plenty of time for regrowth to ripen before cooler weather returns in autumn. Pruned earlier, new growth could be susceptible to frost, and if cut later, say in summer or autumn, the resulting new growth will be soft and sappy, making it vulnerable to damage over winter.

Some evergreen plants can be cut back hard for foliage effect (*see page 103*). For example, eucalyptus plants develop oval leaves on mature growth, but can be pruned

DEADHEADING

Removal of faded flowerheads after flowering, known as deadheading, prevents the plant diverting energy into fruit production. It also improves the look of the plant.

COMPETING SIDESHOOTS

Prune back sideshoots that compete with the main stem, in spring. If a double main stem develops, it can cause a point of weakness.

PRUNING TO STIMULATE SIDESHOOTS

1 **Cut back** the tip of the main stem in spring by just a few leaves to stimulate growth of sideshoots from buds in the leaf bases (*inset*).

2 **Sideshoots develop** in summer, forming a bushier plant. Train the top sideshoot to continue the upward growth of the main stem.

close to ground level each spring to promote lots of new stems that bear plenty of attractive, rounded juvenile leaves. As well as looking good in a mixed border, the new shoots can be cut for indoor display.

Early training of young shrubs

Young evergreen shrubs sometimes need training to help develop a main stem and bushy growth. If the plant has a strong main stem, it may be necessary to reduce the length of any competing sideshoots (*see facing page, left*). Alternatively, if the main stem is weak with very few branches, it can be pruned to encourage the growth of sideshoots; the uppermost sideshoot then takes over as the main stem (*see facing page, right*).

Pruning lavender & heather

If left unpruned, lavender will develop a mass of leggy, woody stems and prove to be difficult to rejuvenate. It is best to keep plants compact, bushy, and attractive by trimming twice a year (*see below*). Heathers need minimal pruning (*see box, right*): lightly trim winter-flowering varieties in mid-spring after they have finished flowering. Prune summer- and autumn-flowering heathers at the same time, as this allows you to enjoy their old flowerheads over winter, which are ornamental.

TRIMMING HEATHER

1 Lightly trim over the plant in mid-spring, removing the old flowerheads just below the base. Use shears, or scissors on small plants, to follow the natural growth of the plant – do not attempt to cut them into shapes.

2 Flowering takes place again the following summer, autumn, or winter, depending on the species of heather. Do not trim again until mid-spring.

PRUNING LAVENDER

FIRST YEAR

1 Prune back young plants quite hard in mid-spring to remove untidy growth, to encourage new branches, and to start to create the required shape.

2 Remove old flowerheads after flowering by giving the shrub a light trim with shears. This improves the look of the plant and prepares it for winter. Avoid the temptation to trim plants back harder at this time.

SECOND & SUBSEQUENT YEARS

3 Trim closely in early spring with hand shears. You can cut back quite hard – it keeps the plants neat and compact – but do not cut back into the older, leafless wood, as this will not rejuvenate.

4 Over the years, lavenders will gradually fill out, despite close trimming each year. Eventually, they will need replacing, as will unkempt or badly shaped lavenders.

Pruning deciduous shrubs

It is a misconception that all deciduous shrubs need to be pruned. All will grow successfully without pruning, but from a gardener's perspective most will quickly begin to look untidy and their displays may lack quality.

It will be necessary, therefore, to prune from time to time. Quite how regularly you do this depends on your needs as a gardener; if you are trying to achieve a naturalistic look, you can ease off a bit and maybe grow shrubs that only need minimal attention (*see page 104*). If you want the maximum performance from each and every one of your garden shrubs, you should prune attentively.

RENEWAL PRUNING

Shrubs that flower on stems produced the previous year can be pruned after flowering to promote a renewed supply of young and vigorous shoots. If done each year, lots of new shoots will grow further down the plant, resulting in flowers nearer the ground, which are easily enjoyed by the gardener.

Renewal pruning not only maximizes the flowering potential of a deciduous shrub, it keeps it within bounds; if left unpruned, especially in a small garden, these shrubs can outgrow their space.

Shrubs that can be pruned by this method form a large group, mostly consisting of spring- or early summer-flowering shrubs like spring-flowering *Ceanothus*, *Deutzia* (*see below*), *Forsythia*, *Kerria* (*see facing page*), *Kolkwitzia*, *Hydrangea* (*see facing page*), *Philadelphus*, flowering currant (*Ribes sanguineum*), *Buddleja alternifolia*, spring-flowering *Tamarix*, *Weigela*, and *Spiraea* 'Arguta'.

If you do not want to prune annually, or if you have the space to let them grow naturally, *Philadelphus*, *Deutzia*, and *Spiraea* can be left to grow for four or five years before chopping them back hard to 15cm (6in) from the ground (*see page 102*). Allowed to grow like this, they will develop an attractive, natural shape that is similar to that obtained by the shrub in the wild; one drawback is that it may take them a couple of years to recover fully.

PRUNING DEUTZIA

FIRST YEAR

1 **Prune away** all weak growth and the tips of all main shoots back to a pair of strong buds on planting in autumn to early spring. Aim to create a balanced, open framework (*see page 94*). Water the roots well and add a thick mulch over the root area.

SECOND & SUBSEQUENT YEARS

2 **Let the plant flower** and develop strong new shoots and branches in its first growing season. These new shoots and branches will become the renewal growth.

3 **Cut back** all the flowering stems to strong side branches lower down the stems as soon as the display is over. Prune out any weak growth and any other badly placed shoots to maintain the open, balanced framework.

4 **In winter**, you will see how the strong side branches have grown to replace the old flowering stems that were removed the previous summer. This is the renewal growth that will flower in the coming year, when the shrub should be pruned using the same method.

PRUNING KERRIA

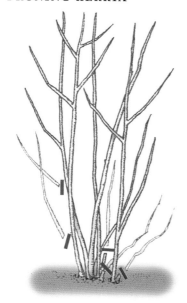

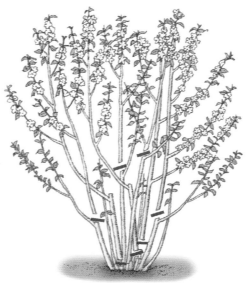

FIRST YEAR

1 **Cut back** all weak growth to a strong bud on planting in autumn to early spring to create a balanced framework (*see page 94*).

2 **Remove all flowered shoots** at the base or low down on the branches where new shoots are forming. Mulch, if necessary.

SECOND & SUBSEQUENT YEARS

3 **Prune after flowering** each year in the same way as in step 2. New shoots that grow form the renewal growth.

Variations on a theme

Deutzia (*see facing page*) is a typical example of a shrub that benefits from renewal pruning. Branches that have flowered are cut back to strong new shoots that then flower the following year.

The new shoots of some shrubs, such as *Kerria* (*see above*), grow from or close to ground level rather than on existing branches. The main point of difference is that after flowering, branches that have flowered are cut right back to the base or to a point low down on the stem where there is vigorous new growth.

Pruning hydrangeas

Lacecap and mophead hydrangeas flower late in the season and they are often mistakenly pruned hard in spring in the belief that the resultant strong growths will flower that same year, as for a butterfly bush (*see following page*). This is not the case.

Only minor pruning is required of a mature hydrangea, and this should be delayed until spring as old flowers left on the plant over winter help to protect the vulnerable buds below from frost. In spring, remove the dead flowerheads back to a healthy pair of buds. Renewal pruning can be done on mature hydrangeas if they have become choked with lots of twiggy growth (*see right*).

PRUNING A MATURE HYDRANGEA

1 **Remove old flowerheads** by cutting them back to a strong pair of buds in mid-spring. On congested plants, remove one third to a quarter of the older branches to their base at the same time; renewal growth will emerge in the coming season. Aim to keep a balanced framework (*see page 94*).

2 **On flowering**, in mid- to late summer, you will notice that new flowerheads form from the strong pair of buds that were below the old flowerheads. The renewal growth will have extended, but this will not flower until the next season.

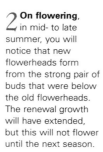

HARD PRUNING

Shrubs that flower on growth that develops during spring and summer can be pruned hard in spring, to produce vigorous new shoots for flowering.

Plants that can be pruned by this method consist of late summer- or autumn-flowering shrubs like butterfly bush (*Buddleja davidii*), autumn-flowering *Ceanothus*, *Caryopteris*, *Ceratostigma*, *Fuchsia magellanica*, *Hydrangea paniculata*, *Leycesteria*, *Perovskia*, *Romneya*, *Spartium*, and all varieties of *Spiraea japonica*.

There are various ways of hard pruning deciduous shrubs. *Leycesteria*, *Perovskia*, and hardy fuchsias, which do not form a woody framework, can be pruned almost to ground level. *Spartium*, autumn-flowering *Ceanothus*, and *Caryopteris* can be allowed to develop a permanent framework of branches and then the old shoots cut back to within a few centimetres or inches of this. Butterfly bush (*Buddleja davidii*), which is extremely vigorous, can be pruned back harder to a lower framework (*see below*).

Hard pruning for winter stems

Deciduous shrubs like *Rubus cockburnianus*, dogwood (*Cornus alba*, *C. sanguinea*, and *C. sericea*), willow (*Salix*), and their many varieties are hard pruned for their colourful winter stems. It is a straightforward procedure that takes place in early spring every year (*see facing page*).

Shrubs grown for their winter stems tend not to be particularly decorative otherwise, so pruning simply consists of cutting down all growth to ground level. New shoots grow vigorously if the plant is growing under the correct conditions, and when the leaves fall in autumn, their ornamental stems are revealed.

This technique of cutting to the ground is known as coppicing. If needed, willows and dogwoods can be pollarded, which means they are grown on top of a short or tall trunk (*see box, facing page*).

Rubus cockburnianus cannot be pollarded as it is a type of bramble. Covered with sharp thorns, it therefore makes an impenetrable barrier, so take care when pruning.

PRUNING A BUTTERFLY BUSH

FIRST YEAR
1 Prune back all shoots by two thirds to vigorous buds or emerging shoots on planting. Remove weak shoots entirely.

2 Vigorous new shoots develop and flower at the tips in late summer. They can be deadheaded to prevent self-seeding.

SECOND YEAR
3 Prune back hard all shoots to 1–2 buds at the base in spring. A permanent woody framework begins to develop.

4 Remove tips of flowered stems in early autumn to prevent self-seeding and damage during winter storms.

THIRD & SUBSEQUENT YEARS
5 Prune back hard all shoots to strong buds at the base in spring, as in step 3. Repeat this process in successive years.

6 Remove sections of the permanent framework with loppers or a pruning saw when it becomes overcrowded.

HARD PRUNING DOGWOOD TO PRODUCE COLOURFUL STEMS

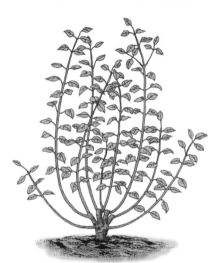

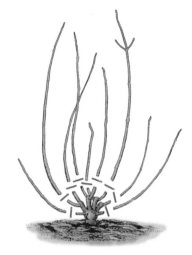

FIRST YEAR

1 **Prune back hard** all shoots close to their base on planting. Mulch the plant and feed around the roots.

2 **Vigorous new shoots** develop in spring and summer. When the leaves fall, the attractive stems will be revealed.

SECOND & SUBSEQUENT YEARS

3 **Prune back hard** all shoots as in step 1. Remove any weak stumps at the base. Feed and mulch well.

Hard pruning for maximum foliage effect

Like deciduous shrubs grown for their winter stems, some shrubs are hard pruned purely for their decorative foliage, which is a feature in summer and autumn.

Shrubs that can be pruned this way include Indian bean tree (*Catalpa bignonioides*), smoke bush (*Cotinus coggygria*), *Cornus alba* (some varieties), sumach (*Rhus typhina*), golden elder (*Sambucus nigra* 'Aurea'), and purple-leaved hazel (*Corylus maxima* 'Purpurea').

Not all shrubs tolerate hard pruning; some will die if given such treatment. Those that can stand it are pruned in the same way as for winter-stem shrubs (*see above*). They will not flower given such treatment, and on most foliage shrubs this is of no importance.

If you want flowers as well as foliage, as you may well do on a smoke bush or a dark-leaved elder, you must prune less harshly; in the case of elders and smoke bushes, revert to minimal pruning (*see following page*).

Indian bean trees (*Catalpa bignonioides*) bear impressive foliage if hard pruned each spring, particularly this golden form 'Aurea'. The leaves are also often much larger than on unpruned specimens.

POLLARDING

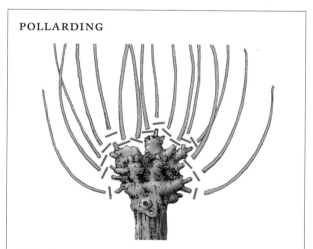

The basic framework of coppiced shrubs can be varied in height if allowed to grow on a trunk, as a pollard. This is useful in raising the height of the display. New shoots are pruned in the same way.

MINIMAL PRUNING

There is a large group of shrubs that develop a permanent framework of branches and require very little pruning once established. Japanese maples (*Acer japonicum* and *A. palmatum*), *Euonymus*, deciduous magnolias, viburnums, cotoneaster, smoke bush (*Cotinus*), *Hibiscus*, witch hazel (*Hamamelis*), and others produce their growth from the perimeter of the framework, unlike other shrubs that make lots of vigorous growth from the base and lower branches. Early training of these shrubs is needed to build up a framework (*see below*), with the aim of creating an attractive shrub with a well-balanced branch structure.

When mature, maintain these shrubs by cutting out any dead, diseased, or damaged branches. Wayward shoots can also be removed to maintain symmetry. If vigorous shoots do grow from the base or lower down the framework, either cut them out or train them in, if this is necessary to replace older branches.

Intricately branched Japanese maples may look like they are the result of attentive pruning, but beyond the creation of the basic framework, they are actually left unpruned. After leaf fall, the shrubs can be inspected for dead, damaged, or diseased branches.

PRUNING A DECIDUOUS MAGNOLIA

FIRST YEAR

1 Remove crossing branches and weak growth on planting in autumn to early spring. Aim to create a balanced, open framework (*see page 94*), here on *Magnolia stellata*.

SECOND YEAR

2 Prune away any badly spaced side branches in spring that have formed after the first season of growth. Leave all the other branches unpruned.

THIRD & SUBSEQUENT YEARS

3 Prune only as required to remove dead, diseased, or damaged branches as they are seen. Crossing branches that emerge must also be removed as this will lead to damage when they rub together.

4 Leave the plant unpruned at flowering time so its display can be enjoyed. The spring flowers and new growth can be seen to emerge at the perimeter of the framework at this time of year.

Pruning a feathered tree

A feathered tree is easily recognized by its main stem which is clad with a series of evenly spaced branches, almost to ground level. This naturalistic method of growth is achievable on many garden trees, and is most often seen on birches, alders, and mountain ash (*Sorbus aucuparia*).

The aim with the early training of a feathered tree is to develop a single dominant top shoot, or leader (*see below*), avoiding a forked or double leader. You do this by removing any competing shoots that may form. Shoots that grow from the base of the tree need to be removed immediately for a similar reason: if they are left, you will end up with a multi-stemmed tree.

As the tree matures, it should form a symmetrical shape without any intervention. You can encourage this by pruning out any branches that ruin the symmetry or are badly crossing during late autumn and early winter. Dead, diseased, and damaged branches can be taken out at the same time. Lower branches that will get in the way of the lawnmower when cutting the lawn or are too overcrowded, can also be removed, if necessary.

A feathered tree can easily be converted into a central-leader standard tree (*see following page*) by cutting back the lower branches over a number of years until the required height of the bare trunk is reached.

PRUNING A FEATHERED TREE

FIRST YEAR

1 On planting, stake and tie in the tree. Allow the tree to grow unpruned in its first spring and summer.

2 Cut back shoots that grow close to the base in mid- to late autumn. If not removed, these may rival the main stem.

SECOND YEAR

3 Remove the stake after 18 months, in summer. Cut out any sideshoots that turn upwards to compete with the leading shoot.

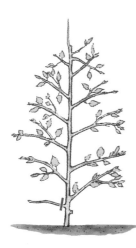

4 Remove any low branches that may interfere with mowing, in autumn.

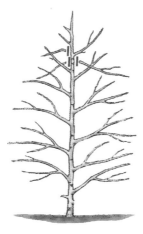

THIRD YEAR

5 Remove any shoots that might compete with the leader, in late winter.

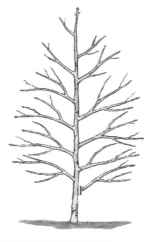

FOURTH & SUBSEQUENT YEARS

6 Let the tree develop naturally, pruning in winter to remove badly placed branches.

Pruning a branch-headed tree

Crab apples, cherries, and many other small garden trees are grown as branched-headed standards. It is the commonest way to grow ornamental trees. These trees have a stem that is clear of branches for the first 2m (6ft) from the ground, followed by a well-branched crown. You can buy young trees from nurseries and garden centres that are already trained with a clear trunk.

These trees are not grown with a dominant central leader, unless they are grown as a central-leader standard (*see box, right*). The type of crown that forms depends on the natural growth of the plant, since there is very little intervention from the gardener.

Early training involves the removal of side branches until the desired length of clear stem has been reached. This stage can be skipped if you have bought a pre-trained standard tree. Thereafter, minimal pruning during late autumn and early winter will keep the tree in good shape – simply remove badly placed or crossing branches, along with any that spoil the symmetry of the tree. Dead, diseased, or damaged branches should be pruned out whenever you spot them. The aim is to create an open crown framework of well-spaced branches.

You should also remove any shoots that emerge on the clear trunk, as well as any vigorous upright shoots within the crown that may try and develop into dominant leaders during the first few years.

CENTRAL-LEADER STANDARD TREES

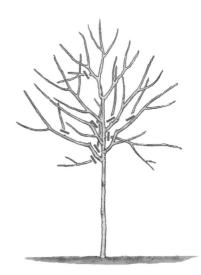

Large trees suit this branch structure. Prune formatively as for a feathered tree (*see previous page*), with lower branches removed gradually each year, until the clear stem is at the desired length.

PRUNING A BRANCH-HEADED TREE

FIRST YEAR

1 **On planting**, stake and tie in the tree. Allow the tree to grow unpruned in its first spring and summer.

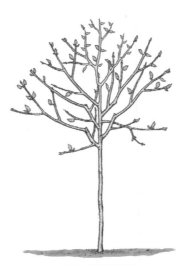

SECOND & SUBSEQUENT YEARS

2 **Allow further branches** to develop in the crown. No pruning is necessary, but if a leading shoot forms, cut it back to a strong bud to encourage branching in the crown.

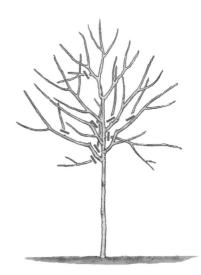

3 **Prune out** crossing or crowded branches in mid- to late autumn to form an open, evenly spaced framework. Remove any shoots that appear on the main stem.

Trees & shrubs *see page 88* | **Hedges** *see page 113* | **Growing fruit** *see page 216*

Shrub renovation

If you inherit a new garden full of neglected shrubs, or you have a plant that has become too large for its position or is choked with branches, you may think that the only answer is to remove the shrub completely and start again. Before making such a decision, it is worth trying to rescue the plant through drastic pruning (*see right*).

This may sound brutal, and sometimes it is, but shrubs have remarkable powers of recovery and many respond well to such treatment. If you have a prized shrub, or one that you feel is not strong enough to recover from such a shock, then you can attempt the renovation over two or more years (*see below*). With evergreens, however, you will find that it is best to tackle the shrub in one go, as partial pruning looks uneven, untidy, and unsightly.

There is a risk that a neglected shrub does not recover from such an operation, for whatever reason. If this is the case, consider it a failed experiment and replace the plant.

When to renovate shrubs

Deciduous shrubs should be pruned in winter while they are dormant. Tackle evergreen shrubs in late spring when they are coming into growth.

A high percentage of deciduous shrubs respond well to hard pruning, but among the evergreen shrubs there are some notable exceptions: most conifers and some woody herbs like lavender and rosemary will not regrow from old wood. Rhodendrons, camellias, mahonias, hollies (*Ilex*), yews (*Taxus*), and cherry laurels (*Prunus*), however, should all recover rapidly.

RENOVATION BY DRASTIC PRUNING

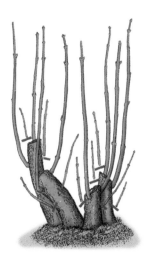

1 **Cut back** all stems to 15–30cm (6–12in) from ground level in winter. Mulch and feed.

2 **Prune out** new shoots that emerge next year, leaving the strongest as renewal growth.

Aftercare

With so much woody material removed, shrubs must be well fed and mulched in spring for several years following renovation pruning. It will also help if you water the plant well in summer, particularly during the first year.

Emerging shoots may be nibbled by rabbits or deer, so protect the plants in gardens where these animals are present. Within three or four years, the renovated shrub should be well recovered.

RENOVATING A DECIDUOUS SHRUB OVER TWO YEARS

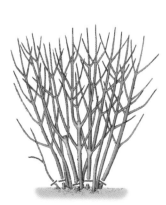
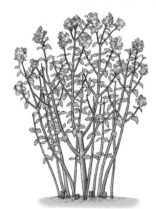
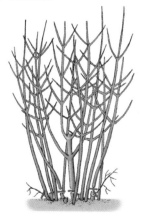

FIRST YEAR

1 **Cut back** half of all old stems back to ground level from late autumn to winter.

2 **New shoots** emerge from the base and the remaining old stems flower. Mulch and feed the plant generously.

SECOND YEAR

3 **Remove the remaining** old stems back to the ground in autumn to winter. Cut back any new growth that is weak.

4 **One-year-old shoots** bear flowers, while new shoots grow from the base. Renovation is complete.

Tree renovation

Large trees in need of renovation must be tackled by a qualified tree surgeon, armed with the right tools and safety equipment to carry out pruning high above the ground. Small trees, however, that have been neglected or poorly pruned in the past can be dealt with by gardeners in late autumn and early winter.

The aim with pruning is to create a well-balanced tree. Most trees can be restored by removing dead, diseased, or damaged branches, followed by pruning out crossing branches and thinning a mass of upright branches to leave an open centre. In some circumstances, it may be necessary to lose one or more large branches. Pruning like this is likely to result in the development of water shoots for several years afterwards, but these can easily be removed by hand (*see above right*).

Corrective pruning

One response to poor pruning is a congested cluster of shoots or knobbly spurs (*see right*). This follows drastic winter pruning in which trees have had all their new growth cut off. It is often seen on apple trees (*see page 267*); it looks ugly and stunts flowering and fruiting.

To restore the balance to trees like this, first remove any dead, diseased, or damaged branches, and any that are crossing or badly placed. Once this is done, you can tackle the knobbly spurs that are left on the branches by thinning out the shoots that grow from them.

Fruit trees are another group of trees that are often inherited in a neglected state. If left to their own devices, they can soon become a mass of twiggy branches with

WATER SHOOTS

Major pruning cuts on large branches often cause the formation of vigorous shoots from around the wound for several years after the cut was made. They should be removed as soon as they appear, at the base.

KNOBBLY SPURS

'Haircut' pruning results in a framework of knobbly spurs. These need careful but heavy thinning over a number of years in order to return the tree to its former glory.

lots of leafy growth but poor yields (*see pages 266–267*). Plums and damsons are commonly encountered in this state. To renovate, prune trees when in growth to avoid infection by silver leaf disease (*see page 272*). Carry out rejuvenation work gradually, over a three year period (*see below*). Feed and mulch all renovated trees well.

RENOVATION OF PLUMS & DAMSONS

FIRST YEAR
1 **Prune back** any dead or diseased branches in summer, and a few that spoil the symmetry. Remove branches from the trunk.

2 **Thin out** some overcrowded side branches at the same time to create an open crown.

SECOND & SUBSEQUENT YEARS
3 **Remove** a few more branches that spoil the symmetry, in summer, and continue to thin out overcrowded branch systems.

PESTS OF WOODY PLANTS

Pests, diseases & other problems *see page 26* | **Rose pests & diseases** *see page 128* | **Fruit pests** *see page 268*

Pests of woody plants

As well as the common pests listed here, woody plants are also vulnerable to aphids, capsid bugs, vine weevil, rabbits, deer, squirrels, and caterpillars (*see pages 35–36*).

Horse chestnut leaf-mining moth

This tiny moth has three generations between early summer and autumn. The caterpillars feed inside the leaves, causing elongated blotch mines that are initially white but later turn brown. By late summer, horse chestnut trees are often so heavily infested that little green leaf area remains. Early leaf fall often occurs.

Horse chestnut trees are too big to be sprayed. With isolated trees it is worthwhile collecting fallen leaves in the autumn and burning them to destroy overwintering pupae. Alternatively, compost the leaves in sealed bags or in heaps kept covered until July of the following year. *Aesculus hippocastanum* is very susceptible; *A. indica* is a resistant species that makes a good alternative tree.

Viburnum beetle

The most susceptible species are *Viburnum tinus* and *V. opulus*, but other species and hybrids can also be damaged. The larvae of this beetle are creamy white with black markings and are up to 7mm (³⁄₈in) long. They hatch from overwintered eggs laid in the stems, then proceed to eat holes in the leaves, often reducing them to a lace doily appearance in mid- to late spring. The greyish-brown adult beetles are 5–6mm (¹⁄₄in) long and cause less severe damage to the foliage in late summer.

Prevent damage by inspecting new foliage as it develops in mid-spring. The appearance of small holes will indicate when larvae are hatching. Spray with an insecticide containing thiacloprid or bifenthrin.

Cushion scale & soft scale

These small, sap-feeding insects are found on the undersides of leaves. Cushion scale attacks evergreen plants including camellia, holly, *Euonymus*, yew, rhododendron, and *Trachelospermum*. Soft scale are flat, oval, yellow-brown creatures also found on a wide range of woody plants, including bay and ivy.

Cushion scale matures in early summer when eggs are laid in broad white bands. These eggs hatch in early to midsummer and the immature nymphs overwinter on the foliage. A sugary honeydew is excreted and this produces a dense coating of sooty mould on the upper leaf surface. Control scale insects by spraying the newly hatched nymphs with imidacloprid or thiacloprid insecticides.

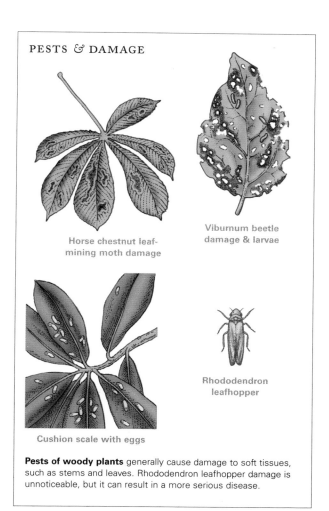

PESTS & DAMAGE

Horse chestnut leaf-mining moth damage

Viburnum beetle damage & larvae

Cushion scale with eggs

Rhododendron leafhopper

Pests of woody plants generally cause damage to soft tissues, such as stems and leaves. Rhododendron leafhopper damage is unnoticeable, but it can result in a more serious disease.

Rhododendron leafhopper & Azalea whitefly

The wingless, creamy white immature nymphs of the leafhopper suck sap from the underside of rhododendron leaves during summer. The adults, 8–9mm (³⁄₈in) long, are turquoise-green with two orange stripes on the wings. They fly up from the plant in late summer.

The leafhopper's feeding activities cause no visible damage, but the females lay overwintering eggs in the scales of next year's flower buds, making small incisions in the process. These provide entry points for a fungal disease called bud blast (*see page 112*). Control leafhoppers by spraying the plants in late summer with an insecticide containing imidacloprid or bifenthrin.

Azalea whitefly are tiny, white, moth-like insects that can occur in large numbers on evergreen azaleas in summer. A sugary honeydew is excreted. Control as for rhododendron leafhopper in early summer.

Berberis sawfly

The caterpillar-like larvae of this insect are up to 2cm (³/₄in) long and creamy white with black and yellow blotches. They feed voraciously on the foliage of some deciduous *Berberis* shrubs, especially *B. thunbergii*, and also *Mahonia* shrubs. There are two or three generations between late spring and early autumn and plants can be defoliated. The shiny black adults, which have black wings and upswept antennae, can be seen between mid- to late spring for the first generation; the second generation is present in mid- to late summer.

Inspect vulnerable *Berberis* and *Mahonia* shrubs between late spring and early autumn for young larvae. Spray with an insecticide containing bifenthrin, pyrethrum, or thiacloprid before an infestation develops.

Box sucker

The overwintered eggs of this insect hatch in mid-spring and the flattened pale green nymphs feed by sucking sap at the shoot tips of box shrubs during the rest of spring. Winged adults develop in late spring and early summer, but these cause no damage.

The feeding of the nymphs stunts normal shoot extension and causes leaves to be cupped, giving a cabbage-like appearance to the shoot tips. A sugary liquid called honeydew is excreted. The droplets are coated with white wax secreted by the nymphs. These droplets cascade out of the shoot tips when disturbed, leaving white smears on the foliage.

Box sucker is only of consequence on young plants that need to be grown taller. On established hedges and topiary that are frequently clipped to maintain a restricted shape, something that reduces the rate of growth is not going to be considered a problem. Where control is required, spray with an insecticide containing imidacloprid or bifenthrin in mid-spring if sucker nymphs are detected at the shoot tips.

Pieris lacebug

The host plants of this sap-feeding insect are *Pieris* species and some rhododendrons. From late spring, the upper leaf surface develops a coarse pale mottling. By late summer, much of the green colour may have been lost.

Lacebugs live on the leaf undersides, which are covered in brown excrement spots. The adults are 3–4mm (¹/₈in) long and their wings, which are carried flat on their backs, are transparent, with a distinctive black H-shaped marking. Check plants in late spring or early summer for recently hatched nymphs or signs of feeding damage on the new foliage. Spray with imidacloprid or bifenthrin.

Adelgids

These aphid-like insects suck sap from various conifers. Some species live openly on the foliage or young stems, where they are covered by a fluffy white wax secreted from their bodies; others develop inside swollen shoot-tip galls. Infestations can be unsightly, but as little damage is caused, adelgids can be tolerated or rubbed off by hand.

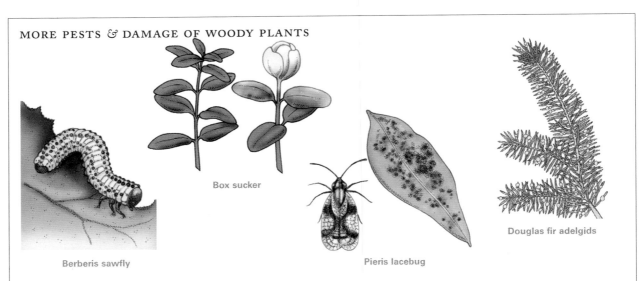

MORE PESTS & DAMAGE OF WOODY PLANTS

Box sucker

Douglas fir adelgids

Berberis sawfly

Pieris lacebug

The severity of pest infestations varies, so you must try to make an accurate identification of a pest before you make a decision about its treatment. Some pests, like box sucker and adelgids, can be tolerated in most cases. Others, like sawfly and lacebugs are more serious in their nature and will need to be dealt with promptly if an infested plant is to survive without too much damage.

DISEASES OF WOODY PLANTS

Pests, diseases & other problems *see page 26* | **Rose pests & diseases** *see page 129* | **Fruit diseases** *see page 271*

Diseases of woody plants

Many diseases can infect trees and shrubs, and some of the most common are listed here. Die-back or death is often attributable to honey fungus, *Phytophthora*, or *Verticillium* (*see page 37*).

Tree rusts

In Britain, rusts are relatively harmless to mature trees, apart from white pine blister rust (*see below*). They predominantly attack the leaves to produce dusty yellow or orange pustules, although some infect the bark and usually alternate between two hosts. Tree rusts that you may encounter include:

Birch rust: This rust alternates on larch. Rust-covered birch leaves will defoliate prematurely.

Poplar rusts: These can alternate on alliums, arums, dog's mercury, larch, or pine. Rust-covered poplar leaves die and remain hanging on the tree.

Willow rusts: These alternate on alliums, euonymus, and larch. The symptoms are similar to poplar rusts.

White pine blister rust: This alternates on currants and gooseberries. Black currants can defoliate severely, but this is usually late in the season and so does not affect plants adversely. This rust affects five-needled pines and infects the bark, forming swellings which can girdle and kill entire branches.

Control is unnecessary, unless the trees are young and getting established. Fungicides that are active against rusts will reduce the severity. Sometimes it is practical to remove a known alternate host to break the life cycle, although other spores can still be blown some distance.

Azalea gall

This common fungal disease can disfigure rhododendrons and azaleas, particularly the Indian azalea. It causes dramatic swellings, or galls, on affected leaves. The green galls become covered in a white spore bloom, which will spread the infection. Remove the galls by hand before they become white.

Wood decay & bracket fungi

Many different fungi can cause wood decay. Some cause rots in upper branches, where airborne spores enter wounds in the canopy and cause branch decay. Others cause root and butt rots, and may be indicated by crown thinning and early leaf loss.

Often the first indication of decay will be the appearance of fungal fruiting bodies. Commonly these are brackets, but toadstools and elaborate structures or

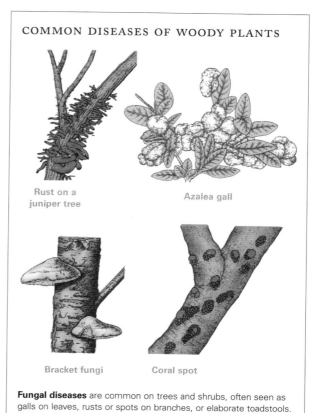

COMMON DISEASES OF WOODY PLANTS

Rust on a juniper tree

Azalea gall

Bracket fungi

Coral spot

Fungal diseases are common on trees and shrubs, often seen as galls on leaves, rusts or spots on branches, or elaborate toadstools.

encrustations are also possible around the tree. Removing the fruiting body does not stop the decay and unfortunately they usually only appear when infection is well established. With an infected tree, it is wise to seek professional advice regarding its safety.

Coral spot

Coral spot is commonly seen on dead twigs of trees and shrubs, or on woody debris such as hazel sticks. It is weakly parasitic and causes problems on plants that are suffering from other stresses; poor establishment, root death, and drought are common factors.

In damp weather, small, pink or red, cushion-like eruptions are evident on affected bark. Vast numbers of spores are produced from these 'coral spots'. They can infect through wounds and once established kill branches rapidly. Magnolias, *Elaeagnus*, maples, figs, currants, and gooseberries are frequently affected.

Good hygiene in the garden will reduce new infections. Careful pruning of your trees and shrubs so that dead wood is removed cleanly is a good precaution against coral spot as it will limit points of entry. If coral spot is a persistent problem, a wound sealant can help. It is also worth investigating plants to ensure that there is no underlying cause that could be corrected culturally.

Willow anthracnose

Small brown spots appear on leaves, leading to early defoliation, and black cankers that cause die-back form on stems. In damp seasons, the disease can be extremely damaging. Trees will recover in drier years and the disease must be tolerated. Weeping willow (*Salix* × *sepulcralis* var. *chrysocoma*) is worst affected.

Bud blast

This fungus kills flower buds on rhododendrons and azaleas, leading to a reduction in flowers. The buds become covered in black pinhead-like structures. This fungus is spread by the rhododendron leafhopper, and control of the insect may reduce new infections. Pick off dead buds as you see them.

Horse chestnut bleeding canker

These trees develop bleeding patches on the bark and they decline in vigour. Traditionally, this was ascribed to *Phytophthora* (*see page 37*), but the epidemic of cases in recent years appears to be caused by a bacterial infection.

Little can be done to halt infection as no antibacterial chemicals are labelled for use on ornamental plants. It is not recommended to cut out infected limbs as this creates new entry points for the bacterium and also spreads the bacterial inoculum trapped in the wood. Unless affected trees are a hazard, in which case it is wise to seek professional advice regarding its safety, they are best left alone and may recover if they have vigorous crowns. Both *Aesculus hippocastanum* and *A.* × *carnea* are susceptible.

Clematis wilt

This disease causes shoots of clematis to wilt and die rapidly, although recovery is possible from healthy tissue. Cut back affected growth to clean tissue, even if this is below ground level. Large-flowered hybrids are most susceptible. Most species forms, including *Clematis montana*, are resistant; *C. viticella* is tolerant of infection.

Cylindrocladium box blight

When infected, box plants develop dark brown spots on leaves and black streaks on stems. The plants drop their leaves and die back. Symptoms are often noticeably worse where water accumulates.

Box blight is extremely difficult to control once present, and so it is most important to avoid introducing infected material. Keep newly purchased plants separate from existing ones for one month to ensure they are clean. All box species are susceptible, but tightly clipped dwarf varieties are the worst affected. If discovered, promptly remove affected plants, carefully clean up fallen leaves, and replace top soil. Fungicides for use on ornamentals have limited success.

Rhododendron powdery mildew

This can appear in winter or spring and discolours leaves. A faint fungal growth on the lower surface corresponds with red or yellow blotches on the upper leaf. Limiting stress brought on by lack of water will help.

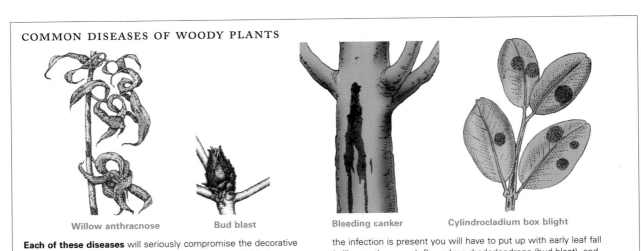

COMMON DISEASES OF WOODY PLANTS

Willow anthracnose   Bud blast   Bleeding canker   Cylindrocladium box blight

Each of these diseases will seriously compromise the decorative qualities of your ornamental plants if they take hold. With the exception of box blight, there is a chance of recovery, although while the infection is present you will have to put up with early leaf fall (willow anthracnose), flowerless rhododendrons (bud blast), and bleeding cankers on horse chestnut trees.

HEDGES

Hedges have many uses in the garden, but their main purpose is to provide an external boundary to your property. They can also be planted to provide shelter and privacy, as well as making a very good windbreak and filter against noise pollution. Within the garden, they can be used as a device to create 'rooms', while dwarf hedges are ideal for intricate parterres or as an attractive border to beds. Formal hedges are often cut several times a year to keep a geometric shape and are grown for their foliage rather than flowers. Informal hedges are mostly left to grow more naturally, with the plants allowed to flower.

Planting a hedge

Deciduous hedges are best planted between late autumn to early spring using bare-root plants. Use container plants for evergreen hedges, planting from mid- to late spring.

Choosing a hedge

What style of hedge you choose largely depends on your style of garden. Formal hedges are kept closely clipped, and hornbeam, beech, box, holly, cherry laurel, yew, and Leyland cypress are commonly used. Informal hedges are allowed to grow more naturally so plants flower or bear fruit. This suits a more relaxed style of garden.

Native hedges consist of several different trees and shrubs that will produce berries, flowers, fruit, and nuts that are attractive to birds, bees, insects, and mammals. They are ideal for a wildlife garden.

Spacing the plants

A single row of plants, spaced 30–60cm (12–24in) apart, is common for most hedges, but in some circumstances where a thicker hedge is required, it may be necessary to plant a double row. Allow 45cm (18in) between rows and stagger plants in the rows, spacing them 90cm (36in) apart.

PLANTING A HEDGE

1 Dig a trench along a planting line marked by a taut piece of string. The trench will need to be 40–60cm (16–24in) wide. Place the excavated soil to one side and remove any weeds as you find them.

2 Fork in well-rotted manure or garden compost into the bottom of the trench, and then return the excavated soil to the trench, mixing it in with the manure or compost as you go. Break up any large clumps of soil with the fork.

3 Tease out the roots from the rootballs of container-grown plants to encourage them to grow outwards after planting. Rake over the soil in the trench and mark planting holes with canes every 30–60cm (12–24in).

4 Firm in the plants after you have dug a hole and planted them at the same depth they were in their pots – or, if they are bare-root plants, to the soil mark on the main stem. Prune back the tips of leggy plants and water each plant in well.

Pruning hedges

To grow into a dense hedge, young plants will need pruning in their early years to encourage thick growth. Formal hedges will need regular clipping to maintain their shape, whereas informal hedges only need clipping once a year to keep them from getting overgrown. Treat wildlife hedges in the same way as informal hedges.

All established hedges are attractive to birds as they provide shelter, so if you can, try to avoid cutting between spring and midsummer, the main nesting time for birds. Always check for nests before you cut.

Tools for hedge cutting

A pair of hand shears is perfect for maintaining a short run of hedge, while longer hedges are easier with a powered trimmer. For most gardens, choose either an electric or lightweight, battery-powered model.

Initial pruning of a newly planted hedge

In the past, hedging plants were pruned hard upon planting, but this is unnecessary. The modern way of thinking is to save the first prune until the second growing season after planting.

Cut back deciduous plants to half their height in winter and evergreen shrubs to about two thirds their height in spring (*see facing page, top*). If you forget to prune a young hedge, it will fail to 'knit' together and there will be a lack of shoots at the base of the hedge.

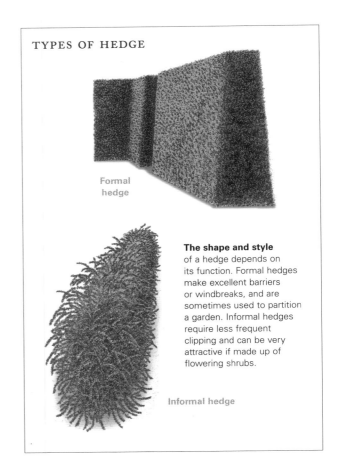

TYPES OF HEDGE

Formal hedge

The shape and style of a hedge depends on its function. Formal hedges make excellent barriers or windbreaks, and are sometimes used to partition a garden. Informal hedges require less frequent clipping and can be very attractive if made up of flowering shrubs.

Informal hedge

GETTING YOUR HEDGE TO THICKEN AT THE BASE

Hedges with no initial pruning tend to grow upwards quickly, forming top branches at the expense of the lower ones. The base remains bare, while the top growth is dense.

Young hedges that are correctly pruned when young form dense growth that is evenly distributed from top to bottom. Such hedges look good and they are effective as boundaries and screens.

FORMATIVE PRUNING OF AN EVERGREEN HEDGE

SECOND YEAR

1 Hard prune only if growth is leggy (shown). Otherwise, cut evergreens by one third in spring; deciduous hedges by a half in winter.

THIRD & FOURTH YEARS

2 Trim back sideshoots lightly in summer and then harder in early spring, starting to form a shape with tapered sides.

SUBSEQUENT YEARS

3 Let the hedge gradually fill out to full size, all the while trimming twice a year to maintain the tapered shape.

Hedges made from shrubs that are naturally bushy at the base, such as hornbeam, hazel, and beech (*see below*), should have their leading shoots pruned lightly in the second growing season after planting, along with some of the longer sideshoots. This should be repeated in the third and fourth years. Prune with a good pair of secateurs, making a slanting cut just above a bud. The angle should be facing away from the bud.

After planting a coniferous hedge (*see following page*), simply trim any untidy side branches to encourage more sideways growth. In subsequent years, trim the sides to get the required shape and only prune the leading shoots when they reach the desired height for the hedge.

In a newly planted hedge, there will be a lot of competition at the roots. Apply a thick mulch of organic matter each year and water the new plants in well.

FORMATIVE PRUNING OF A NATURALLY BUSHY, DECIDUOUS HEDGE

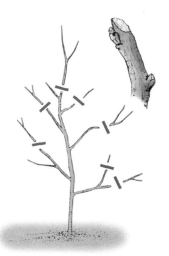

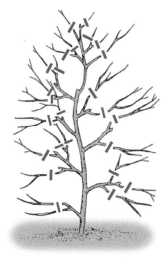

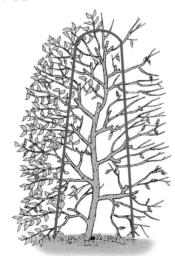

SECOND YEAR

1 Trim back the main stem and side branches by one third between autumn and late winter. Cut to a bud using good secateurs.

THIRD & FOURTH YEARS

2 Shorten all new growth by one third between autumn and late winter. The hedge will begin to thicken.

SUBSEQUENT YEARS

3 Cut the sides with shears in early summer, and again in winter, trimming back to a permanent framework with tapered sides.

Pruning established hedges

Once established, formal hedges are maintained by cutting every four to six weeks in summer, aiming to keep a neat shape with slightly tapered sides. Informal hedges are usually pruned after their display of flowers or berries.

Maintain coniferous hedges by pruning once or twice in summer. Fast-growing hedges like Leyland cypress must be cut regularly or they will get out of control; do not plant these trees in small gardens. In very large gardens, however, they make excellent tall screens and windbreaks.

FORMATIVE PRUNING OF A CONIFEROUS HEDGE

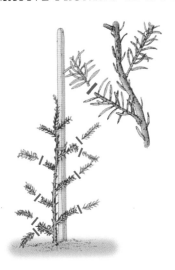

SECOND YEAR

1 **Prune side branches** by about one third in winter. Tie the unpruned leading shoot to a stake as it lengthens.

THIRD & FOURTH YEARS

2 **Trim back** sideshoots in summer, gradually forming a tapered shape. Continue to tie in the leading shoot to the stake.

SUBSEQUENT YEARS

3 **Prune the leading shoot** when the hedge is at its required height. Trim in summer to maintain the tapered sides.

Renovation

Over time or through neglect, hedges can become too wide or overgrown. It is possible to restore these plants through some drastic pruning carried out over a two-year period (*see box, right*).

In the first year, treat one side of the hedge as normal, but cut back the branches on the other hard to the main stems. The following year, if growth on the hard-pruned side has been vigorous, cut the other side back hard and treat the restored side as normal. If new growth is not vigorous, sprinkle a general-purpose fertilizer around the base of the hedge at the recommended rate, mulch thickly with well-rotted organic matter, and wait a further year.

Deciduous hedges can be treated this way in winter, when dormant, while evergreens should be pruned in late winter. Unfortunately, most coniferous hedges will not tolerate such hard pruning as they do not regenerate from old wood; yew is a notable exception. In such cases, it will be necessary to dig out the old hedge and replant with a new one. After pruning, give hedges a boost by watering, feeding, and mulching well.

RENOVATING A HEDGE

Cut back one side of the hedge, then repeat on the other side the next year. Not all hedges respond well to this, but it works with yew, holly, cotoneaster, pyracantha, and many deciduous plants.

Improving the soil *see page 20* | **Garden design basics** *see page 60* | **Trees & shrubs** *see page 88*

ROSES

Of all the garden plants, roses are one of the most versatile. They can be used in a variety of ways to bring colour and fragrance to the garden, from bold displays in summer borders to climbing roses that adorn walls and arches, and rambling roses scaling height into tree canopies. Patio roses may be grown in containers, and groundcover roses will scramble over a bank or trail from a raised bed. The first steps in giving your roses a good start are to buy good stock from a reputable nursery, and to plant correctly. You can then keep your roses flourishing by following the basic maintenance advice.

Buying roses

Buy only vigorous, healthy plants. Bare-root plants are best because they can be prepared and planted easily, between late autumn and late winter. They are wrapped in plastic to reduce drying out; bulk orders are bundled with twine in batches of 10. Plant on a frost-free day when the soil is not waterlogged (*see following page*), and if you are unable to plant the roses at once, heel them in (*see page 92*) into a hole or trench. Do not leave the roses in their packaging.

Containerized rose plants

Roses are available from garden centres in containers all year round. However, if you buy roses in early spring, directly after the bare-root season has finished, they can be up to three times more expensive. You may also find that when you come to tip the plant out of its pot before planting, all of the compost will fall off the rootball. This indicates that the rose is not container grown, but 'containerized', in which case you are essentially paying for a bare-root plant, compost, and pot.

It is preferable to wait to buy containerized roses in midsummer, when their roots have had time to become well established. You will still pay more than for a bare-root plant, but it should establish better than a containerized rose bought earlier in the season.

Alternatively, leave the containerized rose in its pot until early winter, then plant, following the same techniques as for bare-rooted plants.

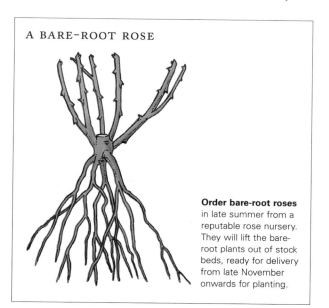

A BARE-ROOT ROSE

Order bare-root roses in late summer from a reputable rose nursery. They will lift the bare-root plants out of stock beds, ready for delivery from late November onwards for planting.

A huge range of roses is available, from bushes and climbers (*shown*) to different flower forms, colours, scents, and forms of rosehip.

Planting roses

Roses are prone to replant disorder, or soil sickness (*see below*). The first measure to combat this problem is deep soil preparation prior to planting. If preparing an old border that previously contained roses, remove the topsoil to a depth of 15cm (6in). Use this soil elsewhere in the garden – as long as you avoid growing roses in it, you should not encounter any problems.

Cultivate the soil by single digging or with a rotavator. Incorporate a generous layer of well-rotted manure, then leave the ground fallow for a few weeks to allow the soil to settle. Planting an intermediate crop of *Tagetes* 'Legend Series' the season before planting will 'clean' the soil and again reduce the risk of soil sickness.

How to plant

Soak the roots of bare-root roses as they will have been lifted for sale using machinery that may have damaged the roots. The graft union (*see page 243*) is typically planted just below soil level; on heavier soils, avoid the risk of rose canker by shallower planting.

1 Prepare the plant by soaking the root system in a bucket of water for about an hour before it is planted. Remove any leaves or hips from the branches, and prune off any long or damaged roots.

2 Dig out a hole about 50cm (20in) deep and wide for each new plant. For a rose against a wall or fence, dig the hole 30cm (12in) away to avoid the soil drying out. Exchange the soil with soil from another part of the garden; mix in well-rotted manure and a handful of general fertilizer.

3 Place the plant in the hole and carefully spread out the roots. On heavy soils, the graft union (*see page 243*) should be planted about 2.5cm (1in) above soil level to prevent rotting. On lighter soils, plant it 2.5cm (1in) below soil level. Check this by laying a cane or spade handle across the hole.

4 Water the rose bush and hole by filling it to the brim and allowing the water to soak away. Once it has drained, start backfilling right away, as a delay could lead to the roots drying out.

5 Backfill the hole with the improved garden soil, firming the soil around he roots as you go. Give the soil a final firm in with the heel of your shoe and rake the soil over to tidy it up. Add a thick mulch.

REPLANT DISORDER

The causes of this disorder are not fully understood. It occurs when a rose is planted into soil previously occupied by roses. An affected rose may display stunted growth or a distinct lack of vigour. If you uncover the roots of the plant, you may see signs of root rot; in severe cases, the plant may die rapidly (*see page 129*).

For most gardeners, the straightforward approach is to avoid planting roses on a site previously occupied by roses. Alternatively, the soil can be well prepared or even replaced with new topsoil. Mycorrhizal fungal spores can also be added to the soil on planting. These are beneficial fungi that form a symbiotic relationship with the plant. They are available from garden centres.

Improving the soil *see page 20* | **Garden design basics** *see page 60* | **Trees & shrubs** *see page 88*

Routine care of roses

Roses are not as difficult to grow and maintain as some people think, but if you want the best display of flowers and a strong, healthy plant, there are a few tasks that you should carry out through the year.

Spring

Remove any die-back on shoots and branches. This may have occurred a few weeks after pruning or during periods of prolonged cold in winter.

Check plants for pests and diseases (*see pages 128–129*). If you intend spraying against pests and diseases, buy a proprietary chemical from a garden centre and follow the instructions and application rates. Alternatively, rely on natural predators, such as lacewings, ladybird larvae, and birds.

New growth on climbing and rambler roses should be tied in as these roses do not have a natural twining habit and benefit from a bit of guidance.

Early to midsummer

Carry out light weeding and hoeing around the roots of your roses, and remove any suckers (*see right*). Remove spent blooms to encourage further flowering (*see following page*). If required, purchase containerized roses now for immediate planting or planting in early winter.

Late summer to early autumn

Tie in new growth on climbing and rambler roses while it is still supple and easy to bend into place. Continue removing spent blooms to prolong flowering.

In early autumn, place orders for bare-root roses, ready for delivery in late autumn, and heel in (*see page 92*) straight away unless you are ready to plant. Lightly prune hybrid tea and floribunda roses to prevent wind rock.

Winter

Begin pruning and tying in climbing and rambling roses in early winter and prepare beds for planting of new roses on days that are frost free and dry.

In late winter, begin pruning hybrid tea, floribunda, standard, shrub, and patio roses. Once pruning is complete, rake over the bed to remove old foliage, rose stems, and old mulch. Apply a dressing of rose fertilizer around the base of each plant, and rake it in lightly. Apply a 8–10cm (3–4in) layer of well-rotted manure around each rose or cover the rose bed completely. This will help to suppress weeds and retain moisture during the forthcoming growing season.

ROSE SUCKERS

Standard roses are prone to suckering on their main stems, which is actually the rootstock of the grafted plant (*see page 243*). As soon as you spot a sucker growing on the rose, put on a pair of thick gloves and pull it off or rub it away with your thumb.

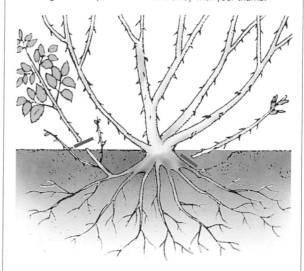

Remove suckers growing from the ground as soon as they are seen. Carefully clear away the soil and trace the sucker back to the roots. Rip it off at its base – if you cut off a sucker with secateurs, you will encourage more suckering growth to develop.

Check roses for suckers during summer. Suckers are shoots that sometimes develop from the rootstock of the rose, below the graft union. If left unchecked, suckers will eventually take over the plant and they become increasingly difficult to remove.

You can distinguish a sucker by its appearance, which will differ from the rest of the top growth. The sucker may have several leaves attached to one shoot or may be different in colour to the rest of the plant. Sometimes a sucker appears from the main stem rather than the roots (*shown top*).

Tools for rose pruning

It is well worth investing in good-quality secateurs: bypass secateurs are used by professionals and can be expensive but should last a lifetime. If expense is an issue, opt for a cheaper pair. Use secateurs only to cut stems with diameters of no more than 1.5cm (²⁄₃in) – about the thickness of a finger. If you want to prune stems thicker than this, use a pruning saw or a pair of loppers.

Loppers come in various styles: select a pair with sturdy handles for good leverage when pruning, preferably with a by-pass cutting blade. Folding pocket saws are great for pruning thicker stems and make a cleaner cut than loppers. They have pointed tips, which allow you to make pruning cuts close to the base of a plant. The blades cut on the pull stroke for efficient pruning.

Pruning techniques

Pruning is a simple operation, but as roses range in size from miniatures, which are less than 30cm (12in) tall, to vigorous climbers, which may reach 10–12m (30–40ft), they require a variety of pruning techniques to keep them healthy, free flowering, and within bounds.

Use sharp tools to cut stems cleanly with no ragged edges to reduce the change of infection. Make a 45-degree sloping cut above a healthy, outward-facing bud to allow moisture to drain away (*see right*), reducing risk of die-back and rot in the bud. This should prompt new shoots to grow outwards from the centre of the bush, avoiding overcrowding of shoots, improving circulation of air, and reducing occurrence of diseases like black spot. If you cut too high above the bud, the stem will die back due to a lack of sap flow.

DEADHEADING

Snap off dead flowers in summer at the abscission layer – the slightly swollen section of stem just below the bloom and the point where the bloom naturally falls off the plant. This technique encourages more flowers over a shorter period and promotes healthy foliage.

PRUNING

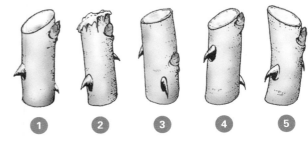

Pruning rules ❶ Make a sloping cut 5mm (¼in) above a bud. **❷** Ragged cuts lead to infection. **❸** Too high a cut leads to die-back. **❹** Cutting too close damages a bud. **❺** A cut towards a bud causes it to rot.

Basic steps of pruning

First cut out all dead, diseased, and damaged wood to leave a framework of healthy wood to prune. Always be mindful of the shape with every pruning cut made and aim to create an open-centred or goblet-shaped plant. Deadhead flowers to prolong flowering (*see above*).

PRUNING A HYBRID TEA BUSH ROSE

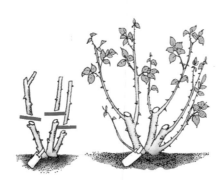

FIRST YEAR

1 Prune a bare-root rose before planting by cutting back the main shoots slightly and pruning long, coarse or damaged roots.

2 Cut back each shoot in late winter or early spring, to leave 2–4 buds or 15cm (6in) of stem above soil level (*left*). By summer, new shoots should have grown (*right*).

3 Trim back flowered stems at the end of the first season's growth to prevent wind rock over winter. Also cut out any soft, unripe shoots.

BUSH ROSES

Garden design basics *see page 60* | **Trees & shrubs** *see page 88* | **Choosing & using secateurs** *see page 398*

Bush roses

The most common types of bush rose grown in gardens are the hybrid tea and floribunda roses, also known respectively as large-flowered and cluster-flowered bush roses. As the names suggest, floribunda roses bear their flowers in clusters, and hybrid tea roses bear them singly.

Pruning bush roses

As with all roses, pruning is a constant process of wood renewal, with the aim of encouraging vigorous new growth and maximum flowering.

Look for potential buds, or eyes, on the shoots when deciding where to cut (*see facing page*). If you examine a rose bush and look closely at the individual buds on the stems, you will notice that the buds are positioned closer together if they are nearer the base of the plant.

In the dormant season, sometimes a bud is not always evident, but if you look closely at the stem you will see a fine line or scar, which indicates where a bud will eventually appear and grow in spring.

New plantings of hybrid tea and floribunda roses should be pruned in the same way (*see below*). Reduce all shoots back to two, three, or four buds – about the same height as a pair of secateurs standing on the ground. This promotes vigorous growth during the first year. After this, prune as for an established plant.

Pruning hybrid tea roses

Stems on new hybrid tea roses are pruned back relatively hard to encourage plenty of well-placed flowering shoots. When pruning established hybrid tea roses (*see below*),

This floribunda bush rose has clusters of flowers, which distinguishes it from a hybrid tea. They thrive on quite hard pruning in late winter or early spring, which promotes new, vigorous growth.

remove all dead, diseased, and damaged wood, then cut back all the remaining shoots, according to their relative vigour. This method ensures that all the old wood in the bush is renewed over a three-year period.

Pruning floribunda roses

Floribundas are more vigorous than hybrid teas, so are not pruned as hard. Remove all dead, diseased, and dying wood, then cut back all remaining shoots to five to seven buds or 15–20cm (6–8in) above the base of the plant.

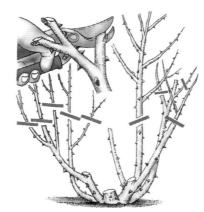

SECOND & SUBSEQUENT YEARS

4 Cut out wood that is dead, diseased, weak, crossing, or inward-growing in late winter or in early spring.

5 Prune strong stems at the same time, cutting them back to 4–6 buds or 10–15cm (4–6in) of stem above soil level. Cut back the less vigorous stems to 2–4 buds.

6 Trim back flowered stems at the end of the season's growth in early autumn. Also cut out any soft, unripe shoots.

Climbing & rambling roses

These are both excellent roses for covering structures like fences and walls. You can also train them to grow into the canopies of mature trees. Ramblers tend to have laxer habits and more pliable stems than climbing roses, and they usually flower only once, whereas climbers repeat flower throughout summer. Ramblers are also more vigorous and produce more basal growth once established. However, no two varieties are the same, so it is worth doing some research before purchasing new plants.

After planting, apply a general rose fertilizer around the base of the plant; work it in with a fork and then apply a generous layer of mulch or well-rotted manure.

Pruning climbing and rambling roses

Most climbers and ramblers require support; this may be in the form of a tripod of posts, a post and rope swag, or a wall or fence. Over the first two or three years after planting, concentrate on developing a basic framework of rose stems, which you can then tie into place on the support structure until it is covered.

Traditionally, climbers were pruned in late autumn when dormant, and ramblers were pruned in late summer directly after flowering. However, you can prune climbers and ramblers at the same time of year, from late autumn to midwinter, to produce plenty of flowers (*see below*). The key is to replace old wood with new wood, while keeping a strong framework of stems.

Before beginning to prune, look carefully at the climber or rambler and identify any dead, diseased, or damaged wood; prune it out. Also look for new rose stems to replace the older stems. At this point, you may decide to remove one or two old stems completely if the rose has produced sufficient new growth since it was last pruned. This is often the case with ramblers.

PRUNING CLIMBERS & RAMBLERS

FIRST YEAR

1 **Prune before planting** to leave 3–4 stems 9–15cm (3½–6in) long. Trim coarse or uneven roots on bare-root plants.

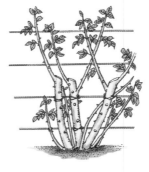

2 **New shoots develop** in the first spring after planting to form the basic shape of the rose.

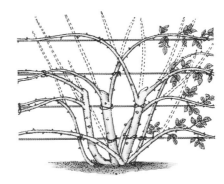

3 **Train the stems** into the supports from early summer to early autumn, to prompt new sideshoots to develop along the stems.

SECOND & SUBSEQUENT YEARS

4 **Tie in shoots** that develop horizontally, from early to midsummer. Flowers are borne on previous year's sideshoots.

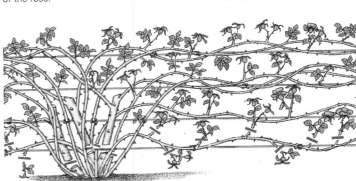

5 **Cut out a few flowered shoots** in late summer or early autumn to the base, leaving some to fill in the framework. Prune sideshoots to 2–3 buds, then tie in all new growth to the supports, keeping the stems horizontal to stimulate more sideshoots.

Next, prune all the remaining sideshoots arising from the main stems. Sometimes these are very vigorous, so it is worth considering them as replacements for older stems. Finally, tie in all pruned stems. Use special rose ties or garden twine looped in a figure-of-eight cross loop (*see box, right*). Cut the tips off the longest stems if they are outgrowing the support.

Climbers and ramblers growing against a fence or wall often tend to have a concentration of rose blooms at the top of the fence or wall. If you regularly bend the stems horizontal during pruning and training, they will produce more flowering laterals lower down on the plant. It is often easier to untie the plant from its support, then bend and twist the stems into place before tying them in with new twine. Take your time to ensure the best result.

Creating a floral wall

It is possible to train roses horizontally to form a fragrant wall. This can be achieved by erecting a series of wooden posts 10cm (4in) wide and 1.5m (5ft) tall, at regular intervals along a boundary. Use several lengths of strong galvanized wire, spaced 40cm (16in) apart, fixed to tension bolts to connect the posts together.

Select fragrant varieties of climbing roses (hybrid musk roses) to plant along the length of the supports. Once the plants are established, train and tie in the stems to cover the support, pruning in the same way as against a wall or fence for a dense wall of flowers in summer.

Roses in trees

When growing roses through mature trees, it is important to provide an initial support, such as a thick rope or wooden stake. Anchor this to the ground and secure into

TYING IN A CLIMBING ROSE

Tie in stems to the support with special ties or soft 3-ply twine, using a figure-of-eight cross loop to cushion the stem. Make sure it is not too tight to avoid the twine cutting into the stem.

the lower branches of the tree to help the rose to establish quickly. Roses growing under trees have to compete with the root system of the tree for soil, water, and nutrients, so they will require the best of care, with regular feeding and watering to help promote strong, vigorous growth.

It is not necessary to undertake any pruning once the rose has grown into the lower branches of the tree – just let it grow and enjoy its beauty.

Summer maintenance

During late summer, loosely tie into the supports any vigorous new shoots that develop on rose climbers and ramblers. At this time of year, you will find that the stems are soft and pliable, making them less prone to damage when you bend them into place.

TRIPOD-TIED CLIMBERS

Train the stems of a climber or rambler growing up a tripod or obelisk by bending them gently and twisting them around the structure. This slows the flow of sap within the stems, encouraging the plant to produce more sideshoots and, eventually, flowers.

WALL-TIED CLIMBERS

Support roses grown against fences and walls with wires, fixed into place with screw, or vine, eyes, and tension bolts. Position the wires horizontally, spacing them about 40cm (16in) apart.

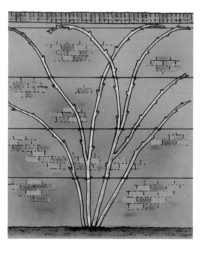

Garden design basics *see page 60* | **Trees & shrubs** *see page 88* | **Tools & equipment** *see page 396*

Species & shrub roses

When choosing a species or shrub rose, take note of the plant's habit and eventual size, because you do not prune these roses as hard as bush roses, so it is not so easy to contain them. Pruning them is a matter of judgement; assess the shape, habit, and growth of each rose as you prune it in early spring year to year.

Prune lightly on planting, pruning the tips of each shoot to a healthy bud. Once they are established, the aim is to maintain a strong, open framework, gradually replacing old wood with new growth over a number of years to promote vigour and encourage flowers.

Continually assess the plant as you prune. Remove all dead, diseased, and damaged wood, and cut out up to three old stems. Prune sideshoots by up to a half. Take care not to remove too much wood, which may spoil the shape of the rose and cause it to splay apart.

Variations on a theme

There are many types of species and shrub rose, all with slightly different flowering and growth habits. They can be divided into three main groups.

Once-flowering shrub roses: This group contains what are known as the old roses, such as alba, centifolia, moss, and damask roses. You can leave these unpruned, but after a few years you will have to thin them substantially in early spring to get rid of older, unproductive wood. Otherwise, prune as for general shrub roses (*see below*).

Repeat-flowering shrub roses: This group contains the 'English Roses', which flower through the summer. Prune these as for general shrub roses (*see below*).

Groundcover roses: To cover large areas of bare soil, peg down strong stems with small wire hoops to prompt rooting. Cut back any upright stems in early spring.

PRUNING A SHRUB ROSE

SECOND YEAR

1 **Cut main stems** by one third and sideshoots by up to a half, in early spring. Remove badly placed shoots.

2 **Flowering begins** in early summer, on the pruned sideshoots. Repeat-flowering shrub roses will flower through the summer.

3 **Prune back the tips** of tall stems in early autumn to minimize wind rock over winter, which loosens the roots.

THIRD & SUBSEQUENT YEARS

4 **Cut main stems** by up to one quarter, and sideshoots by up to a half, in early spring. Remove 1–3 older stems at the base.

5 **Flowering begins** again in early summer, more abundantly this time as there are more sideshoots to flower from.

6 **Prune back tips** of tall stems in early autumn. Prune from now on to maintain a balanced, open framework.

Standard roses

These are hybrid tea and floribunda bush roses that have been budded onto tall-stemmed rootstocks (*see page 243*). They are used to give height to bush roses when they are grown in borders. Given such a position, they can be extremely effective, particularly in a formal context.

Staking standards

Standard roses require some form of staking to help support the top growth. Use 3cm (1¼in) square posts and two rubber tree ties, each with a spacer, for each plant. Position the ties at equal distances along each post.

Pruning standard roses

Follow the pruning techniques as for bush roses, but take care not to over-prune them; if this happens, the suckers from the rootstock can dominate (*see page 119*).

First remove all dead, diseased, and damaged wood; prune healthy stems to outward-facing buds to promote an open centre. Remove any suckering growth on the main stem below the crown, and from below soil level.

To prune a weeping standard (*see box, right*), first remove all dead, diseased, and damaged wood, then prune out two-year-old wood in early spring to leave strong, new, vigorous growth. Prune lightly to shape the canopy.

Pruning patio & miniature roses

Remove all dead, diseased, and damaged wood, and reduce strong shoots by one third in spring. Cut out twiggy growth and prune lightly to shape the plant.

WEEPING STANDARDS

This form of rose is created by budding a climbing rose onto a rootstock with a tall stem. The graft union (*see page 243*) is at the top of the stems, just below the top growth. This produces a weeping standard, with long and attractive, trailing shoots.

PRUNING A STANDARD ROSE

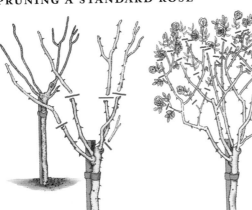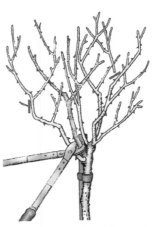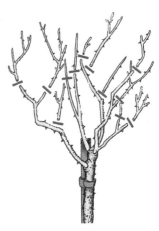

FIRST YEAR

1 Cut back each branch in early spring, to leave 4–7 buds on each branch. Remove spent blooms during summer.

2 Trim back the flowered stems in autumn to prevent wind rock over winter. Also cut out any soft, unripe shoots.

SECOND & SUBSEQUENT YEARS

3 Cut out dead, diseased, or damaged growth, and any badly placed stems, in early spring to create an open centre.

4 Prune branches at the same time, to 4–6 buds. Cut back the weaker stems to 2–4 buds to promote vigour.

Garden design basics *see page 60* | **Trees & shrubs** *see page 88* | **Bush roses** *see page 121*

Rose renovation

Unpruned and neglected roses can flower quite happily for many years; however, after a period of time they will start to become less vigorous and produce weak stems and fewer blooms. Many of us inherit roses in such a state when we move house; this can be daunting, as you may be faced with a large, unruly plant that you need to prune but are unable to identify.

Pruning a neglected rose

Wait until the rose comes into flower, so you can see if it produces good flowers and is worth keeping. If you decide to keep it, try to identify it, perhaps by sending a sample to a local rose nursery or society.

To renovate a rose, aim to prune it in late winter or early spring, then encourage the plant to produce new growth by feeding it with a dressing of rose fertilizer over the soil and lightly raking it in. Apply a mulch of well-rotted manure around the base of the rose and water regularly through summer. Most bush and shrub roses will respond well to renovation pruning.

Neglected roses often have thick stems without any visible signs of buds. Do not be concerned by this when deciding where to cut stems; concentrate on making good, clean cuts with a pruning saw.

Revisit the rose a month after pruning and examine the stems. If your pruning has been successful, you will notice new buds emerging from the remaining stems. This is a good sign, indicating new vigour.

Large roses can be daunting to prune if they are neglected. Many can be restored to their former glory by renovation pruning over 2–3 years; you and the rose can then sit together comfortably.

Continue to monitor the rose throughout summer and if growth still appears to be weak apply a liquid fertilizer at the manufacturer's recommended dose.

Prune again in early spring, and remove one or two old stems, depending on the amount of new growth. Continue with this annual prune over the next few years until all or most of the original old wood is replaced.

RENOVATION PRUNING

FIRST YEAR

1 **Cut out half** the main stems to the base in early spring; leave the youngest and strongest. Cut sideshoots to 2–3 buds.

2 **Flowers should appear** by midsummer on sideshoots of older wood. Vigorous new shoots should grow from the base.

SECOND YEAR

3 **Cut out more** of the old stems in early spring. Prune all sideshoots to 2–3 buds.

4 **Flowers are borne** in early to midsummer on sideshoots. New, vigorous stems replace the old framework of the plant.

Rose pests & diseases

As with other plants, the best protection against rose pests and diseases is to keep them growing strongly. However, some problems appear to be endemic; most of these are unsightly, but few seriously affect the plants. As well as the pests listed here, roses are also vulnerable to aphids, capsid bugs, rabbits, deer, and caterpillars (*see pages 35–36*).

Black spot

Dark brown or black blotches appear on leaves from late spring onwards. Affected leaves usually turn yellow and fall prematurely, which can weaken the plant. Initially, the infection originates in spots on stems in which the fungus has overwintered.

When new infections arise, promptly remove diseased material (*see below*) to slow the spread of the disease. Various fungicides are available; try alternate applications of different active ingredients to find the most effective product for your situation. Spray immediately after early spring pruning, then again when leaves open.

Large rose sawfly

The female has a yellow abdomen with a black head and body. Her eggs are laid in the soft, young shoots of wild and cultivated roses, and hatch into caterpillar-like larvae

that are greenish-white with many black and yellow spots. They feed voraciously and cause extensive defoliation, with two or three generations between early summer and early autumn. Pick off the larvae by hand or spray with bifenthrin, pyrethrum, thiacloprid, or imidacloprid.

Rust

In spring, elongated patches of perennial rust appear on stems and leaf stalks. In summer, leaves become infected, with small, bright orange, dusty spots arising on the undersides of leaves. The spots multiply and turn dark brown by late summer. Often, plants are severely defoliated. The dark spores overwinter on plant debris, soil, and stems. Cut out lesions when you see them on stems and destroy fallen leaves. Various fungicides are available; apply to stems in mid-spring before overwintering spores germinate. You can also spray foliage in summer.

Leaf-rolling sawfly

Small, black-bodied sawflies emerge in late spring and females insert eggs into rose leaves from late spring to early summer. Affected leaflets curl downwards along their lengths until they are tightly rolled. Later, the eggs hatch into pale green, caterpillar-like larvae, which eat the

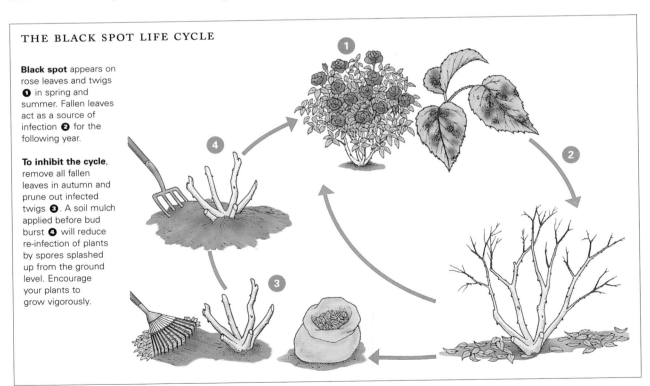

THE BLACK SPOT LIFE CYCLE

Black spot appears on rose leaves and twigs ❶ in spring and summer. Fallen leaves act as a source of infection ❷ for the following year.

To inhibit the cycle, remove all fallen leaves in autumn and prune out infected twigs ❸. A soil mulch applied before bud burst ❹ will reduce re-infection of plants by spores splashed up from the ground level. Encourage your plants to grow vigorously.

ROSE PESTS & DISEASES

Garden design basics *see page 60* | **Pests of woody plants** *see page 109* | **Diseases of woody plants** *see page 111*

PESTS & DISEASES OF ROSES

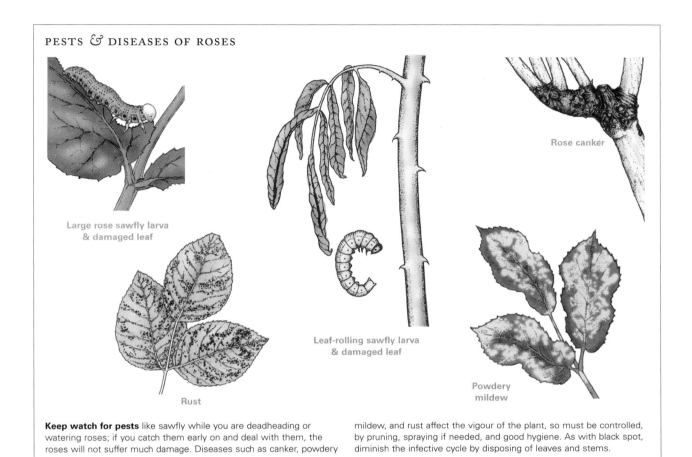

Large rose sawfly larva
& damaged leaf

Rust

Leaf-rolling sawfly larva
& damaged leaf

Rose canker

Powdery
mildew

Keep watch for pests like sawfly while you are deadheading or watering roses; if you catch them early on and deal with them, the roses will not suffer much damage. Diseases such as canker, powdery mildew, and rust affect the vigour of the plant, so must be controlled, by pruning, spraying if needed, and good hygiene. As with black spot, diminish the infective cycle by disposing of leaves and stems.

rolled leaves. It is difficult to prevent female sawflies from causing leaf curling, but you can control larvae by picking off rolled leaves on lightly infested plants. If many leaves are affected, spray with thiacloprid or imidacloprid.

Rose canker

Various fungi cause canker and die-back of rose stems. Most infect through bad pruning cuts or wounds. Plant roses so that their graft unions are not covered by soil and make clean pruning cuts, close above buds. Keep roses vigorous by feeding with rose fertilizers. Prevent drought or waterlogging to avoid die-back.

Powdery mildew

White powdery patches appear on leaves, stems, thorns, and buds. The fungus commonly overwinters around the thorns and in dormant buds. Rambling and climbing roses are particularly susceptible, although this may be as a result of their location – soil near walls often remains

dry and roses that suffer dryness at the roots are always more prone to mildew. Thorough mulching and regular feeding helps to keep plants vigorous. Remove heavily infected stems during spring pruning, and any that appear during the growing season. Various fungicides are available; use them when symptoms appear and alternate active ingredients.

Replant disorder

This results in stunting of plants when they are planted in affected soil; the roots are found to be small and dark (*see page 118*). The rootstock *Rosa canina* is very susceptible. Change the soil before planting beyond the full spread of the roots.

Honey fungus

If established rose bushes suddenly die, inspect them for the presence of honey fungus (*see page 37*). Rose family plants are highly susceptible to this disease.

CLIMBERS & WALL PLANTS

Climbers have adapted to grow vertically, clambering over rival plants in a search of sunshine. This habit is exploited by gardeners to cover unsightly garden features or brighten up dull walls and to add extra height to the garden by training climbers on obelisks or arches. Fences clothed with climbers provide a more natural backdrop to borders. Many shrubs also suit wall training, in particular slightly tender plants that benefit from the warmth and shelter. Climbers and wall shrubs take up very little soil space, which makes them invaluable for smaller gardens where they can show off their foliage, flowers, and berries.

Methods of support

Choose a climber to suit the allotted space or support, thereby reducing the need to prune too often, and the aspect – sun-loving plants become straggly in shade.

Train wall shrubs or climbers on taut, horizontal wires fixed to walls and fences. Use vine eyes to hold the wires about 5cm (2in) away from the vertical surface to allow space for stems to twine and air to circulate.

Space wires 25–45cm (10–18in) apart, depending on the climber. Twining climbers can be trained on trellis or netting, fixed to wooden battens to create a 5cm (2in) gap between the support and wall. Wooden trellis needs to be 30cm (12in) above soil level to prevent rotting. Free-standing screens made from trellis or netting on posts work in sheltered sites; large structures need good anchorage.

GROWTH HABITS OF CLIMBING & WALL PLANTS

Natural clingers hold on to walls and fences by means of aerial roots or sucker pads, so no system of support is needed. Examples include ivy (*Hedera*) and Virginia creeper (*Parthenocissus*). The clinging parts may mark or damage soft brickwork.

Twiners are a large group of plants that climb by means of curling or twining leaf tendrils, leaf stalks, or stems. A support system, such as a trellis or wire lattice, is needed for the tendrils to twine around. Typical plants include honeysuckles (*Lonicera*), clematis, and wisterias.

Scramblers and floppers clamber up neighbouring vegetation by using hooked thorns (roses) or by rapid elongation of their willowy shoots, such as the potato vine (*Solanum crispum*). A support system is needed to which the growth can easily be tied in.

Wall shrubs are shrubs trained on wires fixed to a wall or fence, even though they do not climb naturally. This method is especially useful for growing slightly tender species, such as bottlebrushes (*Callistemon*), on a warm wall.

GROWING CLIMBERS & WALL PLANTS

Garden design basics *see page 60* | **Pests of woody plants** *see page 109* | **Diseases of woody plants** *see page 111*

Growing climbers & wall plants

Most climbers are container grown, but some are available as bare-root plants. Look for healthy plants with well-developed roots and strong stems. Although container plants can be planted at any time of year (as long as the soil is not frozen or waterlogged), plants tend to establish better if planted in autumn or spring.

Avoid planting in summer since plants will require regular watering. More tender plants are best planted in spring. Plant bare-root plants immediately after purchase.

Planting

Fix the support in place before planting. Do not plant right up against it, but leave a 20–30cm (8–12in) gap. Allow a 45cm (18in) gap if planting against a wall or fence to avoid the rain shadow (*see box, right*).

Dig a planting hole twice the size of the existing container and fork the bottom and sides to relieve any compaction. Water the plant well and place in the planting hole at a 45-degree angle, making sure that the top of the rootball is level with the soil surface. A few climbers, such as most clematis, benefit from deeper planting. If the soil is poor, mix in a small amount of well-rotted organic matter before planting, then firm well and water.

Pruning & training

The aim of formative pruning is to create a well-balanced framework that clothes the support. Remove any weak or damaged shoots and train the remaining stems into the support, spacing them evenly. If any stems are too short, tie them to canes fixed to the support. Tie in stems as they grow to cover the required area. Cut back sparse growth to encourage branching. Shorten or prune out stems that are badly placed.

Climbers require regular pruning to stimulate new growth and flowering, as well as to restrict the size. The time of pruning depends on the age of the flowering wood. Early-flowering plants bloom on previous season's wood; prune them straight after flowering. Plants that flower in mid- to late summer on the current season's growth are best pruned in winter or early spring.

General care of climbers

For healthy plants, apply a well-balanced fertilizer each spring around the base of the plant at the manufacturer's recommended rate. Water in dry spells, especially climbers planted against walls. Mulch with organic matter to improve moisture retention and reduce evaporation from the soil, but do not let the mulch touch the stems.

PLANTING CLIMBERS

Walls and fences create a certain amount of rain shadow, and this must be accounted for when planting at their base. Site the plant about 45cm (18in) from the wall or fence. A short stake or cane can be used to guide the young growth so that it bridges the gap between the roots and the support. This can later be removed once the plant has established itself on the support wires of the wall or fence.

Free-standing supports, such as pillars, trellis, or frames, do not create the same degree of rain shadow as a solid structure, so the planting distance needs to be only 20–30cm (8–12in). If you intend to grow a climber into a host plant, such as a tree, the root systems of the 2 plants will compete with each other for food and water, so plant the climber a good distance away from the host plant's roots, and water well to help the climber take root.

Clematis

Clematis are evergreen or deciduous climbers that often use twining leaf stalks to attach to supports. There are also some shrubby and herbaceous clematis. The climbers are very versatile: use them to clothe walls and fences, on pergolas and frames, or to extend seasonal interest and complement other climbers such as roses.

Planting & initial training

Choose a site in full or partial sun, with fertile, moisture-retentive but well-drained soil. Plant the rootball about 5cm (2in) below the soil surface to protect the crown from clematis wilt, a fungal disease (*see page 112*). Evergreen and herbaceous species do not need deep planting. Keep the base of the clematis cool, with shade cast by nearby plants and an annual mulch of organic matter, such as well-rotted garden compost.

To avoid lanky growth and ensure branching from the base, cut all clematis back to 15–30cm (6–12in) after planting (*see box, facing page*). Train in shoots if needed; handle them with care as new stems are brittle. Clematis are split into three groups, according to pruning needs.

Clematis group 1

This group includes evergreen and deciduous species that flower in winter or spring on the previous year's growth, for example *Clematis alpina*, *C. armandii*, *C. macropetala*, and *C. montana*. They do not need regular pruning, apart from trimming of over-long stems and removal of dead, diseased, or damaged wood.

If needed, prune to shape after flowering; prune winter-flowering species in early spring. Older plants may benefit from congested growth being thinned and some older branches cut back to the main framework. You can completely renovate them by cutting them back to 15cm (6in) from the base, after flowering in spring. Do not do this again for at least three years.

Clematis group 2

This group comprises large-flowered, deciduous varieties, such as 'Nelly Moser', 'The President', and 'William Kennet', all of which produce spectacular flowers in early summer on the previous year's growth. A second flush follows in late summer, of fewer medium-sized blooms on the current season's growth.

Prune to establish a framework of older wood and to stimulate new growth. In late winter, remove weak shoots and thin congested growth, and cut about one fifth to a quarter of the oldest stems to 30cm (12in) above the base

Early-flowering clematis, such as these red flowers of 'Constance', are in group 1 and require only minimal pruning.

Mid-season clematis, such as this variety 'H.F. Young', flower in early summer. Being in group 2, they can be renew pruned or left unpruned.

Late-flowering clematis, such as 'Étoile Violette', are in group 3. They should be hard pruned each year in late winter or early spring.

FORMATIVE PRUNING OF CLEMATIS

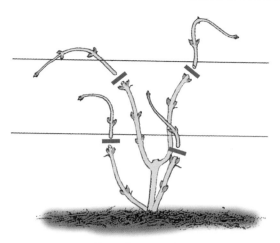

Initial pruning of all clematis

Prune the stem of a newly planted clematis in mid- to late winter, cutting it back to just above the lowest pair of strong, healthy buds. Mulch well around the base of the stem without it touching the stem.

Second-year pruning

Cut back all main stems that have been trained during the previous year, reducing them by half their lengths to a pair of strong buds. Do this in mid- to late winter and mulch well.

to encourage renewal growth. Trim back immediately after flowering to improve the second flush. This type of clematis can be left unpruned and cut hard back to the base every three or four years. The first flush of flowers will be lost, but it should flower in late summer.

Clematis group 3

Clematis that flower from midsummer to autumn on the current season's growth fall into this category, and include 'Étoile Violette', 'Duchess of Albany', and *C. texensis* and *C. viticella* varieties.

The plants become top heavy, with bare bases, tangled growth and fewer flowers high up, if not cut back hard each year. Hard prune to a pair of buds 15–30cm (6–12in) above soil level in late winter or early spring, as the buds begin to break; only buds higher up might show signs of growth – pruning will stimulate breaking of dormant buds close to the base. To extend the season, prune late large-flowered clematis, such as 'Perle d'Azur', 'Rouge Cardinal', 'Star of India', and 'Jackmanii' varieties, by combining pruning methods from group 2; retain some older stems and cut others back to the base, in early spring.

PRUNING MATURE CLEMATIS

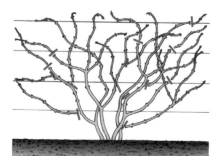

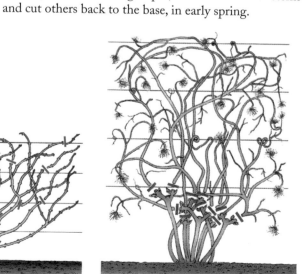

Group 1 clematis only need to be pruned to shape after flowering, in spring. Trim over-long stems and remove dead or damaged growth.

Group 2 clematis are pruned back to an established framework in winter. A few of the older stems are cut back to the base.

Group 3 clematis are hard pruned back each year to 15–30cm (6–12in) above soil level. This keeps them tidy and prolific.

133

Wisteria

These deciduous, woody-stemmed, vigorous, twining climbers flower in spring, producing showy, hanging bunches of flowers that are frequently scented. Occasionally, a few flowers appear in summer.

Wisterias are ideal plants for covering sunny walls or growing on sturdy posts, arches, and pergolas; however, rigorous training and pruning is required to keep them within bounds. If space allows, and with a little help to start them off, they will cover entire structures or climb into large trees, giving a beautiful, naturalistic flowering display in spring in return for very little attention.

Choosing a wisteria

The most commonly grown wisteria is *Wisteria sinensis*. This species, together with the less widely known *W. brachybotrys*, is recommended for training on walls. The flowers are best displayed when a wisteria is trained as an espalier. With its long racemes of flowers, *W. floribunda* is well suited for training on pergolas.

Almost any wisteria, however, will look attractive, regardless of the structure on which it is grown or how it is trained. Where space is limited, try *W. frutescens*, which is one of the less vigorous and slower growing types; it has shorter racemes of flowers later in the season. When buying a wisteria, choose a grafted, named variety. There

A properly trained wisteria over a pergola is not only beautiful, it doubles up as a shady canopy in summer. Although the spring flowers are the main feature, the deciduous leaves are also elegant.

are many to choose from, with flowers in shades of blue, violet, pink, or white. Seed-raised plants are shy to flower, often have inferior blooms, or may not flower at all. Even a grafted, named variety may take three to five years to produce a worthwhile display.

ESPALIER PRUNING OF WISTERIA

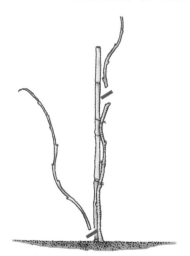

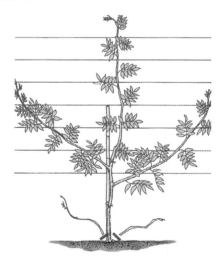

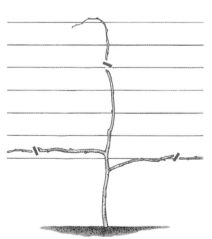

FIRST YEAR

1 **Prune the strongest shoot** after planting, cutting it to 75–90cm (30–36in) above soil level. Tie to a stake, taking care not to damage the plant. Cut back to the base all other shoots. Remove any sideshoots on the main shoot to promote new growth.

2 **Tie in the main shoot** vertically as it grows in summer. Select the two strongest sideshoots, on each side, and train them in at 45 degrees. Trim any secondary shoots on the sideshoots to 15cm (6in). Remove any growth from the base and the remaining sideshoots.

SECOND YEAR

3 **Cut the main shoot** in winter to about 75cm (30in) above the topmost sideshoot. Carefully lower the sideshoots that were at 45 degrees and tie them horizontally to the supports. Cut them back by about one third.

Formative pruning

Wisterias are often trained as espaliers (*see below*), but they can be grown as fans, low standards, or as semi-formal wall shrubs, so initial pruning will differ according to the required habit. It is best to train the main stems horizontally to encourage flowering. If growing an espalier, continue training until the vacant space is covered and the main framework is formed.

Maintenance pruning

Although wisterias flower if left unchecked, flowering on established plants can be encouraged and improved by regular pruning, once in late summer and again in winter, to divert the plant's energy into producing flowering spurs (*see box, below*). This will also help to manage the vigorous extension growth. Even on plants that are trained informally, regular summer and winter pruning is beneficial to encourage flowering.

In late summer, prune back all the current season's growth to 15–30cm (6–12in), unless any growth is needed to extend the existing laterals or to replace damaged branches. Further growth should break from the pruned shoots, and flowering buds will form at the bases of the shoots. These buds should be easily distinguishable because they are rounder and plumper than the slim and pointy growth buds. In late winter, prune back again to the lowest two or three buds from the main branch.

General care

The most common complaint about wisterias is a lack of blooms or poor flowering, despite regular pruning. Poor soil conditions may be to blame. Although established plants benefit from an annual application of well-balanced fertilizer in spring, it pays to avoid overfeeding. The use of high-nitrogen fertilizers will encourage leafy growth at the expense of flowers. Feeding with a sulphate of potash or tomato fertilizer may encourage flowering.

Wisterias are fairly drought tolerant, but they may flower poorly if planted against a wall where the soil is in a rain shadow and very dry. Water the plant well during dry spells in summer and mulch to conserve soil moisture. Wisterias require plenty of sunshine to grow and flower well, making them unsuitable for north- and east-facing sites. Dry conditions, fluctuating temperatures, and frost can cause flower buds to drop in spring.

Neglected plants

Renovation pruning of neglected plants is best spread over several years. In winter, select damaged, old, or unwanted main branches and cut each back to the base of another suitable branch, or remove branches completely at the base. You will probably have to cut and remove long branches in sections to free them from the dense growth without causing damage to the plant. Hard prune to stimulate vigorous growth; flowering may diminish for a while.

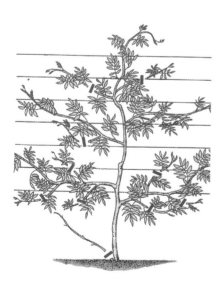

4 **Train the main shoot** vertically as it grows in summer. As in step 2, choose further pairs of sideshoots and tie them in at 45 degrees, and trim secondary shoots. Remove other sideshoots and any growth at the base. Trim sideshoots so they fit the allotted space.

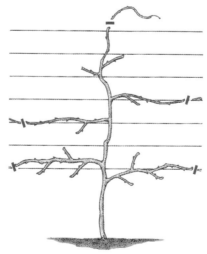

THIRD YEAR
5 **Prune the main shoot** in winter to about 75cm (30in) above the topmost sideshoot. Carefully lower the laterals that are at 45 degrees, tie horizontally, and reduce these and other sideshoots by about one third. Continue each year until the basic framework is formed.

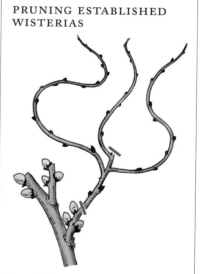

PRUNING ESTABLISHED WISTERIAS

Prune in 2 stages to encourage flowering spurs: in summer, cut extension growth to within 15cm (6in) of the framework (top cut). In winter, cut down again to 2–3 buds (bottom cut).

Honeysuckles

These woody, twining climbers with fragrant flowers prefer full sun but tolerate light shade. After planting, reduce all stems by about a half to stimulate strong growth from the base. As the new shoots appear, train the strongest onto the support and remove the rest (*see below*). Mature plants are split into two groups for pruning.

Vigorous, evergreen honeysuckles like *Lonicera japonica*, *L. henryi*, and *L. hildebrandiana* make up the first group. They produce flowers from summer to autumn on the current season's growth. Established plants do not require regular pruning, but as they quickly fill the allotted space, the growth will have to be controlled.

In early spring, prune back over-long branches, thin out congested growth, and remove weak or damaged shoots. Mature or neglected plants can be renovated by cutting all stems back to 60cm (24in) from ground level in late winter.

Into the second group fall deciduous and semi-evergreen honeysuckles that flower on the previous year's growth in summer. The most commonly grown honeysuckle from this group is *Lonicera periclymenum* (common honeysuckle or woodbine) and its varieties.

Prune after flowering to encourage even growth (*see below*). Alternatively, leave them to scramble over structures or into trees; over time these plants might become an unsightly mass and require renovation.

TRAINING OF HONEYSUCKLES

Initial pruning at planting time is the same for all honeysuckles. Cut all stems by half to stimulate strong growth.

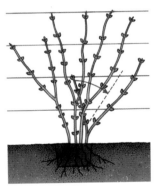

Train and tie in the shoots so that they evenly cover the support. If growth becomes too congested, prune hard in winter.

DECIDUOUS HONEYSUCKLE PRUNING

Prune back by one third after flowering to prevent plants become bare at the base. As for evergreen honeysuckles, they can be renovated in winter by hard pruning all shoots.

Wall shrubs

Shrubs gain an extra dimension if they are grown against a wall or fence. Some, such as pyracantha, daphne, cotoneaster, and variegated *Euonymus*, enliven shady walls. Bottlebrush (*Callistemon*), ceanothus, and *Fremontodendron* all flower well against a warm, sunny wall.

Ceanothus as a wall shrub

Evergreen ceanothus is often grown as a wall shrub for its brilliant blue spring flowers, which form on the previous season's growth. Autumn-flowering ceanothus, such as 'Autumnal Blue' and 'Burkwoodii', flower on the current season's growth in late summer.

After planting in spring, tie in the shoot that is to form the main stem. Space the side branches evenly on the support and remove any badly placed or competing shoots. Lightly shorten over-long branches. You should cut back any branches that are growing inwards, towards the support, or outwards away from it. As growth progresses, tie in the extension growth and trim the unwanted branches to two buds again after flowering.

In following years, tie in the new growth to form the framework. After flowering, trim back all flowered shoots to 10–15cm (4–6in) from the side branches. Shorten longer branches by about one third. Prune back some of the older side branches to a younger branch, which can be used as a replacement.

For autumn-flowering ceanothus, prune the previous season's growth by about one third in spring. Prune all ceanothus regularly as it does not respond to renovation pruning. Neglected plants are best replaced.

PRUNING SPRING-FLOWERING CEANOTHUS

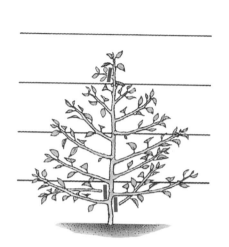

FIRST YEAR

1 **Tie the main shoot** vertically. Spread out the side branches and remove crossing, or inward- or outward-growing branches in spring.

SECOND YEAR

2 **Cut back branches** growing inwardly or outwardly from the support, after flowering. Let the framework fill out, and tie in.

THIRD & SUBSEQUENT YEARS

3 **Trim back all flowered shoots** to 10–15cm (4–6in) after flowering. Shorten long branches by one third at the same time.

Flowering quince as a wall shrub

Making a handsome wall shrub, flowering quince or japonica (*Chaenomeles* × *superba*) flowers in spring on one-year-old and older wood. Though they will grow in a shady situation, flowering is better when planted against sunny walls. They can be trained as an espalier, as described for wisteria (*see pages 134–135*).

To train as a more relaxed wall shrub, follow the basic training as described for ceanothus (*see also right*). Several evenly spaced main stems can be selected instead of just one to develop a multi-stemmed framework.

Pyracantha as a wall shrub

Pyracantha is often used to brighten up walls with its bright yellow, orange, or red fruits. It also bears attractive white flowers in early summer on the previous season's growth, which need to be encouraged for their fruit.

To train pyracantha as a wall shrub, follow the method recommended for ceanothus. After the initial training, shorten extension growth in spring to retain the shape, even though some flowering wood will be pruned off. In late summer, shorten the new extension growth to display the developing berries and to enhance wood ripening. Pyracantha can be renovated in spring, by removing some of the old growth. It can also be trained formally, as an espalier, cordon, or fan.

PRUNING A MATURE FLOWERING QUINCE

1 **Shorten all** flowered sideshoots by pruning back to 3–6 leaves after flowering. On established plants, cut back long extension growth unless it is needed for further development of the framework.

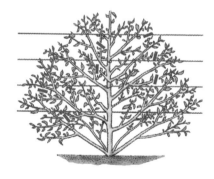

2 **Cut back** badly positioned, dead, diseased, damaged, or crossing branches, as well as any that grow in or away from the support, after flowering. This maintains an open and healthy, permanent framework.

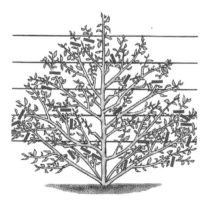

CHAPTER FOUR

GROWING VEGETABLES & HERBS

PREPARING TO GROW 142

SOWING & GROWING 146

SALADS & LEAVES 150

THE CABBAGE FAMILY 162

STALKS & SHOOTS 171

PODS & SEEDS 176

THE ONION FAMILY 184

ROOTS & TUBERS 189

VEGETABLE FRUIT 200

HERBS 206

COMMON PROBLEMS 210

GROWING VEGETABLES CAN SEEM DAUNTING AT FIRST, FROM the jargon of intercropping and rotation, to the bewildering range of pests and diseases that need controlling. There are so many vegetables, each with their own different needs and treatment, that it can be puzzling to know how to fit everything in at the right time. But domestic vegetable growing must be very similar to the earliest farming at the dawn of civilization: clearing weeds, planting seed and tubers, and then with luck, rain, and care, harvesting something you can eat. If the first farmers could do this without seed catalogues, garden centres, or books, think how comparatively easy it is for us. The secret is to start simply and work your way up to more demanding crops.

For many people, it seems a miracle that home-grown food tastes better than that sold in shops. In fact, the relatively hard life of home-grown vegetables contributes to stronger flavours and more pleasing textures than those found in pampered crops grown in the best soils with lavish feeding and watering, which often spend days in cold stores before reaching your plate.

Getting started

The soil is the basis for success. Soil appears to be very ordinary, but it holds water and nutrients, releasing them more or less as plants need them. Any minor variations in soil fertility can be made up for by following the feeding recommendations given for each crop.

Getting seeds, plants, sets, and tubers into the soil is the most crucial stage of vegetable growing. Practice helps: refine your technique by sowing inexpensive lettuce or radish seeds – you can always use the seedlings as mini-leaves in your salads if you don't need the extra plants. If you have 'unkind' soil that won't easily make seedbeds, it is much easier to raise transplants.

There is something especially satisfying in raising plants from seed, and it gives you the widest choice, but you can if you prefer just buy young plants instead – these are sold in nurseries or garden centres, and via mail-order. Most herbs are wanted in only small quantities, so buying plants makes sense; plant them close to the kitchen door, where they can be reached easily.

A successful harvest

Once plants and seeds are in the ground, their main need is water. It is difficult to grow good vegetables without watering, but most gardeners aim to protect the environment and avoid lavish use of tap water. Target water when and where it is needed, and don't be afraid to take your trowel and look at the soil near the roots. Water if it is dry, wait a little if it is moist.

Wildlife can thrive in vegetable gardens with plentiful organic matter, close vegetation, and occasional watering. Naturally gardeners do not want to harm beneficial creatures, but pests and diseases will need controlling. Modern approaches manage rather than eliminate these: try to prevent conditions that favour problems, and treat any that do arise promptly, but don't waste time or money and upset the balance with heavy-handed use of remedies on lost causes. Scrap problem crops and move on to the next – safety lies in variety. Remedies offered to gardeners are safe if used as directed.

Finally, you will need to harvest your crops. However hard you try, there will always be times when there is too much or too little. Store or give away any surplus, and in times of dearth, fall back on the shops to remind yourself how much better your home-grown produce tastes.

PREPARING TO GROW

Preparation of a vegetable and herb plot is not always the most popular task in the gardener's calendar, especially as most of the digging and clearing tends to be done when the weather is wintry and the soil can be cold, lifeless, sticky, and wet. Looking forward to bountiful days ahead, however, makes forward planning a happy antidote to the cold work outside, as seeds are ordered, sowings planned, and beds organized. By spring, soil that has been well dug should merely need superficial attention – raking or a light touch with the fork – in readiness for planting.

Soil preparation

The ideal soil for vegetable crops is open in texture, allowing roots and water to penetrate it and holding moisture well, and is rich in nutrients, not too acid, and free of weeds. Some soil preparation is essential, but the less that is done to achieve the ideal soil the better, both for the soil and for your back.

Raised beds or traditional digging?

Many gardeners find raised beds the easiest way to manage their vegetable garden. Beds should be 1.2–1.5m (4–5ft) across, narrow enough so that you can reach the centre; paths in between will need to be wide enough for a wheelbarrow. Raised beds drain and warm up more readily than in open ground, and need less frequent digging.

To make raised beds, you will need to construct 15–40cm (6–16in) high sides of timber or masonry. Take soil from the paths to fill the beds, avoiding the need to import expensive soil that may contain diseases and weeds.

Double digging or even trenching (*see page 18*) were widely practised in the past. They allow deeper rooting and access to more soil moisture, but they are only essential where compacted soil is encountered below the normal digging depth. Single digging is sufficient for most soils.

If your plot is free of perennial weeds, use a rotavator (*see page 280*) to give quick and satisfactory results, but do not use it when the soil is wet. Clay soils are very vulnerable to damage if rotavated when wet, and raised beds are an especially effective solution for these soils.

CONVERTING GRASSLAND

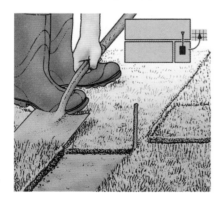

1 **Divide the plot**, nicking a line down the centre and marking out trenches 60cm (24in) wide. Skim the turf from the first trench to a depth of about 5cm (2in) and put it, grassy side up, by the trench at the same end.

2 **Remove the soil** from the first trench to one spade's depth, placing it in a separate heap next to the skimmed turf. Fork over the bottom of the first trench to a depth of 30cm (12in) to break up the subsoil.

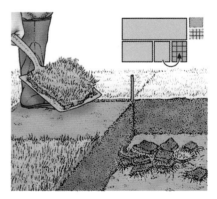

3 **Place the turf** from the second trench in the first and chop it. Dig the soil from the second trench into the first and fork over the bottom. Repeat across the plot, filling the last trench with the turf and soil from the first.

Clearing a new site

A grassy or overgrown site is often rich in nutrients and free of soil-borne pests and diseases, but clearing the plot of its covering of grass or weeds to make a vegetable garden can appear a formidable task.

If you have plenty of time, all weeds can be killed by covering overgrown plots with opaque sheets, such as black plastic, for at least one full growing season. You can also avoid a great deal of hard work by applying a systemic weedkiller containing glyphosate, which will not harm subsequent crops. It must be applied when there is plenty of foliage to take up the weedkiller; some tough weeds may need more than one application. Deep digging and the burial or removal of weeds are also highly effective.

Raised beds are a good way of tackling an overgrown plot, because weeds, turf, and debris can be buried deep in the base of the raised bed. Here they will rot to release nutrients to support crops and will not regrow, although persistent weeds, such as bindweed and couch grass, should be carefully removed.

Enriching the soil

Because crops take nutrients with them when harvested, the soil in a vegetable garden needs fortifying. Enrich the base of raised beds and the soil on top with well-rotted organic matter. If using animal manure, wait several weeks before adding lime to prevent the release of ammonia.

Planning your crops

A constant supply of perfect produce often requires repeated or successional sowings, typically at intervals of two to four weeks. Salads, young carrots, peas, and French or broad beans are examples of crops that can be grown successionally as they soon become over-mature.

Opportunities often arise to fit in crops either before and after the main crop (catch cropping) or between larger slow-growing crops (intercropping). These techniques takes some planning, to avoid the main crop and the catch crop or intercrop getting in each other's way, but they can greatly increase your plot's productivity. For example, you might want lettuces, but there is no need to set aside land for them alone; you can intercrop them between widely spaced courgettes, or grow them as a catch crop after early crops such as early potatoes.

Crops also need to be rotated from year to year (*see box, above*) to prevent the build up of pests and diseases in the soil. You can adapt systems of rotation, catch cropping, and intercropping to meet your individual circumstances.

CROP ROTATION

	Area 1	Area 2	Area 3
Year 1	Potatoes and tomatoes	Roots, peas, and beans, and everything else	Brassicas
Year 2	Roots, peas, and beans, and everything else	Brassicas	Potatoes and tomatoes
Year 3	Brassicas	Potatoes and tomatoes	Roots, peas, and beans, and everything else

Soil-borne pests and diseases can be damaging if susceptible crops are grown repeatedly in the same site. To help prevent this, divide the vegetable garden into sections and grow different crops each year on each section. A typical rotation plan has 3 crop groups, giving a 2-year gap between plantings. Problems can persist in the soil for far longer, but rotation helps to reduce losses; it is also a convenient and efficient way of working a plot.

The deeply dug soil manured for the potatoes is ideal for roots and peas and beans, while the nitrogen-enriched soil from the peas and beans helps the subsequent brassica crop. Brassicas come out in spring in time for planting potatoes.

You may find that strict rotation is impractical in a small area: here, grow crops wherever is most convenient year after year. If troubles arise, and often they do not, grow the affected crop in a new place or in containers of sterile potting media.

INTERCROPPING

The gaps between slow-growing crops that fill their space slowly can be planted with fast-maturing crops that are harvested before they present any competition. Slow-growing leeks and speedy spinach are ideal partners, as are parsnips and radishes.

Preparing a seedbed

Establishing a crop is the most important, yet trickiest part of growing vegetables. Sowing seeds directly into a seedbed is the cheapest method and is essential for crops that transplant poorly, such as carrots and parsnips. Thin out seedbed crops to their required spacing and leave them to grow, or transplant them to their final growing positions.

Working the soil

Prepare your seedbed in spring, but check first to ensure the soil is not wet and sticky. Working wet soil ruins the structure and will reduce crop growth and cause root crops to become distorted. Sometimes it is useful to dig the ground over the previous autumn and expose the rough soil to the winter weather, to help break it down.

If you are worried about compacting the soil you have just prepared, stand on a plank as you work; seedbeds on raised beds are worked from the surrounding paths. To make the soil ready for early sowing, cover open ground with cloches or clear polythene in midwinter to keep the soil warm and dry. By spring, you will have a warm, well-drained soil ready for early cultivation and sowing.

Creating a level surface for sowing

For good results when sowing, level and finely rake the soil surface. The lower layers of the soil need to be firm but not compact so that a drill (a shallow groove for sowing) can be drawn to a constant depth. You achieve this by raking the soil level and then lightly treading the surface if it appears to be 'fluffy'. After treading, rake the soil over again.

Generally, the less soil movement the better, but sometimes the soil has to be broken up beforehand, and debris, weeds, and stones removed. If you have raised beds, a light raking is usually all that is needed.

Raking has the side effect of exposing slugs and other soil pests to both birds and to drying out. It will also break up tiny crevices where pests may be hiding.

PREPARING THE SOIL

1 **Cultivate the soil** during spring. A hand cultivator or rake can be used to break up any large clods. Work to a depth of about 15–20cm (6–8in), using a backwards-and-forwards motion. Remove any surface weeds, debris, or stones as you do so.

2 **Consolidate the soil** by breaking up any remaining clods with the head of a rake. Use the rake to fill any depressions with soil, but do not overwork the soil at this stage. Where possible, do not tread the soil unless it appears to be light and 'fluffy'.

3 **Apply a general-purpose fertilizer** by spreading a base dressing evenly over the newly cultivated soil. Work the fertilizer into the top 10–15cm (4–6in) of soil using a hand cultivator or rake.

4 **Level the surface** with the rake to produce the final, level tilth. Move the rake backwards and forwards with as little soil movement as possible, keeping the teeth of the rake only just in the soil surface.

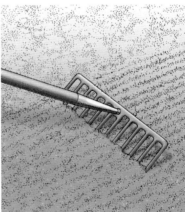

Green manures

Growing crops for the sole purpose of then digging them into the soil seems a waste, but a covering of green manure prevents soil erosion and leaching of nutrients, and also smothers weeds. Dig in green manures when young, before the plants go woody. They are not a substitute for compost or manure, but they can improve soil structure and make the soil easier to work into a seedbed.

When to sow

Most green manures are sown from late summer to early autumn to follow summer crops and cover the soil over winter. Autumn-sown green manures include mustard and fodder radish, which are killed by frost and can be dug in during the winter. Rye, Italian ryegrass, and the leguminous vetches and field beans are green manures that grow all winter. Spring- and summer-sown peas, vetches, lupins, and clovers will add significant amounts of nitrogen to the soil if allowed to grow in summer.

Dig in green manures at least 2 weeks before the ground is needed for planting. Alternatively, add the material to the compost heap or spread it over the soil as a mulch.

GROWING A GREEN MANURE CROP

1 **Sow seeds** in rows or scatter the seed over the ground, They will grow quickly to cover the soil. Choose a green manure to suit the season; most are sufficiently hardy to keep growing all winter in mild weather. Spring and summer sowings may occupy ground better used for vegetable crops.

2 **Chop the foliage** down with a pair of shears or a strimmer when the land is needed or when the green manure is beginning to mature (whichever comes first). Leave the clippings to fall on the ground and wilt before digging them in.

3 **Dig the clippings** into the soil with a sharp spade. As they rot down, they will release nutrients into the soil that can be used by the following crop. Alternatively, leave the clippings on the surface as a mulch. Green manures that have become too mature to dig in easily can be added to the compost heap.

4 **Allow 2 weeks** or more between digging and any further sowing or planting for the green manure to decompose. The interval between cutting and planting should be longer if the green manure has become tough or the soil is cold in winter or spring.

SOWING & GROWING

Fresh, high-quality seeds are an absolute necessity. Seeds that are stale or have been exposed to heat, damp, or sunlight are less likely to make a worthwhile crop than fresh seeds from a reputable supplier or your own garden. The difference between the best varieties and ordinary ones is often marked; choose varieties that have done well in trials, such as those with the RHS Award of Garden Merit. Many newer varieties are F1 hybrids, the result of a carefully controlled cross of two selected parents; unlike the seeds from conventional varieties, the seeds they produce will not be as good if saved and sown the following year.

Sowing seeds

Seeds can be sown either directly into the soil or in containers (*see page 406*). Direct sowing is much less time consuming, but in containers you have more control over the growing environment, where seedlings can be protected from pests, warmed for early crops, or given a head start if they have a long growing season.

Direct sowing into the ground

There are two methods: sowing into shallow grooves called drills (*see below*), or station sowing, also known as space sowing (*see facing page*).

In drills, keep seeds in close contact with moist soil, sown as shallowly as possible. Draw deeper drills for larger seeds with a hoe, and shallow drills of 1–2cm (½–¾in) for small seeds by pressing a length of broom handle into the soil. Stretch a string between two pegs to get a straight, easy-to-hoe drill. Ideally, run rows north–south to provide even light, but this is not essential.

A simple method of sowing fine seeds is to hold a little in the palm of one hand and then take pinches between thumb and forefinger of the other hand and gently trickle them into the drill. Fluid sowing is another method; it helps if the seed is pre-germinated (*see facing page*).

In dry weather, water the bottom of the drill before sowing, and sow a little deeper than normal. Some soils 'cap' or pack down under rain so that seedlings cannot break through. Where soil is prone to capping, cover seeds with peat-free potting compost instead. Finally,

DRILL SOWING

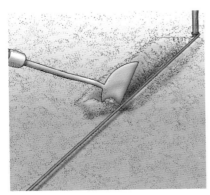

1 **Stretch some spring** tightly between 2 pegs at the ends of the row at ground level. Hold the hoe against the line and draw out a drill with one of its corner edges.

2 **Water the bottom** of the drill and allow to drain. In very wet conditions, lay a line of sand in the bottom instead. Sprinkle seeds thinly and evenly, cover with soil, and firm in.

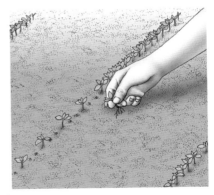

3 **Thin excess seedlings** as soon as possible, to avoid problems caused by overcrowding. Leave the strongest to grow: you may thin a row of seedlings several times.

Looking after your soil *see page 16* | **Preparing to grow** *see page 142* | **Sowing seeds** *see page 405*

VARIATIONS ON SEED SOWING

Station sowing This is ideal for large seeds such as broad beans and sweetcorn. Sow 3–5 seeds per station at their final spacing, and later thin to one seedling.

Fluid sowing Stir small seeds into non-fungicidal wallpaper paste and squeeze from a bag with a corner cut off. It is an easy way to handle small or fine seeds.

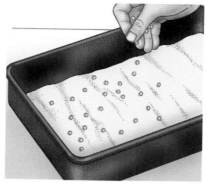

Pre-germination Place seeds on damp tissue paper in an airtight box and keep at 18–22°C (64–72°F) until the first signs of roots are visible, then sow immediately.

firm down the soil with the head of a rake to keep the seeds and soil in close contact. A very shallow raking of the surface then conceals the drill from birds.

When seedlings emerge, thin them by removing surplus plants in stages. At first, leave four times the final number of seedlings, then half, and finally just those plants that are needed for the crop. This means that you must judge how many seeds to sow, which can be tricky. Sow too many and they may spoil from overcrowding before you can thin them, but sowing too few can result in gaps, wasting space and leading to shortfalls.

Thinning seedlings is very slow and tedious, so sowing sparsely is usually best. Sow a few extra seeds at the end of the row in order to give some spares in case any gaps need to be filled; mark the ends of the rows with short sticks to help avoid inadvertent damage later; bear in mind that some root crops do not transplant well.

Station sowing can speed up thinning and wastes fewer seeds. As it is impossible to be certain that each seed will germinate, place three to five seeds a finger-width apart wherever you want a single eventual plant.

If you only have a few, expensive seeds, you can pre-germinate them (*see above*). Only those that germinate are sown, so the seed can be used more economically.

Growing from transplants

Transplanting – either from container-grown plants or those raised in a seedbed – is useful as plants can be raised in a small area before planting out. Transplants make efficient use of space and a small number of expensive seeds, but it is quite a lot of work to raise them, unless you buy them ready prepared from a nursery.

Bare-root transplants are the easiest to grow. These are plants raised in a seedbed outdoors in garden soil. They need to be carefully lifted with a fork and replanted with a trowel and plenty of water. This works well for cabbage family plants and for leeks. Most vegetable transplants, however, are raised in pots or cell trays just as ornamental plants often are; you will find that they are even easier to grow on than most ornamentals.

BRINGING ON TRANSPLANTED SEEDLINGS

Water transplanted seedlings regularly as every day each transplant needs about 150ml (5fl oz) of water until fully established. Use a coarse rose, and water at the base of each plant in the morning or evening to minimize wasteful evaporation.

Protect newly transplanted seedlings on cold spring nights with makeshift tents made from newspaper and pea sticks or canes. Hold the newspaper in place with stones or bricks. Remove the covers during the day as prolonged shade will stunt growth.

147

Watering & weeding

Sometimes you can grow vegetables without watering, but careful watering at key times can greatly improve results. Constantly wet soil from wasteful overwatering often means the plant grows more leaf rather than usable produce, and encourages weeds, diseases, and slugs.

To reduce the need for watering, try wider planting, giving each plant about 50 percent more space. Adding organic matter increases the water-holding capacity of the soil so that on average it holds another two weeks' worth of water. 'Ponding' – drawing up low banks of soil around plants and along rows – can help water to soak in. Weeds will rob vegetables of water, so weeding is vital.

Water according to need

Ideally, you should water your seedbeds 24 hours before sowing, although watering into the bottom of drills is often enough. In dry weather, seedlings and transplants need regular, thorough watering. A fine spray is essential to avoid compacting soil or damaging young plants.

Leafy crops, celery, cauliflowers, calabrese and tender young roots need 10–15 litres (2.2–3.4 gal) per square metre (10 sq ft) every week, but root crops such as carrots and parsnips need watering only in severe dry spells as watering tends to produce foliage rather than root.

Plants that form heads, such as cabbage and lettuce, do fairly well with one good soak when their heads begin to form about two weeks before harvesting. Leave fruiting

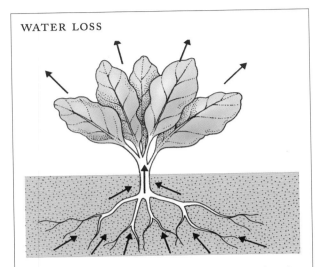

WATER LOSS

The water absorbed from the soil by roots is pulled up through the plant, carrying nutrients and fuelling chemical processes, and is lost through transpiration from the leaves.

vegetables like beans, courgettes, tomatoes, and sweetcorn unwatered once established until they flower, or they will produce leaves but no extra crop, then apply 5 litres (1.1 gal) per square metre (10 sq ft) every three days.

Water early potatoes every 10–14 days in dry weather, but maincrops only when tubers begin to form, when one good soak will greatly boost yields.

WEED CONTROL METHODS

Dig out perennial weeds in winter. Remove every possible fragment of root, or they will regenerate. Annual weeds are easily controlled by hoeing.

Mulch with well-rotted compost after rain or watering to conserve water and suppress weeds. Planting through opaque plastic or paper mulches is ideal for widely spaced crops or those that compete poorly with weeds.

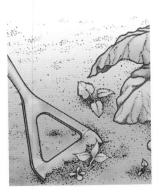

Hoeing is best done on dry, warm days before annual weeds flower and set seed. Slice the stems with a sharp hoe, keeping the blade just below the soil surface and level with it.

Chemically control weeds on plots before a crop is sown or planted. Crops are most vulnerable to weeds in their early stages, so treatment at an early stage, either by chemical or organic means, saves effort later.

Cloches, tunnels & frames

Nothing can equal a good greenhouse for protection, but few of us have enough greenhouse space for all our needs. Cold frames, cloches, and plastic films and fabrics can greatly increase productivity, providing shelter from the wind and a few extra degrees of warmth that can make all the difference to tender plants.

Fabrics & films

Fleece is the most economical and convenient covering material. It keeps off wind and the mildest frosts and adds a little warmth by day. Birds and other pests are excluded, but weeds and slugs thrive if left unchecked. Fleece does not give enough frost protection for tender plants, but can bring on early carrots, peas, and salads. Potatoes can often be started a month early, but will be frosted where they touch the fleece on chilly nights. Plants covered by fleece generally crop about two weeks before uncovered plants.

In summer, fleece can make all the difference for cucumbers, peppers, and early French beans. Perforated plastic films raise temperatures more, but need careful management to avoid scorch. Both fleece and film trap too much heat for hardy crops; use insect-proof mesh instead.

Cold frames, cloches & polytunnels

Cold frames are essentially boxes with a glazed lid that can be opened. They give more protection and much better control of temperature than cloches (*see box below*)

Fleece tunnels suspended over plastic or wire hoops are especially useful for advancing early crops. Often, they also offer protection from pests, such as the carrot root fly – a pest of carrots and parsnips.

and may be heated. They are ideal for raising and hardening off transplants in spring, and for warmth-loving crops, such as cucumbers and peppers in summer.

Polythene tunnels allow you to work under cover, but aren't warm enough to acclimatize young plants in spring. In summer, they suit tall crops like tomatoes and climbing beans; in winter, they keep salads growing and free of rots.

TYPES OF CLOCHE

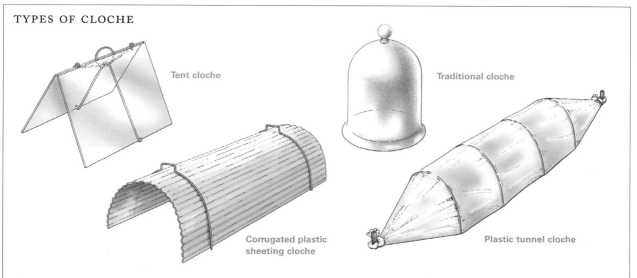

Tent cloche

Traditional cloche

Corrugated plastic sheeting cloche

Plastic tunnel cloche

Glass and plastic cloches make a low tunnel of continuous design, while individual ones are like a hat for each plant. Both give more protection than fleece, advancing early crops by 3–4 weeks and ripening tender crops almost as well as a greenhouse in summer. They cost much more than fleece and covered plants need frequent watering. Like fleece, they are easily blown away in exposed gardens.

SALADS & LEAVES

Salads and leafy plants such as spinach are the very essence of freshness and flavour, and nothing can be fresher than those from your own garden. Salads and leafy crops often quickly 'bolt' or flower, so sowing little and often, weekly in summer, avoids waste and ensures absolute freshness. A 1.5m (5ft) row is usually sufficient for a week's supply. Ready-prepared or 'baby leaf' salads can offer inspiration — the tasty contents of these are very quick and easy to grow yourself, and will be all the better for their freshness. Mini-leaves or cut-and-come-again salads are an easy way of producing these.

Lettuces

You can sow lettuces at intervals so that leaves, if not hearts, may be gathered all year. There is a wealth of different lettuces on offer, in shades of green, yellow, and red, reflecting the varied possibilities of this salad crop:
Butterheads: Very easy-to-grow varieties that form soft, round hearts, with medium flavour.
Cos: Medium or tall, upright varieties are available, with boat-shaped, flavoursome leaves and sweet hearts. They prefer rich, moist soils.

Crispheads: Crisp-leaved varieties, tolerant of dry, hot weather. Includes icebergs, which need much space and water to grow; mini-icebergs are suitable for most gardens.
Little Gem: Sweet and crunchy mini-hearts that are fast-growing and ideal for small gardens.
Leafy lettuces: Many varieties available, with loose and brightly coloured leaves, but often lacking flavour.
Stem lettuce (celtuce): Grown for its cookable stems, but cultivated just like other lettuces.

FROM SOWING TO HARVESTING LEAF LETTUCE

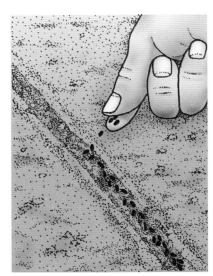

1 Sow in drills about 1cm (½in) deep weekly in mid- to late spring. Thin seedlings as soon as they can be handled, because crowded plants will not form proper hearts.

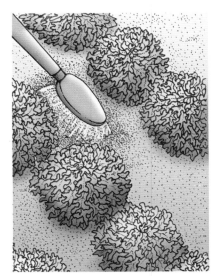

2 Water well in hot, dry weather, applying about 2 watering cans per square metre (10 sq ft) every 10 days to prevent bolting. If water is in short supply, water when the heart is just about to swell for best results.

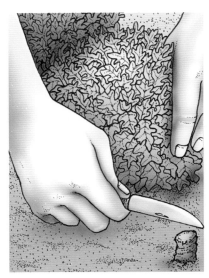

3 Harvest the leaves when still small, usually in 3–6 weeks. Leave a stump of about 5cm (2in) with enough side buds to regrow — another crop can be taken in a few weeks, and usually another after that.

SOWING PROTECTED LETTUCE

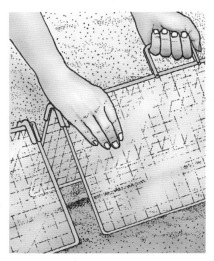

1 **Sow in mid-autumn** in a prepared seedbed, in drills 20cm (8in) apart. Station or space sow, placing 3–4 seeds at 7cm (2¾in) intervals. Protect with cloches.

2 **Thin seedlings** when they are 1cm (½in) high, leaving only the strongest plant growing at each station. Protect young plants over winter, but ventilate them well.

3 **Make final thinnings** when growth begins in spring. Leave a plant every 15–24cm (6–9in), depending on eventual size. Plants should be ready to harvest by mid-spring.

Soil & site

Any fertile garden soil in full sun is suitable; summer crops can tolerate light shade. Before sowing, add half a bucketful of organic matter and 70g (2½oz) of general-purpose fertilizer or 150g (5¼oz) of organic fertilizer, such as dried poultry manure, every square metre (10 sq ft).

Sowing & cultivation

Lettuces sown direct from early spring until late summer are easy to grow (*see page 150*). Sow seeds in drills – 25cm (10in) apart for small lettuces, 30cm (12in) for medium lettuces and 35cm (14in) for large cos and icebergs – and thin seedlings to 15cm (6in), 20cm (8in) or 25cm (10in) respectively. Avoid transplanting, but use surplus seedlings with under five leaves to fill gaps.

For convenience or an early start, sow in module trays using good general-purpose potting compost. Mild, but not warm, conditions and high light levels are essential – a cold frame or cloche will do, but windowsills are seldom suitable. Plant out as soon as the roots bind the compost, and water well before and after planting.

From autumn to spring lettuces are trickier to grow. Seeds sown in late summer can be harvested in early winter if protected by cloches or frames (*see above*). Especially hardy lettuces can be sown in early autumn for crops in mid- to late spring. Cover with cloches or frames for earlier, better and more reliable crops. Mini-leaves are most successful; hearted lettuces really need a greenhouse.

Common problems

Slugs and snails are the most damaging pests. Vigilant hygiene is the only control for caterpillars and viruses. You can control aphids with an organic insecticide, but try resistant varieties if root aphids cause wilt and stunted growth. In wet periods, downy mildew attacks older leaves; sow resistant varieties for autumn crops.

Loose-leaved lettuces bring varied colour and texture to the salad bowl, and there is some evidence that the red-tinted types are less prone than most lettuces to slug and snail damage.

Endive

The leaves of this very bitter salad plant can be cut when young to add a different note to mixed salads (*see page 156*). Alternatively, it can be blanched to reduce the bitterness (*see below*). The curled and plain-leaved forms are both grown in the same way.

Any fertile garden soil in full sun is suitable. Before sowing, promote fertility and moisture-holding in the soil by adding half a bucketful of well-rotted organic matter and, unless the ground was enriched for a previous crop in the same season, 25g (1oz) of general-purpose fertilizer every square metre (10 sq ft).

Mild, but not warm, conditions and high light levels are essential for sturdy plants. A covering of horticultural fleece after sowing can advance harvesting by as much as two weeks. Spring sowings benefit from a site in partial shade, which will help to prevent them from bolting to seed. If growth is slow and leaves pale, apply additional fertilizer and water it in.

Common problems

Endive is easy to grow and suffers few significant problems. Slugs and snails are the most damaging pests and are dealt with as for other crops.

Endives may succumb to grey mould and other fungal diseases in wet weather, especially when the plants are covered for blanching. Good ventilation around the plants can help prevent this from happening, but prompt disposal of affected material is the only remedy.

FROM SOWING TO HARVESTING BLANCHED ENDIVE

1 **Sow the seeds** directly into the ground 12mm (½in) deep in drills 30cm (12in) apart. Sow at fortnightly intervals from mid-spring to late summer so that leaves can be gathered from summer until winter.

2 **Thin emerging seedlings** when the first 4 leaves appear, so they are 25cm (10in) apart. Water the growing plants regularly, especially during hot, dry weather, to prevent the plants from running to seed.

3 **Loosely tie the plants** around their stems with raffia when they are fully grown – about 3 months after sowing. The raffia tie keeps the lower leaves off the ground, which reduces the risk of rotting.

4 **Begin to blanch** about 4 months after sowing, covering each plant with a large, light-proof container. Blanch 2–3 plants at a time for a supply over a long period, because blanched plants tend not to last long.

5 **Cover any holes** to exclude light. A slight gap between the rims and the soil allows for ventilation to prevent rotting. The blanched leaves should be free of bitterness within 2–3 weeks in mild weather.

6 **Harvest blanched plants** by cutting just above soil level. Use blanched endive immediately, because it does not keep well in the kitchen. Harvesting can be extended by growing varieties of winter endive.

Chicory

There are various types of chicory. Radicchio and other hearting chicories form firm heads with a bitter flavour that are used in salads, while sugarloaf chicory has only moderately bitter leaves. Roots of Belgian or witloof chicory are stored for forcing in winter to produce buds of mild-tasting, firm leaves called chicons (*see below*).

Sowing, cultivation & harvesting

Any fertile garden soil in full sun is suitable. Before sowing add half a bucketful of organic matter and 25g (1oz) of general-purpose fertilizer every square metre (10 sq ft).

Sow all chicories either directly where they are to grow in containers at fortnightly intervals, so that the leaves can be harvested from summer until winter. Thin the seedlings as soon as they can be handled. The leafy chicories are suitable for growing as cut-and-come again salad leaves (*see page 156*), and these should be thinned to just 1cm (½in) apart; thin other types to 20cm (8in)

spacings. Plant out seedlings raised in as the roots bind the compost, and both before and after planting.

Radicchios form heads about four months after sowing, but this period can be shortened by covering with fleece. Chicories have deep roots, and watering is only necessary for young plants during very hot, dry weather; apply two watering cans' worth of water every square metre (10 sq ft) every 10 days. Fertilize if growth is slow and leaves are pale.

Harvest chicory when the hearts are firm or the leaves are usable. Cut-and-come again crops can make an interesting, bitter addition to salads, and a second crop may regrow from the stumps. Picking young leaves does not have an adverse affect on the development of Belgian or witloof chicory roots for forcing.

Chicory is easy to grow and suffers from no significant pest or disease problems, although netting to prevent attacks by pigeons is often required.

FROM SOWING TO HARVESTING FORCED BELGIAN OR WITLOOF CHICORY

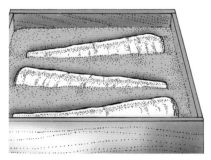

1 **Sow the seeds** directly into the ground 12mm (½in) deep in rows 30cm (12in) apart from mid-spring until late summer. Remove surplus plants when large enough to handle, allowing 20cm (8in) between plants.

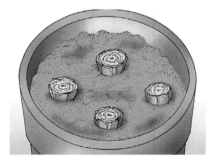

2 **Lift the roots** in autumn when the leaves start to die down. Discard any thin or forked roots and retain those that are 1–3cm (½–1¼in) in diameter at the top, because these are the most suitable for forcing.

3 **Cut off remaining leaves** to within 1cm (½in) of the crown and discard unsuitable, damaged or diseased roots. Shorten the roots to 23cm (9in) and remove any side roots with a sharp knife.

4 **Half-bury prepared roots** horizontally in boxes of dry sand so they are not touching. Keep in complete darkness in a cool but frost-free place, until mid- to late autumn.

5 **Plant a few roots** in a pot of soft sand or light garden soil, keeping 1cm (½in) of the crown above the surface. Water sparingly and keep in darkness. Creamy white chicons will appear in just a few weeks.

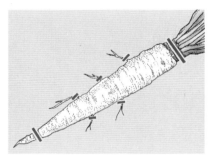

6 **Cut or snap off** the blanched chicons about 4 weeks after planting. Use them immediately in winter salads. After harvesting, the roots will produce several smaller shoots that can be blanched in the same way.

Spinach & spinach beet

Spinach is a useful crop, but there are similar, easier-to-grow crops that have their own special qualities. Any fertile garden soil in full sun or light shade is suitable. Before sowing add half a bucketful of organic matter and 100g (3½oz) of general-purpose fertilizer, or 200g (7oz) of organic fertilizer such as chicken manure, every square metre (10 sq ft) to ensure good leaf production.

Spinach

You should sow spinach where it is to grow, 2cm (¾in) deep in rows 30cm (12in) apart, from late winter until early autumn. Gradually thin the plants to 15cm (6in) apart; the thinnings can be eaten. As spinach quickly runs to seed, sowing little and often is best – a 1.5m (5ft) row at one sowing provides plenty.

Apply two watering cans per square metre (10 sq ft) every 5–10 days in hot, dry weather to reduce bolting. After about 60–80 days start cutting, removing no more than half the leaves at a time. A final sowing of hardy spinach in late summer or early autumn will grow slowly over winter for gathering in spring.

Slugs and snails can be controlled by removing all old foliage and weeds. Greenfly sometimes need treating with an approved insecticide. Downy mildew may infect plants in wet weather; resistant varieties are available.

Spinach beet, New Zealand spinach & chard

These all make good alternatives to spinach, and crop abundantly. New Zealand spinach is a robust sprawling plant suitable for any soil in full sun, or even hanging baskets. Pests and diseases seldom trouble these crops.

Cultivation is as for spinach beet (*see below*) and they are ready for harvest just as soon as leaves become big enough. Like spinach, spinach beet and chard make good mini-leaves sown in rows 15cm (6in) apart with 1cm (½in) between plants. Pick the leaves as soon as usable.

FROM SOWING TO HARVESTING SPINACH BEET

1 Sow 3–4 seeds at 20cm (8in) intervals in 2cm (¾in) deep drills from late winter for spring crops, during mid-spring for summer crops, and again in late summer for picking the following spring. For crops of mini leaves, sow seeds in rows 15cm (6in) apart with 1cm (½in) between plants.

2 Thin the seedling clusters when each seedling is big enough to handle. Leave 1 seedling per station. Thinning can be done over several weeks as the thinnings are useful eaten either cooked or raw.

3 Hoe regularly between the rows during the growing season. Water the growing plants liberally, approximately two watering cans per square metre (10 sq ft) every 5–10 days in hot, dry weather.

4 Harvest a few of the largest leaves after 60–80 days or as soon as the plants are large enough, picking or cutting them off as close to the ground as possible. Gather the the leaves regularly to encourage further production.

Rocket & exotic salad leaves

Rocket is now a 'must-have' crop for any vegetable grower, but it has only become popular in recent years. This is surprising, given that it is so easy to grow and so well suited to the smallest gardens, even if confined to a large pot. Many other 'exotic' salad leaves are now available as seed, and are well worth trying for their interesting flavours. Mixed seed packets are available; they are very easy to grow as cut-and-come again (*see below*) and in summer make a superior and cheaper alternative to mixed salad from the supermarket.

Growing rocket

Any fertile garden soil in full sun or light shade is suitable. Before you sow, apply half a bucketful of organic matter and 25g (1oz) of general-purpose fertilizer, or 100g (3½oz) of organic fertilizer, such as chicken manure, every square metre (10 sq ft).

Sow every two weeks, ideally direct in the ground, from mid-spring until late summer for a continuous supply. If space is limited, sow in module trays using general-purpose potting compost and plant out as soon as the roots bind the compost, watering in well. Sow seeds 25mm (1in) apart in drills about 1cm (½in) deep and 10–20cm (4–8in) apart; reduce spacing by 10 percent on raised beds. There should be no need to thin.

In hot, dry weather, apply two watering cans of water every square metre (10 sq ft) every 10 days to reduce bolting. If growth is slow and leaves pale, give extra

Special seed mixtures for cut-and-come again crops can be bought. Each leaf type should grow at the same rate and will provide a spicy or Mediterranean flavour. Try experimenting with your own mixtures.

fertilizer. Take a few leaves from each plant as soon as they can be handled; the plant will grow more. Leaves can be punctured by flea beetles; fleece usually excludes the beetle and liquid fertilizer helps plants to outgrow the pest.

FROM SOWING TO HARVESTING CUT-AND-COME AGAIN SALAD LEAVES

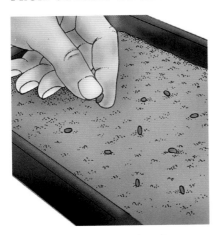

1 **Sow salad seeds** direct where they are to grow in a container. Growing bags are ideal. Sow every 2 weeks for a steady supply of young leaves throughout summer.

2 **Lightly cover and water** and keep in a light, airy place; raise the container on bricks to deter slugs and snails. Plants take 3–6 weeks to produce the first usable crop.

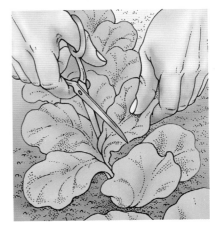

3 **Cut the leaves** as required and leave the stumps to regrow. Water lightly to keep plants growing; they should produce further crops at 3–6 week intervals.

Cucumbers

Greenhouse cucumbers (*see below*) are familiar supermarket salad plants, but outdoor cucumbers have shorter, rougher, and prolific fruits with a more robust flavour.

Growing outdoor cucumbers

Any fertile soil in full sun is suitable. Before sowing, add a bucketful of organic matter and 100g (3½oz) of general-purpose fertilizer every square metre (10 sq ft); double this if using an organic fertilizer. Sow seeds at 20–25°C (68–77°F) in mid-spring in small pots, with the soil just covering them. Plant them out 90cm (35in) apart in early summer. Cloches or cold frames are helpful in cold regions. To save space, grow trailing varieties up a trellis or wigwam.

Pollination

Outdoor cucumbers: These need both male and female flowers for pollination. Many fruit will be shed; this is normal as more are set than the plant can take to maturity.

Greenhouse cucumbers: Remove any male flowers produced as the female flowers they fertilize will grow into misshapen, bitter fruit. Pollination is not necessary. Female flowers have a miniature fruit at the base of the flower; the male flowers do not, making them to easy to identity. Old varieties have many male flowers.

Common problems

Outdoor cucumbers are usually problem free. In greenhouses, typical pests – such as glasshouse red spider mite, thrips, whitefly, and aphids – are best controlled by using biological controls well before outbreaks become a problem. Sticky yellow traps give early warning of whitefly and aphids. Severe attacks can be reduced by several applications of oil or fatty acid (soap) based insecticides a few days apart. These do no significant harm to biological control organisms. Powdery mildew can be prevented by dusting with sulphur and choosing resistant varieties.

FROM PLANTING TO HARVESTING GREENHOUSE CUCUMBERS

1 **Plant 2 plants** into a standard-sized growbag in mid-spring. Large pots or border soil can also be used, with one plant per pot or 70cm (28in) between border plants. Cucumbers thrive in peat-free media. If using border soil, add 100g (3½oz) of general fertilizer per square metre (10 sq ft) and plenty of compost. Shade the plants in hot weather and liquid feed regularly.

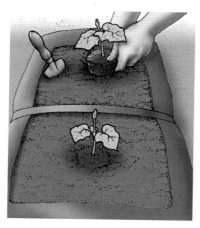

2 **Support the plants** by tying them to bamboo canes as they grow. Remove the growing points between thumb and forefinger when the main stems reach the greenhouse roof. Maintain a temperature of 18–25°C (64–77°F). Modern greenhouse varieties produce only female flowers and set fruit without pollination (*see above*).

3 **Allow side branches** to develop, but pinch out their growing tips between thumb and forefinger once they have formed 2 leaves. The first fruits will develop on the main stem, followed by fruit on the sideshoots.

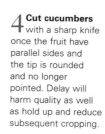
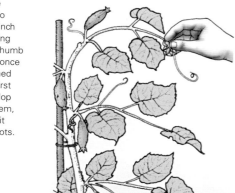

4 **Cut cucumbers** with a sharp knife once the fruit have parallel sides and the tip is rounded and no longer pointed. Delay will harm quality as well as hold up and reduce subsequent cropping.

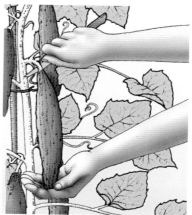

Tomatoes

In mild, especially urban, areas good tomatoes can be grown outdoors in late summer, although if you grow them in a greenhouse the yields will be bigger, tastier, and less disease-prone. Most tomato varieties grow as either vines or bushes:

Vine varieties: These must be tied to a supporting stake or string every 20–30cm (8–12in), and sideshoots should be removed from every leaf junction to produce one fruiting stem. They are easier to grow well in greenhouses, and some varieties will not fruit in the cooler conditions outdoors.

Bush varieties: These are shorter, and they are more often chosen for outdoor cultivation because they can be protected with frames, cloches, and fleece; smaller varieties can even be grown in hanging baskets. Sideshoots do not need to be removed.

Growing tomatoes from seeds

Sow seeds indoors at 18–25°C (64–77°F) in late winter or early spring for greenhouse crops and mid-spring for outdoor crops. Sow thinly in shallow pots of multi-purpose or seed compost, and lightly cover the surface with vermiculite or grit, and water with a copper-based fungicide to prevent damping off (*see page 390*).

Greenhouses or conservatories provide sufficient light for tomatoes, but windowsills are less suitable. If you do not have such facilities, a wide range of tomato varieties are available as young plants from most garden centres.

Tomatoes are delicious summer treats and they come in a huge range of flavours, shapes, and sizes. Some varieties make compact growth and can be grown in hanging baskets.

Choices in the greenhouse

The easiest option is to plant tomatoes straight into the border. Border soil is largely trouble free, requiring only to be kept moist. Enriched with a bucketful of organic matter and 70g (2½oz) of general-purpose fertilizer or 100g (3½oz) of organic fertilizer per square metre (10 sq ft), border soil will provide all that tomatoes need unless disease strikes, when you will need to replace it.

FROM SOWING TO TRANSPLANTING TOMATO PLANTS

1 **Plant up seedlings** as soon as they have their first 4–5 leaves. Plant in individual small pots of multipurpose compost and grow in bright light, at 12–18°C (54–64°F), spacing the plants so that their leaves do not touch.

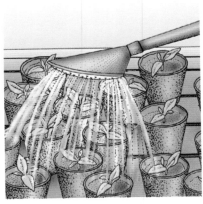

2 **Water plants** regularly, keeping plants moist but never soggy. Give liquid fertilizer every week from 6 weeks after potting or if the plants become pale.

3 **Plant out** once the first flowers begin to show or when the plants are 15–23cm (6–9in) tall. Water well before and after planting in their final position.

GREENHOUSE GROWING SYSTEMS

Greenhouse tomatoes are easily grown in border soil ❶, but pests and diseases can build up from year to year. Large 10–15 litre (2.2–3.3 gal) pots ❷ are an alternative, as are ring pots ❸ or straw bales ❹ (from fields that have not been sprayed with hormone weedkillers) stood on pebbles or ashes on a sheet of polythene. Growing bags ❺ are popular, but need very frequent watering.

Containers, especially growing bags, have a very limited water-holding capacity and may need watering several times a day unless you have an automatic watering system installed. Large pots filled with growing bag media only need watering twice a day as they do not lose water quite so rapidly. Infrequent drenching is no substitute for careful, frequent watering and will stress plants, causing disease and crop failure. Containers can also easily run out of nutrients, so fertilize regularly.

Cultivating greenhouse tomatoes

When growing indoor vine tomatoes (*see next page*), you should train them up wire supports or canes by tying in regularly with soft string. The weight of the crop, about 5kg (11lb) per plant, will not break canes because there is no wind to rock the plants. Snap off any leafy sideshoots as they form in the angle between leaf stalk and stem, or snip out larger shoots. Avoid jagged breaks or tears, which may allow infection. When the plants reach the top of the cane, usually 1.5m (5ft), remove the growing tip.

Ventilate and shade your greenhouse or conservatory to keep the temperature constant at around 20°C (68°F); do not allow it to exceed 25°C (77°F). Never allow your pots or growing bags to dry out; keep them moist but never saturated, and apply tomato fertilizer every week from 30 days after planting. Border soils are less vulnerable to over- or underwatering or feeding. Your tomatoes are ready to pick when they are ripe and evenly coloured.

Choices outdoors

Outdoor tomatoes need a sunny, sheltered location. Patios and balconies are ideal. Enrich the soil with a bucketful of organic matter and 70g (2½oz) of general-purpose fertilizer, or 100g (3½oz) of organic fertilizer per square metre (10sq ft). Use crop rotation to avoid any build-up of soil problems; potatoes and tomatoes occupy the same space in a rotation because they are related and share the

Companion planting tomatoes with African marigolds is often seen in gardens and greenhouses, with the purpose of controlling greenfly, whitefly, or soil nematodes. The strong marigold smell is said to either repel the insects or attract them away from the tomatoes.

159

GROWING GREENHOUSE TOMATOES

1 Set out plants in early spring 45cm (18in) apart and with the top of the rootball level with the compost or soil. Water thoroughly and keep the rootball moist to help the roots explore the surrounding compost or soil.

2 Tie soft string loosely around the stem of each plant and tie one end to a wire stretched above. Twist the string around the growing stem. Alternatively, use canes, tying in every 20–30cm (8–12in) with soft string.

3 Spray the flowers with a fine droplet spray or tap the canes on sunny days. This shakes the plants and helps to move the pollen from male to female parts of the flower so the flowers set fruit.

4 Remove lower leaves once the plants are 1.2–1.5m (4–5ft) tall to make watering easier. Remove any dead or diseased growth immediately, and sideshoots that grow from the leaf axils.

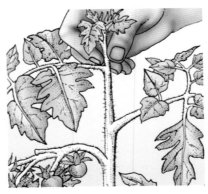

5 Remove the growing tip 2 leaves beyond the last fruit cluster (truss) once the plants reach the roof. In garden greenhouses, 6 or 7 trusses can be expected to ripen.

6 Pick the fruit individually as they develop full colour, taking each one with the stalk intact. At the end of the season, pick unripe fruit as whole trusses and ripen indoors.

same pests and diseases, especially cyst eelworms. Growing bags or containers can be used if fertile garden soil is not available, but they do need more watering and feeding.

Cultivating outdoor tomatoes

When growing outdoor tomatoes (*see facing page*), you can suppress weeds and keep your crop cleaner by planting through a black polythene sheet mulch, although this makes watering more difficult. Bush tomatoes don't need a stake, although it may be helpful; you'll need to make a strong support for vine tomatoes, enough to support the weight of a good 4kg (8½lb) crop per plant.

Water well every 10 days in dry spells. Feeding with a tomato fertilizer is less essential, so long as the soil was enriched well before planting. You should water very lightly if rain is expected, to avoid overwatering.

Common problems

Aphids can be common early in the crop. Outdoors, control them immediately with approved insecticides or by hand, as they can badly damage young plants. Greenhouse whitefly can be controlled by early introduction of biological controls. Organic insecticides based on oils or soaps can reduce infestation if the whitefly are too numerous for biological controls. Caterpillar damage can occur in late summer. Picking off the few caterpillars usually present is the best control measure.

Tomato blight is a fungal disease that requires water on the plant and warm conditions to spread. It is seldom troublesome indoors if there is good airflow and leaves are kept free of moisture. Outdoors, and in polythene greenhouses where condensation is unavoidable, plants are at high risk of infection in wet weather from early

GROWING OUTDOOR TOMATOES

1 Plant out in early summer, once the risk of frost has passed, into well-cultivated and fertile soil. Choose a sunny, sheltered spot and space plants 45–60cm (18–24in) apart. Water well before and after planting.

2 Support bush tomatoes with a short cane to promote air flow through the plant and reduce disease. Support vine tomatoes well: a sawn timber stake 2.5cm (1in) square is ideal.

3 Snap sideshoots as they appear on vine tomatoes: bush tomatoes do not need this treatment. Early morning is the best time, because the shoots are turgid and snap easily. Avoid pulling and leaving untidy wounds.

4 Remove the growing tip when 4 clusters of flowers (trusses) start to form fruit, 2 leaves beyond the last truss. More trusses are unlikely to ripen outside in a typical summer.

5 Spray with fungicide to protect plants against blight infection. Continue to water and feed plants regularly and snap out any new sideshoots that develop as a result of stopping the main growing tip.

6 Use cloches over bush tomatoes for earlier and more reliable crops. In early autumn, vine tomatoes can be untied and laid down under cloches for late-ripening fruit, or remove the trusses and ripen indoors.

summer to mid-autumn. If such conditions prevail, apply fungicide every 10 days (five days in very wet weather), thoroughly coating every part of the plant.

Good airflow and an absence of condensation will prevent or limit other fungal diseases, which are largely a problem in greenhouses. If diseases do occur, promptly remove affected foliage or even whole plants if necessary.

Contamination with hormone weedkillers can cause twisting and distortion of young foliage. It is often very difficult to track down the source, but common culprits are lawn weedkiller residues in sprayers or watering cans, drift from agricultural land, or compost and growing media derived from treated grass mowings or cereal straw.

In greenhouses, excessive temperature fluctuations cause leaf rolling and distortion of young shoots, almost identical to aphid damage, and the fruit may be distorted.

Uneven watering can lead to blossom end rot, in which a lack of calcium in the fruit results in black markings where the flower was attached to the fruit.

Hard, under-ripe areas within fruit or on the upper surfaces of fruit, often called white wall or greenback, are due to insufficient potassium and excess heat and light. Better ventilation, more shading, and potassium-rich fertilizers are the only remedies. Lack of magnesium can lead to yellow leaves starting at the bottom of the plant. Make a solution of Epsom salts with 200g/11 litres (7oz/2½ gal) and apply as a spray to the foliage in the evening every two weeks until the foliage is normal.

Mottling, streaking, and stunted growth may indicate viral diseases. There is no remedy, and early removal of infected plants is advisable as the viruses are spread from plant to plant on hands and tools.

THE CABBAGE FAMILY

Plants of the cabbage family are also known as brassicas. They are a varied group of crops, ranging from leafy cabbages and kale to broccoli and cauliflowers cultivated for their flowers. They even include swedes (*see page 194*), found among the root crops. Their long growing season and pest protection requirements combine to make them seem a great deal of trouble. But with a little forward planning, you can use brassicas to extend the productive season in the garden into winter and early spring and provide healthy and tasty greens when plentiful summer and early autumn crops come to an end.

Growing brassicas

Brassicas crop abundantly in mild, wet climates, and are useful because young plants can be raised in a small space and transplanted to fill in after another crop has finished. With a few exceptions all are grown in the same way: home-raised or bought young plants should be planted in fertile soil and protected from their numerous enemies.

Any fertile garden soil will support brassicas; if in doubt, add a bucketful of well-rotted organic matter and 70g (2¹/₂oz) of fertilizer or 100g (3¹/₂oz) of organic fertilizer per square metre (10 sq ft) at least four weeks before planting. Alternatively, apply 100g (3¹/₂oz) fertilizer or 150g (5¹/₄oz) of organic fertilizer per square metre (10 sq ft) two weeks before planting. Check the soil pH (*see page 17*) and add lime if it is less than pH 6.5 to limit the severity of clubroot; avoid liming within two weeks of applying fertilizer. Try to rotate plantings with at least two years between brassica crops.

Raising plants

Bring on young plants in containers filled with multipurpose compost. Summer cauliflowers and cabbages often mature so quickly that only a handful of plants are needed. Sow twice as many seeds as you need for large plants, such as Brussels sprouts, and transplant seedlings into 9cm (3¹/₂in) pots as soon as they can be handled. If many plants are needed, as with spring cabbages, sow two seeds per cell in module trays and discard the weaker one. Transplant seedlings when they have grown four or five leaves (*see right*).

To exclude pests, especially cabbage root fly, cabbage whitefly (*see page 28*), and mealy cabbage aphid, cover containers with fleece until late spring; after this, fleece

may overheat the plants, so use insect-proof mesh. Flexible mats or collars protect against cabbage root fly. Brassicas are seldom badly damaged by their many leaf diseases, but where disease is a problem, resistant varieties are available. Fungicides are not available. Pick off caterpillars by hand or use an approved insecticide.

TRANSPLANTING BRASSICAS

1 **Transplant when** the roots bind the potting media firmly together. Firm the soil, watering 24 hours before transplanting if it is dry, and rake level. Water, then ease out the seedlings. Set in the soil up to the lowest leaves and firm in very well. Water regularly until growing strongly.

2 **Fit root collars**, at least 10cm (4in) wide, around the neck of the young plants to exclude cabbage root fly, which lays its eggs in the soil near the roots of the plant. The collars are simply a barrier and can be made out of any thick, flexible material, such as carpet underlay or roofing felt.

Cabbages

In their first growing season, cabbages form a head of edible leaves. This is actually a giant bud that will flower the following year. If you sow cabbage seeds too early, they can flower in the first year, ruining the crop.

Types of cabbage

Cabbages are bred to be sown and then crop at particular times of year for a continuous supply:

Summer cabbages: These are sown from late winter to mid-spring for cropping from early to late summer.

Autumn cabbages: Sown in late spring, crop in autumn.

Winter cabbages: Sown in late spring and early summer, crop in winter. Red cabbages and crinkly leaved Savoy types, both of which also crop in winter, take longer to grow than green winter cabbages, so plant these a little earlier.

Spring cabbages, or spring greens: Sown in late summer; these grow through winter and are ready for harvesting from early spring until early summer.

Chinese cabbage: Ready to eat in as little as six weeks. Although bolt-resistant varieties can be used for earlier sowings, the most reliable way of raising these cabbages is to sow in midsummer.

Assorted cabbages are available: spring and winter cabbages are useful seasonal greens, summer and Chinese cabbages are light and can be eaten as salad, and red cabbage is a popular winter ingredient.

FROM PLANTING TO HARVESTING SPRING CABBAGES

1 Pull up a little soil around the base of the young plants about 2 weeks after planting in late summer. This protects against wind rock in winter, which can loosen the roots and cause problems in later months. Firm any plants loosened later by adverse weather.

2 Hoe between the growing plants regularly from late winter to keep the rows free from competing weeds and maintain a good tilth to the soil. Some of the young cabbages can be cut from early spring if early greens are desired.

3 Spread fertilizer around the developing cabbages in early spring to encourage rapid growth and hearting. Use a dressing of a nitrogen-rich dressing, such as sulphate of ammonia, following the instructions on the pack.

4 Cut mature spring cabbages as required from mid-spring to early summer. Clear away the stumps and roots as this breaks the cycle of the whitefly pest, which may otherwise move on to other brassica plants in summer (*see page 28*).

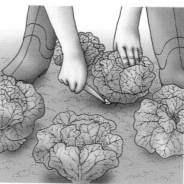

HARVESTING & STORING CABBAGE

1 **Lift winter cabbages** for storing as entire plants in late autumn and early winter. If they are carefully stored and regularly checked, some varieties can last through winter.

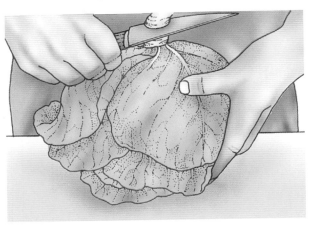

2 **Trim off** the roots and the bottom of the stem. Remove the coarse outer leaves to leave a clean, solid head. The tightly packed, almost white Dutch cabbages are most suitable for long storage.

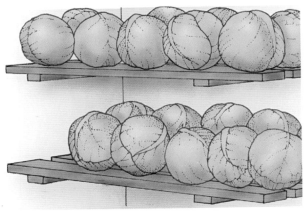

3 **Store the heads** in a cool but frost free place, such as a garden shed. Slatted shelving allows air to circulate, and the cabbages can be stacked if necessary. Check for blemishes every few weeks.

Raising & planting out

Start young plants in module trays or pots, bearing in mind that summer cabbages soon become over-mature, so sowing little and often is ideal. Spring, autumn, and winter cabbages stay in good condition for many weeks and sowing in larger batches gives good results. Plant out into very fertile soil. Space summer cabbages about 40cm (16in) apart, and allow 45cm (18in) between autumn and winter varieties. Spring cabbages (*see previous page*) are a special case; allow 30cm (12in) between rows, but only 15cm (6in) between plants. In spring, gather alternate plants as soon as they are usable as greens, then take the remaining plants as they form good hearts a few weeks later.

Chinese cabbages need very fertile soil. They can be raised in module trays, but sowing where they are to grow is usually better. Sow 2cm (¾in) deep, 5cm (2in) apart, in rows 30cm (12in) apart, and thin to 20–25cm (8–10in) apart as soon as they can be handled.

Cultivation & harvest

As your plants grow, 'topdress' them by sprinkling extra nitrogen-rich fertilizer around the base if growth appears to be fading. Apply at about 25g (1oz) every square metre (10 sq ft); apply organic fertilizers at 70g (2½oz) every square metre (10 sq ft). Ideally, water your cabbages so that the soil is constantly moist in dry spells, but if water and time are in short supply, the most economical use of available water is to give a good soak when the head is just forming. Chinese cabbages in particular must be kept well watered in dry spells or they will run to seed.

You can cut heads whenever they are usable, although it is best to wait until firm, solid heads have formed. When the hearts are truly solid, cut and use immediately or keep in the salad compartment of the fridge. Some cabbage varieties, including some red ones, are especially solid and can be cut in autumn and stored in a frostproof shed until late winter. After the heads are cut, scoring a cross with a knife on the top of the stump can result in a useful crop of greens within a few weeks.

Common problems

Caterpillars can be very damaging; control them by thorough hand-picking, application of an approved insecticide, or covering with insect-proof mesh, which will form an effective barrier to the egg-laying adult butterflies without the need for pesticides. Mesh provides protection against all flying pests, but it can act as a hiding place for slugs. Minimize club root by liming, improving drainage, rotating crops, and by growing resistant varieties; Chinese cabbage is particularly susceptible.

Cauliflowers & calabrese

Both cauliflower and calabrese are related to broccoli. They only do well in very fertile, moisture-retentive soils, especially cauliflowers, and they are highly susceptible to club root, although resistant varieties are sometimes available. Grow in a well-limed, neutral to alkaline soil with a high level of organic matter, and apply a dressing of fertilizer before planting.

Types of cauliflower & calabrese

Summer and autumn cauliflowers: The tightly packed flower buds or curds of these are cut as a single head and tend to mature in gluts. Late summer and early autumn types are available in green, orange, and purple as well as the traditional white; romanesco types have minarets of pale green curds and a robust texture and flavour.

Biennial cauliflowers: Sown in late spring or early summer for cutting from midwinter until the following early summer, these are often confusingly called broccoli. They are unreliable in cold regions, but do well in mild areas.

Calabrese: This forms a large central head with smaller sideshoots and is also called heading broccoli, but it is less hardy than sprouting broccoli (*see page 167*). It can mature as little as 12 weeks after sowing, so late-summer sowings crop well into autumn.

Raising & planting out

Sow little and often, in module trays or small pots to minimize potential damage from club root, from late winter until early summer for cauliflowers and until late summer for calabrese. Crops of summer cauliflowers and calabrese can be sown in autumn in a greenhouse for crops in early summer or spring. Sow biennial cauliflowers from late spring until early summer and plant out in midsummer for sturdy, frost-resistant plants.

Summer cauliflowers (*see following page*) can be planted 45cm (18in) apart, but often need much less watering if planted 60cm (24in) apart. Space autumn cauliflowers 50cm (20in) apart; some vigorous varieties are ideal for less-than-perfect sites, and they do best at spacings of 70cm (28in). Biennial cauliflowers need to be spaced 75cm (30in) apart so they can develop to full size, essential for enduring winter. Plant calabrese 45cm (18in) apart.

Cultivation & harvest

Keep your cauliflowers and calabrese moist during dry spells, but if time is short, soak well two to three weeks before harvest. Topdress your plants with extra nitrogen-rich fertilizer if growth appears to be fading, at about 25g

Calabrese is more convenient than cauliflower for the home gardeners as it gives a reasonable period of summer cropping rather than a brief glut. This is because after the main head is harvested, the sideshoots develop and can be gathered for several weeks.

MINI-CAULIFLOWERS

Small but perfectly formed mini-cauliflowers are ideal for small households or for freezing. Plant out or station sow (*see page 147*) 15cm (6in) apart in rows 25cm (10in) apart. Seed suppliers offer suitable varieties, but you will need to sow in small batches, as they all have a tendency to mature in a rush, creating a glut.

(1oz) every square metre (10 sq ft), or 70g (2½oz) every square metre (10 sq ft) if using organic fertilizers. Any stress or setback, such as growing for too long in containers, poor planting, or a lack of water, can lead to premature flowering and disappointingly small curds or heads, called 'buttons'.

Cut the curds, head, or sideshoots as soon as ready. On loose-leafed varieties, cover developing cauliflower curds with cut leaves to preserve the colour. In 'self-blanching' varieties, the leaves stay wrapped over the curds.

Common problems

To exclude cabbage root fly, cabbage whitefly, and other flying pests, cover plants with horticultural fleece, insect-proof mesh, or – in the case of cabbage root fly – tightly fitting mats at the base of the plants (*see page 162*). Clear away stumps and roots of old crops before planting new crops to deter whitefly and mealy cabbage aphids.

Caterpillars can be controlled by regular hand-picking, by applying an approved insecticide or by covering the plants with insect-proof mesh.

FROM SOWING TO HARVESTING SUMMER CAULIFLOWER

1 **Cultivate the soil** deeply in winter, and dig in plenty of well-rotted farmyard manure or garden compost.

2 **Rake in additional fertilizer** if the soil is still poor, in early to mid-spring, and add lime if necessary to increase pH. Do this 1–2 weeks before sowing or planting out.

3 **Plant out seedlings** at desired spacings. Water both seedlings and site the day before transplanting, and puddle plants in well.

4 **Water in** a dressing of nitrogen-rich fertilizer in late spring for transplanted crops or in midsummer for those sown direct.

5 **Water weekly** in dry weather, applying about 2 watering cans worth per square metre (10 sq ft). If this is not possible, water 2–3 weeks before harvest, as the curds form.

6 **Cut cauliflowers** as they mature and as needed. The curds should be firm and well developed, but not yet beginning to open.

Preparing to grow *see page 142* | Sowing & growing *see page 146* | Common problems *see page 210*

Broccoli

This versatile vegetable is now available for nearly half the year. Modern plant breeding has greatly extended the season of cropping from late winter to late spring, and autumn-cropping varieties are available that will produce sprouts all winter in mild areas.

Sprouting broccoli (*see below*) is extremely hardy and will survive winter in areas where cauliflowers would not. It produces abundant tasty spears in early to mid-spring. Both purple and white varieties are available, but the white types have benefited less from advances in plant breeding.

An equally hardy crop, and closely related to broccoli, is purple cape broccoli. This produces a small cauliflower-type head in late winter and early spring, but has a texture and flavour closer to broccoli than cauliflower.

Sowing & transplanting

Sow seeds for autumn crops in mid-spring. Sow those for late winter and spring cropping, including purple cape broccoli, in late spring and early summer.

Spring-cropping varieties flower in response to winter cold, but need to be quite large plants to do so. If sown too early, however, excessively large plants will form; they will flower prematurely in summer and die before winter.

Raise young plants in module trays or pots and plant out 75cm (30in) apart in late spring or early summer. These crops grow best in only moderately fertile soil, which should be prepared as for most brassica crops, but using only half the amount of fertilizer. Omit fertilizer altogether if bulky organic matter was applied during preparation of the soil.

Cultivation & harvest

There is no need to water broccoli lavishly. In fact, the soft growth that will be produced in response to heavy watering is not as frost-hardy as the firmer growth of plants watered sparingly.

Cut the shoots as soon as they can be handled, typically when they are about 10cm (4in) long, and before the buds open. Purple cape always produces just a central head, with no sideshoots, while broccoli often forms a large central head with many sideshoots; harvest the head first, and then return for further crops. Frequent picking of sideshoots will prevent any of them from becoming overmature, and will prolong cropping for several weeks.

Common problems

Broccoli is significantly less susceptible to pests and diseases than cauliflowers or calabrese, but you should grow it in alkaline soil with protection from cabbage root fly. Overwintered crops are a favourite food of pigeons during cold weather and must be carefully netted, with the net suspended 30cm (12in) above the crop so that the birds cannot land on the net and feed through it and foul the crop with their droppings.

FROM PLANTING TO HARVESTING SPROUTING BROCCOLI

1 **Set out transplants** in their final position in early to midsummer, in space left empty by earlier crops. Keep weed-free and water regularly, as needed.

2 **Begin to harvest** by taking any central head that forms, or the topmost shoots. Watering in of a general-purpose fertilizer can be helpful at this stage.

3 **Continue to pick** any sideshoots that develop further down the stem. Harvest them every few days for as long as possible.

Brussels sprouts

Brussels sprouts are deservedly popular and are ideal even for small gardens because they crop over a long period. Modern plant breeding has created some excellent F1 hybrids with greatly improved flavour, disease resistance and weight of crop.

Three varieties – early, mid-season, and late – will provide you with a good succession of cropping from late summer to early spring, but at a pinch a mid-season variety on its own will cover most of the sprout season. Although Brussels sprouts can be bought as young plants, only early or mid-season types are usually offered.

Sowing, raising & planting out

In cold or exposed regions, you will need to start all sowings in a greenhouse or cold frame. In milder regions, covering with horticultural fleece or cloches is sufficient. Fleece is best as it excludes mealy cabbage aphid, cabbage whitefly, and cabbage root aphid, which can all severely damage this crop. Early sowings in late winter or early spring, for all varieties, produce the best crops.

Sow twice as many seeds as you need in small pots and transplant into 9cm (3½in) pots – or 15cm (6in) pots where clubroot is a problem – as soon as they can be handled. Plant into their final positions as soon as the roots bind the potting media. Because they take time to fill out, intercrops of salads, spinach and beetroot can be grown between the rows.

Although it is not true that planting in loose soil results in fluffy sprouts, you should firm in well after planting to encourage good growth; when the leaves are gently tugged, you should not be able to uproot the whole plant.

Harvesting

Break off sprouts as soon as they are firm and before they become loose. They mature from the base upwards. The tops can be cut for use as greens, but only after most of the sprouts are gathered as the leaves provide protection from severe weather. Remove and destroy spent crops promptly in spring to prevent the carry-over of whitefly and mealy cabbage aphids.

FROM PLANTING TO HARVESTING BRUSSELS SPROUTS

1 **Transplant young plants** into a well-prepared soil that has been treated with a general-purpose fertilizer. Space the plants at about 60cm (24in) apart in rows 75cm (30in) apart. Plant them firmly with the lowest leaf at soil level.

2 **Puddle in the** young plants and check that they are firmly planted by tugging each top leaf gently. Firm planting is essential, especially on light soils, as the plants can become top-heavy and planting them in firmly helps them become more stable.

3 **Protect young plants** from cabbage root fly by positioning a tightly fitting root collar around the base of each plant at transplanting time. The collar prevents the female laying eggs in the soil.

4 **Continue to water** the young plants through late spring and early summer until they are well established. Further watering will not be necessary after this, unless they begin to suffer during prolonged dry weather.

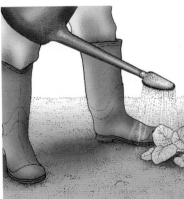

Common problems

Brussels sprouts can be tall and top-heavy and need staking in exposed gardens or where the soil is light. Deep and firm planting, however, as well as drawing soil into a low ridge around the base of the plants in summer will often be enough to steady them in sheltered gardens.

All parts of the crop are a favourite food of pigeons during lean times and plants need careful netting, with the net strongly suspended 30cm (12in) above the crop. Caterpillars are a serious pest and should be controlled by thorough hand-picking, application of an approved insecticide, or covering with insect-proof mesh, which will keep out other flying pests.

Mealy cabbage aphid and cabbage whitefly can build up in late summer and are best controlled with an approved insecticide, such as fatty acids or oils. Prevent reinfection of new crops the following spring by removing all old brassica crops before the new plants are introduced.

Young transplants are susceptible to cabbage root flies; in spring and early summer, it is essential to place root collars around the necks of the plants, or cover with fleece or insect-proof mesh, as no pesticides are available.

BRUSSELS SPROUTS VARIETIES

Conventional varieties (*right*) compare poorly to modern F1 hybrids (*left*). They produce fluffy, poor-quality sprouts that are less abundant and have less resistance to disease.

Brussels sprouts are very susceptible to club root. Grow in well-drained, neutral to alkaline soil with a little lime placed in the planting hole. Raise transplants in 15cm (6in) diameter pots to obtain large root systems able to withstand infection. Do not compost any infected material.

5 Draw up some soil around the base of each stem during summer in light soils or exposed sites to make the plants more stable. Hoe around the plants regularly to keep them free from weeds.

6 Apply a nitrogen-rich fertilizer around the base of the plants during midsummer at a rate of about 30g (1oz) per square metre (10 sq ft), or 70g (2½oz) for organic fertilizers. To protect the crop from flying pests, such as cabbage white butterflies and pigeons, cover with a fine mesh netting.

7 Remove loose or open sprouts from the lower stems, and any yellowing leaves, from late summer onwards, consigning them to the compost bin. This will help reduce foliage disease and suppress slugs.

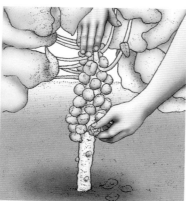

8 Gather the sprouts as soon as they are firm, harvesting them as required, starting from the bottom of the stem. The leafy tops of the plants can also be removed for eating, but not before most of the sprouts have been collected.

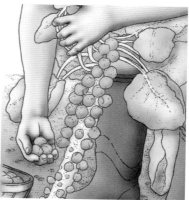

Kale

The dark green, crinkly leaves of kale can be harvested from late autumn to mid-spring. As it is extremely hardy, and the flavour is enhanced by frost, kale is a very useful winter vegetable. Edible kales are usually green or red, although 'black' kales are also available. Brightly coloured ornamental kales are botanically identical but are considered unrewarding to eat. Some quick-growing flowering types are available for summer harvesting.

Kale is much less prone than other brassicas to pests and diseases, including club root and cabbage root fly, although mealy cabbage aphid may require control.

Sowing, cultivation & harvest

Sow plants for autumn cropping in mid-spring, followed by winter crops in late spring, and spring crops in late spring and early summer. Raise young plants in cell trays or pots and plant out 40–50cm (16–20in) apart, depending whether dwarf or tall varieties are being grown. The soil need be only moderately fertile; use half the fertilizer needed for other brassicas, omitting fertilizer altogether if bulky organic matter is applied.

Kale seldom suffers from drought so there is no need to water lavishly, except on planting. Firm planting is required and drawing soil up around the stem in late summer will help to steady the crop in exposed gardens.

You can keep kale in reserve in case other winter brassicas are destroyed by especially severe winter weather. Young leaves and shoots can be gathered as needed, and old yellow foliage consigned to the compost bin. As spring approaches, sideshoots are produced continuously, but by early spring, flowering starts and you should discard the plants and clear the plot to make way for summer crops that follow in the rotation.

HARVESTING KALE

Pick only young leaves and shoots, pulling off and discarding yellowing or tough old leaves. Sideshoots will form in response; again, harvest when young, from the top downwards.

KALE VARIETIES

Red curly kale is a curly, dark purple variety with ornamental qualities. 'Redbor' is a tall F1 hybrid that overwinters well.

Italian black kale is famed for its delicious strong flavour and revered by cooks. 'Nero di Toscano' is a popular variety.

Red winter kale has purple stems with red frilly leaves. Useful for salads or stir fry. It is very hardy.

STALKS & SHOOTS

There are few edible stalks, as stems have to be robust to support foliage in a potentially hostile environment and are therefore usually stringy and unrewarding to eat. What few there are, however, make a delicious addition to the vegetable patch. Asparagus and rhubarb, like many plants, put on a spurt of growth in spring to grab as much light and space as they can before the competition catches up. Until they toughen with age, the young shoots of these crops are tender and tasty. By lavish feeding and watering, celery stems (technically petiole or leaf stalks) can be grown to a crunchy but 'stringless' texture.

Asparagus

You could describe asparagus as the perfect vegetable crop: it produces delicious shoots from mid-spring until early summer when little else is available; it is expensive to buy in the shops; and it is a long-lived perennial, so it does not need sowing each year.

Preparing the site

Find a sunny site with good drainage. Raised beds provide perfect conditions where the soil is heavy or badly drained. Once asparagus is growing it is nearly impossible to remove perennial weeds, so choose a weed-free site or devote a season to eradicating all perennial weeds.

Thorough cultivation is essential, since the crop is likely to be in place for at least 10 years. Dig in 10kg (22lb) of organic matter every square metre (10 sq ft) to get the crop off to a good start, adding lime, if necessary, to ensure the pH is 6.5–7. As asparagus grows up to 1.5m (5ft) tall, choose a sheltered spot. The young spears are easily damaged by frost so avoid frosty parts of the garden.

Planting & cultivation

Modern F1 hybrid varieties are very vigorous and are 'all male'. Male plants produce heavier crops than female plants and do not set seed, avoiding the problem of hard-to-remove seedlings between the rows. In fact, occasional female plants sometimes occur even where 'all-male' varieties are grown. Traditional, non-F1 varieties are much less productive and often lack redeeming attributes such as good flavour.

Planting one- or two-year-old 'crowns' (dormant roots) is the traditional way of starting asparagus, although modern hybrids grow very strongly and raising

from seeds (*see below*), or as young plants in small pots, is often cheaper; raising young plants in pots can bring a bed into production more quickly than by using crowns.

Crowns are bought in winter or more commonly in spring. Space them about 40cm (16in) from each other in trenches 1.2m (4ft) apart. Where space is short, you can use closer planting, but this will result in a shorter-lived plants. Spears must not be cut until the third season after

FROM SOWING TO THINNING ASPARAGUS

1 **Sow the seeds** thinly in 1.5–2cm (½–¾in) deep drills, 45cm (18in) apart, in spring. Keep the bed completely free from weeds and water in dry weather. Seed varieties advertised as F1 tend to be more vigorous and productive than traditional, non-F1 varieties.

2 **Thin the seedlings** when they emerge until they are eventually 15cm (6in) apart. The seedlings can be transplanted to the permanent bed the following spring, but if you wait a year it allows you to identify and remove any less-productive female plants when they produce their berries.

GROWING ASPARAGUS: THE FIRST YEAR

1 Cultivate the ground to the depth of one spade blade in winter. Dig in plenty of well-rotted organic matter, and add lime as required so that the soil pH is between 6.5 and 7. Ensure the ground is clear of weeds before you plant.

2 Dig a trench about 30cm (12in) wide and 20cm (8in) deep, in spring. Lightly rake into the trench 100g (3½oz) of general-purpose fertilizer every square metre (10 sq ft) – use double the quantity for organic fertilizers. Make a ridge 10cm (4in) high at the bottom of the trench.

3 Plant the crowns in spring at 40cm (16in) intervals. They have spidery roots that can be spread evenly over the ridge, with the pointed bud facing upwards. Carefully pull back soil into the trench over the roots so that the top of the crowns are only just covered. As the plants grow, gradually fill in the trench.

4 Cut back in autumn once the stems turn yellow and add to the compost heap. Remove any weeds by hand; do not dig too deeply as asparagus roots are easily damaged. Finally, apply a 5–8cm (2–3in) layer of well-rotted manure or compost into the top of the trench and mound it up over the row.

planting, as eventual heavy cropping depends on a slow build-up of crown size, starting with the all-important first two seasons, when no cutting should be done.

Thorough weeding and watering in dry spells is essential in the first year to help really strong plants develop. You will need to weed and water the following year as well, taking great care not to damage the shallow roots when hoeing or lifting out weeds. Give a further dressing of general-purpose fertilizer in spring.

By the third spring you can cut a light crop from the emerging spears of the young plants for six weeks from mid-spring. In succeeding years, a full crop can be taken.

Harvesting a mature crop

Asparagus spears are the emerging shoots that grow from the roots as they break dormancy in spring. From the fourth year, spears can be cut for about eight weeks from mid-spring to early summer without harming the following year's crop. Use a small, sharp knife to carefully sever each one just below soil level, bearing in mind that other shoots are probably underground growing very close by; if they are damaged they will not produce spears.

Every shoot needs to be cut, even the thin ones called 'sprue' (which are good for soup), as any shoots that are allowed to grow big will suppress further cropping. Avoid cutting after early summer, as it will weaken the plants and reduce their shoot production the following year.

Subsequent management

Management of a mature crop is very easy. Remove any weeds by hand or carefully ease them out with a trowel as soon as they appear. Often it is possible to spot-treat perennial weeds with a ready-to-use preparation of a glyphosate-based weedkiller. This works its way into the roots killing the weed completely. If it gets on the asparagus plant, however, the asparagus will be badly damaged and perhaps killed.

A mulch of weed-free, well-rotted organic matter, such as spent mushroom compost, can be very effective in preventing annual weeds growing in the crop. It will also help feed the asparagus. An annual application of general-purpose fertilizer will be necessary as well; sometimes this is supplemented with an extra dressing immediately after the last spears are harvested.

MANAGING AN ASPARAGUS BED

1 Topdress the bed with 100g (3½oz) of general-purpose fertilizer every square metre (10 sq ft) in early spring to feed the coming growth. Double the quantity if you are using organic fertilizers.

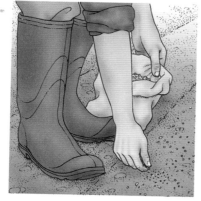

2 Cut the spears with a sharp knife in mid-spring when they are 12–15cm (5–6in) above soil level. Cut each spear obliquely 2.5–5cm (1–2in) below the soil surface. Take care not to damage any underground shoots as you do so.

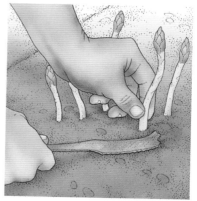

3 Apply a post-harvest dressing of general-purpose fertilizer in early summer after harvest, at the same rate as in spring. This extra dose of fertilizer is not essential, but it ensures a high level of fertility as the plant builds up its energy levels for the next harvest. Allow the plant to grow unhindered.

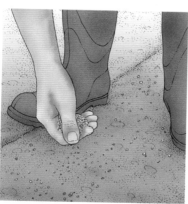

4 Cut down the yellowed stems and foliage in autumn and add to the compost heap. Remove weeds by hand or with a trowel, then apply a mulch of well-rotted manure or compost.

After harvesting, leave the stems to grow, supported with stakes and string if necessary. In autumn, the top growth turns yellow and straw-like; remove this by cutting near to soil level, and add it to the compost heap. At this stage the plant's resources are stored in the roots ready to support spear production the following spring. Before winter, apply a thick mulch to improve the soil and smother weeds. For additional weed control, before mulching, you can draw up soil with a hoe from between the rows of plants to form a ridge of earth over the crowns.

Common problems

Asparagus is largely trouble free, but asparagus beetles can strip foliage in summer. On a small scale, these red beetles can be removed without resorting to approved insecticides, either by hand or with a carefully directed jet of water. Slugs sometimes feed on the emerging spears in spring and will need controlling.

Leaf and root diseases occasionally reach significant levels in asparagus; burning any infected foliage in autumn and removing and destroying plants found to have diseased roots are the only remedies.

HOW ASPARAGUS GROWS

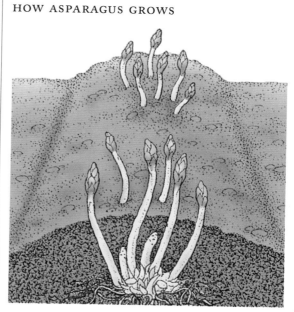

Emerging shoots or 'spears' grow from a rootstock deep underground. The plant dies back to this rootstock over winter.

Celery

In its first growing season, celery forms an edible clump of strong leaves and fleshy stalks. It flowers the following year, though it readily flowers if stressed in its first year, which ruins the crop. Modern green-stemmed celery is well-flavoured, tender, and rich in vitamins; older varieties need blanching to produce pale stems, which many consider to be the finest. Self-blanching varieties, if closely planted, provide naturally pale stems.

Sowing & cultivation

Sow the fine seed indoors in early spring at 15°C (59°F); temperatures below 10°C (50°F) may induce bolting. As soon as the seedlings are easily handled, transplant them into small pots. By early summer, strong plants can be set out in highly fertile soil. Add at least 10kg (22lb) of organic matter every square metre (10 sq ft) and apply a general fertilizer. Growing in a trench aids watering and promotes lush growth, ideal for raising blanched celery.

Never let plants dry out, and add 25g (1oz) of nitrogen-rich fertilizer every square metre (10 sq ft) once they are growing well. For tender, sweet stems, exclude light by earthing up (*see below*), by using light-excluding collars, or by placing boards along the rows of stems.

Celery leaf spot is the most damaging disease; buy treated seeds to prevent serious problems. Celery leaf mining fly looks worse than it is; remove affected leaves.

FROM SOWING TO HARVESTING CELERY

1 **Dig a trench** 40cm (16in) wide and 30cm (12in) deep in early to mid-spring, in full sun. Fork manure into the bottom and refill.

2 **Transplant young plants** grown from seed once they have a few leaves and are large enough to handle.

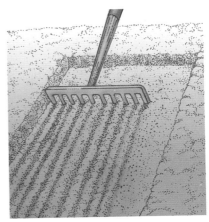

3 **Rake fertilizer in** at a rate of 100g (3½oz) per square metre (10 sq ft) just before planting. Double this rate for organic fertilizers.

4 **Plant out** self-blanching types 25cm (10in) apart in a block for mutual shade, others 40cm (16in) apart in rows 45cm (18in) apart.

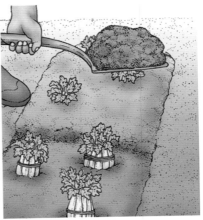

5 **Exclude light** to blanch the stems by tying them and earthing them up; or simply wrap collars of opaque material around the stems.

6 **Cut whole heads** at the base in late summer and early autumn. Celery rapidly becomes pithy or rots as winter approaches.

Rhubarb

This long-lived crop can remain productive for many years without replanting. In summer, its broad, lush leaves build up resources that, after the leaves die down in autumn, are stored in the roots over winter. In spring, buds expand rapidly into long leaf stalks that are cut for use.

Cultivation

Although container-grown plants are available from garden centres, it is very easy to take an offset from any mature plant. A very few varieties can be grown from seeds, but the plants are variable and seeds are seldom used.

Rhubarb grows on any good garden soil in full sun or light shade. Because it remains in the same place for several years, you should improve the soil before planting. Leave new plants uncut for the first year. Once they are growing well, pull stalks of a worthwhile size in spring. Continue to fertilize and mulch each spring.

Although rhubarb may occasionally be damaged by viruses, honey fungus, or crown rot, most failures result from excessive shade and lack of generous feeding.

FORCING RHUBARB

The best and earliest stalks are produced in the dark. Cover the crown of the plant with a light-proof container at least 50cm (20in) high in late winter, and gather the stalks as soon as they are large enough, generally within 5–6 weeks. You can try piling rotting manure or other organic matter around the container to speed up stalk growth. Leave the plants to rebuild their reserves uncovered and unpicked for 2 years after forcing them. Fertilize well in spring and add a thick mulch around the stems.

FROM PLANTING TO HARVESTING RHUBARB

1 Take offsets with a strong bud from the edge of a parent plant during winter or early spring. Replant 1m (3ft) apart in soil enriched with 10kg (22lb) of organic matter and 100g (3½oz) of general fertilizer (double this quantity for organic fertilizer) every square metre (10 sq ft). Plant the offset with the bud just above the surface.

2 Feed plants in spring with 100g (3½oz) of general fertilizer or 150g (5¼oz) of organic fertilizer per square metre (10 sq ft), water well in dry spells, and keep weed-free. An 8cm (3in) deep mulch of well-rotted organic matter in spring will help prevent weeds and improve growth.

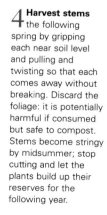

3 Remove the old leaves in autumn, once they have turned brown and helped to build up reserves in the root. Apply a general-purpose fertilizer, to each plant.

4 Harvest stems the following spring by gripping each near soil level and pulling and twisting so that each comes away without breaking. Discard the foliage: it is potentially harmful if consumed but safe to compost. Stems become stringy by midsummer; stop cutting and let the plants build up their reserves for the following year.

PODS & SEEDS

Bean and pea plants, otherwise known as legumes, are varied, attractive, and rewarding to grow. Some are eaten as pods, such as runner beans and French beans, others grown for their protein-rich seeds, like broad beans and peas. All these plants share one characteristic: thanks to specialized bacteria in nodules on their roots, they can 'fix' nitrogen from the air. This means they need less nitrogenous fertilizer than other vegetables, and when the season is over, their remains make a valuable addition to the compost heap. Given sun and support, they provide crops from late spring to late autumn.

Garden peas

Peas are hardy annuals that are available in a sometimes bewildering range of types, but all are easy to grow and are highly nutritious and tasty.

Traditional garden peas are 'shelled' and the immature peas eaten. Some varieties, however, have pods succulent enough to be eaten whole, for example sugarsnap and mangetout peas.

Plant densely because each pea plant will only produce a few pods, so many closely spaced plants are needed for a worthwhile crop. Successive sowings will also be needed to ensure continuity of supply throughout summer.

Round-seeded peas are starchy, while wrinkle-seeded types are richer in sugar and especially sweet. Although of lesser flavour, round-seeded peas are less susceptible to rotting when sown in cold, wet soils. Very small-seeded varieties called 'petit-pois' are claimed to be especially tasty, but round peas harvested at the right stage are just as sweet and succulent – and much less trouble to pick and shell.

Some peas have tendrils instead of leaves. They grow perfectly well and are less affected by bird damage than leafy peas, but do not suppress weeds as leafy varieties do.

Early peas are quick growing, 45–60cm (18–24in) tall, and ready to pick about 12 weeks after sowing, while slow-maturing maincrop peas are 75–120cm (30–48in) tall and ready in 14–16 weeks; peas of intermediate maturity are known as second early, and are 60–70cm (24–28in) tall. Edible-podded peas are ready more quickly than shelled peas because they are gathered before the peas swell.

Growing conditions
You will need to provide fertile, well-drained soil in full sun, although acceptable results are possible in very light shade. Acid soils less than pH 6 are unsuitable. If growing where fertilizers or manures have been applied for previous crops, peas will need no extra fertilizer, but if in doubt, apply 50g (2oz) of low-nitrogen fertilizer or 5kg (11lb) of well-rotted organic matter every square metre (10 sq ft).

Successive sowing
As a rule of thumb for successive sowing, sow when the preceding sowing is 5cm (2in) high. In autumn or late winter in mild regions, or early spring elsewhere, sow early, round-seeded peas for early summer crops. Sowings of

FROM SOWING TO HARVESTING PEAS

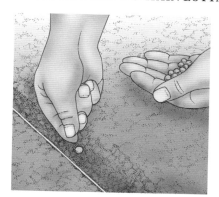

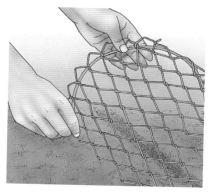

1 **Sow seeds** at about 1cm (½in) spacings in drills 5cm (2in) deep and as far apart as the expected final height of the peas. This gives a high plant population but still allows easy weeding and picking.

2 **Cover the drill** by raking the soil back over it gently. Firm down with the head of the rake to ensure that the seeds are held in close contact with the soil.

3 **Place wire netting** curved into tunnels over the rows immediately after planting. This will help to prevent birds from digging up the seeds or seedlings, although mice may still present a problem.

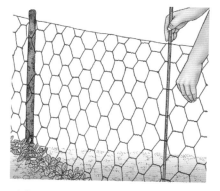

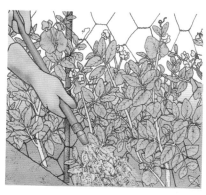

4 **Erect netting support** on posts and wire when the plants are 8–10cm (3–4in) tall. The netting should be at least as high as the expected height of the plants. Twiggy sticks or canes and string are other options.

5 **When plants flower**, water thoroughly and protect against pea moth (*see below*). For the best crops, never allow peas to dry out while in flower or when the pods are swelling.

6 **Pick the pods** about 4 weeks after flowering, when well filled but still young and tender. Pods at the base of the plant develop first. Harvest regularly to keep the plants producing more flowers and pods.

early peas in late winter usually suffer heavy losses from root disease, although protection with cloches greatly increases your chance of success.

In mid-spring, sow second early peas for midsummer crops, and maincrop types at the same time for a late summer harvest. Late spring and summer harvests are lower yielding than first earlies and are prone to powdery mildew. Even later crops, sown from late spring to summer, tend to be light and suffer badly from pests and diseases. French and runner beans make a better late crop.

The numbers of plants needed makes raising seedlings in pots a lot of work. One way round this is to sow peas in sections of roof guttering, sliding the seedlings off into pre-prepared trenches when the roots hold the potting compost together. Although laborious, this is often the only way to get early pea crops where the soil is wet and cold in spring.

Cultivation & harvest

You only need to water once the peas flower. A thorough soaking when flowering begins and again two weeks later ensures a good crop in dry spells. Gather edible-podded varieties as soon as the pods are big enough, and shelled peas when the seeds have swollen but before they turn floury. When cropping is over, compost the plants.

Pea moth caterpillars can ruin later crops by feeding on seeds within pods; early peas escape attack, and edible podded peas do not suffer noticeably if gathered as soon as ready. Applying insecticides at flowering is highly effective, but organic gardeners can protect plants with insect-proof mesh. Greenfly and thrips can be damaging, but treatment of pea moth will reduce damage from these. Powdery mildew can only be effectively countered by growing resistant varieties and watering in dry periods.

Broad beans

There are three good reasons for growing broad beans: they are extremely easy to grow, they crop early when few other vegetables are ready, and they are sweet and delicious.

Broad beans are robust annuals that grow in any well-drained, fertile garden soil in full sun, with a pH no lower than 6. If grown where previous crops have been fertilized and manured there should be no need to add more nutrients; if in doubt, give the soil a boost with 50g (2oz) of low-nitrogen fertilizer or 5kg (11lb) of organic matter for every square metre (10 sq ft).

Sowing

In sheltered regions, you can sow the hardiest broad bean varieties in late autumn for a late spring or early summer crop. For an early to late summer crop, sow seeds in early to mid-spring as soon as the soil is dry enough. Late spring sowings are less worthwhile, producing lighter crops and being susceptible to pests and diseases.

Unless the soil is heavy, cold, and poorly drained, sow broad beans straight into the ground. Otherwise, raise plants in small pots or large cell trays of multipurpose compost indoors, and delay planting out until mid-spring.

The easiest way to grow broad beans is in two rows 25cm (10in) apart, making drills 7cm (2¾in) deep and sowing beans 20cm (8in) apart. Sow a few extra at the end of each row in case you need some spare plants to fill in gaps. Leave 70cm (28in) between double rows. Dwarf varieties, at 50cm (20in) tall, are useful for small gardens and windy sites. Sow these 20cm (8in) apart in single rows 25cm (10in) apart. This recommended spacing will allow easy access from the paths for staking, weeding, pest control, and picking. It also ensures good ventilation.

Cultivation & harvest

Hoe out weeds as the beans grow and, if necessary, support plants with stakes and string. If the soil is dry when the beans are flowering, they will go on to produce fewer pods. In dry spells, give the ground a thorough soaking as the beans come into flower. Broad beans seldom need watering until flowering begins.

The flowers are produced in succession from the bottom of the plants. When production slows down or stops, remove the growing tip to direct the plant's resources into pod formation. The tip of the plant is

FROM SOWING TO HARVESTING BROAD BEANS

1 **Sow seeds** 7cm (2¾in) deep, every 20cm (8in) in double rows set 25cm (10in) apart. This wide spacing ensures good air circulation between plants to discourage fungal disease.

2 **Hammer strong stakes** into the ground at each end of the row to support tall plants in exposed areas. Run lengths of string along the row and attach it to the stakes. You may need extra stakes if the rows are particularly long.

3 **Weed between the rows** with a hoe, taking care not to damage the bean plants. If left to grow, weeds compete with your crop for nutrients, moisture, and sunlight. They also reduce ventilation and may harbour pests.

usually where blackfly (black bean aphid) start an infestation; prompt removal can prevent problems, often until the crop is finished.

As soon as the beans are big enough to use you can gather them. You can harvest the immature pods, when 10–15cm (4–6in) long, as if they were runner beans, or you can wait until the beans have swollen. If you pick too late, however, the pods will harden and become fibrous, making the beans hard and starchy. Broad beans cross-pollinate easily, but if you are only growing only one variety you can save seeds for the following year.

Common problems

Black bean aphid can be very damaging, especially to later sown crops. Treat them with an approved insecticide as soon as you spot them. Products based on oils, soap, or fatty acids are effective and are likely to spare natural predators. Application needs to be thorough and all the blackfly must be drenched when spraying.

In mild, wet weather, the fungal disease chocolate spot can be damaging, but it is usually only significant for overwintered beans. The only remedies are promoting air flow by wider spacing, a more open position, and increasing ventilation if you are using cloches.

BROAD BEAN TOPS

Pinch out the tips of broad bean plants once they have flowered to deter blackfly. They can be eaten as 'greens' and are something of a delicacy. Lightly steamed, they taste a little like spinach.

4 **Soak the ground** if the weather is dry when the flowers first appear. Repeat 2 weeks later. This will help the flowers go on to produce a good yield of pods.

5 **Harvest broad beans** after 28–35 weeks for autumn-sown crops, or 12–16 weeks for spring-sown crops. Dry the beans for storing – dig up a plant, shake off the soil, and hang it upside down in a frost-free place until dry.

6 **Dig spent plants** into the soil. Like other legumes, broad beans are a valuable resource as they fix nitrogen in small nodules on their roots – digging old plants into the soil will boost nutrient levels for the next crop.

Runner beans

These climbing beans are actually tender perennials, although they are grown as an annual crop as they do not survive cold winters. They do well in cool climates, and thrive in any good garden soil in full sun or very light shade. You are likely to have poor results on acidic soils with a pH lower than 6. A sheltered position is essential as strong, gusting winds will easily topple these tall plants, damage developing pods and impair pollination – the flowers are pollinated by flying insects, such as bees, which are deterred by windy sites.

Success also depends on lush growth, which can only be achieved with plenty of moisture. Runner beans like a rich start in life; dig 10kg (22lb) of well-rotted manure or garden compost into each square metre (10 sq ft) of soil. You could also prepare a planting trench enriched with organic matter (*see facing page*). In addition, apply a general-purpose fertilizer at 100g (3½oz) per square metre (10 sq ft), or double this if using organic fertilizer.

Sowing

Sow runner beans outdoors in late spring or early summer after all danger of frost has past. In mild areas you can make a second sowing in mid- to late summer for an autumn crop. Plants can be raised indoors in small pots of multipurpose compost from mid-spring; this is essential where the soil is cold, heavy clay. It is tempting to try for an early crop, especially if indoor-sown plants are speeding ahead, but French beans (*see page 182*) are a safer bet to precede a main crop of runner beans.

By late spring the roots will be binding the compost and in mild districts the plants can be set out beneath a covering of fleece or under cloches. In colder areas, delay planting out until early summer.

Supporting runner beans

Make a wigwam with one cane at each corner of a 1m (3ft) square, sowing three seeds 7cm (2¾in) deep at the base of each cane. Later, remove one plant to leave two per cane. Alternatively, make two parallel drills, 60cm (24in) apart and 7cm (2¾in) deep. Space the seeds 15cm (6in) apart, thinning plants when they emerge to one every 30cm (12in). Push a 2–2.5m (6–8ft) cane beside each plant, crossing and tying the poles at the top, then join them all together by tying a horizontal cane along the ridge (*see facing page*). In sheltered gardens, you can replace some of the canes with netting or string. Allow 1m (3ft) between

With their pretty flowers and fast growing habit, runner beans make an attractive and productive, temporary screen for the ornamental garden. Within a matter of weeks, these vigorous climbers will have scrambled to the tops of their 2.5m (8ft) supports.

SOWING & PLANTING OUT

Plant out young plants raised indoors, at the base of each cane support, as soon as the risk of frost has passed. As they will already be growing strongly, the crop will get off to a fast start. A second sowing from midsummer can give a extra crop in autumn.

wigwams and 1.2m (4ft) between double rows. Dwarf varieties do not need support. Sow seeds every 15cm (6in) in rows 70cm (28in) apart, and thin to 30cm (12in).

Cultivation & harvest

Hoe between plants to remove weeds, and if the shoots need encouragement to climb their supports, gently twine them against the canes or tie them in. When the plants reach the top of the canes, pinch out their growing tips.

Unless the growth is very green and lush, add 30g (1oz) of nitrogen-rich fertilizer (double this amount for organic fertilizer) to every square metre (10 sq ft); you should do this when the young plants are thinned.

When the plants are flowering, never let the soil dry out as this results in a poor yield of pods. You may need to water as often as every three days. Warm nights can also hinder pollination of the flowers. Under heatwave conditions, you may find that the cooling effect of misting the flowers with water at night and watering the soil will help the flowers to form pods.

Harvest the pods when they are about 18cm (7in) long. Unlike peas, broad beans, and French beans, runner beans will crop over a long period if you keep them well watered during dry spells. The plant will stop cropping if any pods are allowed to mature. Where only one variety is grown, the seeds can be saved for next year's crop.

Common problems

Runner beans are free of significant pests and diseases, but you may need to treat blackfly. Drench the affected areas with an insecticide based on oils, soap, or fatty acids, which are likely to spare natural predators.

FROM SOWING TO HARVESTING RUNNER BEANS

1 **Dig a trench** and enrich the soil with plenty of organic matter, such as well-rotted garden compost. Runner beans are deep rooting and like a moisture-retentive soil.

2 **Rake the soil level** and firm it in by treading over it lightly. Add a dressing of general-purpose fertilizer.

3 **Sow seeds** in drills 7cm (2¾in) deep, 15cm (6in) apart. Make a parallel drill 60cm (24in) apart. When young plants emerge, thin them to 1 plant every 30cm (12in). Stake each plant.

4 **Tie the canes** together to form a length of triangular supports. Secure them at the top where they cross over, and lay a cane across the ridge, tying it to each support to give it rigidity. Alternatively, you could form a wigwam.

5 **Feed young plants** with an extra dressing of nitrogen-rich fertilizer, unless the growth is very green and lush.

6 **Harvest the beans** after 13–17 weeks when the pods are around 18cm (7in) long. Pick frequently to encourage and stimulate continued cropping.

French beans

Once regarded as the poor relation of other beans and peas, an amazing range of varieties of French beans is now available. This range includes both dwarf and climbing types, as well as those with unusually coloured pods and seeds. They are all equally easy to grow and have the delicate flavour and texture that makes this such a rewarding crop to have in the vegetable garden.

French beans are a tender annual. They need the same soil conditions and preparation as broad beans (*see page 178*), but they will not overwinter. If you are not sure about the fertility of your soil, apply a general-purpose fertilizer at 70g (3½oz) per square metre (10 sq ft); double this quantity if you are using organic fertilizers.

Sowing & planting out

Begin sowing indoors in mid-spring at a temperature of 18–25°C (64–77°F). Use small individual pots or large cell trays filled with multipurpose compost. The seedlings grow quickly and as they cannot be planted out until the outdoor air temperature stays consistently above 10°C (50°F) – usually from late spring – only sow as many plants as you have space to keep frost free until then.

Once all danger of frost has passed, you can start sowing directly outside. Successional sowing every three weeks until late summer will ensure a continuous crop until early autumn. If you also grow runner beans, you may find that an early sowing to precede runner beans is all that is needed, because the runner beans will take over

Dwarf French beans grow well in containers. With their pretty flowers, lush foliage, and slender pods, they give good value in summer as a decorative and productive plant.

SUPPORTING CLIMBING BEANS

Like runner beans, climbing French beans need a strong support. The simplest structure is a wigwam (*shown far right*) of 4 canes, one pushed into the ground at each corner of a 1m (3ft) square, but more elaborate or decorative structures can be used. Secure the canes at the top with a binding of string. Sow 3 seeds 5cm (2in) deep at the base of each cane, later thinning to leave 2 plants per cane. Alternatively, hammer 2 strong wooden stakes into the ground at each end of the row of beans and stretch netting across (*shown right*). As the beans grow, they will make an attractive and productive screen for summer. Spacing is the same for runner beans: 15cm (6in) apart, thinning plants to 30cm (12in).

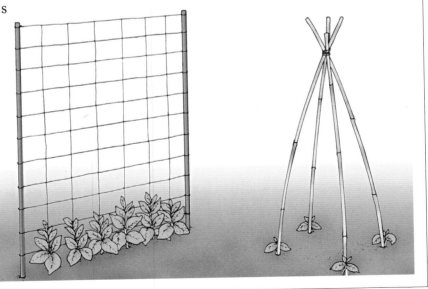

production until autumn. It is worth noting that the cropping period of French beans is quite a bit shorter than runner beans, which is why you sow successionally.

If sowing directly outside, sow seeds of dwarf French beans 5cm (2in) deep, at 15cm (6in) intervals, in rows 50cm (20in) apart. Climbing French beans are sown at the same depth, but you will need to space the plants as for runner beans (*see page 180*).

By late spring the roots of pot-sown beans will be binding the compost together. In mild districts, the plants can be set outside under fleece or cloches; in colder areas, it is advisable to wait a few more weeks until early summer, when temperatures are consistently warmer.

Cultivation & harvest

As soon as the beans are growing well discard every other plant to leave a final spacing of 30cm (12in). At the same time, if the beans are anything less than green and lush it is advisable to feed them with 30g (1oz) of nitrogen-rich fertilizer every square metre (10 sq ft); double the quantity if you are using an organic fertilizer. Support is not essential for dwarf varieties of beans, but a few twigs pushed in among the plants will stop them flopping. Climbing varieties will need to be grown up a robust support (*see box, facing page*).

French beans are less sensitive to dry soil at flowering time than other beans and peas. However, thorough watering every 10 days during dry spells will greatly increase the quantity and quality of the crop.

Pick the beans as soon as they are usable and be sure not to let any mature on the plant as this inhibits further cropping. Varieties grown for their dried seeds should be gathered as late as possible, then dried, shelled, and stored. Like peas, French beans are self-pollinating so seed can be saved for the following year.

Common problems

French beans are largely free of pests and diseases, but blackfly can be a problem. Use an oil, soap, or fatty acid insecticide, as they do least harm to natural predators.

FROM SOWING TO HARVESTING FRENCH BEANS

1 **Sow seeds** in drills 5cm (2in) deep at 15cm (6in) intervals. Grow in fertile soil in full sun with a pH no lower than 6. If grown where previous crops have been fertilized, there should be no need to add extra nutrients. Wait until after the last frost before sowing outdoors.

2 **Hoe plants** regularly to remove weeds before they compete with your crops for nutrients, moisture, and sunlight. Take care not to damage the roots or top growth of the young plants.

3 **Water the soil** well every 10 days during dry spells. While dry soil at flowering time is less of a problem for French beans than other types of beans and peas, boosting the moisture will help increase the crop.

4 **Harvest beans** regularly to encourage plants to keep producing pods. The young pods are delicious, but French beans also dry well – pull up a whole plant, hang it by the roots to dry in a dry, frost-free place, then remove the dried beans from the pods.

THE ONION FAMILY

The onion family, which includes garlic, leeks, onions, and shallots, are all easy to grow. They either store well or, in the case of leeks, are very hardy, which makes them valuable in winter when other vegetables are in short supply. Their distinctive flavour comes from sulphur compounds produced by enzymes released when the plant tissue is cut. These compounds are not only flavoursome but are also claimed to have medicinal properties. As all the onion family are susceptible to onion white rot, a persistent soil-borne disease, never grow them on the same piece of ground two years in a row.

Onions

Bulb onions are two-year plants. Initially, they concentrate their efforts on sending up leaves, then, when a certain critical day length is reached in late spring, the process of bulb formation is triggered. It isn't until the second year that the bulb sends up flowers and sets seed. Unfortunately, if sown or planted too early, onion plants 'mistake' cold weather in spring for winter, causing them to 'bolt', which means they will flower in the first year. Your aim, therefore, is to plant onions out as early as possible to make a strong plant by mid-spring, but not so early so that bolting occurs.

Sowing & planting

Choose a site in full sun in fertile, well-drained soil. Onions will not grow well on acidic soils with a pH of less than 6. Before sowing, add 10kg (22lb) of organic matter, then 100g (3½oz) of general fertilizer for every square metre (10 sq ft). Double the amount if using an organic fertilizer or if you have been unable to manure the plot.

In most gardens, onion sets are the best way to grow onions, but only a limited range of varieties are offered compared to seeds. Sets are miniature onion bulbs that are too small to form flowers if subjected to cold.

FROM PLANTING TO HARVESTING ONION SETS

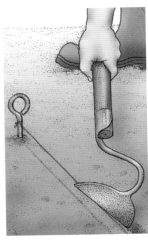  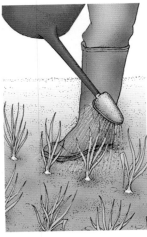 

1 **Make a drill** 2cm (¾in) deep. To help keep it straight, run the edge of a hoe along a length of string held taut between two pegs knocked into the ground.

2 **Plant sets** 5–8cm (2–3in) apart. Push each bulb firmly into the soil, burying it so only the tip is visible. Cover with fleece to deter birds and warm the crop.

3 **Water plants** during dry spells. They need little water at other times, but they are easily swamped by weeds, so hoe around the plants regularly.

4 **Harvest onions** after 12–18 weeks. Pull them as needed. For onions to store, wait until their leaves bend over before digging up. Leave to dry for about 10 days.

FROM PLANTING TO HARVESTING SPRING OR SALAD ONIONS

1 **Sow seeds** every 3 weeks a finger's width apart in rows 10cm (4in) apart from early spring to summer for a continuous crop. Seed can be sown from late winter in mild areas, under a cloche. Alternatively, sow the seeds at the same spacing in 7cm (2¾in) wide blocks set 15cm (6in) apart.

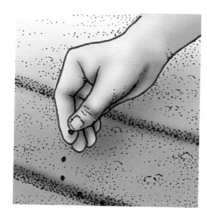

2 **Thin out** the developing onions to 2.5cm (1in) apart. The thinnings can be used in a salad. Spring onions are ready to harvest just 8 weeks after sowing. Lift them gently with a hand fork.

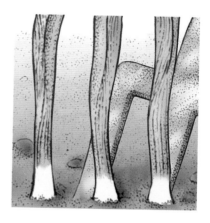

Plant onion sets in spring every 5–8cm (2–3in) in drills 2cm (¾in) deep. Make the rows 25cm (10in) apart. Bury the sets so that only their tips show. To prevent birds from dislodging them, cover your sets with fleece until they are firmly rooted; the extra warmth will speed up growth.

In mild regions, onions can be raised from seeds sown outdoors (*see right*) in early spring in drills 1cm (½in) deep. Space seeds a finger-width apart and in rows 25cm (10in) apart; thin to 5–8cm (2–3in) between plants.

Seeds sown indoors in late winter in cell trays of multipurpose compost, however, are more reliable. Sow either two seeds per cell and thin later to one plant, or sow six or seven seeds per larger cell to get a clump of four to five plants. When the plant roots start to bind the compost, the cells can be planted out. Allow 25cm (10cm) spacing between clumps of plants in the larger cells.

In mild regions, special bolt-resistant onion varieties can be grown over winter. They are available as onion sets or as seeds. Sets are especially reliable; plant them in early autumn, 5–8cm (2–3in) apart in drills 2cm (¾in) deep, spaced in rows 25cm (10in) apart. Sow seeds in late summer into a prepared seedbed in drills 1cm (½in) deep, with 1cm (½in) between seeds and in rows 25cm (10in) apart. Aim to grow these plants to 10–15cm (4–6in) tall before winter weather sets in; any larger and they may bolt, any smaller and they may succumb to cold, wind, and rain. In early spring, thin these plants to their final spacing: 5–8cm (2–3in) between plants.

Cultivation

Onions have limited root systems so thorough watering after planting out and in dry spells is essential. To encourage strong growth in spring, scatter 30g (1oz) of nitrogen-rich fertilizer for every square metre (10 sq ft). Onion leaves cast little shade, so the ground around them is quickly colonized by weeds. Hoe and hand weed carefully around the plants, especially in the early weeks when the young onions are vulnerable to competition.

Harvesting & storing

As the bulbs mature in summer, the foliage topples; let this happen naturally. Once the tops have toppled, the bulbs will not swell further and the crop can be lifted for drying. Loosen their roots with a fork if you intend to dry

SOWING ONIONS OUTDOORS

1 **Sow seeds** in soil that has been previously enriched with organic matter and fertilizer. Mark out a drill 1cm (½in) deep and sow seeds about 1cm (½in) apart. The rows should be 25cm (10in) apart. Sow bolt-resistant varieties in late summer, other varieties in early spring.

2 **Feed plants** in spring with 30g (1oz) of nitrogen-rich fertilizer. This will ensure bigger bulbs. Thin out plants to a spacing of 5–8cm (2–3in) apart. By late summer your onions will be ready to harvest.

185

DRYING & STORING ONIONS

1 Loosen ripe onions with a fork on a sunny day and let them dry for about a week. Onions are ripe once the foliage flops over. Let this process happen naturally; if you attempt to speed things up by toppling the foliage yourself, it will let in disease.

2 Lift onions and spread them out to dry in a well-ventilated cold frame or greenhouse if the weather is damp or wet. If you have room indoors, bring them in to dry on trays. It can take up to 2 weeks.

3 Inspect each onion, checking whether the skins feel papery. If not, leave them for a few more days to dry out. Any onions with thick necks or those showing the first signs of rot should be used immediately for cooking; only store blemish-free onions.

4 Store onions by placing them carefully in layers in an open-sided wooden box. Place the box somewhere well ventilated. Cold will not harm them, but dampness and poor air circulation will lead to rapid deterioration. Examine them regularly and discard any onions that are blemished or showing signs of deterioration.

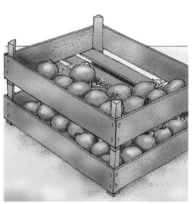

them in the sun, but in wet weather you should lift the bulbs and dry them under cover, as better bulbs will result. Once dried, onion bulbs should be stored in cool, dry, airy conditions (*see above*).

Common problems

Onions are damaged by onion fly and onion thrips, although these rarely prove too much of a problem in gardens. Insect-proof mesh will keep onion fly at bay. There are no reliable controls for onion thrips, but well-watered and well-fed crops seldom suffer serious damage.

In mild, persistently wet weather, onion downy mildew may develop on damp foliage. No fungicides are available, but crop rotation, removal of all infected material, avoiding growing perennial onions nearby, and using autumn onion sets that send up leaves only after any infected crops have been cleared away, should reduce damage. Growing onions under cloches is also a option.

Onion white rot persists in the soil, so careful crop rotation and removal of all infected material is necessary to allow crops to grow. In severe infestations, grow in raised beds or pots filled with sterile potting compost.

Onion harvests are usually dried as they are the ideal crop for storing for use in the kitchen through the winter. Put aside any damaged or less-than-perfect onions for immediate consumption.

Garlic & shallots

Both garlic and shallots are easy to grow. They are usually problem free, but onion white rot can be damaging (*see facing page*). Prepare soil as for onions (*see page 184*) but use half the fertilizer. If growth seems weak in spring, scatter 30g (1oz) of nitrogen-rich fertilizer per square metre (10 sq ft). Garlic and shallots seldom require watering. Weeding, however, must be regular as their leaves cast little shade and weeds soon exploit the space around them.

By early to midsummer their foliage yellows and dies back. The bulbs can then be eased out of the soil and dried and stored as for onions (*see facing page*).

Growing garlic

Split your garlic bulbs into separate cloves and plant them out in early to late winter or, for certain varieties, in early spring. Depending on the planting time, they take 16–36 weeks to mature. Grow in rows 35–45cm (14–18in) apart, with 15–20cm (6–8in) between plants. Bury your cloves 2.5cm (1in) deep so the tip is just visible, then firm them in to prevent them being dislodged by frost or birds. Rust occasionally covers and destroys the foliage – the only remedy is crop rotation, which prevents it building up.

With its mild flavour and thick stem, it may not be such a surprise to learn that 'elephant' garlic is related to the leek rather than to garlic. Grow it in the same way as garlic, but plant the bulbs in early autumn to prevent solid single bulbs forming instead of a bulb made up of individual cloves. Save a few cloves for replanting.

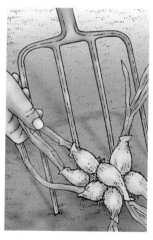

PLANTING GARLIC

Use your fingers to pull a garlic bulb apart, gently separating the individual cloves; damaged bulbs are susceptible to rotting. When planting, position the cloves pointed end up.

Growing shallots

Shallots are exceptionally easy to grow (*see below*). Although they can be raised from seeds – sown as for onions (*see page 185*) – this is an unnecessary complication compared to the ease of planting small seed bulbs.

Plant seed bulbs in early to late winter or, for certain varieties, in early spring, in drills 2cm (¾in) deep. Plant the bulbs 15–20cm (6–8in) apart, barely covering them with soil but firming them in to prevent them becoming dislodged by birds and frost. Make the rows 25–30cm (10–12in) apart, then cover with fleece. Onion downy mildew can be damaging (*see facing page*).

FROM PLANTING TO HARVESTING SHALLOTS

1 Plant shallot seed bulbs with their tips just showing. By early summer each set will develop into a clump.

2 Hoe regularly between rows to keep the weeds at bay. You only need to water during prolonged dry spells.

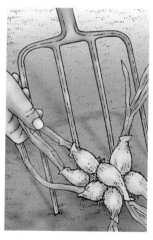

3 Harvest shallots with a fork when the leaves die down and the bulbs are a good size.

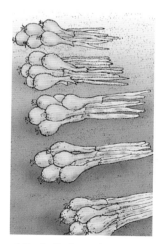

4 Dry bulbs for storing by spreading them out on the ground in the sun for a few days. If it rains, dry them under cover.

Leeks

Among the easiest vegetables to grow, leeks are valuable for the gardener because they crop abundantly, stay in good condition through the hardest winter weather, and are relatively expensive in the supermarket. They are grown from seeds in the same soil conditions as onions. In small gardens F1 seeds are worthwhile for a heavier crop, but open-pollinated seeds are almost as good.

Sowing & cultivation

Sow seeds outdoors in early spring, a finger's width apart in drills 1–1.5cm (½–³⁄₈in) deep and 20cm (8in) apart. Indoor sowing is often more convenient, and essential for early autumn crops. Sow in modules, either two seeds per small cell, thinning to one, or five to seven seeds per larger cell to make a clump of four to five plants. Plant out into a seedbed once the roots bind the compost together. After thinning in early to midsummer, transplant the seedlings when they are at least pencil thickness into deep planting holes.

Leeks are traditionally blanched by planting into deep holes 10cm (4in) deep and 10–15cm (4–6in) apart in rows 30cm (12in) apart. It is easier to plant leeks from cells in the base of a drill, and space clumps 30cm (12in) apart. Draw soil around the plants in drills; watering washes enough soil into holes to cover the roots, and the hole gradually fills. As the leek grows, pull soil around the plant to exclude light. As much as possible, avoid trimming leaves and roots for ease of handling; this sets the crop back.

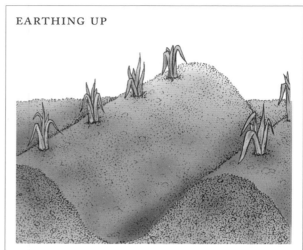

EARTHING UP

Leeks grow perfectly well planted on the level, but excluding light increases the length of the tender white stem and controls weeds. Blanching with a collar of opaque material, such as cardboard, can supplement or even replace earthing up.

Leeks appreciate generous watering in dry spells. Add nitrogen-rich fertilizer at 25g (1oz) per square metre (10 sq ft) in midsummer if growth appears to be flagging.

Earthing up controls weeds, but careful weeding is needed in the early stages. Leeks can be affected by onion white rot, but usually only suffer from rust, and this seldom causes severe losses. Partially resistant varieties are available.

FROM SOWING TO HARVESTING LEEKS

1 **Sow** in a prepared seedbed in early spring.

2 **Thin** to 2–3cm (¾–1¼in) between plants in early summer, and firm back the soil around remaining plants.

3 **Plant out** from early to midsummer. Mulch around the plants or, for longer white stems, earth up (*see box, above*).

4 **Harvest** from late autumn. Cover a few with several layers of fleece so that you can lift them even during heavy frost.

Preparing to grow *see page 142* | **Sowing & growing** *see page 146* | **Common problems** *see page 210*

ROOTS & TUBERS

Roots are not the most glamorous occupants of the vegetable patch, and gardeners with very limited space may feel inclined to omit them altogether. But most root crops can be grown in containers, and short-term crops such as carrots, early potatoes, and turnips can make good use of space, allowing for two harvests a year from the same ground. Young, freshly lifted roots are quite different from the fare found in the shops. Root crops come from a wide range of plant families and have varied requirements, but some needs are common to all: well-cultivated soil and crop rotation.

Carrots

Carrots are biennials, forming a fleshy root in the first year and flowering in the second. They might seem boring and everyday, but gardeners have an amazing range of carrots to choose from. Carrots are usually orange, but recently white, yellow, red, and purple roots that were once common have been reintroduced:

Paris Market types: Round, golf-ball-sized roots that are especially good for containers and give early crops.

Amsterdam types: Thin, cylindrical carrots bred for early crops and also good for containers.

Nantes types: General-purpose carrots with cylindrical roots, suitable for both early and late crops.

Autumn King types: Late-cropping varieties with conical roots, among the longest of all carrots.

Berlicum types: Late cropping, with thick cylindrical roots.

Chantenay types: Stubby, conical roots lifted in summer and autumn, claimed to have the best flavour.

Imperator types: Very long, thin roots, widely grown commercially, and claimed to be ideal for eating raw.

Sowing, cultivation & harvest

Any friable, well-drained, sunny soil will support carrots. Dig over heavy soil in winter, or loosen lighter soils with a fork in spring, removing as many stones as possible to help reduce the number of 'fanged' roots. Soil fertility need only be moderate; while there is little evidence that adding organic matter causes forked roots, it is best avoided. Ideally, plant on ground that had been manured for a preceding crop, and rake in 50g (2oz) of general fertilizer per square metre (10 sq ft), or double this if using organic materials, before sowing. Carrots dislike acid soils, and a pH of 6.5–7 is ideal.

Sow carrots in drills 10–15mm ($\frac{1}{2}$–$\frac{3}{8}$in) deep, spacing seeds about a finger's width apart. Sow in rows 20cm (8in) apart for early carrots, and 30cm (12in) apart for later, larger carrots. Gardeners in mild areas who do not flinch from risk can try sowing in mid-autumn, but the first sowing is usually made in early spring, where the soil is light enough, to give a crop that is lifted in midsummer.

Carrots have been bred in orange shades in the West for centuries, but the wider range of colours originally found is now being bred again. Red carrots in particular have 'superfood' status.

Gardeners with sticky clay soil can use tubs, ideally kept in the greenhouse, for early spring sowings, using Nantes carrots and other short-rooted varieties. Sow in the ground in mid-spring for late summer and early autumn lifting. The larger varieties are sown in late spring for use in winter.

Thin carrots as soon as possible, to 2cm (¾in) apart for early carrots, 10cm (4in) for mid-season ones and 15cm (6in) for winter carrots. Watering is usually unnecessary, but in really dry spells a thorough soak every 10 days will help swell the crop. Regular and careful hand weeding and hoeing are required.

Carrots can be used as soon as roots are a worthwhile size. Although they can be lifted and stored in boxes of sand over winter use, this is only worthwhile on wet,

sticky clay soils; it is better to leave the crop in the ground and cover it with a frost-excluding layer of cardboard, topped with polythene sheeting to keep the carrots dry.

Common problems

Garden carrots usually only suffer significant damage from carrot fly. Although resistant varieties are available, these are limited to Nantes types. Covering with fleece will exclude carrot fly, but the fleece must be replaced with insect-proof mesh from early summer, as the heat trapped by fleece could harm the crop. Alternatively erect a barrier 60cm (24in) high around the carrot patch and no more than 2m (6ft) across; this will largely exclude carrot fly, because this weak flyer is unable to surmount the barrier or if it does, cannot descend within 2m (6ft).

FROM SOWING TO HARVESTING CARROTS

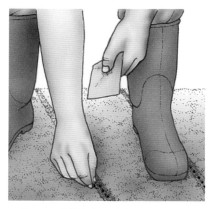

1 **Sow seed** thinly in drills from early spring after raking the ground to a fine tilth. Fleece coverings exclude carrot fly and greatly improve the reliability of early sowings.

2 **Thin seedlings** to the appropriate spacing when the first 4–5 leaves appear. Remove thinnings promptly and cover crops; the smell of bruised leaves attracts the carrot fly.

3 **Water in dry spells** and hoe between the rows to keep down weeds, because the feathery foliage of carrots is not effective at suppressing them.

4 **Harvest carrots** from summer onwards as they are ready and required. Early sowings are usually best harvested young and tender.

5 **Protect from frost** with a loose mulch of straw in mid-autumn if your soil and local conditions allow you to leave crops in the ground. The foliage will die back naturally.

6 **Lift for storage** if necessary. Twist off foliage and store sound roots in boxes of dry sand, spaced so that they do not touch, in a cool but frost-free place.

Parsnips

These biennials form thick, sweet roots in the first year and flower in the second. They may be conical, wedge-shaped, or bulbous – the last are often preferred for clay soils, being easier to lift in winter. Hybrid varieties are especially reliable for difficult sites or where parsnip canker is troublesome. Parsnips must be sown early for good crops, but after that are very undemanding.

Sowing, cultivation & harvest

Any friable, well-drained soil in full sun is suitable; a pH of 6.5–7 is ideal, but parsnips are not fussy. There is little evidence that adding organic matter causes forked roots but it is best avoided; choose instead ground that has been manured for a preceding crop. Buy fresh seeds every year, because parsnip seeds are short-lived, and sow in early spring, as soon as the soil is warm and dry enough. Gardeners with clay soils might have to delay sowing until mid-spring. Watering is seldom necessary, but in really dry spells a thorough soak every 10 days will help swell the crop. Harvest as needed from late autumn.

Parsnips can be damaged by carrot fly; control these as for carrots (*see facing page*). Where parsnip canker rots roots, use resistant varieties, exclude carrot fly to minimize damage to roots, and apply lime. Leaf-miners cause damage that is more cosmetic than significant, and picking off the worst affected leaves is all that is required.

FROM SOWING TO HARVESTING PARSNIPS

1 **Dig heavy soils** in winter or loosen lighter soils with a fork in spring to provide the right structure. Remove as many stones as possible to help reduce 'fanged' roots.

2 **Rake in general fertilizer** at 70g (2½oz) per square metre (10 sq ft), or double this if using organic materials. Covering soil with clear plastic from midwinter helps germination.

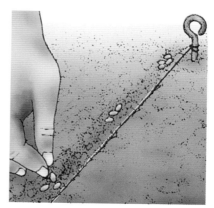

3 **Sow seeds** 10–15mm (½–⅜in) deep a finger's width apart, or station sow at 10cm (4in) intervals, in rows 35cm (14in) apart. Covering with fleece will improve germination.

4 **When 4–5 leaves appear**, thin seedlings as soon as possible to 10cm (4in); if seeds were station sown, remove weaker seedlings to leave one strong plant at each station.

5 **Hoe and weed** by hand, taking care not to damage the 'shoulders' of the swelling roots because damage encourages canker. The thick foliage will suppress weeds.

6 **Lift in autumn** for storage when the foliage dies down. Alternatively, cover the crop with a layer of cardboard topped with plastic sheet to repel rain, and lift as needed.

Radishes

Summer radishes are a well-known salad crop, while larger-rooted, hot-flavoured winter radishes can be grated into salads, soups, or casseroles, and immature seed pods can be eaten raw. Oriental radishes, often called mooli or daikon, are grown in the same way as winter radish.

Sowing & cultivation

All radishes belong to the brassica family, but summer radishes grow too fast to suffer from soil-borne diseases. They can be grown in any part of the rotation, or as catch crops and intercrops. Slow-growing winter radishes are grown with the brassicas. Any fertile garden soil in full sun is suitable; if in doubt treat as for turnips (*see page 194*).

Sow summer radishes from late winter to late summer in drills 1–2cm ($\frac{1}{2}$–$\frac{3}{4}$in) deep and 15cm (6in) apart, leaving about a thumb's width between seeds. Protect early sowings before mid-spring with cloches or fleece. Thin seedlings to 2–3cm ($\frac{3}{4}$–$1\frac{1}{4}$in) apart if necessary. Water in dry spells: quick growth gives tender crisp roots, and dry soils produce poor-quality roots. To produce seed pods, just let plants run to seed, which they do very quickly in summer. Long-podded varieties are available for the best seed pods – grow these as you would winter radish.

Sow winter radish in late summer, as for summer radishes but leaving 30cm (12in) between rows and thinning to 25cm (10in).

Common problems

Cabbage root fly is the only significant pest. Protect winter radish with insect-proof mesh; summer radishes may need protection but often grow too fast for serious damage. Flea beetles and aphids can cause minor damage.

FROM SOWING TO HARVESTING SUMMER RADISHES

1 Sow seeds in drills where they are to grow, or for early crops, sow indoors in multipurpose compost. Radishes soon become coarse and unpleasantly fiery, so sow every 2–3 weeks for mild, tender roots.

2 Thin seedlings as soon as they can be handled, as they emerge rapidly in warm weather.

3 Lift roots regularly when they are 2cm (¾in) in diameter. This takes 6–8 weeks for early sowings, or as little as 3–4 weeks by midsummer.

FROM SOWING TO HARVESTING WINTER RADISHES

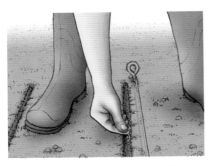

1 Sow seeds in drills in late summer. The seeds can be station-sown (*see page 147*) in groups of 3–4 seeds at 25cm (10in) intervals.

2 Thin seedlings as soon as they can be handled, leaving one plant at each station if the seeds were station sown. Water the seeds afterwards.

3 Lift for storage in mid-autumn in cold regions. Elsewhere, winter radishes are very hardy, though you should protect Oriental winter radishes with a double layer of fleece.

Beetroot

These biennials are grown for the sweet roots formed in the first year. They are quick growing and almost free of pests and diseases, so can be used as catch crops without upsetting rotations. Less familiar than the typical red beetroot are varieties in white and yellow, or with bands of colours in their flesh, giving a range of options for the adventurous cook. Round beetroot are most common, but there are also cylindrical and long, pointed varieties, although these tend to be slower growing. Hybrid varieties are especially reliable and productive where space is limited.

Sowing & cultivation

Any well-drained, fertile, sunny soil that is not acid (below pH 6) is suitable. If possible, add 10kg (22lb) of organic matter every square metre (10 sq ft), then rake in 110g (4oz) of general fertilizer, or double this quantity if using organic materials or if the plot is not manured. Into this, sow beetroot in drills 2cm (³⁄₄in) deep, spacing seeds about a thumb's width apart. Sow in rows 35cm (14in) apart. Most seed is 'multigerm', producing several seedlings; monogerm seeds will produce only one plant per seed.

On clay soils or in colder regions, raise plants indoors in module trays. Sow two seeds per cell, thinning to one plant as soon as possible and planting out under fleece in late spring. Follow with successional sowings every three weeks until late summer. Thin beetroot as soon as possible, with final spacings according to the variety size. Watering in really dry spells with a thorough soak every 10 days will help to swell the crop.

Leaf mining flies are the only significant pest: control by removing infested leaves as soon as seen. Aphids may sometimes need controlling with an approved insecticide.

FROM SOWING TO HARVESTING BEETROOT

1 Prepare the ground from early spring and rake to a fine tilth ready for sowing or planting in late spring.

2 Sow thinly or station sow (*see page 147*) as soon as the soil is warm and dry enough. Protect earlier sowings with fleece.

3 Thin seedlings when 4–5 leaves appear. Spacings vary, from 8cm (3in) for small beetroots to 15cm (6in) for large ones.

4 Hoe very carefully or pull weeds by hand to avoid damaging the roots. The thick foliage helps to suppress weeds.

5 Harvest roots from late summer for immediate use or storage. Lift carefully, and avoid breaking the skin.

6 Store only undamaged roots in boxes of potting compost or sand for a ready-to-use, winter supply.

Swedes & turnips

These biennials form roots in the first year and flower in the second. Although the roots are the main edible part, the leaves can also be eaten, and turnips are often sown in early autumn for their succulent spring leaves or 'tops'. Kohlrabi is grown as for turnip, but the edible portion is actually part of the stem. Being members of the cabbage family, all are grown in the cabbage part of your rotation.

Turnips are quick growing but easily spoilt by frost. Young roots are amazingly succulent and sweetly flavoured, older roots woody and coarse flavoured. Swedes grow slowly but are very hardy. They have harder, yellower flesh with a distinctive sweet flavour, and their leaves usually arise from a 'neck'. Both are badly affected by drought; swedes in particular grow best in moist, cool soil. Kohlrabi is considered to be much less drought-sensitive.

Site & soil

These crops are usually sown where they are to grow, but where convenient they can be grown in module trays sowing three seeds per cell and singling the seedlings as soon as possible. Any seed or multipurpose potting compost can be used, including peat-free formulations.

Any fertile, well-drained garden soil in full sun suits swedes and turnips, while light shade is acceptable for turnip tops. Dig in 10kg (22lb) of rotted organic matter per square metre (10 sq ft). For the best yields, rake in general-purpose fertilizer at 70g (2½oz) every square

SWEDE SHOOTS AS GREENS

Swedes can be lifted in midwinter, trimmed, and packed into boxes of compost or soil. Kept in a shed or garage in semi-darkness, they will produce blanched greens.

metre (10 sq ft), or 110g (4oz) if using organic fertilizer or where organic matter has not been dug in. Acid soils promote club root; where this disease is present liming to at least pH 6.5 is the best way of reducing damage. You can grow a resistant variety, but these are often resistant to only some club root strains and are therefore still occasionally infected.

FROM SOWING TO HARVESTING TURNIPS

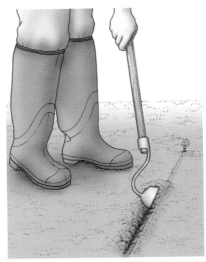

1 **Prepare the ground** and water the day before sowing. Draw out drills and water the base of the drill if the soil is at all dry.

2 **Sow thinly**, allowing about a thumb's width between seeds. Cover the drill, firm the soil, and gently rake over.

3 **Thin seedlings** to 8cm (3in) as soon as they are large enough to be handled. Water after thinning, especially if the weather is dry.

Sowing, cultivation & harvest

Sow summer turnips (*see below*) from late winter until midsummer, initially protecting with cloches or fleece. The earliest sowings, gathered in early summer when few other vegetables are available, are the most valuable, but later sowings make good use of space at the end of summer. Sow a short row every few weeks for tender young roots.

Sow seeds a thumb's width apart in drills 10–15mm (½–³⁄₈in) deep and 30cm (12in) apart. Start thinning as soon as possible. Where crops are not doing well, after thinning apply nitrogen-rich fertilizer at about 25g (1oz) per square metre (10 sq ft), or double this for organic fertilizers. Water in dry spells and ideally do not allow the soil to dry out. Pull roots as soon as they are usable, from about golf-ball size. Store turnips for winter use in boxes of potting media or sand in a frost-free shed.

Slower-growing swedes are sown from late spring to early summer in the same way as turnips, but allowing 40cm (16in) between rows and thinning to 25cm (10in). The roots are ready to use from late autumn. Water in dry summer weather to swell the roots and help to prevent powdery mildew, which is especially damaging to drought-stressed crops. Swedes often survive unprotected in the soil in mild regions; elsewhere, store as for turnips.

Common problems

These crops suffer from the same pests and diseases as other brassicas. Cabbage root fly larvae in particular will kill young plants and tunnel into maturing roots, making

TURNIP TOPS AS SPRING GREENS

The roots of early autumn sowings will not swell before winter, but they will survive the winter to produce a crop of early greens in spring. These will sprout again to produce a further crop.

them unuseable. Covering initially with fleece, and then with insect-proof mesh in summer, prevents damage. Fleece also excludes flea beetles, which can damage young plants from mid-spring, and aphids and caterpillars, but slugs thrive beneath fleece and mesh and usually need to be controlled. Weeds also thrive under covers, which must be pulled aside for weeding.

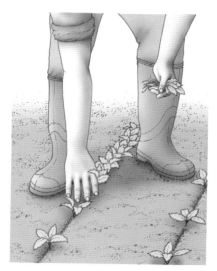

4 **Thin plants again** to 15cm (6in) when their leaves begin to touch those of their neighbours in the row. Firm the soil after.

5 **Hoe between rows**, taking care not to damage the developing roots. Ensure that the plants never dry out.

6 **Harvest young turnips** as needed, or by late autumn in all but the mildest areas. Store in sand or dry soil in a frost-free shed.

Potatoes

These are half-hardy perennials that use starch-rich tubers to survive adverse conditions. The foliage is killed by even the lightest frost, but in the four to five months that potatoes grow in a temperate climate they produce more nourishment for a given area than any other crop. Potatoes are a major source of energy in most people's diets and contain low levels of high-quality protein and useful amounts of vitamins, especially vitamin C. It is well worth growing your own, not only for the best flavour but also for the substantial savings on shop-bought organic crops.

Types of potato

Earlies and second earlies: Gathered in early summer and mid-summer respectively. Earlies are indispensable for their exquisite texture and flavour in early summer, but you can be more relaxed about later potatoes. On wet soils or where slugs are a problem, second earlies are best, being lifted before slugs do much damage in summer. They store well, and most gardeners plant them if they have any room remaining after planting enough earlies.

Early maincrop and maincrop: These mature in mid- to late summer and early autumn respectively. Maincrop potatoes only give their best if they are protected against potato blight, which can be damaging in early autumn; earlies and second earlies have an advantage in this respect.

Salad potatoes: Smallish tubers with superb flavour and high dry-matter content, these remain firm when cooked and are ideal for salads and recipes that call for firm potatoes. These are grown as you would other potatoes and are available in early, second early, and maincrop

FROM PLANTING TO HARVESTING EARTHED-UP POTATOES

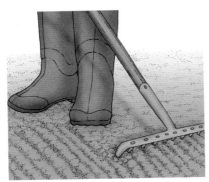

1 Prepare the ground well in advance with manure and fertilizer, and cultivate the fine tilth needed for earthing up.

2 Dig drills 10–15cm (4–6in) deep, spaced appropriately for the type of potatoes you are planting: earlies are closest, maincrops most widely spaced.

3 Place the tubers in the drills with the shoots of the rose end (*see facing page*) uppermost. Space the tubers according to the type of crop.

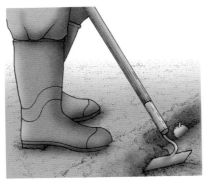

4 Cover the drills using a draw hoe to pull back the earth. Mound it over the drills into a ridge 10–15cm (4–6in) high.

5 Water during dry weather through the growing season, particularly at the start of summer and when the plants flower. Hoe out weeds, and after midsummer apply fungicide.

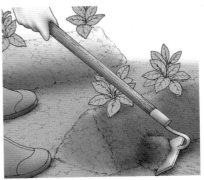

6 Earth up rows regularly, drawing soil up from the furrow between, until the ridges are 30–38cm (12–15in) high.

varieties. Unfortunately, they seldom have the same degree of disease and pest resistance that is found in conventional tubers and need more care to grow.

Seed potatoes & chitting

Potatoes are usually raised from 'seed potatoes', which are small tubers carefully grown under official supervision to be free of significant levels of viruses, which would greatly reduce the yield. Always buy certified seeds; this should be indicated on the label. Although good crops may be raised from ordinary bought potatoes or from tubers you have saved from your previous crop, they will seldom be as successful and are often badly diseased.

Seed tubers are packed with starch. The starch store is to feed the buds, called 'eyes', present on the tuber. Most of the eyes are found at one end, called the 'rose end'. The buds are dormant when the tuber is harvested but over time they become active, and they are ready to start growing by spring when tubers are bought. Seed potatoes are chitted by placing them in good light. This stimulates them to produce sturdy little shoots, giving an invaluable headstart early in the season and leading to early maturing crops. If kept in the dark, they grow into thin, etiolated shoots, and it is hard to plant these out without damaging them. Although chitting is very worthwhile, it is not absolutely essential if time is against you; unchitted tubers will still produce a good crop.

Microplants or 'mini-tubers' are also sometimes available. These are grown in a laboratory to be free of viruses, and they are rather expensive. The best use of them may be to grow them in a pot to produce your own seed potatoes for planting out the following year. They must be protected with insect-proof mesh to ensure they are kept scrupulously free of virus-carrying aphids.

CHITTING POTATOES

Buy seed tubers as early as possible. Tubers the size of hen's eggs are best. Large seed tubers have numerous eyes and can produce masses of crowded shoots; they grow better if you can rub off all but 4–5 of the eyes.

After purchasing, place each tuber pointed end uppermost in a tray or shallow box, rejecting any that are damaged. Place them in a cool, frost-free place in good light. Tubers soon get into a tangled mess if neglected and left in their packaging.

Site & soil

Any fertile, well-drained garden soil in full sun suits potatoes. Unlike most vegetables they don't object to acid soils, but common scab disease can disfigure potatoes grown in alkaline soils. Choose scab-resistant varieties where the soil is chalky, lies over limestone, or has been limed to obtain a high pH to control brassica club root disease. Aim to leave at least two, and preferably three full years between potato crops on the same soil to prevent build-up of soil-borne pests and diseases.

7 **Lift early potatoes** in early summer, when the flowers are fully open. Using a flat-tined fork will help to avoid damage.

8 **Lift second early** and maincrop potatoes from midsummer onwards, when the foliage tops begin to die down.

9 **Store the tubers** in a frost-free place. Use sacks or trays, but make regular inspections and remove any rotten tubers.

Plenty of organic matter will not only feed the plants but also help to prevent scab and hold moisture, so greatly increasing the yield. Dig in 10kg (22lb) per square metre (10 sq ft) over winter. Before planting, scatter 110g (4oz) of general fertilizer every square metre (10 sq ft) or 150g (5¼oz) of organic fertilizer. If you cannot get hold of enough manure or compost in advance, double the amount of general fertilizer applied instead.

Planting & cultivation

Plant early potatoes in early to mid-spring, second earlies in mid-spring, and maincrops from mid- to late spring. Allowing for the risk of late-spring and early-summer frosts, aim to plant all potatoes by mid-spring for the best crops. Autumn and winter 'new potatoes' can be raised from late-summer plantings in areas where blight and early frosts are not severe.

Space early potatoes at 30cm (12in) apart in rows 60cm (24in) apart, second earlies and early maincrops 35cm (14in) apart in rows 70cm (28in) apart, and maincrops 40cm (16in) apart in rows 75cm (30in) apart.

Tubers should be set in drills 10–15cm (4–6in) deep (*see page 196*). Cover the tubers and make a slight ridge over the drills, so you know where the potatoes will emerge and can hoe weeds without harming the plants. As the shoots grow, lightly cover them with soil every week or before a frost is forecast. This kills any weeds, encourages tubers to form at the stem base, and ensures tubers are always covered with soil and protected from both light and blight spores falling from infected foliage. Exposure to light will cause potatoes to turn green and accumulate toxins in their skins. Although earthing up gives spring frost protection, be ready to protect with fleece when late frosts occur, because frosted plants seldom fully recover.

GROWING POTATOES UNDER BLACK POLYTHENE

1 Push the seed potatoes into the soil in spring after watering the ground. Space the tubers according to the type of crop.

2 Cover the potatoes with soil, mounding it slightly. Apply slug controls – pellets or nematodes – over and around the mounds.

3 Cover the bed with a black plastic sheet. Mound earth over the the edges of the sheet to hold it down securely.

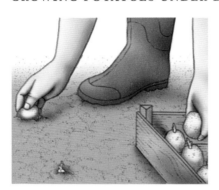

4 Cut crosses in the plastic sheet over each mounded-up tuber. Do not make these too large, or the tubers will be exposed to light and weeds will grow through.

5 As the shoots grow, they push through the slits in the plastic sheet. The sheet suppresses weeds, retains moisture, and protects tubers.

6 Harvest the tubers at the same time as for earthed-up potatoes, but instead of digging and lifting the crop, simply pull back the plastic sheet to expose the tubers.

Alternatively, plant through black plastic sheet (*see facing page*), which suppresses weeds and avoids the labour of earthing up. If using this method, however, remember to apply slug controls before laying the plastic sheeting.

A thorough soak in early summer if the weather turns dry can lead to more tubers being formed and will help to reduce scab infection. Ideally, potatoes should never be allowed to suffer from drought, but in practice this can be difficult to achieve. A second good soak if it is dry when the potatoes are in flower gives fair results and is feasible for most gardeners.

Harvesting

As soon as early tubers are usable – usually when they are about the size of a hen's egg – they can be dug, and when they have finished the second earlies will be ready to lift. Second earlies can be dug and stored when their foliage dies back and as soon as their skin 'sets'. Test this by pressing the skin firmly with finger and thumb – it should resist being rubbed from the flesh. Leave maincrop potatoes as long as possible to 'bulk up'.

When the time comes to lift, cut off remaining foliage and leave for two weeks to let the skin harden and any blight spores decline. Then ease the tubers from the soil with a fork, taking great care not to pierce them with the fork or bruise them by careless handling. Leave to dry on the surface for two hours before storing. Store sound, disease-free tubers in jute or paper sacks, keeping them dry and cool but frost free and inspecting every month to remove any diseased tubers. Diseased tubers should be burnt or consigned to the rubbish.

Potted potatoes & winter crops

Potatoes grow very well in containers. Plant up to three tubers in a large pot or plastic bag about 45–70cm (18–28in) in diameter, half filled with compost from a growing bag or potting medium; peat-free compost is ideal. In a greenhouse, planting can begin in late winter; a midwinter crop can be planted in late summer. As the potatoes grow, add more potting compost until the pot is nearly filled. The tubers can often be gathered by careful exploration by hand, and after the container is finally emptied to gather the tubers, it can often be replanted to give a second crop. If plants fail to grow lushly, apply a potassium-rich liquid fertilizer to raise yields.

Common problems

Potato blight (*see page 214*) is the greatest threat. Organic growers who cannot use fungicides can try planting blight-resistant potatoes, but these may not be to

Patio potatoes growing in pots may be the only alternative for those who have limited free soil. Any pot deep enough to allow earthing up is suitable, and potato flowers, while not showy, are attractive.

GROWING POTATOES IN POTS

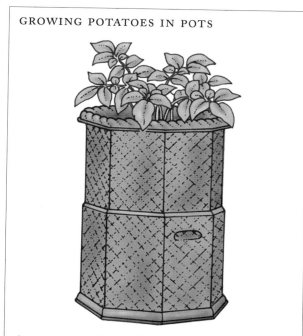

Growing potatoes in specially made containers is often the best way to satisfy the needs of these underground crops. All-in-one kits are advertised in spring and are available by mail order.

everyone's taste. Varieties with reasonable resistance to common scab (*see page 214*) are also available. Slugs can ruin crops left in the ground after late summer. Apply slug controls in midsummer or use second early varieties that are lifted before the slugs become damaging. Potato cyst eelworms (*see page 212*) can also be damaging, particularly on allotments. Resistant varieties are available.

VEGETABLE FRUIT

Fruiting vegetables are some of the tastiest on offer and often highly ornamental, so they are an asset in the garden. It is true that they usually need plenty of space and do not appear to be very productive for the area given, but they suffer relatively little from pests and diseases, so there is no need to be strict about their place in your rotation. Fruit only forms in warm and sunny conditions, so these are crops for the summer, which in cooler regions usually need at least a start in the greenhouse and often do best under protection. However, some fruits store well and greatly extend the winter vegetable supplies.

Courgettes, marrows, pumpkins & squashes

These members of the cucumber family are closely related and, in the case of winter squash and pumpkins, will interbreed freely. Their cultivation and harvest differ.

Courgettes, marrows, and summer squash produce soft, watery fruit that are usually consumed in summer as tender, immature fruit with a delicate flavour and texture. You can store marrows for short periods.

Pumpkins and winter squash produce solid, robust, and often ornamental fruit that can be stored during winter or, for winter squash, until spring.

Courgettes and marrows all used to be elongated and cylindrical in shape, the distinction being that marrows were much bigger than the immature fruit called courgettes. You can now buy spherical courgettes. Summer squash come in bottle shapes, with or without a neck, or as scalloped disc-like fruit. The flowers are also edible.

Winter squashes and pumpkins are rewarding to grow, and pumpkins are of special interest to children. Their attractive, brightly coloured fruit add a range of flavours and textures to winter meals.

FROM PLANTING TO HARVESTING COURGETTES, MARROWS, PUMPKINS & SQUASHES

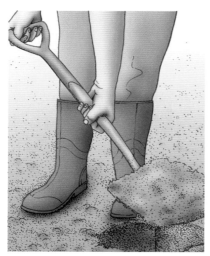

1 **Dig holes** before planting out at a spade's width and depth at the desired spacings for either bush or trailing varieties.

2 **Water the soil** thoroughly once the holes have been filled with well-rotted manure or compost. The excavated soil can be used to create a ridge around the planting hole, which can be used as a reservoir for water.

3 **Transplant young plants** into the top of the prepared soil once the risk of frost has passed. Alternatively sow 3 seeds, and when 4–5 leaves develop, remove plants as necessary so that 1 plant is left to grow.

Site & situation

All of these plants are grown in the same way (*see below*) and can have either a trailing or a bushy habit. They need a position in full sun and fertile, well-drained soil that is not too acid, with a pH greater than 6.

If possible, add to every square metre (10 sq ft) at least 10kg (22lb) of organic matter, and rake in 70g (2½oz) of general fertilizer before sowing; double this if you are using organic fertilizer or if you have been unable to manure the plot. One traditional and very effective way of producing large fruit is to grow marrows, pumpkins, and squashes on old compost or manure heaps.

Sowing seed

Early crops can be grown from seeds sown indoors in mid-spring at 20–25°C (68–77°F). Sow in small pots or large module trays, allowing one seed per pot and placing the seed on its thin edge. Any multipurpose potting compost is suitable, including peat-free materials. The large seeds produce large, vigorous plants that will be ready to set out in early summer when the risk of frost is past. They are ready for transplanting when the roots hold the compost together and each plant has four or five leaves.

In mild areas, you can sow the seeds where they are to grow in early summer. Sow three seeds per station and remove surplus plants later. A second sowing in midsummer for early autumn crops of courgettes can also be productive; sow seeds directly into the ground or in pots.

Growing courgettes, marrows & summer squash

Plant or set seeds of bush varieties 75cm (30in) apart in rows 1m (3ft) apart, and trailing types 1m (3ft) apart in rows 1.5m (5ft) apart. Closer planting may suppress fruit formation. You could try growing trailing varieties up a fence or wigwam – this is a very effective use of space in small gardens and is highly ornamental.

Planting or sowing through a black plastic sheet mulch is a good way to prevent weeds. In cool areas and for early crops, cover your plants with cloches or horticultural fleece to greatly increase growth. Weeding will be needed until the foliage spreads, but later the leaves will suppress most weeds. Watering every 10 days in dry spells will improve cropping and prevent powdery mildew.

Male flowers are formed before the females, and they can be removed and stuffed or fried. Female flowers follow, but they may spontaneously abort until the plant is large and growing well. Regular watering and scattering 25g (1oz) of nitrogen-rich fertilizer every square metre (10 sq ft) will increase growth and reduce loss of fruit.

Cut the fruit as soon as it is usable. Young courgette fruit are easily missed, and if allowed to mature will suppress further fruit formation. Removing some older leaves will help harvesting. Cut marrows for storing in early autumn, after the foliage dies down. Keep maturing marrows free of soil contamination by placing them on tiles or pieces of wood, and for the best shape turn the fruit occasionally.

4 **Water developing plants** regularly, and begin to feed as soon as the first fruit start to develop. Liquid feeds are useful as they can be applied while you water.

5 **Pinch out the tips** of all sideshoots of trailing varieties once they reach 60cm (24in) long. Train all of the trailing stems evenly around the plant.

6 **Harvest the fruit** as soon as ready. Pick courgettes regularly when young and tender, marrows as required. Leave pumpkins and winter squashes to ripen in the sun and gather once the foliage has died down.

VARIED FRUIT

Traditional marrows are elongated and hard skinned, with either plain or striped skins. Expect 2–8 fruit per plant.

Pumpkins are usually trailing varieties. Allow at most 4 fruit per plant; the fewer there are, the larger they will be.

Courgette plants produce about 12 fruit in a season; they are best when no more than 10cm (4in) long. The flowers are edible, too. Surplus crops can be grated and frozen.

Growing pumpkins & winter squashes

These crops can be sown outdoors like courgettes and marrows, but they need the longest possible growing season for the best results, and much better results are obtained from raising plants indoors from mid-spring for planting out when the risk of frost has passed.

Plant out bush and trailing varieties in the same way as courgettes and marrows, either weeding until the foliage spreads or growing through a black plastic sheet mulch. A sheet mulch has the added bonus of protecting the fruit from damage caused by soil contact. If not using a mulch, place maturing fruit on tiles or pieces of wood, turning occasionally for the best shape and even ripening.

If growth appears weak, scatter 25g (1oz) of nitrogen-rich fertilizer every square metre (10 sq ft), though be aware that excessive feeding can reduce cropping. The male flowers are produced first, and female ones follow often as much as several weeks later. Pumpkins and squashes often respond to close planting by failing to fruit. Consider growing trailing varieties up fences or a trellis, or in other situations where they can wander.

Harvesting pumpkins & winter squashes

You can tell when the fruit are mature when they develop stout and woody stems and a fully coloured and firm skin, and they ring hollow if gently tapped. Gather them as late as possible: typically, the first chilly nights of autumn kill the foliage and expose the fruit, which can then be collected. If a very hard frost is expected, either cover the fruits with straw or similar material or bring then indoors before they freeze, because frozen fruit rot quickly. Fruit that are not fully coloured can sometimes ripen if kept indoors at 12–20°C (54–68°F).

Store the fruit in a dry, airy, and frost-free place. If possible, store for a two week 'curing' period at about 15°C (59°F) to heal any wounds, then at 10–12°C (50–54°F). You will need to use your pumpkins by midwinter, but many winter squashes will keep until early spring.

Common problems

Greenfly or aphids often infest young courgette and marrow plants; wash them off or use an insecticide. Viral diseases are spread by aphids and any affected plants should be immediately removed; resistant varieties are available. Powdery mildew often attacks plants in late summer, especially where plants are short of water. Fungicides give some protection, but watering and improving the soil with plenty of organic matter are more effective. Pumpkins and squashes are largely trouble free, but can suffer from the same pests and diseases.

Sweetcorn

Recent breeding has resulted in more succulent cobs, which has increased sweetcorn's popularity. Traditional varieties contain up to 10 percent sugar and are the earliest to crop. Supersweet varieties contain up to 35 percent sugar, but the kernels are of a less melting texture, and the sugary seeds also rot easily in wet soil. Sugar-enhanced sweetcorn has up to 25 percent sugar, tender kernels and more reliable seeds. You should grow each type, particularly supersweets, in blocks of a single variety to prevent the flavour suffering because of cross-pollination.

Cultivation

Grow in any well-drained, fertile soil that is not too acid (ideally pH 6.5–7). Sow early maturing varieties in mid-spring for planting out in early summer when the risk of frost has passed. In mild areas, sow again outdoors in late spring and early summer for autumn crops.

Keep the site free of weeds and water in very dry spells. Soak the soil when the corn's silk tassels appear; the cobs are ready to be pollinated and watering now improves the quality of the cobs. There are few pests and diseases.

FROM SOWING TO HARVESTING SWEETCORN

1 **Dig in** well-rotted organic matter in winter. Add 100g (3½oz) fertilizer per square metre (10 sq ft); double this for organic fertilizer.

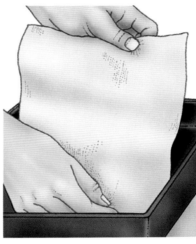

2 **Scatter seeds** on moist tissue paper in a closed container in mid-spring. Keep in a warm place for 2–3 days, until sprouted.

3 **Sow pre-germinated seeds** in individual pots. If sowing direct, sow 3 seeds at a depth of 3cm (1¼in) in late spring.

4 **Plant sweetcorn** in blocks rather than rows to assist pollination. Space plants 40cm (16in) apart, in each direction.

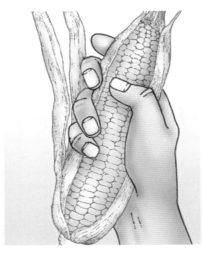

5 **Harvest ripe cobs** in late summer, when the tassels have withered and pressing a nail into a kernel yields creamy white juice.

6 **Twist the cobs** downward and pull away from the stem to detach them. Eat as soon as possible; the sugars soon turn starchy.

Peppers

All peppers need hot, sunny conditions and are killed by frost, so they are usually grown as tender annuals. Even in mild areas, peppers do best under the protection of a greenhouse, cold frame, cloche, or even fleece. They will happily grow with cucumbers or tomatoes in a greenhouse. Ideally, aim for a temperature range of 18–25°C (64–77°F).

Planting & cultivation

You can raise peppers from seeds in spring as for tomatoes, but they need even more warmth and light. Many gardeners prefer to buy 'plug plants' by mail order or larger plants from garden centres. The range is less extensive than seed, but there are plenty to choose from.

Any fertile garden soil is suitable for peppers. Unless previously manured, add 10kg (22lb) of rotted organic matter every square metre (10 sq ft) and rake in 70g (2½oz) of general fertilizer before sowing. Double the quantities if using an organic fertilizer. Most gardeners grow their peppers in containers. Growing bags are highly suitable, and growing bag compost is also ideal for filling pots and tubs, which are easier to keep adequately watered. Peat-free compost works well.

Plant into the final position as soon as the young plants begin to flower, or after the risk of frost if planting outdoors; after six weeks, start to liquid feed every week. Use a general-purpose fertilizer if growth appears weak, and tomato fertilizer if it is lush. Fruits form from midsummer indoors and by late summer outdoors.

Common problems

Peppers are largely trouble free, but biological controls or insecticides are sometimes needed for aphids. Pick off caterpillars at night when they come out. Late-season fruits can rot; keep indoor fruits dry by careful ventilation. Lack of water, especially in container-grown and indoor peppers leads to dark sunken patches (blossom end rot).

FROM PLANTING TO HARVESTING PEPPERS

1 Pot up young plants, whether grown from seeds or bought, into 24cm (9in) pots in a bright, warm place. Space them 45cm (18in) apart each way for growth. Water the plants regularly.

2 Pinch out the main growing point on each plant once it has reached 20–25cm (8–10in) in height, leaving 3–4 branches to make a bushy plant. Provide canes to support the branches if necessary. Outdoor plants will not grow as tall as those in greenhouses.

3 Combat pests such as aphids or red spider mite in greenhouses with biological or chemical controls. Pick off caterpillars by hand. Continue to water, keeping plants moist but never soggy.

4 Harvest the fruit as required from mid- to late summer. Fruit left to ripen to red become richly flavoured but will temporarily suppress formation of more fruit, so for the maximum crop harvest the immature green fruit.

Tomatoes *see page 160* | **Common problems** *see page 210* | **Growing under glass** *see page 364*

Aubergines

These ornamental fruit are tender annuals that need hot and sunny conditions. They grow outdoors in summer, but only fruit well given the protection of a greenhouse, tunnel, or cloche. In mild areas, outdoor plants are helped by fleece, and in urban hot spots they thrive on the patio. Indoors they grow like peppers at 18–25°C (64–77°F).

Cultivation

You can raise plants from seeds in spring, as for peppers. A very limited range can be bought as young plants, but a bigger and more interesting range is offered as seeds.

Any fertile garden soil suits outdoor plants. Unless already manured, add 5kg (11lb) of rotted organic matter and 50g (2oz) of general fertilizer per square metre (10 sq ft); double the quantities for organic fertilizer. Growing aubergines in containers avoids verticillium wilt infection. Growing bags are suitable, and growing bag compost is ideal for filling pots and tubs, which are easier to manage.

Water container-grown plants to keep the soil moist, but never soggy. Feed weekly with liquid tomato fertilizer from about six weeks after planting out. Use a general-purpose fertilizer on plants that are growing weakly.

Fruit will form from midsummer indoors and outdoors by late summer. Allow only one fruit per stem to avoid numerous small fruit with thick skin and little flesh.

Common problems

Aubergines are often attacked by aphids, whitefly, and red spider mites. Biological controls for use in greenhouses are highly effective if introduced early, and oil- or soap-based insecticides can be used at the same time as they leave no harmful residues.

Verticillium wilt, a soil-borne fungal disease, is very damaging; growing aubergines in containers filled with potting media is the only remedy. Late-season fruit often rot, so aim to keep indoor fruit dry by careful ventilation.

FROM PLANTING TO HARVESTING AUBERGINES

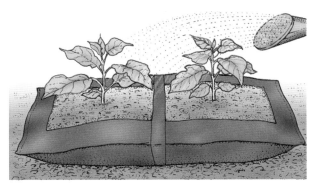

1 **Plant up when** flowers form. Allow 1 plant per 30cm (12in) pot, 2 to a growing bag, or space 60cm (24in) apart in the ground.

2 **Pinch out growing** tips when they reach 20–25cm (8–10in) tall to make a bushy, freely cropping plant. Support plants with canes.

3 **Remove excess fruits** to leave only 5–6 on each plant, evenly spaced for good growth. Pinch out any further flowers.

4 **Gather fruits** by cutting the stem with a sharp knife when they are large enough to harvest and showing full colour.

HERBS

Nothing can compare to herbs fresh from the garden. Most thrive best in full sun with plenty of drainage and with shelter from the worst weather. Imagine a sun-drenched Mediterranean hillside with a coarse soil where deep roots sit out the summer heat and drought. If you can mimic this, your herbs will thrive; try the herb wheel on page 208. If there is nowhere in your garden with at least six hours of sun in midsummer, the range of herbs you can grow will be limited, although a windowbox might be suitable. Herbs grow very well in pots, and it is easy to make containerized herb gardens on patios and balconies.

Growing herbs

Easy access to your herbs is essential if you want to use them in the kitchen. Formal gardens edged with low-growing herbs are a traditional favourite, but in less formal gardens the herbs can be planted though gravel, perhaps with paving slabs for walking. Gravel suits herbs as it keeps soil from being splashed onto leaves by rain. Clay and other wet soils are often too badly drained for herbs to really thrive. Raised beds are the ideal solution.

Herbs are ideally grown for convenience near the kitchen door or on or under windowsills, near windows, or next to patios and seated areas for their summer scent. Many grow well in pots and can be positioned all around the garden for an interesting display.

Propagating herbs

Many herbs, such as parsley, are easily raised from seeds sown where they are to grow or in module trays. They will need to be replaced at least annually: make several sowings each year for a regular, fresh supply. These herbs fit in well in the vegetable garden as intercrops and catch crops.

Other herbs, such as thyme, are perennial and need to be replaced every few years. These are easily raised from semi-ripe cuttings (*see page 435*) taken in late summer and early autumn and placed in equal parts multipurpose compost and coarse grit. Some herbs, such as mint, can be grown from divisions of older plants simply pulled off and replanted.

Cultivation

Most soils, especially sandy ones, benefit from the addition of 5kg (11lb) of organic matter per square metre (10 sq ft). Low-nutrient composted bark helps to open up clay soil; grit can help if the clay content is not too high, but too little grit can make matters worse. Try it in a small area first. Add lime, if necessary, to achieve a pH of at least 6.5.

Start with a weed-free plot, treating with glyphosate-based weedkiller in summer or covering the site for at least one growing season with black plastic sheeting. In established herb gardens, remove weeds rigorously, spot treating perennial weeds as soon as they are seen.

Herbs seldom need feeding or watering, but seedlings or new plants need water for their first few weeks. If growth is poor try a potassium-rich liquid fertilizer. Pests and diseases rarely cause problems. Soap, fatty-acid, or oil-based insecticides will eliminate most pests and leave no residues. Remove diseased foliage or plants as soon as seen.

MAKING A HERB WHEEL

1 **Mark a circle** with pegs and string to a diameter of 60–120cm (24–48in), which is the traditional size for a herb wheel. However, you can tailor the size and sections, or even the shape, to suit your own needs.

2 **Dig out the circle** to a depth of half a brick's length. Place the bricks, stood on end, around the edge. This forms a slightly raised bed, which provides the warmer and better-drained conditions that many herbs enjoy.

3 **Divide the bed** into sections with double courses of bricks. Too many divisions will make the spaces both hard to build and small and fiddly to plant, so aim for no more than 6. A short section of ceramic drainage pipe makes an ideal centre that can be planted. Mortar the bricks in place and leave for a day to set.

4 **Fill the sections** with soil. You can adjust the soil in each to suit different herbs, but your plants should be well matched in their size, vigour, and needs if the wheel is to look good for more than a season. Lining a section with weed-proof membrane will constrain mint roots.

Harvesting & drying

Plants that resist the nibbling of goats on Mediterranean hillsides have no problem with frequent harvesting. In fact, the more you cut herbs the healthier the plants will be, as long as you don't cut into older woody stems.

For the best flavour, gather 5–10cm (2–4in) stems, ideally on warm, sunny days and just before flowering begins. Cut with a sharp knife or scissors and aim to leave the plant with a pleasing, balanced shape. Always keep different harvested herbs apart to avoid flavours and scents mingling. Some herbs, like fennel and dill, are best used fresh and do not store; basil is best stored in oil.

You should dry herbs in the dark in a warm, airy place such as a darkened spare room. Store dried herbs in airtight jars in the dark and check for mould from time to time. Herbs can also be chopped and frozen in plastic bags ready to be added, straight from the freezer, to dishes. This is often a better alternative for the softer herbs, such as coriander, parsley, or chervil, and preserves green colour.

Garden-grown herbs that have been subject to natural stresses often have a better flavour than commercial crops that are grown with perfect watering regimes and rich soil.

Popular herbs

Basil (*Ocimum basilicum*): Tender annual, 30cm (12in) tall. Sow with heat in early spring, plant in multipurpose compost or soil when the risk of frost has passed. Cut to prevent flowering. Bring plants in before the first frosts.

Bay (*Laurus nobilis*): Evergreen tree, usually pruned to shrub size. Grow from cuttings in a sheltered site and bring indoors in harsh winters. Cut as needed all year.

Borage (*Borago officinalis*): Hardy annual, 60cm (24in) tall. Sow in poor, well-drained soil or pots in spring and summer. Cut flowers and leaves as needed. Self-seeds.

Chives (*Allium schoenoprasum*): Hardy perennial, 30cm (12in) tall. Divide in spring and water well in first year. Cut leaves near ground level as needed. Cut flowers to encourage fresh foliage. Feed if foliage yellows.

Coriander (*Coriandrum sativum*): Tender annual, 60cm (24in) tall. Sow in situ from mid-spring to late summer. Water if dry. Pick leaves in summer, seeds in late summer.

Dill (*Anethum graveolens*): Hardy annual, 60cm (24in) tall. Sow from mid-spring, away from fennel. Water if dry. Pick leaves in summer, seeds in late summer.

Fennel (*Foeniculum vulgare*): Hardy perennial, 1.5m (5ft) tall, spreads to 60cm (24in). Grow from seeds, away from dill to keep a clear flavour. Gather leaves in summer.

Lemon grass (*Cymbopogon citratus*): Tender perennial, 1m (3ft) tall. Sow in spring with heat. Grow in pots and bring in when frost threatens. Cut as needed or freeze.

Marjoram (*Origanum majorana*): Tender perennial, 30cm (12in) tall. Grow as an annual in poor, well-drained soil.

Mint (*Mentha spicata*): Hardy spreading perennial, 45–60cm (18–24in) tall. Grow in fertile, moist soil in a bottomless container to prevent spreading. Pick leaves as needed. Cut back in summer to encourage fresh foliage.

Parsley (*Petroselinum crispum*): Hardy biennial, 45cm (18in) tall. Sow in mid-spring and late summer. Grow in pots or rich soil. Use fresh, dried, or frozen.

Rosemary (*Rosmarinus officinalis*): Evergreen shrub, 1.5m (5ft) tall. Grow from cuttings in a sheltered site with low-fertility soil. Cut as needed all year. Prune lightly in spring.

Sage (*Salvia officinalis*): Evergreen perennial, 60cm (24in) tall. Grow from seeds or cuttings in poor soil and a sheltered site. Cut as needed, and protect in winter.

Tarragon (*Artemisia dracunculus*): Tender perennial 75cm (30in) tall, spreads to 50cm (20in). Grow from divisions in spring in a site sheltered from winter weather. Remove flowers in summer. Protect from winter frosts.

Thyme (*Thymus vulgaris*): Evergreen perennial, 30cm (12in) tall. Grow from seeds or cuttings, in pots or poor, well-drained soil in a sheltered sites. Cut as needed.

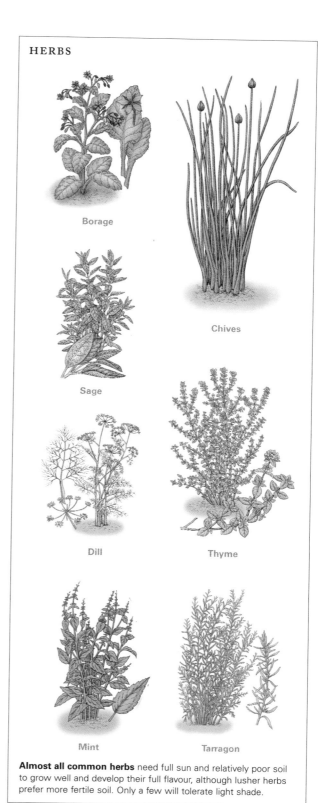

HERBS

Borage

Chives

Sage

Dill

Thyme

Mint

Tarragon

Almost all common herbs need full sun and relatively poor soil to grow well and develop their full flavour, although lusher herbs prefer more fertile soil. Only a few will tolerate light shade.

COMMON PROBLEMS

It can seem at first that vegetables are vulnerable to a host of pests and diseases, and that growing them will be an unrelenting and unwinnable struggle. It is true that there are many creatures keen to enjoy your harvest before you do, and each year some plants will be lost or damaged by disease, but the problems are not really so great. With good cultivation techniques and some defensive measures, losses will be minimal. The key is to watch plants carefully, spot potential problems early, and act promptly, ideally before any damage is done. In the vegetable garden, as everywhere else, prevention is better than cure.

Pests

Some pests, such as slugs, will attack almost any plant in the garden and are familiar to every gardener; these are discussed in Chapter One. Other pests are specific to certain crops, or even a single crop.

Bay sucker

The flattened, greyish white nymphs of this pest live under leaf margins at the shoot tips. They suck sap from the foliage and secrete chemicals into the tissues, causing the margins to thicken and curl over during summer. The affected parts are pale yellow but later dry up and turn brown. Fully grown nymphs emerge from the galls and turn into tiny, greenish-brown winged insects. Control light infestations by removing affected leaves; if heavy infestations have built up in previous years, spray with thiacloprid as soon as signs of galling appear on new foliage in spring or early summer.

Sage leafhopper

These yellowish-grey, tiny sap-feeding insects cause a coarse, pale mottling of the leaves of thyme, rosemary, mint, sage, oregano, and basil. By late summer, the foliage

Makeshift bird scarers like old compact discs are often used to keep birds away from crops. Most are not that effective. Vulnerable crops need to be netted with the net suspended well above the crop.

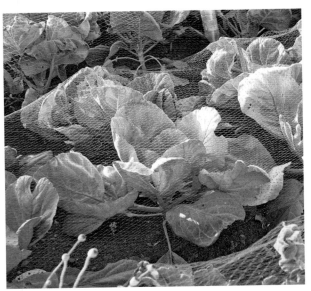

Brassicas are a favourite food of caterpillars, which can cause extensive defoliation if left uncontrolled. Insect-proof netting or mesh is an effective and environmentally friendly control.

IDENTIFYING VEGETABLE PESTS

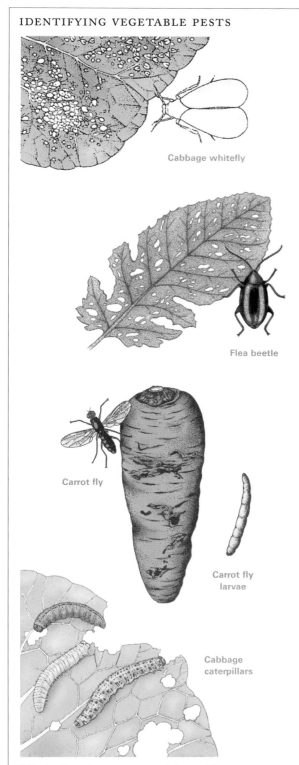

Cabbage whitefly

Flea beetle

Carrot fly

Carrot fly larvae

Cabbage caterpillars

Tell-tale signs of some pests are obvious, while you may never see others at all because they are very small or hide well. Learn to recognize the typical damage they leave behind.

may be extensively marked but growth and flavour are little affected. Damage can be tolerated, but if necessary spray with pyrethrum or thiacloprid.

Cabbage whitefly
These small insects cluster under brassica leaves and suck sap. Direct damage is minor, but their sugary excrement, called honeydew, encourages sooty moulds. Whitefly are difficult to control; remove all old plants in spring before planting anew to limit reinfection. Spraying with bifenthrin or pyrethrum will reduce infestations but the effect may be short lived. Damage is mainly confined to outer leaves, discarded before cooking, so this pest can be tolerated.

Flea beetles
Brassicas and allied plants, such as radish, turnip and rocket, are prone to attack from these tiny beetles. They are black, sometimes with yellow stripes, and jump from plants when disturbed. They eat small holes in leaves in spring and late summer. Seedlings can be killed or retarded. Keep seedlings watered so they quickly grow through the vulnerable stage. If necessary, spray with bifenthrin or thiacloprid.

Carrot fly
This pest attacks carrots and, to a lesser extent, parsnip, celery, and parsley. The maggots, up to 1cm ($\frac{1}{2}$in) long, leave brown tunnels in roots, which are vulnerable to rots and taste unpleasant. Most damage occurs in late summer. There are no pesticides for garden use: grow under fleece or in a 75cm (30in) high enclosure to prevent the low-flying females from laying eggs, and try less susceptible varieties such as 'Resistafly', 'Flyaway', and 'Maestro'.

Cabbage caterpillars
Brassicas are host plants for several caterpillars. Those of the large cabbage white butterfly are yellow and black and feed mainly on the outer leaves. Those of the small cabbage white and cabbage moth are green and tend to bore into the cabbage hearts. Remove them by hand as soon as seen, or grow plants under fleece or netting to prevent eggs from being laid on the plants. Bifenthrin or pyrethrum will control small caterpillars.

Pea & bean weevil
Small, greyish-brown weevils eat U-shaped notches in leaf margins of peas and broad beans in early summer. The growth of seedlings may be checked, but otherwise little significant damage occurs. Encourage growth by watering seedlings well. If necessary, spray plants with bifenthrin.

Rosemary beetle

This southern European pest of rosemary, lavender, thyme, and sage extended its range northwards in the 1990s. The beetles are 6–7mm ($\frac{1}{4}$–$\frac{3}{8}$in) long and have metallic purple and green stripes. They feed little until late summer, when they begin laying eggs, and both adults and the greyish-white grubs eat the leaves until late spring. Heavily infested plants become shabby, with many damaged and discoloured leaves. Collect beetles and larvae by spreading newspaper under the plants and tapping the stems to dislodge them, or spray with pyrethrum or thiacloprid in late summer.

Pea moth

This moth lays its eggs on pea plants flowering in midsummer. Caterpillars eat the seeds in the pods. Sow quick-maturing varieties early or late to avoid flowering during the moth's flight period, or grow under fleece. Otherwise spray with bifenthrin about seven days after the start of flowering to control newly hatched caterpillars.

Cabbage root fly

The white maggots of this pest, up to 8mm ($\frac{3}{8}$in) long, attack the same plants as flea beetles. In late spring to early summer, the root systems of seedlings or transplants can be destroyed. Established plants can tolerate the root damage. No insecticides are currently available for garden use. Grow young plants under fleece or place collars of roofing felt, carpet underlay, or board, about 15cm (6in) wide, around the base of the stems to prevent female flies laying eggs in the soil near the plants.

Asparagus beetle

The beetles and their creamy grey grubs feed on asparagus foliage and bark. The adults are 7mm ($\frac{3}{8}$in) long and have black wing cases with yellow squares. They emerge in late spring to lay greyish black eggs on stems and leaves. Heavy infestations cause defoliation and stems turning yellowish brown and drying up. Hand-pick, or spray with pyrethrum at dusk, if in flower, to avoid harming bees.

Potato cyst eelworms

Heavy infestations kill plants and produce marble-sized tubers. Leaves yellow and dry up, starting at the bottom of the stems. Young nematodes feed within the roots; mature females burst through the wall to form tiny white cysts. Cysts of golden cyst eelworms turn pale yellow, then brown, while those of white cyst eelworms turn directly brown. No pesticides are available. Eggs can remain viable in the soil for up to 10 years. Some potato varieties are resistant.

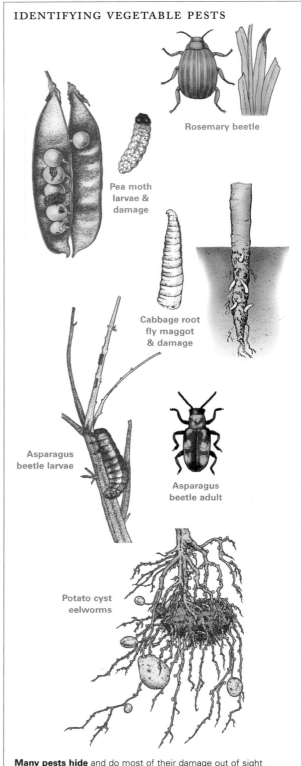

IDENTIFYING VEGETABLE PESTS

Rosemary beetle

Pea moth larvae & damage

Cabbage root fly maggot & damage

Asparagus beetle larvae

Asparagus beetle adult

Potato cyst eelworms

Many pests hide and do most of their damage out of sight before you notice what is going on. The first sign that something is wrong may be when you spot the adults or begin harvesting.

DISEASES

Pests, diseases & other problems *see page 26* | **Taking action** *see page 32* | **Common diseases** *see page 37*

Diseases

Most plant diseases affecting crops are fungal or viral. Airborne fungal infections are spread by spores, so good spacing and airflow help to reduce incidence, but some are spread in the soil and are harder to combat. Viruses are mainly spread by handling, or by sap-sucking insects.

White blister

This fungus is common on many brassicas. White chalky pustules develop on the underside of leaves, and the upper surface is sometimes distorted and discoloured. It is unsightly, but not serious. Remove affected leaves, and reduce incidence by spacing plants well and using rotation.

Onion white rot

Roots and basal tissues develop white fluffy growth and rot, sometimes causing plants to fall over, and leaves to yellow and die. Dig up and destroy affected plants. The fungus produces black spores that can survive in soil for 15 years. Grow alliums elsewhere or replace the soil: do not spread it.

Onion downy mildew

Onion leaves wither and collapse. If humid, an off-white mould develops. The bulbs do not store well. Destroy affected plants and avoid growing onions on the site for five years. Control weeds to encourage good airflow.

Leaf spots

Several fungi cause brown spots, particularly on older leaves and in wet seasons. Diseased tissue may fall out to leave shot holes. Destroy affected leaves and if necessary remove alternate plants to improve airflow.

Club root

This can affect all the brassica family. Plants are stunted and leaves may wilt on hot days, recovering overnight. On lifting, the roots are thickened and distorted. This is a slime mould, usually introduced on brought-in seedlings, and possibly manure from cattle fed on diseased plants. It can survive in soil for 20 years, and is worst on acid, wet soils. Liming and improving drainage will help, as will raising seedlings in pots and planting out when larger. No chemicals are available, but there are resistant varieties.

Leek rust

This fungus forms elongated pustules of orange spores on leeks, onions, garlic, and shallots. Severe infections can cause dying of leaves and small bulbs. Late season foliage is normally healthy. Applying sulphate of potash is claimed to help, as will clearing infected material and crop debris, good drainage, wide spacing, and using a long rotation. Resistant varieties are available.

IDENTIFYING VEGETABLE DISEASES

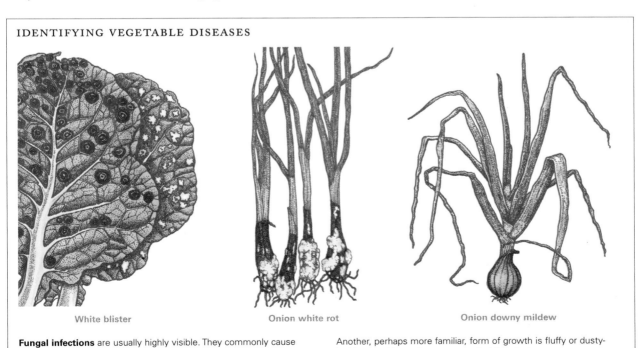

White blister   Onion white rot   Onion downy mildew

Fungal infections are usually highly visible. They commonly cause pustules, from which spores are released to infect other plants.

Another, perhaps more familiar, form of growth is fluffy or dusty-looking mould growing on any part of the plant.

213

Bean rust

Dark brown pustules appear on leaves, stems, and pods of runner and French beans. The white cluster-cup stage of the fungus may develop later in the season. Destroy affected tissue when seen.

Sclerotinia

This disease (*see page 38*) affects many vegetables including beans, potato, tomato, and celery. Late planting of potatoes sometimes helps limit infection as there are fewer dying leaves at the time of spore release.

Potato common & powdery scabs

Common scab: This is caused by a bacterium and scabby spots with irregular edges develop on the skin. Although unsightly, the damage is not very serious. Common scab occurs on light soils lacking organic matter and is worst in dry years. Dig in organic matter and ensure a regular supply of water when the tubers are forming, from two to three weeks after emergence, continuing for at least four weeks. Liming can encourage common scab, so avoid growing potatoes on ground limed for a previous brassica crop. Resistant varieties are available.

Powdery scab: This fungal disease causes irregular brown depressions with raised margins, containing dusty masses of spores. Badly affected tubers are swollen and worthless. It is worst on wet soils and in wet years. Plant tubers that have as low a level of infection as possible. Some varieties are more resistant than others.

Foot & stem rots

Several fungi can cause these rots, and some vegetables such as tomatoes and those of the cucumber family are prone to infections. The roots or stem base rot, and the plant collapses. Irregular watering or a poor root system exacerbate the problem. If caught early, foliar feeding may encourage new root production. Destroy severely affected plants and replace the soil around the roots.

Potato & tomato blight

Potato blight and tomato blight are caused by *Phytophthora infestans*. Brown dead patches appear at the leaf tips and enlarge to kill the leaf. In dry weather the infection may slow, but in wet weather it spreads rapidly.

Potato blight: Spores can be washed onto the ground where they infect the tubers. The rot is a hard, reddish-brown patch that extends into the tuber. Secondary bacteria often infect these wounds to cause a slimy soft rot. Affected tubers will not store.

For infection to take place, there must be a period of 48 hours above 10°C (50°F), with at least 11 hours of relative humidity above 89 percent each day. The airborne spores can infect plants over wide ranges. Foliage must be sprayed with a protectant fungicide before blight appears. If blight arrives late in the season, it is best to remove the stems and leaves so that the tubers do not get infected.

Powdery mildews

Some vegetables, such as the cucumber family and peas, are particularly susceptible to powdery mildew infection (*see page 38*), which is most severe on dry soil.

Mint rust

This common, sometimes serious disease of mint and related plants turns stems and leaves pale and distorted before erupting as masses of orange pustules that turn black. Leaf tissue dies and plants are defoliated. The fungus is perennial in garden mint, but spores also overwinter in the soil. Use a flame gun to remove debris in the autumn and kill spores on the soil.

Viruses on tomatoes

Typically, viruses cause mottling and distortion of leaves, stunting, and poor fruit yield, but some symptoms are very similar to those caused by herbicide exposure or cold damage. Tomato mosaic virus (TMV) is highly contagious and serious. Fruit may not set and young fruit are 'bronzed' or streaked. Destroy affected plants immediately; extensive spread may have occurred but not yet be obvious. Clean tools and hands well, and control pests. Some varieties are marketed as resistant to TMV.

Tomato blight

Outdoor tomatoes are particularly at risk from this bacterium. Infected fruit are discoloured brown and rot rapidly. Keep fruit picked from diseased plants for five days: if no rot develops, it is safe to eat. In a dry year, spray plants once they have set the desired number of trusses and been pinched out. In a wet year, spray as soon as the first truss has set and then at 10-day intervals.

Smut on corn

This disease is common in warmer regions, and seen in hotter summers elsewhere. Plants may be stunted. Cobs, flower tassels, stems, and occasionally leaves develop dramatic ashen malformations, from which a dark spore mass later erupts to cause new infections or survive in crop debris or soil. Destroy all infected material and grow no sweetcorn on the site for five years.

DISEASES

Pests, diseases & other problems *see page 26* | **Taking action** *see page 32* | **Common diseases** *see page 37*

IDENTIFYING DISEASES OF VEGETABLES CROPS

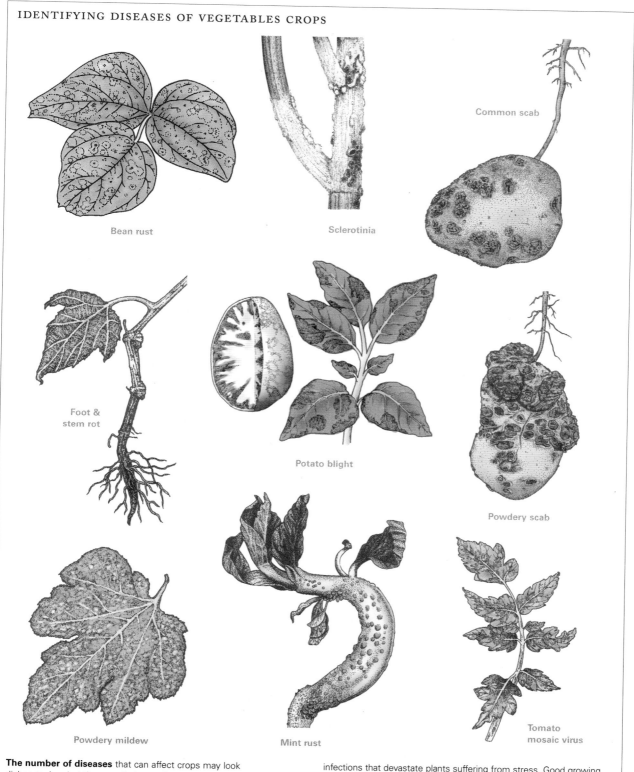

Bean rust

Sclerotinia

Common scab

Foot & stem rot

Potato blight

Powdery scab

Powdery mildew

Mint rust

Tomato mosaic virus

The number of diseases that can affect crops may look disheartening, but the overall vigour of a plant can go a long way towards preventing serious damage. Healthy plants may fight off infections that devastate plants suffering from stress. Good growing practices and frequent checks on crops, so that any problems are dealt with promptly, are important to reduce the incidence of disease.

CHAPTER FIVE

GROWING FRUIT

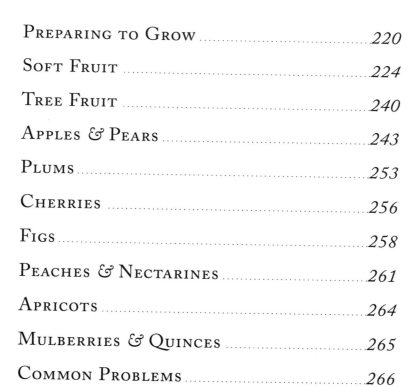

PREPARING TO GROW *220*

SOFT FRUIT *224*

TREE FRUIT *240*

APPLES & PEARS *243*

PLUMS *253*

CHERRIES *256*

FIGS *258*

PEACHES & NECTARINES *261*

APRICOTS *264*

MULBERRIES & QUINCES *265*

COMMON PROBLEMS *266*

PICKING YOUR OWN FRESH FRUIT STRAIGHT FROM A PLANT IN the garden, whether a juicy strawberry or a crisp apple, is one of life's great pleasures. Not only do you get the satisfaction of eating the fruit of your labour (quite literally), but the taste of home-grown fruit will be far superior to anything you can buy from a shop. Shop-bought fruit can be very expensive, too, and growing your own is certainly cost-effective, especially if you choose a variety that fruits over a long period of time – you can expect an apple tree, for instance, to give you a decent yield for many years.

Concern for the environment makes many people feel uneasy about the distance fruit has to travel around the world – its so-called food miles – before it reaches our plates. In a perfect world, all our fruit would be picked a few steps outside the kitchen door, and you can achieve this to a limited extent by growing your own. This will help, too, to put you back in touch with the seasons, and can also encourage children to think about where the fruit they eat comes from and when they should expect to see it on their plates. Add to this the year-round pleasures that growing your own fruit provides – blossom in spring, luscious and nutritious fruit in summer, colourful autumn foliage, and the structural shapes of fruit trees over winter – and the rewards are plain to see.

Where & what to grow

Fruit can be grown in any garden, whether you have a small balcony or the space to plant an orchard. If you have a tiny garden, the trick is to choose your varieties carefully and use training techniques to maximize the space. Many fruit plants can also be grown in containers: you can find more information in the Container Gardening chapter.

There are many plants to choose from, ranging from apples and other tree fruit to soft fruit such as black currants and raspberries. The golden rule is to grow fruit that you like to eat, though you will also need to consider your local climate, growing conditions, and available space – most fruit prefer a sunny site if the crop is to ripen well. When buying, it pays to choose a reputable fruit specialist who can supply quality plants that are certified free from pests and diseases; many such specialists will supply by mail order.

How to grow fruit

Once you have decided what to grow, this chapter will help you to get the best from your plants, with details on how to raise, plant, prune, train, and care for many traditional fruit, along with others that are becoming more widely grown, such as figs, melons, and blueberries.

The information in this chapter is written for gardeners in cool-temperate climates, and gives advice on how to assess the microclimates and conditions that affect fruit in such conditions. It also covers choosing the perfect site and how to take any necessary protective measures against pests, diseases, and cultural problems. If you live in a cold or exposed area, you may need to wait two or three weeks longer than the times recommended here to carry out some tasks. Growing fruit under protection, in a polytunnel, cloche, greenhouse, or cold frame, can extend the growing season.

Very few chemical sprays are available for home fruit growers today, so the emphasis needs to be on prevention of pests and diseases rather than control. Buy fruit varieties with natural resistance, for example, and protect fruit from birds with strong netting.

PREPARING TO GROW

Growing fruit is very enjoyable, but rather than purchasing plants on impulse, take your time to choose, basing your decision on conditions within your garden. This ensures that whatever you decide to grow will thrive and reward you with an excellent crop. It is essential to consider your local climate, which will play a large part in determining what you can grow. The most important aspects of climate are rain, wind, and temperature. The amount of rain and exposure to wind may be tempered by cultivation techniques or protective structures. However, crops may fail or even die in unfavourable temperatures.

Choice of site

Most fruit do best in a sunny, sheltered position, where heat and light encourage formation of fruit buds and allow the crop to ripen. Although it may affect the yield, many types of fruit still do well in slight shade, but only if they can bask in sun for at least half the day.

Also consider your garden's altitude. Generally, the higher the altitude, the cooler the climate, and the shorter the growing season. Microclimates within your garden, such as a warm, south-facing slope, may temper these elements and still allow fruit to grow.

The minimum temperature for fruit is 6°C (43°F). Some fruit, such as melons, need consistently higher temperatures. Generally, the 'growing season' is considered to be the number of frost-free days between spring and autumn. Some crops, such as grapes, need a long growing season, while others, such as strawberries, only need a short season to fruit well.

Rainfall

Moisture is vital for the healthy growth of fruit plants, but very wet conditions and high humidity provide the perfect conditions for fungal diseases, while waterlogged soil can cause the roots to rot. Good drainage is crucial in such conditions. Too little rainfall or drought in summer can affect the yield or quality of fruit. Apply a mulch to seal in moisture and water if necessary.

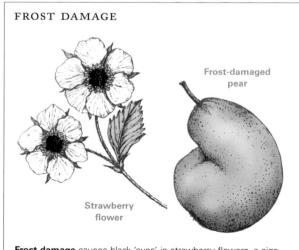

FROST DAMAGE

Frost-damaged pear

Strawberry flower

Frost damage causes black 'eyes' in strawberry flowers, a sign that the ovaries are dead and will not produce fruits. Pears become distorted by frost, but they are still edible.

A sheltered, sunny spot is the best site for a fruit garden. In any garden you can improve conditions for fruit, ensuring that the plants thrive and produce a good crop every year.

CHOICE OF SITE

Climate & your garden *see page 12* | **Looking after your soil** *see page 16* | **Pests, diseases & other problems** *see page 26*

WIND TURBULENCE AND WINDBREAKS

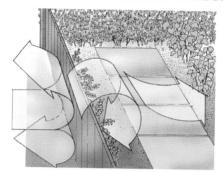 

Wind turbulence is very strong on both sides of a solid barrier, such as a fence or evergreen hedge, and can severely damage fruit plants.

Open windbreaks on exposed sites filter wind and slow it down without causing turbulence. A deciduous hedge is attractive, but competes with the fruit for shade, water, and nutrients. Effective artificial barriers include a picket fence, trellis, or robust netting on posts.

Wind

Strong winds can blow blossom or fruit off a tree and scorch leaves, snap branches, and prevent pollinating insects reaching the plants. If needed, erect a windbreak (*see box, above*) or consider a barrier of fast-growing deciduous trees, such as poplar, alder, or willow.

Frost

Spring frosts can damage buds, flowers, fruit, and shoots, so protect crops under glass with a heater. You can build structures around fruit trained against walls or fences and use cloches or mini-tunnels over smaller plants in the ground. Fleece can also be draped over compact forms of tree fruits in containers or small groups outdoors; you can even buy fleece 'jackets' that can be slipped over plants.

Alternatively, try growing late-flowering fruit, such as hardy varieties of black currant, raspberry, and blackberry, or fruit that is known for its blossom hardiness, including many varieties of apple.

Soil

It is possible to grow fruit on most reasonable soils, although a fertile, well-drained soil that is slightly acidic (about pH 6.5) is ideal. Very damp soil can cause roots to rot, so if your soil is heavy and has pools of standing water after rain, improve it by digging in plenty of well-rotted manure before planting. If the soil is waterlogged, do not plant until you have installed a drainage system. Improve a lighter soil that dries out fast by adding plenty of organic matter to help retain moisture, and apply regular mulches.

IDENTIFYING FROST POCKETS

Frost pockets are small patches of cold air, often trapped on a slope or at a bottom corner (*shown far left*). Avoid such areas when planting. If there is no choice, improve air flow in the area to help cold air to escape, by using a porous barrier for example (*shown left*). Alternatively, grow only larger trees at the bottom of the pocket, so that the blossom is above the level of the coldest air, or grow smaller plants higher up the slope.

Planning

The lifespan of a fruit tree may be 20–50 years and many soft fruit plants have a life of 10–15 years, so planting a fruit garden, or even a single tree, is a long-term venture. Plan carefully before buying any plants and ask the fundamental question: do you have space for a dedicated fruit garden with a mixture of soft, cane, bush, and tree fruit, or just a single fruit tree? Make a scale plan of your outdoor space on squared paper; include all fences, walls, and hedges and all existing large plants. Also note the aspect – most fruit thrives in full sun or light shade; cold, shaded sites result in slow growth and very poor yields.

Where to place plants

Take note of the correct spacings for your chosen fruit, to avoid buying too many plants and allow each one room to develop to its maximum cropping potential. Often two fruit trees are needed to pollinate their blossom.

Whatever the size of the garden, exploit any fences, walls, trellis, or other vertical structures that provide a sunny and sheltered aspect as supports for fruit plants. Fix training wires to the vertical supports and use them to raise grape vines, blackberries, raspberries, and trained forms of apples, pears, gooseberries, as well as more exotic fruit such as figs, apricots, and peaches. Vertical supports also make it easy to secure a blanket of fleece for frost protection or to add netting in spring to baffle birds.

When planning a fruit garden, consider whether you want to include some permanent structures, such as fruit cages to prevent birds from stealing or damaging the crop, or supports, such as fencing or trellis, on which to train fruiting canes or restricted tree forms (*see box, right*).

FRUIT TREE FORMS

Oblique cordon

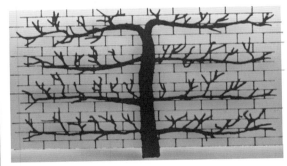

Espalier

Fan

Standard tree with a clear stem

Half-standard with a 1m (3ft) stem

Bush with little or no stem

Restricted trees, such as fans, espaliers, and cordons, are ideal in limited space. Freestanding trees may be pruned into different shapes, but this can affect accessibility for picking the crop.

SOFT FRUIT

'Soft fruit' is the general term used to describe a diverse group of perennials or low-growing shrubs that bear soft, juicy fruit. It includes currants, gooseberries, blueberries, raspberries, strawberries, grapes, and melons. Unlike tree fruit, which can need a lot of room to grow happily, soft fruits are ideal for a sunny or slightly shaded position in a small garden because they do not need too much space to thrive. Some can even be grown in containers, making them perfect for patio gardens. Another advantage of soft fruits is that they bear crops soon after planting, in some cases within the same year.

Red currants, white currants & gooseberries

All three of these shrubs are popular bush fruit for the small garden as they all grow best in the sheltered, sunny positions these gardens can provide. They also tolerate partial shade, even against a cold and shady wall, although this will result in a deficiency in the flavour of the currants and gooseberries. Ideally, the soil should be slightly acid or neutral, well-drained, and fertile. Red currants are tolerant of most soils.

PLANTING A RED CURRANT, WHITE CURRANT, OR GOOSEBERRY BUSH

1 **Clear the ground** of weeds and dig in an 8cm (3in) layer of well-rotted manure or compost, then rake in a general-purpose fertilizer at 50g (2oz) per square metre (10 sq ft) in early autumn.

2 **Plant from late autumn** to early spring. Dig a hole sufficiently deep and wide to spread out the roots. Plant the bush at the same depth as it was planted at the nursery, using the soil mark on the stem as a guide. Fill in and firm gently.

3 **Feed each year in** late winter or early spring with a general-purpose fertilizer applied at the same rate as before planting (*see step 1*). Also add 15g (½oz) per square metre (10 sq ft) of sulphate of potash. If the soil is light, apply a 5cm (2in) mulch around each bush.

4 **Protect the fruit buds** from birds during late winter. In spring, use netting or fleece to protect the blossom against spring frosts; remove the covers during the day to allow access to pollinating insects.

PRUNING A RED CURRANT, WHITE CURRANT, OR GOOSEBERRY BUSH

FIRST YEAR

1 Maintain a clear stem, or leg, on newly planted bushes. The first branches should start about 10–15cm (4–6in) above ground level. In winter, use sharp secateurs to remove any growth that has formed below this point.

2 Cut back, in winter, each branch that will form the framework by a half, to a bud that faces the centre of the bush and points upwards. This formative pruning helps to develop an upright, open-centred bush.

SECOND YEAR

3 Shorten the leading shoots by a half to one third in late autumn to inward- and upward-facing buds. Select well-placed side branches to form further permanent branches; cut them back by one third. Remove any low stems at the base.

THIRD YEAR

4 Shorten again the leading shoots by a half from late autumn to early spring to a bud facing in the required direction. Cut out any shoots crowding the centre. Shorten any sideshoots that are not needed for the framework to about 5cm (2in).

5 Thin gooseberry fruits in late spring by removing every other one; use them for cooking. Leave the rest to ripen and develop their full flavour. Cover the bush with netting to prevent birds from stripping the remaining crop. Currants do not need thinning.

SUBSEQUENT YEARS

6 Prune sideshoots produced that season to 5 leaves, in midsummer. Do not prune the leading shoots. Leave these until winter, then cut them back by a half; also cut sideshoots pruned in the previous summer to about 2 buds in winter. Prune out dead, diseased, and crowded growth.

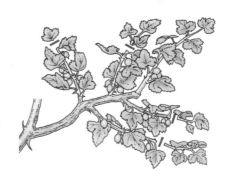

Planting & spacing

Plant bare-root currants and gooseberries between late autumn and early spring, and container-grown plants at any time, avoiding waterlogged or frozen soil. Allow 1.5m (5ft) between bushes and 1.5m (5ft) between rows.

Pruning & training

Red and white currants and gooseberries give good yields when trained as open-centred, goblet-shaped bushes (*see above*), with well-spaced branches above a short leg, or main stem, 10–15cm (4–6in) tall. The pruning regime for all three crops is similar.

Aftercare

Spread a general-purpose fertilizer around plants in late winter or early spring (*see facing page*). Water well in dry weather and keep the soil free of weeds. The flowers suffer in hard frosts, but a covering of fleece will protect them. Birds find the fruit buds and brightly coloured currants irresistible, so cover the bushes with strong netting.

Harvesting & storing

Red and white currants and gooseberries are ready to eat in early to midsummer. They often crop heavily, and excess fruit can be put into polythene bags and frozen.

Black currants

These currants are very easy to grow and reward you with lots of tangy fruit in the second summer after planting. They are best planted from bare-root stock (*see below*); look for plants that have three or more shoots. Some bushes reach 2m (6ft) so need plenty of space, but they may provide you with high yields for up to 15 years.

Black currants are tolerant of many soils, but they prefer their roots to be in slightly acidic, fertile, moisture-retentive yet well-drained soil. They tolerate partial shade but prefer a sunny, sheltered position

The flowers of black currants appear in early spring, so they are vulnerable to hard frosts. Cover the crop with fleece at such times, remembering to lift it during the day to allow pollinating bees access to the flowers, or buy a hardier or later-flowering variety.

Once established, black currants have a simple pruning regime, but they do need plenty of feeding to thrive. Plants also need watering regularly in dry weather, and as the roots are shallow, keep the area free of weeds using a hoe rather than a fork, which can disturb the roots.

PLANTING & PRUNING A BLACK CURRANT BUSH

FIRST YEAR

1 Dig in an 8cm (3in) layer of manure or compost in autumn, then rake in a balanced fertilizer at 85g (3oz) per square metre (10 sq ft). Between late autumn and early spring, plant each bush 5cm (2in) deeper than it was at the nursery, with its roots spread out.

2 Cut down all the shoots to within 5cm (2in) of the soil surface. Allow 1.5m (5ft) spacing between bushes, or 2m (6ft) if they are a vigorous variety, and 2m (6ft) between rows. Lightly firm the soil around the roots and water in well.

SECOND YEAR

3 Apply fertilizer in the second winter, by which time strong new shoots will have appeared; they do not need pruning yet. Use a general-purpose fertilizer at a rate of 85g (3oz) per square metre (10 sq ft). Protect the emerging fruit buds from birds with strong netting.

4 Apply sulphate of ammonia a month later at a rate of 25g (1oz) per square metre (10 sq ft). Repeat this feeding regime, followed by a mulch, every year thereafter. In midsummer, the bush fruits best on 1-year-old wood.

THIRD YEAR

5 New growths develop at the base of each bush. Thin out weak shoots in late autumn. Also remove any branches that are too low, or if they are broken or show signs of mildew.

SUBSEQUENT YEARS

6 Prune out one-third of the bush every winter, cutting older stems first back to the point of origin or to a strong shoot. Also remove badly placed or damaged stems. Remember to feed and mulch black currants each year.

Looking after your soil *see page 16* | **Preparing to grow** *see page 220* | **Common problems** *see page 266*

Blueberries

Blueberries are an incredibly popular late summer fruit, largely because they are regarded as a 'super food' with a high content of vitamin C in the berries. The many varieties of blueberry are easy to grow in the garden and have the added bonus of being attractive plants, boasting dense clusters of pretty spring flowers and showy fruit. Commonly grown blueberries are mostly varieties of the 'high bush' blueberry *Vaccinium corymbosum.*

Blueberries are hardy down to -28°C (-18°F) and come in many shapes, from compact forms that are only 60cm (24in) tall to shrubs that reach over 2m (6ft).

Where to grow blueberries

Moist, well-drained acid soils, with a pH of 4–5.5, are perfect for blueberries, although acidic clay or sandy soil can be improved by digging in plenty of composted bark or pine needles before planting. The plants will not tolerate alkaline soil or even soil that is only mildly acid.

Choose a sunny or slightly shaded spot, avoiding frost pockets, since a frost-free season of about five months is necessary for a good crop. You can grow dwarf blueberries in large containers filled with ericaceous (acidic) compost. Although blueberries are considered self-fertile, it is best to grow at least two different varieties to ensure good pollination and therefore a good crop.

Aftercare & harvesting

Blueberries need plenty of moisture in summer. In dry weather, water them copiously, preferably with collected rainwater, which has the right pH.

Regular pruning is not needed, but old bushes become dense. Thin them by removing the oldest, least-productive stems back to ground level or to a strong bud.

Pick the berries when they are blue-black with a whitish bloom and starting to soften. Eat them fresh and put the rest in polythene bags for freezing.

PLANTING & PRUNING A HIGH BUSH BLUEBERRY

1 **Dig out** a 30cm (12in) square hole before planting. Fill it with a mixture of composted bark or leafmould and soil. Mound it slightly and then leave for a few weeks to allow the soil to settle.

2 **Plant bushes** from container-grown stock 1.5m (5ft) apart, in rows 2m (6ft) apart in autumn or spring. With a trowel, make a hole large enough to accommodate the rootball. Fill the hole around the roots and firm the soil.

3 **Apply a dressing** of sulphate of ammonia at 15g (½oz) per square metre (10 sq ft) in spring, and repeat for subsequent years. At the same time, mulch with a substance suitable for acid-loving plants, such as leafmould, sawdust or pulverized bark.

4 **Cut back** fruited branches that have become thin and twiggy to a more vigorous shoot, between late autumn and late winter. Cut out any damaged or dead branches close to their base.

Raspberries

These tasty berries grow on canes and are some of the most productive plants you can grow. Raspberries are excellent for growing in cool climates and do well in most soils, although they prefer moisture-retentive, well-drained soil that is slightly acidic. Give them a sunny, sheltered spot to prevent the canes from being damaged.

Except for autumn-fruiting varieties, raspberry canes are vegetative in their first year, bear flowers and fruit in their second year, then die back. New stems grow as suckering shoots (*see page 97*) from ground level.

The best way of supporting canes in a small space is a single fence system using 2.2m (7ft) tree stakes spaced 4–5m (12–15ft) apart. Drive each one 60cm (24in) into the ground. Fix 14-gauge galvanized wire to the end posts, using straining bolts with U-staples on intermediate posts. Stretch single wires horizontally between the posts at heights of 75cm (30in), 1m (3ft), and 1.5m (5ft). Tie in canes individually to train them vertically on the wires.

Raspberry varieties belong to the same group of plants as blackberries and hybrid berries. More unusual types include this autumn-fruiting raspberry 'Fallgold', with golden fruit.

PLANTING RASPBERRY CANES

1 Dig out a trench in early autumn in prepared ground that is 3 spade blades wide by 1 spade blade deep. Cover the base with an 8–10cm (3–4in) layer of well-rotted manure or compost and fork it in thoroughly.

2 Return the soil to the trench and roughly level it. Then fork in a general-purpose fertilizer at a rate of 85g (3oz) per square metre (10 sq ft). Leave the soil to settle for a few weeks before planting.

3 Plant the raspberry canes between late autumn and early spring, at 45cm (18in) intervals. Spread out the roots of each cane and plant to a depth of about 8cm (3in). Cut every planted cane to a bud about 25cm (10in) above the soil.

4 Dress the soil around the canes in early spring with sulphate of ammonia, at 15g (½oz) per square metre (10 sq ft), at least a few weeks after planting. Mulch with a 5cm (2in) layer of garden compost; take care to keep it clear of the canes.

RASPBERRIES

Looking after your soil *see page 16* | **Preparing to grow** *see page 220* | **Common fruit problems** *see page 266*

MAINTAINING RASPBERRY CANES

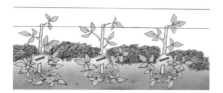 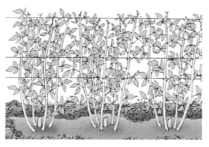 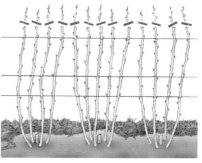

FIRST YEAR
1 Cut down the stumps to ground level in spring, when the new canes appear; do not remove the new growth.

2 In summer, tie in the new canes to the support wires as they develop. Keep the canes spaced about 10cm (4in) apart.

SECOND & SUBSEQUENT YEARS
3 Cut each cane back to a bud about 15cm (6in) above the top support wire in late winter. Mulch around the bases of the plants.

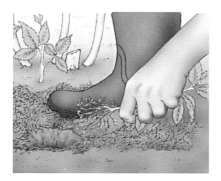 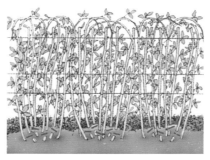 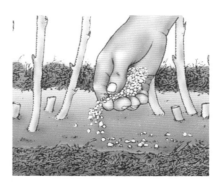

4 In midsummer, pull out shoots growing away from the row and thin out the weakest new growth to leave canes 10cm (4in) apart.

5 Cut down fruited canes to the ground after fruiting in summer. Tie in new canes, 10cm (4in) apart. Loop over vigorous canes.

6 Feed plants with 25g (1oz) sulphate of potash per square metre (10 sq ft) in winter. Every 3 years, apply 50g (2oz) superphosphate.

AUTUMN-FRUITING RASPBERRIES

Unlike summer-fruiting varieties, these raspberries fruit at the tops of stems produced in the current season, generally ripening between late summer and the first frosts. The plants prefer full sun and are planted in the same way as summer-fruiting varieties. However, they are best trained on parallel wires that allow the canes to grow between the supports. The canes do not need tying in unless the garden is exposed. To construct supports, drive 2m (6ft) posts 45cm (18in) into the ground and 4–5m (12–15ft) apart. Fix two crossbars 75cm (24in) long and 5cm (2in) wide to the end posts and to intermediate posts. Set the crossbars at 90cm (3ft) and 1.5m (5ft) from the ground. Stretch parallel wires, 60cm (24in) apart, between the crossbars.

Cut down all canes to soil level in late winter, and train new canes between the wires from spring. Control spread by pulling out any canes growing outside the row.

Blackberries

These very vigorous, often thorny canes are sometimes known as brambles; they are frost hardy and do best in well-drained, fertile soil in a sunny spot. Hybrid berries, such as the boysenberry, tayberry, and loganberry, are grown in a similar way, but generally are less rampant.

Planting & spacing

Blackberries should be planted between late autumn and early spring, as for raspberries (*see page 228*). Space less-vigorous varieties, such as tayberry and boysenberry, 2.5m (8ft) apart, loganberries and blackberries of medium vigour 3m (10ft) apart, and vigorous varieties 4–4.5m (12–15ft) apart.

Pruning & training

Growing canes on a support keeps the fruit clean and stops vigorous forms from taking over the garden. To make a support, drive 2.5m (8ft) posts 75cm (30in) into the ground at each end of the planned row. Between the end posts, align intermediate posts every 4m (12ft). Attach restraining bolts to the end posts and stretch four wires between them, the first fixed 80cm (32in) from the ground and the others above it, spaced 30cm (12in) apart.

Less vigorous varieties can be fan trained; but for other types, the weaving system (*see below*) allows you to make the most of the long canes and ensure a good harvest, although it requires a lot of handling.

Aftercare & harvesting

In late winter, apply a general-purpose fertilizer at a rate of 50g (2oz) per square metre (10 sq ft), followed by a thick mulch, keeping it off the canes. Water during dry spells; avoid wetting the canes to minimize fungal diseases.

Pick the fruit when it is fully coloured and soft in summer. At this time, the crop may need protecting from birds with a cover of strong netting.

PLANTING & TRAINING A BLACKBERRY CANE

FIRST YEAR

1 Tie the young canes as they appear to the wire supports in summer. Train them vertically at first, then weave the extension growth in and out of the bottom three wires.

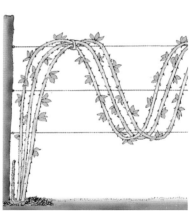

3 Cut out all the fruited canes to the base of the plant in mid-autumn, after fruiting. If there are not very many new canes to bear next year's fruit, retain the best of the old canes to supply some extra blackberries.

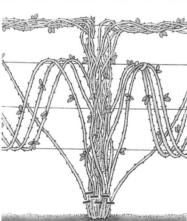

SECOND YEAR

2 Train the new canes in summer up through the centre of the bush and along the top wire so that they do not cover the previous year's canes. The old canes will carry this year's fruit.

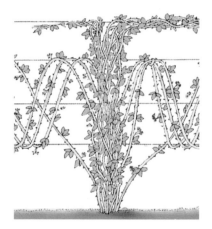

4 Untie the current season's canes at the same time and carefully weave them around the lower 3 wires and tie them in. In late winter, prune any damaged tips from the young canes back to healthy buds.

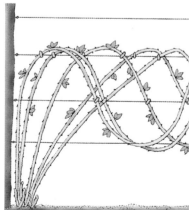

STRAWBERRIES

Looking after your soil *see page 16* | **Preparing to grow** *see page 220* | **Common fruit problems** *see page 266*

Strawberries

The common, summer-fruiting strawberry usually has a single, heavy flush of fruit anytime from late spring to late summer, depending on the variety. Perpetual types fruit sporadically from late summer until mid-autumn. Alpine strawberries (*Fragaria vesca*) produce tiny, but intensely flavoured berries for months. If you grow some plants under cover (*see page 384*), you can pick strawberries for many months of the year.

Summer-fruiting strawberries

Give these strawberries slightly acidic, well-drained soil in a frost-free, sunny place (they tolerate light shade), and each plant should produce about 250g (9oz) of fruit. You can grow them as annuals, planting new runners each year (*see page 233*), but mature plants have larger harvests and a productive life of up to four years. A month before planting, remove perennial weeds and dig in well-rotted manure at 6.5kg (14lb) per square metre (10 sq ft).

Plant bare-rooted strawberries from midsummer to early autumn for cropping the following year. You can plant rooted runners in early spring, but they may crop poorly in their first year – remove blossom as it appears so that the plant can put its energy into getting established. Plant pot-grown plants at any time; they will fruit the same year if planted in spring. Space the plants 45cm (18in) apart in rows 1m (3ft) apart.

Perpetual strawberries

As these fruit later in the year, you will need to protect crops by placing cloches over them in order to extend the season into autumn. Unlike summer varieties, which crop for several years, perpetual strawberries run out of steam after the first crop so are best replaced. Plant in spring, summer, or autumn, and remove any early-season flowers. Grow these plants at the same spacing as for summer-fruiting strawberries.

PLANTING & PROTECTING A STRAWBERRY PLANT

1 Fertilize the soil just before planting by forking in a balanced granular fertilizer at 85g (3oz) per square metre (10 sq ft). Plant the strawberries 45cm (18in) apart with 90cm (36in) between rows. Spread out the roots, keeping the crowns level with the surface. Firm the soil.

2 Water regularly for the first few weeks after planting and in dry spells in the growing season. To avoid risk of fungal diseases, such as botrytis, do not wet ripening berries. A trickle irrigation system with a programmable timer, set to water several times a day, is helpful.

3 Scatter slug pellets along the rows when the fruit begins to swell. Cover the ground beneath the berries and between rows with barley or wheat straw to keep the ripening fruit clean and stop weeds growing.

4 Protect the fruit from birds with some anti-bird netting stretched over cloche frames. Alternatively, make low cages by supporting the nets on posts that are at least 45cm (18in) tall – cover the post ends with jars or pots to protect your eyes when bending down to harvest the fruit.

Water crops in pots regularly, especially during sunny, dry weather. Once flowers appear, feed weekly with a fertilizer that is high in potash until the fruit starts to turn red.

Lay 150-gauge plastic over 8cm (3in) ridges of moist soil, 15cm (6in) apart. Plant through slits at 38–45cm (15–18in) intervals.

Place individual mats around single plants like collars so that the swelling fruit rest on the mats and are protected.

Alpine strawberries

These fruit sparsely and are best grown as edging plants or in containers and hanging baskets. They tend not to produce runners, so are best started from seed sown in spring or bought as young plants.

Their soil requirement is the same as for summer-fruiting strawberries. Space plants 30cm (12in) apart with 75cm (30in) between the rows.

Aftercare & harvesting

To promote flower formation, feed plants in early spring with sulphate of potash at a rate of 15g (½oz) per square metre (10 sq ft) alongside each row. Keep all types well watered during dry weather and protect the fruit with straw (*see page 231*), plastic, or matting (*see box, above*).

If you can, harvest the fruit in the morning, when it is fresh and cool, removing each fruit with its stalk and handling carefully to give it a longer shelf life. Once you have picked all the fruit in late summer, dispose of the straw and clear up the bed by shearing the leaves off the plants and weeding (*see facing page*). In late winter, tidy up by removing leaves damaged during winter.

Growing crops in pots

You can grow single plants in 20cm (8in) pots of multipurpose compost, or six plants per growing bag. You will get a better, trouble-free crop by raising growing bags off the ground, where they are less likely to be discovered by slugs and snails. Place them on a plank supported by crates or bricks at each end to improve air flow around the plants and drainage. Fruit can trail down the sides without touching the ground. Water containers regularly as they dry out quickly in hot weather.

Protected cropping

For an earlier crop and to protect the fruit from birds, you can grow outdoor strawberries in a cold frame (*see facing page*) or under a polytunnel or cloche. You can expect strawberries under glass to be ready three weeks earlier than unprotected plants, while crops grown under polythene will be ready two weeks earlier. Put cloches in place in early spring.

You can grow any variety of strawberry this way, but for an especially early crop, try an early-fruiting summer variety. Plant the runners in the normal way, but spacing them 30cm (12in) apart with 75cm (30in) between rows. Remember to ventilate at flowering time.

Alternatively, you can cover the plants with aerated plastic, which prevents a build-up of high temperatures while allowing insects to enter and air to circulate. Immediately after harvesting, remove the protection and clean up the strawberry beds before winter.

PROPAGATING STRAWBERRIES FROM RUNNERS

1 **Select 4 or 5 runners** from vigorous and disease-free cropping strawberries, from early to late summer.

2 **Peg each runner** with a U-shaped wire firmly into an 8cm (3in) pot of potting compost sunk into the soil or into open ground.

3 **Sever from the parent plant**, close to the runner, after the runner has rooted, which should take 4–6 weeks.

4 **Lift out each potted runner** or knock it out of its pot, plant into a new bed and water. Transplant runners rooted in open ground.

Growing in the greenhouse

You can grow strawberries for early spring in a cool greenhouse (*see page 384*). Start with rooted runners and pot on into 15cm (6in) pots. Keep the soil damp and feed the plants every week until early autumn. At the end of autumn move them into a cold frame to protect them from frost, and in early winter bring them into the greenhouse, giving them plenty of space to allow air to circulate.

Propagation

Most strawberries produce masses of runners. You can propagate from these after harvesting to start new beds or replace worn-out plants (*see above*). Keep the runners well watered until they root, and cut back and discard any surplus runners. Most alpine and some perpetual strawberries do not form runners, but you can propagate these by division (*see page 422*).

COLD FRAMES

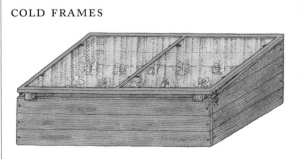

Place plants in a cold frame from in early spring for an early crop. Ventilate at flowering time to allow in pollinating insects and to stop plants overheating. At night, close the vents.

CLEARING UP THE BED

After cropping, cut off old leaves along with surplus runners using shears. Fork up compacted soil between the rows.

233

Grapes

Vines grown for their grapes crop heavily for many years with care and attention. There is a bewildering amount of varieties to choose from, usually with green or dark purple fruit. Dessert grapes are best for eating fresh, while others are bred for turning into wine. Generally these contain more sugar than dessert grapes. Depending on the variety, you can raise vines outdoors or under the protection of a greenhouse. They are usually ready to harvest from late summer until mid-autumn.

GROWING GRAPES OUTDOORS

Choose a sheltered, sunny site, either against a sunny fence or wall, which is ideal for cooler areas, or in the open, in a row. If you have the space, a sunny slope with the row running north to south allows both sides of the row to receive plenty of light.

Grapes thrive in deep, slightly acid, well-drained soil, but it is not worth attempting to grow them if the soil is soggy or very chalky (alkaline) because this can result in chlorosis caused by nutrient deficiency.

Before planting, you will need to prepare the soil and erect a system of supports. Start by removing perennial weeds from the site and dig over the soil in the planting area two to three weeks before you plan to plant. Finish by applying a general-purpose fertilizer, at a rate of 50g (2oz) per square metre (10 sq ft) and rake into the surface.

Erecting supports

If you are training vines on a wall or fence, attach three heavy-duty, horizontal wires 25–30cm (10–12in) apart, held by vine eyes or straining bolts.

In open ground, construct a freestanding support system using wires stretched between stout posts. Set 2m (6ft) posts 2.5–3m (8–10ft) apart and drive 60cm (24in) into the ground. Stretch one 12-gauge wire between the posts, 40cm (16in) above the ground. Add two 14-gauge wires at 30cm (12in) intervals above the first wire, weaving the wires around alternate sides of the posts.

Planting & training

One-year-old vines are best planted between mid-autumn and early spring (*see below*), as long as the ground is not frozen. If planting a bare-root plant, dig a hole that is wide enough for the roots to spread out fully and deep enough for it to be planted at the same level as before it was lifted. If the variety has been grafted onto a rootstock, ensure the graft union (*see page 243*) is above the surface of the soil. Plant pot-grown vines so that the surface of the compost is just beneath soil level.

If planting vines against a wall or fence, make sure that the plants are about 25cm (10in) away from the wall or fence and spaced 1.2m (4ft) apart. In the open, space vines 1.2–1.5m (4–5ft) apart in rows 1.8–2m (6ft) apart.

PLANTING & PRUNING AN OUTDOOR GRAPE VINE

FIRST YEAR

1 **Erect a support** from mid-autumn to early spring. Insert a cane for each plant.

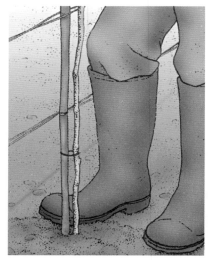

2 **Plant each vine**, then firm, water, and tie in to the support. Cut the main stem back to 2 good buds above soil level.

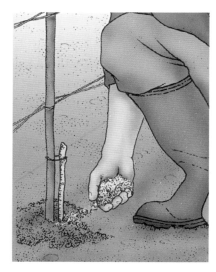

3 **Feed each winter** with a general-purpose fertilizer and mulch well. Also add a dressing of sulphate of potash.

GRAPES

Climbers & wall plants *see page 130* | **Preparing to grow** *see page 220* | **Common fruit problems** *see page 266*

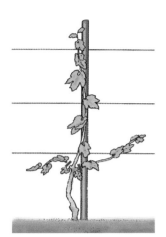

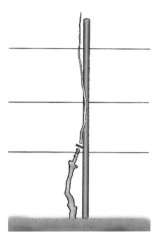

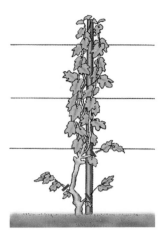

SECOND YEAR

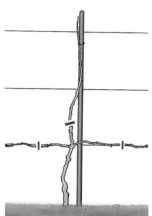

4 **Allow 1 branch** to develop from each plant in the first growing season. Train it vertically up the cane. Pinch back any other branches to just 1 leaf.

5 **Cut down** the main stem of each plant to within 40cm (16in) of ground level in late autumn. Make sure that you leave 3 good buds.

6 **Train the 3 new branches** vertically from mid-spring to late summer. Pinch back to 1 leaf any branches that develop.

7 **Tie 2 of the new branches** to the lowest wire in opposite directions in autumn. Cut both back to 60–75cm (24–30in). Prune the upright branch to 3 good buds.

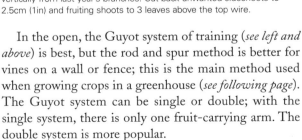

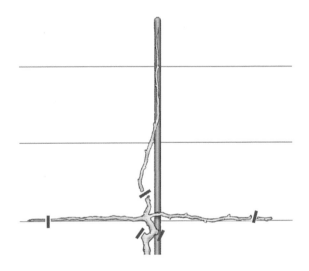

THIRD & SUBSEQUENT YEARS

8 **Train the 3 new branches** that will grow up the central support, in summer. Allow several well-spaced, fruit-bearing shoots to grow vertically from last year's branches. Cut back unwanted sideshoots to 2.5cm (1in) and fruiting shoots to 3 leaves above the top wire.

9 **Cut off** both the arms of the vine each year in late autumn. Take the 3 new central branches and tie 2 of them horizontally and cut back to 60–75cm (24–30in). Prune the remaining shoot to 3 good buds.

In the open, the Guyot system of training (*see left and above*) is best, but the rod and spur method is better for vines on a wall or fence; this is the main method used when growing crops in a greenhouse (*see following page*). The Guyot system can be single or double; with the single system, there is only one fruit-carrying arm. The double system is more popular.

Aftercare & harvesting

Every late winter, dress the soil with 50g (2oz) general fertilizer and 15g (½oz) sulphate of potash per square metre (10 sq ft). Then mulch with well-rotted manure or garden compost. Once a week during the growing season, feed dessert grapes with a general liquid fertilizer until the fruits ripen. Plants grown against walls need regular watering since the soil tends to dry out quickly.

Remove some leaves around bunches in late summer to allow air to circulate and light to penetrate the fruit. If any grapes are wizened, mouldy, or damaged, remove carefully with scissors. When harvesting, cut the branch above the bunch to avoid damaging the fruit or marking the white bloom on some varieties.

GROWING GRAPES INDOORS

In cool climates, a greater choice of grape varieties can be grown in a cool or heated greenhouse. They can be planted in the greenhouse, either in the border soil or in a large container, or outside the greenhouse, with the main stem threaded inside through a low hole. Planting outside allows the vine to be partly irrigated by rainfall, but indoors, the soil inside warms up quickly in spring, giving earlier growth. When digging a planting hole, replace the soil with loam-based John Innes No. 3 compost.

In a large greenhouse, vines should be trained in the rod and spur method (*see below*) against a series of 12-gauge wires. The wires should be about 40cm (16in) from the glass, about 25cm (10in) apart, with the highest one approximately 45cm (18in) below the ridge. In a small greenhouse, plant the vine near a corner and train it horizontally along a wire, letting branches grow vertically. Alternatively, plant it against the far gable and train it upwards and along the ridge of the greenhouse roof. Plant indoor vines as for outdoor types (*see page 234*).

PLANTING & PRUNING AN INDOOR GRAPE VINE

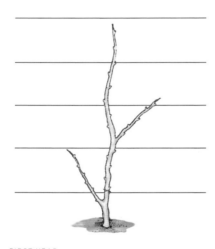

FIRST YEAR
1 **Plant a vine** from late autumn to early winter, in loam-based potting compost.

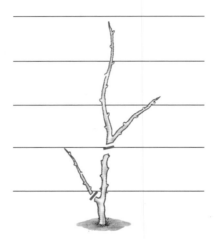

2 **Cut back the main stem** by two thirds immediately after planting. Cut any remaining side branches to just one bud.

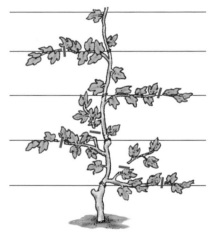

3 **Let the main stem** reach 3m (10ft) in the first summer. Cut back side branches to 5 leaves and sub-side branches to 1 leaf. Tie in.

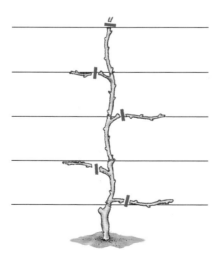

4 **In late autumn** after leaf fall, cut back the main stem by two thirds. Prune each side branch on the main stem to 1 good bud.

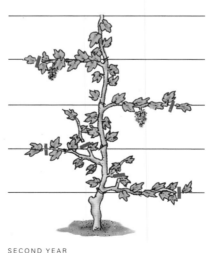

SECOND YEAR
5 **Cut back side branches** in summer to 2 leaves after the first flower truss and tie in. Cut back sub-side branches to 1 leaf.

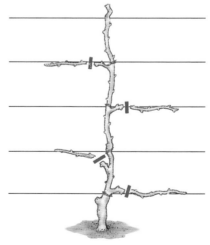

6 **Shorten new tip growth** on the main stem by a half in early winter. Cut back each side branch to 2 good buds.

GRAPES

Climbers & wall plants *see page 130* | **Common fruit problems** *see page 266* | **Gardening under glass** *see page 364*

Aftercare

When plants start into growth in late winter or early spring, soak them well so water penetrates to the roots. Mulch with well-rotted manure and water every week in hot weather. A vine planted outside the greenhouse may also need watering in hot, dry weather. As the grapes ripen, reduce watering to avoid splitting the fruit.

You should feed the vines when growth begins; apply a tomato fertilizer every fortnight. Feed weekly when flowers appear in spring until the fruit changes colour.

To help the grapes set fruit, tap the flowers daily to disperse some pollen. Some varieties, such as muscats, need more care: gently stroke the flowers with your cupped hands to transfer the pollen to the stigmas.

When the fruit appears, thin bunches in midsummer to allow each grape room to grow. Avoid handling the fruit; snip out smaller grapes from the centre of congested clumps with scissors to leave a pencil-sized gap between each grape. Open the vents or doors on sunny days to stop the air becoming too hot or humid.

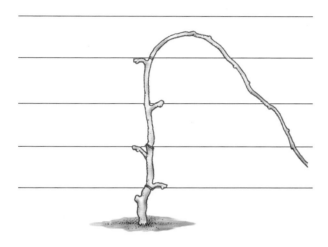

7 **Undo the ties** in midwinter, except for one about one third up the main stem. Bend it over so it almost touches the ground. Once the buds begin to swell, tie the main stem back into position.

THIRD & SUBSEQUENT YEARS

8 **Cut back growing tips** 2 leaves beyond the flower trusses as they appear in spring. Tie in each fruiting side branch as they develop. Remove sub-side branches to 1 leaf. In summer, thin the fruit.

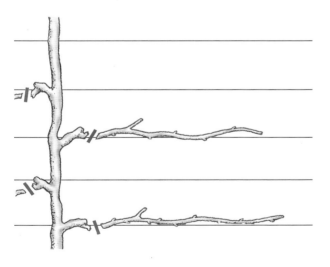

9 **Remove the growing tip** of the leading shoot in summer; in midwinter cut it back to within 2.5cm (1in) of the new growth. Cut back to 1 bud all side branches produced that year.

Productive grape vines are limited in choice in cool climates, but you can overcome such restrictions by growing vines under the protection of a cool or heated greenhouse.

Melons

Sweet melons are trailing or climbing tropical plants. They can be grown successfully as annuals in cool climates from seed sown in spring in a warm greenhouse, or outdoors if given some protection. There are three main groups: cantaloupes usually have thick green or orange, rough skins that are often ribbed; musk melons have netted skins; while winter melons (also called honeydews) have smooth skins that are often bright yellow.

GROWING MELONS OUTDOORS

Cantaloupe varieties, such as 'Charantais', are slightly tougher than other melons, making them ideal for raising outdoors under cloches or in unheated polytunnels and cold frames. Start them from seed sown indoors in mid-spring for planting out into fertile, well-drained soil in late spring and for picking at summer's end. They need plenty of care – water and feed them regularly. You will also need to train the stems, thin the fruit, and ventilate the crop.

There are many melon varieties to choose from; ones that are mildew resistant are a good choice. You can train them over archways, or let them trail from raised beds or growing bags.

GROWING A MELON IN A COLD FRAME

1 Plant each seedling melon with the soil ball 2.5cm (1in) above ground in late spring. Make the hole deep and wide enough for the rootball. Space the plants 1–1.2m (3–4ft) apart. Water in, but avoid wetting the stems.

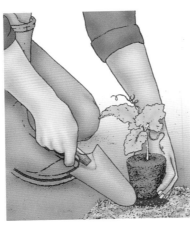

2 Remove all but the 4 strongest shoots in early summer, then train each of these shoots in opposite directions. Keep well ventilated in warm weather and when the flowers need to be pollinated, in summer.

3 Remove all but the best 4 fruit when they are about the size of gooseberries. Cut back the sub-sideshoots at 2 or 3 leaves beyond the retained fruit. Pinch out the growing points on all 4 stems.

4 Protect each developing melon from the soil and prevent it from rotting by placing it on a tile or on a piece of wood. Through summer, keep the plants thoroughly watered. Feed the fruit every 7–10 days with diluted liquid fertilizer. The fruit ripen from late summer, when circular cracking appears near the stalk and they smell sweet.

Pollination *see page 241* | **Container gardening** *see page 338* | **Gardening under glass** *see page 364*

GROWING MELONS IN A GREENHOUSE

A heated greenhouse with a minimum night temperature of 16°C (61°F) is perfect for growing musk and winter melons. Traditionally, young melon plants would have been planted directly into the border, but it is now easier and more flexible to plant two per growing bag.

The plants are grown as single cordons up canes, with the side branches trained along a network of horizontal support wires until they reach the top of the greenhouse. A structure that has a height of no less than 2m (6ft) up the side wall and to the eaves is perfect.

To guarantee a good indoor crop, it is best to pollinate the fruit by hand. Brush a male flower over four female flowers. You can identify a female flower by the embryonic fruit behind the flower. Do this in summer when there are at least four female flowers on separate side branches.

When ripe, melons have the typical melon scent and circular cracking appears near the stalk. The end farthest from the stalk should yield slightly to finger pressure. They should part easily from the stalk when lifted.

SUPPORTING RIPENING MELONS

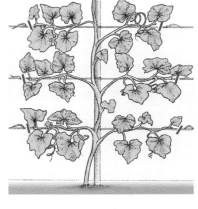

To stop the melons from breaking off under their own weight, provide slings as supports. Use melon nets made from squares of 5cm (2in) netting, and tie them to the roof rafters or to wires when the fruit are the size of tennis balls.

GROWING A MELON IN A GREENHOUSE

1 Plant seedlings raised in a heated greenhouse from late winter onwards. Space them 38cm (15in) apart, with the tops of the rootballs 2.5cm (1in) above the soil surface. Do not firm the soil. Keep at 16°C (61°F) and damp down the paths regularly to keep up the humidity.

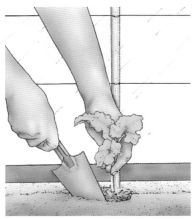

2 Tie the central stem of each plant onto a cane for support as it grows. Remove the growing point at 2m (6ft) in order to encourage side branches to grow, then tie these to horizontal wires and cut back each one at 5 leaves.

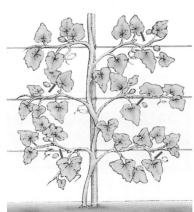

3 Cut back the resulting sub-side branches to 2 leaves beyond the flower. When the flowers need pollinating in summer and as the fruit begins to ripen, ventilate fully to maintain a drier atmosphere.

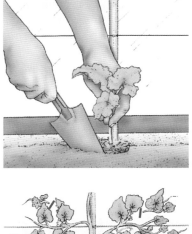

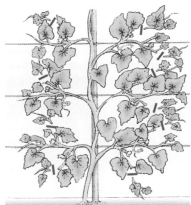

4 Thin the fruit when they are the size of walnuts to 4 of the same size on each plant, removing all the others. Water thoroughly and give a liquid feed every 7–10 days, or every time you water if in a growing bag. Support the fruit as necessary (*see above*). The fruit ripens from summer to early autumn.

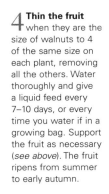

239

TREE FRUIT

Tree fruit encompass some of the most popular fruit grown by gardeners. Also referred to as top fruit in the horticultural industry, this large group includes plants that if left to their own devices grow into trees or very large shrubs. Apples, pears, plums, and cherries, along with others that once were considered exotic but are now grown more widely, such as figs, peaches, nectarines, and apricots, are all tree fruit. Many tree fruit can be raised in containers, making growing fruit possible for anyone, whatever the space available; lots of dwarf and compact varieties are bred specifically for containers.

Fruit trees in the garden

If you have space, you can establish an orchard of full-size trees, but it is more likely that your choice will be restricted to compact varieties or restricted forms, grown as fans, cordons, or espaliers and trained on horizontal wires fixed to a fence or a wall.

In a cool climate, the shelter of a wall can be beneficial to some tree fruit, and it helps the fruit to ripen effectively before the end of the growing season. Indeed, a warm, sunny wall in a sheltered garden is necessary for the more tender fruit to thrive.

All fruit trees require pruning for three reasons: to restrict growth, remain productive, and to keep an attractive shape. Thinning of fruit also ensures that the best possible fruit is obtained.

Most fruit trees do best in a sunny site free from severe frosts, especially when plants are in blossom; hardier plants include the Morello cherry. They all prefer well-prepared, free-draining, moisture-retentive soil. Tender tree fruit, such as nectarines or peaches, may be raised in cooler gardens in a warm or unheated greenhouse.

Fruit trees in the open garden can be very ornamental as well as productive. They do not require a great deal of space if you choose a suitable variety and appropriate rootstock.

Restricted forms of fruit trees, such as fans, cordons, or espaliers, make good use of vacant spaces on walls and fences, and they can also be used to create decorative screens or barriers in the garden.

Pollination

For fruit to be produced, flowers need to be pollinated. This is the process in which pollen is transferred from the male part of a flower (anther) to the female part (stigma) in order to fertilize the ovule.

More often than not, pollination is carried out by bees or other insects, although pollen can also be transported by the wind. In some circumstances, it may be necessary to carry this out yourself to ensure that fertilization has taken place in as many blossoms as possible.

Fertilization

Peaches, nectarines, and some plums and apricots are self-fertile and can be pollinated by their own flowers. Apples, pears, and most sweet cherries are self-incompatible, which means that they will not set fruit without being pollinated by a different variety of the same fruit. The other variety should flower at the same time and be planted nearby to enable both trees to fertilize each other.

Pollination groups

To enable you to choose an appropriate partner for your chosen fruit tree, apples, pears, plums, and cherries are split into different pollination groups, depending on when they flower. Pollination group 1 includes the earliest-flowering trees. Varieties in the same pollination group can be grown together, as can varieties in adjacent groups, as long as the flowering periods overlap. When selecting fruit trees, take your time to research different varieties and ask a specialist nursery to recommend two or more types that can be grown together successfully.

Incompatibility groups

Although plenty of varieties of the same fruit can cross-pollinate, there are some pears, cherries and plums that will not, even if grown with a variety from the same pollination group. This quality is known as cross-incompatibility and the varieties are divided into incompatibility groups. If you choose a plant that is in an incompatibility group, it will cross-pollinate only with a variety that flowers at the same time from a different or adjacent group.

Ineffective pollinators

Even though not strictly cross-incompatible, some fruit trees are poor pollinators. This can be due to a number of reasons, including the genetic make-up of the plant or its irregular flowering. A successful harvest can be achieved from such a plant by growing it with two other suitable varieties to provide the necessary pollen.

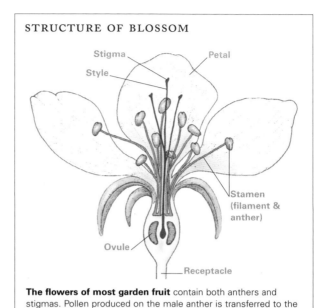

STRUCTURE OF BLOSSOM

The flowers of most garden fruit contain both anthers and stigmas. Pollen produced on the male anther is transferred to the female stigma, and travels down the style to fertilize the ovule.

HAND POLLINATION

1 **Test if pollen** is being shed by drawing a fingertip over the anthers; they should deposit yellow grains. When it has been warm and dry for 2–3 days, pollinate at midday. Transfer pollen gently from the anthers to the stigmas with a soft camel-hair brush or cotton wool on a matchstick.

2 **If compatible flowers** are on separate plants, strip the petals from a ripe flower, then press its centre against the centre of another flower to pollinate it. Hand pollinate every day, if possible, until flowering is over.

Planting fruit trees

Plant dormant bare-root fruit trees – available from good garden centres and specialist fruit nurseries – from late autumn to early spring. If the plants cannot be planted right away, heel them into the ground (*see box, right*) until you are ready. Container-grown trees are available, and can be planted, all year round. There are several different tree forms (*see page 222*).

How to plant

First weed and dig the soil, preferably four weeks before planting. Dig a square metre (10 sq ft) area for each tree rather than the entire site, unless trees are being planted very closely. Add plenty of organic matter if the soil is heavy or sandy. Just before planting, rake in a balanced general fertilizer at 50g (2oz) per square metre (10 sq ft).

You can use angled or upright stakes to support fruit trees. Angled stakes are ideal for bush trees or those bought container grown, but bare-root fruit trees prefer vertical stakes (*see page 91*). Both should be hammered into the ground before planting – at least 60cm (24in) deep on light soils. For vertical stakes, standard trees need them 2.5m (8ft) long; half-standards 2m (6ft) long; and bush trees 1–1.2m (3–4ft) long.

HEELING IN FRUIT TREES

Plant bare-root trees as soon as possible, but if a delay is unavoidable, dig a shallow trench and lay the tree in the trench at an angle. Cover the roots with moist soil.

Use soft ties for young trees and buckle ties for larger trees. Put a single tie, 2.5cm (1in) from the stake top, for bushes; two ties, at the top and halfway down, for standards and half-standards; and three ties for pyramidal forms.

PLANTING A FRUIT TREE

1 **Trim off** broken or long taproots, using secateurs. If the roots are dry, soak them for an hour before planting.

2 **Stake appropriately** for the type of tree (*see above*) – here, a rootballed plant. Do not plant too deeply.

3 **Replace the soil** and firm gently. Water well and mulch.

Apples & pears

These favourite tree fruit can be grown as a restricted form against a wall or fence, such as a cordon or espalier (*see pages 246 and 248*), or as a freestanding tree (*see below*).

Where to grow apples & pears

Both fruit prefer a well-drained, slightly acidic loam but tolerate a wide range of soils. Cooking apples like heavier soils, as long as they are not waterlogged. Improve light, sandy soils with organic matter; avoid thin soils over chalk. The trees thrive in a sunny, sheltered, frost-free location. If necessary, use windbreaks, or train plants against a wall.

Choosing trees & rootstocks

Apples and pear varieties are grafted onto rootstocks – a special root system – which control the tree's growth rate and its eventual size. The place at which they join, on the main stem, is called the graft union. The main apple rootstocks, in order of size of tree they produce, are M27 (1.2–1.8m/4–6ft), M9 (1.8–3m/6–10ft), M26 (2.4–3.6m/8–11ft), MM106 (3.6–4.5m/8–14¾ft), MM111 (4–4.5m/12–14¾ft), and M25 (over 4.5m/14¾ft). The main pear rootstocks are Quince C (2.4–3.6m/8–11ft), EMH (2.7–3.3m/9–10½ft), Quince A (3.6–4.5m/8–14¾ft), and Pyrus (6m/20ft).

Choose a rootstock to suit the size of your garden and how you will train the tree. Smaller rootstocks are good for restricted forms, but need fertile soil and plenty of water. Larger rootstocks are better for freestanding trees and large gardens, giving higher yields.

Freestanding trees

Freestanding trees include dwarf bush, bush, half-standard, and standard trees; all need to be trained as open-centred plants (*see below*). Dwarf pyramid trees

FORMATIVE TRAINING OF A FREESTANDING APPLE OR PEAR TREE

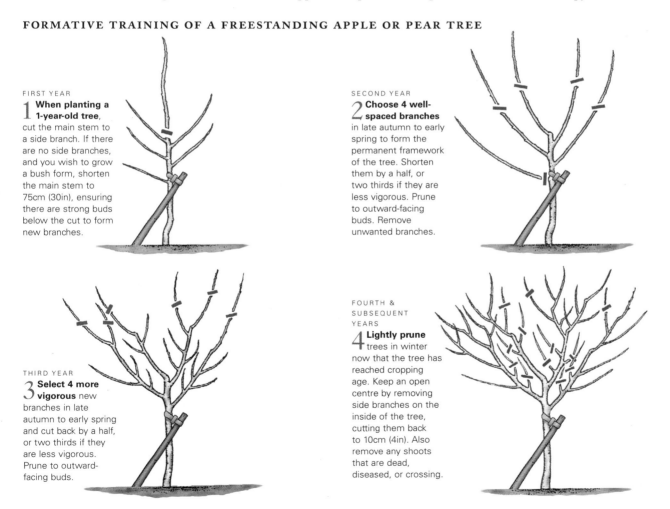

FIRST YEAR

1 When planting a 1-year-old tree, cut the main stem to a side branch. If there are no side branches, and you wish to grow a bush form, shorten the main stem to 75cm (30in), ensuring there are strong buds below the cut to form new branches.

SECOND YEAR

2 Choose 4 well-spaced branches in late autumn to early spring to form the permanent framework of the tree. Shorten them by a half, or two thirds if they are less vigorous. Prune to outward-facing buds. Remove unwanted branches.

THIRD YEAR

3 Select 4 more vigorous new branches in late autumn to early spring and cut back by a half, or two thirds if they are less vigorous. Prune to outward-facing buds.

FOURTH & SUBSEQUENT YEARS

4 Lightly prune trees in winter now that the tree has reached cropping age. Keep an open centre by removing side branches on the inside of the tree, cutting them back to 10cm (4in). Also remove any shoots that are dead, diseased, or crossing.

(*see page 250*) are an anomaly as they are freestanding but grown as a restricted form. The spacing of freestanding apples and pears varies according to tree form, assuming that an appropriate rootstock is chosen for the form of tree. Restricted tree forms are discussed later in the chapter (*see pages 246–251*).

For bush forms, space plants 2.5–3m (8–10ft) apart if they are dwarf forms; otherwise set at 3–5m (10–15ft) apart, or more for a larger rootstock like MM106 or MM111. For standard and half-standard trees on large rootstocks like M25, space at least 6m (20ft) apart.

Plant pears that are on Quince C rootstocks 2.7m (9ft) apart. Varieties on EMH or Quince A stocks should be 3.5m (11ft) apart, those on Pyrus stocks 6m (20ft) apart.

Pruning for fruit

Once the formative training stage is over, it should not be necessary to prune the branch framework. On a cropping tree, the only pruning required is the careful management of fruit buds and the branches they grow on.

Most apples and pears fruit on short, stubby spurs found on two-year-old wood. You therefore need to maintain a mixture of side branches at different stages of growth to be cut back after fruiting. This is achieved by spur and renewal pruning (*see boxes, below*). Renewal pruning is best reserved for the tree's outer branches where there is space for extra growth, while spur pruning is most useful for restricted forms. Branches will also need to be removed if they are dead, diseased, or crossing.

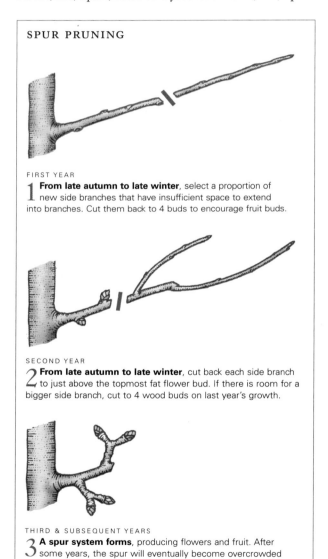

SPUR PRUNING

FIRST YEAR
1 **From late autumn to late winter**, select a proportion of new side branches that have insufficient space to extend into branches. Cut them back to 4 buds to encourage fruit buds.

SECOND YEAR
2 **From late autumn to late winter**, cut back each side branch to just above the topmost fat flower bud. If there is room for a bigger side branch, cut to 4 wood buds on last year's growth.

THIRD & SUBSEQUENT YEARS
3 **A spur system forms**, producing flowers and fruit. After some years, the spur will eventually become overcrowded and need to be thinned in winter (*see page 248*).

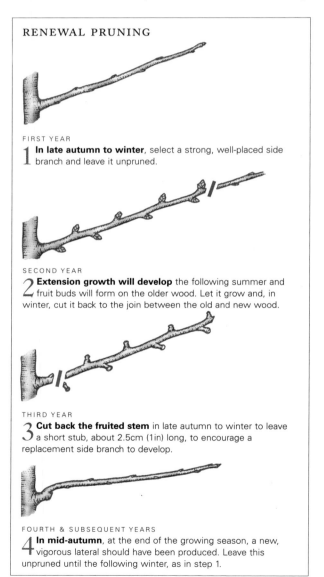

RENEWAL PRUNING

FIRST YEAR
1 **In late autumn to winter**, select a strong, well-placed side branch and leave it unpruned.

SECOND YEAR
2 **Extension growth will develop** the following summer and fruit buds will form on the older wood. Let it grow and, in winter, cut it back to the join between the old and new wood.

THIRD YEAR
3 **Cut back the fruited stem** in late autumn to winter to leave a short stub, about 2.5cm (1in) long, to encourage a replacement side branch to develop.

FOURTH & SUBSEQUENT YEARS
4 **In mid-autumn**, at the end of the growing season, a new, vigorous lateral should have been produced. Leave this unpruned until the following winter, as in step 1.

APPLE & PEAR CORDONS

Usually planted at an angle, cordons consist of one or more stems with many spurs (*see page 244*). Several cordons can be squeezed into a tiny garden, making it easy to overcome problems of cross-pollination.

Choosing rootstocks & plants

On fertile soils, apples grown on M9 rootstocks are ideal. For less fertile soils, choose vigorous rootstocks such as M26 and MM106. Quince C is the best rootstock for pear cordons on fertile soil, while Quince A is more tolerant of poorer soils. Partially trained one- or two-year-old trees are sold by nurseries, which can reduce the time taken to establish a cropping tree. They also make a more instant screen if the cordons are to be grown along a boundary.

Spacing apple & pear cordons

Cordons need to be spaced about 75cm–1m (2½–3ft) apart. Use the wider spacing on poor soils. The plants receive the best light if planted in a row that runs north–south.

Planting & supporting cordons

If you are using a fence or wall, secure three horizontal, heavy-duty, 12-gauge wires held parallel between straining bolts 60cm (24in) apart to make the permanent support.

On planting, leave 15cm (6in) between the wire support and the tree, and ensure the graft union (*see page 243*) is above soil level when you plant with the stem at the required angle. Lean each tree into the vertical support and tie to a 2m (6ft) bamboo cane, which should be secured at the required angle to the wire support.

Pruning & training

In their first few years, pruning concentrates on forming the cordon framework (*see below*). You should remove all flowers in spring from a cordon in its first two years so that the tree can put its energy instead into growing new branches and filling the framework.

Once the framework is in place, prune cordons through the growing season to encourage fruiting buds and to keep the trees within limits (*see facing page*). If there is too much

FORMATIVE PRUNING OF A CORDON

FIRST YEAR

1 Plant the 1-year-old tree from late autumn to early spring against a bamboo cane secured at 45 degrees to wire supports. Cut back any side branches to 4 strong buds. Do not prune the central stem.

SECOND & SUBSEQUENT YEARS

2 Remove flowers in spring to stop the tree fruiting in its second year. Stubby shoots called spurs should have formed on the previously pruned side branches. In subsequent years, do not remove the flowers.

3 Cut back side branches longer than 23cm (9in) arising from the central stem to 3 good leaves in late summer, ignoring the basal cluster of leaves. Prune sideshoots arising from existing spur systems to 1 leaf beyond the basal cluster.

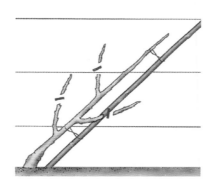

4 Just before leaf fall, if any new growth develops from the pruned shoots, cut it back to the old wood.

CORDON FORMS

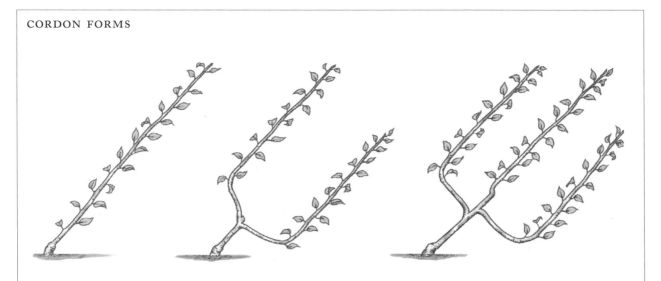

Cordons may be single or multiple, with 2, 3, or more arms, trained vertically or at an angle. Train a multiple cordon initially in the same way as the first horizontal arms of an espalier. Then treat each arm as a

single cordon. Vertically trained cordons are usually more vigorous and less fruitful than those trained at 45 degrees. The angle can be lowered further to increase fruit-bud formation or to check vigour.

secondary growth after late summer pruning, delay to early autumn instead. This secondary growth will be damaged by frost if not removed in autumn, but if too much is removed it will weaken the tree.

Winter prune to renovate cordons if they have made poor growth. The central stem can be pruned back by one third to promote the development of extra side branches. This time of year is also best for thinning out overcrowded spur systems (*see following page*).

Cordons are ideally suited to smaller gardens because they can be grown against a wall or fence, or planted against a wire fence in the open to create a fruiting barrier or divider in the kitchen garden.

MAINTAINING A FRUITING CORDON

1 **In late spring**, cut back new extension growth on the main stem to its origin when it passes beyond the top wire and reaches the required height of about 2.2m (7ft).

2 **In late summer**, remove the new leading shoot that has grown in its place at the tip of the central stem, cutting it back to 2.5cm (1in). Prune back to 3 leaves all mature side branches longer than 23cm (9in) growing directly from the main stem. Cut back sideshoots from existing spurs to 1 leaf beyond the basal cluster.

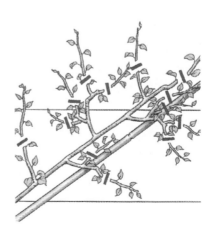

APPLE & PEAR ESPALIERS

These restricted tree forms consist of a central stem with tiers of horizontal, fruiting arms trained either side. Grown against a fence or wall, or on wires stretched between stout, vertical posts, they make an attractive garden feature, providing verdant colour for many months of the year, flowers in the spring, and attractive, delicious fruit in autumn. The good looks of the espalier make it more ornamental than the cordon, but it does require more space and maintenance.

Choosing rootstocks & plants

If you have reasonable soil in the garden, espalier apples grafted onto M26 rootstocks are best. For a site with poorer soil, or if you want to grow a slightly more vigorous plant, choose trees that have been grafted onto MM106 rootstocks. To clothe larger walls, trees grafted onto MM111 rootstocks grow to a bigger size. Pear rootstocks can be chosen as for cordons (*see page 246*).

You can start espaliers off from one-year-old trees or save time and buy partially trained trees. Many specialist fruit nurseries supply older trees, often with two tiers and a main stem, ready for the gardener to train further arms. You will have less choice of varieties, but it reduces the time taken to establish a cropping tree and it also creates a more instant feature or screen.

Espalier fruit trees, like this pear, are some of the most elegant and decorative of tree-fruit forms. They can be grown in small spaces and may be incorporated into a wide range of potager, formal, or town gardens. Harvesting the fruit is very easy.

OVERCROWDED SPUR SYSTEMS

On older trees, spur systems can become overlong, overlapping or congested. Thin out the weaker buds first, and cut back some spur systems to 2 or 3 fruit buds, from late autumn to late winter.

Spacing apple & pear espaliers

Space espaliers that have been grown on M26 rootstocks 3–3.5m (10–11ft) apart, trees on MM106 rootstocks 3.5–4.5m (11–14ft) apart, and apples on MM111 rootstocks 4.5–5.5m (14–18ft) apart. Plant pears on Quince A rootstocks 3.5–4.5m (11–14¾ft) apart and those on smaller Quince C rootstocks 3–3.6m (10–11½ft) apart.

Planting & supporting espaliers

Before planting the trees, first construct a support system using 10-gauge galvanized wires stretched between straining bolts. If you are buying partially trained trees, use the arms of the trees to guide the placing of the horizontal wires; usually these should be between 38–45cm (15–18in) apart.

To allow room for the trunk to grow, make sure that each tree is planted 15cm (6in) away from the supports, leaning slightly towards the support. Also check that the graft union (*see page 243*) remains above ground.

Pruning & training

To form espaliers, prune your trees in winter to encourage shoots that can form new tiers (*see facing page*). On planting, a one-year-old tree should be cut down, leaving three buds that are well placed to form a central vertical leader and two arms extending in opposite directions.

In the first growing season, train the first two 'arms' temporarily on canes at an angle to encourage extension growth; laid horizontally, branches fruit well but are less vigorous. If the arms are weak, you can angle them slightly more upright to prompt more extension growth.

FORMATIVE PRUNING OF AN ESPALIER

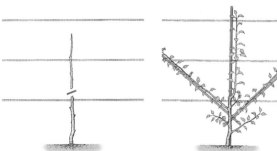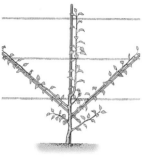

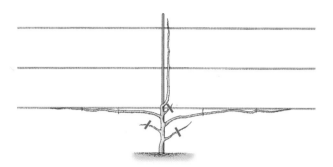

FIRST YEAR

1 Cut down to 38cm (15in) after planting in late autumn to early spring. Keep 3 good buds.

2 Train the top bud shoot up a vertical cane and the 2 lower shoots at 45 degrees in summer.

3 Lower the 2 side branches to the horizontal in late autumn, and tie them carefully to the wires with soft twine. Cut back surplus side branches on the main stem to 3 buds.

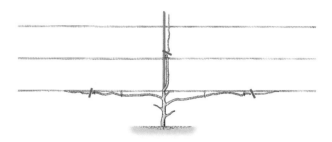

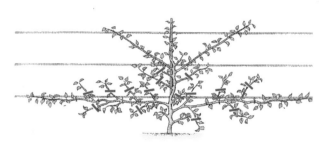

4 Cut back the central stem in winter to within 45cm (18in) of the lower branch and at a wire, keeping 3 good buds. If growth is weak, prune back the 2 branches by up to one third, cutting to downward-pointing buds.

SECOND & SUBSEQUENT YEARS

5 Train the next tier the following year from midsummer to early autumn, as in step 2. Cut back sideshoots growing from the central stem and horizontal branches to 3 leaves.

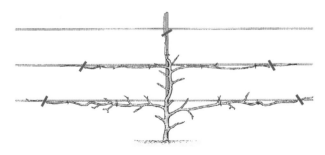

6 Cut back the central stem in winter, as in step 4. Tie down the new horizontal branches, as in step 3. Prune back the branches by up to one third, cutting to downward-pointing buds.

7 Cut back new tip growths to old wood in late spring, when the espalier has filled its allotted space. Maintain thereafter as for cordons (*see page 247*).

Continue formative pruning and training until the desired number of arms, usually between four and five tiers, have been produced on each espalier. In a good year, if growth is strong, you could leave the central stem unpruned so that more tiers are formed next season.

Once the espalier has reached its mature shape, the new terminal growths on the horizontal and vertical arms should be cut back to their origins, where they join the old wood, every year in late spring. From then on, carry out summer pruning of the side branches in the same way as for mature cordons (*see page 247*). Prune in winter to renovate cordons, if necessary.

After a few years of fruiting, the spur systems can become complicated and should be simplified by thinning weak buds, or by removing those on the shaded side of the system (*see facing page*).

APPLE & PEAR DWARF PYRAMIDS

The dwarf pyramid was developed by commercial fruit growers as an easier method of producing apples and pears intensively. The pear, in particular, when grown on Quince rootstocks, responds well to this method of training. With apples, M9 and M26 rootstocks are ideal.

The aim is to produce a tree about 2.2m (7ft) tall with a branch spread of about 1.2m (4ft) at the base of the canopy, which tapers to the top to form a pyramidal shape.

It is vital to keep such a closely planted and compact tree form under control – by summer pruning, early cropping, complete removal of vigorous, upright shoots, and by growing on the right rootstock.

Planting, spacing & supporting dwarf pyramids

Use single stakes if planting one or two trees. Support a row of trees by running two horizontal wires between two posts, one at a height of 45cm (18in) and the other at

FORMATIVE PRUNING OF A DWARF PYRAMID

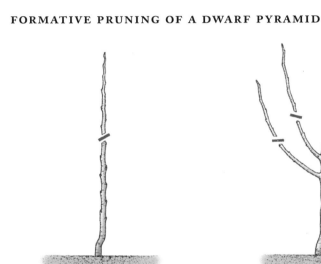

FIRST YEAR

1 Cut back one-year-old trees to a bud within 50cm (20in) of soil level at planting.

SECOND YEAR

2 Cut the central stem to 23cm (9in) of its new growth, to a bud. Prune the main branches to 20cm (8in) of their new growth.

3 Cut side branches not required for the tree framework to 3 leaves in late summer. Cut sideshoots to 1 leaf after the basal cluster.

THIRD & SUBSEQUENT YEARS

4 Cut the central stem in winter to a bud on the opposite side to the previous pruning. Otherwise repeat as for step 2.

5 Prune side branches and sideshoots in late summer, as in step 3. Cut back the tips of the main branches to 6 leaves.

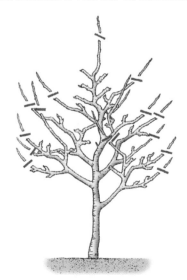

6 Prune the central stem in winter, as in step 4. Shorten main branches as needed to downward-facing buds to keep them horizontal.

THE MATURE DWARF PYRAMID TREE

When the tree has reached a height of about 2.2m (7ft), cut back the central stem to its origin each year in late spring. Maintain the central stem and retain the pyramid shape by pruning and removal of vigorous shoots. Thin spurs as necessary (*see page 248*).

Dwarf pyramid forms of apple and pear trees make a very ornamental feature and are especially suited to smaller spaces if grown singly. The pyramid or conical shape makes it very easy to pick the ripe fruit.

90cm (36in). Tie the trees to the wires with soft string or tree ties. Pyramids on M26 or Quince C rootstocks should be spaced 1.2–1.5m (4–5ft) apart, and those on M9 or Quince A rootstocks 1.5–2m (5–6ft) apart. Adopt the wider spacing on fertile soils. In large gardens or orchards, space rows of trees 2.2m (7ft) apart.

Pruning & training

On planting, prune to encourage four or five vigorous shoots to grow (*see facing page*). Cut them back in the second winter to begin forming a pyramid shape; when pruning the central leader, cut to a bud that points in the opposite direction to the first pruning. Summer prune side branches to encourage the formation of fruiting spurs. Winter prune in subsequent years to maintain a dwarf pyramid shape by cutting the branches to downward-facing buds. Thin sideshoots to stop the tree being crowded with branches. Every summer, shorten sideshoots back to three leaves.

CARE OF APPLES & PEARS

Besides pruning, apples and pears need year-round attention to keep them healthy and productive (*see following page*). If your garden suffers from severe late frosts, protect flowers and emerging fruitlets in spring with fleece, where practical.

Harvesting

There is no exact time for picking apples and pears, since this is dependent on variety, the season, and the location of your garden. Generally, you can tell when a fruit is ready to pick by holding it in the palm of your hand, lifting upwards, and twisting it away gently. If the fruit comes off the spur easily, without leaving behind any damaged wood, then it should be ready to pick. Test this further on apples by cutting a fruit open to see whether the pips have turned from white to brown.

Fruit that falls naturally from the tree, known as windfalls, is another indicator that fruit is ready, as is a

MAINTAINING AN APPLE OR PEAR TREE

1 In early spring, feed with a general-purpose fertilizer at a rate of 50g (2oz) per square metre (10 sq ft) over the root area and rake in. Lack of nutrients may hamper the formation of fruit buds, leading to a poor crop.

2 In mid-spring, mulch newly planted and young trees with a 5cm (2in) deep layer of well-rotted manure or garden compost. Spread it over the root area to a radius of about 45cm (18in), keeping it clear of the stem to prevent it from rotting.

3 In summer, water young and newly planted trees copiously every 10 days in drought. Lack of moisture can affect yields and formation of next year's fruit. Carry out any summer pruning as necessary.

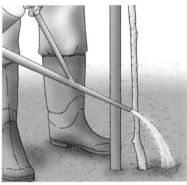

4 In summer, thin overcrowded fruit clusters to avoid small fruit. Trees shed some fruit naturally in early summer, but you may have to thin later in midsummer. First remove small or misshapen fruit, including the large, central king apple if it is damaged. Less thinning is necessary on pear trees.

5 Before harvest, maypoling is a way of supporting a bumper crop of fruit on a small tree, to stop the branches bowing and possibly breaking. Support each branch with a rope attached to a central, stout post.

6 In winter, maintain a weed- and grass-free circle, 60cm (24in) in diameter, around the base of each tree. Carry out any winter pruning as necessary. The maintenance cycle then begins again in early spring with feeding around the roots.

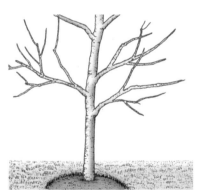

change in colour. Generally, pears turn from a dark to lighter green, while apples tend to become brighter.

As a rule of thumb, fruit is best picked when under-ripe – just after midsummer for early-season pears, late summer for mid-season pears, and early autumn for late-season pears. Early apples may be ready as soon as midsummer, while later varieties are on the tree in mid-autumn. To avoid bruising, handle the fruit gently and collect it in a container lined with soft material.

Avoid storing ripe or early fruit, which are best eaten fresh. Keep fruit in a cool (3–7°C/37–45°F), dark place where air flows freely, such as a garage, cellar, or shed. Wrap apples in newspaper, but leave pears unwrapped, and place them in old fruit crates or a purpose-built storage unit (like a chest of drawers with slatted trays). Check the fruit regularly and remove any that are damaged or rotting.

Biennial bearing

Poor yields often follow the year after a heavy crop, and trees can get into a pattern of biennial bearing. To prevent this, try removing half of the fruit buds in the spring after a poor crop. This causes the tree to produce a more modest crop, leaving enough energy to form sufficient fruiting buds for the following year.

Plums

Plums and closely related fruit, such as gages, bullaces, damsons, mirabelle plums, and cherry plums can be grown as freestanding bushes, half-standards, or standards (*see page 222*). In smaller gardens, plums can be grown in a restricted form, such as a fan against a wall or fence, or as a pyramid (*for both, see following page*). They are not suitable for growing as cordons or espaliers.

Where to grow plums

Plums prefer a moisture-retentive, well-drained soil with a pH of 6.5–7.2 in a sunny, sheltered site. Gages in particular need lots of sun to produce tasty fruit so are best trained against a warm and sunny wall. Plums tolerate some shade, but will not grow on a cold wall.

As many plum varieties flower early, choose a sheltered, frost-free site. In frosty areas, grow the tree against a vertical structure, such as a wall, which makes it easy to cover the frost-prone flowers and developing fruit.

Choosing trees

Plum trees are grafted onto rootstocks (*see page 243*), and it is therefore necessary to select a rootstock based on the local soil conditions, the space available in your garden, and on how you intend to grow the tree.

Best for growing as a bush, fan, or pyramid form in a small garden is Pixy, a dwarfing rootstock. It requires fertile soil and frequent watering during dry periods. St Julien A is a semi-vigorous rootstock and will thrive in most soils. It is ideal for bushes, fans, and half-standards. If you have an orchard, the Brompton rootstock produces a very vigorous, standard tree.

If you intend to grow a standard, half-standard, bush, or fan plum, you can buy a partly trained, two- or three-year-old tree from the nursery, which saves time. Pyramid plums are best started from a one-year-old tree. Trees grown on a Pixy or St Julien A rootstock can be expected to begin producing fruit between their third and sixth year.

PLANTING & THINNING A PLUM TREE

1 Prepare the soil in autumn, clearing away any perennial weeds. Lightly fork in 85g (3oz) of a general-purpose fertilizer and 50g (2oz) of bonemeal per square metre (10 sq ft).

2 Drive in a stake if the tree is to grow in the open. Use an upright stake for bare-root trees, or a stake at 45 degrees for container-grown trees or those with a rootball. For fan-trained plums, construct a system of wires on the wall. Plant the tree between late autumn and early spring and tie it to the stake or wire support.

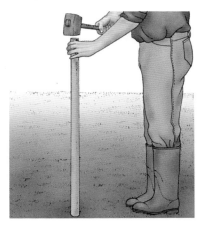

3 Mulch around the tree with a 2.5–5cm (1–2in) layer of well-rotted garden compost or manure after planting. Apply a general-purpose fertilizer at 110g (4oz) per square metre (10 sq ft). A month later, apply sulphate of ammonia at 25g (1oz) at the same rate.

4 After 3–6 years the first crop will form in late spring. Thin heavy crops when they are the size of hazelnuts and once the stones have formed within the fruit. Repeat when the fruit are twice this size, to leave them 5–8cm (2–3in) apart on the branches – or slightly more for larger varieties.

FORMATIVE PRUNING OF A PYRAMID PLUM TREE

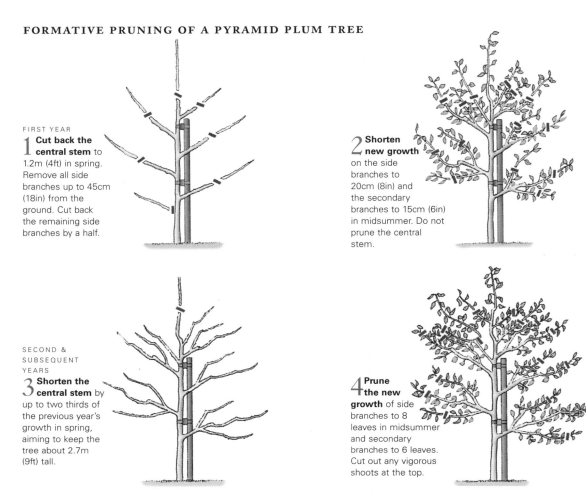

FIRST YEAR

1 Cut back the central stem to 1.2m (4ft) in spring. Remove all side branches up to 45cm (18in) from the ground. Cut back the remaining side branches by a half.

2 Shorten new growth on the side branches to 20cm (8in) and the secondary branches to 15cm (6in) in midsummer. Do not prune the central stem.

SECOND & SUBSEQUENT YEARS

3 Shorten the central stem by up to two thirds of the previous year's growth in spring, aiming to keep the tree about 2.7m (9ft) tall.

4 Prune the new growth of side branches to 8 leaves in midsummer and secondary branches to 6 leaves. Cut out any vigorous shoots at the top.

Planting & spacing

If planting a fan-trained plum or gage, first install a series of horizontal training wires to the wall or fence, spacing them 15cm (6in) apart. Standard plums and gages grafted onto Brompton rootstocks should be spaced 5.4–6m (18–20ft) apart, while bushes, half-standards, and fan-trained plums on St Julien A stocks can be planted every 3.5–4.5m (11–14ft). Allow 3–3.5m (10–11ft) between plums on Pixy stocks, and the same distance for pyramids on St Julien A rootstocks.

Pruning & training

To avoid silver leaf disease, to which plums are particularly prone (*see page 272*), never prune when dormant in winter. Wait until bud break in spring.

The process for pruning and training a pyramid plum is shown above. If growing a bush, half-standard, or standard plum, cut back the central stem of a one-year-old tree to a bud – at a height of 90cm (36in) for a bush, 1.5m (5ft) for a pyramid, 1.35m (4½ft) for a half-standard, and

2m (6ft) for a standard. To thicken up the stem, cut all side branches back to 8cm (3in), and in midsummer select four or five of these and cut the rest back to four or five leaves. When pruning side branches for a pyramid plum, always cut to downward-facing buds to keep growth of new branches horizontal.

In early spring of the following year, prune the selected branches left unpruned from last year, cutting back each by a half to an outward-facing bud. Cut back all other side branches to the main stem.

In summer, pull up any suckering shoots that appear from ground level (*see page 97*) and snip out any shoots on the trunk below the first set of main branches. In subsequent years, repeat this process, but allow more secondary branches to develop to fill the space. You should eventually aim for about eight, well-spaced branches growing from the main trunk.

The formative pruning of a fan-trained plum is the same as for a peach fan (*see page 262*), but changes as the tree matures (*see facing page, above*). The aim is to

FORMATIVE PRUNING OF A PLUM FAN

FIRST THREE YEARS

1 Prune as for a peach fan, extending the framework to fill in the wall space (*see page 262*). Prune only when the tree is in growth to reduce the possibility of silver leaf disease.

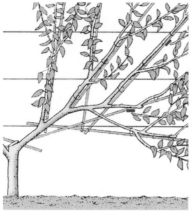

FOURTH & SUBSEQUENT YEARS

2 As growth begins in spring, pinch out shoots growing directly towards or away from the wall between your thumb and forefinger, leaving only those that grow in the direction of the fan, parallel to the wall.

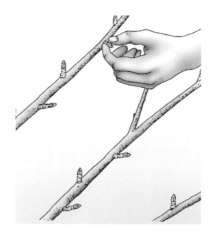

3 Pinch out the growing points of shoots not wanted for the framework when they have made 6 or 7 leaves, from early to midsummer, as new shoots appear. This begins to form the fruit-bearing spur system.

4 Cut back the pinched-out shoots to 3 leaves between late summer and early autumn. This encourages fruit buds to form at the bases of the pinched-out shoots in the following year.

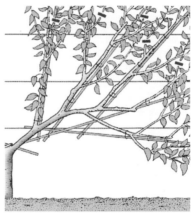

encourage fruit bud formation and, in later years, to replace worn-out branches by cutting out a proportion of the old wood back to young replacement branches in spring.

Pollination

Most plums are self-fertile so do not require a pollinator, but check your chosen variety. Hand pollinate to improve the chances of a good crop (*see page 241*), as plums flower at a time of year when pollinating insects are scarce.

Aftercare

In late winter, spread a general-purpose fertilizer over the root area at a rate of 110g (4oz) per square metre (10 sq ft) and rake in, then spread a 5cm (2in) layer of mulch in early spring, leaving it clear of the stems. Water during dry periods in the growing season to avoid a check in growth; irregular, heavy watering causes fruit to split.

Plums can be vulnerable to frost because they flower early in the year when frosts are harsher and more prevalent. The flowers and young fruit are most at risk.

Protect trees growing against walls or fences with fleece. Fruit buds and developing leaf buds are irresistible to birds; if possible, protect trees with netting.

To avoid the risk of biennial bearing (*see page 252*) and to preserve the flavour, thin fruit to ensure that they have enough room to develop (*see page 253*). Do this first when they are about the size of hazelnuts and again when they are about twice this size. Tugging off the fruit may tear away next year's fruit buds, so cut them off with scissors or secateurs, leaving a single plum every 5–8cm (2–3in).

Heavily laden branches on young trees can easily be damaged by the weight of fruit. These can be supported by using the maypoling technique (*see page 252*).

Harvesting & storing

Depending on the weather, local climate, and variety of plum, fruit should be ready for picking any time from midsummer to late autumn. Pick ripe fruit with their stalks. Plums do not store, but those picked when slightly under-ripe will keep for a few weeks in a cool place.

Cherries

There are three main types of cherry: sweet cherries are most popular, and generally fruit from early to mid-summer; acid or sour cherries, such as the famous morello, are harvested in late summer and early autumn; and duke cherries taste like a cross between the two.

Where & how to grow cherries

Cherries will grow on light soil if you improve it before planting and then feed, mulch, and water regularly, but they fare best in well-drained, deep, loamy, soil. Give them a sunny, sheltered site away from frost pockets; they flower early in the year and are vulnerable to cold snaps. Hardier acid cherries can be grown on cold, shady walls.

Cherries are usually grown as fans against a wall or fence, but they can also be grown as freestanding bushes, or half-standard or standard trees (*see page 222*). In the past, they always made large trees – too big for a small garden – but most are now grafted onto a dwarfing Gisela 5 rootstock to form a fully grown tree that is only 2m (6ft) tall. Although the bulk of old varieties need a pollinator, many of the new types do not; they are self-fertile.

Planting & spacing

If training cherries as a fan, you will need to construct supports with horizontal, 14-gauge wires spaced 15cm (6in) apart. Even on a Gisela 5 rootstock, each fan needs

Birds love cherries and can strip a tree clean before you have a chance to pick them. A restricted or dwarf form, shown here, is much easier to protect from birds, so you can gather a good crop.

plenty of wall space – about 3.5m (11ft) wide by 2m (6ft) high – to grow. Freestanding bushes and trees on the same rootstock need planting 2.5–3m (8–10ft) apart. Cherries on other, more vigorous rootstocks, such as Colt, can only be grown in large gardens as they need at least 5m (15ft) between freestanding bushes, trees, or fans.

FORMATIVE PRUNING OF A FAN-TRAINED CHERRY TREE

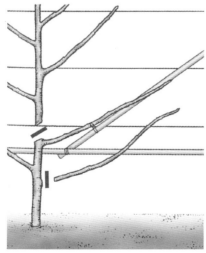

FIRST YEAR

1 **Tie 2 strong side branches** to canes on wires at a 35-degree angle in spring. Cut the central stem back to the uppermost of the selected branches. Remove all other branches.

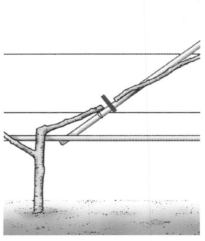

SECOND YEAR

2 **Shorten each branch** to about 30cm (12in) in spring. Cut to a bud that points in the direction of the fan. This encourages shoots to develop that will be used as the ribs of the fan.

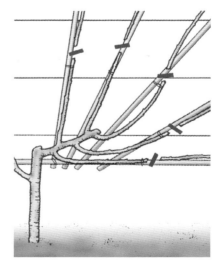

THIRD YEAR

3 **Cut back all the new** secondary branches to suitable buds in spring, leaving 45–53cm (18–21in) of new growth.

Pruning & training

Sweet and duke cherries fruit on two-year-old and older wood and are usually trained as fans from one-year-old trees (*see below*) against a wall or fence. Prune acid cherry fans hard to obtain lots of new shoots; training is similar to that of peaches and nectarines (*see page 262*).

To grow cherries as a freestanding bush, half-standard, or standard tree, prune the upper branches to three or four buds in spring to develop a head of branches in the same way as for an open-habit apple or pear tree (*see page 243*). Prune in spring to avoid silver leaf disease, and instead of removing the lower branches to form a clear trunk, pinch them off to four leaves, then in the summer of the second year, pinch out their growing points. These lower branches should not be removed until the fourth year, because they help stiffen the main stem. In the first year, remove any flowers so the tree concentrates its energy on vegetative growth. Cut out dead, diseased, dying, or badly placed and crossing branches each year in midsummer.

Aftercare

Soil around fan-trained trees can dry out quickly, so water little and often, especially once the fruit have started to form; a sudden deluge after drought can split the fruit.

In late winter, spread 85g (3oz) of a general-purpose fertilizer every square metre (10 sq ft) over the soil and rake in. In early spring, spread an 8cm (3in) mulch of well-rotted garden compost or manure over the root area.

A mature, fan-trained cherry makes an attractive tree and takes up little space in the garden, being vertically trained. It boasts pretty spring blossom, followed by bright and tasty, marble-sized fruit, which are commonly red, although varieties in different colours are available.

If frost is predicted, protect the flowers with fleece. You may also need to protect the winter buds and summer fruit from birds by netting the tree.

Harvesting & storing

When the fruit is ripe in summer, cut off your cherries with their stalks intact to discourage brown rot (*see page 272*). Eat them when fresh as they do not store well.

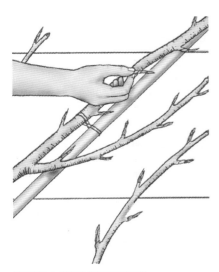

FOURTH & SUBSEQUENT YEARS
4 Remove any new shoots that grow directly towards or away from the wall. Do this in spring, when most of the wall space has been filled.

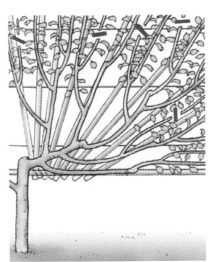

5 Cut to 6 leaves any secondary branches not needed for the framework, in midsummer. Cut stems that reach the top of the wall to a weak branch just below, or bend and tie it down.

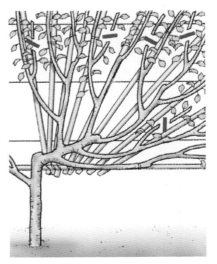

6 Cut back to 3 leaves the branches that were pinched out in midsummer, in early autumn. This encourages fruit buds to form at the bases of the shoots for the next year.

Figs

Common in Mediterranean regions, figs are a gourmet fruit that can be grown successfully in cooler climates. As well as tasty fruit, many fig trees have showy foliage, some with long and extended, lobed leaves. Many varieties, with much variation in the shape, colour, and taste of the fruit, are readily available. Figs are parthenocarpic, which means that the fruit develop without needing to be pollinated.

How figs fruit

Figs produce up to three crops a year, depending on where they are grown. In tropical regions, they bear three flushes of fruit, in subtropical areas they crop twice, while in cool-temperate regions they produce two crops, but only one will ripen successfully.

Outdoors in cool climates, the first crop appears in early summer, but as there is not enough time for the fruit to ripen, they are still green by autumn and so should be removed before winter. The second crop appears in late summer; these are carried over the winter as pea-sized embryo fruit. Provided these are not destroyed by cold, they develop the following spring and summer to ripen in late summer and early autumn.

Where to grow figs

As a native of warm-temperate climates, the fig prefers a warm, sunny wall or fence for a fan, or a warm, light corner for a bush. They are happy in most well-drained soils. Rather than plant straight into the soil, dig a specially prepared pit to restrict the roots (*see above right*). This stops the plant from getting leggy and improves cropping.

PLANTING A FIG TREE

1 **Dig a hole** about 0.4 square metres (4 sq ft) in size and 60cm (24in) deep, in late autumn to early spring. Line it with concrete slabs so that they stick out 2.5cm (1in) above the soil surface. Tightly pack the base with 20cm (8in) of rubble.

2 **Plant the tree** to the same depth as it was at the nursery and spread out the roots. If the tree is being trained on a wall, plant it 20cm (8in) away from the wall. Backfill the hole with a good loam-based compost, such as John Innes No. 3. Firm well and water in.

Supports & planting

To train a fig as a fan against a wall or fence, you will need to construct a series of horizontal support wires, spaced 30cm (12in) apart, using heavy, 14-gauge galvanized wire. To obtain a fan 2m (6ft) tall by 3.5m (11ft) wide, excavate a planting pit 0.4 square metres (4 sq ft) in size.

FORMATIVE PRUNING OF A FAN-TRAINED FIG TREE

1 **Prune the tree** after planting to stimulate 2 strong side branches to develop. In summer, tie new side branches onto angled canes.

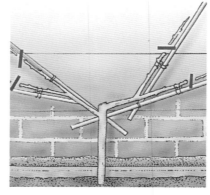

2 **Cut back the new side branches** by one third in late winter to early spring so more will grow to form the framework.

3 **Tie in shoots** that radiate from the centre. Remove shoots growing towards or away from the wall.

PRUNING A MATURE FAN-TRAINED TREE

1 Remove the growing points in early summer of one half of the young shoots carried by the main framework branches. This encourages new shoots and embryo fruit. As the shoots develop, tie them to the wires.

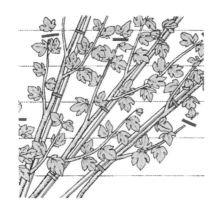

2 Prune half the fruited shoots in late autumn to 2.5cm (1in) to encourage new shoots from the base. Tie in remaining shoots parallel with the wall 23–30cm (9–12in) apart. Remove any crossing shoots or those growing into or away from the wall.

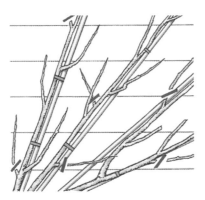

The size of the planting pit determines the eventual size of the fig tree. If raising a fig as a freestanding bush, half-standard, or standard – only really suitable for larger gardens – prepare a planting pit in the same way. Partially trained trees are available to buy, lessening the time you have to wait for the first crop.

Pruning & training

Formative training of a fig fan (*see facing page*) follows the same principle as for a peach fan (*see page 262*), aiming to fill the wall space with a strong framework of branches. This should take three to four years; thereafter, prune it as for a mature, cropping fan (*see above*) to encourage a plentiful supply of young shoots and – in cool climates – a mixture of ripe and embryonic fruit each autumn.

Bush, standard, and half-standard fig trees need little pruning after the first year (*see right*), except to remove dead, damaged, diseased, or badly placed branches. On old figs, where branches have become gaunt and bare, cut out a proportion of old wood in late winter to a young shoot or, if there are none, to a 2.5cm (1in) stub, to encourage fresh young growth.

If you inherit a fig that has not been planted to restrict the roots, the growth may be extremely leggy, resulting in poor fruit. Rejuvenate overgrown plants by pruning out a number of branches every late winter until the tree achieves a satisfactory shape.

Aftercare

Figs are capable of dealing with dry conditions, but in drought are unlikely to produce a decent crop of fruit. Plants can sometimes shed their entire crops of fruit if they become too stressed through lack of water. Start to water when the fig comes into growth in early spring, daily from midsummer for figs in pots. When the figs are ripening, do not water too much to avoid causing the fruit to split.

PRUNING A BUSH, STANDARD, OR HALF-STANDARD TREE

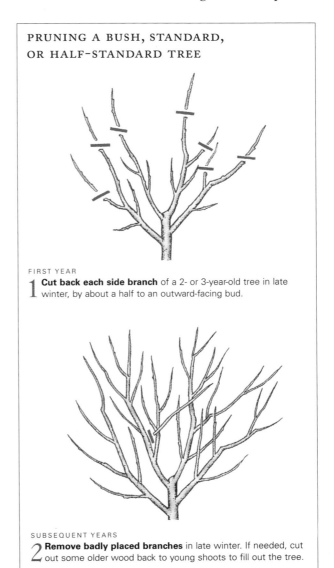

FIRST YEAR
1 Cut back each side branch of a 2- or 3-year-old tree in late winter, by about a half to an outward-facing bud.

SUBSEQUENT YEARS
2 Remove badly placed branches in late winter. If needed, cut out some older wood back to young shoots to fill out the tree.

PLANTING & PRUNING A FAN-TRAINED FIG TREE IN A GREENHOUSE

1 **Dig a hole** 0.4 square metres (4 sq ft) in size and 60cm (24in) deep in winter (*see page 258*). Fill with a mixture of rubble and soil to create free-draining conditions.

2 **After planting the tree** (*see page 258*), hang 15cm (6in) wire netting or erect support wires 30cm (12in) away from the glass, to allow room for leaves and shoots.

3 **Water the plant** twice a week in summer. When the temperature reaches 15°C (59°F), spray the stems and foliage to discourage red spider mite and damp down the floor daily.

4 **In a heated greenhouse**, after fruiting, cut back about a half of the fruited stems to 2 leaves. Repeat after every crop.

In a cold greenhouse, pinch out secondary branches at the fourth leaf in early summer. In autumn, thin out the fruited stems.

5 **Apply a topdressing** of well-rotted manure or compost and 2 or 3 handfuls of bonemeal fertilizer each winter.

In early spring, spread 50g (2oz) of a general-purpose fertilizer over the soil in the planting pit. Once the embryonic fruit begin to swell, feed weekly with a liquid tomato fertilizer or sulphate of potash to obtain plump, juicy figs. Do not overfeed figs – it can lead to rampant growth at the expense of fruit.

Many figs are hardy down to −10°C (14°F), but the branch tips that carry the embryo fruit are vulnerable to frost. If there is a risk of frost, protect the embryo fruit by covering the branches with horticultural fleece or by thatching them loosely with straw or bracken. Remove the protection when the risk of hard frost has passed. This may only be practical for fan-trained figs.

Harvesting & storing

Test if figs are ripe and ready for harvesting by giving each a gentle squeeze to see whether it is soft. A drop of nectar at the base of a fruit is another sign that it is ripe. Figs are best eaten when they are fresh, but they will keep for a couple of weeks if kept in a cool place.

FIGS IN THE GREENHOUSE

In cool climates, you can obtain heavier crops of higher-quality fruit in a greenhouse, and if you can heat the greenhouse, you can expect more than one crop a year. A fan needs a 2–3m (6–10ft) wide area, such as the back wall of a lean-to greenhouse; plant it in a pit, as for outdoor figs. Plant a freestanding bush fig in a container.

Caring for indoor figs

For two or more crops a year, you need a minimum temperature of 13°C (55°F) from midwinter onwards. Ventilate only if the temperature tops 24°C (75°F).

Formative pruning is the same as for outdoor figs (*see previous page*). Pruning of mature, cropping figs differs according to whether they are grown in a heated or unheated greenhouse (*see above*).

After the last crop in autumn, leave the greenhouse open until midwinter to give the figs a cool resting period before they start into growth next year – close the greenhouse in frosty weather to prevent damage.

Peaches & nectarines

Peaches and nectarines were once seen in cool climates only within the protected environment of a greenhouse, but they are now becoming more widely grown outdoors. Most garden varieties are grafted onto St Julien A rootstocks, and this is perfectly adequate for most sites. You can plant a single tree if desired, since these tree fruit are self-compatible, which means that another tree is not needed for pollination (*see page 241*).

Where to grow peaches & nectarines

Both fruit are best fan-trained against a warm, sunny wall or fence in moisture-retentive, well-drained soil. Ideally, peaches and nectarines like a slightly acidic or neutral, loamy soil. Neither crop grows well in light, sandy soil.

Avoid planting them in frost pockets because they flower early in the year and the crop will be reduced if the blossom is damaged. Choose the most sheltered site possible. In warm areas, it may be possible to grow peaches and nectarines in the open, as freestanding bushes, or half-standard or standard trees.

Planting & spacing

Fan-trained trees need a vertical support. Erect a series of horizontal training wires, set about 15cm (6in) apart, starting from 30cm (12in) above the level of the soil. As you train the fan, you will need to tie canes at an angle to the support wires with thin wire (*see following page*).

Space trees for fan training 3.5–4.5m (11–14ft) apart and 15–20cm (6–8in) from the vertical support, angling the plant towards it slightly. Space freestanding trees 5–6m (15–20ft) apart. Partially trained young trees are often available, otherwise grow from a one-year-old tree.

A mature, fan-trained peach or nectarine produces a yield on average of 13.5kg (30lb) of fruit; a bush form produces 13.5–45kg (30–100lb), but yield varies according to the size of the tree and conditions.

Pruning & training

Peaches and nectarines are never pruned when dormant because of the risk of silver leaf disease and bacterial canker (*see page 272*). Prune them from late winter onwards, while the sap is rising in the plant, which is effective in preventing spores from entering the tree.

For freestanding trees, prune formatively as for an open-centred apple or pear tree (*see page 243*), but make all pruning cuts in spring rather than in winter.

THINNING

When the fruitlets are about the size of large peas, start thinning them. Remove poorly placed, small, or misshapen fruit to leave one fruitlet every 15cm (6in) or so. This should encourage good-sized fruit to form.

HARVESTING

Pick the fruit from late summer onwards, when the flesh feels soft at the stalk ends. Hold each fruit in the palm of the hand, lift and twist it slightly. A ripe fruit should come away easily; do not try to tug off the fruit – you will tear the bark.

FORMATIVE PRUNING OF A FAN-TRAINED PEACH OR NECTARINE TREE

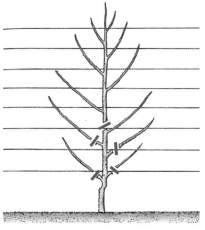

1 Cut back the main stem of a 1-year-old tree to a side branch at about 60cm (24in) from the ground, in late winter. Cut other side branches back to 1 bud.

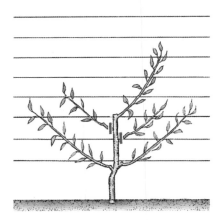

2 Select 3 side branches in early summer. Tie into the wires the topmost branch and the lower branches to the left and to the right. Remove all other branches from the main stem.

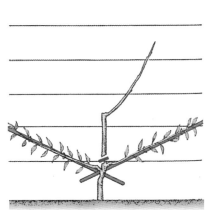

3 Tie the lower side branches to canes, set at an angle of 45 degrees, in early or midsummer. Late in summer, cut out the central stem.

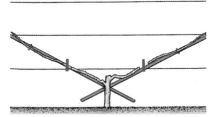

SECOND YEAR

4 Cut back the 2 side branches in late winter to a wood or triple bud (*see below*) at 30–45cm (12–18in) from the main stem.

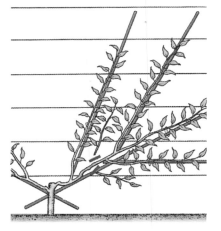

5 Remove all but 4 secondary branches on each side branch in summer to form the ribs. Tie them to canes attached to the wires.

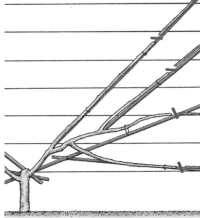

THIRD YEAR

6 Shorten the tip of each rib by one-third in late winter, cutting to a downward-facing wood bud.

For a fan-trained peach or nectarine, start with a one-year-old tree with 5–12 evenly arranged side branches (*see above*), or start with a partially trained tree with several well-trained, evenly spaced side branches (or ribs).

On one-year-old trees, if there are no suitable side branches to prune back to, cut back to a wood bud, which is slender and pointed. If in doubt, cut to a triple bud, which consists of two round flower buds and one pointed wood bud. Once the buds have grown on, select three branches and remove the rest, cutting them back to the main stem (*see above, step 2*), then continue as shown.

In the second year, aim to develop eight ribs on the fan, keeping the centre clear. In the third year, allow the ribs to extend and increase the spread. To fill in the framework, train three shoots on each rib: remove those that grow into or away from the wall; let others grow on every 10cm (4in).

From the fourth year, the tree will cover the allotted space. Fruit is borne on one-year-old wood, so you will need to remove fruited stems and encourage new ones to replace them. In late spring, prune the side branches of every rib so they have three shoots: one at the base (a replacement shoot), one in the middle (in reserve, in case

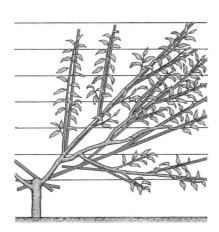

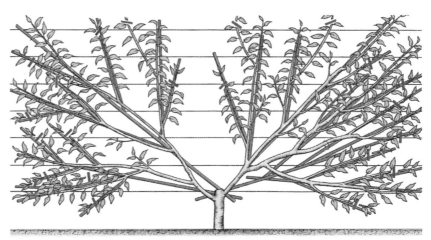

7 **Train 3 shoots** outwards on canes from each of the ribs. Leave other shoots every 10cm (4in); remove the rest.

8 **Remove the growing points** of each shoot once they have made 45cm (18in) of growth, unless they are needed to extend the

framework. This encourages the formation of fruit buds. In late summer, tie in the cut-back shoots to canes on the wires.

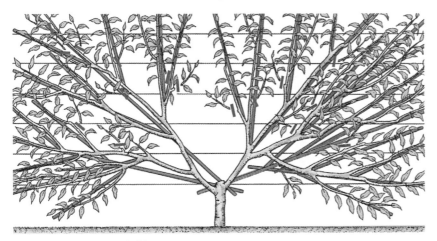

FOURTH & SUBSEQUENT YEARS

9 **Prune each year** in late spring to renew fruiting wood and maintain the framework. First remove shoots growing directly towards or

away from the wall or fence (*above*); if any have rounded flower buds at their base, cut them back to 1–2 leaves. Prepare for renewal by

pruning the side branch of each rib to 3 shoots (*top*) in late spring. Cut back after fruiting (*bottom*) to the replacement shoot.

the base shoot fails), and one at the tip (for extension growth); cut other shoots back to two leaves. When the base and middle shoots are 45cm (18in) long and the leader extension has six leaves, cut off the tips. After fruiting, cut each side branch back to the basal shoot.

Aftercare

You may need to protect the early flowers from frost by draping each tree with fleece or hessian at night. As there are few pollinating insects around when the trees flower, you may also need to hand pollinate the flowers. As the

fruit develop, thin the fruitlets (*see page 261*) and protect them from birds and squirrels. Feed over the root area with a general-purpose fertilizer at 85g (3oz) per square metre (10 sq ft) in late winter, and from late spring with sulphate of potash. Water well, particularly in dry periods, but not while the fruit is ripening to avoid skins splitting.

Harvesting & storing

The summer fruit is ripe when it has a reddish flush on the skin and you can pull it off easily with a gentle twist of the hand. They are best eaten fresh.

Apricots

Fan-training is a popular way of growing apricots, against a warm, sunny wall or fence. They will not grow well in light, sandy soil or in frost pockets; choose a moisture-retentive, loamy, neutral to alkaline soil. Apricots will fruit as single trees because they can pollinate themselves.

Planting & spacing

Start with a partially trained, three-year-old tree. Before planting, erect a support of strong horizontal training wires against the vertical support; set them 23cm (9in) apart, with the lowest one 30cm (12in) above soil level. Space fans 4.5m (14ft) apart, 15cm (6in) from the support.

Pruning & training

Once your fan-trained apricot is trained (*see below*), prune as for a fan-trained sweet cherry (*see page 256*), thinning the fruit as they appear. Remove poorly placed, small, or misshapen fruit when they are each about the width of your little fingernail, to leave one fruit approximately every 8–10cm (3–4in).

Aftercare

In late winter each year, use a general-purpose fertilizer to feed the tree, spreading 85g (3oz) per square metre (10 sq ft) over the root area. From late spring onwards, apply sulphate of potash to promote fruit formation.

Water well during periods of dry, sunny weather, but avoid excessive watering when fruit is ripening as this can cause the skins of the apricots to split.

The flowers appear very early on in the year, so protect them and the young fruit from frost by draping fleece over the fan. At this time of year there are also very few pollinating insects around, so it is best to carry out pollination by hand. Later, as the crop develops, protect it from birds and squirrels using strong netting.

Harvesting & storing

Apricots ripen from midsummer to early autumn, depending on the variety. They are ready to pick when they are fully coloured and come away easily from the tree. Apricots are best eaten fresh, but can also be dried.

PLANTING & PRUNING A FAN-TRAINED APRICOT TREE

FIRST YEAR

1 Dig a hole in prepared soil in autumn, large enough for the roots. Plant at the same depth as at the nursery. Mulch well.

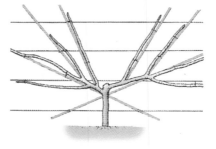

2 Tie in secondary branches, here of a 3-year-old fan-trained tree, to canes fixed at angles to the horizontal support wires.

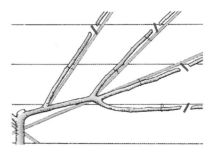

3 Shorten each secondary branch by one third to a bud pointing in the direction of the fan, in late winter.

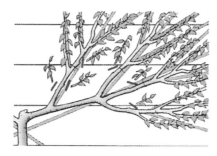

4 Select and tie in 3 shoots that develop from each secondary branch in mid- to late summer. Remove all remaining shoots.

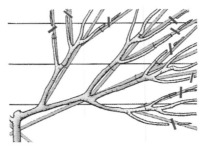

SECOND & SUBSEQUENT YEARS

5 Remove buds pointing towards or directly away from the wall or fence in spring. Prune the tips of all sideshoots by one quarter.

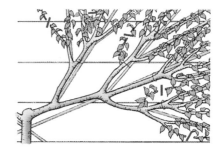

6 Cut sideshoot tips back to 6 leaves in midsummer. After cropping, prune them by a half. Every 4–6 years, cut out some old shoots.

PRUNING A WALL-TRAINED MULBERRY

1 Start with a 3–5-year-old tree, as mulberries grow slowly. Cut out any branches growing towards or away from the wall at the same time. Train in the remaining side branches to a support of strong horizontal wires in summer.

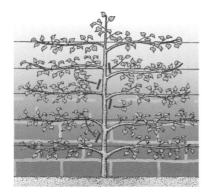

2 Stop the side branches once they have reached their required length, by cutting them back to one bud on the previous year's growth in spring. In midsummer, prune the sideshoots that grow from the side branches to 4–5 leaves.

PRUNING A QUINCE

FIRST YEAR

1 Cut back the main branches in winter by about one third of the previous year's growth, to outward-facing buds. Remove any weak and badly placed branches back to 2–3 buds.

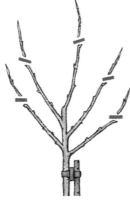

SECOND & SUBSEQUENT YEARS

2 Prune back the main framework branches in winter by about one third of the previous year's growth, to outward-facing buds. Cut back any weak and badly placed laterals to 2–3 buds.

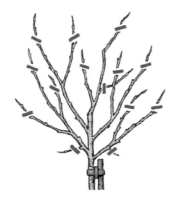

Mulberries

When buying, look for the black mulberry (*Morus nigra*) to avoid confusion with the inedible white mulberry. Mulberries can be grown as freestanding trees if you have a warm and sunny, sheltered garden. In cooler sites, train them against a sunny wall or fence. They thrive in rich, moisture-retentive yet well-drained, slightly acid soil.

Since these deciduous trees can take up to 10 years to produce fruit, it is easier to save time by buying a three- to five-year-old plant from the nursery. Wall-trained mulberries will need a support network of strong horizontal wires, spaced 23–38cm (9–15in) apart, installed before planting, and they should be planted at a distance of 15cm (6in) from the wall.

Prune freestanding plants in winter, aiming to create an attractive shape by reducing side branches that are not needed for the main framework to four or five buds. Prune wall-trained plants in spring and summer (*see left*).

Make sure that the trees are watered thoroughly in warm, dry weather. In late winter, apply a general-purpose fertilizer to the soil, spreading 50g (2oz) per square metre (10 sq ft). Mulch with well-rotted farmyard manure or garden compost in spring. Mulberries are ready for picking in late summer.

Quinces

Requiring very little attention when established, the quince is an attractive and compact tree with spreading branches. In autumn, it is festooned with highly perfumed, large, pear- or apple-shaped fruit.

Quince trees prefer a warm, sunny, and sheltered site in most soils as long as they are deep, light, fertile, and moisture-retentive. When you buy, look for a goblet-shaped tree, or choose a partly trained, three- or four-year-old standard or half-standard. Before planting, drive a stake into the ground to provide support, ensuring that the top will be just beneath the lowest branches. Water in dry, sunny weather and apply a general-purpose fertilizer over the soil at 85g (3oz) per square metre (10 sq ft) in late winter. Mulch well in spring.

Quinces should be pruned in winter (*see left*), but after four years very little trimming is required, apart from removing suckering shoots that emerge from the base (*see page 97*) and cutting out overcrowded branches. The fruit grow on spurs or on the tips of the previous summer's growth and are usually ready for harvest from mid-autumn – leave them on the tree as long as possible.

COMMON PROBLEMS

Perhaps you have a well-loved fruit tree that has been healthy, vigorous, and high-yielding for many years but has suddenly succumbed to a pest infestation or an outbreak of disease. Or maybe you have acquired a new garden or allotment with a badly neglected tree that is in dire need of remedial action. It is inevitable that you will encounter problems from time to time as a fruit gardener, and it is worth keeping an eye out for early signs of infection or infestation, so that you can control them swiftly before you are overwhelmed.

Stunted, over-vigorous & neglected trees

Apart from looking awful, trees that have been pruned poorly or have not had any tender loving care for some time will probably furnish you with misshapen, small, or unpleasant tasting fruit. They may also have outgrown their allotted space, become stunted, or have diseased growth. Assess the tree and decide if it can be rescued; it makes sense to remove a tree that is badly diseased, but others can be restored to their former glory over two to three years by undertaking remedial action.

Stunted trees

A tree can become stunted for a variety of reasons: the ground around it may have become overgrown with weeds, resulting in competition from the weed roots for soil moisture and nutrients; the tree may have been planted badly and failed to anchor itself effectively in the soil; there may be insufficient light reaching the foliage because of other trees nearby; or the tree may have been damaged by pests or diseases.

Aim to restore a stunted tree's vigour by removing competing weeds, feeding with a general-purpose fertilizer, and mulching around the root area with an 8cm (3in) layer of well-rotted farmyard manure or garden compost, leaving a gap between the trunk and the mulch. If any pests and diseases are present, treat them as necessary.

If the tree has not been staked, drive one or two strong stakes into the ground – avoiding damage to the roots – and secure with a tree tie. This will prevent the roots of the tree from being rocked in heavy winds.

Use secateurs or loppers to remove any dead, diseased, or dying branches. If the head of the tree is a congested mass of spurs, thin these out, while shortening any young

RENOVATING A STUNTED TREE

1 **Remove weeds** and grass all around the tree at a distance of 1.2m (4ft), then mulch. Drive in a stake and tie in with a tree tie.

2 **Thin out overcrowded spurs**, if needed, in winter. Prune hard any young wood. This admits light and air and prompts new shoots.

3 **Remove most or all** of the fruitlets in spring, for 1 or 2 years. Feed and mulch well each year and control pests and diseases.

RESTORATIVE PRUNING OF AN OLD, BADLY PRUNED APPLE TREE

1 Inspect the tree in winter, when the branches are bare, to determine the work that needs to be carried out. This apple has areas of congested growth, particularly around pruning cuts made 2–3 years ago.

2 Thin out strong shoots around congested wounds where major branches were once removed. Cut them out at the base, taking care to leave the collar intact so that the wound can heal cleanly (*see page 96*). Do not prune out more than one third of such growth in a single year. Remove crossing branches.

3 Aim to leave a healthy, evenly balanced framework of branches that are 60–90cm (24–36in) apart. Continue the pruning over 2–3 years, starting each winter by removing any dead, diseased, or damaged branches to keep the tree healthy.

4 In summer, a more graceful and balanced open crown will develop with productive new growth. Feed, water, and mulch, then resume normal pruning and maintenance once renovation is complete.

wood to allow air and light into the tree. For the next couple of years, remove any fruit as it forms to allow the tree to regain its vigour. After this, carry out a normal pruning and maintenance programme.

Over-vigorous trees

Excessive feeding, very fertile soil, or being grafted onto a vigorous rootstock could result in a tree having rampant top growth and very poor yields of fruit. If the trees are in an orchard, seed it with grass and withhold fertilizers that are high in nitrogen until the vigour is under control.

Plums and other stone fruit can be root pruned. To do this, dig out a circular trench around the trunk of the tree during late autumn or early winter. Cut the trench 1.5m (5ft) away from the tree, or farther out if it is particularly large. Use a pruning saw to cut back any thick roots, then refill the trench with soil and firm down.

Neglected trees

An unpruned tree may produce plenty of blossom, but have small, pest-ridden, or diseased fruit. Prune out dead, diseased, or dying branches, and any that are badly placed, crossing, or that spoil the shape. Reduce the number of side branches on main stems. Then feed, water, and mulch.

Renovating apple & pear trees

Masses of vegetative growth on apple and pear trees is usually the result of over-enthusiastic pruning. Any further trimming aimed at stemming this vigorous growth often exacerbates the problem because hard pruning prompts more non-fruiting extension growth.

To curtail the vigour of such a tree, the first step is to grass over the root area and feed moderately until the tree is fruiting well. Then carry out restorative pruning from late autumn to early spring, while the tree is dormant (*see above*). It is important to spread this renovation work over a two- to three- year period to lessen the shock to the tree. Winter pruning stimulates extension growth, whereas summer pruning checks it, so only a proportion of the overgrown stems should be removed each winter and the resulting new shoots then pruned again in summer to encourage formation of fruit buds.

If possible, steer clear of cutting back horizontal shoots because these usually produce more fruiting spurs. Young vertical shoots, which tend not to fruit, can also be bent over and tied down, or looped one over the other, to encourage production of fruit-bearing spurs. After three years or so, the tree should begin to produce better fruit and you can resume a normal maintenance regime.

Fruit pests

Correct cultivation and good weed control will help to keep the plants healthy, but the best protection against fruit pests is vigilance – inspect the plants regularly to spot signs of infestation early on so that you can take prompt action to control any pests.

Codling moth

Maggoty apples are caused by codling moth caterpillars. The female moths lay eggs on or near the fruitlets in early summer. A single caterpillar then bores into a fruit and feeds in the core before tunnelling out of the fruit in late summer. Apple is the main host plant for the codling moth, but pears are also affected.

Small apple trees can be sprayed with bifenthrin in the middle of early summer, with a second application three weeks later. A codling moth pheromone trap can be placed in the tree in late spring to give more accurate timing of control measures. The trap attracts and captures male codling moths, giving an indication of when the females are active and laying eggs. On isolated trees, a pheromone trap may capture enough males so that the females are unable to produce viable eggs.

Woolly aphid

Apples, including ornamental crab apples, are the main host plant for woolly aphid, but it also attacks pyracanthas and *Cotoneaster horizontalis*. The brownish-black aphids are covered in fluffy, white, waxy fibres secreted from their bodies. This makes colonies on stems and branches look like a mould. In early spring, woolly aphid occurs mainly on the trunk and larger branches, particularly near splits in the bark or on pruning wounds. Later in summer, the infestation spreads to the young shoots, where aphid feeding induces soft, knobbly swellings in the bark.

The waxy coating of woolly aphids helps to protect them from contact sprays. A systemic insecticide, such as thiacloprid on edible apples or imidacloprid on the ornamental varieties, gives better results. You can sometimes control woolly aphid on small trees by scrubbing colonies with a stiff-bristled brush in spring.

Plum moth

This moth has pink caterpillars that feed inside the ripening fruit of plums, damson, and gages. None of the pesticides available for garden use on plums is likely to be effective. A plum moth pheromone trap can be used to capture males, which may reduce the females' mating

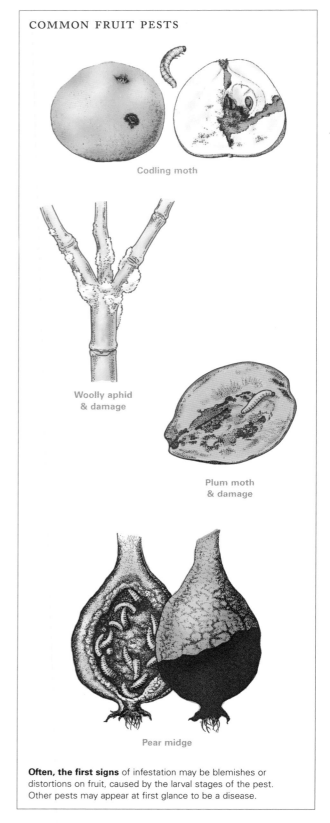

COMMON FRUIT PESTS

Codling moth

Woolly aphid
& damage

Plum moth
& damage

Pear midge

Often, the first signs of infestation may be blemishes or distortions on fruit, caused by the larval stages of the pest. Other pests may appear at first glance to be a disease.

Pests, diseases & other problems *see page 26* | **Weed control** *see page 39* | **Preparing to grow** *see page 220*

success on isolated trees. Infested fruit ripen prematurely, so early pickings may all have maggots; later ripening fruit are likely to be less affected.

Pear midge

When blossom is at the white bud stage, the pear midge, a tiny fly, lays its eggs on the buds. The orange-white, tiny maggots feed inside pear fruitlets, which become abnormally enlarged but soon blacken and drop from the tree in late spring or early summer. Sometimes nearly all the young fruit are lost. Pick and destroy any blackening fruitlets before the larvae go into the soil to pupate. Some control can be achieved on small trees by spraying at the white bud stage with bifenthrin.

Gooseberry sawflies

The caterpillar-like larvae of several species can defoliate gooseberries and red and white currants. There may be two or three generations from mid-spring to mid-autumn. The larvae are up to 2cm (³⁄₄in) long and pale green, sometimes with many black spots. Carefully check the plants, particularly inner parts, from mid-spring onwards to detect larvae before they cause serious damage; remove them by hand or spray with pyrethrum.

Pear blister mite

These microscopic mites overwinter under bud scales and emerge to infest new foliage in spring. The leaves develop slightly raised, pale green or pinkish-red blisters where mites are feeding inside. The blisters turn brownish-black later. The tree will survive and still produce fruit. There are no effective pesticides available for garden use. On lightly infested trees, it is worthwhile removing affected leaves or shoots in the spring. If many leaves are infested, the presence of the mites has to be tolerated.

Black currant big bud mite

Microscopic mites feed inside the buds, causing them to become abnormally swollen and rounded over the winter months. Infested buds often dry up and fail to produce any growth in spring. Mites emerge from the buds in late spring to seek out new buds to infest. They can spread a virus-like disease called reversion, which further reduces the vigour and productivity of affected plants. There are no effective pesticides for garden use. On lightly infested plants, pick off and destroy enlarged buds in winter. If plants are heavily infested and fail to produce a good crop, dig up the plants after picking the fruit and put in new stock in autumn. A mite-resistant black currant variety, 'Ben Hope', is available from some nurseries.

COMMON FRUIT PESTS

Gooseberry sawfly

Pear blister mite damage

Black currant buds infested by big bud mite

Pests may not harm the fruit crop if caught early – pick them off and destroy them and burn affected plant material. If allowed to get a hold, they can cause more serious problems.

Raspberry beetle

Whitish-brown larvae, up to 8mm (³⁄₈in) long, feed on raspberry, blackberry, loganberry, and other cane fruit. They start at the stalk end, causing it to dry up, then move inside to feed on the core. The pale brown adult beetles lay eggs in late spring to midsummer, so autumn-fruiting raspberries are less affected. When pink raspberry fruits first appear, spray against the larvae with pyrethrum and again two weeks later. Spray loganberries as the petals fall and blackberries when the first flowers open. Spray at dusk to avoid harming bees.

Raspberry leaf & bud mite

These microscopic mites suck sap from the undersides of raspberry leaves from late spring to early autumn, causing yellow blotches on the upper leaf surfaces that look like a virus infection, but unlike viruses, growth is not stunted. Lower leaf surfaces become darker green instead of silver-green. A heavy infestation distorts leaves. No amateur pesticide controls this mite. Plants may appear unhealthy, but still fruit. Less susceptible varieties are 'Glen Prosen', 'Glen Magna', 'Gaia', 'Leo', and 'Terrie Louise'. Prone varieties are 'Glen Ample', 'Glen Shee', 'Malling Jewel', and 'Malling Enterprise'.

Currant blister aphid

Black, red, and white currants form puckered or blistered leaves at shoot tips in mid- to late spring. Those on red currants are pinkish-red; those on black currants are yellow-green. Pale yellow aphids can be seen beneath the puckered leaves; in early to midsummer, they develop wings and fly away to wild flowers called hedge woundwort, returning in autumn to lay overwintering eggs on currant stems. The symptoms can look alarming, but the aphid has little impact on growth or fruiting, so can be tolerated. As soon as leaf distortion is seen in spring, you could spray leaf undersides with pyrethrum.

Winter moth

Wingless females emerge in late autumn to midwinter to lay eggs on tree fruit twigs. Pale green caterpillars then hatch to eat the foliage, blossom, and fruitlets in spring. In early summer, the caterpillars go into the soil to pupate. Put sticky grease bands around trunks in late autumn to stop female moths climbing up. Control caterpillars by spraying with bifenthrin or pyrethrum at bud burst.

Other pests

Other pests that may affect fruit include aphids, vine weevils, rabbits, deer, and squirrels (*see pages 35–36*).

COMMON FRUIT PESTS

Raspberry beetle, grub & damage

Raspberry leaf & bud mite & damage

Currant blister aphid & damage

Once you identify the pest and know a little about its life cycle, it is possible to take action to control it at a time that has most effect on the pest and prevents further harm to the crop.

Pests, diseases & other problems *see page 26* | **Weed control** *see page 39* | **Preparing to grow** *see page 220*

Fruit diseases

Many fruit diseases are caused by fungal infections; contact fungicides only check or prevent attacks so should be applied before the disease appears. Systemic fungicides, absorbed by the fungal tissues, have short-lived effects and may cause resistant strains to occur if used too often.

Nectria canker

This serious fungal disease of apples and pears causes elliptical, concentric rings of shrunken bark near buds or wounds. The bark usually swells around the wound. White pustules form in summer and red fruiting bodies in winter. Infection can occur anytime through wounds. Prune out and destroy small cankered branches; chisel back cankers to green wood on larger limbs. Spray in autumn after harvest with a copper fungicide and again after half the leaves have fallen.

Apple & pear scab

Brown scabby blotches form on the skins of young fruit; in severe cases fruit may be distorted. If the skin cracks, rot can occur. Felty brown blotches appear on leaves, which defoliate; shoots may also be affected. Crab apples suffer in particular. Remove diseased tissue, thin overcrowded branches, and rake up fallen leaves. Some varieties are more resistant to scab than others. You can also use targeted sprays.

Pear & plum rusts

Bright orange blotches appear on pear leaves in summer; fruit and twigs are also sometimes infected, but the disease is rarely serious. The fungus also lives on juniper, causing swellings on branches that release spores in spring. Removing affected junipers helps, but spores can still be blown some distance. Trees treated for scab infection are rarely affected by rust. Plum rust appears in late summer as abundant, tiny, yellow pustules on leaves, which may fall, but the disease rarely affects tree vigour. Rust overwinters on stem cankers, fallen leaves, and garden anemones, so hygiene is vital.

Blossom wilt

Many fruit trees suffer from this disease, which is worse in damp springs. Usually the flowers wilt and turn brown and the fungus may grow into the spurs to kill leaves or form cankers on branches. Spores blow in from overwintering infections to attack the flowers as they open. It is important to cut out any diseased tissue in summer and remove any fruit suffering from brown rot.

COMMON FRUIT DISEASES

Nectria canker

Apple scab

Pear rust

Blossom wilt

Fungal diseases such as canker, scab, rust, and blossom wilt are caused by spores carried in the air, so it is important to prune at the right time and to watch for early signs of infection.

Cane fungal diseases

Cane spot: Small, elliptical purple spots appear on raspberry and hybrid berry canes in early summer, and sometimes on leaves and fruit. The spots split into shallow pits and can cause tip dieback. Remove affected tissue and use copper oxychloride as a control.

Cane blight: In summer, raspberry canes suddenly die back; brown lesions appear at stem bases, the bark ruptures, and stems are brittle. Cut back diseased wood to healthy tissue. Prune carefully to avoid infection through wounds, avoid waterlogging, and improve airflow between canes.

Spur blight: In late summer, purple patches appear around buds of new raspberry or loganberry canes and kill many buds, making canes unfruitful. They enlarge and pale over autumn. Small, black fruiting bodies release spores in late spring to infect new canes. The blight thrives on overfed or overcrowded plants. Remove affected canes and spray with copper oxychloride. Some varieties show resistance.

Peach leaf curl

On peaches, nectarines, and close relatives, red or pale green blisters form on new leaves. These become swollen and curled and later covered in white spores. Some spores overwinter on dormant shoots. Apply copper fungicide as the buds begin to swell in late winter, a fortnight later and before leaf fall. Remove diseased tissue promptly and feed affected trees well. Covering wall-trained forms from late winter to late spring helps to avoid infection, but you will need to hand pollinate.

Bacterial canker

In this serious disease of cherries, plums, peaches, nectarines, and apricots, long lesions occur on branches, often on one side, and tissue dies above those points. Large amounts of gum may seep from the canker (less common on plums). In late spring, small brown spots may form on leaves and fall out to leave 'shot holes'. In late autumn, rain splashes bacteria from the leaves onto the bark to form new cankers. Prune during active growth to reduce infection. Spray trees with Bordeaux mixture in late summer, early autumn, and mid-autumn to avoid bark infection. Some plum and cherry varieties are resistant.

Silver leaf

This serious disease affects many trees, particularly apples and cherries. The leaves become silver and branches die back. Small, purple bracket fungi appear on dead wood, which is stained brown within. Save infected trees by cutting branches back 15cm (6in) beyond the staining. Do not prune these trees when dormant.

Fireblight

Leaves of affected branches wilt and brown, as if scorched. Bacteria spread from old infections or by insects travel down the inner bark to form sunken cankers, with reddening of the growth tissue. It can occur in warm, sunny but wet conditions. Swiftly prune out affected branches and sterilize your tools. It is often mistaken for diseases with similar symptoms; apples and pears are affected but not cherries.

Brown rot

Many fruit trees can be affected. Spots of soft brown rot develop on fruit and rapidly enlarge; rings of buff spores appear on this tissue and initiate more infections. The disease also spreads to any fruit that are touching. Rotten fruit becomes mummified on the tree. The fungus can invade the spur, so it is vital to prune out diseased spurs and remove all rotten fruit. Avoid damaging fruit to reduce infection. Brown rot can affect stored fruit, so store only perfect, dry fruit and check it regularly.

Crown gall

On examining a struggling woody plant, a large gall at soil level or on the roots indicates infection by crown gall. Soil-borne bacteria parasitize injured or diseased roots or the stem, causing the gall to grow. Grow potatoes on the area and avoid replanting with susceptible species.

Powdery mildews

Gooseberries and apples are worst affected. Powdery white patches on leaves and young shoots cause leaves to die and stunt shoots. The fruits of gooseberries also suffer. Prune out infected tissue; if the disease advances, grow resistant varieties. Fungicides are available. Avoid overuse of nitrogen-rich fertilizers and prune plants to improve airflow. Keep well watered and mulched in dry periods.

Stigminia shot hole

This fungus causes tiny spots on leaves of cherries, plums, peaches, nectarines, and apricots. The dead tissue falls away to leave 'shot holes'. It is most severe where high humidity and rainfall occur at a time when young growth is present. Ensure the tree is watered, mulched, and fed well and use chemical remedies as for bacterial canker (*see left*).

Quince leaf blight

Irregular brown spots blacken quince leaves, which fall early. Shoots or fruit may also be affected. Remove and burn all infected tissue and fallen leaves. The variety 'Aromatnya' is supposedly more resistant.

FRUIT DISEASES

Pests, diseases & other problems *see page 26* | **Weed control** *see page 39* | **Preparing to grow** *see page 220*

COMMON DISEASES OF FRUIT

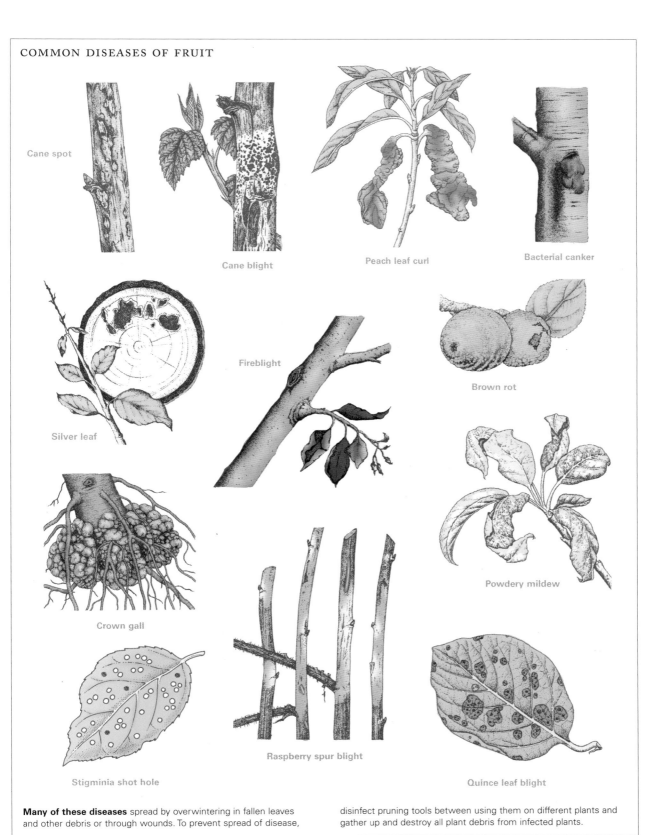

Cane spot

Cane blight

Peach leaf curl

Bacterial canker

Silver leaf

Fireblight

Brown rot

Crown gall

Powdery mildew

Stigminia shot hole

Raspberry spur blight

Quince leaf blight

Many of these diseases spread by overwintering in fallen leaves and other debris or through wounds. To prevent spread of disease, disinfect pruning tools between using them on different plants and gather up and destroy all plant debris from infected plants.

CHAPTER SIX

LAWNS

PLANNING THE LAWN 278

PREPARING THE SITE 280

SEED OR TURF? 282

SOWING A LAWN 283

LAYING TURF 284

LAWN MAINTENANCE 286

COMMON PROBLEMS 294

EVERYBODY LOVES THE SMELL OF FRESHLY MOWN GRASS. A lush, green carpet of lawn is often considered to be an essential feature of a garden, whether it be a small town patch or a large country plot. Every lawn contains thousands of little plants, all of which contribute to a cleaner environment and reduce the build-up of carbon dioxide. Long grass also increases local biodiversity by creating a home for a huge range of wildlife, as well as providing food and nesting material for other creatures, such as birds. By laying a lawn you are laying the future for a cleaner and healthier world.

Lawns & their place in the garden

Grass is a much cheaper means of surfacing a garden than using materials such as patio slabs and the ever-popular decking. Its soft texture makes it ideal for children to play on or for adults to relax and sit on and its flexibility makes it easy to lay following contours and slopes.

For enthusiasts, a lawn can be a feature in its own right. For others, areas of turf may be used to define specific areas in a garden or to bind together all the disparate elements of the garden. A lawn may soften the contours of hard landscaping or act as a neutral backdrop for borders and other features.

Lawns may be incorporated to suit many styles of garden – from the sharply defined, structured symmetry of formal gardens, to the sweeping, informal contours of wildflower meadows. With a little imagination, you can cut a lawn into any shape or pattern you wish, simply by using a half-moon edger.

However, a lawn does require maintenance if it is to look good all year round. Frequent mowing – sometimes twice a week – during the growing season is essential; other maintenance tasks such as reseeding of bare patches, clearing of autumn leaves and annual feeding, aeration, watering, and scarification will help to keep a lawn at its peak. The constant demands of keeping up a lawn can be an uphill struggle for people with busy lives. Other disadvantages of lawns are that they can become slippery and muddy in winter and wear rapidly if well trodden.

Choosing the type of lawn

Nearly all lawns are composed of a selection of different grasses and the skill of the gardener lies in selecting the best combination. Specialist suppliers offer a huge range of grass seed mixtures for different styles of lawns, including customized mixes for individual clients. Mixtures are also available to suit particular environmental conditions, such as slow-growing grasses for sunny sites, or varieties that are suitable for shaded, damp, or dry soils.

High-quality lawns are most often seen in formal, symmetrically planned gardens; they usually have immaculately mown strips and are seldom walked upon. Such lawns are composed of fine grasses, such as bents (*Agrostis* species) and fescues (*Festuca* species).

The most common lawns are utility lawns. Typically, this is the standard family back garden lawn that undergoes frequent wear from children playing, garden furniture and so on. These lawns can still look good if well maintained, but they usually contain a high proportion of rye grass (*Lolium perenne*), which is hard-wearing and resilient but fairly coarse and less attractive. Plant breeders have now developed a less vigorous rye grass, which is still fairly durable but lacks the coarseness of the commonly used species.

PLANNING & PREPARATION

Creating a lawn requires careful planning before you open the shed and reach for the gardening tools. It is easiest to plan a lawn on a new plot that offers a blank canvas, but more often than not you will have to deal with an existing garden and have to work around features such as trees, flower beds, and ponds. So a little time spent planning will help to avoid time-consuming and laborious alterations later. Once you have plotted out the lawn, it is important that the ground is properly prepared to enable the new grass, whether sown from seed or laid from turf, to establish well and achieve the result that you desire.

Planning the lawn

It is much easier to sketch and change a rough outline of a lawn on paper than digging out a design in the garden, and a well-planned sketch will act as an incentive to put your plans into action. Use graph paper to give you an idea of scale. Only once you have considered the points below, and are happy with your design, should you begin the physical work of putting your plans into action.

To maximize the potential from your existing site, walk into the garden and work out what you want from your lawn. Will it be formal with straight lines or informal with long sweeping curves? Draw up a list of existing features, such as trees, ponds, or paths, in the garden, and decide which you want to keep and which should be scrapped.

Site & aspect
Consider the garden's aspect. Most lawns prefer sunny, well-drained soil, although there are seed mixes of grasses that cope with shade and damp conditions. Bear in mind

Circular lawns work well in a small garden because they distract the eye from the straight lines of the boundaries. If it mirrors circular features, such as a water wheel (*above*), the lawn unifies the space.

On a long, narrow lawn, place medium-sized or large shrubs at the apex of each indentation to break up the long edges. Partially obscuring parts of the garden in this way also creates intrigue.

Creating a wildflower area *see page 52* | **Seed or turf?** *see page 282* | **Lawn maintenance** *see page 286*

that if your garden receives sun first thing in the morning, it probably will not get any sun in the afternoon. The ideal site receives sun for most of the day, although a lawn will still grow in a site that is shaded for most of the day.

Avoid laying lawn in deep shade cast by overhanging trees, particularly evergreens. Shallow-rooted trees such as beech (*Fagus*) deprive grass of water and nutrients. Smaller specimen trees can be tolerated by creating square or circular beds around their trunks. Low or overhanging branches in the middle of the lawn can be a nuisance when you are trying to mow.

Shaping the lawn

Square and rectangular swards are easiest to mow and edge, and are most used in formal gardens, but these shapes can look dull and unimaginative. Make sure that there is plenty of room for planting around the lawn; a classic mistake is to install one large, dominant lawn with very narrow beds squeezed along the boundaries. Consider wide flower beds, perhaps running horizontally or diagonally across the lawn. This can divide the garden into more interesting and balanced spaces.

A long, narrow garden can be made to look wider by a lawn that flows in large, sweeping curves. Alternatively, run paths across the width of the lawn – this will encourage the eye to travel between the sides of the garden, rather than be drawn directly to the end of it.

Short, wide lawns can also be problematic. A sward that sweeps diagonally across the width of the garden will make it appear longer. Growing taller plants towards the back of the garden and lower ones at the front will also give the illusion that the lawn is longer than it really is.

Practical considerations

If the lawn is going to be regularly walked on, avoid narrow entrances since these will accelerate the wear in a small area and cause compaction. Installing several access points onto the lawn may alleviate some of the problem. Make sure that the access point is wide enough to get the mower through. If the lawn is raised above the path and patio, ensure that there is one easy access point – petrol mowers are extremely heavy and not easy to drag up steps. You will be exhausted before you even start up the mower.

Unless it is an essential part of the overall design of the garden, it is best to avoid creating small patches of grass that are going to be awkward to mow. Narrow strips will allow the mower to move only in one direction and can cause compaction. Tight corners also make it difficult to manoeuvre a mower, so consider making the edge of the grass curved instead. Also avoid taking the lawn right up to the edges of fences and walls, as it will not be possible to get the mower close enough for a clean cut. Leave a small gap of 10–15cm (4–6in) between the edges of the lawn and the boundaries.

Rectangular lawns can be made more interesting by allowing more room for planting around the edge. This approach is best suited to informal gardens and larger plots. Note that a few large curves are often better than lots of small undulations, which can appear fussy. Large borders also make space for more ornamental planting, although the larger they are, the more maintenance they require.

Preparing the site

Preparation for creating a lawn should begin at least eight weeks before laying turf or sowing seed. This gives the soil a chance to settle and you time to get the weeds under control. For autumn sowing or winter turfing, you should begin preparing in summer. For spring sowing, begin in autumn, or in summer if levelling is to be done.

Clearing the site

The first stage is to clear the site of any rubbish (*see right*) before levelling can begin. This includes removing any builder's rubble and any stones and bricks. You will also need to dig out tree stumps, removing as much of the root system as possible. Leaving them in the soil will encourage fungi and other diseases. Most stumps can be removed using a pickaxe and spade, but for really large ones it might be necessary to hire an excavator and driver.

All weeds need to be removed, either manually or by chemical means. When digging it is essential you remove all the roots as well as their top growth.

Preparing the soil

You should now dig over or deeply rotavate the soil (*see box, below right*), as this reduces the compaction and allows air into the soil. Grass prefers a well-drained loamy soil to a depth of at least 20cm (8in). Add sharp sand to poorly drained soil, and if the soil is too well drained then incorporate well-rotted organic matter. Most soils should be within the pH limits of 5.5–7; if your soil is not, it is worth seeking professional advice.

If the soil is waterlogged, seek professional advice about installing drainage. Alternatively, reconsider the project and find plants and a design more suited to the conditions. In milder cases it may be possible to remedy the problem by spreading an 8cm (3in) layer of sharp sand onto the surface. This requires a brick or metal edge to hold the sand together and level. A week before the seed or turf is placed, well-rotted organic matter is then spread over the surface to encourage rooting.

Grading & levelling the site

The term grading means the elimination of surface irregularities. Levelling is the process whereby a sloping site is made level (*see box, facing page*). Both jobs can be expensive and on larger sites need not be necessary as gentle slopes or undulations can be visually pleasing. Minor irregularities can be corrected by adding a little topsoil. Do not take this from higher points on the site, as this can leave it very thin in places, causing bare patches.

CLEARING THE SITE

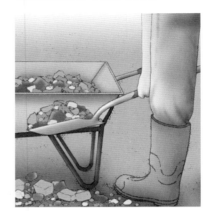

1 Remove any debris, including any waste left by builders, such as rubble and bricks. If builders have left heaps of subsoil, remove that as well, since the fertility of subsoil is low. Tree stumps, roots and all weeds will also need to be removed.

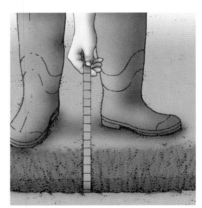

2 Test the depth of the topsoil and, if necessary, purchase extra from a local supplier to bring it up to a minimum depth of 15cm (6in). Recently vacated building sites may have lost much of their topsoil.

USING A ROTAVATOR

Large areas of ground are best cleared and cultivated with a rotavator (rotary cultivator). These chop up perennial weeds rather than remove them, so weed control will still be necessary.

Final site preparation

The soil should ultimately be broken down into a fine tilth. Use a metal rake or reversed garden fork to break up clods of soil and to level out any bumps or dips. Work the soil to a fine crumbly texture. It will need to be fairly dry to do this as wet soil sticks to tools.

Soils that are heavy may be very rough after digging. These need to be weathered for up to a year before they can be worked to the right consistency.

Firm the soil evenly to remove any air pockets (*see below*), then rake it over. This can be repeated a number of times, but be careful not to compact the soil too much. After this is done, check the levels and make the appropriate changes if necessary.

Allow several weeks for the site to lie fallow, during which time weed seedlings can be killed periodically by light hoeing or spraying with herbicide. Fallowing is less important on sites where turf is to be laid. About a week before seeding or laying turf, a base dressing of compound granular superphosphate fertilizer can be added to the soil at a rate of 150–200g (5¹⁄₂–7oz) per square metre (10 sq ft), then raked in.

FIRMING THE SOIL

1 Lightly tread evenly over the site, taking short or overlapping steps and with the weight of the body on the heels. The purpose is to remove air pockets. Any stones that are discovered as you work over the site should be removed.

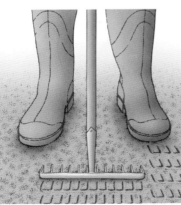

2 Tamp down the soil with the back of a rake, as an alternative to treading, then use the rake to lightly groom the soil back into a fine tilth. The site can be trodden down 2 or 3 times more and raked, although be careful not to compact the soil too much.

LEVELLING THE SITE

It is not essential to have a perfectly level site; a gentle fall is quite acceptable and has the advantage of assisting surface drainage. Many people will try to level the ground by eye, but to produce a fine ornamental lawn it is best to do the job properly. To do so, you will need to create a level grid of wooden pegs, each one with a mark 10cm (4in) from the top. One of these is the master peg, from which all the other pegs take their guide. You will need to add or remove soil to the level on each peg, only removing the pegs once all the soil is evenly firmed.

1 Hammer the pegs into the soil in a grid system 2m (6ft) apart. If the garden has an existing path or patio then make sure that the mark on the master peg is level with it.

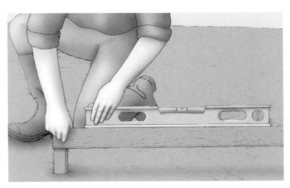

2 Use a straight plank and spirit level to ensure that the pegs are level, working away from the master peg. Adjust the height of the secondary pegs until all are level with the master.

3 Add or remove topsoil, firming it down so that the surface is level with the mark on each peg. Fill in any dips or bumps.

Seed or turf?

One factor in determining whether to use turf or seed is the time of year. Turf (pre-grown strips of grass) can be laid at any time except during frosty or extended dry periods, although it is usually laid from early autumn to late winter to avoid the need for copious watering. Grass seed is normally sown in early autumn or mid-spring, but it will germinate in summer, as temperatures are too low in winter.

Advantages of seed

Seeds are far cheaper than turf and are less bulky and so easy to store. They have a long shelf life, allowing the gardener to wait for suitable weather conditions. Different seed mixes allow the lawn to be tailored to the function, style, and conditions of the garden. Sowing seed is also lighter work than laying heavy rolls of turf.

Disadvantages of seed

It can take months before a seed-sown lawn is ready for use; even then it might still be patchy and need more work. After sowing, you will need to prevent birds eating the seeds. Weed seeds may blow onto the site and compete with the seedling grass for nutrients and water.

Advantages of turf

Turfing is a more appealing proposition for someone who wants to brighten up the garden instantly. The lawn may be used fairly soon – six weeks for light wear – after it has been laid. Turf can be laid in winter when there are fewer other jobs to be done in the garden.

Disadvantages of turf

Turf is far more expensive than raising a lawn from seed. Be wary about the quality of the turf: inexperienced gardeners may fail to notice the difference between good- and poor-quality turf (*see page 284*).

Advance notice will be needed if the turf is delivered. Once delivered or purchased, the turf must be laid within a few days. If the weather turns wet or cold, it will be very difficult to lay the turf properly, resulting in a loss of turf – and money.

Laying turf is hard work. It involves carrying and handling heavy rolls of turf, often from the front garden around to the back garden. If it does not rain, the turf will need constant watering after laying to help it root down into the soil – not an environmentally friendly option.

Seedling grass is very delicate and should not be walked on at all for at least 10 weeks and not used much for the first growing season, to allow it to establish a good root system.

Recently laid turf, if it is kept well watered, will root together and into the soil quickly and can be used much sooner than seed-sown lawns. It is still wise to avoid heavy wear of the turf in the first 6 months.

Planning the lawn *see page 278* | **Lawn maintenance** *see page 286*

Sowing a lawn

The best time to sow seed is early autumn when the soil is still warm and the rainfall keeps the soil moist. You can also sow in spring, but the grass has to compete with weed seedlings, and cooler soil and early spring frosts will hinder germination and growth. Summer sowing is possible but the lawn will require constant watering during dry periods.

Grass seeds need a slightly moist soil to germinate successfully. If the soil is dry, lightly water it a couple of days before sowing, then rake the soil over again.

Choose a calm day for sowing – any wind will blow the seeds about and result in uneven distribution. Do not sow in wet conditions because the wet soil and seeds will stick to boots and the wheels of the seed distributor. Rake over the site just before sowing to break up any surface capping of the soil and ensure that the seeds settle well.

Check the sowing rate for the seed mix to avoid any problems. The usual rate is 50g (2oz) per square metre (10 sq ft), but this can vary depending on the mix. Sowing too much seed increases the surface humidity, which encourages damping off disease. Sowing too thinly leaves bare patches of lawn which allows weeds to establish.

Sowing grass seed by hand
Divide the area up and calculate how much seed is needed to fill each grid section. Use a measuring cup to portion out the seeds. Sow in two directions for an even distribution (*see above, right*). To get a sharp edge to the lawn, cover the perimeter of the site with plastic or hessian to stop any seeds falling outside the area. Alternatively, an edge could be cut with a half-moon edger once the grass has established.

Sowing grass seed with a seed distributor
A distributor spreads seeds evenly at the required rate. As with hand sowing, the edges may be covered to obtain a straight edge. Push the machine onto the sheeting at the end of each row to stop seeds falling out as you turn.

Aftercare
It is important to keep the soil moist, so if the weather remains dry, water frequently using a sprinkler system with a fine spray. Avoid dragging a hose over the site as this will disturb the seeds. Protect the area from birds by placing a net over the site, or use a scarecrow for larger areas. Seedlings should appear 7–21 days after sowing. When they reach about 6cm (2½in), lightly cut the grass with a rotary mower (a cylinder mower will rip out the seedlings). Repeat mow at the same height into the growing season.

SOWING GRASS SEEDS

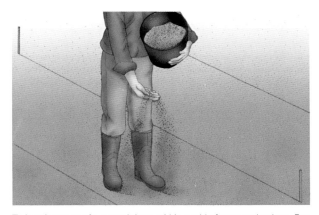

To hand sow seeds, spread them within a grid of pegs and strings. For each area, scatter half the amount needed in one direction over the soil. Sow the other half of the seeds at right angles to the first spreading.

To use a seed distributor, fill the machine with half the required amount of seeds for the plot and push it up and down the area lengthways. Refill the machine and repeat, walking across the plot.

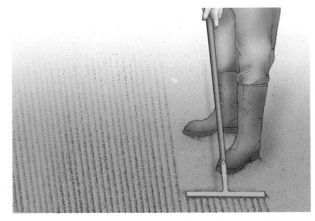

After sowing the seeds, lightly rake over the seedbed to bed the seeds gently into the soil. Work backwards to avoid treading on the raked soil and do not bury the seeds too deeply since this inhibits germination.

Laying turf

Lightly water the prepared site a couple of days before laying the turf if there has been no rain, but do not saturate the soil because this will make it too sticky and unworkable. A light level of moisture in the soil will encourage the roots downwards and will also allow the soil to settle before the turf is laid.

Initial checks

Turves are relatively expensive to buy and it's best to inspect them before purchasing to ensure that the grass is of a good quality. The soil should be of a loam consistency with a well-established root system and few stones. The thickness of the rolls of turf should be consistent; if they are of uneven thicknesses, achieving a level lawn will be almost impossible and all the hard work that has gone into site preparation will go to waste. The grass should be uniform in appearance with no weeds. Be prepared to send the turf back if the quality is not up to scratch.

If you cannot place the turves immediately after delivery, stack or lay them out individually (*see box, facing page*). The turves should be laid as soon after delivery as possible, as they quickly deteriorate.

LAYING TURVES

1 Apply a pre-turfing fertilizer to the prepared soil unless it is already very fertile. This fertilizer can be purchased from most garden centres. Follow the manufacturer's instructions for the rate of application.

2 Rake the soil before laying the turf. Start by positioning the turf at the edge of the site, ideally along a long, straight edge such as a path or against a patio.

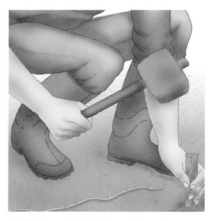

3 Mark out the first line with wooden pegs and garden twine if there is no straight edge. To lay turf, work facing the prepared site and avoid standing on it; always use a plank whenever you need to stand on the site.

4 Lay the first row of turf out along the line, butting the edges of each piece right up to the next. Start the second row by cutting a strip of turf in half and use one half as the first piece before continuing with full-sized turves.

5 Avoid using small strips of turf at the end of a row, as these will dry out. If a short piece is needed to finish a row, move a full-size turf section to the end of the row, lay another over the gap so that it overlaps, and trim to fit.

6 Firm each turf to avoid air pockets by tamping it down gently with the back of a rake. Keep a bucket of sandy loam with you and work some into any hollow that may have formed; firm to produce a level surface.

CHECKING & STORING TURVES

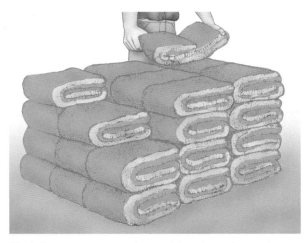

Check the turves as soon as they are delivered, to make sure that they are healthy and of good quality. The turves can be stored for 2–3 days by stacking them, rolled or folded, 3–4 turves deep.

Lay out each turf section in a shaded position and keep well watered if you need to store them for more than 3 days. If you allow them to dry out, the exposed roots will dry out, shrivel and die.

Laying turves

When laying the turf, it is important to avoid walking on the prepared soil or the newly laid turves. Use wooden planks to stand on as you lay the turf and as pathways to fetch new pieces. This helps to distribute the weight and avoid compaction and indentations. Lay the rows so that the joins between turves are staggered, as in brickwork, to create a stronger bond. Make sure that each row is tightly butted up against the previous one.

Avoid turfing right up to the edges of fences and walls, as this will be difficult to cut cleanly with a mower and will need strimming. Leave a space of about 30cm (12in) and fill the gap with paving slabs or another hard surface; ensure they are just below the height of the lawn. Never turf right up to a tree to avoid damaging the tree with the mower. It is best not to turf banks as they are hard to mow and dangerous if using a ride-on mower.

Aftercare

Water frequently if the weather remains dry. Wait for the grass to start growing before you mow, then cut with the mower on a high setting. You can walk on the new lawn right away, but full use should be postponed until the roots have knitted into the soil.

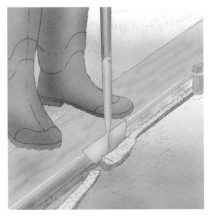

7 **Trim the edges** of the finished turf with a half-moon edger. Stand on a plank of wood and use it as a guide to make sure that the cut is straight. Use a hose pipe laid on the turf as a guideline to create curving edges.

8 **Scatter a sandy topdressing** (1 part organic matter to 3 parts sand and 3 parts loam) across the surface of the lawn and lightly work it into the joins with a broom, back of a rake or a lute.

9 **Firm the new lawn** with a light roller to eradicate any remaining air pockets. Do not roll the turf if it is wet; instead, wait until the turves have grown together. Water thoroughly.

LAWN MAINTENANCE

Once a lawn is established, it will need regular upkeep to keep it healthy and looking good all year. A little and often maintenance is the key to achieving a lawn that is lush and green. On the other hand, long periods of neglect rapidly cause problems, resulting in the lawn looking tatty or even dying off in parts. As well as mowing, you will need to feed the grass and water when needed, and carry out an annual overhaul involving scarifying, aerating, and topdressing the lawn. These processes promote healthy, strong, growth, giving the grass a greater capacity to combat attacks from pests, diseases, mosses, and weeds.

Feeding lawns

The three main plant nutrients are nitrogen, phosphorus, and potassium, often seen expressed as a ratio N:P:K on fertilizer packets. Iron (Fe) is also a key ingredient; it helps to 'green up' the grass without stimulating growth, making it useful in autumn feeds. Other essential minerals are required for healthy growth, but in far lower quantities. The one disadvantage with feeding lawns is that the grass grows faster and needs cutting more often.

USING A FEED DISTRIBUTOR

Lawn fertilizer may be applied using a belt- or drop-spreading machine; push it up and down the lawn as if it were a mower. Take care to distribute the feed evenly; apply half a batch in one direction and the other half at right angles to it.

Proprietary mixes

A lawn should be fed in spring or early summer and again in autumn. Spring feeds, high in nitrogen for lush growth, are applied as the grass starts to grow. Feeds given in autumn, as growth of the grass slows, are lower in nitrogen – late, vigorous growth encourages lank grass prey to fungal diseases – and higher in phosphate to encourage good root systems. Most proprietary mixes blend slow- and fast-release compounds; they act quickly and have a continuing effect. Blends of fertilizer and weedkiller are available, such as lawn sand (sulphate of ammonia, iron sulphate, and fine sand), which kill mosses and some weeds but also provide nutrients for growth.

The organic approach

Natural phosphate may be added by sprinkling bonemeal over the lawn in autumn. If you leave grass cuttings on the lawn after mowing, they take nitrogen into the soil as they break down. Alternatively, rake in well-rotted, friable compost to add nitrogen and potassium in spring.

Application methods

Over-application of fertilizer can damage the lawn so read the instructions carefully. Feeds should be applied in dry weather when rain is predicted in the next couple of days. If no rain appears, gently water in the fertilizer, using a hosepipe. Application by hand is simplest. Measure out the required amount of feed for the size of lawn and divide in half; spread the first batch crossways and the second batch lengthways for an even distribution. Always wear gloves when handling chemicals. Spinner-type feed distributors are useful for large areas, but spread unevenly.

Making compost *see page 23* | **Lawn weeds** *see page 294* | **Lawn pests & diseases** *see page 296*

Scarifying

Scarifying involves slightly aerating the soil surface and removing excess thatch (*see right*) from the lawn. A small amount of thatch is fine, but heavy thatch impedes the development of new blades of grass, shades out sunlight, and encourages moss. It can also stop fertilizers reaching the grass roots, and it absorbs moisture during damp periods, harbouring fungal diseases, as well as preventing water from penetrating the soil in drought.

Apply lawn sand before scarifying to kill off any moss. To scarify, vigorously scrape a rake over the lawn surface, keeping the tool well pressed down so that the tines penetrate the soil. Work across the grass from one edge, scraping towards yourself. Once you have raked all the lawn, rake it again, working at right angles to the original direction. Mow the lawn afterwards to remove any loose pieces of thatch. Add all the thatch to the compost heap. Scarifying should also remove any blackened, dead pieces of moss. You may need to reseed any bare patches. Scarifying with a rake is tiring work, so you may prefer to use a scarifying machine. Scarifying attachments for some types of lawnmower are effective.

The best time to scarify is early autumn, when the growth of the lawn starts to slow. This is when the grass starts to thicken and send out shoots from new stolons

Thatch is the springy remains of dead grass and other fibrous material that accumulates among the blades of grass; a small amount retains moisture during drought and protects the lawn from wear.

(spreading stems) and rhizomes (creeping underground stems). Scarification can also be done in spring, but this can leave bare patches and it can take the lawn a long time to recover. If it is essential to scarify in spring, do it lightly with a spring-tined rake.

SCARIFYING TOOLS

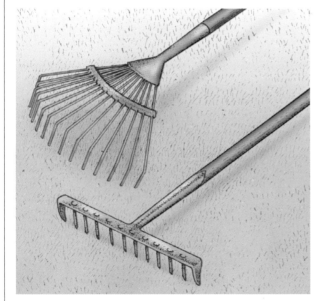

A spring-tined rake (*see top*) is preferable to a standard garden rake because the flexible wire tines penetrate and aerate the soil without lifting it up or dragging out the grass roots.

A scarifying machine is useful for larger areas of lawn. These usually pick up the thatch as they travel across the lawn, but it is best to mow afterwards to tidy the lawn up and pick up any remaining debris.

Aeration

Over time, lawns become compacted by foot traffic, games playing, garden furniture, or even frequent mowing. Unnecessary compression with a lawn roller is also a cause. Compaction can result in major problems for the health of the lawn by impeding the flow of air and water into the soil.

Grass roots, as in all other plants, rely on air to assist with the uptake of water and nutrients. In compacted soils their growth is physically restricted. Water drains poorly, causing surface waterlogging, and in drought, irrigation water cannot penetrate. Compacted lawns soon weaken and become infested with tougher weeds. If air cannot reach the roots, the grass begins to starve, ultimately turning brown and dying.

Regular aeration in autumn reduces compaction and encourages strong root growth. In the aeration process, channels are created in the lawn to allow the air and water to penetrate deeply into the soil.

Methods of aeration

Scarifying forms part of the aeration process by removing the thatch. True aeration, however, needs to penetrate deeper into the soil, making holes to a depth of at least 6.5cm (3in) but ideally 10–15cm (4–6in).

A hollow-tined fork, which gives better results on clay soils than a standard fork, can be used to aerate small areas of lawn. Hand-operated or powered aeration

AERATING MACHINES

An aerating machine cuts through the thatch on the surface of the lawn and creates parallel slits or holes that sink up to 8–10cm (3–4in) into the soil. This allows air and water to penetrate.

machines, with hollow or solid tines, are best for larger areas. On sandy soils, aeration is ineffective as the holes quickly collapse, but sandy soils usually drain adequately.

Aerate in early autumn, at the same time as scarifying. Begin in one corner of the lawn and work backwards to avoid walking on the aerated areas. Fill the holes with sharp sand or a sandy topdressing. Do not aerate during wet weather as the plugs will stick to the tines.

AERATING LAWNS MANUALLY

Hold a fork with the tines curving towards you and drive it into the ground. Move the fork back and forth slightly to enlarge the holes, and remove it without lifting the turf. Repeat across the lawn.

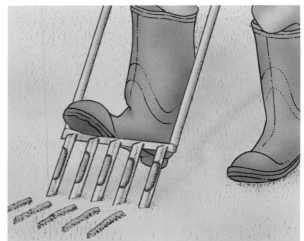

Drive a hollow-tined fork into the ground to remove small plugs or cores from the lawn. Each time you sink the fork into the soil, the previous plugs will fall out. When you have finished, remove the plugs.

Topdressing

A lawn is improved by a layer of specially prepared fine soil. Light soils, for example, benefit from added organic matter and loam, and the drainage of heavy soils is improved by extra sand. The process also encourages new basal growth from the grass, creating a much denser lawn. Lastly, topdressing is used to fill any hollows that have developed over the year.

When to topdress

High-quality turf or lawns on poor soils benefit from topdressing annually; topdress other lawns every two or three years. Aerating the soil prior to topdressing is recommended, particularly on heavy soils, because this will make it easier for the topdressing to penetrate the soil.

The process should be carried out in early autumn, while the grass is still growing, after aerating and scarifying, otherwise the topdressing will be disturbed or removed. After completion, new shoots will appear through the topdressing.

Making topdressing mixes

Ready-made mixes are available from garden centres, but it is easy to make up your own mix. Lawn topdressing has three ingredients: loam, sand, and organic matter. Do not use builder's or sea sand as these may be very alkaline. The organic matter is traditionally peat, but leaf mould or garden compost is fine. A typical mix contains 3:3:1 parts

of sand, loam, and organic matter, but the blend may be modified to suit individual soil types. Pass the mix through a 5mm (¼in) mesh sieve to remove lumps.

The amount of topdressing required will vary depending on the state of the lawn and the type of soil. For example, more may be used if the lawn has been hollow-tined, as there will be holes to fill. An average lawn requires 1.5–2kg (3–4lb) per square metre (10 sq ft).

USING A LUTE

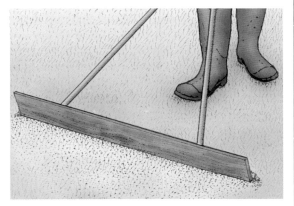

A lute may be used to level a lawn surface after it has been topdressed. Drag it over the ground to work the topdressing into the soil and level out any ridges or bumps. You can make a lute from a 1.5m (5ft) wooden plank and a pair of poles for the handle.

APPLYING A TOPDRESSING

1 **Spread the topdressing** as evenly as possible with a shovel, once an appropriate amount has been measured.

2 **Work as much topdressing** as possible into the soil by pushing it over the surface with the back of a rake. Remove any excess.

Alternatively, brush the lawn, using a broom with stiff bristles, to work the topdressing into the soil. Again, remove any excess.

Watering

During periods of summer drought, a lawn can suffer badly from lack of water. Most garden lawns, however, can withstand drought and will recover in autumn when the rains return. Only water your lawn during shortages of water if absolutely necessary. You can help grass to survive a drought by cutting the lawn less often and on a much higher setting than usual. Lawn maintenance such as scarifying, aerating, and topdressing contributes to a healthy, deep root system that can withstand drought.

When & how to water

To reduce wastage from evaporation, water in the early morning or early evening. Late evening watering may leave an excess of surface water, encouraging diseases and moss. During drought, water only if it is essential to maintain a green sward. Your soil type will affect how frequently you should water. Avoid light, daily watering that soaks just the top layer of soil, as this draws the roots up towards the surface. As a rule of thumb, a high-quality turf on loamy soil needs watering once a week in a drought. Light, sandy soil struggles to hold on to moisture so requires more watering. Heavy, moisture-retentive soil needs far less.

Use a hosepipe fitted with a spray gun or a sprinkler if you need to water. The water should penetrate to a depth of 10–15cm (4–6in); dig a small hole to monitor the water level so that you can determine how long the

First symptoms of drought in a lawn include dulling of colour and slowing growth. The leaves then turn yellow and brown. Eventually, the grass shrivels up and begins to die back, allowing weeds to invade.

sprinkler takes to dampen the soil at the required depth. Do not waste water by placing a sprinkler so that spray falls on paths, patios, or fences. Runoff can occur if the surface is crusty or the lawn is sloping; turn the sprinkler off and allow the water to soak down before switching it back on. Hard, crusty surfaces can be spiked with a fork so that water can penetrate.

WATERING EQUIPMENT

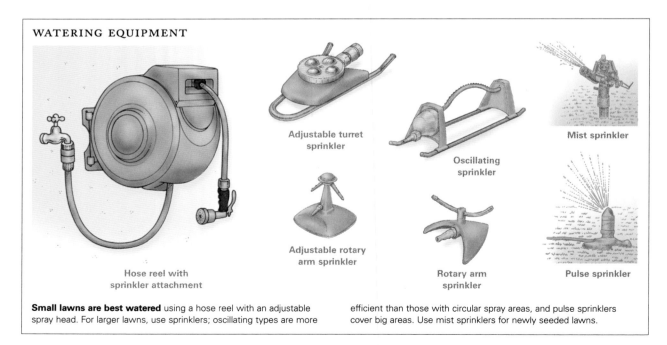

Adjustable turret sprinkler

Oscillating sprinkler

Mist sprinkler

Adjustable rotary arm sprinkler

Rotary arm sprinkler

Pulse sprinkler

Hose reel with sprinkler attachment

Small lawns are best watered using a hose reel with an adjustable spray head. For larger lawns, use sprinklers; oscillating types are more efficient than those with circular spray areas, and pulse sprinklers cover big areas. Use mist sprinklers for newly seeded lawns.

Lawn tools & mowers

There are two basic types of mower: rotary and cylinder. Rotary mowers are most popular: they have horizontal blades that spin beneath a motor and are ideal for less formal grass areas, uneven ground, and longer grass. They do not cut as cleanly as a cylinder mower, but some petrol models have a heavy roller behind the blades to produce stripes. More expensive rotary mowers are self propelling. Hover models have a rotary blade and float over the lawn on a cushion of air, making them light to handle. Always disconnect the power supply before inspecting the blades.

Traditional cylinder mowers give the best cut. The blades are mounted around a cylinder that revolves as the mower moves forward, slicing the grass between the blades and a stationary bar that lies parallel to the ground. There is usually a roller behind the blades to create formal stripes. With hand-driven cylinder mowers, the pushing action spins the cylinder; they are light, easy to use, and the most environmentally friendly option. Petrol-driven powered cylinder mowers usually have a wider cutting width than electric ones. Costlier options include ride-on mowers, suitable only for large lawns, and automatic mowers.

Petrol-driven or electric mower?

Mowers that run on petrol are more powerful, more expensive, and heavier than electric mowers and may be rotary or cylinder, self-propelling or require pushing. They are suitable for larger gardens because their range is

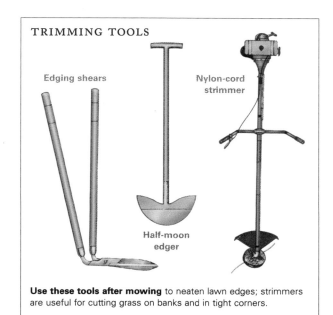

TRIMMING TOOLS

Edging shears

Half-moon edger

Nylon-cord strimmer

Use these tools after mowing to neaten lawn edges; strimmers are useful for cutting grass on banks and in tight corners.

not restricted by a cable, but some may find them too heavy to manoeuvre. They last longer than electric mowers but need regular maintenance.

Electric mowers are light, easy to manoeuvre, and good for small spaces. They are also quieter than petrol mowers. Some are battery powered or cordless, so you do not need to worry about cables.

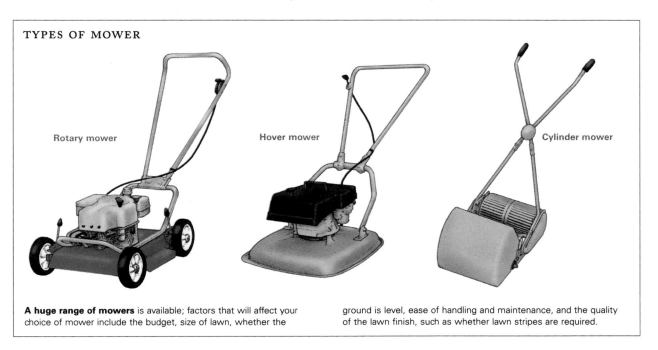

TYPES OF MOWER

Rotary mower

Hover mower

Cylinder mower

A huge range of mowers is available; factors that will affect your choice of mower include the budget, size of lawn, whether the ground is level, ease of handling and maintenance, and the quality of the lawn finish, such as whether lawn stripes are required.

Mowing lawns

Regular mowing, using a good technique, encourages healthy new grass growth and a strong root system that enables the grass to survive periods of drought or prolonged rain. It should be an easy and satisfying job. Mowing also helps prevent a build up of pests and diseases and keeps down weeds and removes their seedheads. Uncut grass looks unsightly and allows coarser grasses to dominate and weeds to invade the turf. Most lawns should be cut frequently but not too closely.

The correct height

Cutting a lawn to an appropriate height at the correct time of year is vital for a healthy lawn. If cut too low, the surface of the lawn will dry out too quickly, making it susceptible to drought, and moss may encroach into the short sward. Cutting grass so short that it scalps the lawn will leave unsightly bare patches of soil as well as blunt the blades. Grass cut too high results in poor, weak, and lank growth that lacks vigour and thickness. With the exception of meadows, it is unwise to try to save time by leaving the grass to grow long and then giving it one major chop.

When to cut

Grass should be cut during the main growing period, beginning in early to mid-spring. Never mow when it is wet or raining because the grass sticks to the blades,

Frequent mowing makes the job easier and quicker, with fewer clippings to remove. It results in an attractive and healthy lawn – an important factor in giving a garden a well-maintained appearance.

giving a poor cut. Avoid mowing early in the morning if dew is on the ground. Instead, knock the dew into the grass by running a bamboo cane or besom broom across it and mow a few hours later. Leave the grass to grow slightly longer in prolonged dry periods as this will help it to survive and reduce the need for watering.

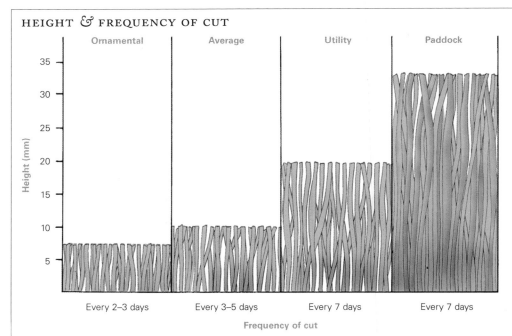

HEIGHT & FREQUENCY OF CUT

	Ornamental	Average	Utility	Paddock
Frequency of cut	Every 2–3 days	Every 3–5 days	Every 7 days	Every 7 days

Height (mm): 35, 30, 25, 20, 15, 10, 5

This chart indicates the heights to which different lawns should be cut from late spring to early autumn, as well as how often they should be cut. Allow the grass to grow 1–2cm (½–¾in) taller outside the peak growing season.

When the grass starts to grow in spring, the first few cuts should be made slightly higher than the optimum height for the lawn type, and gradually reduced down to the correct height for the rest of the growing season.

Utility lawns are standard back-garden family lawns which undergo frequent wear and foot traffic.

Factors such as the season, weather conditions, the health of the grass, irrigation, and weeds all influence the rate at which grass grows, and a good gardener will adapt the mowing methods accordingly. Mow under trees less often and leave the grass taller. The lawn may be mown in winter during mild spells, to tidy the garden and remove fallen leaves; raise the cutting blade to a high setting. Never mow in frosty conditions or when cold winds are blowing as this will scorch leaf tips.

Removing grass clippings

Generally, it is best to remove clippings from the lawn, particularly from fine grass, since they look unsightly. Weed seeds remain on the surface of the lawn and will germinate if not collected up. Even chopped stems from white clover (*Trifolium repens*) and speedwell (*Veronica* species) will regenerate. Clippings may also smother the grass by stopping air reaching the soil and, in damp autumns, cause an increase in surface humidity, which will encourage fungal diseases. Finally, damp clippings encourage unsightly worm casts.

There are, however, some benefits to leaving clippings on the lawn. It makes mowing much easier and quicker, as you do not have grass clippings to collect or a grass box to carry and empty, and it returns nitrogen to the soil, increasing the fertility, greenness, and lushness of the grass. In dry periods, the clippings act as a mulch by helping to retain moisture and slow down the rate of evaporation from the lawn. Some mowers have a built-in mulcher, which chops the cuttings into tiny pieces before dropping them back onto the grass. This is a good compromise, but it will still spread weed seeds.

You can compost clippings by adding them in layers to a compost heap (*see box, right*). As they contain large quantities of moisture, they will decompose into a slimy mass if you simply heap them into one big pile. Dried clippings can also be used as a mulch around the garden, but they can contain large quantities of lawn weed seeds.

Mowing techniques

Before mowing, remove all debris; stones, twigs, and pet droppings can fly out from under the mower and harm the operator as well as the blades of the mower. Brush fine turf before mowing to ensure that the grass blades are standing upright and will be cut at the correct height. Brushing also removes any wormcasts that would otherwise leave brown patches of soil on the lawn after being crushed under the mower.

Plan the direction of mowing before starting to avoid getting stuck in corners, making tight turns, or repeatedly

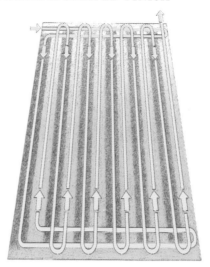

PRODUCING A STRIPED FINISH

For a formal lawn, with contrasting dark and light stripes, use a lawnmower with a rear roller. Mow in parallel rows, with each row in the opposite direction to the next. This effect cannot be obtained if the grass is too long, so frequent mowing is required.

COMPOSTING GRASS CLIPPINGS

Add small quantities of grass clippings to the compost heap in thin layers, alternating them with layers of other garden and organic waste. If you have large quantities of clippings, it is useful to let them dry out first by spreading them out thinly.

mowing the same areas of grass and causing compaction. Mow at 90 degrees to the direction of the previous cut, to smooth out irregularities in the grass.

After mowing, tidy up edges with edging shears and steep banks or awkward corners with a strimmer (*see box, page 291*). Once or twice a year, neaten border edges, if necessary, with a half-moon edger.

COMMON PROBLEMS

Lawns may be invaded by a wide range of weeds. However, the degree to which you need to control them depends on the effect required. A fine display lawn has no place for weeds and moss, but a practical family lawn may be less pristine; some lawn weeds may form part of a wildflower garden. Pests and diseases are much easier to control if dealt with at an early stage, but before you do so make sure you have the diagnosis correct; the most common problem in lawns is discoloured grass, which could be caused by pests or diseases but is often a sign of problems such as poor mowing, pet damage, or drought.

Lawn weeds

The best way to keep weeds out is to encourage lawn grasses to thrive, producing a dense, healthy sward in which weeds cannot establish. Light, well-cultivated soil, good drainage, reasonable fertility, and an open, sunny position are ideal, together with regular mowing.

Weeds exploit poor conditions such as compacted ground, poor drainage, shade, lack of water or nutrients, and grass that has been mowed too short. Trees, especially if they have overhanging branches and are shallow rooted or evergreen, provide such conditions as they deprive grass of water and nutrients. A solution for smaller specimen trees is to cut a circular or square bed around them, which can be planted with shade-tolerant plants.

Main types of lawn weed

Rosette-forming weeds: These form a flattened whorl of leaves, smothering the grass beneath and escaping mower blades. Daisies (*Bellis perennis*) are an example.

Creeping weeds: These colonize gaps in turf, outgrowing grass in poor conditions. The stems lie lower than mower blades. White clover (*Trifolium repens*) is an example.

Weed grasses: These include coarse species like Yorkshire fog (*Holcus lanatus*) and grass relatives like field woodrush (*Luzula campestris*). They cause uneven colour and texture.

Mosses, liverworts and lichens: These are most often a problem in lawns where the soil is compacted, poorly drained, or very shaded. Moss is almost always present, to

COMMON PERENNIAL LAWN WEEDS

Yarrow (*Achillea millefolium*) is able to survive drought and mowing. It has spreading roots and forms mats on free-draining soils. The flowers appear from early summer to late autumn.

Mouse-ear hawkweed (*Hieracium pilosella*) has a basal rosette. It prefers dry, sunny places, spreading by rooting stem tips (stolons) and flowering from late spring to mid-autumn.

Broad-leaved plantain (*Plantago major*) has a large rosette and long straight roots from a short rhizome. It survives in well-trodden areas and flowers from early summer to mid-autumn.

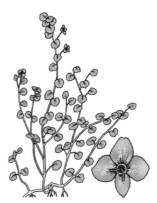

Slender speedwell (*Veronica filiformis*) is a low, creeping weed that forms dense mats and can root from stem fragments. It thrives in grassy terrain, flowering from mid-spring to early summer.

Creating a wildflower area *see page 52* | **Lawn maintenance** *see page 286* | **Repairing neglected lawns** *see page 299*

SPOT TREATMENT

Use a chemical spot weeder if you have only a few weeds in the lawn, especially weeds that form basal rosettes or small patches of creeping weeds. Some are available in the form of an aerosol or ready-to-use spray.

Spot weeders are also available as a solid, waxy stick or as a liquid applied by roller ball. Some weeds, such as plantains, will succumb after 1–2 applications of weedkiller; other weeds may require several treatments over 4 to 6 weeks.

BROAD APPLICATIONS OF WEEDKILLER

Lawn weedkillers may be applied in a variety of ways. Concentrated liquids require dilution before use and should be applied using a watering can and dribble bar, or a sprayer on a coarse setting to reduce the risk of spray drift.

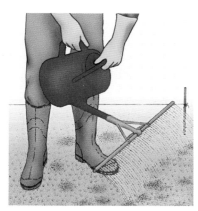

Granular products are applied dry and are more economical over large areas. Scatter the granules by hand or with a hand-held spreader.
 A wheeled spreader is useful and can be hired. Usually you need to water in the granules if it does not rain within a few days of application – check the instructions for details.

a certain extent, but too much can smother fine grasses and weaken the turf's resilience to wear. Liverworts and lichens make the soil slippery.

Chemical lawn weedkillers

These target broadleaved weeds but do not harm grass if used correctly. Some weeds are resistant to particular weedkillers, so most products contain a blend of active ingredients. You may need to repeat the application; if some weeds persist, use a product with different active ingredients. A few weeds, such as slender speedwell, resist all lawn weedkillers. Dig them out, or use a general-purpose weedkiller – which will also kill the grass – and reseed or returf the affected area. Mosskillers are often combined with lawn weedkillers and fertilizers.

Removing grass weeds manually

Lawn weedkillers do not affect weed grasses, which you will need to remove by hand. For large areas, the only option may be to returf or reseed the affected lawn. You can remove moss by scarifying in spring. Lichens and liverworts may be raked or scraped off the soil.

HAND WEEDING

Ease out rosette-forming weeds with a small tool called a daisy grubber or cut the taproot with an old knife and lift the weed out. Tackle creeping weeds when they first invade as they are much easier, and cheaper, to control at this early stage.

295

Lawn pests & diseases

Fortunately, there are not many pests and diseases that attack lawns, but the few that do can cause unsightly damage. As with any problem, prompt action at the correct time will be the most effective.

PESTS

There are two categories of lawn pest: those that feed on grass roots, weakening the turf, and those that deposit soil on the lawn, which is unsightly and hinders mowing.

Chafer grubs

The curved grubs of the chafer beetle destroy grass roots, making it easy for foxes, badgers, and crows to dig up the turf as they feed on the grubs. Damage is visible from autumn to spring, although the larvae start feeding in early summer. Apply imidacloprid or a biological control (the nematode *Heterorhabditis megidis*) in early summer.

Leatherjackets

These tubular larvae eat grass roots and can kill areas of lawn during late winter to summer. The adults, known as crane flies or daddy-longlegs, emerge and lay eggs in early autumn. Control the newly hatched larvae with imidacloprid or use a biological control (the nematode *Steinernema feltiae*) in early or mid-autumn.

Wormcasts

Earthworms feed on dead plant material in the soil. They are beneficial animals because their tunnels provide drainage and aeration passages through the soil. Some species of earthworms, however, deposit their muddy excrement in small heaps on the surface. These worm casts get smeared when the lawn is mown or walked on, spoiling the appearance of fine lawns and allowing the establishment of weeds. There are no chemical controls currently available to amateur gardeners. Break up and disperse the casts by brushing or raking them when dry.

Ants

These cause little direct damage to plants but can be a nuisance. They bring soil to the surface when they extend their nests and create an uneven sward. Brush away the excavated soil when it is dry. Where mounds have built up over time, restore a level surface by peeling back the turf and removing the excess soil. It is easier to do this in winter when ants are less active. Insecticides deal with ants on the surface, but usually fail to eliminate nests in the soil. The presence of ants often has to be tolerated.

Moles

As they search for worms and insects to eat, moles create an underground tunnel system. Soil excavated from the tunnels is deposited as molehills on the surface. There are many repellent devices available, but they are not always effective. Mole traps are cheaper and, provided that they are set correctly, are more reliable. Live-capture traps are available for those who do not wish to kill moles.

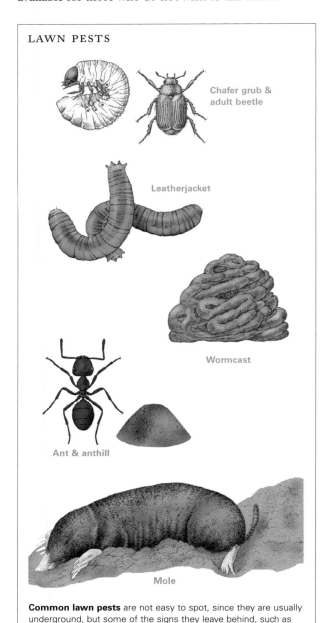

LAWN PESTS

Chafer grub & adult beetle

Leatherjacket

Wormcast

Ant & anthill

Mole

Common lawn pests are not easy to spot, since they are usually underground, but some of the signs they leave behind, such as wormcasts and molehills, are very obvious and unattractive.

Lawn maintenance *see page 286* | **Lawn weeds** *see page 294* | **Repairing neglected lawns** *see page 299*

Rabbits and other animals, such as badgers, squirrels and foxes, can spoil a smooth sward by burrowing or digging for grubs or nuts.

Molehills look unsightly, kill off grass and interfere with mowing. All the molehills on a lawn may be caused by one solitary mole.

Dead patches can be caused by drought, poor aeration, dog urine, buried debris, and fertilizer scorch, as well as various pests and diseases.

DISEASES

There are several turf diseases that can kill, weaken, or disfigure large areas of turf, most of them caused by fungi and some encouraged by humid conditions. Avoid them by keeping the lawn well maintained.

Fairy rings

Several soil-borne fungi disfigure lawns by forming fairy rings – one or more rings of lush green grass, sometimes with toadstools at the periphery in appropriate weather conditions. The rings or bands may be continuous or broken. The most serious form of fairy ring is also accompanied by an area of dead grass between the lusher grass. This results from a dense mat (mycelium) of fungal growth (*Marasmius oreades*), which extends as deep as 45cm (18in) into the soil; it repels moisture and competes with the grass for water and nutrients, resulting in an area of dead grass, killed by drought and starvation.

No chemical controls are available to amateur gardeners. Dig up affected grass and topsoil to a depth of at least 30cm (12in) and the same distance beyond the edge of the ring. Fill with fresh soil and reseed. If the fairy ring is very large, aerate the grass in the ring before soaking it well with a slowly dripping hose and a small amount of detergent. The mycelium declines in persistently wet soil. It may be worth employing the services of a professional gardener or specialized contractor. If mushrooms or toadstools appear, dispose of them. Take care to limit contamination of the remaining lawn with thatch or soil from the excavated ring.

Other fungi may appear in lawns that do not stimulate grass growth, as above. They may feed on woody material in the soil; to treat, find the food source and remove it.

Ophiobolus or take-all patch

This disease occurs in late summer or autumn. Circular bronze-coloured depressions a few centimetres across appear and increase in size each year. Grass dies off in the centre. The disease is fostered by wet conditions, high soil pH, and heavy liming. Avoid it by ensuring good drainage and aeration, and feeding with sulphate of ammonia in spring and summer. Returf small affected areas.

FAIRY RINGS & OPHIOBOLUS PATCH

Fairy rings

Ophiobolus patch

Fungal diseases can cause fairy rings and disfiguring patches. Returfing or reseeding are often the only remedies.

MORE LAWN DISEASES

Fusarium patch

Slime moulds

Red thread

Pythium blight

Moulds and fungi are the causes of most of the common lawn diseases. Some are not treatable by fungicides, so good aeration and drainage are the best way of preventing them.

Fusarium patch

This serious disease is commonly called snow mould, because it may be associated with areas of grass that were walked on when covered in snow. Usually it becomes evident during mild, moist weather in spring or autumn when small patches of yellow, dying grass appear. These turn brown and increase in size. In humid conditions, white or pink fungal growth may mat the blades of grass. Lawns containing annual meadow grass (*Poa annua*) are worst affected, but red fescues (*Festuca rubra*) are also susceptible. The disease is worsened by poor air movement and late applications of nitrogenous fertilizer.

No fungicides are available to amateur gardeners for control, but cultural measures will limit its spread. Scarify the turf or spike the surface of the lawn to improve aeration, and prune back overhanging shrubbery. Remove heavy dew with a besom broom or bamboo cane to reduce moisture on grass blades. Nitrogen-rich fertilizers should not be applied after late summer. Iron sulphate can reduce the severity of the disease; it toughens the grass and acidifies the turf, which discourages the fungus.

Slime moulds

These harmless organisms often coat blades of grass in late spring or early autumn. They vary in colour but are commonly white or yellow; they develop into grey, round, spore-bearing structures. Slime moulds are superficial and short lived, so no control measures are necessary. They can be easily washed away if desired.

Red thread

Fine turf is frequently affected by this fungal disease, which is most troublesome in late summer and autumn. Infection is most apparent after heavy rain. Reddish patches of grass appear and pink, gelatinous fungal structures grow among the blades. When dry, these can be easily spread by foot to cause new infections. Many grasses are susceptible, but fescues are worst affected. Although it is unsightly, the grass usually recovers.

No fungicides are available to amateurs to control the disease. Improve the aeration of the turf to help affected grass to recover and apply nitrogen-rich fertilizers (such as sulphate of ammonia) in spring and summer.

Pythium blight

This serious turf disease causes dead patches. Often, as new grass attempts to recolonize the dead areas, the young seedlings rot at their base and topple over. The organisms responsible for this blight thrive in waterlogged conditions, so improve the drainage to reduce the problem.

Repairing neglected lawns

Without regular care and attention, lawns can rapidly fall into disrepair. Surfaces can become uneven and weeds take hold where the grass has struggled to establish itself. General wear and tear from children playing, badger activity, collapsing mole tunnels, and severe weather conditions are all causes of lawn deterioration.

Most neglected lawns can be reinstated to their former glory in a relatively short period of time. First, thoroughly examine the lawn and decide if any fine grasses remain. Where fine grasses dominate, with weeds and coarse grasses appearing only in patches, renovation is definitely worthwhile. Spring is a good time to start a renovation programme (*see below*), as there are several months of active growth ahead. If faced with a neglected lawn in summer, you can still begin renovation, but do not apply an autumn turf fertilizer.

On neglected lawns where coarse grasses and weeds dominate, it is probably worth stripping off the turf and starting again; this means levelling the whole area and then reseeding or returfing.

PROGRAMME OF RENOVATION

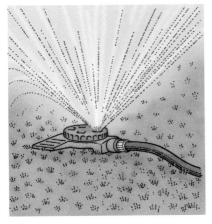

1 **Mow the lawn** with a rotary mower set at a cutting height of 5cm (2in), or with a strimmer, to remove the dead grass as well as weed stalks and seedheads. Mowing too closely at this stage will weaken the grass.

2 **Rake off the mowings**. After a week, cut the grass again, if possible with a cylinder mower, set at the highest cut. Repeat over the next 2–3 weeks, reducing the cut height to a level appropriate to the type of lawn.

3 **Feed the grass** with a general-purpose spring turf fertilizer, and follow it with a treatment of lawn weedkiller 10–14 days later. Take care to avoid any recently seeded areas – the new grass may get scorched.

4 **Water the lawn** in spring in dry periods. Reseed any bare patches and keep well watered. In midsummer and at least 5–6 weeks after the spring feed, apply sulphate of ammonia to keep the grass growing strongly.

5 **Examine the lawn** in early autumn for weeds and poor growth; fork out areas of coarse grasses and reseed ready for next year. Scarify and aerate the turf where required in the usual way to keep it healthy.

6 **Apply a topdressing** of sandy loam after completing the scarifying and aerating. Add an autumn lawn fertilizer to the topdressing. The following spring it should be possible to return to a standard lawn maintenance routine.

LEVELLING BUMPS & HOLLOWS

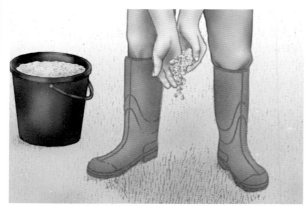

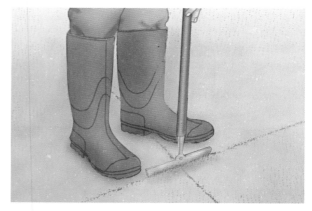

Small bumps and hollows are simple to repair. Very small bumps can be reduced to a level surface by using a hollow-tined aerator on the area and removing the cores. Small hollows can be filled by gradually adding a light topdressing, to a depth of no more than 1cm (½in) at a time. Continue until the hollow is filled.

For a large bump or hollow, first cut a cross into the turf, right across the bump or hollow using a half-moon edger. Fold the 4 flaps back, making sure that the turf does not tear or break. Add or remove topsoil as needed and replace the turf, tamping it down gently with the back of a rake. Fill in any gaps with topdressing and water well.

Repairing broken edges

A sharp edge can contribute greatly to the overall appearance and attractiveness of a lawn. Ideally, there should be a 5–7cm (2–3in) drop, or gully, around the boundary of the lawn, to prevent grass from rooting into the beds. Broken or uneven edges ruin the overall shape of a lawn and look unsightly. You can create or reinstate sharp edges by using a half-moon edger – never use the back of a spade because it tends to have a slight curve to it.

To repair a broken edge, first cut out a patch of turf that includes the broken edge, then follow the method shown below. Alternatively, remove the piece completely, turn it around and place it back into the hole so that the good edge is facing outwards. There will now be a hollow left by the broken edge in the middle of the grass. Fill it with topsoil and reseed it or fill the hole with a new piece of turf. This method works only if the turf is cut precisely, with straight edges and right-angled corners.

REPAIRING BROKEN EDGES

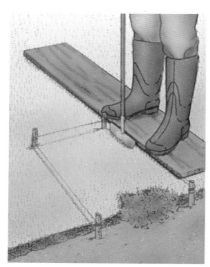

1 **Mark out a rectangle** of turf to include the broken edge. Cut it out with a half-moon edger, using a plank edge as a guide.

2 **Loosen the piece of turf** carefully by slicing underneath it with a sharp spade blade, cutting it to a uniform depth.

3 **Gently push out** the piece of turf along the ground until the damaged part is clear of the edge of the lawn.

REPLACING BARE PATCHES

1 **Cut a straight-sided piece** of turf that includes the bare patch using a half-moon edger. Loosen with a spade blade, and lift out.

2 **Use a fork** to loosen the soil before replacing the turf with fresh pieces cut to the same size as the hole.

3 **Fill in the cracks** between the pieces of turf with a sandy topdressing and brush it in. Keep the new turf watered until it roots in.

Bare patches

If there is a bare patch in the lawn, it is wise to determine why the area has become bald before undertaking any repairs, otherwise the problem may recur. You can then take appropriate measures to rectify the cause of the problem, as well as repairing the bare patch. For example, you may need to control a lawn pest or take measures to improve the drainage and aeration of the turf to combat disease. If the baldness is a result of heavy foot traffic, it may be worth considering embedding stepping stones into the lawn or even installing a proper path. Other causes of bare patches include weed removal, bitch marks (scorching by female dog urine), and spilled oil or petrol.

The best time to repair a bare patch, either with turf or by reseeding, is in autumn, or spring if necessary. If you decide to sow seed, measure out enough seed, according to the recommended rate, to fill the area. Water the sown patch gently, taking care not to wash away the seeds.

4 **Lay the plank across** the damaged turf so that it aligns with the lawn edge. Cut off the damaged area, using the plank as a guide.

5 **Cut a fresh piece** of turf to fit the gap left in the lawn and lay it into the hole. Check it is level, then tamp down and water well.

SOWING BARE PATCHES

Sow fresh grass seeds as an alternative to laying new turf. Remove the damaged turf, top up the hole with topsoil, then sprinkle the seeds.

CHAPTER SEVEN

WATER GARDENING

SITING & DESIGN 306

LINERS & CONSTRUCTION MATERIALS 309

PUMPS, FILTERS & HEATERS 310

LIGHTING 311

FOUNTAINS 312

MARKING OUT 313

INSTALLING A PRE-FORMED POND 314

LAYING A POND LINER 316

MAKING A BOG GARDEN 318

MAKING A WILDLIFE POND 319

PLANTING WATER PLANTS 320

POND CARE 332

PERHAPS YOU HAVE PLANS FOR A LARGE WILDLIFE POND, OR you might only have space for a simple barrel water feature. Maybe you have an awkward, naturally damp piece of land in your garden that could take on new life if transformed into a pond with a bog garden at the edge. Whatever the choices available, there is no doubt that water can become an important part of your garden.

The benefits of water in the garden

Moving water can add life to a static space. The gentle trickle of a stream or the gurgle of a bubble fountain can help you to unwind and mask unwanted noise, while plunging cascades or waterfalls add drama. Features such as rills can lead the eye from one area to another, connecting different garden areas. Still water can be exploited for striking visual effects. Specimen plants, statues, or buildings near the edge will be reflected, and a large body of water can also create the illusion of greater space by reflecting the sky.

A pond provides the opportunity to grow a wider range of plants, from floating waterlilies to marginal plants, and a bog garden allows an even greater variety. A water feature in your garden will also encourage wildlife. Birds will visit a simple bubble fountain to drink or bathe, while a well-planted pond can become a magnet to frogs, toads, newts, birds, and insects, or even an important watering hole for hedgehogs, deer, and foxes.

The secrets of success

The success of a pond depends on the interaction of the water, air, nutrients, plants, temperature, and wildlife that make up its complex ecosystem. The right balance means clear water and thriving fish and plants, while imbalance leads to algae growth, suffering fish, poor plant growth, and weeds.

For a pond to work well, it needs plenty of oxygen. Plants in a pond produce this, while animals in the water consume oxygen and turn it into carbon dioxide. You can promote a healthy level of oxygen in your pond by incorporating both running water and submerged oxygenating plants. Plants are also essential to prevent the growth of algae, which pollutes and colours the water. Since algae spreads rapidly in sunlight and in water with high nutrient levels, surface-covering plants help to limit its development by providing shade and taking up the nutrients.

A healthy community of micro-organisms is also essential for clean water and a food chain that supports many creatures. Fungi, snails, and bacteria that feed on decaying plants will be eaten by dragonfly larvae and water beetles, which in turn will become food for frogs, toads, and fish.

Creating a healthy pond

The design of your pool will have an impact on the ecosystem. Areas of deep water will remain frost-free in winter and cool in summer, keeping micro-organisms alive through extremes of temperature. Shallow water, however, can heat up quickly, providing the perfect environment for algae.

How you look after your pool can also have a huge effect on the life it sustains. You should prevent pesticides or fertilizers from entering the water, and avoid cleaning too often, as this disrupts the natural balance, which is very delicate and can take many seasons to restore. Try and keep your pond at a neutral pH and avoid sudden changes or extremes of pH, which can happen when replacement water is added to the pond.

305

SITING & DESIGN

When building a pond or water feature, you are aiming to create a healthy underwater world, where creatures and plants thrive. To ensure that a pond develops to its full potential, think carefully about its size and shape, along with where it is constructed in relation to the house and other major features, such as trees. There are many different kinds of water feature that you might consider, ranging in style from formal pools to wildlife ponds, and in size from wall fountains to swimming ponds. To ensure that a water feature adds beauty and interest it is important that it works well with the rest of your garden.

Pool designs

A formal pool or canal with a few key plants is a classic feature for a restrained or minimalist space. It may be circular, square, or another regular shape, perhaps echoing features such as neatly clipped topiary. Use materials that match other hard landscaping features, such as paths or walls. This is particularly important for raised ponds, which are usually formal and make perfect focal points.

An informal pond should look like part of the natural landscape and not a construction. Its outline should be sweeping curves, rather than straight lines, and it should be well-planted, allowing for the introduction of fish.

An informal pond will attract many creatures, but you can maximize its potential by turning it into a wildlife pond. Fill it with many native species of plants, and ensure that the edges provide access and plenty of cover so that visiting creatures feel protected. If you have the space, a modern alternative is the swimming pond, planted to be a magnet to wildlife, but big enough to allow swimming.

Many water features require a large garden, but even a small space can accommodate a bubble fountain or a wall-mounted fountain with a small pool below. Small aquatic plants like pygmy waterlilies fit barrels and tubs.

Informal cascades are one of the more difficult features to design and build, but when successful, they look stunning.

Even the smallest feature can add variety and life to a garden. This fountain will attract birds even without a large accessible pool.

Formal symmetry does not have to limit your creativity, as demonstrated here by the use of mixed materials and a topiary peacock.

SITING PRACTICALITIES

Gardening with the environment *see page 15* | **Methods & materials** *see page 309* | **Planting water plants** *see page 320*

Siting practicalities

Aquatic plants thrive in sunlight, so you should avoid siting a pond in an area of the garden that is heavy shaded throughout summer. A spot that receives partial shade is ideal, as too much sun can promote the growth of algae, while too much shade will result in low oxygen levels in your pond. If possible, plan your water feature in summer when deciduous trees are in full leaf, so you can avoid densely shaded sites, but remember to take into account buildings, which will cast more shade in winter because the sun is lower in the sky. Unfortunately, some small gardens remain shady all year round. A pond will not thrive under such conditions, but there are several bog-garden plants that do well in lower light levels and will make a great alternative.

As well as casting shade, trees can cause other problems. Tree roots can damage the pond liner, and falling autumn leaves will clog the pool. Some trees, such as horse chestnut, laburnum, and yew, have poisonous leaves or seeds that could damage pond life. Ideally, you should site your pond 5m (15ft) from any trees.

Windswept sites are not attractive to visiting wildlife, so ensure that your site has some shelter and is not in a frost pocket. Shelter will also prevent strong gusts from lifting plants in pots from the marginal shelf of a pond, and it also means less water will evaporate from your pond in summer, so you will not have to top it up so often. In winter, the surface will be less likely to freeze over.

Avoid any area with a high water table, which could lift a pre-formed pond or alter the shape of a liner. There is also a risk that water from the soil, which may contain fertilizers or pesticides, could enter the pond.

If you are uncertain about the height of your water table, dig a hole in the proposed site in late winter when the ground is saturated. If the water table is within 60cm (24in) of the planned level of the pond floor, choose a different site if possible. Alternatively, you could drain the site; seek professional advice in such cases.

SAFEGUARDING CHILDREN

Water is a hazard so site the pond close to the house where children can be supervised. It can also be made safer with a fence or grille. Secure grilles placed over the pond or just beneath water level are one of the least obstructive methods; they should be able to take the weight of an adult.

RAISED PONDS & FLAT PONDS

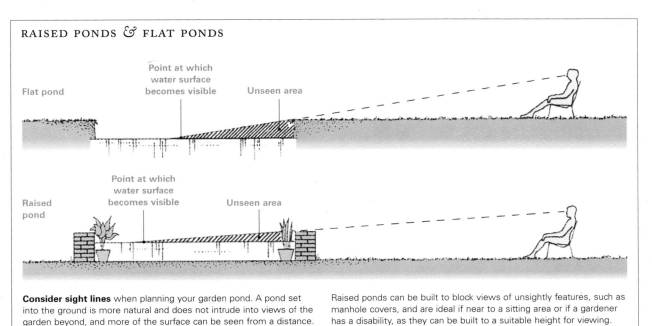

Flat pond

Point at which water surface becomes visible

Unseen area

Raised pond

Point at which water surface becomes visible

Unseen area

Consider sight lines when planning your garden pond. A pond set into the ground is more natural and does not intrude into views of the garden beyond, and more of the surface can be seen from a distance.

Raised ponds can be built to block views of unsightly features, such as manhole covers, and are ideal if near to a sitting area or if a gardener has a disability, as they can be built to a suitable height for viewing.

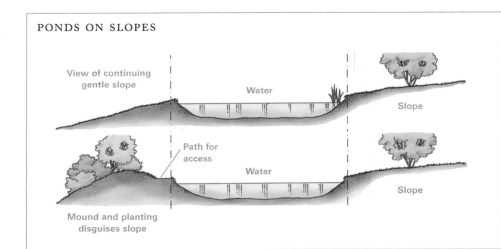

PONDS ON SLOPES

View of continuing
gentle slope

Water

Slope

Path for
access

Water

Slope

Mound and planting
disguises slope

Sloping sites are at first glance less promising than flat sites for ponds. A gently sloping piece of ground is easy to level, but steeper sites may need retaining walls to contain a water feature on the lower side.

Artificial ponds are not convincing if a slope can be seen to continue beyond. To disguise this, use soil dug from the pond to create a natural-looking mound on the down-sloping side of the pond, and plant it up with trees and shrubs. Use some evergreens for year-round screening.

Suiting the site

When designing a pond think carefully about how the area of water will be viewed from the main seating area of the garden or from the house – it will look different when sitting or standing, as well as from different distances. Also consider how to make the pond appear an integral part of the garden design, rather than an afterthought.

From plan to perspective

After deciding where you want to site the pond, trickle sand onto the ground to outline its shape, then go to the area of the garden where you spend most time, or step inside the house to gaze from a window. Look at the shape on the ground and it will give you a good idea of what the finished pond will look like.

Also try to imagine what the pond will look like with plants, because these will conceal some of the water from your view; taking a few photographs and drawing in plants on printouts may help. If you think the shape you have laid out on the ground will not enable you to see as much water as you would like, try altering it by making it longer from front to back.

Linking features

To help marry the pool to the rest of the garden, you could create a bog garden to accompany it (*see page 318*). These are planted with species that like moist soil, but not standing water. They can be made in any shape, but tend to look best with bold, sinuous lines.

In a larger garden, you could link several separate water features together with moving water. A geometric rill is perfect in a formal garden, while a meandering stream would suit a more naturalistic setting.

THE EFFECTS OF PERSPECTIVE

Island

Planting

Planting

Position
of viewer

1

Plan view

Unseen

2

View as seen from standing

3

View as seen from sitting

Seen as a plan ❶ your pond may look like a large expanse of water, but it will not be viewed from this perspective once built. When you are standing ❷ the surface appears much smaller, and areas beyond the pool are obscured by planting. Viewed from a seating area ❸ the surface becomes smaller still and much of the pond itself can be hidden by foreground planting.

METHODS & MATERIALS

Once you have planned the look and position of your pond, there are decisions to be made about its construction. You can choose from a variety of different flexible or rigid liners, depending on the shape and size of pool you want. Unless you live in a very mild region, heaters may be necessary in cold weather and if you plan to incorporate moving water, you will need to equip your pond with a pump and filter. Last but not least, carefully placed lighting can really enhance your pond and ensure that it remains an attractive feature until long after darkness has fallen.

Liners & construction materials

Pools can be constructed from a variety of flexible and rigid materials, each with advantages and disadvantages in durability, ease of laying, and cost.

Butyl rubber: A popular flexible material – strong, easy to fit to any shape, and simple to repair. Available pre-packed or cut to length; sheets can be welded for a large pond.

PVC: Less durable than butyl, this flexible liner is still tough, cheap, and easy to mould. Usually supplied pre-packed; coloured and pebbled versions are available.

EPDM: The most expensive flexible liner, this is very tough and used for commercial projects.

Polythene: Easily damaged by light, this is not suitable for pools but can be used to line bog gardens.

Pre-formed ponds: Usually fibreglass, these come in many rigid shapes and sizes, and can incorporate streams and waterfalls. However, installation is time-consuming, design is restricted, and repair is not as easy as for flexible liners.

Concrete: This can make a tough base for a simple shape, but may need to be constructed by a professional. If properly prepared, it needs little or no repair work for many years; if badly prepared, it cracks and flakes, especially in frosty periods, and is not easy to repair.

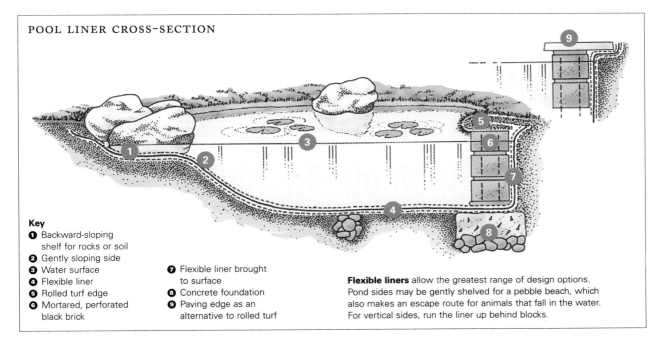

POOL LINER CROSS-SECTION

Key
1. Backward-sloping shelf for rocks or soil
2. Gently sloping side
3. Water surface
4. Flexible liner
5. Rolled turf edge
6. Mortared, perforated black brick
7. Flexible liner brought to surface
8. Concrete foundation
9. Paving edge as an alternative to rolled turf

Flexible liners allow the greatest range of design options. Pond sides may be gently shelved for a pebble beach, which also makes an escape route for animals that fall in the water. For vertical sides, run the liner up behind blocks.

Pumps, filters & heaters

All artificial ponds need a pump to keep the water moving and a filter to keep the water clean. A floating heating device is not always needed, but is a good idea if your pond is likely to freeze over in winter.

Pumps & filters

Pumps are either submersible or placed on the surface. Submersible pumps (*see right*) are the most popular. Surface pumps are more powerful, used for high jets or faster flows over larger-scale features. They must be kept in a dry chamber at a level just below the water level of the pond.

Filters remove impurities, such as algae, from the water, but they are not a substitute for a properly maintained and planted pond. They are either mechanical or biological. Mechanical filters are the simplest option (*see right*). You might not need a filter if you have a naturally balanced pond, but if you keep fish, a biological filter is a necessity as they neutralize harmful fish waste as well as clean the water of algae and debris. Biological filters are sited outside the pond, at the highest point.

Pool heaters

A simple floating heater will help to keep a small area free of ice (*see page 333*). Koi carp owners sometimes use specialized heaters for temperature control of water, but these are not necessary for most other fish.

SUBMERSIBLE PUMP

Easy to install, quiet, and with enough power to operate most small-scale, gently moving water features, these pumps are popular and competitively priced. You simply place them on the bottom of the pond.

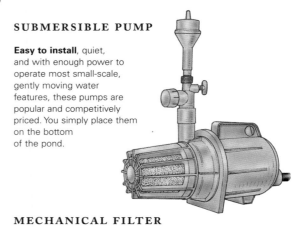

MECHANICAL FILTER

A simple structure consisting of a foam filter covered in charcoal or gravel and housed in a plastic box, these filters are sited on the pond floor and connected to the pump.

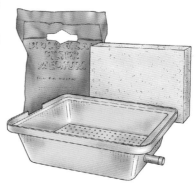

WATER FLOW USING A WATERFALL PUMP

Key
❶ Electrical power connection
❷ Steep pond sides show water loss more than shallow sides
❸ Lowest point of pond
❹ Submersible pump, raised off bottom of pond and placed inconspicuously close to wall
❺ Water pipe
❻ Pump outlet
❼ Disguising plants or rocks
❽ Water pipe diameter determined by pump size

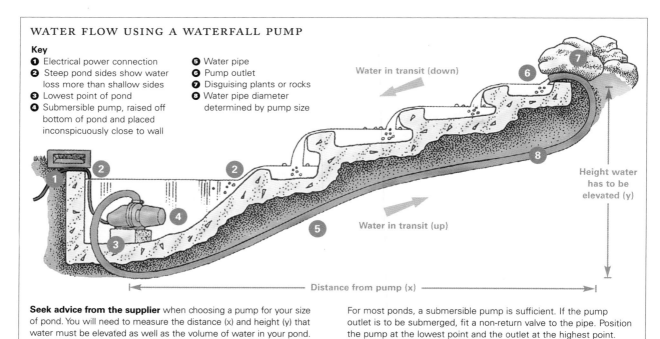

Water in transit (down)

Water in transit (up)

Height water has to be elevated (y)

Distance from pump (x)

Seek advice from the supplier when choosing a pump for your size of pond. You will need to measure the distance (x) and height (y) that water must be elevated as well as the volume of water in your pond.

For most ponds, a submersible pump is sufficient. If the pump outlet is to be submerged, fit a non-return valve to the pipe. Position the pump at the lowest point and the outlet at the highest point.

Lighting

You can create many effects with both submerged and above-water lights, but for the best and least intrusive show, use them sparingly and avoid your pond resembling an airport landing strip at night.

Above-water lights can be bought individually or in packs of three or more. Placed around the edge of your pond, spotlights can pick out a sculpture, waterfall, or specimen plant. Placed behind a feature, floodlights will silhouette it and illuminate the marginal plants and area around it, leaving the water a sheet of black.

Underwater lights give a ghostly glow to the pond or, placed on the surface of the pond, glance upwards towards a plant. Traditional white lights are popular, and coloured filters can look out of place in some gardens.

Another option is to simply light the water itself. Floating or permanently submerged lights, which sit just beneath the surface of the water, provide a mysterious look and are perfect in a contemporary garden. An illuminated fountain can look magical – these are available as kits, with a spotlight that sits beneath the fountain head and illuminates the jet of water. White, single-coloured, and multicoloured lights, as well as colour-changing filters, are all widely available.

A simple alternative to electric lights is to create a mood by using floating candles. There are even some that are moulded, to resemble waterlilies for example.

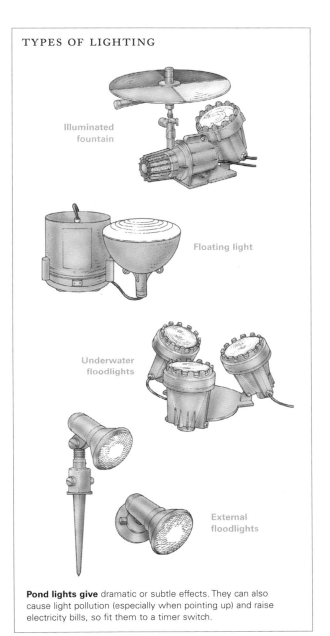

TYPES OF LIGHTING

Illuminated fountain

Floating light

Underwater floodlights

External floodlights

Pond lights give dramatic or subtle effects. They can also cause light pollution (especially when pointing up) and raise electricity bills, so fit them to a timer switch.

Lighting is most effective when the source of the light is concealed. Here the water and the wall glow, but the bulbs are hidden behind the wall and below the bridge, or obscured by the falling water.

SAFETY

Pond lighting kits are designed to be safe and easy to install. They contain lights attached to a length of cable, a low-voltage transformer and a plug that can be used in a protected outdoor socket or routed through a wall to a socket inside; make sure that there is always an RCD (residual current device). Low-voltage cables can be clipped along a wall or buried in a shallow trench (fed through a length of hosepipe for protection). Any electrical work beyond the simple installation of such a kit should be undertaken by a qualified electrician.

Fountains

Water fountains can transform your pond or pool into a spectacular focal point, or simply add sound and movement to the garden. All fountains work in the same way: a fountain head is attached to a pump that drives water up and through the head. The fountain head controls how the water is released (*see box, below*), and some are adjustable, so you can vary the effect.

Choosing & installing

Before adding a fountain, think carefully about whether it will suit your garden and fit within the constraints of your pool. Your pool should be large enough to contain the spray of water and capture drift, which could be considerable on a windy day. As a rule of thumb, the pond should be twice as wide as the spray is high.

Choose a spray effect that suits your style of garden. A natural-looking bubble fountain suits modern and smaller gardens, while a plume is best in a grand garden with a large pool to capture the spray. A bell fountain suits a classical space and again needs a large pool, as do high jets or columns of water and fountains with several tiers.

ORNAMENTAL FOUNTAINS

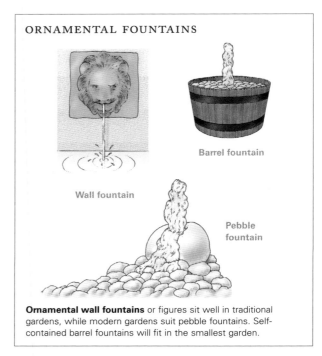

Wall fountain

Barrel fountain

Pebble fountain

Ornamental wall fountains or figures sit well in traditional gardens, while modern gardens suit pebble fountains. Self-contained barrel fountains will fit in the smallest garden.

POSITIONING THE FOUNTAIN PUMP

If the fountain head is directly attached to the pump, set it 8cm (3in) above the water level. Raise the pump on a brick if necessary, and place a piece of old carpet or geotextile beneath the brick to prevent damage to the liner.

A separate fountain head on a length of pipe can be threaded through an ornamental figure or sculpture to produce a spray above the pond. The pump can sit on the bottom of the pond if it makes it less visible.

FOUNTAIN SPRAYS

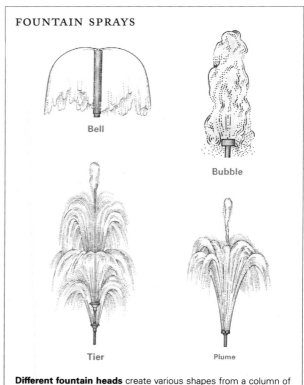

Bell

Bubble

Tier

Plume

Different fountain heads create various shapes from a column of water to a classical tiered spray. The height of the jet should be adjustable; remember that spray drifts further than solid water.

Wildlife ponds *see page 50* | **Siting & design** *see page 306* | **Planting water plants** *see page 320*

Marking out

Marking out level ground before installing a pre-formed pond or laying a liner is quite easy. All you need are some 30cm (12in) pegs, a sharp stake, string or hosepipe, some bricks, a hammer or mallet, a plank, and a spirit level.

Marking out irregular shapes

Place your pre-formed pond on the ground and raise it up on bricks by 8cm (3in), keeping it horizontal (*see below, top left*). To mark out its perimeter, place a spirit level vertically against the rim of the pond with its lower end on the ground. Mark the position on the ground by hammering a stake in to a depth of 10cm (4in). Repeat this at 30cm (12in) intervals around the pond.

If installing a liner pool, first draw your design on paper so you have a plan to work from. Then mark the desired shape on the ground by hammering in stakes 10cm (4in) deep, every 30cm (12in). When you are happy with the outline, join up the stakes using sprinkled sand or a length of string or hosepipe (*see below, top right*), then score the ground with a sharpened stake.

Levelling & excavating

Once the shape has been planned on the ground, remove the string or hosepipe. Next, use a spirit level and mallet to ensure that the top of the stakes are all level by choosing a starting peg and placing a plank between it and an adjacent peg.

Check with the spirit level and knock the adjacent peg in or move the other out slightly if necessary. Continue to measure around the outline. Once all the pegs are level, make any adjustments needed to the ground level so that the same length of peg is visible all round. This ensures the pond edge sits level and the liner will not be exposed. Now you can start to excavate (*see below, bottom*).

MARKING OUT A PRE-FORMED POND

For pre-formed ponds, support the unit on bricks, making sure that it is level when you start. If it is not, the shape you mark on the ground will be distorted. Take vertical readings from the perimeter down to the ground and mark their positions all around the pond. Alternatively, mark a rectangular area that will fit your pond (*see following page*).

MARKING OUT A LINER POND

For pond liners or concrete pools, mark the outline with pegs. Use a hosepipe, string, or sand to show the outline clearly. Take into account both the width or length and the depth of the pool when buying a liner. If you dig before buying you will have accurate measurements, but check the sizes and costs of liners before you start.

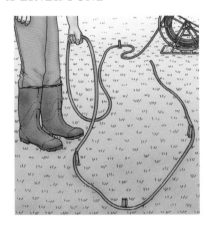

EXCAVATING

1 Use a spirit level on a plank to check that the tops of the pegs, and the surface of the ground, are level. Measure from peg to peg around the edge and straight across for added certainty. You may have to build up one side of the edge or excavate the other to achieve a level rim.

2 Start by digging a trench inside the pegs. Excavating by hand is far more accurate than using a digger. For lined ponds, make sure any sloping sides are no steeper than 20 degrees to avoid instability. If you decide to include a marginal shelf make it at least 23cm (9in) deep and wide.

Installing a pre-formed pond

Pre-formed pools can be easier to install than lined ponds as they are already moulded into shape. The installation is a job for two people, however, as the shell can be awkward to handle. Fibreglass ponds tend to be more rigid than plastic shells, which can distort as they fill with water.

Underlining

After excavating the hole (*see previous page*), prepare the base of the hole and any marginal shelves so that they will cushion the shell when it is full of water. Even though the pre-formed ponds are quite rigid, they can still be damaged if not properly supported or if they come into contact with sharp objects as the pond is filled.

Remove any large stones, twigs, or debris and roughly level the base with a rake. Use your feet to tamp down the soil, then spread a 2.5cm (1in) layer of damp builder's sand over the base. To get an even layer across all surfaces, use a rake and then a builder's trowel.

Installing the pond

With assistance, place the liner centrally in the hole. Make sure it is firmly embedded in the sand, and if any shallow areas of the base are not well supported, shore them up with flat stones or bricks so that it is held firmly.

Check that the pool is level by placing a spirit level on a plank laid across the rim from side to side, and from end to end (*see facing page, step 5*). Add or remove supporting material as necessary, then add 10cm (4in) of water to the base of the shell and check the levels again.

Slowly start to backfill the excavation with a gardener's trowel (*see facing page, step 7*). If the excavated soil is too stony or lumpy to flow in around the pond easily and provide good support all around, it may be worth buying pea shingle or builders' sand instead. Firm in the soil with your hands as you go to prevent the pond from moving later and changing the water level. Keep checking the levels and fill up to the lip of the pond.

INSTALLING A PRE-FORMED POND

1 **Mark a rectangle** or contoured shape that completely encloses the outline of your pond (*see previous page*) with space to spare around the edges for backfilling. Remove the soil, digging the hole 2.5cm (1in) deeper than the pond.

2 **Remove sharp objects**, such as roots or stones, from the floor of the hole. Rigid ponds are stronger than flexible liners, but they can still be damaged. Tread down the bottom of the hole until it is flat and level.

3 **Lay damp sand** on the floor of the excavation in a 2.5cm (1in) layer. The sand will support and cushion the pond when it is installed.

4 **Position the pond** in the hole. Build up bricks or flat stones under areas that are not touching the ground and so are not supported, such as the planting shelves.

Siting & design *see page 306* | Liners & construction materials *see page 309* | Planting water plants *see page 320*

EDGING WITH PAVING

1 Lay a bed of mortar around the edge of the unit after making any necessary adjustments to the ground around the pond so that it meets the level rim of the pool. The mortar should be about 2.5cm (1in) deep.

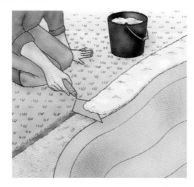

2 Lay each paving edge so that it is firmly supported on the mortar but overhangs the edge of the pool slightly. Point the joints between the paving and leave to set completely before carrying out any further work.

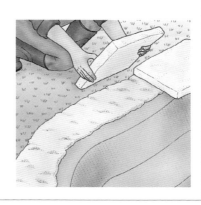

Laying the edging

Stone, paving, plants, or turf (*see page 317*) are ideal for masking the edges of a pre-formed pond. If you are planning on using stone or slabs (*see box, above*), start by laying a 2.5cm (1in) thick bed of mortar. This should be five parts builder's sand to one part cement, with added waterproofing compound. Bed the slabs into position, about 5mm (¼in) apart. They should overhang the pool by at least 5cm (2in) to conceal the rim.

If you are planting up the area around the edge of the pond instead, use garden plants rather than aquatics, to help your pond to marry with the rest of the garden.

5 Check that the pond is absolutely level in the excavation using a spirit level laid on a plank across the rim. Remember to check in both directions. Adjust the sand beneath the pond if necessary; any slope will be obvious once the pool is filled.

6 Fill the pond with water to approximately 10cm (4in) before starting to backfill around the pre-formed pond. This weight gives the unit stability while the earth is filled in around the sides, helping to ensure that it stays level.

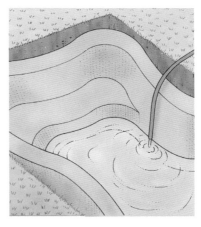

7 Backfill with soil around the pond with a gardener's trowel. Start by laying a 15cm (6in) layer, firming it in as you go. Build up the layers, making sure that you work the soil well into the contours of the pond.

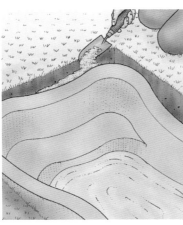

8 Keep checking that the pond is level. Backfill in layers, ensuring good contact with all parts of the pond unit. Work all the way around the pond and check that it is still level before starting the next layer.

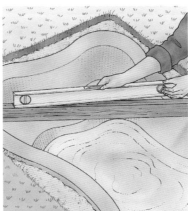

Laying a pond liner

The most popular way of creating a pond is to use a liner. Flexible liners are ideal if you want a custom-built pool and do not want to be confined by the range of shapes and sizes that are available with pre-formed pools. Although more preparation work is required than when installing a pre-formed pool, it is a straightforward job as long as you have prepared the ground well and calculated the right amount of liner needed.

Although liners are versatile, some pond shapes are simpler than others. It is easier to lay a liner when the shape is full of sweeping curves and not intricate, geometric lines and angles, which will cause you problems when trying to smooth out folds and wrinkles in the liner. To prevent soil slippage, make the marginal shelves fairly wide.

Calculating the liner size

There is a simple formula for calculating the amount of liner you need for a square, rectangular, or irregular shaped pond. The same technique can also be used to calculate the amount of liner needed for a stream.

First double the maximum depth of the pool. Add this figure to the length of the pool to find the total length of liner needed. Then add double the maximum depth to the width to give the total width of liner needed. Multiply your two figures together to find the total area of liner. This will allow you to estimate the cost. Liners are widely sold in pre-cut sizes, but for an unusual shape there are suppliers who will cut to order; individual sheets can also be welded together.

INSTALLING A LINER

1 **Mark out the shape** of the pond and excavate the hole. Incorporate a marginal shelf to maximize planting, and make sloping sides no steeper than 20 degrees for stability.

2 **Remove any sharp** sticks, roots, or stones from the walls and floor of the hole. If left, they could puncture the liner. Rake over the floor and shelf to smooth the surface.

3 **Lay an underliner** in the hole. This non-woven fabric will protect the liner. It can be cut to fit awkward areas – as long as all the surfaces are covered.

Alternatively, spread sand 2.5cm (1in) deep to protect the liner. It may be hard to make it stick to all but the shallowest slopes.

4 **Centre the liner** over the pond. Spread it out and weigh down the edges. Try to arrange any excess liner into neat folds.

5 **Slowly fill the pond** and remove the weights as the water pulls the liner taut. It is now ready to be edged (*see facing page*).

LAYING A POND LINER

Siting & design *see page 306* | **Liners & construction materials** *see page 309* | **Planting water plants** *see page 320*

EDGING WITH PAVING & STONES

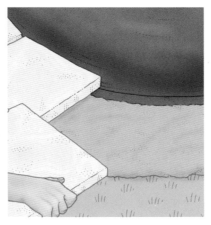

1 **Trim the excess** liner away using scissors, leaving at least 15cm (6in) all around. Dig out the soil around the pond to at least 8cm (3in) and bury the edge of the liner.

2 **Lay a bed** of mortar 2.5cm (1in) deep for slabs. Lay the paving edges on it and point between them with more mortar. Natural stone may need a deeper bed of mortar than paving to accommodate its irregular contours.

EDGING WITH TURF

Grass gives a natural look to a pond edge. Bury the liner edge, ensure that the soil is level and compact, then lay closely butted turfs. Do not use fertilizers or herbicides on the lawn, as these can disrupt the pond ecosystem, and clear away all clippings, which can discolour water and add unwanted nutrients.

Excavating & underlining

After excavating your pond, remove any large stones, sticks, or other debris that could puncture the liner from the sides and floor. Although the liner may seem tough, it can become vulnerable with the weight of water pushing down on it and out against the sides. Rake the base of the hole level, then add a sheet of fleece, geotextile, or polyester matting to act as a protective underliner. Calculate how much of this you need, employing the same formula used for working out the area of liner required, because the sides as well as the bottom of the pool will need cushioning.

Place the underliner in the hole and push it in so it fits the contours. Alternatively, for a smooth underlining you could spread a 2.5cm (1in) layer of damp builder's sand over the base of the hole, but you may still need to use material at the sides, where sand is unlikely to stick.

Installing the liner

If at all possible, spread the liner out in the sun for a while before laying it in the pond, because the warmth will make it more flexible. Once you are ready to install it, fold or roll the sides of the liner in to the middle so that it is easier to handle.

Unroll or unfold the liner over the excavation, keeping it placed as central as possible – it will make life easier if you have at least one other person to help you. It may take considerable adjustment to position the liner correctly for an irregularly shaped pond. When you have found the right position, hold the edges of the liner in place by weighing them down with bricks or paving, and try to smooth wrinkles together into a few larger folds or pleats. Slowly fill the liner with water from a hosepipe.

Allow the weight of the water to pull the liner down into the hole, removing the weights as necessary, while at the same time trying to ease out any creases. At the end of filling, the liner will be pressed into the outline of your excavation perfectly, and should have the minimum of wrinkles showing at the edge.

Finishing the edge

After the pond has been filled with water, work out how much liner to leave for edging and cut away the excess. If you are planning on using turf, stones, or paving, leave 15–38cm (6–15in), or double this if you want to fill the area around the edge of the pond with plants.

For stones, paving, or turf, you will need to cover the edge of the liner with soil at least 8cm (3in) deep (*see above*). Stones and paving give a pond a formal look and should be set in a 2.5cm (1in) bed of mortar, placed so that they overhang the pond by at least 5cm (2in).

If you intend to plant around the edge of the pool, dig around it to a depth of about 15cm (6in) and bury the liner, keeping it in place with bricks. You could use this opportunity to enrich the excavated soil. Plant with normal garden plants rather than water or bog plants, because the soil will only be as moist as the rest of your garden. Choose plants that are in keeping with your style of garden but complement the pool planting to provide a visual 'bridge' between the two.

Making a bog garden

Bog gardens can be constructed either on their own or integrated with a pond. Creating one at the same time as a pond is excavated helps to ensure that the two features marry together in the garden. All bog gardens will need topping up regularly by hand to prevent the soil from drying out and the plants from perishing.

Preparing the bog garden

Make a bog garden no bigger than the surface area of any pool to keep it in scale with the rest of the water garden, and dig it to a minimum depth of 30–45cm (12–15in) to prevent it from drying out too quickly. An integrated bog garden should be no more than 10cm (4in) away from the pool, with an interconnecting wall 8cm (3in) lower than the pool edge. Excavate the hole, remove any sharp stones or debris, and add an underliner. Next, cover with a liner (you might need two), weigh down the edge with bricks, and fill the pond.

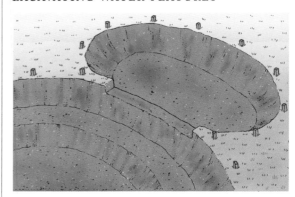

EXCAVATING WATER FEATURES

An integrated bog garden should be created at the same time as the pond and will initially draw most of its water from it. Dig out both features to the required depth and leave a wall where they join that is lower than the edge of the pond. This will allow water to flow into the bog garden from the pond.

MAKING A BOG GARDEN

1 Dig and line your bog garden in the same way as a pond with a liner (*see page 316*). If it joins a pond, aim to lay a single large liner over both areas if possible. A wall must separate the pond from the bog garden (*see box, above*). Fill the pool to just below the level of the wall between it and the bog garden.

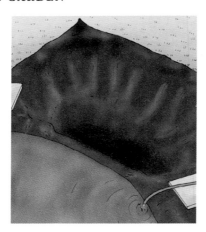

2 Lay gravel 3cm (1¼in) deep in the bog garden, top with soil, and soak well. Then place large, heavy stones along the wall. The gravel provides drainage, and the heavy stones will keep the wall stable.

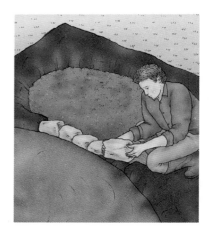

3 Top up the soil until it is level with the surrounding ground and place a strip of fine-mesh plastic netting along the barrier, on the bog garden side. This will prevent any soil or debris from the bog garden entering the pond. Firm the soil into place behind the wall.

4 Fill the pool with water and allow it to seep through the barrier into the bog garden. Once the soil in the bog area is damp it can be planted up with your chosen plants. Remember to check the soil regularly and top up with water when necessary.

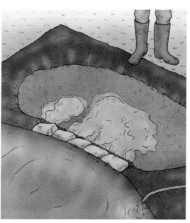

Making a wildlife pond

A well-designed and richly planted wildlife pond will act as a magnet to all sorts of creatures. The design will need to be slightly different to that of an ornamental pond to ensure that the pond appeals to wildlife.

Design tips

The best wildlife ponds will have a simple shape that includes a peninsula or inlet to provide a secluded spot for wildlife, and are about 90cm (36in) deep in the centre.

Make approximately one third of the edge a beach with gently sloping sides at about 20 degrees, to allow easy access to the pond for drinking or bathing. The remaining perimeter should be steep, about 75 degrees, with wide marginal shelves.

If your pond is larger than 6 square metres (65 sq ft), you can add an island to act as a refuge for wildlife. This should be built at the same time as the pool (*see box, right*).

Filling the pond

Cover the floor and marginal shelves with a layer of soil and arrange pebbles on the beach (*see below*). Then trickle water into the pond slowly to prevent it from disturbing the soil too much. Plants can still be grown in baskets (*see page 321*) in a wildlife pond, but a layer of soil in the bottom gives a more natural look, allows native plants to establish themselves, and acts as a habitat for wildlife.

BUILDING AN ISLAND

1 Lay the liner and then build the island before filling the pool. Fill hessian sacks with soil and place them on the floor of the pond to form a ring. The island should cover about one eighth of the surface area of the pond.

2 Fill the centre of the island with soil or gravel in the lower layers, and compact it. Continue to lay sacks until the desired height has been reached. Fill the top 15cm (6in) of the island with good quality, heavy soil.

CONSTRUCTING A WILDLIFE POND

1 Lay an underliner after excavating the site and removing any stones or debris. Place a liner on top and smooth out any wrinkles until it fits the contours of the pool. Bury the edges in 8cm (3in) of soil.

2 Add a layer of soil 10cm (4in) deep to the bottom of the liner and any marginal shelves. Spread the soil part of the way up the gently sloping part of the sides.

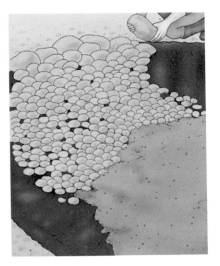

3 Make a pebbly beach on gently sloping areas. Use larger stones around the edge and smaller pebbles and gravel as you work down the slope. Aim to build a ramp from the edge to the floor of the pond.

PLANTING WATER PLANTS

Generous planting not only looks attractive, but it will help to keep the water free of algae, which prospers in light. Aim to cover a least one third of the surface of the pond with foliage. Submerged oxygenating plants will also keep to the pool ecosystem balanced. Once you have equipped the pond with functional plants, you can choose more decorative ones to plant around the edges. When the planting becomes established you can expect the pond to become a magnet to visiting wildlife.

Planting basics

There are six different groups of aquatic plants: deep-water plants that root at the bottom of the pond and send their flowers and some of their leaves to the surface; submerged plants, which are useful oxygenators; floating plants; marginal plants; waterlilies; and bog plants.

For a long season of interest, choose a mixture of plants with assorted flowering times. For a wildlife pond, choose native plants that provide food and nectar, and a few taller marginals for visiting birds and insects. If you are planning to keep fish, introduce them a few weeks after planting.

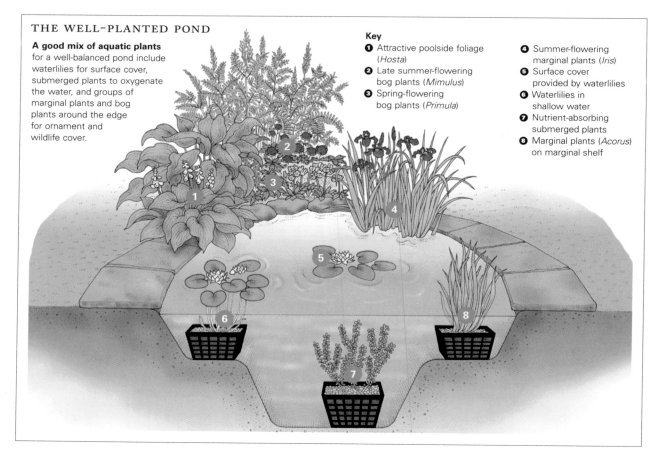

THE WELL-PLANTED POND

A good mix of aquatic plants for a well-balanced pond include waterlilies for surface cover, submerged plants to oxygenate the water, and groups of marginal plants and bog plants around the edge for ornament and wildlife cover.

Key
❶ Attractive poolside foliage (*Hosta*)
❷ Late summer-flowering bog plants (*Mimulus*)
❸ Spring-flowering bog plants (*Primula*)
❹ Summer-flowering marginal plants (*Iris*)
❺ Surface cover provided by waterlilies
❻ Waterlilies in shallow water
❼ Nutrient-absorbing submerged plants
❽ Marginal plants (*Acorus*) on marginal shelf

Growing in baskets

In most garden ponds, aquatic plants should be grown individually in mesh basket containers. There are several reasons for this: water can flow freely in and out through the mesh sides, allowing the plant to take up nutrients from the water; the confinement of the container prevents the plant roots from spreading too far and invading the territory of other plants; and growing in baskets also makes it easy to move individual plants around to change the display or to lift them out of the pond when they need tidying up or dividing.

Square, round, and elongated baskets are available in many different sizes. Choose ones that are large enough to accommodate the eventual size of the plant and to keep it stable as it grows. If you have a pre-formed liner, you can also find curved baskets that are designed to fit the contours of your pond. More recently, planting bags made from rot-proof textile have become available. These are flexible enough to mould to the shape of uneven shelves, but should not be used where there might be sharp stones on the floor.

SOIL STRUCTURE TEST

Aquatic plant compost is widely available, but you can make your own. Take soil from an area where healthy plants grow, but no fertilizers or pesticides have been used recently. Sieve it to remove any large stones and debris, then test the soil structure. Dry a small amount of the soil and crumble it into a jar half filled with water. Put the lid on and shake to mix. Leave until the water is clear – about 5 days. There will be layers of sand, clay, water, and floating organic material. If the clay layer is twice as deep as the sand layer, with very little organic material, then it is ideal.

PREPARING A BASKET

1 Place the basket on a piece of lining material and cut out a square twice the size of the basket so that the fabric will come right the way up the sides. You can also buy pre-cut lining squares, but cutting your own is more economical.

2 Line the basket with the fabric, folding excess neatly in the corners. If you are planting tall marginals, it is a good idea to weight the basket with a brick for stability, but if you do this you will need to choose a larger basket to make up for the soil volume that will be lost.

3 Fill the basket with aquatic compost or suitable soil to within 2.5cm (1in) of the rim. Firm the soil lightly with your hands and trim off any excess lining fabric from around the edges of the basket.

4 Soak the soil thoroughly and evenly. To avoid displacing the soil, use a watering can with a very fine rose attached. The water will fill all the spaces in the soil and drive out all the air.

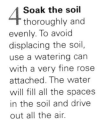

PLANTING A BASKET

1 **Make a hole** that is large enough to accommodate the roots of your chosen plant, using a trowel. If you are planting a small division, it may be less fiddly to just make the hole by hand. Place the plant in the hole.

2 **Cover the roots** and firm the soil around them. If you are planting container-grown plants, it may be easier only to half fill the basket at first. Sit the plant rootball on the soil and then fill in more soil around it. Water in after firming the soil.

3 **Cover the surface** of the soil with a layer of pea gravel 1cm (½in) deep. This is essential to keep the soil in the basket, preventing the surface from being washed away whenever the water of the pond is disturbed.

4 **Water the basket** thoroughly before lowering it into the pool to drive out any pockets of air in the planting medium. If they are left in, they will rise to the surface to escape when the basket is submerged, and this will disturb the plant roots.

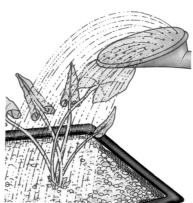

To prevent soil from being washed through the sides of baskets and clouding the water, most baskets will need to be lined before planting (*see page 321*). Squares of hessian or plastic mesh are both suitable and sometimes sold cut to the appropriate size. Lining is unnecessary for micro-mesh containers with fine perforations or planting bags.

Placing the plants

Once you have planted up your baskets (*see above*), you can place the plants. Aim for a natural look when placing marginal plants. This is best achieved by placing plants slightly closer than their optimum spread, which will allow the foliage to knit together quickly.

Baskets need to be at the correct depth to ensure that the plants will thrive. In some circumstances they may need to be raised up on bricks to reach the desired position. If this is necessary, remember to put a piece of underliner or other cushioning under the bricks to protect the liner from rough edges.

In shallow ponds, baskets can easily be lowered in by hand, but if the water is deep, you may need to thread string through the basket (*see above, step 5*). If the basket

5 **Lower the basket** into position. If the level it is being planted at is beyond easy reach, use lengths of heavy duty string to lower it in. Make sure that you thread string through each side or corner and hold them all, or the basket will tilt and spill soil.

is heavy, enlist a second pair of hands to help out. To place a container in the centre of the pond, it may be necessary to lay a plank over the pond to work from.

To remove baskets from a shallow pool, you can simply reach in and retrieve them with ease, aiming to keep the container upright at all times. In deeper pools, you may need to wear chest-high waders to take them out by hand. As this will disturb the water, plant life, and any wildlife, aim to do it as infrequently as possible.

Siting & design *see page 306* | **Methods & materials** *see page 309* | **Container gardening** *see page 338*

Small ponds & containers

Even if you only have a small pond or a container water feature, you can still include plants. The range will inevitably be more limited than in a large pond, and you may not be able to vary the planting levels much.

If the container is large enough to accommodate small mesh baskets, a selection of different aquatics can be planted in these and then added to a container just as they would be to a large pond. For example, many barrels are large enough to accommodate several plants arranged on the base of the container. If necessary, secure a waterproof liner inside the container with galvanized tacks, leaving a gap of about 2cm (³⁄₄in) between the top of the liner and the rim, so the liner will remain hidden as much as possible. Next, add your plants, using bricks if necessary to provide different planting heights. Once your plants are arranged, put a hose over the side and fill slowly to avoiding disturbing the plants and soil. The surface of the water should be just below the top of the liner.

If the container is too small for baskets, plant with the rootballs wrapped in hessian tied loosely around the neck. You can also plant directly (*see below*), a method usually avoided with vigorous plants in a large pond, because they might spread aggressively and become tangled if their roots are not kept in check. The more restrained plants suitable for small water features should not present a problem.

When planting small ponds, use exuberant planting around the pond to compensate for a restrained choice within it. Avoid vigorous plants, or you will have to remove them more often than is good for the pond.

PLANTING A SMALL POOL OR CONTAINER

1 Spread a layer of aquatic compost or suitable soil about 10–15cm (4–6in) deep on the floor of the container. Soak it gently but thoroughly using a watering can fitted with a fine rose.

2 Plant your chosen aquatic plants directly into the soil. Once they are all in place, cover the surface with a layer of pea gravel 1cm (½in) deep to keep the soil in place.

3 Lay a plastic bag flat on top of the plants and soil and lay the end of your hosepipe on the bag. Turn the water on at a very low pressure so that it flows gently from the hose across the plastic bag.

4 The bag spreads the water out and protects the plants and soil from any disturbance. It will float up as the container slowly fills. Once the water is at the required level, the bag can be removed.

Hardy waterlilies

Waterlilies are the most elegant and dramatic of all aquatic plants and are available in a wide range of colours, shapes, and sizes. Although they are primarily grown for their flowers, which appear from early summer until the first frost of autumn, their foliage provides useful cover for wildlife and helps to shade out algae.

Some waterlilies are vigorous and fast-growing, suitable for only the largest pool, while diminutive types are ideal for a container pond. All prefer sunny, fairly still water.

Preparing plants

If you buy from an aquatic nursery, you are most likely to find bare-rooted plants. Before planting into a mesh basket, these will need some preparation. Most waterlilies grow from a log-like rootstock that has shoots and leaves at the top and a ruff of roots just beneath them. Remove any long-stalked, floating leaves and any flowers from the top of the rootstock with a knife, because they will die anyway, but leave shoots that were submerged in place. This allows the rootstock to form new leaves and stems that suit the depth of your pool. At the same time, trim back the roots and the old rootstock (*see box, below right*). Prevent fungal infection by dipping the rootstock in flowers of sulphur, and plant into a mesh basket.

Container-grown waterlilies should be removed from their pots and planted into mesh baskets before being put in the pond. If the compost falls away when they are removed from the pots, treat them as bare-rooted plants.

NYMPHAEA & NUPHAR

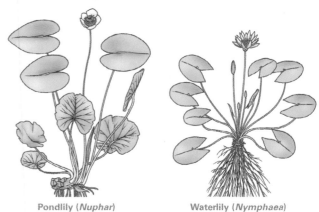

Pondlily (*Nuphar*)   Waterlily (*Nymphaea*)

Although they look similar, waterlilies (*Nymphaea*) and pondlilies (*Nuphar*) grow differently. Many waterlilies are ideal in small ponds, but pondlilies (*see page 326*) are more vigorous, needing large areas of water.

Planting depths

Waterlilies can be divided into three groups based on their ideal planting depth (*see box, below left*). Hardy dwarf and pygmy waterlilies like *Nymphaea* 'Aurora' and *N.* 'Caroliniana' suit shallow pools 15–45cm (6–18in) deep. Mid-depth waterlilies such as *N.* 'Gonnère' and *N.* 'James Brydon' will thrive at 45–75cm (19–30in), given a surface area of 4 square metres (43 sq ft) or more. If the pool is up to 3m (10ft) deep with a surface area of over 9 square metres (97 sq ft), plant deep-water waterlilies.

WATERLILY PLANTING DEPTHS

The depth that a waterlily prefers to grow at also governs its vigour. The leaves of the deeper types spread to a far greater diameter at the surface.

Key
❶ **Deep 1.8m (6ft)**: spreads to 75cm–3m (2½–10ft) across
❷ **Mid 60cm (24in)**: spreads to 45–75cm (1½–2½ft) across
❸ **Shallow 30cm (12in)**: spreads to 15–45cm (6in–1½ft) across

---

PREPARING WATERLILIES FOR PLANTING

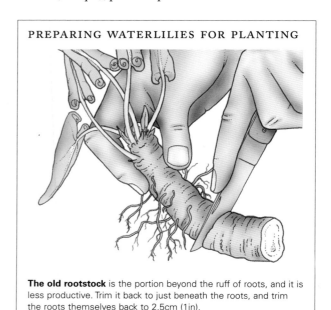

The old rootstock is the portion beyond the ruff of roots, and it is less productive. Trim it back to just beneath the roots, and trim the roots themselves back to 2.5cm (1in).

Deep-water plants

Plants that have their roots at the bottom of the pool and their flowers and some of their leaves above the surface are known as deep-water aquatic plants. Most love to grow in sun, although the pondlilies (*Nuphar* species) will tolerate a certain amount of shade.

This is a useful group of plants, especially if you are planting a stream, because some tolerate moving water. Their leaves provide shelter for wildlife, and their shade helps to inhibit unwanted algal growth. All of these plants need a minimum depth of 30cm (12in) of water to thrive, and the spread of their foliage is roughly one to one-and-a-half times the depth at which the plant grows, although this is also influenced by the size of the planting basket.

What to grow

Water hawthorn (*Aponogeton distachyos*): Also known as Cape pondweed, this plant will provide your pond with a reliable show of white flowers from early spring until autumn. The highly scented, forked blooms float on the water among green leaves that are often splashed purple. It needs a depth of 30–90cm (12–36in), and is not reliably hardy below -5°C (23°F).

Pondlily (*Nuphar lutea* subsp. *advena*): Most pondlilies are not as attractive as waterlilies, but this is a worthy rival. It has large yellow flowers with purple or green tints in summer, held above oval, floating leaves. Although it will tolerate growing in the shallows, it prefers water at least 45cm (18in) deep. This vigorous species will grow at depths of 1.5m (5ft) and spreads to fill as much space as it is allowed unless it is constrained by planting in a mesh basket.

Golden club (*Orontium aquaticum*): Thriving in moving water, this plant produces pencil-like spikes of yellow flowers in late spring, which stand proud of the water between slender leaves. Although it is sometimes grown as a marginal, it is much more successful if planted at a depth of around 45cm (18in).

Water violet (*Hottonia palustris*): This pretty plant is recognizable for the slender spike that hold its white or lilac flowers above ferny foliage in summer. Not particularly easy to grow, it prefers to be planted in a pool that has been established for some time. Plant in water 30–45cm (12–18in) deep.

Water crowfoot (*Ranunculus aquatilis*): A useful hardy plant for moving water, with lots of white flowers with yellow centres in early summer. It bears clover-like leaves that float on the water and grassy leaves beneath the surface. Grows at a depth of 30–45cm (12–18in).

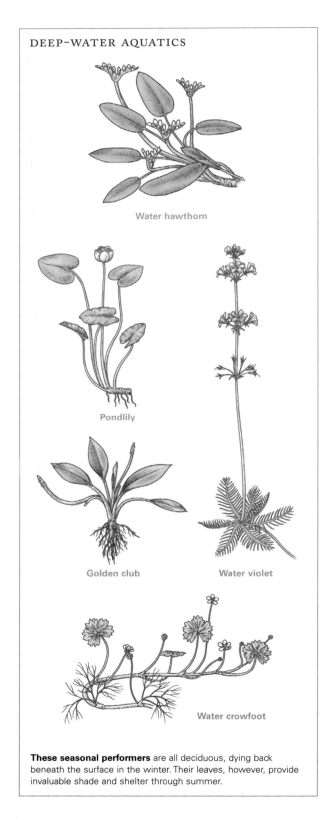

DEEP-WATER AQUATICS

Water hawthorn

Pondlily

Golden club

Water violet

Water crowfoot

These seasonal performers are all deciduous, dying back beneath the surface in the winter. Their leaves, however, provide invaluable shade and shelter through summer.

Wildlife ponds *see page 50* | **Siting & design** *see page 306* | **Pond care** *see page 332*

Submerged plants

Submerged plants help to keep ponds clear of algae, oxygenate the water, and provide shelter for pond life. Plant them no more than 90cm (36in) deep in sun or light shade, adding a bunch for every square metre (10 sq ft) of surface area. Simply push them into a mesh basket of soil, firming in well to prevent them from floating free. They can spread widely, so be ready to remove excess plants.

What to grow
Curled pondweed (*Potamogeton crispa*): Translucent foliage and tiny purple and white flowers in summer.
Hair grass (*Eleocharis acicularis*): Good in formal pools as it remains under the surface at all times.

Hornwort (*Ceratophyllum demersum*): Ideal for shady, deep ponds, it has brittle stems and bristly leaves.
Spiked milfoil (*Myriophyllum spicatum*): Whorled leaves, along with spikes of red and yellow flowers.
Whorled milfoil (*Myriophyllum verticillatum*): Fern-like foliage and small yellow flowers in summer.

Plants to avoid
Some submerged plants outcompete native plants if they escape, and deprive some wildlife of food. Never plant parrot's feather (*Myriophyllum aquaticum*), Canadian pondweed (*Elodea canadensis*) or curly waterweed (*Lagarosiphon major*, sometimes sold as *Elodea crispa*).

Curled pondweed has submerged leaves but carries purple and white flowers just above the surface of the water.

Hair grass is a diminutive plant that gives the appearance of an underwater lawn if its roots spread through a soil-bottomed pool.

Hornwort floats to the surface during summer. Buds break off in autumn and sink to the bottom, where they take root.

Spiked milfoil turns from green to bronze before summer. Do not confuse it with parrot's feather, a close relative but an invasive weed.

Floating plants

Unlike other aquatic plants, you will not have to plant these into baskets. Simply float them on the surface of the water. They can be highly decorative and play an important role in ponds by reducing the risk of invasion by algae, as they absorb mineral salts that are necessary for its growth and provide surface cover, reducing the amount of sunlight that falls into the water.

All floating plants have the potential to be invasive. Be a responsible water gardener and dispose of them carefully by composting – never put them into drains or local water courses. Do not buy any of the 'plants to avoid' listed below, and only buy properly labelled plants that give both Latin and English names from a reputable supplier.

What to grow

Most aquatic nurseries will have a good choice of non-invasive floating plants that are ideal for ponds.

Water soldier (*Stratiotes aloides*): Among the most dramatic of the floating plants, this forms a rosette of upright leaves that resembles the top of a pineapple, and produces small white or pinkish flowers in summer.

Fairy moss (*Azolla caroliniana*): This small floating fern spreads across the surface of the pond; its green leaves turn purplish red in autumn. Avoid the very similar *A. filiculoides* (*see page 331*), an invasive weed; if you doubt the correct identity, do not buy this plant.

Water chestnut (*Trapa natans*): This produces white summer flowers and triangular leaves marked with purple, then a nut-like fruit in autumn, which sinks to the bottom of the pool and germinates in spring.

Frogbit (*Hydrocharis morsus-ranae*): Kidney-shaped leaves and pretty, three-petalled white flowers in summer.

Plants to avoid

Conservationists advise against growing the following plants, due to their ability to colonize natural waterways with great speed if they escape from the garden.

Water fern (*Azolla filiculoides*): This may be hard to distinguish from *A. caroliniana* (*see above*).

Floating pennywort (*Hydrocotyle ranunculoides*): This plant is sometimes mislabelled as the non-invasive marsh pennywort (*H. vulgaris*).

Water lettuce (*Pistia stratiotes*): Invasive in frost-free areas.

New Zealand pygmy weed (*Crassula helmsii*): Sometimes this is sold as Australian stonecrop, *Tillaea helmsii*, or *T. recurva* (*see page 331*).

Water hyacinth (*Eichhornia crassipes*): A problem in areas with mild winters; hardier strains are starting to appear.

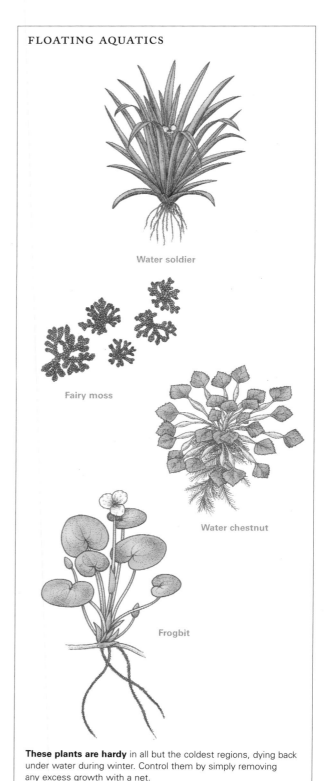

FLOATING AQUATICS

Water soldier

Fairy moss

Water chestnut

Frogbit

These plants are hardy in all but the coldest regions, dying back under water during winter. Control them by simply removing any excess growth with a net.

Wildlife ponds *see page 50* | **Pond care** *see page 332* | **Overcoming problems** *see page 337*

Marginal plants

Grown around the pond edge on purpose-built marginal shelves, these plants soften the transition from water to land and are essential for an attractive pond. They also provide cover, food, and a place to perch for wildlife. Growing 15–60cm (6–24in) in height, they like to have their roots in wet mud or several centimetres of water, and most will tolerate up to around 15cm (6in) of water. Plants bought in traditional plant pots will need to be trimmed back for planting (*see box, below*). Place the planted baskets on the marginal shelves of your pond.

What to grow
There is a rich selection to choose from.
Dwarf reed (*Typha minima*): Ideal for even small pools, this reed has grassy leaves and dense 'bulrush' spikes of brown flowers in late summer.
Corkscrew rush (*Juncus effusus* f. *spiralis*): Grown for its curiously curled leaves.
Bog arum (*Calla palustris*): Bears white flowers in summer.
Water forget-me-not (*Myosotis scorpioides*): Bright blue flowers bloom in early summer.
Blue flag (*Iris versicolor*): The flowers are violet-blue and gold; those of the variety 'Kermesina' are plum purple.
Sweet flag (*Acorus calamus*): This has similar foliage to irises, but less showy, yellow flowers.

Pickerel weed (*Pontederia cordata*) has spikes of soft blue flowers in late summer, but the less common form *albiflora* is white-flowered.

Arrowhead is the name given to several species of *Sagittaria*, due to their leaf shape. They have white flowers in summer.

PREPARING MARGINALS FOR PLANTING

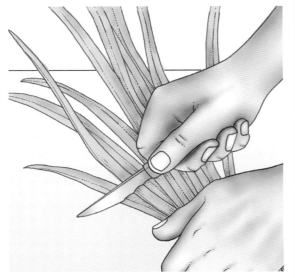

Trim back roots to within 2.5cm (1in) of the crown. If planting mature plants from midsummer onwards, trim back the top growth by two thirds, using a sharp knife or pair of secateurs.

Water irises, such as *Iris pseudacorus* and *I. laevigata* and its striped variety 'Variegata', are hard to beat in summer.

Bog plants

Acting as a bridge between your water feature and the rest of the garden, bog plants provide colour and interest from early spring until autumn. They range in height from creeping ground cover to towering specimens, so choose plants that will fit your garden. Bog plants thrive in damp soil but they will not survive long in standing water.

Preparing & planting

Bog plants are planted directly into the soil like any other perennial. If planting from midsummer onwards, remove any fading flowers and reduce the height of vigorous, clump-forming plants by about one third before planting. Water well while still in their pots, an hour before planting if possible. Dig a hole wider than the pot but at the same depth, remove the pot, and place the plant in the hole. Backfill with soil, firm, and water, ensuring that the crown is slightly proud or at the same level as the soil.

What to grow

Giant rhubarb (*Gunnera manicata*): If space is not an issue, nothing is more dramatic than this foliage plant. The huge, deciduous leaves grow swiftly and it easily makes a 3m (10ft) clump.
Bugle (*Ajuga reptans*): Bears low spikes of blue flowers.
Primrose (*Primula*): These give essential colour in spring and summer and many types suit bog gardens: *P. rosea* has red flowers in early spring, and *P. bulleyana* is a candelabra type with orange-yellow flowers in summer.

Broad swathes of bog plants visually extend a pond and anchor it in its surroundings. They are essential to creating an informal, natural look.

Astilbe (*Astilbe*): Attractive foliage topped by plumes of flowers up to 1.2m (4ft) in summer.
Daylily (*Hemerocallis*): These statuesque plants have showy yellow flowers in summer, like the scented blooms of *H. lilioasphodelus*.
Monkey flower (*Mimulus*): Compact forms, such as yellow *M. luteus* and *M. guttatus*, are ideal. Their bright flowers liven up late summer.

Royal fern (*Osmunda regalis*) is a stately architectural plant with an upright habit and large, leathery fronds up to 1.8m (6ft) long.

Drumstick primula (*Primula denticulata*) flowers from mid-spring to summer. Reddish and white-flowered varieties are also available.

Ferns and grasses and the large, heart-shaped, blue-green leaves of a hosta such as *H. sieboldiana* provide a lively mix of textures.

Aquatic weeds

Ponds can provide ideal growing conditions for vigorous plants, which may outgrow their welcome. Planting in baskets helps to control them by restricting the roots, and makes it much easier to lift and divide plants.

Over-vigorous natives such as bur-reed (*Sparganium erectum*), white waterlily (*Nymphaea alba*), and bulrush or reedmace (*Typha*) can rapidly fill smaller ponds. Small amounts of duckweed (*Lemna*) can look attractive at first, but can spread to spoil the pond's appearance and hide fish.

Invasive non-natives, such as New Zealand pygmy weed (*Crassula helmsii*) and water fern (*Azolla filiculoides*), are sometimes introduced for decorative effect or as oxygenators. They can become a nuisance in the pond, but cause far more serious problems if they escape. They can choke natural ponds and waterways, crowd out native vegetation, and displace the wildlife that depends on it.

Controlling native plants

Remove large, invasive plants rooted in the sides or base of the pond and replace with less vigorous species. Autumn is the ideal time for this work, and it is easier if you can lower the water level of the pond before you start.

Limit regrowth by reducing the nutrient levels in the pond, and make sure that fertilizers introduced on other parts of the garden cannot seep in from surrounding areas. Keep out falling leaves, avoid overfeeding fish, and top up the pond with rainwater, rather than tap water. There are no weedkillers approved for amateur use in ponds.

REMOVING DUCKWEED

The plants of duckweed are tiny, but they are simple to remove if you use a fishing net. If the pond is too large to reach the middle, use a hose to drive the weed to the sides first.

Controlling non-native plants

Prevention is better than cure, so avoid buying plants known to be invasive. Always check newly acquired pond plants for unwanted 'hitchhikers' – these problem plants can develop rapidly from small fragments. If you already have them in your pond, pull up, rake out, or scoop off excess plants. Never take the debris out of the garden; compost the plants or bury them.

New Zealand pygmy weed or Australian stonecrop looks harmless, with its dainty white flowers, but it is very difficult to control.

Water fern is pretty but spreads vigorously. Think twice before introducing this or any other species of *Azolla*.

Reedmace flower spikes are a classic pond plant, but for large, natural ponds only. Elsewhere, treat it with caution.

POND CARE

If left to its own devices, a healthy pond can all too easily become an eyesore, with overgrown plants, murky water, and a build up of algae or unwanted pond weeds. Almost no other area of the garden will show neglect so quickly or so dramatically. To keep a pond in good shape, it is important to treat it like any other part of the garden and carry out seasonal jobs so it remains an attractive and valuable feature. If your pond is carefully sited, properly constructed, and sensibly planted, maintenance should be straightforward, but unfortunately it cannot be avoided altogether.

Seasonal care

Like every other part of your garden, a pond has its own annual cycle of maintenance. These tasks range from weed control to plant division, and from water replenishment in summer to frost protection in winter.

Spring
Remove any heating devices from the pond once all danger of frost is over. Take filters, pumps, and lights out of storage, check that they are working and place them back in the pond. Every few years it may be necessary to empty and thoroughly clean a pond (*see page 334*), but avoid frequent cleaning because it will upset the pond's ecosystem. Feed your pond plants as they are coming into growth with an aquatic fertilizer (*see page 336*).

In winter, the pond and surrounding area should be clear of all debris. Keep a small patch free of ice to protect the pond (*see facing page*).

KEEPING A POND CLEAR OF AUTUMN LEAVES

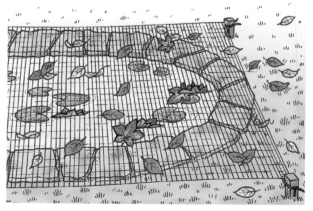

A net stretched over the surface of a pond and secured to the ground with pegs is essential if deciduous trees overhang the water, but clearing leaves from the centre can be tricky on large ponds.

A net fence around ponds can be put in place in less vulnerable sites, where leaves are likely to be blown in from the ground. Secure with wire to stout canes spaced 60cm (24in) apart around the perimeter.

Summer

Perhaps the biggest problem in a long, hot summer is the pond's water level dropping through evaporation. Top it up once a week or more in hot weather. If possible, use rainwater captured in a water butt, but if none is available use tap water. If using tap water, top up little and often to prevent the shock of the colder water disturbing fish.

To keep the water clean over summer, regularly deadhead flowers and remove dying foliage to prevent it from rotting in the pond. Twirl out blanketweed with a stick and leave it on the side before disposing of it so that any creatures within it can find their way back to the water.

Autumn

Leaves fall for many weeks over autumn, and many will find their way into your pond, where they will look unsightly and discolour the water. If there are trees directly over the pool, stretch a net over it (*see facing page*). If the trees are farther away, you could construct a low fence around the perimeter instead. The netting can be left in place over winter or until all the trees are bare. Autumn is also the time to remove dead, dying, and tatty foliage from waterside plants and to divide overcrowded clumps.

Winter

Some pond equipment is at risk from damage over winter, so remove any lights, filters, and pumps. Clean them and store in a dry place until spring.

Ponds are at great risk from freezing over in winter. Expanding ice can cause concrete to crack, and fish can die as the air between the surface of the water and the ice is replaced by the gases from decaying vegetation.

AVOIDING A FROZEN SURFACE

Expanding ice can cause concrete pond liners to crack, so it is very important they are not allowed to freeze over completely. Reduce the risk by floating a rubber ball or a piece of wood on the surface – as the water freezes the softer ball or wood will absorb the pressure and prevent fractures.

The easiest solution is to add an electric pool heater to the pond. This generally consists of a brass rod with a heating element in it, which is attached to a float. Although it will not prevent the whole surface from freezing over, it will keep a small patch of water free from ice. This is all that is needed to allow oxygen to enter and let toxic gas escape from the water.

If your garden generally remains frost free, you can use simpler methods. For instance, float a rubber ring from a pet shop in the pond. If the surface freezes, it is easy to melt the area inside the ring. A floating ball will keep an area free of ice; pour boiling water over the ball and lift it out to create a ventilation hole. Alternatively, sit a saucepan filled with boiling water to melt a hole in the ice. Never simply break ice, as the shock can kill any fish.

CREATING A VENTILATION HOLE IN WINTER

Fill a saucepan with boiling water, put the lid on, and sit it on the ice. Several refills may be needed to melt a hole in thick ice.

A floating ring will freeze in place. Treat it as a well: the ring will hold boiling water in one place, so the ice there can be melted.

Electric pool heaters will keep a small area free of ice, and may be the best solution if you are unable to check on your pond regularly.

Cleaning ponds

From time to time you will need to completely clean out your pond. This is necessary to remove any sediment that has built up on the floor, causing the water to turn murky, and to reduce the tangle of old underwater plants.

The best time to give your pond an overhaul is in spring, because this gives the pond plants plenty of opportunity to re-establish themselves before summer. Although it is hard work, it is not something that needs doing often; every five years or so if the pond is small and every 10 years with larger ponds.

Removing water

Before you can clean the pool you will need to empty it of water. You should direct the water onto a border; never empty it into a drain or water course as this cans cause potentially invasive water plants to escape into the wild.

If part of the surrounding land is lower than the pool, you can try siphoning out the water using a piece of hosepipe. The pull of gravity should help most of the water drain from the pond and any that is left in the bottom can be removed with a bucket. If siphoning is not possible, you will have to pump or bail out the water.

Removing plants & pond life

Be careful not to throw away fish when you are draining a pond. Most will remain in the wet soil on the pool floor. Use a net or mug to remove them to bowls of clean pond water and add a few pieces of submerged aquatic plant to provide shelter and food. Remember to feed fish with their usual dried food if they remain in the buckets for a few days. Dispose of snails with tall, spiral shells, which eat plants, but keep snails with flat shells, which eat algae.

Put marginal plants in a shady place and keep all other aquatics in buckets, bowls, or tanks of pond water. Ensure that submerged plants are completely covered with water. If any plants have outgrown their containers, now is a good to time to repot and divide them.

Cleaning the pond

Remove any mud, taking care not to damage a flexible liner. You can use a spade with care, but scraping with an empty pot is safer. When dry, the mud can be mixed into your garden soil. Scrub the sides and floor of the pool with a stiff brush and clean water, and finish by removing all traces of water added to the pool while cleaning.

CLEANING A POND

1 Empty your pond by siphoning off the water with a hosepipe, bailing out with a bucket, or pumping out. Take care where you empty the water; some plants become invasive and aggressive weeds can, if they are allowed to, enter natural water courses via drains.

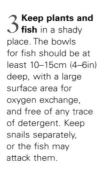

2 Bail out the last of the water with a bucket. Remove plants as you go, and scoop out any fish or other livestock as you see them. Be careful not to bail out small fish or snails with the mud accidentally.

3 Keep plants and fish in a shady place. The bowls for fish should be at least 10–15cm (4–6in) deep, with a large surface area for oxygen exchange, and free of any trace of detergent. Keep snails separately, or the fish may attack them.

4 Empty the mud from the floor, being very careful if your pond has a liner. Remove dirt and algae by scrubbing the pond vigorously with a brush and fresh water, then bail this out. Never use detergent, because any trace left behind will cause problems.

Pond repairs

While a pool is empty you can make good any damage to the liner. Make sure that any repair work is dry before water, fish, and plants are returned to the pond.

Butyl liners are repaired with a special kit (*see below, top*), while a concrete pond will need more dextrous treatment to mend cracks or areas that have deteriorated (*see below,*

bottom). Pre-formed fibreglass pools can be mended with a car body repair kit, but the whole liner is best removed and patched from underneath. Plastic liners do not repair well. If you have a rigid pond of any kind that cannot be repaired, the best alternative may be to treat the pond as an excavated hole, lay a butyl liner in it, and make a new edge.

REPAIRING A BUTYL LINER

1 **Clean any dirt** or traces of algae from the damaged area to ensure the repair patch will stick.

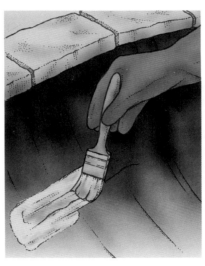

2 **Roughen the area** with sandpaper. Use a paintbrush to spread adhesive over a wide area around the damage.

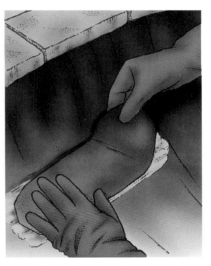

3 **Lay the patch** down on the damaged area once the adhesive becomes tacky. Press firmly, and leave for at least 12 hours to dry.

REPAIRING A CONCRETE POND

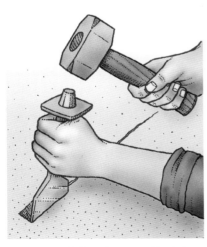

1 **Hammer a V-shaped groove** with a bolster chisel along the crack, at least 2.5cm (1in) deeper than the depth of the crack.

2 **Mix the concrete** and waterproofing compound. Fill the channel and smooth it level using a plasterer's trowel or float.

3 **Treat with sealant** once the concrete has dried, mixing and applying it according to the manufacturer's instructions.

Feeding plants

Aquatic plants are essentially the same as any other plants in the garden, and they will do best if they are supplied with nutrients. Waterlilies, especially, are very hungry plants and require plentiful nutrients to perform well.

Testing your water

Extremes of acidity or alkalinity can affect the growth of water plants. Iron, an essential trace element, cannot be absorbed by plants in alkaline water, while plants in very acid conditions do not respond to fertilizers, and the foliage of waterlilies can even turn brown. The only option in such conditions is to empty the pool, clean it, refill with fresh water, and stock with new plants.

Use a test kit to check the pH value of your pond water. Simply take a sample from the pond and pour it into a tube, mixing it together with the solution that is supplied with the kit. Checking the colour against the supplied chart will tell you its pH value (*see page 17*).

Adding aquatic fertilizers

Feed aquatic plants when they are just coming into growth; once a year in spring is ideal. Some marginal plants will need to be divided and replanted in fresh growing medium instead. Generally, aquatic fertilizers arrive in perforated packets that are pushed into the growing medium among the plant roots.

It is possible to make your own fertilizer 'balls' from a mixture of heavy soil or clay and coarse bonemeal (*see below*). If you have a lot of aquatic plants, this is sometimes a more economical way to feed them.

Looking after the nutrient balance

Inevitably, some nutrients will leach into the water. These will be taken up by floating aquatics, because aquatic plants absorb nutrients through their leaves as well as their roots. Too much fertilizer in the water, however, will encourage algal growth, so do not overfeed.

ADDING AQUATIC FERTILIZER

1 Push fertilizer sachets into a planting basket, after peeling off the protective tape. Place it close to the crown of the plant so the maximum amount of fertilizer reaches the plant instead of leaching out into the water.

2 Cover the sachet over with a handful of pea gravel. This makes doubly sure that the nutrients go where they are supposed to and are not leached out. The gravel also covers the disturbed soil so that it stays in place when the basket is returned to the water.

HOMEMADE FERTILIZERS

1 Take a handful of moist clay or heavy soil; it should hold together in a ball fairly well when rolled and squeezed. Crumble the soil and add approximately 5ml (1tsp) of coarse bonemeal to each handful.

2 Roll the mixture into pellets the size of golf balls between the palms of your hands. Insert these into the growing media, next to the crown of the plant, just as you would a proprietary fertilizer sachet (*see left*).

Overcoming problems

Ponds are generally trouble free, but there may occasionally be problems. If you inherit a neglected pond with too many problems, give it a complete overhaul. Drain and clean it and make repairs if necessary. You may need to restock it with plants, but save any in good condition.

Problems in the water

Algae is a common problem, although a well-balanced pond discourages it. Twirl out mats of algae on a cane or stick, leaving it on the sides of the pool so that pond life can crawl back into the water. A filter with an ultraviolet clarifier causes cloudy algae to clump together so it can be sieved out. Top up the pond with rainwater, rather than tap water, as it is less likely to upset the pH balance of the pond, which can take a long time to put right. Algacides are a quick fix if used carefully, but do not cure the causes.

Muddy water is usually a result of fish disturbing planting baskets in search of insect larvae to eat. Soil builds up on the pond floor and swirls up when a fish passes. Always topdress containers with pea gravel to minimize this; clean out the pond in severe cases.

Pond defences

Plastic herons around the pool together with netting close to the water's surface or a low fence will deter herons. To keep cats away, grow strong marginals and ensure that any paved edge has an overhang for fish to hide underneath (*see box, right*).

PROTECTING THE POND

Key
❶ Bird bath to draw birds away from the pool
❷ Thick marginal planting to discourage herons and to keep cats from the water
❸ Fence of fishing line on canes 15cm (6in) high to discourage herons
❹ Planting baskets covered with 1cm (½in) of pea gravel to minimize soil disturbance by fish
❺ Overhang of 8cm (3in) to prevent cats from fishing
❻ Fish over 15cm (6in) long are safe from kingfishers

Perhaps the greatest predators of ponds are herons, which will quickly pick off your fish until you are left with an empty pool. Local cats also pose a problem, and even wildlife we are usually pleased to see, such as kingfishers, will take smaller fish.

SEASONAL CHANGES

Algal growth may be rife in spring when aquatics are starting into growth and the filter has not been put back into the pond after winter. The condition of the pond is likely to improve in summer when the plants flourish and the filter is reinstalled.

Key
❶ Blanketweed
❷ Filamentous floating weed
❸ Suspended free-floating algae
❹ Overwintered floating and submerged aquatics
❺ Reduced water level due to evaporation
❻ Surface cover provided by waterlilies
❼ Collected rainwater to top up pool
❽ Clear water free from algae
❾ Filter and pump

CHAPTER EIGHT

CONTAINER GARDENING

CHOOSING CONTAINERS *342*

RAISED BEDS *348*

PLANTING *349*

PLANTING HANGING BASKETS *352*

BEDDING PLANTS *353*

BULBS & CORMS *354*

PERENNIAL PLANTS *355*

TREES, SHRUBS & CLIMBERS *356*

VEGETABLES & HERBS *358*

FRUIT *359*

AFTERCARE & MAINTENANCE *360*

P LANTING CONTAINERS FOR SEASONAL OR PERMANENT displays can be great fun, and it provides an excellent opportunity to experiment with planting combinations. You can create some eye-catching and unusual displays, in the knowledge that replacing them is easy if they fail to live up to your hopes.

Container displays make great garden props, not dissimilar to scenery or stage sets inside theatres; they are an intrinsic element of the overall beauty of our gardens and open spaces. Containers filled with attractive plant combinations can enhance the plainest of environments, brightening up patios and balconies. They can also help to soften hard landscaping and provide height and living architecture in a variety of garden situations.

We often think of planted containers as a small oasis for plants, but they also provide habitats for beneficial insects in environments where there is very little in the way of natural habitat. This can be seen in urban areas where large-scale planters, rather than plants in the ground, are prevalent.

Planting trends

Over recent years the availability of a range of plant material and of different and unusual styles of container have both increased dramatically, providing ever-greater opportunities for gardeners to experiment creatively and imaginatively. The trend with regards to using plants has been to move away from traditional annual bedding towards plants that either extend the growing season or provide a more permanent display that can be used, perhaps with variations, over a number of years.

Plants that have become more popular include herbaceous perennials, tender perennials, grasses, bulbs, shrubs, and trees. One advantage of these plants is that they provide an opportunity for more sustainable gardening.

For example, herbaceous perennials can be planted in container displays for a couple of seasons and then removed from the container, divided, and re-used either in the container or planted out in a permanent site in the garden. Alternatively, tender perennials planted in containers can be propagated in late summer to produce plants for future displays.

Annual plants are still popular, but they tend today to be used to enhance permanently planted container displays containing trees, shrubs, grasses, or herbaceous perennials, where their vibrant colours provide a welcome addition. Although they are short-lived, this trait means that annuals provide an opportunity to make small-scale seasonal planting changes to rejuvenate displays when they start to fade.

Types of container

There are many different styles of container on the market, designed to suit all tastes and pockets. The types of container available are boundless, ranging from traditional terracotta or rustic wood to modern, contemporary designs constructed out of glazed ceramic, metal, plastic, and recycled materials. Your vision need not be limited to the designs available specifically for plant use: with a little imagination almost any vessel can be used to create a versatile planter.

Whichever containers, materials, and plants you decide to select, always keep an open mind. Enjoy the experience, be creative, and most importantly have some fun. If you keep this in mind, whatever planter you create will be a unique expression of your personality.

CHOOSING CONTAINERS

Always buy the best containers you can afford. From a practical point of view it is better to buy one or two large containers rather than three or four small ones, because the more space you have for the plant roots, the more choice you will have when it comes to selecting suitable plants, and the easier it is to keep plants adequately watered and fed. Remember that sleek modern styles are unlikely to suit a traditional garden, and classical urns may look out of place on an urban balcony.

Types of container

Once you have decided on the size and style of container, the next consideration is what it is constructed from. Each material has its advantages and disadvantages: heavy concrete may be needed for stability in a windswept position, while lighter fibreglass or metal can be moved around as displays fade or for winter protection.

Terracotta & clay

Traditional terracotta pots are used in many container gardens. They are aesthetically pleasing, come in a variety of shapes and sizes, and age and weather gracefully. Their porous nature allows for the evaporation of water, which helps to reduce overheating when weather conditions are

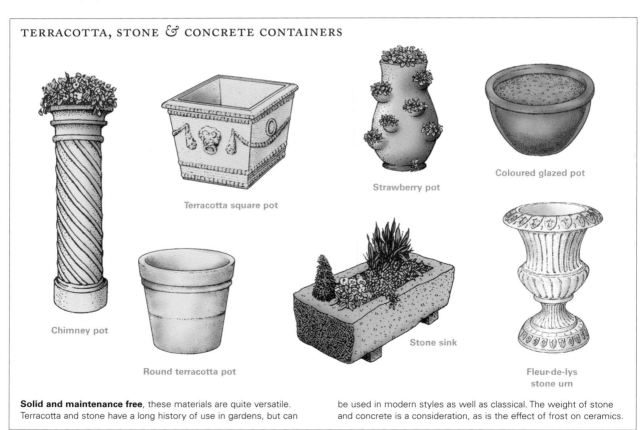

TERRACOTTA, STONE & CONCRETE CONTAINERS

Chimney pot

Terracotta square pot

Strawberry pot

Coloured glazed pot

Round terracotta pot

Stone sink

Fleur-de-lys stone urn

Solid and maintenance free, these materials are quite versatile. Terracotta and stone have a long history of use in gardens, but can be used in modern styles as well as classical. The weight of stone and concrete is a consideration, as is the effect of frost on ceramics.

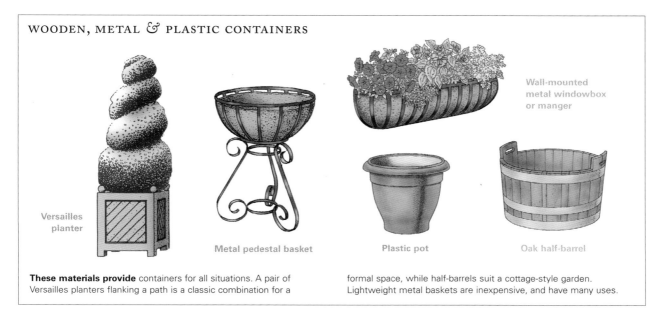

WOODEN, METAL & PLASTIC CONTAINERS

Versailles planter

Metal pedestal basket

Wall-mounted metal windowbox or manger

Plastic pot

Oak half-barrel

These materials provide containers for all situations. A pair of Versailles planters flanking a path is a classic combination for a formal space, while half-barrels suit a cottage-style garden. Lightweight metal baskets are inexpensive, and have many uses.

hot but also makes them less water retentive. Not all are frostproof. Other ceramics have coloured glazes, which both improve their water-retaining and frost-resistance qualities and provide an opportunity to design creative colour combinations with a variety of plants.

Stone & concrete

The advantage of both these materials is their durability. Stone containers are not as popular as they once were. They can be heavy and difficult to move, and are a considerable investment. However, they are often seen in larger, traditional gardens, with ornate decoration and sculpted design in keeping with the setting.

Concrete is versatile, with various finishes available, so you will be able to find something in keeping with your garden's environment. Very large containers made out of concrete are often used in urban areas, while on a smaller scale, concrete is often used for relatively inexpensive garden containers, which are sometimes clad with other materials to enhance their appearance.

Plastic & fibreglass

Gardeners today are looking for containers that offer ease of use and value for money, without compromising on appearance. As a result there are a wide range of plastic and fibreglass containers on the market. The advantages of these materials are that they are lightweight, durable, and also relatively inexpensive. The best of them can also be attractive in their own right or a remarkably realistic simulation of more expensive materials, such as terracotta, glazed ceramics, stone, lead, and wood.

Metal containers

Another modern trend is the increased use of metals, such as galvanized steel, copper, and zinc. These containers provide a contemporary twist on planting design and are surprisingly lightweight due to their thin-skinned, often double-walled, construction. Their main disadvantage is that they rapidly absorb heat from the sun, which in turn accelerates the drying out of the compost. The only solution is to water regularly and attentively and maybe restrict their use to shady areas.

Recycled materials

It is becoming easier now to purchase containers made from a variety of recycled materials, including wood, plastic, and pre-moulded synthetics. These make fine alternatives to buying traditional materials. It is also often rewarding to see what you can recycle yourself or create with a little bit of effort (*see pages 346–347*).

Wooden containers

Wooden containers are very versatile and can range in style from rustic half-barrels to square Versailles boxes. Unlike some of the other materials described here, they provide a cool environment for the roots of plants to thrive in, and they retain moisture exceptionally well. When planting it is advisable to use a waterproof liner inside the wooden planter to help protect its interior from decay. Even half-barrels benefit from this, because today very few are reused hardwood casks. When buying wooden containers, make sure that the timber is properly certified as being harvested from a renewable source.

Baskets & windowboxes

Hanging baskets and windowboxes make a great addition to any garden container display as they make it possible to suspend colourful plants and decorative foliage in doorways, porches, pergolas, and conservatories. A well-planted basket or box is a living, cascading flower arrangement, constantly changing as it grows.

With careful plant selection and maintenance you can achieve stunning results. A good lesson to learn when first caring for any container display (but particularly baskets and boxes) is the need to water frequently: long-handled watering lances provide a longer reach to make this easier. Another tip is to check on the quality of the chain that is supplied for suspending a hanging basket. Consider the weight of the compost, plants, and water once it is planted to avoid a potential calamity.

Wire baskets

Wire baskets are one of the more popular and traditional types of hanging basket available. They are usually made out of plastic coated wire. Mangers that can be used beneath windows tend to be heavier. Both need liners to contain the potting compost (*see facing page*).

Always consider the shape and the size of the spaces in the wire frame, as you may want to plant through the sides. There is nothing more frustrating, or damaging, than trying to squeeze a plant through a very small hole when planting up a hanging basket. The best baskets overcome this problem by having large gaps in the sides so plants can be positioned freely.

Wood & terracotta

Wooden baskets or windowboxes are natural alternatives to wire ones, and in themselves can be decorative. It is also possible to construct your own by recycling scrap timber, the obvious benefit of this being that you can tailor the size and shape to suit your needs.

Terracotta bowls or half bowls tend to be displayed fixed to walls or fences. They make attractive planters, and are a natural-looking alternative to wire or plastic.

Plastic baskets

Over recent years there has been an increase in the variety and quality of plastic hanging baskets. These may be solid with built-in saucers, which provide a useful water reservoir and help to catch any drips, or have removable sides and slots to allow for easier planting. It is helpful to have a built-in reservoir, but they cannot be relied upon to give sufficient watering for more than a short time.

A windowbox with summer and winter displays can provide an oasis of colour to look out on and enjoy from the comfort of your home.

Wicker & fibre baskets

Wicker baskets are attractive and relatively inexpensive, and have become a very popular choice. Often conical in shape, they have a basic wire frame interwoven with a natural wicker weave. They are usually only planted at the top, so plant selection is important and needs to include

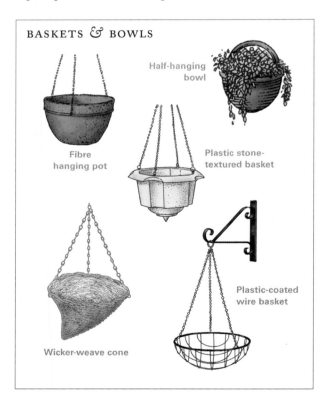

BASKETS & BOWLS

Half-hanging bowl

Fibre hanging pot

Plastic stone-textured basket

Wicker-weave cone

Plastic-coated wire basket

When choosing a basket, remember that it will look different once planted. Some designs look attractive in themselves, but plainer structures will need to be concealed by foliage and flowers.

a combination of flowers and trailing plants. Only expect wicker to last for a couple of seasons: it tends to degrade quickly with constant watering and drying out.

Fibre hanging baskets are expensive and made from compressed fibre shaped into a bowl. These are strong enough to last a season, or can be used as a liner.

Basket liners

Moss raked from lawns is a traditional liner, but there are other materials that are just as effective (*see box, right*). Biodegradable liners include shoddy, a by-product of the wool industry, and coir. Foam or plastic sheet liners are generally concealed by straw or home-harvested moss sandwiched between them and the basket mesh.

Hanging & fixing

Baskets come with a chain or rope, but you can buy spring-loaded suspension devices, which enable you to raise and lower the basket for maintenance. Always make sure you have a strong metal bracket, securely screwed into a solid structure. Windowboxes need strong fixing, and placing a batten behind them to maintain an air gap between them and the wall is also a good idea.

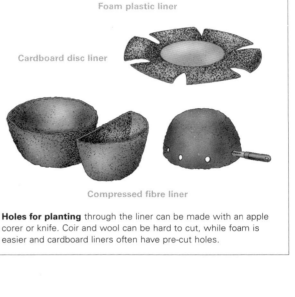

BASKET LINERS

Foam plastic liner

Cardboard disc liner

Compressed fibre liner

Holes for planting through the liner can be made with an apple corer or knife. Coir and wool can be hard to cut, while foam is easier and cardboard liners often have pre-cut holes.

MAKING A WOODEN HANGING BASKET

1 **Make the base** by screwing several slats to 2 outer ones, using wood of at least 2cm (¾in) either way. Use 2 screws at each end for rigidity. Brass or decking screws will last longest, and drilling pilot holes prevents splitting.

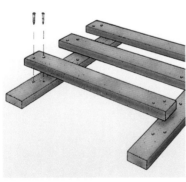

2 **Drill a hole** in each end of the 2 outer slats. This should be large enough to fit a galvanized wire about 2mm (⅟₂in) thick (14 gauge), which will run through the basket corners.

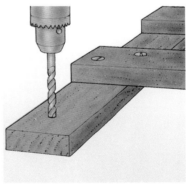

3 **Thread a wire** through each corner, bending over the bottom end, and build up the basket with slats in alternating directions, each drilled to fit over the wire. Too shallow a basket will dry out quickly, but a deep basket is heavy.

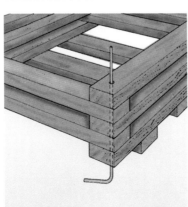

4 **Bend the wire** into loops at the top of the basket with pliers. Hang the basket on chains attached to the loops at each corner. This basket will need some kind of liner inside it; you can make holes for plants to grow out between the slats.

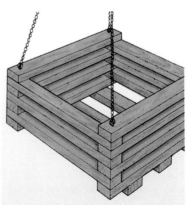

Improvised containers

When designing container displays you can often come up with exciting and imaginative plant combinations. However, many planting schemes are let down by the style and shape of their containers, particularly if these are of inferior quality or design.

If you want to design your container displays with imagination and flair, there is nothing better than recycling a potential container that has the merits of being a little bit out of the ordinary. Aim to raise a smile with your ingenuity and imagination, and you can achieve some stunning displays.

If you open your eyes to new possibilities, practically anything can be used as a container. The important considerations are that there must be adequate drainage and the container must provide sufficient space for the roots of plants to grow and develop healthily. You can also tailor your plant selection to suit your improvised container shape and colour.

Recycling smaller containers

There are many ceramic objects that can be used as containers, including chimney pots with plant pots wedged into the top, or lengths of drainage pipe with one end sunk into the ground. Terracotta plant pots can even be stacked on top of each other to make a strawberry planter (*see page 359*). Secure the pots together using a metal rod or heavy-gauge wire through the drainage holes.

Wooden wine boxes, wicker baskets, or galvanized watering cans all present planting possibilities. Discarded chicken wire can be shaped into a variety of sculptural forms for the garden; this technique can be adapted to make versatile containers.

An old pair of boots makes an unusual container for alpine plants. All you need to do is drill a series of drainage holes through the rubber soles and fill the boots with suitably gritty, free-draining compost.

Creating larger containers

Old sinks have long been used as alpine troughs, sometimes with a coating to simulate stone, but defunct household goods can provide more modern styles as well. Garden centres today sell a variety of metal containers, but these are often expensive; consider using the stainless steel drum out of an old washing machine as a suitable container instead. With a little care and patience the drum can be removed from the frame, and it has several

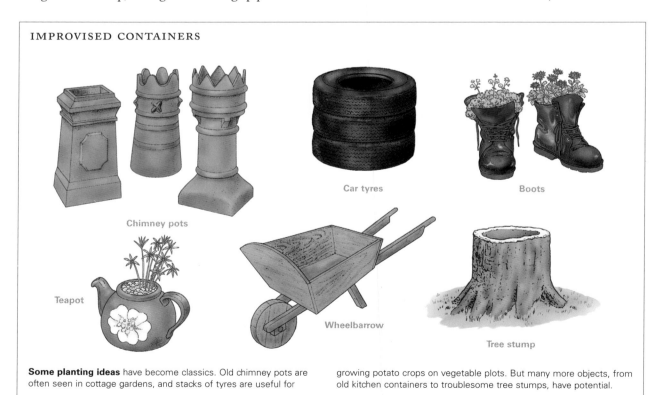

IMPROVISED CONTAINERS

Chimney pots

Car tyres

Boots

Teapot

Wheelbarrow

Tree stump

Some planting ideas have become classics. Old chimney pots are often seen in cottage gardens, and stacks of tyres are useful for growing potato crops on vegetable plots. But many more objects, from old kitchen containers to troublesome tree stumps, have potential.

advantages: plenty of holes mean there is always adequate drainage, it has good depth and width for planting, and being stainless steel, it will not rust.

Sometimes recycling can be more whimsical. Even an old porcelain toilet bowl can be planted up with a variety of plants, and you will never have to worry about providing drainage for them.

Recently, planting bags of strong woven plastic have become popular, particularly for crops. Similar in construction but more generous in size are the disposable 'dumpy' bags used by builder's suppliers to deliver materials such as sand. They are incredibly tough and durable and can be recycled into large containers that look good and are simple to construct (*see below*).

MAKING A DUMPY BAG CONTAINER

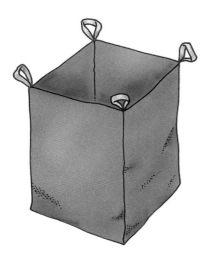

1 **Measure your bag** to work out the dimensions. You can fold in the tops and sides to smaller dimensions if you prefer. With a knife, make slits for drainage at the bottom.

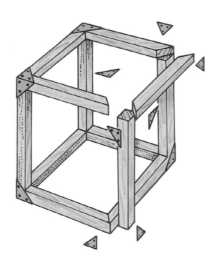

2 **Make a simple crate** to the dimensions of your bag, perhaps from scrap timber such as wooden pallets. Triangular metal plates provide strength and stability at the corners.

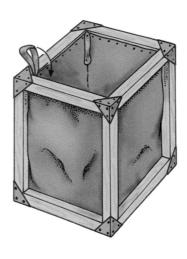

3 **Position the bag** inside the crate and attach it with nails or staples around the top. Remove or fold down the handles.

4 **Design facing panels** to your own taste. You can use wood, metal sheets, woven willow, or plastic. Interchangeable panels can give your planter a versatile appearance.

5 **Fill your planter** to one third of its depth with lightweight drainage material, such as expanded polystyrene. Lay landscape fabric over this, top up with compost, and plant.

ALTERNATIVE USE OF A DUMPY BAG

The flexible fabric of dumpy bags mean they can be used to line structures of almost any shape, such as this pyramid.

Raised beds

Versatile raised planters in keeping with your garden style can be built from wood or brick, and are ideal for growing crops. You can adapt the size of the beds to fit your garden and growing needs and the height to allow easy access. They are easy to protect with cloches and frames, and are a good way to encourage children to grow vegetables on a small scale. Always use a good-quality loam-based compost to fill the bed, and if your planter is on paving, you will need to provide drainage holes.

Wooden beds

Thick posts or railway sleepers can easily be painted or stained, but try to avoid materials that have been treated with harmful preservatives or, if they are recycled, contaminated in some way. It is not necessary to use a liner to prevent rot on hardwood or treated timber.

Brick planters

As these require more preparation, they must be carefully sized and sited. It is important to get the height of the bed right to allow for easy maintenance; about 1m (3ft) is adequate in most gardens. For drainage, make a number of weep holes in the bottom course of bricks, about 1m (3ft) apart, and add rubble in the base (*see box, right*).

Raised bed kits

There are a number of flexible and versatile kits for building beds to size. Some consist of plastic units, others of pre-cut and treated wooden blocks, and they are either slotted together or secured with pegs.

Prominently placed beds form part of the garden landscape, so they need to be thoughtfully integrated if they are not to look unsightly.

A BRICK RAISED BED

Key
❶ Coping on walls to protect brickwork
❷ Soil-based potting compost or good garden topsoil
❸ Old grass turves laid upside-down
❹ Rubble for drainage

When planning the height of a brick bed, bear in mind that it is well worth part-filling the raised bed with broken bricks or rubble to benefit drainage, so you should allow for some extra depth.

JOINING PLANKS OR SLEEPERS

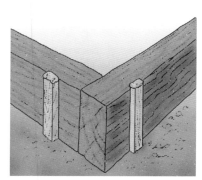

Heavy duty stakes driven into the ground at the corners of a bed can hold a bed of planks or sleepers together. Short tree stakes are ideal for this purpose.

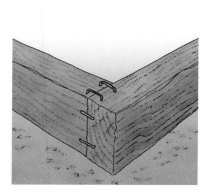

Large staples can be hammered into the corners. Alternatively, you can use large screws or wooden pegs. Beds will be most durable if built from planks at least 5cm (2in) thick.

Growing ornamentals *see page 56* | Growing vegetables & herbs *see page 138* | Aftercare & maintenance *see page 360*

PLANTING

Always buy the best plants you can afford: it is better to have a few well-grown plants than an array of miserable specimens. When making your selection, be aware of not only the colour, but the texture and height of the plants, choosing those that will contrast or complement each other and the container you have in mind. Once you have bought your plants, give them the best possible chance of creating a successful and long-lasting display. Plant them in a suitable growing medium, incorporating any additional ingredients to improve either drainage or water retention.

Preparing for planting

When selecting plants for container displays, visit your local garden centre or nursery to see what is on sale. Take a basket or trolley and see what captures your eye. Start with an open mind, and if you favour a particular colour scheme, assemble a group of plants based on this. Select your favourite plants from the group and return the rest to their stands. Avoid plants that are discounted as there is likely to be something wrong with them.

When choosing plants, be aware of texture and height, and if they are to share a pot, consider whether they have compatible needs. Check that they look healthy, with no signs of disease or damage. It is always worth carefully lifting a plant out of its pot or growing tray and checking that the plant is not root-bound and the root system is healthy. You are looking for strong white roots that have penetrated through the compost and hold it together.

Schemes with bulbs need to be well planned in advance, using the pages of a catalogue as a guide rather than the plants themselves. Many suppliers now sell combinations of bulbs to make planning easy.

Colour comes first in almost any display because it is the first thing we notice. But do not neglect the shape and texture of plants because these are what draw the eye back a second or third time.

349

Potting compost

There are a variety of named brands and formulations (*see below*), but just two main types: loam- or soil-based, and soilless composts. You can use either in containers. Loam-based composts are heavy, but they retain moisture and nutrients well, making them useful for raised beds and long-term plantings. Soilless types are lighter, which makes them good for containers and baskets, but they tend to dry out quickly and only suit short-term bedding displays.

John Innes: A loam-based formulation available in three different blends: No. 1 is used for seedlings and cuttings, No. 2 is used for repotting and season-long planting, and No. 3 is high in nutrients for mature shrubs, trees, and other long-term plantings.

Ericaceous compost: A loam-based compost for plants that need acidic soil conditions.

Multipurpose compost: This generally contains peat or a substitute and nutrients, and is for general use.

Bulb fibre: Reduced-peat compost for bulbs, containing oyster shell and wood charcoal to maintain the right pH.

Container and basket composts: Usually reduced peat, with plenty of nutrients and water-retaining granules.

Useful additives

Water is vital for flourishing containers. Water-retaining granules that expand to hold water and slowly return it to the compost can be incorporated into your mix, delaying the need to water. Always follow the packet instructions.

You can reduce the weight of a container by half filling it with perlite. These lightweight granules are pH neutral, free draining, and used in the nursery industry as a lighter alternative to grit for blending free-draining composts.

MOVING CONTAINERS

Moving large pots can be risky, for both the pots and the toes or back of the mover. If you have pots you move regularly, invest in either a trolley or a platform on castors to make the job easier and safer.

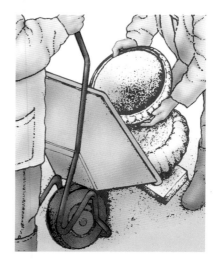

Moving heavy pots is a job for 2 people. They can be moved in a wheelbarrow: raise the handles so the wheelbarrow is almost vertical, tilt the container into it, and lower the handles. Reverse the process to unload.

PROVIDING DRAINAGE

Drill drainage holes in the base of any container that lacks them. Turn the container over and drill 2–3 holes – each with a minimum diameter of 1cm (½in) – in the base.

Fill the base of the container with broken pot pieces or large chunks of polystyrene. This prevents water-logging because water collects in the drainage material instead of the compost if the flow out of the holes is slow.

Planting containers

Containers are like stage sets for plants – with a bit of careful planning and planting, you can create spectacle, drama, and intrigue. Group your plants together on the floor, still in their individual pots, before you go ahead and plant them. This gives you the chance to move them around and decide which arrangement works the best.

You often see containers planted up with a mix of plant types, and this is an excellent way of extending the season and display. However, in too many cases you will see a large plant, perhaps a shrub or a tree, planted in the centre of the container with smaller plants grouped around it. This is a safe and reliable arrangement, but can become dull, and there is a more dynamic approach for those willing to experiment.

In a successful stage set, painting, or photograph, the main feature is often offset, so try placing the largest plant in your display away from the centre of your container. Then mix plants with varying heights around the largest plant, rather than following a simple gradation from the tallest down to the shortest around the container

edge. By using this approach, you will achieve a better visual result, particularly when you are grouping a number of containers together informally.

How to plant

Before planting, water the plants and leave them to drain. Ease them out of their pots or trays and carefully tease away some of the compost from around the neck of each plant. This is useful because the area around the neck may contain weed seeds or surplus compost that is best removed at this stage. If you have limited space in your container, you may want to tease away some of the compost from around the roots of each plant as well, and gently compress the rootball to allow easier planting.

Once the plant is in the soil, make sure you fill in any gaps remaining around the plants with compost and firm in gently. If the container is relatively light you can tap it firmly on a hard surface, which will help settle the compost down. A good soak from a watering can with a fine rose fitted will also help to eliminate any air pockets.

PLANTING FROM POTS OR BOXES

1 **Water the plant well** then remove it from its pot by turning it upside down with your fingers spread to either side of the plant stem, and tapping the base of the pot firmly. Plantlets in module trays can be pushed out from below with a pencil.

2 **Dig a hole** in the compost large enough for the rootball of the plant, and place the plant in it. For ease of working, start with the plants at the centre of the container and work outwards to the edge.

3 **Firm the compost** around the plant to eliminate air pockets. You can do this with the end of the trowel handle, or you may prefer using your fingers. It is important not to over-compact the compost.

4 **Plant the rest** of the container in the same way, finishing with the plants at the edge. Level the surface of the compost and then give the container a thorough soaking.

Planting hanging baskets

Hanging baskets can be planted up for summer displays any time from mid-spring and kept in a greenhouse until they are well established and the risk of frost has passed.

Good basket displays tend to be the ones where you cannot see the basket's wire or plastic structure, so with that in mind allow for plenty of plant material. Select young plants based on colour, texture, and trailing habit. Most baskets are hung at or above eye level, perhaps in a porch or a conservatory, so plants that have a tendency to trail will naturally be an ideal choice. Choose a basket that suits your location and the plants you are intending to grow, and allow for good-sized planting holes that will help to minimize damage to plants when planting up.

How to plant

Most baskets have rounded bottoms, so use a large pot to stand the basket in while filling. This will provide a supportive base from which to work.

Line your basket with your preferred liner (*see page 345*) and part-fill with compost (*see page 350*). This needs to be lightweight, so avoid loam-based composts. At this stage you may want to add some water-retaining granules to the compost; these are particularly useful for hanging baskets, which contain many plants in a small amount of compost.

Insert your young plants through the slots of the basket, remembering to handle them carefully. Cup the stems or foliage with your fingers or wrap them in paper to avoid damage. Gradually work your way around the the basket, placing young plants in the planting slots at intervals, then firming in additional compost. If using loose lining material, infill with more between each plant's collar and the inside of the basket.

Once you have reached the top of the basket, firm in with a little more compost and finish planting the top. Dust off any compost that has fallen on the plants and give the basket a thorough watering.

PLANTING A HANGING BASKET USING A MOSS LINING

1 **Line the basket** to one third of the way up with damp moss or an alternative lining. It is worth placing a piece of plastic sheet or a shallow dish in the bottom of the basket over the liner, to help retain water, before filling with compost.

2 **Insert the plants** that are to trail from the basket. It may be easier to put the rootball through the hole from the outside, or the foliage through from the inside: if the latter, it is often worth wrapping the leaves in paper to protect them. Continue around the basket sides.

3 **Fill the basket** with compost to about 2.5cm (1in) below the rim. This small gap will prevent the basket from overflowing when it is watered. Plant up the top of the basket, using your fingers to make holes without damaging the roots of the plants below. Pack the rim with more lining material.

4 **Water in well**, using a watering can with a fine rose to avoid disturbing the compost. Some liners will absorb water so allow for this by leaving the basket to stand and then watering again, to ensure that the compost is thoroughly moist throughout.

Growing ornamentals *see page 56* | **Aftercare & maintenance** *see page 360* | **Propagating plants** *see page 392*

Bedding plants

Garden centres often supply bedding plants from early in the season. Many of these have been grown with heat, and are insufficiently hardened off and so prone to frost damage. If you have a heated greenhouse at home, you can allow the plants to establish undercover and then bring them out once the risk of frost is over. Alternatively, you can select larger plants from which you can later propagate. When the display is over, bedding plants are usually disposed of on the compost heap.

Annuals grown from seed provide vibrant displays of short-lived colour, mainly for summer display. There are a number of seed companies that supply a wide range of varieties of the plants listed below, and new varieties are constantly being introduced. It is worth registering with seed companies for inclusion on their mailing lists to see these first. Alternatively, you can visit company websites and order either seed or plug plants online as well as looking in local suppliers.

Cosmos keeps flowering for weeks if old flowers are removed frequently, and the flowers occur in shades of pink and white.

Some types of begonia are grown as summer bedding, although they are actually perennials. They cost a little more, but make showy plants.

Trailing nasturtiums are usually easier to incorporate in container displays than the bushy types.

BEDDING PLANTS SUITABLE FOR CONTAINERS

- African marigold (*Tagetes*)
- *Ageratum*
- *Agrostis nebulosa*
- *Alyssum*
- *Amaranthus*
- *Antirrhinum*
- *Bassia scoparia* f. *trichophylla*
- Basil (ornamental)
- *Begonia* (shown)
- *Bellis*
- *Bidens* (trailer)
- *Brachyscome*
- *Briza maxima*
- Cabbage (ornamental)
- *Calceolaria*
- *Calendula* (marigold)
- *Celosia*
- *Cerinthe major* 'Purpurascens'
- *Cheiranthus*
- *Chrysanthemum*
- *Cineraria*
- *Cleome*
- *Cobaea scandens*
- *Convolvulus*
- *Cosmos* (shown)
- *Dianthus*
- *Dimorphotheca*
- *Eccremocarpus* (climber)
- *Felicia*
- *Gomphrena*
- *Heliotropium*
- *Impatiens*
- *Isotoma*
- *Lagurus*
- *Limonium*
- *Lobelia*
- *Lotus*
- *Mimulus*
- *Mina lobata* (climber)
- *Mirabilis*
- Morning glory (climber)
- Nasturtium (trailer) (shown)
- *Nemesia*
- *Nicotiana*
- *Nierembergia*
- *Nolana*
- Pansy (*Viola*)
- *Petunia*
- *Rhodochiton* (climber)
- *Ricinus*
- *Rudbeckia*
- *Salvia*
- *Sanvitalia*
- Sunflower (*Helianthus*)
- *Thunbergia* (climber)
- *Tithonia*
- *Verbena*

Bulbs & corms

Bulbs are a fabulous addition to any container for spring display, providing exuberant colour at a drab time of year when it is most welcome in the garden. Bedding plants are limited during winter, so bulbs make an excellent alternative. Once a display is past its best you can lift the bulbs and plant them out in the garden for next year.

Containers can be planted in layers to provide flowers in succession. By using different types of bulbs you can have flowers from midwinter through to late spring from the same container. For example, plant a layer of lilies at the bottom followed by tulips and finally a top layer of anemones and crocus; they should be layered according to the depth they need to be planted (*see box, below*), rather than their order of flowering times.

Buying & keeping bulbs

Always buy from a reputable source: most garden centres carry a good range of bulbs from early autumn. Check for firm bulbs with no signs of rot. Most bulbs remain in the soil year after year where they gradually increase.

Lilies are ideal bulbs for containers. When in flower, they can be placed on show, then moved away once they fade until next year.

BULBS SUITABLE FOR CONTAINERS

Early spring displays
- *Crocus*
- *Chionodoxa*
- *Convallaria*
- *Cyclamen coum*
- Daffodil (*Narcissus*)
- *Erythronium*
- Grape hyacinth (*Muscari*)
- Hyacinth (*Hyacinthus*)
- *Ipheion*
- *Iris reticulata*
- *Scilla*
- Snowdrop (*Galanthus*)
- Tulip (*Tulipa*) (early-flowering varieties)
- Winter aconite (*Eranthis*)

Late spring & summer displays
- *Allium*
- *Anemone*
- *Dahlia*
- *Dracunculus*
- *Fritillaria*
- *Gladiolus*
- Lily (*Lilium*) (shown)
- Tulip (*Tulipa*) (late-flowering varieties)

Autumn displays
- Autumn crocus (*Colchicum*)
- *Cyclamen hederifolium*
- *Sternbergia*

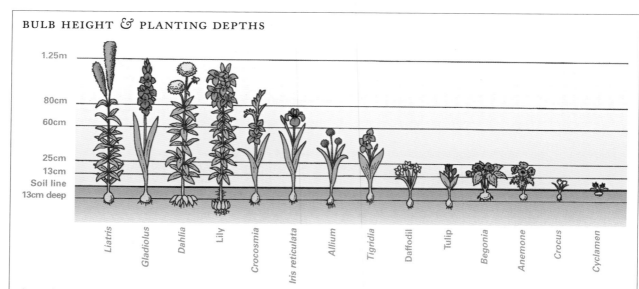

BULB HEIGHT & PLANTING DEPTHS

1.25m
80cm
60cm
25cm
13cm
Soil line
13cm deep

Liatris · Gladiolus · Dahlia · Lily · Crocosmia · Iris reticulata · Allium · Tigridia · Daffodil · Tulip · Begonia · Anemone · Crocus · Cyclamen

As a rule of thumb, plant bulbs 3 times their own depth, so smaller bulbs are planted shallowly, while larger bulbs with greater reserves of energy are planted more deeply. You need not be too precise; bulbs can use their roots to 'fine tune' their position if it is roughly correct.

Use a suitable compost, either a specialist bulb fibre or loam-based compost such as John Innes No. 2. Position the bulbs close to each other but make sure that they do not touch each other or the sides of the pot, because this contact could encourage rotting.

Perennial plants

Perennials are a welcome group in any garden and work particularly well in both containers and raised beds, either mixed with other types of plants, such as trees or shrubs, or as a perennial-only display. Once they outgrow their space, many are easily refreshed by division (*see page 79*).

Buy small plants in pots; they bulk up very quickly, especially when grown in containers where they receive plenty of food and water. New or slightly frost-tender plants may need some cover early in the year (*see below*).

Grasses

In recent years, grasses have become a popular choice for containers. They are exceptionally versatile, combining well with all types of plants, and add an air of naturalistic beauty to a display. Grasses provide both movement and a transparent quality that enhances companion plants.

It is worth researching the types of grasses available via specialist books and nursery websites. Most grasses like to be in sun and they prefer free-draining compost, so they adapt well to container conditions.

FROST PROTECTION IN RAISED BEDS

Drape newspaper over plants, supporting it on hoops or sticks, to give protection from mild frosts. These are short-term covers only as they stop sunlight reaching the plants.

Use cloches to protect young plants in raised beds. If a severe frost is forecast, add a layer of weighted-down hessian or fleece.

Geraniums can give long-lasting colour in summer, and their low, spreading habit means that they can be planted among taller plants.

PERENNIALS SUITABLE FOR CONTAINERS

- Achillea
- Acanthus
- Aeonium
- Agapanthus
- Alchemilla mollis
- Anthemis tinctoria
- Artemisia lactiflora
- Aster
- Astrantia
- Bleeding heart (*Dicentra*)
- Campanula
- Canna
- Catmint (*Nepeta*)
- Cosmos atrosanguineus
- Crocosmia
- Daylily (*Hemerocallis*)
- Echinacea
- Echinops
- Eryngium
- Euphorbia polychroma
- Gaura lindheimeri
- Gazania
- Geranium (shown)
- Geum
- Hellebore (*Helleborus*)
- Helenium
- Helichrysum petiolare (trailer)
- Heuchera
- Hosta
- Knautia macedonica
- Kniphofia
- Melianthus major
- Persicaria
- Phlox

- Pink (*Dianthus*)
- Primula
- Rudbeckia fulgida var. fulgida
- Salvia
- Sedum
- Sisyrinchium striatum
- Verbena bonariensis
- Zantedeschia

Grasses & grassy plants
- Acorus
- Briza maxima
- Calamagrostis brachytricha
- Carex
- Chionochloa rubra
- Deschampsia
- Elymus magellanicus
- Eragrostis airoides
- Festuca
- Hakonechloa macra
- Hordeum jubatum
- Imperata cylindrica 'Rubra'
- Juncus 'Curly-wurly'
- Luzula nivea
- Miscanthus
- Molinia
- Nassella trichotoma
- Ophiopogon planiscapus 'Nigrescens'
- Panicum
- Pennisetum
- Phormium
- Stipa
- Uncinia uncinata

Trees, shrubs & climbers

Small trees, shrubs, and climbers can be planted to give height and structure to a container display. When purchasing trees and shrubs for containers, bear in mind where their final planting position will be, because trees and shrubs will inevitably outgrow the largest pot over time and need moving to the open ground.

Planting up

Container-grown trees and shrubs can be planted at most times of the year, but early autumn or late winter is generally best. Select a large pot with a suitable diameter to accommodate the rootball of the plant and allow an 8–10cm (3–4in) gap between the plant and the pot.

Place a good layer of drainage crocks in the base of the pot and fill with loam-based compost, such as John Innes No. 3. Before planting, check that the rootball of the plant is thoroughly soaked by immersing it in a bucket of water for several minutes. Plant and firm in well. Once planted, give the container a good watering to settle the plant and the compost down.

Until the plant develops roots, some support may be required. Use a stake with a good finish because it will be very visible in a container. A short stake encourages the tree to develop a stronger stem and root system by allowing the upper part to move with the prevailing wind.

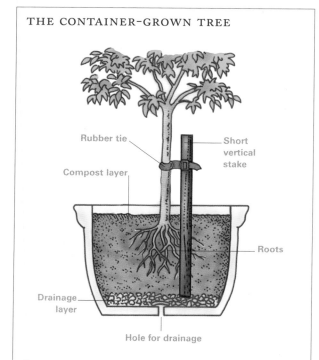

THE CONTAINER-GROWN TREE

Rubber tie

Compost layer

Short vertical stake

Roots

Drainage layer

Hole for drainage

Trees that stay in containers for long periods need high-nutrient, loam-based compost and large pots to allow the roots room to grow over time. A heavy pot balances top growth to give stability.

Some container displays rely solely on foliage effect to make an impression. Potted box topiary is a popular element of formal gardens, often repeated regularly along a path or around a space.

The exuberant display of a rhododendron in flower will only last a few weeks. The advantage of growing in containers is that when the flowers fade, the shrub can be swapped out of a prime position.

TREES, SHRUBS & CLIMBERS SUITABLE FOR CONTAINERS

- *Aucuba*
- *Ballota*
- Bay (*Laurus*)
- *Berberis*
- Box (*Buxus*) (shown)
- *Camellia*
- *Caryopteris*
- *Ceratostigma*
- *Chaenomeles*
- *Chamaecyparis*
- *Chamaerops humilis* (palm)
- *Choisya*
- *Cistus*
- *Clematis* (climber) (shown)
- *Clerodendron*
- *Cotoneaster*
- *Cycas*
- *Danae*
- *Daphne*
- Dogwood (*Cornus*)
- *Elaeagnus*
- *Erica*
- *Euonymus*
- *Fatsia*
- x *Fatshedera lizei*
- *Fuchsia*
- *Forsythia*
- *Hebe*
- Holly (*Ilex*)
- *Hypericum*
- Jasmine (*Jasminum*) (climber)
- Juniper (*Juniperus*)
- Ivy (*Hedera*) (climber)
- Lavender (*Lavandula*) (shown)
- *Lonicera* (climber)
- *Magnolia stellata*
- Maple (*Acer*)
- Myrtle (*Myrtus*)
- *Nandina*
- Olive (*Olea*) (shown)
- *Osmanthus*
- Periwinkle (*Vinca*)
- *Perovskia*
- *Phlomis*
- *Pittosporum*
- *Potentilla fruticosa*
- *Rhododendron* (shown)
- Rose (*Rosa*)
- *Santolina*
- *Sarcococca*
- *Skimmia*
- *Trachycarpus* (palm)
- *Trachelospermum* (climber)
- *Vaccinium*
- Willow (*Salix*)
- *Wisteria* (climber)
- Yew (*Taxus*)
- *Yucca*

Some Mediterranean trees are particularly suited to growing in containers. Olives do well in a free-draining compost, and can be moved or protected if heavy frosts threaten.

Many lavenders are hardy, but some of the most fragrant types will not survive a cold winter in the ground. These Mediterranean shrubs take well to pots, and can be overwintered under glass.

Patio areas often leave no planting space. The solution here is to grow bold plants in large pots, such as trees or shrubs, or climbers on tall, strong supports, such as this clematis on an obelisk.

Vegetables & herbs

Vegetables and herbs both make ideal container plants, particularly if they are planted in pots near a door, where they can be picked fresh, ready for immediate use. You can plant a pot with a selection of salad crops or three or four herbs that you use on a regular basis. This type of container gardening is a great way of encouraging children to grow and eat fresh produce.

Vegetables and herbs can be bought in as young plants or they can be raised from seed by sowing them directly into pots. This provides an ideal opportunity to grow successional crops for harvesting as you need them.

Planting

Select a large container with a good depth, ideally no less than 45cm (18in). Fill with a loam-based compost that has been mixed with well-rotted organic matter, which will help retain moisture. Herbs will grow in shallower containers with good drainage (*see page 206*).

VEGETABLES & HERBS SUITABLE FOR CONTAINERS

Vegetables	Herbs
• Beetroot	• Basil
• Beans	• Chamomile
• Carrots	• Chives
• Courgettes (shown)	• Coriander
• Kohlrabi (shown)	• Fennel
• Lettuce	• Marjoram
• Marrows	• Mint
• Onions and shallots	• Parsley
• Peas	• Rosemary
• Peppers	• Sage
• Radish	• Tarragon
• Tomatoes (shown)	• Thyme

The swollen stem of kohlrabi grows above the soil and is harvested young and tender. Purple varieties are particularly ornamental, and all types grow well in raised beds.

Tomatoes are well suited to growing in containers, being started from seed or young plants every year. An underplanting of basil makes a perfect aromatic and culinary combination.

Highly productive courgettes grow quickly and need to be checked and harvested daily to be enjoyed at their peak. Containers in a sunny spot near the kitchen are therefore an ideal place to grow them.

FRUIT

Growing vegetables & herbs *see page 138* | **Growing fruit** *see page 216* | **Choosing containers** *see page 342*

Fruit

Fruit plants can be included in any ornamental container display; they tend to be long lived so require more care and attention from one year to another. Consider what types of containers will best suit what you want to grow. Trees need large containers that hold enough compost to act as a buffer during dry conditions, particularly important when fruit is swelling and ripening. Strawberry pots look decorative and are space-saving; hanging baskets planted with three strawberry plants per basket are also a possibility. You will need to turn the pots and baskets from time to time to ensure even ripening.

You can create a Mediterranean look in your garden by planting up figs and citrus trees in pots. Figs prefer to have their roots constricted, so they can be planted in relatively small containers. This helps to reduce vigorous foliage and promote fruiting. Citrus fruit will need winter protection in a frost-free greenhouse or conservatory.

Apples in tubs are a popular choice. Choose a large container and a good-quality, loam-based compost, such as John Innes No. 3. Select two-year-old trees that have been grafted onto dwarfing rootstocks such as M27 or M9 (*see page 243*). To ensure good pollination (*see page 241*), grow several compatible varieties and in separate pots, or grow a family tree where three or four compatible varieties are grafted onto the same rootstock.

FRUIT SUITABLE FOR CONTAINERS

- Apples
- Blueberries (shown)
- Citrus (shown)
- Gooseberries
- Figs
- Peaches
- Red currants
- Strawberries (shown)

Strawberries in pots are easy to care for as the delicate fruit are raised off the ground. There are several container stacking systems on the market, but terracotta pots stacked in decreasing size work well.

Blueberries need acid soil (*see page 17*), so in many gardens growing them in containers filled with ericaceous compost is the only option. Grow a few varieties for the best pollination and fruiting.

All citrus fruit prefer their soil warm, moist and well-drained, making terracotta the perfect container material for them. Constriction keeps the plants compact – essential if you want to overwinter them indoors.

359

AFTERCARE
& MAINTENANCE

Unlike plants in the open ground, plants in containers are entirely dependent on you to fulfil their needs. No water can seep from surrounding earth to refresh them or bring additional supplies of nutrients, and little rain will fall on the small surface area of their compost. Their roots are far more constricted than those of plants in the ground, so their needs are even more urgent. Above the ground, they have no neighbouring plants to shelter and support their growth. There are various types of equipment available that can help with maintenance, but regular attention is the most important aspect of plant care.

Watering & feeding

An established basket or container will need to be watered at least twice a day during hot weather. Drip irrigation systems allow water to be trickled to each container without waste. It is worth investing in a timer device to automate your watering system, particularly during periods of absence for holidays.

Hanging baskets are particularly vulnerable to drying out, because they are usually packed with plants and water can evaporate from the sides as well as the top. A long-handled lance with a curved tip and rose allows easy watering, as will a rise-and-fall device (*see box, facing page*).

Growing bags are often blended using a peat-based compost and pose a challenge when watering because they tend to dry out very quickly. One solution to this is to place deep collars cut from old plastic pots around the plants when small and secure to the growing bag with tape. These create reservoirs for each plant and allow the water to soak into the growing bag rather than running off.

As always with irrigation, avoid watering during the hottest part of the day, when much of the water will simply evaporate. Instead water in early morning or evening when conditions are cooler.

WATERING HANGING BASKETS

Use a hose on a low flow rate for baskets you can reach; high flows will displace compost.

An extension or lance is almost essential for high baskets unless you use a ladder.

A watering can with a long spout is an option, but it is heavy and time-consuming.

Feeding

The nutrients in most potting composts will only last about four weeks after initial planting. After this the plants will need feeding either weekly or every two weeks depending on their needs. Fertilizer products for container plants range from slow-release pellets, which you push into the compost, to liquid feeds that are applied when you water and come in a variety of formulae to suit the plants that you are growing. Liquid feeds can be applied through a diluter connected to a hose or tap, which dilute granular or liquid feed at a set ratio; alternatively, use a watering can and mix according to instructions.

As a general rule, if a fertilizer contains a higher proportion of nitrogen, it will be beneficial for plant foliage growth, and if it has a high potash content it will be beneficial to flower production (*see page 20*).

RISE-&-FALL BASKET FIXING

A special pulley mechanism allows a basket to be pulled from a high position to a low one for watering or maintenance. A gentle push on the bottom of the basket returns it to the high position.

Staking & supports

Many plants grown in containers require some form of staking to help provide them with support. There are a number of products on the market, many of which make attractive additions to your container display in their own right. These include woven willow wigwams, wooden or metal obelisks, or modern spiral stakes (*see below*). If you want to make your own supports, you can use bamboo canes, plastic-covered wire stakes, galvanized mesh, plastic netting, twiggy sticks, or heavy stakes for trees.

All supports need to be installed at planting time or while the plants are young as this allows the plants to grow over and through the support, disguising it. By summer, this will lead to the impression that no staking is in place. If you are using twiggy sticks, they are best collected from deciduous trees like birch in late winter when they are without leaves, and so are ready to use when you plant up your containers in spring.

Climbers that are to be grown in containers for many years can be placed against a wall or fence and supported on training wires, as can wall shrubs and restricted fruit trees (such as cordons and espaliers). Woody plants will need a robust support. Consider the growth habit and pruning needs when choosing plants as this will affect the type of support you choose.

METHODS OF SUPPORT

Cane tripods are simple but beware of sharp cane ends.

Twiggy sticks blend in quickly. Push them in and trim neatly.

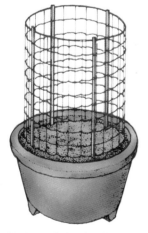

Netting cylinders held by canes provide sturdy support.

Modern supports include spiral stakes made of metal.

Wind & frost protection

Container displays can be prone to wind and frost damage because they often lack the shelter of surrounding trees and shrubs. In late autumn, move containers on exposed patios to a sheltered spot next to a wall or hedge, positioned so that the container will benefit from winter sunshine. Alternatively if you have a conservatory, greenhouse, or even just a shed with windows, move containers under cover.

Protect your plants

Heavy and cumbersome containers, and plants in raised beds, cannot be moved, so it will be necessary to protect them from frost individually where they are growing. This can be done by wrapping or covering plants with fleece, straw, or hessian sacking (*see page 14, page 355, and below*).

Tree ferns need to have their crowns protected from both wind and frost, but their trunks can remain exposed. Wrap the top section of the plant with horticultural fleece, covering the fronds and protecting the crown; fleece bags make this easy work as they simply need to be slipped over the top of the plant.

Compost in smaller containers may freeze entirely if they are left outside over winter, killing the plant roots and ultimately the entire plant. If such plants cannot be moved under cover, keep them away from frost pockets and wrap the containers with hessian or bubble wrap.

Protect your pots

It is easy to forget the containers themselves, but if you have unglazed terracotta pots or other containers that are not frostproof, lift them off the floor and support them on pot feet or something similar. This allows water to drain away, helping to avoid damage. Wrap containers in hessian sacking, bubble wrap, or fleece. If they are empty, move them into a shed to keep them dry. You can save yourself a lot of expense by siting pots carefully.

WIND & FROST PROTECTION

Wrap fleece or hessian around free-standing plants. Push four canes into the edge of the container and secure the wrapping around these. Plastic sheeting gives less protection and can cause condensation and encourage mould.

Form a cage of plastic mesh or galvanized chicken wire around the plant and stuff it with straw or bracken. This method can be used quite easily to protect plants that are growing against a wall, making them difficult to wrap.

Put a sack over the plant and container for protection. This can be done to give added warmth to tender plants that are already under cover. Traditionally hessian sacks were used, but today bags made from fleece are also available.

Plunge pots into the soil in a sheltered spot to protect the roots from freezing. Stuff bracken or straw between the branches, holding it in place with twine or any supports already in place.

Climate & your garden *see page 12* | Choosing containers *see page 342* | Planting *see page 349*

Potting on & replanting

Autumn is a good time to make changes to long-term displays and start thinking about the following year. Many plants benefit from being removed from their containers and potted into something larger (*see below*). By spring they will be healthy and ready to be planted into the garden for new or existing displays.

Sprucing up displays

Once a container display has passed, it is tempting to pull out the plants and replant into the same compost to save money, but the old compost will be spent and may also be harbouring pests and diseases that could be harmful to a new planting. It is far wiser to remove the old compost from the container, and start afresh to give the new plants the best possible start.

After a time you may have to repot existing trees and shrubs in order to reinvigorate the display. This is not always the easiest of tasks due to their weight and size. The best technique is to roll the container onto its side and enlist a second pair of hands. Once the plant is out of its pot, use a garden fork to tease away the old compost and free up the root system. If you are potting back into the same container, or one of a similar size, remove some of the outer roots with secateurs to provide space for the new compost. Place the plant back in the pot and firm in fresh compost around the sides. Finish off by giving the plant a thorough watering.

KEEPING PLANTS TIDY

Cut back overlong stems that spoil the shape of a plant or threaten to grow out of bounds. This also encourages sturdy, bushy growth. Use a knife, sharp scissors, or secateurs.

Remove dead flowers or dying leaves as soon as seen. This not only improves the general appearance of the plant but is good hygiene, and the practice – known as 'deadheading' – often stimulates production of fresh flowers.

If you have a large container with long-term planting that is difficult to move and replant, it may be worth top-dressing it with fresh compost to add nutrients. To do this, remove the top layer of existing compost from the the pot, using a hand fork to loosen it. Then apply a fresh layer of a loam-based John Innes No. 3 potting compost.

POTTING ON

1 **Water the plant** thoroughly and leave it to drain before removing it from the container.

2 **Choose a container** 2 sizes larger than the one the plant is currently in. Turn the plant upside down and tap it from its container.

3 **Place the rootball** in the new container. Trickle fresh compost into the space around the sides. Firm with your fingers and water in.

CHAPTER NINE

GARDENING UNDER GLASS

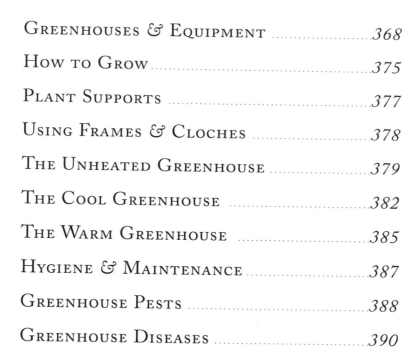

GREENHOUSES & EQUIPMENT 368

HOW TO GROW 375

PLANT SUPPORTS 377

USING FRAMES & CLOCHES 378

THE UNHEATED GREENHOUSE 379

THE COOL GREENHOUSE 382

THE WARM GREENHOUSE 385

HYGIENE & MAINTENANCE 387

GREENHOUSE PESTS 388

GREENHOUSE DISEASES 390

ONE OF THE MOST SATISFYING ASPECTS OF GARDENING under glass is being able to grow a whole range of plants that would otherwise be too sensitive to grow outdoors. Gardeners who have just a limited experience and knowledge of growing plants under protection should not be daunted by what may first appear a technically demanding and time-consuming operation. There is an enormous range of greenhouses, polythene tunnels, frames, and garden cloches to suit the needs and aspirations of any gardener, and with just a bit of thoughtful preparation and some basic understanding of plant needs, you can quickly learn the necessary techniques and establish a routine. Investing in a greenhouse can be a rewarding and profitable addition to any garden.

Meeting plant needs in a greenhouse

It must be understood from the outset that plants growing under protection depend on you, the gardener, to manage their environment: the fundamentals of plant growth – light levels, correct temperature, and moisture and humidity – must be carefully controlled to ensure the right conditions for your plants to grow and flourish. As a result, your approach to growing plants in a greenhouse will be influenced by the external environment: weather conditions and seasonal changes. The fluctuating climatic conditions outside the greenhouse are greatly magnified inside, and it is up to you to manage them. Manipulating the environment to suit your plants' needs is at the heart of greenhouse gardening.

Springtime often brings variable weather conditions; the greenhouse will require careful attention to ventilation so that plants are not subject to rapid rises and falls in temperature. As summer approaches, it may be easier to predict weather conditions, so ventilators can be opened earlier and left open for longer; plants may also require shading from the intensity of the sun and the greenhouse floor sprayed with water to raise humidity. The short days of autumn and winter mean that all plant functions slow down and the demand for watering and feeding is dramatically reduced; care will be needed to manage ventilation and heating to ensure the atmosphere of the greenhouse does not become stagnant and heavy with moisture.

Today there is plenty of scope to automate a great deal of these greenhouse tasks, including ventilation, shading, watering, and humidification. This does attract some significant additional costs but may be considered worthwhile where time available to work in the greenhouse is limited.

Growing in a greenhouse

Growing under glass allows the gardener to cultivate a wide range of tender ornamental plants, fruits, and vegetables that would not normally thrive in the open, such as late summer and winter bulbs, acacias, fuchsias, bougainvillea, winter-flowering chrysanthemums, orchids, and other exotics and, of course, a delicious variety of fruit, vegetables, and herbs.

The protection that glass offers, even in an unheated greenhouse, allows you to extend the cropping season for many food plants, as well as bring on ornamental plants so that they can be established early in the garden. It is easy to raise plants from seeds, cuttings, or by other propagation methods, whether they are for bedding, for sale, or for the kitchen garden. As you bring your tender plants into the greenhouse for overwintering in autumn, you will see how quickly you have come to rely on it; for each month of the year a greenhouse has its use.

GREENHOUSES & EQUIPMENT

Many factors influence the size and style of greenhouse you should buy, as well as the type of equipment you are going to need. The primary consideration must be the needs of the plants, but affordability comes a close second, as well as the amount of space you have in your garden for a greenhouse. Most enthusiasts agree that it is best to purchase the largest structure that will fit comfortably into your garden, but even then you must think about where it is going to be placed in order to make the most of the sun. Furthermore, you must also think about shading, ventilation, heating, and electrical connections.

Basic requirements

The varied prices of greenhouses are usually reflected in their style, quality, and degree of equipping. The key features to look out for are a well-braced structure that is easily secured to a base, a glazing system that makes the house as airtight as possible, and a sufficient number of vents in the roof sections for cooling, preferably with an equal area of side vents (*see page 371*).

Head room, shelving, and doorway space are also important. If you want to grow plants in borders, beds, or growing bags, the greenhouse should be fully glazed. If your greenhouse is to be benched for growing potted plants and propagation, then the sides can be timber or brick up to bench height, for better insulation.

Structural materials

The framework of a timber greenhouse needs to be quite bulky in order to provide structural strength, and it may need to be regularly painted to preserve the wood. Steel or aluminium frames are much lighter and require minimum maintenance.

The standard glazing material is horticultural grade glass, but safety glass or a rigid transparent plastic or polycarbonate is used where greenhouses are positioned in a vulnerable situation or are used as plant rooms or conservatories. Twin-walled polycarbonate is light, strong, and more thermally efficient than glass, but it can be scratched and it degrades more quickly. Polythene sheeting is used to cover walk-in structures and tunnel cloches. It can be used as a temporary fix if a glass panel is broken.

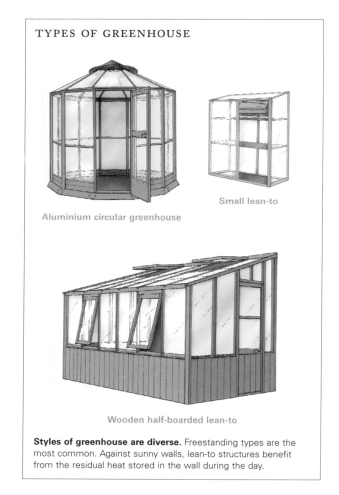

TYPES OF GREENHOUSE

Aluminium circular greenhouse

Small lean-to

Wooden half-boarded lean-to

Styles of greenhouse are diverse. Freestanding types are the most common. Against sunny walls, lean-to structures benefit from the residual heat stored in the wall during the day.

Frames, cloches & tunnels

If you do not have room or the inclination to buy a greenhouse, there are many alternatives on offer, ranging from wooden cold frames for the back garden, to polythene tunnels (polytunnels) for the allotment.

Frames & cloches

There are many variations on the traditional cold frame, which is simply a case or box made from brick or timber with a sloping top over which a glass-glazed frame is placed. It is very functional, has a huge number of applications, and can easily be made at home to fit any space, substituting glass with polycarbonate to make the tops light and easy to handle. Some modern frames might also be glazed with acrylic or polycarbonate, but this can make them so light that you will have to anchor them to prevent them blowing away. Well-constructed frames can undertake many of the functions of a greenhouse.

Cloches and low tunnels (*see page 149*) are versatile structures that can be employed throughout the garden, particularly where plants require simple protection from the elements, as in the vegetable and fruit garden during spring. You can also use them to protect weather-sensitive ornamental plants through the winter months. Cloches and tunnels made from acrylic or polycarbonate may need to be weighted down.

Mini greenhouses can be used like a cloche or frame. They can be flimsy, but properly secured they will house a number of tender plants, even in the smallest garden.

Polythene tunnels

Walk-in polythene tunnels are made up of a number of large galvanized steel hoops fixed to the ground and covered with a heavy-duty polythene film. They are simple to put up and easily moved around, but they can be unsightly and are best positioned in out-of-the-way places, such as on an allotment.

Polytunnels warm up and cool down quickly. They are also difficult to ventilate and depend on air flowing through doors and windows at the ends of the tunnel. Nor are they efficient at retaining heat; artificial heating is not viable for tunnels. Nevertheless, they allow good light penetration and like other unheated structures they are immensely productive in the kitchen garden and ideal for early spring production of vegetables and fruit.

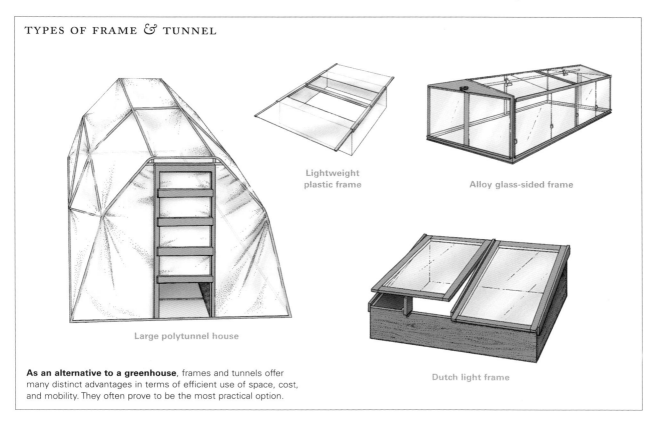

TYPES OF FRAME & TUNNEL

Lightweight plastic frame

Alloy glass-sided frame

Large polytunnel house

Dutch light frame

As an alternative to a greenhouse, frames and tunnels offer many distinct advantages in terms of efficient use of space, cost, and mobility. They often prove to be the most practical option.

Site & situation

An ideal situation for a greenhouse is one in which it receives good light levels all year round, is sheltered from cooling winds and is close to a tap and a power point.

Before siting your greenhouse, you should consider the microclimate of your garden, which is influenced by the topography of the surrounding area as well as nearby trees and buildings. An exposed site increases air movement and therefore greater heat loss; even a modest breeze of 15mph (24kmph) will double the amount of heat drawn from the greenhouse. Use a windbreak, such as a hedge, to mitigate this problem. You should also assess your site for shade cast from buildings, walls, fences, and trees. If your greenhouse is in shadow for long periods, plant growth will be poor, particularly in late winter and spring when new growth is starting.

Base, foundation & construction

Build your greenhouse on a level and firm site on ground that is not prone to waterlogging. Small greenhouses can be secured by ground anchors in concrete. Larger structures will require footings and a concrete foundation.

If your greenhouse has a brick base, it needs to be set out to the exact measurements specified by the manufacturer. At an additional cost, manufacturers usually offer an erection service as long as you clear and

A well-sited greenhouse should not only be in an accessible position, but also in a sheltered site that receives adequate light. In summer, some shade may be welcome, but not in late winter and early spring.

prepare the site ready for immediate assembly. Standard metal-framed houses are delivered in their component parts together with instructions for assembly. Timber-framed greenhouses usually arrive in unglazed sections allowing the framework to be erected quite quickly. Glazing takes place after the framework is assembled.

SHELTER FROM THE WIND

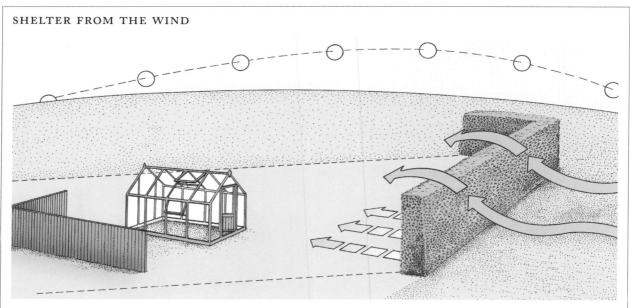

The creation of a sheltered, sunny site for your greenhouse can be achieved by cutting the force of the prevailing wind, using semi-permeable walls, fences, or hedges. These windbreaks must be carefully sited so they do not shade the greenhouse. To check if a site is likely to be shaded, find out the lowest angle of the winter sun so you can estimate which trees or buildings will cast shade.

Shading & ventilation

When the sun shines on a greenhouse the air inside heats up rapidly, and you will need to control the temperature within using a combination of ventilation and shading. Ventilation also brings in fresh air and controls humidity.

Ventilating the greenhouse

Generally, the more ventilation a greenhouse has the better, but as a minimum, the area covered by vents in your greenhouse roof should be the equivalent of at least 20 percent of the total floor area, in order to allow rising hot air to escape easily. Additional side vents, covering an area equal to the roof vents, speeds up air changes in the greenhouse creating a chimney effect (*see box, right*).

In spring and autumn, you must take care when opening and closing vents as increased sunlight causes inside temperatures to rise, but the outside temperatures remain very low. At such times, open roof vents partially to regulate the temperature, but keep side vents closed so that cold air is not directly introduced on to the plants.

Air movement can be strong on windy days and create unwelcome draughts. For this reason, vents are usually found on both sides of the greenhouse so you can close those on the windward side when cold winds are blowing.

Before you buy a greenhouse, check that your chosen model has enough vents – often they do not. You can use the door as an emergency vent on hot, still days, but this is not standard practice as it negates the chimney effect.

Automated vents & extractor fans

Vents are hand operated in small greenhouses, but in larger structures, where the vents may be out of reach, various mechanisms are seen. These too can be hand operated, but more often than not they are controlled automatically by a thermostat, and calibrated to open and close at set temperatures.

Automated vents are a worthwhile investment as they take care of ventilation whenever you are away or too busy to take care of matters yourself, and if you forget you can easily lose vulnerable plants.

Extractor fans are an alternative to the passive movement of air through vents. The size of the fan and inlet area needs to be proportional to the volume of the greenhouse. Fan ventilation systems do not operate efficiently if combined with other venting methods.

THE CHIMNEY EFFECT

Ventilation expels hot air from greenhouse roof vents and introduces cooler fresh air from side vents. This flow of air allows plants to 'breathe' and is vital for a healthy growing environment.

METHODS OF VENTILATION

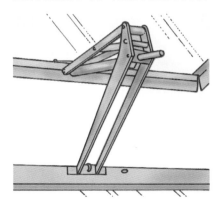

Hydraulically driven vents lend themselves to automatic or remote-control systems.

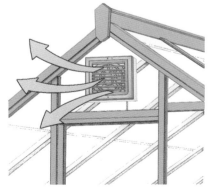

Extractor fans circulate fresh air and should be placed above the door in small greenhouses.

Louvred vents are often seen on side panels. Check they are draught-free when closed.

Shading

In summer, ventilation alone will not be enough to maintain the interior temperature of your greenhouse at a comfortable level for your plants. The strong summer sunshine through glass will also overheat and scorch your plants, and only those adapted to such harsh conditions, such as cacti and succulents, will escape damage.

To prevent this from happening, you will need to provide the necessary degree of shading for the type of plants you are growing and their stage of development. Specialist plants like orchids and ferns require plenty of shade for many months of the year. Seedlings and young plants growing in spring can be shaded from the short periods of strong sunshine in the middle of the day by draping a layer of horticultural fleece over them.

Into summer, mature plants need longer periods of shade, as well as protection from extreme temperatures. You can provide this effectively using shade paint or external covers or screens (*see below*). Internal blinds provide adequate shade, but they tend not to be so effective at reducing temperatures, and plants can get in their way, making it hard to open and close them.

METHODS OF SHADING

Shade paint should be thinly applied on to the outside of the glass in spring.

Interior blinds can be neat, but tend to be less effective than exterior shading.

Improvised shading can be made from netting or thin cloth. It must not exclude light.

Electricity & heating

When electrical power is required for a greenhouse, be it for lighting, propagators, heaters, or fans, it must be fitted by a certified professional electrician. You will need to have waterproof sockets and switches installed, as well as suitable cabling; make sure you choose equipment that is designed to be durable and safe to use in a greenhouse environment.

Before you add supplementary heating, first consider ways to conserve heat and reduce heating bills. Ensure that draughts are minimized, and fix a temporary insulation material of clear polythene or bubble plastic (*see box, facing page*) to the glass panels of the greenhouse from late autumn until late winter. Select a thermostatically controlled heater that has the capacity to maintain the required temperatures in your size of greenhouse. It may be feasible to heat a smaller area of your greenhouse by compartmentalizing it, or by making a temporary screen to close off the roof space at night.

Sources of heating

Electrical fan heaters are the easiest and most versatile heating system to install. Their power rating is usually between 2kW and 4kW, which suits most small to medium greenhouses. Better-designed fan heaters have an adjustable heat output and a fan that can be run separately from the heating system, which is useful in helping to cool the greenhouse in summer. Some efficient fan heaters have a pipe that recycles rising air from the roof section of the greenhouse.

Tubular heaters rely on convectional air movement to circulate their heat; position them under benches where the plants can benefit from the rising warm air, but keep trailing plants clear of the pipes, which get very hot and can scorch the leaves.

Where electricity is not available, you can run a gas heater from bottled gas. Place large gas bottles outside of the greenhouse so they do not take up valuable space.

TYPES OF GREENHOUSE HEATER

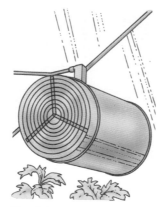

Gas heaters connect to bottles kept outside the greenhouse. To avoid running out of gas, always have a spare bottle at the ready.

Oil heaters are the least efficient heat source and therefore the most expensive to run. Their heat output depends on the number and size of wicks.

Electric fan heaters are ideal for the average greenhouse. Position them so that warm air circulates without obstruction to the coldest parts of the greenhouse.

Electric tubular heaters are fixed to brick or wooden side walls close to ground level. The tubes get very hot and will scorch hands and plants that touch them.

Oil heaters heat less efficiently than the other heat sources. Their wicks require regular maintenance to ensure the paraffin is burnt cleanly; the by-products of combustion are water vapour and carbon dioxide as well as other gases, some of which are not tolerated by many plants. The better application for paraffin heaters, therefore, is to provide frost protection to tolerant groups of plants like salad crops, vegetables, and half-hardy annuals. These plants will actually benefit from the additional carbon dioxide being given off, if the heaters are run during the daytime while photosynthesis is taking place.

Alternative forms of energy like wind turbines and solar panels are becoming more viable as technology advances, but the feasibility of such devices depends on your heating requirements. Conservatories and lean-to structures can be heated either directly or indirectly by domestic central heating systems.

Greenhouse heaters are measured in kilowatts (kW). To calculate what power you will need for your greenhouse, you first need to determine your temperature lift (*see box, below*). Temperature lift is the difference between the average coldest temperature in your region and the temperature you want to maintain in your greenhouse. For example, if your greenhouse is to be maintained at 5°C (41°F), and the average coldest temperature in your area is -7°C (19°F), then the temperature lift required would be 12°C (54°F). It pays to buy a slightly more powerful heater than you need, so that you have extra heat in reserve.

INSULATING A GREENHOUSE

Bubble plastic fixed to glass panels during winter is a simple way to reduce heating bills by insulating against heat loss and excluding draughts. Fit it to the sides only if you need to maximize light.

HOW MUCH HEAT DO YOU NEED?

Calculate the total surface area of the greenhouse sides, ends, and roof sections in square metres. Multiply this figure by 7 to account for heat lost through the glass. Multiply this second figure by the temperature lift required (*see above*) in °C. The resulting figure shows the number of watts required to warm your greenhouse for temperatures down to -7°C (19°F). Divide this figure by 1,000 to achieve the same figure in kilowatts (kW), and round up to a whole kW. Choose a heater with a kW rating the same as your greenhouse heat requirement, or a bit higher.

Water supply & watering

As greenhouse plants cannot benefit directly from rainfall, it is essential to have a reliable water source to hand, most typically from a domestic mains supply.

Watering cans are a very practical way of watering a small greenhouse. Allow the water to reach ambient greenhouse temperature before watering to prevent chilling root systems of pot plants, particularly in spring.

METHODS OF WATERING

Watering cans are heavy when full, so choose a suitable size. A well-fitted rose is essential when watering seedlings and young plants.

Capillary matting suits pot plants of all sizes. Keep the absorbent mat moist, and use pots with a substantial number of drainage holes.

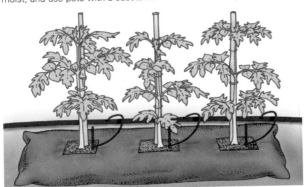

Trickle irrigation is good for watering pots and growing bags. They connect to a low-pressure source, such as a raised water butt.

Managing the water requirements of individual plants as they grow and develop is a learned skill. Overwatering will easily kill your plants, while underwatering will result in stunted growth and poor yield.

During the growing season many greenhouse plants require daily watering; it is best to do this in the morning so that the plant is turgid during the day when water is needed for transpiration and photosynthesis. When using a watering can, aim to fill the space at the top of the pot; this should be sufficient to moisten the compost all the way through.

Watering can be automated using timing devices to turn irrigation on and off for preset durations. Trickle and drip nozzle systems are also useful, but they must apply sufficient water to moisten the whole profile of the compost. If water penetration is too slow then it will evaporate before reaching the roots.

Sprinkler systems and misting nozzles are used for propagation, providing moisture and humidity to seedlings and young plants. They are driven by mains water or a pumped water source.

Raising humidity

Hot, dry conditions are stressful for plants. During hot weather, damp down the greenhouse floor so that the evaporating water cools the air temperature around the plants. This may need to be done several times a day.

WATER HARVESTING METHODS

Gutter systems can be led to a water tank inside the greenhouse, or water butts on the outside. Such a system will help reduce your dependency on mains water and is useful during times of drought and water restrictions. Rainwater is beneficial for watering acid-loving plants and orchids.

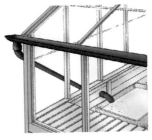

Water butts should have a tight fitting lid and a strainer to trap organic matter before it enters the butt. To be independent of a mains water supply, butts should be sized to meet the water needs of the greenhouse or garden. You may need more than one butt.

Container gardening *see page 338* | Hygiene & maintenance *see page 387* | Propagating plants *see page 392*

GROWING UNDER GLASS

Of all the disciplines of gardening, growing under glass is the most specialized. Not only are greenhouse plants dependent on you to provide a comfortable environment in which they can flourish, but you also need to give them something in which to grow. Plants under glass have access to lower levels of soil nutrients than do plants in the open garden, so soil in beds needs to be enriched, and special composts or mixes are required for containers. If you follow good growing practices, you will find that your greenhouse is visited less regularly by pests and diseases, as this is the most important means of controlling them.

How to grow

You should use as much of the greenhouse space as possible for cultivating plants. Potted plants can be grown on benches and shelves, with additional shelves attached to the sidewalls, and the space under benches used for holding or resting dormant plants in large pots or tubs.

Greenhouse growing systems are based either on open beds or some form of container to restrict root run. The size, type, and site of the greenhouse, and the choice of plants to be grown, will determine which kind of growing system you should use. If you intend to use your greenhouse for propagating plants, benches and shelves will be needed so you can work at a comfortable height.

Growing in containers

Containers are the best growing system if a large number of different plants are to be grown in a greenhouse, as they can be moved and resited as the plants grow, thus freeing space for further plant raising.

Growing bags are useful for short-term crops. They usually contain about 30 litres (6½ gallons) of peat or peat-free compost, which can become quite compressed in the manufacturing and transporting processes. Before laying the bags down on the greenhouse floor it is important to ensure the compost is loosened and aerated, so you will need to shake and pummel the unopened bag.

THREE DIFFERENT WAYS TO GROW PLANTS IN THE GREENHOUSE

Growing bags are a convenient way to grow a range of greenhouse plants, particularly short-term crops like tomatoes, cucumbers, salads, and strawberries.

Large pots and tubs maximize the growing space in a greenhouse. Small batches of plants can also be started off under protection and moved outside as weather conditions improve.

Border soil is ideal where the greenhouse is fully glazed (glass to ground) and is suitable for both short-season crops or long-term plants, such as fruiting and ornamental trees or vines.

USING GROWING BAGS

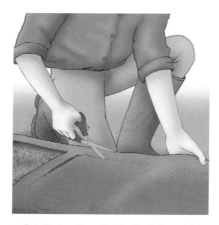

1 **Cut the bag** to make planting holes, which are often pre-marked. Make drainage slits near the bottom of the bag with a knife.

2 **Water the compost** thoroughly and let it soak in overnight so that the compost is moistened throughout before planting.

3 **Feed and water** the plants regularly during the growing season. They dry out rapidly during hot weather if neglected.

The effect will be that the volume of compost in the bag will appear to double. After cutting out planting holes, moisten up the compost and allow it to soak overnight so that the compost is uniformly moist.

Because of the limited rooting volume in containers, you must take great care when watering to ensure that roots do not become saturated or dry out. Give small amounts of water frequently, to match the weather conditions and stage of plant growth. All containers need drainage holes; in growing bags, cut horizontal slits just above the bottom to allow excess water to escape.

Growing in the soil

Where plants are to be grown directly in the greenhouse border soil, a deep, well-cultivated soil is required to produce healthy plants and good yields. It is important, therefore, to keep the soil in good condition by digging in deeply plenty of well-rotted organic matter to improve the structure, drainage, and water-holding capacity.

A soil pH of 6.5–7 is best for vegetables and salad crops. If you are going to be using your borders intensively, it is advisable to measure the soil nutrient level and pH status each year, as additional fertilizers will be required to replace the large amount taken up by the crops. Before planting and sowing, ensure the ground has been well watered, thoroughly incorporate a dressing of general-purpose fertilizer, and produce a firm level finish with a fine tilth using a rake.

If plants are to be grown in the greenhouse border soil for a number of years, consider containing the beds behind 10–15cm (4–6in) wide bed boards. This will contain the soil and allow you to add soil improvers, such

Utilize your greenhouse space efficiently by making use of different growing systems. Here, young plants and seedlings grow on shelved staging, with larger ornamental plants growing in the border soil.

as garden compost, on top of the soil without them spilling over. This helps provide a well-aerated rooting zone for long-term plants.

You can grow plants in open-bottom pots set on top of border soil. In the early stages, the pot provides a warmer rooting zone than the border soil. As the roots grow into the border soil, the plant is buffered from changes in moisture levels that might occur in a container.

PLANT SUPPORTS

Looking after your soil *see page 16* | **Climbers & wall plants** *see page 130* | **Sowing & growing** *see page 146*

Plant supports

You will need to provide a range of support and training systems in your greenhouse so that plant growth can be managed efficiently. These range from simple canes and string systems for short-term crops like tomatoes and cucumbers, to netting and wires permanently fixed to the inside of the greenhouse to support perennial climbers and woody plants like trained fruit trees.

There are many plant support aids available for greenhouse plants, most of which do a tidy and reliable job. They include moulded plastic hooks, clips and spacers, special metal bolts and eyes that fix into glazing bars, and a range of adjustable soft plant ties. Hoops and adjustable plant rings can also be used to support bushy or tall plants.

Temporary plant supports

A stake or bamboo cane driven into the soil provides a very quick and easy rigid support for tomato vines. Tie the plants in at regular intervals, preferably just below a leaf junction, using soft twine or one of several types of moulded plastic clips.

You can use strong twine as a support for climbing plants to twist around. Loosely tie the twine around the bottom of the plant stem and run a length up to the greenhouse roof. Fix it there, allowing considerable slack so that as the plant grows the string is gently twisted around the head of the plant. Make sure that the twist is under a leaf junction to prevent the stem slipping down the string as its length and weight increase. There is always a chance that the head may be snapped off in this operation, so use a light touch and do not attempt it in the early morning when the plant is very turgid.

Permanent plant supports

Long-term plantings of trees, shrubs, and climbers need a robust and permanent plant support system. The first step is to secure a framework of wooden battens to the greenhouse wall or frame, onto which netting, wire, plastic mesh, or other fixings can be attached.

Tie climbing plants, fan-trained shrubs, and fruit bushes onto plastic mesh or netting using soft twine or plastic clips, allowing some slack for the stems to expand. Tall plants or those with heavy crops, such as melons, will need a strong support covering a large area.

Galvanized wires set out horizontally at regular intervals are essential for restricted plants like grape vines (*see page 234*). Selected side branches should be tied in at regular intervals along the horizontal wire. Wires can also be used for other climbing plants.

TYPES OF PLANT SUPPORT

Canes and stakes are pushed into the soil. Tie or clip the plant to the support, under the leaf junctions.

String and twine fixed to the roof makes a good support for tomatoes to climb on to.

Mesh or netting is a versatile support and can be adapted for most greenhouse plants.

Tall plants need a comparably tall support. If heavy crops are formed, make the support strong.

Cordon grape vines need to be trained along horizontal wires to support their side branches.

Walls in lean-to greenhouses can be covered in supports for the cultivation of climbing plants.

Using frames & cloches

Beyond the greenhouse, frames, mini greenhouses, cloches, and tunnels (*see page 369*) can be used to great advantage in producing edible crops, raising plants for the garden and for temporary protection of plants in winter months.

Cold frames & mini greenhouses

These provide enough protection during early spring to grow early crops of radish, lettuce, spinach, carrots, and spring onions. At this time of year weather conditions can be very variable so it is important to manage the environment in the frame to protect the developing plants.

When outside temperatures are forecast to fall below freezing point, drape extra insulation over the frames at night. Layers of horticultural fleece are useful as an insulating blanket folded over the plants inside the frame and can remain in place if frost persists during the daytime. Reduce the incidence of fungal diseases by partly opening up the frame each morning for ventilation. When the daytime weather conditions are dry and temperatures rising, you can ventilate the frame fully for an hour or two in the middle of the day.

Frames and mini greenhouses are also used to wean greenhouse plants from warm to cool, outdoor conditions (*see below*), and later in the year to extend the growing season by providing protection to late summer and autumn salad crops. Slightly frost-tender plants, or those that require protection from high winter rainfall, can also be overwintered in these structures.

Cloches & tunnels

Low polytunnels and garden cloches are a versatile growing aid, easily moved from crop to crop providing protection from the elements and creating a microclimate that can induce speedy growth and better quality. Cloches require careful watering, as well as ventilation to avoid

HARDENING OFF IN AN UNHEATED FRAME

1 Place boxes or pots of greenhouse-reared young plants into the cold frame in spring. The purpose is to gradually acclimatize these plants to the outdoor environment. Sudden exposure can kill plants. Frost-hardy plants can be introduced to the outdoors much faster than those that are tender to frost.

2 Open up frames partly during the day for ventilation during the first week, but only during mild spells of weather. Close the window each night as cold, frosty air may harm the young plants.

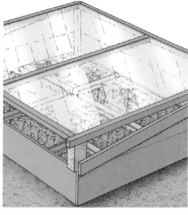

3 Leave frames open during the day as the weather warms up from mid-spring. They can also be opened a little at night. Remove the cover completely towards the end of spring, except in windy weather.

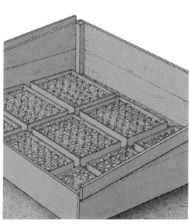

4 Remove plants from the frame and plant in their permanent positions in the garden once the risk of frost has passed. By this time, the young plants should have doubled in size and will grow on uninterrupted.

Bulbous plants *see page 83* | Frames, cloches & tunnels *see page 369* | Sowing seeds *see page 405*

The unheated greenhouse

Unheated greenhouses and walk-in polytunnels are used to extend the growing season, particularly in spring when the garden soil temperature is low and cold winds can chill and dry out soft plant growth. Such greenhouses are, in effect, no more than a protective covering against extremes of cold, wet, and wind.

Growing vegetables

The range of vegetables and salad crops that you can grow under protection is extensive: salad leaves, lettuce, bunching carrots, salad onions, radish, and spinach are all reliable early vegetables, and there are great opportunities to experiment with others. Choose quick-maturing varieties; this information is found on the seed packet.

You should sow the earliest crops directly into the greenhouse border soil or into suitable containers from late winter, having some fleece to hand to protect young plants should the temperatures fall below freezing. For continuity of supply, raise further plants ready for transplanting into the garden as weather conditions improve.

Tomatoes, peppers, cucumbers, melons, and aubergines are all commonly grown in unheated greenhouses through summer. All are easy to raise from seeds, or you can buy them as young plants from a garden centre. As these crops are sensitive to low temperatures, delay planting until mid-spring when night temperatures do not fall below 8°C (46°F) during the daytime. Close ventilators early in the afternoon during these early stages to keep the greenhouse warm in the evening and hasten growth.

Growing tree fruit

You can grow tree fruit such as peaches, nectarines, and citrus trees in a greenhouse that is kept just frost-free, but it will be necessary to hand pollinate the flowers (*see page 241*). As container-grown plants, they can spend summer outside and then be brought in again in early autumn for protection from winter weather. For a late-spring crop of strawberries, bring outdoor-raised container plants into the greenhouse in early spring; earlier crops can be had in a cool greenhouse (*see page 384*).

GROWING HYACINTH BULBS FOR EARLY FLOWERING

1 **Plant bulbs** in containers in early autumn. Choose bulbs that are of equal size and plant them in multipurpose potting compost so that the top half of the bulbs is left exposed. In large pots, you can sow more than one bulb per container.

2 **Plunge the containers** up to their rims into the border soil once they are all potted. This can be done either in a greenhouse or a frame. Cover the bulbs with more potting compost, grit, or weathered ashes. Keep the compost around the bulbs moist.

3 **Remove the containers** from the plunge bed 6–8 weeks later when shoots begin to appear. Stand the containers in a cool and shady, frost-free place, such as beneath the greenhouse shelving.

4 **Move into full light** 1 week later and let the bulbs grow. Flowering will take place in early spring, at which time the plants can be moved for indoor display. After flowering, keep the bulbs cool and slightly shaded while the foliage dies away and store for next year.

Growing ornamentals

Spring bulbs such as narcissi and hyacinths (*see previous page*), potted in early autumn and brought into a greenhouse, will provide colour and interest long before the bulbs perform in the garden. Early bulbs make excellent gifts for indoor display if grown in ornamental pots.

An unheated greenhouse can also be a place to bring on early seeds (*see below*) as well as being a winter home for garden plants that are sensitive to winter weather. Camellias, for example, are perfectly hardy except for their flowers, which are easily damaged by frost and wet; to enjoy them in an unheated greenhouse, move your container-grown camellias into the greenhouse in mid-autumn, keeping them as cool as possible to avoid the flower buds dropping. Early-flowering rhododendrons and azaleas can be treated in the same way. Keep watering to a minimum and ventilate the greenhouse for part of the day, every day, if outside temperatures permit.

The most important limitation of the unheated greenhouse is that of temperature. If the outside temperature drops below 0–3°C (32–37°F), it is likely that there will be several degrees of frost inside the greenhouse; in such instances, frost-sensitive plants will need further protection.

GROWING ANNUALS FOR SPRING FLOWERING

1 **Sow seeds** in early autumn in sterilized seed compost, following the instructions on the packet for exact timing and handling.

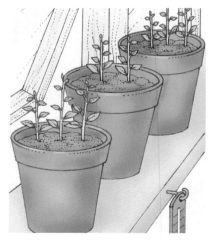

2 **When the seedlings appear**, place the container on the greenhouse staging, or well-lit windowsill or shelf. Keep the compost just moist and ventilate carefully.

3 **When large enough to handle**, transfer the individual seedlings into small pots of well-drained multipurpose potting compost.

4 **Pot the seedlings on** into larger containers from late autumn as they increase in size.

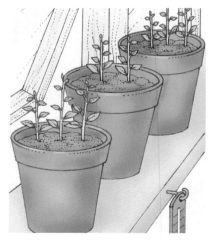

5 **Ventilate young plants** carefully over winter, whenever outdoor temperatures allow, and water sparingly.

6 **Pot on** into final containers, in late winter, into a loam-based potting compost, such as John Innes No. 2. Plant out in spring.

The cool greenhouse

By providing some artificial warmth to a greenhouse – with a minimum temperature of 4.5°C (40°F), even on the coldest night of the year – you can ensure that it will be full of interest year round. Nearly all of the plants from the world's temperate zones will grow under such conditions.

Growing ornamentals

Bulbs from South Africa are satisfying to cultivate in a cool greenhouse, as they provide a welcome splash of colour from late autumn to early spring. *Nerine sarniensis* hybrids flower in autumn, veltheimias in late winter, and lachenalias from midwinter into early spring, according to the species. You need to feed and water these bulbs from when they start into growth in late summer until the foliage begins to die back after flowering. You should then allow the dormant bulbs to rest in their pots throughout summer, keeping the compost just moist. Only repot the bulbs when they have outgrown the space in their containers. Other bulbs to try include freesias, gladioli, ixias, and sparaxis.

GROWING SUMMER BEDDING PLANTS FROM SEED

1 **Sow seeds thinly** onto a lightly firmed surface of seed compost in a seed tray. Small seeds can be mixed with fine, dry sand to make sowing easier.

2 **Sieve potting compost** over medium-sized or large seeds so that they are just covered with a layer of fine compost. Small seeds do not need covering.

3 **Water well** after sowing. Dilute fungicide into the water to prevent fungal infections, such as damping off.

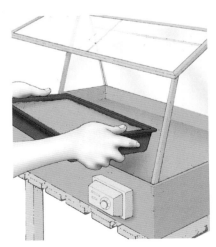

4 **Place the tray** into a propagating case at 21°C (70°F), or in a warm place indoors. Check each day for signs of germination.

5 **Place the tray** in good light as soon as the first seedlings emerge. Keep the seedlings well ventilated and warm.

6 **Transplant seedlings** into individual pots as soon as they are large enough to handle, into a loam-based seedling compost.

Plumbago capensis and *Mandevilla sanderi* are two examples of free-flowering climbers that are easily contained in a tub and grown up a greenhouse frame or wall, but there are many others to choose from, including hoyas (wax flowers), passion flowers, and scented jasmines.

Cacti and succulents enjoy a frost-free greenhouse, and many cacti produce hugely flamboyant flowers in the late spring as well as growing into wonderful geometric shapes. *Agave*, *Aloe*, *Rebutia*, and *Echinopsis* hybrids are easily obtainable and are good plants to start with. To grow unblemished specimens, you will have to keep the atmosphere of your greenhouse dry, thoroughly watering the rootball once a fortnight from spring, adding a dilute liquid feed at the same time. Almost no water at all is needed in winter.

Grow winter-flowering chrysanthemums (*see below*) as outdoor pot plants in summer and then transfer them to the cool greenhouse in autumn for late autumn and winter flowering. They are available in a huge range of forms and colours and are useful as cut flowers.

Raising plants

Sow annuals for greenhouse display, such as tender primulas, schizanthus, and cinerarias, in pots in late summer for flowering in early spring. Pot them on frequently as they grow so that you end up with a large specimen plant of good quality at flowering time.

The cool greenhouse is an ideal place to raise summer bedding plants (*see previous page*). Their rate of growth determines when you should sow them; devise a monthly sowing plan, starting in late winter for the slowest-growing types. Specific instructions will be given on the seed packets. Even in a cool greenhouse, development will be slow at first because of low light levels in winter.

In late spring, when the young bedding plants are big enough and there is no chance of frost, you should gradually introduce them to the outdoor environment by placing them in a cold frame to harden off (*see page 378*), or by turning off the greenhouse heating system. Gradually increase the ventilation, by day and then night, before moving them outdoors permanently.

GROWING WINTER-FLOWERING CHRYSANTHEMUMS

1 **Take softwood cuttings** (*see page 432*) of new growth from existing plants in late winter. Root the cuttings in a propagating case. Once rooted, transfer the rooted cuttings into small pots in early spring. Alternatively, buy new plants from a specialist nursery in spring.

2 **Pot on** the rooted cuttings into larger pots of soil-based potting compost, such as John Innes No. 3, in mid-spring. Move the plants to a cold frame or cold greenhouse to harden off, closing the vents only in frosty weather.

3 **Transfer each plant** to a large pot and stand the pots in a sheltered place outdoors in early summer. Stake each plant with a timber post or strong cane so they do not topple over in the wind. Alternatively, run a series of horizontal wires between wooden stakes and secure the plants in a line to the wires with string.

4 **Bring the plants** into the cool greenhouse in early autumn and place in a well-lit position. The plants will flower from late autumn to midwinter. After flowering, cut the plants back to about 60cm (24in). In late winter, cut the old stems down to 5–8cm (2–3in) from soil level and begin the process of taking stem cuttings again.

Trees & shrubs for the cool greenhouse

Container-grown trees and shrubs can significantly enhance the internal landscape of both cool greenhouses and conservatories. *Acacia dealbata*, for example, is an almost hardy tree that makes a great late-flowering container plant as a small standard tree or shrub; prune it after flowering in late winter to control its size. Check before buying trees and shrubs for the cool greenhouse as many can grow to enormous sizes and are not so easy to control by pruning.

Bougainvilleas are happy to grow in a cool greenhouse trained on a wall trellis or metal frame. Water them sparingly in winter and prune back overlong stems in early spring as growth commences. They may be deciduous in a cool greenhouse.

Citrus trees make very attractive evergreen trees and shrubs with the additional benefit of fragrant blossom and edible fruits. They respond well to quite heavy watering and feeding with long intervals in between, so that the compost reaches a drying out stage before watering again.

Growing fruit & vegetables

As well as growing popular crops, such as tomatoes, cucumbers, and peppers, you can use a cool greenhouse to grow more tender and exotic vegetables, such as okra, and fruit, like oranges and lemons – if space allows. Strawberries (*see below*) and melons are also good plants for the cool greenhouse as the extra warmth means that you can get crops from early spring for strawberries, or early summer for melons.

Widening the range

Even though there are very many plants that you can grow easily in a cool greenhouse, it is worth experimenting to test your limits. Some plants thought to need a higher temperature than a cool greenhouse can provide, can in fact be acclimatized to such conditions – so long as the temperature does not fall below 4.5°C (40°F), at which point plant cells can be physically damaged. A lot depends on avoiding extremes and sudden changes in the heat, humidity, and ventilation of the greenhouse.

GROWING EARLY STRAWBERRIES

1 Bring rooted plants into the cool greenhouse in early winter, giving them plenty of space to allow air to circulate freely. Keep the temperature just above freezing for the first fortnight. Liquid feed twice a week with tomato fertilizer.

2 Raise the temperature after 2 weeks to 7°C (45°F). When flower trusses appear in late winter, raise it again to 10°C (50°F). Ventilate and damp down the floor if temperatures reach 24°C (75°F) or more on sunny days. Continue to feed and water the plants.

3 Pollinate the flowers daily with a paint brush when the flowers open, and turn the heat up to 13°C (55°F). Continue to ventilate the greenhouse and to feed and water the plants.

4 When the fruit changes colour stop feeding, but continue to water plants and damp down and ventilate the greenhouse. Support the developing fruit trusses with forked twigs inserted in the pots to keep the fruit off the soil and unblemished.

The warm greenhouse

The variety of plants that can be grown in a warm greenhouse is staggering; tropical plants, including flowering trees, shrubs, and climbers, can be grown all year round. The cost of heating a greenhouse to a minimum night temperature of 13°C (55°F), however, can be very high, which is an important consideration.

The atmosphere of a warm greenhouse is different from a cool or unheated house, as you are not just enhancing the outdoor environment but creating an entirely artificial one. Although the way a warm greenhouse is gardened varies from gardener to gardener, the overall look and feel will generally be lush and tropical, with many of the plants grown purely for ornament. Foliage plants, such as ferns and palms, create the backdrop for exotic flowering plants like orchids, African violets, and Cape primroses.

Most orchids should be considered to be plants with special requirements and so left to the hands of the expert. There are still many types, however, that are fairly easy to

GROWING EPIPHYTIC ORCHIDS ON BARK

Make a hole in a piece of bark or branch big enough for the orchid roots. Press the rootball into the hole, with some damp compost, pack moss under the crown and secure with wire.

GROWING CYMBIDIUMS

1 Plant the bulbs in a compost made up by volume of 1 part fibrous loam, 1 part ground bark, 1 part moss and 1 part sharp sand, plus a small amount of bonemeal fertilizer. Pre-prepared composts are available from specialist suppliers.

2 Add liquid feed to the irrigation water once every 14 days when the plants are growing strongly and flowering. Cymbidiums require ample water during the growing season, in both the growing medium and the atmosphere around the plant.

3 Provide shade on hot summer days to prevent sun scorch damage to the plants. Good light is still important, however, so keep the plants well lit by making sure the shading material is not too dense.

4 Damp down the greenhouse floor frequently during the growing season to maintain the necessary humidity. Reduce damping down after flowering – usually between autumn and late winter – and remove all faded blooms.

grow in a warm greenhouse. These include cymbidiums (*see previous page*), some odontoglossums, and dendrobiums, although it is best to consult a specialist nursery for advice on growing requirements before you buy.

Many orchids are epiphytic, meaning they grow on tree bark and require a special compost (*see previous page*). Their root systems have evolved to absorb moisture and nutrients from the air, and therefore you need to keep the atmosphere around the plant humid, and feed them only at a very dilute strength. Although many orchids come from warm parts of the world, they still require shading and cooling, through ventilation, in summer.

Climbers suitable for a warm greenhouse or conservatory include *Allamanda cathartica*, which makes a stunning flowering climber given the support of a trellis or back wall of a conservatory, producing buttercup yellow flowers continuously throughout the year, and *Brunsfelsia paucifolia*, a medium-sized flowering shrub for a large pot or tub that produces an abundance of simple blue flowers and is rarely out of flower.

Foliage plants suitable for a warm greenhouse include *Aphelandra* (zebra plant), colourful-leaved begonias (*see below*), and *Codiaeum*, *Maranta*, *Peperomia*, and many plants grown as house plants.

GROWING TUBEROUS-ROOTED BEGONIAS

1 **Plant tubers** 8cm (3in) apart in a large seedtray filled with moist multipurpose potting compost, in late winter. The compost should reach the top of the tuber.

2 **Pot up the tubers** 2–3 weeks after planting, when the first leaves are 5cm (2in) long, into individual containers at the same depth as they were in the tray.

3 **Water plants** infrequently at first, then more regularly as they establish. Do not allow the compost to dry out or the developing flower buds may fall off.

4 **Shade the greenhouse** in summer to prevent sun scorch, and damp down the floor regularly to keep humidity high.

5 **Tie in** the plants to a stake as they grow, from early summer onwards. Feed plants with a liquid fertilizer as flower buds develop.

6 **Lift and store** the tubers after flowering, once all the foliage has died back. Stop watering before you lift the bulbs.

Sowing & growing *see page 146* | **Growing under glass** *see page 375* | **Propagating plants** *see page 392*

HYGIENE & MAINTENANCE

To maintain the best environment for plants to grow, you must ensure that your structure is kept in good, clean condition. Keep paintwork in good order, heaters and fans serviced, and roof gutters clear, and make sure doors and vents are well lubricated to prevent them seizing up. It is worth making an annual checklist, but deal with structural defects, like broken glazing, immediately. Keep spare glass panels to hand, cut to size, to avert potential disaster. Cleaning is important as it keeps pests and diseases at bay; despite your best efforts, however, you are still likely to encounter problems from time to time.

Keeping clean

Tidiness is part of the greenhouse routine, helping to reduce the conditions that might promote diseases and harbour pests. Each year, thoroughly wash down your greenhouse both inside and out (*see below*) with warm soapy water. Do the same with your containers and tools; secateurs and pruning knives need to be sterilized.

You will notice that through the year the transparency of a greenhouse is reduced by a build up of dust and other pollutants, and the more dirty the glass becomes, the less light can penetrate. In such conditions plant growth will be poor, particularly in the early months of the year.

Remove unhealthy plants as soon as they are spotted, as they may be infected, and take all plant debris and spent compost to the compost heap for prompt disposal. Used pots and containers are best put outside the greenhouse ready to be cleaned. Potting compost deteriorates quite quickly if allowed to become too wet or dry, so keep it in its original bag inside a lidded bin, and remember to buy fresh compost every year. Some products, like rooting hormones, pesticides, and packets of seeds, will quickly deteriorate in a greenhouse so must be stored safely in a cool building away from direct sunlight.

CLEANING THE GREENHOUSE IN AUTUMN

Scrub down the framework to remove pests and diseases that may overwinter.

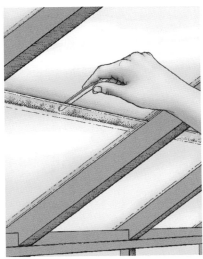

Wash the glass thoroughly using a non-toxic detergent, especially where panes overlap.

Scrub all surfaces including the floor and walls to remove algae or any other deposits.

Greenhouse pests

Good greenhouse hygiene is an essential starting point in the avoidance of pests. Listed below are the most common pests you are likely to encounter, with recommended controls. Other common greenhouse pests are vine weevil, aphids, slugs, and snails (*see pages 35–36*).

Glasshouse whitefly
These small white-winged insects and their whitish-green nymphs suck sap from the underside of leaves of many indoor ornamental plants and vegetables. Honeydew is excreted, making the foliage sticky and coated with sooty mould. Adult whitefly readily fly up from plants when disturbed. They breed throughout the year.

From spring to early autumn, control whitefly biologically with the parasitic wasp *Encarsia formosa*, which kills the nymphs. Pesticide-resistant whitefly occur so insecticides containing bifenthrin or pyrethrum may be ineffective. Systemic insecticides, such as imidacloprid and thiacloprid, generally give good results. Plant oils and fatty acids can also be used but need frequent application.

Tortrix moths
Carnation tortrix moth and light brown apple moth have pale green caterpillars that feed on a wide range of plants. The larvae bind leaves together or curl over the leaf margin with silk threads, and the caterpillars graze on the bound-up leaves. Tortrix moths breed throughout the year on indoor plants. Squeeze bound-up leaves to crush any caterpillars that are concealed within. Insecticides are less effective as the caterpillars are hidden.

Scale insects
Several species of these soft-bodied, sap-feeding insects occur: soft scale is common on *Citrus*, *Ficus*, *Schefflera*, and bay trees; brown scale attacks peaches and grapes; oleander scale infests many ornamental plants. The insects are covered by scales and are immobile for most of the time, attached to the stems and leaves. Some species excrete honeydew and make the foliage sticky and covered in a sooty mould. Wipe them off the foliage and stems or spray with imidacloprid or thiacloprid, which will be absorbed by the scales when they feed. Fatty acids and plant oils give some control of newly hatched scale nymphs.

Glasshouse leafhopper
Both the adult leafhopper and their creamy nymphs suck sap from the lower leaf surface of many plants. This causes a coarse pale mottling of the upper leaf surface.

Leafhoppers are active all year round in greenhouses. They can be controlled with bifenthrin, pyrethrum, imidacloprid, or thiacloprid.

Sciarid flies (fungus gnats)
These small greyish-black flies cause no damage but are a nuisance; put up yellow sticky traps to capture them. Their larvae live in the soil where they feed mainly on dead plant material, but they also damage seedlings or soft cuttings. The predatory mite *Hypoaspis miles* is a biological control that can be used to control them. Help seedlings and cuttings through the vulnerable period by providing good growing conditions.

Mealybugs
Mealybugs are small sap-feeding insects that are often hidden under fluffy white waxy fibres. Cacti and succulents are commonly attacked but many other indoor ornamental plants and grapevines are susceptible. Heavily infested plants lack vigour and may be soiled with a sugary excrement (honeydew) and sooty mould.

Use the ladybird *Cryptolaemus montrouzieri* as a biological control in summer. Otherwise use a systemic insecticide, imidacloprid or thiacloprid, on ornamental plants, or fatty acids and plant oils on grapevines.

Chrysanthemum leaf miner
This small fly lays eggs on the leaves of chrysanthemums and related plants. The maggots bore into the leaves, eating wiggly tunnels. Several generations can occur each year. For light infestations, remove affected leaves or squeeze the tunnels to kill the larvae. Otherwise, spray with imidacloprid or thiacloprid when damage is seen.

Glasshouse red spider mite
Barely visible to the naked eye, this pest is orange-red during autumn and winter and yellowish-green at other times. The mites suck sap from the lower leaf surface, causing the upper surface to develop a fine pale mottling. Leaves become increasingly discoloured as the infestation builds up, causing premature leaf fall. A fine silk webbing may be seen on heavily infested plants. Many indoor plants are susceptible, as well as some outdoor plants during the second half of summer.

Biological control with *Phytoseilus persimilis* is effective from spring to early autumn. Otherwise, spray with bifenthrin, plant oils, or fatty acids. Thorough application is required, especially on the underside of leaves.

GREENHOUSE PESTS & DAMAGE

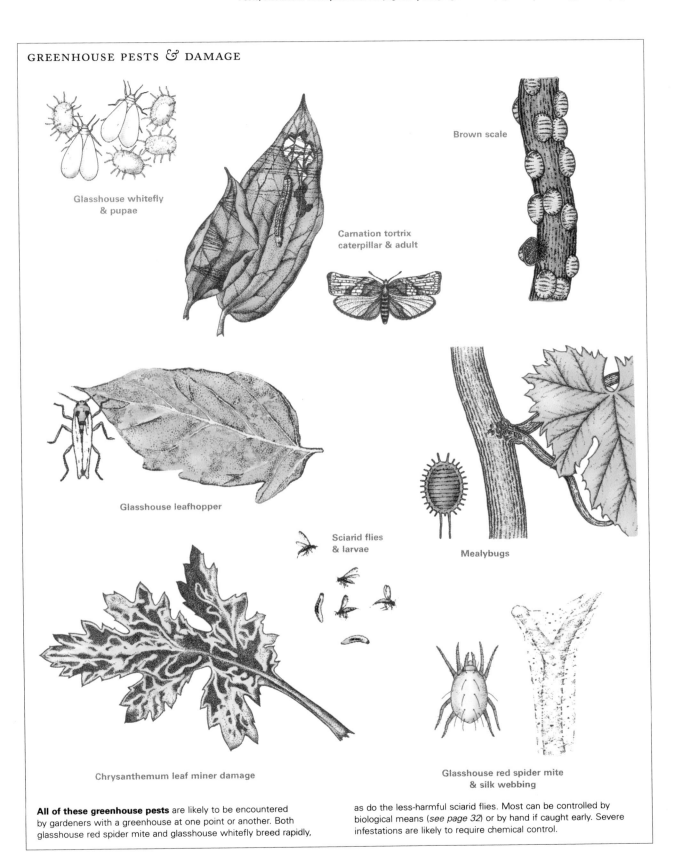

Glasshouse whitefly & pupae

Carnation tortrix caterpillar & adult

Brown scale

Glasshouse leafhopper

Sciarid flies & larvae

Mealybugs

Chrysanthemum leaf miner damage

Glasshouse red spider mite & silk webbing

All of these greenhouse pests are likely to be encountered by gardeners with a greenhouse at one point or another. Both glasshouse red spider mite and glasshouse whitefly breed rapidly, as do the less-harmful sciarid flies. Most can be controlled by biological means (*see page 32*) or by hand if caught early. Severe infestations are likely to require chemical control.

Greenhouse diseases

You can avoid most diseases in the greenhouse by growing things well. Lapses in potting on, ventilation, feeding, watering, temperature control, and other routine tasks will expose your plants to infection.

Damping off

This disease causes seedlings to collapse at soil level, often all at once, and the roots may be decayed. To reduce incidence, use sterile compost and equipment, sow seeds thinly, and water with tap water. Provide adequate light but not excessive heat. Discard affected seedlings and water the remainder with copper oxychloride.

Viruses

Plants exhibit a range of symptoms when infected by viruses, with yellowing patches on leaves the most commonly seen. These patches often take the form of mosaic, ringspot, or mottled patterns. Dead patches can also result, and an infected plant may appear stunted when placed next to a healthy one. Viruses are most often seen in plants that are propagated by division or cuttings, such as dahlias and cannas. Insects usually transfer viruses, but some viruses are highly contagious and can spread by contact between a plant and a surface on which virus particles are present. Under glass, three viruses are very common, and all have a wide host range:
Cucumber mosaic virus: Common on begonias as well as cucumbers, it causes ringspots or mosaic patterns.
Impatiens necrotic spot virus: This can affect a huge range of plants, causing diverse symptoms.
Tomato spotted wilt virus: Common on tomatoes and their relatives. Affected dahlias have 'oakleaf' ringspots.

Viruses cannot be cured and affected plants must be destroyed. To help prevent infection, keep pests under control and sterilize cutting tools when propagating.

Wirestem

This disease affects brassica seedlings, especially cauliflowers. Stems shrink at ground level and then topple. Prevent by sowing thinly in sterilized compost and avoid overwatering. There is no treatment.

Leafy gall

This bacterial disease causes soil-level tissue to proliferate, forming a mass of stunted and distorted shoots. Sweet peas, dahlias, chrysanthemums, and pelargoniums are particularly prone. Destroy affected plants and their soil, and sterilize hands, tools, and, if necessary, work surfaces.

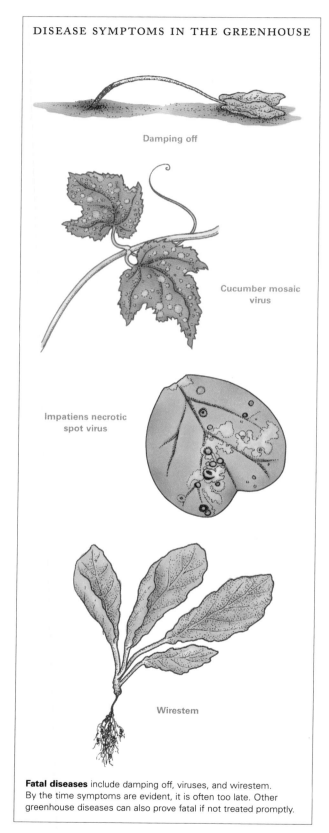

DISEASE SYMPTOMS IN THE GREENHOUSE

Damping off

Cucumber mosaic virus

Impatiens necrotic spot virus

Wirestem

Fatal diseases include damping off, viruses, and wirestem. By the time symptoms are evident, it is often too late. Other greenhouse diseases can also prove fatal if not treated promptly.

Grey mould

Affected plant tissue rots and becomes covered in grey fluffy mould, and the flowers may develop small brown spots on the petals. As grey mould can spread very rapidly by contact between diseased and healthy tissue, ensure that dead plant material is promptly removed. Keep your greenhouse well ventilated and water in the morning to reduce humid conditions, which encourage the fungus. Grey mould can be a problem on grapes under glass, often infecting through the scar tissue produced by powdery mildew disease. Try to limit powdery mildew infection on greenhouse grapes.

Downy mildews

These mildews affect many plants, indoors and out. In a greenhouse, they are most likely to infect brassica and lettuce seedlings. An off-white mould forms on the underside of leaves, which may be outlined by the veins, with corresponding yellow blotches on the upper leaf. Downy mildew spreads rapidly through seedlings. Lettuce downy mildew is the only form that can be treated with a fungicide. Remove diseased plants on sight and improve ventilation. Avoid overhead watering as moisture on leaves encourages the disease. Resting spores can persist for years, so change soil in beds where the disease is established.

Arum corm rot

This rot can develop rapidly on plants in the arum family when corms are planted, causing plants to collapse. Investigation reveals brown areas on the corms with rotting roots. The tissue can be very soft and smelly. If a small area of corm is affected, cut it out and treat with sulphur dust. Otherwise destroy badly affected corms and replace the soil in which they were growing. Inspect bulbs before planting or storing.

Chrysanthemum rusts

Chrysanthemums can be affected by both white and brown rust. White rust is a serious disease, typified by dirty white pustules on leaf undersides and pale craters on the uppersides. Brown rust causes dark brown pustules on leaf undersides and pale green spots on the uppersides. Severe infection causes defoliation and a reduction in flowering. Destroy affected plants immediately, and spray neighbouring chrysanthemums with a fungicide labelled for control of rusts on ornamentals. As a precaution against brown rust, strip lower leaves from cuttings when they are taken and when transplanted, and avoid wetting leaves when watering. Many modern varieties of chrysanthemum are resistant to brown rust.

MORE DISEASE SYMPTOMS

Grey mould on cane

Grey mould on grapes

Downy mildew

Fluffy moulds are typical of downy mildew and grey mould. Both spread rapidly through host plants, and both can be discouraged by providing adequate ventilation in the greenhouse.

CHAPTER TEN

PROPAGATING PLANTS

TOOLS & EQUIPMENT 396

CONTROLLING THE ENVIRONMENT 398

CONTAINERS 400

POTTING COMPOSTS 401

WATERING 402

GOOD HYGIENE, PESTS AND DISEASES 403

METHODS OF PROPAGATION 404

SOWING SEEDS 405

ROOTS, BULBS, CORMS & TUBERS 411

DIVISION 422

STEMS 425

LEAVES 439

GENERATING NEW PLANTS, WHETHER BY RAISING THEM from seed, or by creating divisions or taking cuttings from an existing plant, is one of the most challenging, but rewarding aspects of gardening. If you choose the best technique for the plant you want to propagate, carry it out at the optimum time of year, and follow the procedure with care, you will have done all you can to give your vulnerable young plants the best chance of survival.

Methods of propagation

Some methods of propagation apply to many plants, others to only a few. You can raise almost any plant from seed, but it may not be the best method for slow-growing plants. Also, seed-raised plants may turn out to be very different from their parents. Seeds from highly bred plants, such as varieties of roses and fruit, and F1 hybrids of flowers and vegetables, are likely to produce inferior offspring. To avoid this genetic variability and produce mature plants more quickly, you can use vegetative propagation – growing on new plants from parts of an existing, or parent, plant. Some of these techniques, like division, mirror natural processes; others, such as cuttings, are more artificial, but they can yield large numbers of new plants.

Propagation basics

Propagation begins with choosing suitable parent plants, which may need special treatment to encourage them to produce good propagating material. The material then needs suitable conditions in which to regenerate and to grow on into a self-supporting plant. Often, the optimum conditions for regeneration are not the best for growing on, so the switch from one to the other must be carefully timed.

Selecting suitable plant material

When collecting seeds or vegetative material, it makes sense to do so from healthy plants with the characteristics you want, such as the largest, brightest blooms or good crop yields. The capacity of a plant to regenerate vegetatively is affected by the age of the parent plant and the growth from which it is taken. Material from the current year's growth regenerates more easily than older tissue, and the best response is gained from juvenile plants that have not yet flowered or fruited. Old plants regenerate much less readily.

Plants of the same variety that have been increased vegetatively over many years will all be genetically identical clones, and physiologically the same age, so even a young plant of an old variety may be difficult to propagate.

For some propagation techniques, it is worth stimulating the plant to produce suitable propagation material, for example by pruning it to encourage new shoots or starting the parent plant into growth earlier in the season by providing additional heat and light.

Providing suitable conditions for regeneration

Once you have collected and sown your seeds, and prepared your cuttings or divisions, they will need the optimum conditions in which to thrive and grow into healthy new plants. You can create the most favourable environment by choosing an appropriate compost, providing appropriate levels of warmth and moisture, and controlling pests and diseases. Once the new plant has established and started to grow on, you will need to gradually acclimatize it to outdoor conditions so it can grow on by itself.

PROPAGATION BASICS

You can start propagating plants without any special equipment at all – a few basic garden items will enable you to tackle many propagation techniques. Just as important to success are observing good hygiene and providing appropriate conditions for the plant material. So it is worth choosing the most appropriate container and compost, paying attention to watering, and doing what you can to create a favourable environment for fragile new plants, such as seedlings and cuttings. A heated propagator will make many tasks easier and extend the range of plants from which you can propagate.

Tools & equipment

For many propagation tasks, you do not need any special equipment at all – a few seed trays and plant pots, some multipurpose compost, some plastic bags, a decent garden knife, or your secateurs will do. If you want to try some of the more advanced techniques, or take material from plants that are more difficult to propagate, then you may want to invest in a few extra tools or try out some specialist containers and composts.

A heated propagator is a very useful tool as it will make it easier for you to control the environment of the plant material and encourage germination of seeds or rooting of the various types of cuttings.

If you are lucky enough to have a dedicated area such as a garden shed where you can propagate plants, then it is worth setting up a workbench at the proper height (*see box, below left*) and allocating shelf space to keep all your propagating kit together. This will help you to work quickly and efficiently, which in turn will reduce the stress on the plant material and increase your chances of success.

Otherwise, you can use a greenhouse bench or an area in the kitchen. Wherever you work, it is helpful to first get all your equipment ready and to make sure that the area is clean and brightly lit. After using propagation tools and equipment, clean and, if needed, service them.

ADJUSTING THE WORKBENCH

To prevent backache, it is well worth adjusting your workbench to the correct height. To establish this, stand up straight in front of the bench, drop your arms to your sides, then lift your forearms at right angles to your body and drop your wrists. Your fingertips should just touch the bench top.

CUTTING HARD WOOD

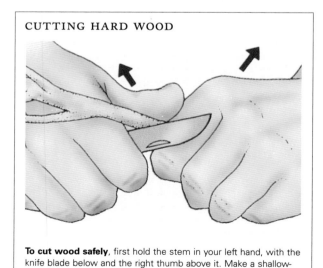

To cut wood safely, first hold the stem in your left hand, with the knife blade below and the right thumb above it. Make a shallow-angled cut from beneath by drawing the right forearm backwards and maintaining a gap between the right thumb and the blade. Avoid cutting up towards your thumb.

Choosing & using a knife

A well-made knife with a sharp blade and comfortable handle is a pleasure to use and will cut plant material cleanly with the minimum of damage to the plant tissue. If plant material is bruised it is more likely to die, as this provides an opportunity for diseases like rot, which will infect your cuttings and spoil your efforts.

Gardeners' knives are available in a range of designs. You should choose one that has a stainless-steel blade, is well balanced, and sits in your hand nicely. Check that it is easy to open and that the shoulder of the blade is set back into the handle when in use (*see box, below*). This reduces play from side to side and prevents the blade from working loose; this is especially important when using knives on tough material such as woody cuttings.

Knife blades may be ground to a cutting edge on one or both sides (*see right*). Both types of blade are equally effective, but while one-sided blades are either left handed or right handed, two-sided blades can be used by either hand. Blades may also be flat ground or hollow ground: a flat-ground blade is more concave and needs to be sharpened at a steeper angle.

It is best to keep one knife for propagation and not use it for other garden tasks. Use the knife to prepare and trim plant material, cutting soft wood against a clean pane of glass laid flat on the workbench. Cut hardwood carefully while holding it securely (*see box, facing page*).

The easiest way to keep a good edge on your knife is with a broad, flat sharpening stone. In time, the knife blade will inevitably become clogged with plant sap or resin, which reduces cutting efficiency. Clean the blade with a rag dipped in a solvent, such as petrol or surgical spirit, or with a fine grade of emery paper.

A scalpel or craft knife, with disposable blades, or a safety razor blade in a solid metal holder, can be very useful for cutting very soft material, such as dahlia or chrysanthemum cuttings.

SHARPENING A FLAT-GROUND BLADE

1 **Lay the blade** on the stone at the end nearest you. While applying a slight, even pressure on the edge, draw the blade along the stone towards the opposite end. Repeat the movement several times. If necessary, turn the blade over and sharpen the other side of the edge.

SHARPENING A HOLLOW-GROUND BLADE

1 **Lubricate the coarse side** of the stone with oil or water, according to the manufacturer's recommendation. Hold the blade at one end of the stone so it faces forwards at an acute angle to the surface of the stone.

2 **Push gently along** the whole length of the stone, while maintaining the angle between the blade and the stone. Lift it off and repeat several times. Give a final rub to the blade along the fine side of the stone. Repeat with the other side of the blade if it has also been ground.

CHOOSING A KNIFE

Side view showing blade

Top view showing tang

The most important quality of a good gardening knife is that it should be sharp, so choose one with a blade that has a straight cutting edge. This should be easier to sharpen. Another point to look for in a good knife is a full-length tang; that is, where the steel extends the full length of the handle to give the knife better strength and stability when being handled. The back end of the blade, or shoulder, should also be set well back into the handle when opened. A general-purpose gardening knife has a rounded tip (*see above*), whereas the tip of a budding knife is pointed.

Choosing & using secateurs

Secateurs can be used to collect tough material for cuttings more quickly and easily than a knife and, if sharp enough, they can be used to prepare the cuttings.

There are two basic designs of secateur (*see box, right*): anvil and bypass. Anvil types have one sharp, thin, straight-edged blade at the top. Its cutting edge is usually hollow ground on both sides and cuts against a broad, flat surface – the anvil – at the bottom, crushing the tissue. Bypass, or scissor, secateurs also have just one sharp blade, but it is heavy, curved, and flat ground only on the inside edge. It cuts with a shearing action, like scissors, by sweeping past the lower, unsharpened anvil blade, so it makes a cleaner cut than anvil secateurs and causes less bruising.

When choosing a pair of secateurs, ensure that the size and handles are comfortable in your hand. Get a spring-loaded pair, which reopens after each cut automatically. When collecting propagating material from a shrub, follow the same rules as when pruning to make a clean cut and avoid leaving snags (*see pages 94–108*).

Maintaining secateurs

Secateurs are much more effective when they are well maintained, especially when they are used for precision work like propagation. Ensure the blades are always clean

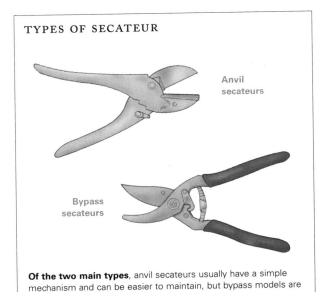

TYPES OF SECATEUR

Anvil secateurs

Bypass secateurs

Of the two main types, anvil secateurs usually have a simple mechanism and can be easier to maintain, but bypass models are generally preferred for propagation as they make a cleaner cut.

of sap and other residues, and keep the moving parts lightly oiled. Sharpen the blades as required to keep them cutting cleanly. Some models can be sent back to the manufacturers for maintenance; with other models, follow the manufacturer's instructions.

Controlling the environment

The main challenge in propagation is to ensure the survival of propagated material, be it a seed, cutting, or piece of root, until it becomes an independent, young plant. This requires controlling the environment – above and below ground – to create optimum conditions for plant growth while reducing risk of drying out or rotting.

A favourable aerial environment produces minimum water loss from plant material, has cool air temperatures, enough light for photosynthesis, and adequate ventilation. Below ground, the ideal is warm, moist, but well-drained soil or compost, with an open, aerated structure, neutral pH, and low nutrient levels. The softer or less hardy the material, the more environmental control is needed. While most propagation methods happen under cover, sowing hardy seeds, taking hardwood cuttings, or dividing herbaceous perennials can take place entirely outdoors.

Cloches

The most basic type of cover is the cloche. These are available in many different designs, as individual rigid units, in glass or plastic, or as tunnels. Make these by

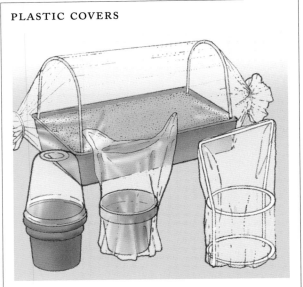

PLASTIC COVERS

There are various covers that will create a closed environment, from plastic bags or sheeting supported on wire hoop or frames to specially designed, individual pot cloches.

CONTROLLING THE ENVIRONMENT

Pruning & training *see page 94* | **Frames, cloches & tunnels** *see page 369* | **Using frames & cloches** *see page 378*

WINDOWSILL PROPAGATOR

This type of propagator, with individual, miniature seed trays and covers on a heated base, may be all you need to raise a few tender seedlings and take small numbers of cuttings.

THERMOSTAT-CONTROLLED PROPAGATOR

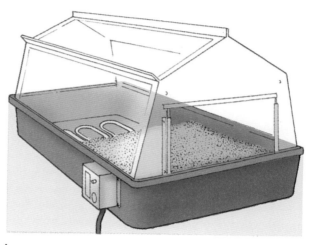

Larger propagators have a heated base, sometimes covered with sand to spread the warmth and hold moisture, and a tall, transparent cover, which may be divided into 2 or more units.

supporting clear plastic sheeting or horticultural fleece on wire hoops, pegging down or burying the edges, and closing up the ends. Cloches aid growth by warming the air and soil and by keeping out cold and drying winds and flying pests. Fleece allows more air movement and is good at keeping out frost. Clear plastic gives better light transmission and raises humidity. All types of cloche can be easily moved. One disadvantage is their relatively small sizes and, at least with some designs, awkward access.

Cold frames

Essentially, these are boxes with glass or clear plastic lids and sides, with a wood, metal, or plastic frame, or with solid wood or brick sides. You can make a serviceable cold frame from second-hand materials like old bricks and windows, or you can buy a ready-made frame. Choose one that is large enough to hold all the plants you want to grow and heavy enough to withstand strong winds. It should be easy to access and to fix the lid open, closed, or ajar for ventilation. Plastic is usually lighter and safer than glass, but glass conserves heat more effectively, so is a better choice for use from late autumn through to early spring.

A cold frame, like a cloche, keeps plants warmer and more sheltered, in increased humidity. You can insulate it on cold nights with a layer of old carpet or bubble wrap. If it gets too hot on sunny days, partly open the lid or cover it with greenhouse shading. Position the cold frame over a bed of soil if you want to bring on plants where they are to grow, or over solid surfaces like paving or concrete if the plants are in pots.

Homemade plastic covers

If you propagate indoors, you can better control the environment and keep a close eye on developing plants. Maintaining humidity is still important, but cheap and simple arrangements are sufficient for easily propagated plants (*see facing page*). Simply place a clean, clear plastic bag over a pot of seeds or cuttings, support it with one or two canes, or a loop of wire, then seal with a rubber band around the pot. Translucent food containers also make suitable pot covers. For seed trays, make a mini-tunnel by supporting a length of clear plastic sheeting over wire hoops. Fasten the ends with a rubber band or clothes peg.

Windowsill propagator

If you need additional warmth for your seeds or cuttings, a heated propagator is the most straightforward solution (*see above*). It also creates a closed environment to maintain humidity. Locate it on a well-lit windowsill, out of direct sunlight to avoid overheating.

Use a propagator with a heating unit and thermostat to maintain a steady temperature. This is normally pre-set to 18–21°C (64–70°F), which is the preferred germination temperature of many tender garden plants. Some have an adjustable thermostat, although you will need a thermometer to check the settings. Most propagators require a background temperature of at least 5°C (41°F) and preferably 10°C (50°F) in order to maintain a compost temperature of 18–21°C (64–70°F). Larger propagators can be used in the house if there is sufficient light, but they are better in a greenhouse or conservatory.

Containers

Most gardeners accumulate a motley collection of plastic pots and trays when buying plants. If they are clean and about the right size (pots smaller than 7cm (2¾in) across dry out too quickly), they are fine for propagation, as are plastic food containers with added drainage holes. If you buy containers, you will need a mixture of pots and trays.

Choosing containers

You only need a few different types for most purposes. Wide, shallow pots are useful for seeds and small cuttings that do not need very deep compost, and long pots are good for deep-rooted plants. Pots with almost vertical sides have greater stability and hold more compost. Seed trays should be 5–6cm (2–2½in) deep; shallower trays dry out too quickly and deeper ones use too much compost. Modular trays (*see right*) are useful for large numbers of seeds, but they may be rather flimsy and can be awkward to fill with compost and difficult to clean.

Modular trays keep the rootballs of the young plants separate and are easier to move than lots of individual pots.

SEED CONTAINERS

Most seed containers, whether seed trays (*shown top*), modular trays (*centre*), or shallow or deep pots (*bottom*), are made of plastic, and are cheap, lightweight, durable, and easily washed and stored. They retain moisture better than clay or wood containers.

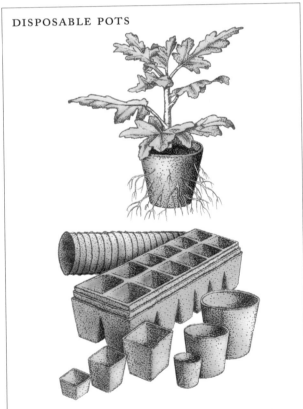

DISPOSABLE POTS

Biodegradable containers are usually made from processed organic material, such as compressed peat. They allow plant roots to penetrate, so you can plant out the pot and its contents with little disturbance to the roots. The pot eventually rots away.

Potting composts

Some types of propagation, including layering and division, take place outdoors, direct into the soil. In most cases, however, garden soil is not a suitable growing medium; you need to use a good, sterile potting compost.

Soil-based composts

John Innes composts are based on loam mixed with sand, peat, lime, and fertilizer in precise amounts. Gardeners can make up a simple formula themselves (*see right*) or buy it ready made. John Innes No. 1 compost is formulated for seeds and cuttings.

Soilless composts

Peat-based composts are now more widely used than soil-based ones, because good loam has become harder to find and peat is lighter and easier to standardize. More recently, concerns have arisen over the extraction of peat for horticulture because it destroys important natural habitats. Many alternatives to peat are now available, including coir (the outer husk of coconuts), composted green waste, bark, and other timber residues.

Composts for propagation

Most compost sold is multipurpose, suitable for seed raising, taking cuttings, and other forms of propagation, as well as growing plants on. This inevitably makes it a bit of a compromise, but for most purposes it is perfectly adequate. Cuttings need the growing medium kept permanently moist to prevent them from drying out, and to have an open structure so that air can circulate within the compost. If you are using multipurpose compost, therefore, add a handful of grit to every four handfuls of compost to improve drainage and reduce the risk of rot.

Seeds require similar conditions but may be more sensitive to the nutrient and chemical content of compost. Multipurpose compost may be too coarse, or contain too much fertilizer, for some finicky or fine seeds. For these, specialist seed compost may give better results.

Mixing composts

When mixing compost materials, you must do it evenly. For large quantities, do this on a clean solid floor with a clean shovel. Make sure all ingredients are sterile.

MAKING YOUR OWN COMPOST

- 2 parts sterilized loam
- 1 part peat or peat substitute
- 1 part coarse sand

to each 9-litre (2-gallon) bucket of mix, add:

- 10g (2 tsp) superphosphate fertilizer
- 5g (1 tsp) ground chalk

Mix all the ingredients thoroughly and store, covered, in a cool, dry place. To sterilize loam, put it in a broad, flat, heat-proof container, such as a meat tin, cover with aluminium foil, and put in the oven at 80°C (180°F) for 30 minutes. For seed compost, sift the peat, or peat substitute, through a 6mm (¼in) sieve.

USING HORMONE ROOTING POWDER

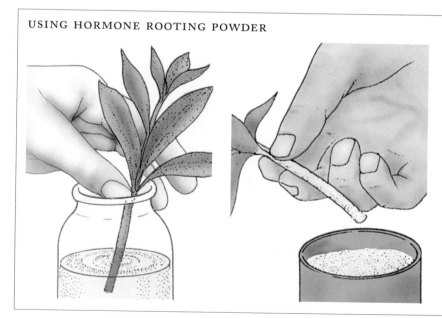

Plant growth is controlled, in part, by naturally occurring hormones. You can encourage a shoot to produce roots by applying hormone rooting powder to the cut surface. If it is dry, dip the end of the cutting in water first. Avoid getting powder on the outside of the stem; it is wasteful and may even inhibit root development.

Hormone rooting powder does not keep well. Buy it fresh each season and store in a cool, dry place. When using it, tip a little into a small dish, then discard any surplus to avoid contaminating the main stock. Hormone rooting powder is effective only on cut stems; it does not aid rooting of root or leaf cuttings. Rooting hormone is also available in gel form.

Watering

Watering is much easier if you start with compost that is already moist – dry compost can be hard to re-wet. Check the compost by taking a handful and squeezing it. When you open your hand, the ball of compost should crack open in just one or two places. If it remains in one lump, it is too wet and, if it all falls apart, it is too dry.

It is possible to water from above, but if the water drops are too large, you may displace seeds or cuttings. For very small seedlings, a sprayer is the best watering device. Watering from below takes longer, but does not disturb seeds or plants. Standing containers in water works well and is the best way to re-wet containers that have dried out. If the compost is overwatered, stand the containers on newspaper to draw out excess moisture.

Capillary systems

An alternative way to water from below is with a capillary system. Stand the containers on a permanently damp base so that the compost can absorb moisture by capillary action continually, but without becoming so wet that the compost becomes waterlogged. The great advantage of this system is that you are unlikely to overwater and only need to top up water in the base material, rather than to one container at a time. Plants may dry out if there is poor capillary contact, especially if they are moved around a lot. You can set up a system with capillary matting, but sand is the most reliable base material (*see right*).

Water via a sand bed to reduce the risk of the compost drying out. Choose a tray with raised sides and good drainage, and line it with plastic sheeting. Stab holes in the sheeting about 1cm (½in) below the required surface level, then fill the tray with fine sand. Level the surface, then water well and allow to drain. Set the containers firmly on the sand bed so that there is no air between the sand and the compost to impede the uptake of moisture from the sand into the pot. Keep the sand moist by adding water from time to time.

WATERING FROM ABOVE

This is a quick way of watering, but it needs a steady hand and a fine, upturned rose that does not drip. Start pouring the water away from the container; once you get an even flow, direct it over the compost. Move the spout away from the container before stopping the flow.

WATERING FROM BELOW

A shallow bath of water – a cat-litter tray is ideal – provides the simplest way of watering containers from below. Stand them in the water bath and, as soon as moisture appears on the compost surface, remove the containers and leave them to drain.

GOOD HYGIENE

Pests, diseases & other problems *see page 26* | Watering & feeding *see page 360* | Hygiene & maintenance *see page 387*

Good hygiene, pests & diseases

Recently propagated plants are especially vulnerable to pests and diseases, so extra care must be taken to protect them. Good hygiene is the first line of defence. All pots, trays, tools, and work surfaces used for propagation should be scrupulously clean. Garden disinfectants are useful allies. If you use a greenhouse, give it a good clean in early winter. Bag up unused compost for reuse on established container plants or put it on the compost heap, rather than leaving it lying around. Also, it is important to check your plants frequently – daily if possible – and remove dead or dying leaves. Take action quickly if you spot any pests or diseases.

Common pests

Glasshouse whitefly: Small, white, moth-like adults and greenish-white, scale-like larvae suck the sap and excrete a sugary substance (honeydew), which makes foliage sticky and feeds growth of sooty mould (*see page 388*).

Sciarid flies: The small, greyish-white larvae of these tiny black flies (also called fungus gnats) eat roots of young plants. They like wet compost, so do not overwater. Catch the flies on yellow sticky traps or use a predatory mite, *Hypoaspis miles*, which is a biological control.

Slugs and snails: These wreak havoc among seedlings and soft cuttings. Check hiding places regularly, such as under pots and between modules (*see page 35*).

Spider mites: You can detect these by their wispy webs and the yellow mottling of affected leaves. Control is difficult, but high humidity discourages them. Discard badly affected plants (*see page 388*).

Vine weevils: The adults lay their eggs in soil or compost; the grubs are C-shaped, cream with dark heads, and feed voraciously on roots and stem bases. Such plants may be killed during autumn to spring (*see page 36*).

Common diseases

Grey mould: This thrives in cold, damp conditions. A brown area of rot anywhere on a seedling or cutting, in time, develops a covering of greyish mould. Promptly remove infected material, ventilate where possible, and provide warm conditions. There is no chemical treatment.

Damping off: Soil- and water-borne fungi kill tissues near soil level, so seedlings keel over and die. Always use fresh compost and clean trays, do not sow densely, give seedlings plenty of light, air, and warmth, and do not overwater.

Foot and root rots: These rots are caused by soil- and water-borne fungi. Practice good hygiene and growing practices to promote strong root growth.

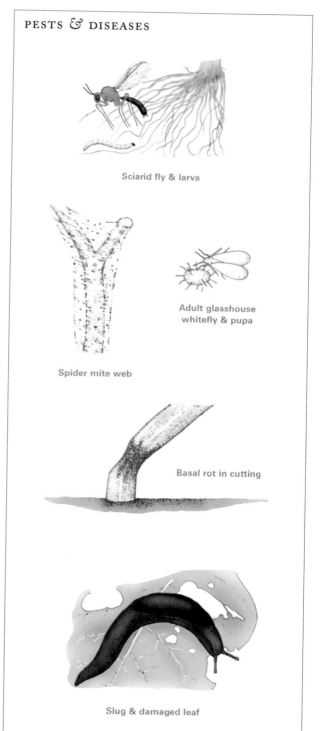

PESTS & DISEASES

Sciarid fly & larva

Spider mite web

Adult glasshouse whitefly & pupa

Basal rot in cutting

Slug & damaged leaf

If you learn to identify the most common pests and diseases that affect newly propagated material and inspect your plants regularly, you can nip any attack in the bud.

Methods of propagation

Some plants increase readily, others may be propagated in several ways, and some are much more difficult than others. You will increase your chances of success if you choose an appropriate method for the plant. The chart below gives an indication of the best methods of raising some common garden and house plants; other examples are discussed in the following pages. Most plants may be increased by means of one or more of the methods described here and, as you gain in confidence and experience, you will discover which you prefer.

PLANT	METHOD OF PROPAGATION
Acanthus	root cuttings
Acer japonicum, A. palmatum	air layering
African violet (Saintpaulia)	leaf cuttings
Agave	offsets
Anemone x hybrida	root cuttings
Aster	division
Aubrieta	division
Bamboo	division
Bellflower (Campanula)	division
Berberis	heel/mallet cuttings
Bergenia	rhizomes
Black currant	greenwood/hardwood cuttings
Bottlebrush (Callistemon)	softwood cuttings
Box (Buxus)	division
Canna	rhizomes
Cape primrose (Streptocarpus)	lateral vein/midrib cuttings
Cardiocrinum	bulblets
Catmint (Nepeta)	rhizomes
Ceanothus	greenwood/evergreen cuttings
Choisya ternata	semi-ripe/evergreen cuttings
Christmas box (Sarcococca)	division
Clematis	layering, leaf-bud cuttings
Coleus (Solenostemon)	softwood cuttings
Convallaria majalis	rhizomes
Cotoneaster (large hybrids)	hardwood cuttings
Crassula	offsets
Cypress (Cupressus)	conifer cuttings
Daphne	evergreen cuttings
Daylily (Hemerocallis)	division
Delphinium	division, greenwood cuttings
Dogwood (Cornus)	layering, semi-ripe/hardwood cuttings
Echeveria	offsets
Elaeagnus	evergreen cuttings
Escallonia	evergreen/semi-ripe cuttings
False acacia (Robinia)	suckers, root cuttings
False cypress (Chamaecyparis)	conifer cuttings
Fleabane (Erigeron)	division
Flowering currant (Ribes)	semi-ripe/hardwood cuttings
Flowering quince (Chaenomeles)	softwood cuttings, suckers
Forsythia	greenwood/semi-ripe cuttings
Fuchsia	softwood cuttings
Geranium	division
Gesneria	leaf cuttings
Gladiolus	cormlets, scoring
Gloxinia	tubers, leaf cuttings
Gooseberry	greenwood/hardwood cuttings
Hebe	evergreen cuttings
Helenium	division
Hibiscus	softwood cuttings
Honeysuckle (Lonicera)	leaf bud/hardwood cuttings
House leek (Sempervivum)	offsets

PLANT	METHOD OF PROPAGATION
Hydrangea macrophylla	division, semi-ripe cuttings
Hydrangea petiolaris	layering, softwood cuttings
Hypericum calycinum	division
Incarvillea	division
Ivy (Hedera)	leaf-bud cuttings, layering
Juniper (low-growing types)	conifer cuttings
Kalmia	layering
Kerria japonica	suckers, hardwood cuttings
Lady's mantle (Alchemilla)	division
Lavatera	semi-ripe cuttings
Lemon (Citrus limon)	air layering
Lilac (Syringa)	air layering
Loosestrife (Lythrum)	division
Lupin	division
Magnolia	layering, air layering
Mahonia	leaf bud cuttings
New Zealand flax (Phormium)	division, offsets
Pampas grass (Cortaderia)	division
Passion flower (Passiflora)	semi-ripe cuttings
Pelargonium	greenwood cuttings
Peony	rhizomes
Peperomia	leaf cuttings
Philadelphus	greenwood/semi-ripe cuttings
Phlox	root cuttings, division
Pieris	layering
Pileostegia	softwood cuttings
Poppy (Papaver)	root cuttings, division
Potentilla (herbaceous species)	runners
Primula	division
Pyracantha	evergreen cuttings
Red and white currant	hardwood cuttings
Rhubarb	division
Rose (species and hybrids)	hardwood cuttings
Rudbeckia	division
Saxifraga	offsets
Sea holly (Eryngium)	root cuttings
Sea lavender (Limonium)	root cuttings, division
Sedge (Carex)	division
Smoke bush (Cotinus coggygria)	layering, suckers
Solomon's seal (Polygonatum)	rhizomes
Spider plant (Chlorophytum)	runners
Spiraea	hardwood cuttings
Spotted laurel (Aucuba)	evergreen cuttings
Sumach (Rhus)	root cuttings, suckers
Sun rose (Cistus)	semi-ripe cuttings
Trumpet vine (Campsis radicans)	layering, root cuttings
Virginia creeper (Parthenocissus)	layering
Waterlily (Nymphaea)	tubers, leaf bud cuttings
Wax flower (Hoya)	leaf-bud/softwood cuttings
Willow (Salix)	hardwood cuttings
Witch hazel (Hamamelis)	layering, air layering
Yew (Taxus)	conifer cuttings

SOWING SEEDS

A seed consists of a miniature plant or embryo, a food supply, and a protective seed coat. Outside this may be other layers, such as fleshy fruit (like on a plum) or a tough skin. The embryo consists of an undeveloped root, an undeveloped shoot, and short section of stem between them. Attached to this embryo stem are seed leaves (cotyledons). These may remain in the soil or emerge above ground when a seedling germinates. They are usually simply shaped and may be quite unlike the plant's true leaves. The seed's food reserves come from the cotyledons or from a separate food store.

Collecting & storing seeds

You can grow many annual and perennial flowering plants, and many vegetables, successfully from seeds that you collect yourself. Avoid collecting from highly bred hybrids, especially those labelled F1 in seed catalogues; these seedlings will not grow true to type and are likely to give disappointing results.

Seeds need to be collected as it becomes ripe but before it is dispersed (*see below*). This means keeping a careful eye on the plants and, as soon as the dead flowers start to break up or the seedheads start to dry out, collect what you need. Do your collecting on a fine, dry day. Snip off small seedheads, pods, or capsules from plants when they are nearly dry; they often fade to brown and become papery when ripe. Place the seedheads in an open paper bag or in a tray and leave to dry further. Alternatively, you can collect the entire flower stem. Break up dried seed capsules, and clean the seeds by sieving or just picking out the debris.

Provided that you dry the seeds properly and then keep them cool and dry, you can store most flower and vegetable seeds for two or three years. A good way to do this is to place the seed packets in a sealed plastic container, with a sachet of silica gel to absorb any moisture, and store it in the salad drawer of the fridge.

COLLECTING & STORING FLOWER SEED

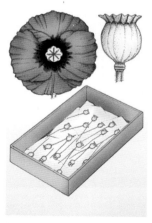

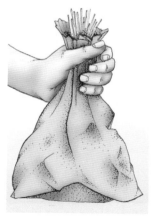

Spread fleshy seed capsules on tissue or kitchen paper in a tray or shallow box. Leave to dry in the sun or a warm place.

Bunch together stems of whole flowerheads, then enclose the heads in a paper bag – avoid plastic bags because they trap moisture that can lead to rotting.

Tie the neck of the bag and hang up in a dry, airy place. Shake the bag occasionally to help release the seeds into the bag.

Label bags or envelopes with the plant name and date, and place the seeds inside once they are properly dried and cleaned of any chaff. Store in a cool, dry place.

Sowing in containers

Before choosing a container, consider the needs of the seeds. How many seeds are you sowing, and how large will the seedlings grow before they are transplanted? Seed trays or wide, shallow pots are best for small seeds, but you can improvise with food-packaging trays if they have plenty of drainage holes. Larger seeds often germinate more successfully since they have large food reserves. You can sow them evenly spaced in trays, but it is better to sow singly into small pots or modular trays.

Preparing containers

Make sure that any container is scrupulously clean before you start. Always use fresh compost, ideally that is newly bought; older or second-hand compost can be used safely on more mature plants. Multipurpose compost should be adequate for the great majority of seeds. Specialist seed compost contains less fertilizer and may be better for some seeds that are sensitive to high nutrient levels. Seeds of acid-loving plants are best sown in ericaceous compost.

SOWING SEEDS IN CONTAINERS

1 Soak large seeds in water for 12–24 hours before sowing so that they can absorb the necessary moisture more easily.

2 Fill a container with compost until it is heaped above the rim, then tap it on the work surface to settle the contents.

3 Firm the compost gently into the corners and base, using the tips of the fingers to eliminate air pockets.

4 Level off excess compost with a sawing action, using a presser board or a piece of wood, so that the compost surface is level with the container rim.

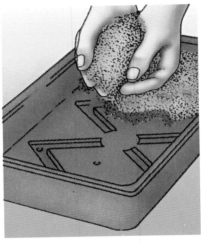

5 Firm the compost lightly to 0.5–1cm (¼–½in) below the rim, using a presser board that fits the container or any flat piece of wood. This creates space for watering.

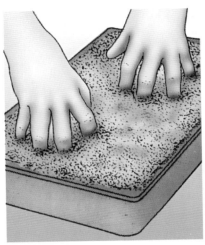

6 Sow half the seeds as evenly as possible right across the surface, keeping your hand low to prevent the seeds from bouncing.

SOWING IN CONTAINERS

Growing under glass *see page 375* | **Potting composts** *see page 401* | **Methods of propagation** *see page 404*

Before sowing your seeds, it is important to ensure that the compost surface is smooth and level. If the surface is uneven, seeds can drop into gaps and end up buried too deeply. In addition, moisture tends to become unevenly distributed through the compost. Sieve very coarse compost, or pick out large fibrous pieces, before use. A presser board – a flat piece of wood with a handle – made to fit the container, makes it a great deal easier to firm the compost evenly. A useful alternative is an empty, flat-based seed tray or pot of the same size. Take care not to compact the compost when firming it.

Sowing seeds

Scatter the seeds in two directions across the compost to get an even spread over the surface. If the seeds are very fine, it is easier to distribute them evenly, and see where they are sown, if you mix them thoroughly with some dry, fine sand first. Cover the seeds with a uniform thickness of sieved compost. Some seeds, often fine seeds, requires light to germinate so should be left uncovered; check the recommendation on the seed packet. Once sown, cover the container (*see below*) and leave it in a warm place to germinate, or put uncovered in a dark, warm place.

7 Turn the container through 90 degrees and sow the remaining seeds evenly across the compost.

8 Cover the seeds to no more than their own depth by sieving compost over them.

9 Label the seeds with their full name and date of sowing. Soft pencil is often the longest-lasting marker to use for this.

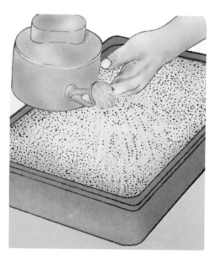

10 Water the seeds using a watering can with a fine rose (*see page 402*). Alternatively, stand the container in a tray of water for 15 minutes, then allow it to drain.

11 Cover the container with a pane of glass or a sheet of kitchen film to keep the seeds moist. Normally, this can be left in place until the seeds germinate.

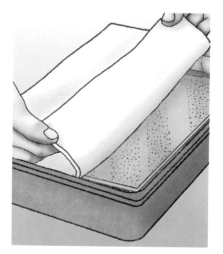

12 Place a sheet of paper over the glass or film to minimize temperature fluctuations. Stand the container in a warm place – around 21°C (70°F) suits most plants.

The developing seed

Once sufficient water has penetrated the seed coat, the warm, moist compost environment sets off a series of chemical reactions in the seed. These release nutrients from the seed's food store, giving the embryo the energy to start developing and to emerge through the seed coat to become a seedling. This is the process known as germination.

In broad terms, the higher the soil temperature, the more quickly germination will occur. However, forcing the seed to develop rapidly can lead to weak seedlings if light levels are low – as they often are in spring. In this situation, it is better to maintain a lower soil temperature to encourage slower, sturdier growth. Seed packets will generally give you a good idea of the best temperature range for any particular seed.

THE GERMINATING SEED

As a seed germinates, the embryo develops an initial root system below ground and a shoot system above. The seed leaves, or cotyledons, may stay under, or emerge above, the soil surface. They are usually simply shaped and rarely bear any resemblance to the plant's true leaves.

CARING FOR SEEDLINGS

1 Uncover the container as soon as the seedlings appear and place it in a well-lit area. Spray the seedlings with water as necessary, but do not get them waterlogged.

2 Transplant the seedlings, once they are large enough to handle, to move them on and give them more room. Using a dibber or similar small tool, loosen a group of seedlings, then gently lift one free. Handle seedlings by their leaves; never touch the fragile stems.

3 Hold each seedling in one hand and make a hole with the dibber in fresh compost in a prepared container. This may be another seed tray, an individual pot, or modules, depending on the plant's requirements.

4 Lower the seedling roots into the hole and firm the compost gently with the dibber. If the stem is a bit long, insert it a little deeper than it was before. Aim for 24–40 seedlings per tray.

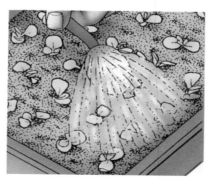

5 Water the seedlings once the container is filled, to settle the compost and allow to drain. Place the container in a warm, well-lit area to re-establish – a temperature of around 21°C (70°F) suits most plants.

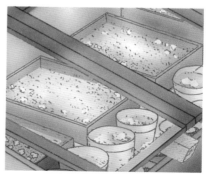

6 Harden off the seedlings once they start to grow again, to acclimatize them to outdoor conditions. Move them to a cool site, such as a cold frame, unheated greenhouse, or well-lit windowsill in a cool room. Raise the cold frame lid on sunny days, but close and insulate it overnight if severe frost threatens.

Seed sowing troubleshooter

Raising plants from seeds is one of the easier methods of propagation and should be straightforward, but if things go wrong the cause may not be obvious. This guide to the commonest problems affecting seeds and seedlings will help you to diagnose the problem and avoid it in future. You should maintain good hygiene, use sterile compost, and provide suitable conditions, usually warm, moist, and light – but not too hot, wet, or humid.

PROBLEM	CAUSE	SOLUTION
Seeds do not germinate	Seeds not viable (dead)	Buy fresh seeds. Most seeds can be stored for no more than three years in a cool (max 10°C/50°F), dry place.
	Compost too dry or too wet	Sow in moist compost. Water and drain after sowing. Water with a sprayer only if it is dry below the surface.
	Wrong temperature	Seeds can rot if too cold or cook if too hot. Check the temperature needed for your seeds (for example on the seed packet) and use a max–min thermometer to monitor the ambient temperature.
	Seeds requires special treatment	Unusual seeds may need different treatment; check the seed packet for special requirements.
Seeds germinate but do not emerge (dig some up to check)	Capping – the seedlings are unable to push through a crust of dried compost	Do not overheat the container and check seedlings daily. If the dry surface of the compost is heaving, use a sprayer to re-wet it so the seedlings can push through.
	Seeds sown too deep	Use fine vermiculite to cover very fine seeds – they often need light to germinate and vermiculite lets it through. Also it is easier to cover the seeds thinly.
Seedlings emerge in patches	Uneven conditions in compost	Firm and level compost carefully before sowing and water the compost from below.
	Uneven sowing	Mix small seeds with fine vermiculite or sand so that you can see where you have just sown them.
	Seeds naturally variable	Some seeds, such as that of wild flowers, germinate erratically. Home-saved seeds may also be variable.
Seedlings are etiolated (thin, pale, and drawn)	Too much heat and not enough light	If you cannot provide more light, keep them at a lower temperature.
Seedlings are lopsided	Uneven light	Rotate the container daily so they are evenly exposed.
Seedlings wither	Not enough moisture	Check daily and water just enough to keep moist.
	Too much heat, often from direct sun, can wither leaves even if the compost is moist	Maintain a humid atmosphere around newly emerged seedlings and shade them from direct sunlight.
Seedlings collapse	Seedlings affected by damping off (which rots the stems near the base)	This can occur soon after germination, or after pricking out, and is caused by a fungal infection (*see page 390*).
Seedlings fail to grow on	Too little warmth	Newly germinated seedlings require similar temperatures to those for germination – harden them off slowly to avoid a check in growth.
	Too few nutrients	Seed composts contain only enough nutrients for germination: prick out seedlings promptly or liquid feed.
	Too much water	Do not overwater small seedlings in large pots or newly pricked-out seedlings that may have damaged roots.

Raising trees & shrubs from seed

You can grow many trees and shrubs from seeds, and surprisingly rapidly in good growing conditions. Sow your own collected seeds as soon as they are ripe; they may germinate immediately or in the next spring. If you let the seeds dry out, they may become dormant and germinate far less readily. This is a survival mechanism to avoid the seeds germinating in unfavourable conditions, but it can be frustrating for the gardener.

There are ways to overcome seed dormancy. Seeds of trees and shrubs used to cold winters may need a period of chilling at 1–3°C (34–37°F). With home-saved seeds, sowing in autumn and placing the pot outdoors is often enough. You can also store and chill seeds in the fridge over winter for a spring sowing (*see below*). Chill bought seeds for six to eight weeks before sowing.

Hard seed coats

A tough coat may delay germination, perhaps for years. Pea-family seeds, such as laburnum, can be soaked for 24 hours in a vacuum flask of warm water; rinse the flask well after use as some of these seeds are poisonous. The seeds are ready to sow when they sink. You could also abrade the seed coats: line a jam jar with sandpaper, add seeds, replace the lid, and shake for 10 minutes or so.

CHILLING SEEDS

1 **Sift leafmould**, peat, composted bark, or vermiculite through a coarse sieve after measuring out by volume about 4 times as much of this medium as you have seeds. On its own, vermiculite does not need sifting.

2 **Add sufficient water** to the compost in a waterproof container to make the growing medium exude a little water when it is lightly squeezed in the hand. If it is too wet, the seeds may rot.

3 **Sprinkle the seeds** evenly over the surface of the damp growing compost.

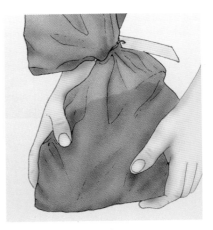

4 **Mix in the seeds** well. If the mixture looks too dense to hold enough air, add 1 part by volume of horticultural grit. Transfer the mixture to a plastic bag.

5 **Label the bag** and leave it in a warm place for 2–3 days. After this, chill the seeds by placing the bag in the fridge for up to 18 weeks, depending on the species.

6 **Check the bag** weekly: remove any germinating seeds and turn and shake the bag to keep the seeds aerated – most will not germinate until sown in warmer conditions.

ROOTS, BULBS, CORMS & TUBERS

Most gardeners will be familiar with the idea of propagating plants from sections of shoot, but many are unaware that the same process can also be carried out using roots. Some plants naturally produce buds and shoots from their roots as a way of spreading out and colonizing new ground. Other plants produce buds and shoots from severed sections of root, for example when plants are damaged by burrowing animals or land slips. These natural processes can also be exploited to propagate modified stems that grow underground, including rhizomes, tubers, corms, and bulbs.

Woody shrubs with suckers

Some woody plants produce suckers – shoots arising from the roots at a distance from the main stem (*see page 97*). You can sever these from the parent plant and transplant them. They are used to propagate raspberries and a number of other plants. Suckers generate a new plant quickly and with little effort. The drawback is that you have to wait for them to appear naturally, although many suckering plants can also be propagated by root cuttings.

Plants that sucker freely, such as sumachs, can be a nuisance – the suckers are difficult to control and may emerge far from the parent. Some plants, especially budded or grafted roses, plums, cherries, and lilacs, sucker from grafted rootstocks (*see page 243*). These suckers are often quite vigorous, and because they emerge from the rootstock, and not the top growth, they are unlikely to exhibit the same properties if propagated.

PROPAGATING WOODY SHRUBS FROM SUCKERS

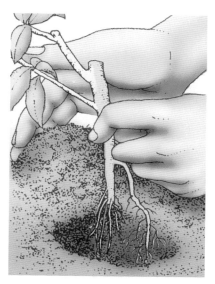

1 **Lift isolated suckers** from woody shrubs during the dormant season.

2 **Trim the roots** and cut back some of the top growth to reduce stress on the roots.

3 **Replant the trimmed sucker** immediately, to the same depth, and water in well.

411

Root cuttings

Relatively few plants propagate by root cuttings; the technique is used most often on a small number of herbaceous perennials but a number of trees, shrubs, and climbers can also be propagated in this way.

Root cuttings can be easier to care for than stem cuttings and are less likely to dry out, but they can be relatively slow to develop and the process is more stressful for the parent plant. You can greatly increase your chance of success by preparing the parent plant in the previous year (*see below*) to encourage plenty of new root growth from which you can take cuttings.

When to take root cuttings

A few species readily produce new plants from root cuttings at any time of year. Horseradish (*Armoracia rusticana*) is a notorious example, as any piece of root broken off at any time will quickly grow into a new plant, and it can easily become an invasive weed. Many troublesome weeds such as bindweed (*Convolvulus arvensis*) and ground elder (*Aegopodium podagraria*) also regrow readily from underground fragments, but these are not roots – they are modified underground stems known as rhizomes.

PREPARING THE PARENT PLANT FOR ROOT CUTTING MATERIAL

1 **Lift a healthy plant** from the ground during its dormant season.

2 **Cut back** any top growth. Shake any excess earth from the roots.

3 **Wash the roots** in a bucket of water, or hose them clean.

4 **Cut off the large roots** close to the crown, using a clean, sharp knife, and leave the fine roots.

5 **Replant the trimmed rootstock**, at the same level as it was before, to grow on.

6 **Allow the plant** to re-establish during the growing season; it should develop plenty of vigorous, new roots ready for propagation.

With most plants, however, the best time to take root cuttings is in the middle of the plants' dormant season. In the case of most herbaceous and woody plants, this will be during winter. Some hardy, herbaceous perennials, however, such as pasque flower (*Pulsatilla vulgaris*), start into growth as early as midwinter and are fully dormant in late summer and early autumn.

Trimming root cuttings

Root cuttings are sometimes potted up so that they lie horizontally in the compost. Much better results are obtained by inserting the cuttings vertically, but they must be the right way up. To make sure that you never plant your cutting upside down, always make a straight cut at the upper end, so that the top is flat, and a sloping cut at the lower end, so the bottom is tapered.

Size of the root cuttings

Once separated from the parent plant, the root cutting must have sufficient stored food in its tissues to survive and produce shoots and leaves. The minimum size of cutting needed will depend on the ambient temperature.

At lower temperatures, the cutting develops shoots and leaves more slowly, so it needs more stored food. It must therefore be larger than a cutting that is rooted in warmth. As a rule of thumb, if you are propagating your

OBTAINING CUTTING MATERIAL

1 **Trim off any top growth** that remains on the parent plant in the middle of the dormant season. Lift the plant carefully.

2 **Wash the soil from the roots** and take cuttings (*see below*) from the newly formed roots close to the crown.

3 **Return the parent plant** to its usual position in the garden and leave to grow on and develop more new roots for next year.

PREPARING A ROOT CUTTING

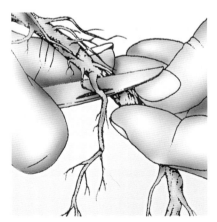

1 **Select roots** that are firm, plump, and undamaged. Cut off any side roots, with straight cuts close to the main root.

2 **Trim each root cutting** by first making a straight cut across and just below the severed top of the root cutting.

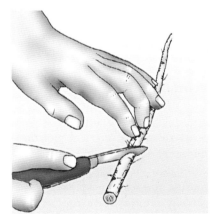

3 **Use a sloping cut** to remove the tapering, thin end of the root, to leave a cutting of uniform thickness.

STARTING ROOT CUTTINGS

1 **Fill a pot** with moist compost, and firm to 1cm (½in) below the rim. Make a hole with a dibber. Plant the cutting vertically, so that the flat end is uppermost and just flush with the compost surface. Space the cuttings 2.5–3.5cm (1–1½in) apart in the pot.

2 **Cover the top** of the compost with horticultural grit. This stops the tops of the cuttings drying out, but it is less moist than compost, which could promote rotting.

3 **Label and date** the pot after levelling off the grit using a ruler or piece of wood. Place the pot in a cold frame or propagator out of direct sunlight, or in a sheltered, shaded position outdoors.

4 **Keep watering** to the absolute minimum, but just enough to maintain a humid atmosphere, until the new plants are established and have developed new roots, then apply a liquid feed. Move the pot to a well-lit position once shoots appear, and gradually increase watering.

root cuttings outdoors, they will need to survive for up to 16 weeks before establishing and should be no less than 10cm (4in) long. In a cold frame, rooting should occur in about eight weeks and so cuttings should be no less than 5cm (2in) long.

In a warm greenhouse or propagator at a temperature of 18–24°C (64–75°F), the cuttings should establish in as little as four weeks, so they need be only 2.5cm (1in) long. If there is plentiful propagating material, however, make them a little longer than necessary to ensure success.

Starting root cuttings

Insert the prepared cuttings into 9cm (3½in) pots (*see above*). Use a multipurpose compost, which will retain a good balance of air and moisture and provide some nutrients once the cuttings start to grow. Unlike stem cuttings, root cuttings do not respond to hormone rooting powder; in fact, it has an adverse effect and actually inhibits formation of buds. If you space the cuttings evenly, you can fit seven into a 9cm (3½in) pot. Cover the cuttings with grit to keep the latent buds at their tops moist and aerated, but do not water them.

Care of the new plants

Often the first new shoots appear from root cuttings before they send out any new roots. Watering at this stage can cause rotting, so do not water the cuttings until you can see signs of rooting, such as the new roots emerging through holes at the base of the pot.

Once the cuttings are established, you can plant them directly in the ground if the soil is reasonably light, or in a cold frame in soil that has been improved by the addition of sand, peat, or peat substitute. However, unless you are dealing with very large numbers, it is usually more convenient to grow on the cuttings singly in pots. Cuttings that have been rooted in a heated environment will need to be hardened off before they are moved to a cooler area or planted outdoors.

Root cuttings of some plants, such as tree poppy (*Romneya coulteri*), do not like being dug up and having their roots disturbed. In such cases, it is best to place only one or two cuttings in each pot and treat them as a single plant. When transplanting out the new plant, once it has grown to a reasonable size, handle the rootball carefully and avoid disturbing the roots as much as possible.

TUBEROUS ROOTS

Growing under glass *see page 375* | **Propagation basics** *see page 396* | **Methods of propagation** *see page 404*

Tuberous roots

Some plants store food in swollen areas on their roots. This enables them to survive through dormant periods and provides a ready source of nutrients when growing conditions improve. In temperate climates, the dormant season is in winter, and the plants start to grow in spring, but in other parts of the world the dormant season may be at other times of year, when there is drought for example. Tuberous roots are often loosely called tubers, although true tubers are swollen underground stems, such as potatoes and Jerusalem artichokes (*see following page*). Tuberous roots may be annual or perennial (*see box, right*).

Dividing tuberous roots

Tuberous roots are propagated by division, but it is crucial to make sure that each portion has at least one healthy bud attached. On annual tuberous roots, the buds will be in the crown at the base of the old shoots; the tuberous part of the root alone does not have any buds and cannot reproduce itself. On perennial tuberous roots, there should be a cluster of buds in the centre of the crown; divide up the buds between slices of the tuberous root. Dust all cut surfaces with a fungicide powder.

After potting up the pieces of root individually, leave them in a frost-free place. Do not water them. Move the containers to a well-lit position once new shoots appear, to grow on. You can begin watering the plants normally. They may be planted out after all risk of frost is past.

TYPES OF TUBEROUS ROOT

Begonia
(perennial roots)

Dahlia
(annual roots)

Perennial tuberous roots from plants like begonias consist of just one, large, central, tuberous root, from which the shoots and fibrous, feeding roots emerge in the growing season. This type of tuberous root persists and grows in size sideways from one year to the next.

Annual tuberous roots from plants like dahlias grow every year in a cluster around the crown. The energy stored in these tuberous roots is used in the following year to produce new growth; as this happens, the old tuberous roots disintegrate and die.

DIVIDING ANNUAL TUBEROUS ROOTS

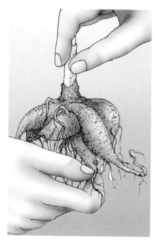

1 **Lift a plant**, here a dahlia, in autumn. Clean the crown thoroughly. Dust the entire crown with fungicidal powder, such as powdered sulphur.

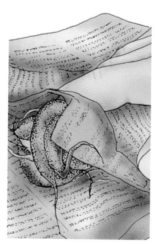

2 **Wrap the crown** in a sheet of newspaper. Store in a cool place at about 3–5°C (37–41°F) until the buds swell in spring.

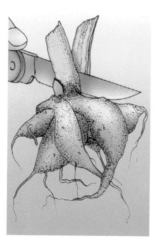

3 **Divide the tubers** into pieces, each with at least 1 crown bud. Dust all cut surfaces with fungicide. Leave in a dry, airy place at 20°C (68°F) for 2 days.

4 **Once the cut surfaces** have developed a corky protective layer, pot up each piece in moist, multipurpose compost. Keep in a frost-free area, in light or dark.

Tubers

True tubers develop on modified underground stems, usually annually, to help the plant get through periods of harsh weather, such as drought or cold. Potatoes have large numbers of tubers; most other plants with tubers, for example angel wings (*Caladium*) and waterlilies, produce very few. Several plants, including Jerusalem and Chinese artichokes, have edible tubers. On washed potato tubers you can clearly see the many buds, or eyes, on their skins. These rapidly develop into new shoots when the environmental conditions are right.

Dividing tubers

When growing tubers as a food crop, it is normal to plant the whole tuber and allow each plant to develop a number of shoots. However, if you have only a few tubers and want more plants, they can be divided.

Tubercles

A few plants produce miniature tubers (tubercles) above ground, in the leaf axils. If left, they fall off and develop into new plants. You can remove mature tubercles – they should come away easily – and plant them at twice their own depth to grow on. Plants that form tubercles include *Achimenes*, *Begonia grandis* subsp. *evansiana*, Chinese artichokes, and yams (*Dioscorea batatas*).

POTATO TUBERS

Tubers are storage organs that develop as roundish, swollen areas on modified underground stems, usually at the tips.

DIVIDING TUBERS

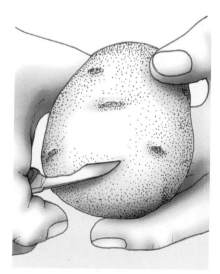

1 **Cut the tuber**, here a potato, into pieces with a clean, sharp knife, just before growth begins in spring. Ensure that each piece has at least 1 good bud or eye. Eyes usually consist of several buds close together.

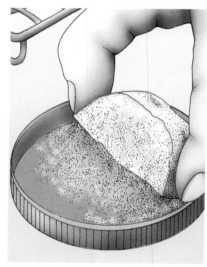

2 **Dust the cut surfaces** with a fungicide, such as powdered sulphur, to reduce risk of rot. Stand the pieces on a wire rack in a dry place, like an airing cupboard, at 20°C (68°F) for 2 days, until the cut surfaces scab over.

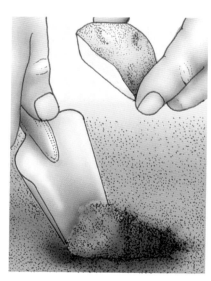

3 **Plant the pieces** in the open ground in a hole that is twice the depth of the tuber. Do this as soon as the cut surfaces form a protective corky layer. If you leave them too long, they will start to dry up.

Rhizomes

A rhizome is a modified stem that grows more or less horizontally, on or just below the soil surface. Since they are modified stems, they readily produce new shoots and leaves and most have roots already, or will produce them if separated from the parent plant. They are therefore highly suitable for propagation.

Some rhizomes, such those of bearded irises, are used by the plant mainly as storage organs. They are relatively short and fat, and grow in recognizable sections year by year. The plant tends to spread outwards, then die off in the centre as the oldest rhizomes deteriorate. To maintain the vigour and appearance of the plants, propagate them regularly from new rhizomes and discard the older ones.

Other plants produce much thinner, longer, rhizomes. Although they often have some food-storage function, these rhizomes are mainly used by the plant to help it spread out and colonize new ground.

Many troublesome weeds, such as couch grass and ground elder, and some garden plants like mints and bamboos, are invasive because of their rhizomatous habit. As well as being very efficient colonizers, they use stored nutrients to develop new plants rapidly from broken rhizomes. Luckily, you can also benefit from the regenerative ability of rhizomes to increase such garden plants as arum lilies (*Zantedeschia*), bergenias, cannas, catmints, and rodgersias.

DIVIDING RHIZOMES

1 **Divide mature rhizomes**, here a bearded iris, after flowering, when old roots die back and new rhizomes start to form.

2 **Lift a clump** using a garden fork, and carefully knock as much soil as possible from the roots.

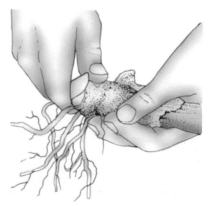

3 **Carefully cut away** and discard any old rhizomes from the clump, leaving the current season's growth.

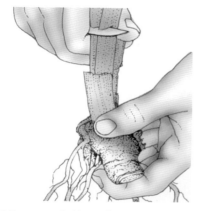

4 **Prepare each rhizome** by shortening the leaf blades (or stems in other plants) by about half. This will reduce wind rock and water loss until the new roots are established. Cut back the existing roots to 5–8cm (2–3in).

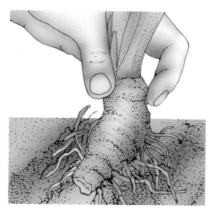

5 **Replant each rhizome** at the same depth as it was before. For irises, this is at the surface: plant the rhizome on a ridge of soil, and spread out its roots in small trenches on either side.

6 **Firm back soil** over the roots. With irises, leave the rhizome itself barely covered. Label and water to settle the soil in place.

Corms

Corms look similar to bulbs and both store food while the plant is dormant. However, they have evolved from different structures. Unlike bulbs, corms are modified underground stems composed of solid tissue and usually flattened in shape. Thin, fibrous modified leaves enclose the corm to protect it from injury and drying out. One or more buds at the top produce leaves and, if the corm is large enough, one or more flowers. Roots develop from the often concave base.

When the leaves die down at the end of the season, new corms develop at the base of each shoot. These form on top of the previous year's corm, which gradually withers. In this way, one corm naturally divides into several over time. If it is necessary to increase corms more quickly, they can be propagated by division (*see below*).

Dividing corms

Cut a large, healthy corm into several pieces in autumn and replant each section (*see below*). For small corms, or those that have too few buds, remove the main stem by snapping it off or cutting it out with a knife to induce the side buds to produce shoots; at the end of the growing season, you should have several small corms or a large corm with several buds that can be cut up.

PROPAGATING FROM CORMELS

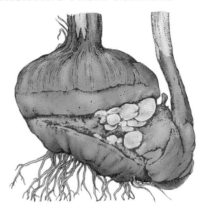

Cormels are miniature corms that sometimes form between the new corm and the old, disintegrating corm. The number produced can vary widely, and will increase the deeper the corm is planted – a gladiolus corm may produce as may as 50 cormels.

To use cormels for propagation, lift the parent corm at the end of the growing season and separate all the cormels. Store them in an environment that is dry, well-ventilated, and frost free but cool – below 5°C (41°F). Plant out the following spring – soak them first for 24 hours if they have become dried out. Cormels are likely to take at least 2 years to reach flowering size.

DIVIDING CORMELS

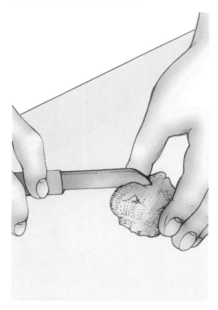

1 **Cut each corm** into several pieces, ensuring that each piece has at least one bud, just before planting time in autumn. Use a clean knife to avoid contamination.

2 **Dust the cut surfaces** with fungicidal powder to reduce the risk of rotting. Leave the pieces on a wire rack in a warm, dry place for a day or two to seal the cut surfaces.

3 **Once the pieces have formed** a corky protective layer over the cut surfaces, plant each singly in a pot of multipurpose compost, or in open ground. Label and date clearly.

Bulbs

Bulbs propagate themselves naturally by division, forming new bulbs either side of the parent bulb at the end of the growing season. The large parent bulb either persists, as in daffodils and amaryllis, or disintegrates after flowering, as with tulips and bulbous irises. The bulbs can be dug up and separated at the end of the growing season, and planted at twice their own depth. For many vigorous garden bulbs, this is the ideal method of propagation, since it is quick and easy.

BULBLETS & BULBILS

A small number of bulbs, particularly lilies, form tiny bulbs called bulblets on their stem underground. All of these have the potential to grow into new plants. Lilies that produce bulblets can be encouraged to produce more from their leaf bases by burying the plant (*see below*).

Bulbils are tiny bulbs that develop in leaf bases of some lilies and in the flowerheads of some alliums. After flowering, pot up the bulbils (*see bottom*).

PROPAGATING FROM BULBLETS

1 **Select a suitable lily** in flower. Pinch out any buds and flowers. Twist the stem out of the bulb, leaving the bulb in the ground.

2 **Dig a sloping trench** two thirds as long as the stem, 15cm (6in) deep at one end. Lay the stem in the trench, with the top protruding; fill with sand or free-draining compost and label.

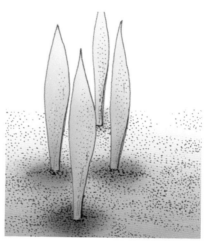

3 **Dig up the remains** of the stem in autumn. Bulblets should have formed in the leaf axils on the lower stem. Detach them and replant at twice their own depth to grow on.

PROPAGATING FROM BULBILS

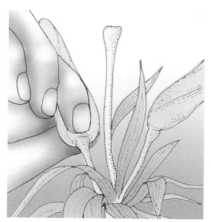

1 **Remove all the flower buds** just before they start to open, from a suitable lily species, such as *Lilium bulbiferum*, *L. canadense*, *L. longiflorum*, and *L. pardalinum*.

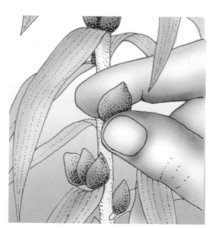

2 **Bulbils should develop** in the leaf axils. Fully developed bulbils often darken and are pulled away easily. Fill a pot with multipurpose compost, including loam for long-term structure.

3 **Set the bulbils** about 2.5cm (1in) apart and one third buried. Cover with grit. Place in a cold frame, cold greenhouse, or sheltered site to bulk up. Plant out in autumn of the next year.

BULB SCALING

You can bulk up virtually any lily species and other scaly bulbs, such as fritillaries, by scaling. Use bulbs freshly lifted at the end of the growing season for the best plump, healthy bulbs. You can use pre-packed bulbs, but they are often not available until spring and are therefore in poorer condition. To reduce disturbance to the parent plant, you can simply dig down carefully next to the parent bulb where it is growing and snap off a few scale leaves. Replace the soil, wash the scales free of soil, then place them in bags of compost to form new bulblets (*see below*).

BULB SCALING

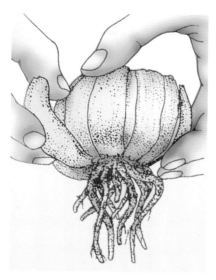

1 **Remove a few scale** leaves from the bulb before planting, one at a time, by pressing them outwards until they snap or cutting them off close to the base plate. The remaining bulb can then be planted normally.

2 **Place the scale** leaves in a bag filled with fungicidal powder, such as sulphur; shake vigorously. Put them in another bag and mix with 4 times their volume of damp vermiculite, or 50:50 sand and peat or peat substitute.

3 **Blow into the bag**, then tie around the neck. Store in a warm place at 20°C (68°F), such as an airing cupboard, so that new plantlets can develop.

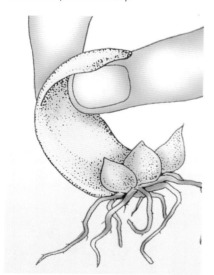

4 **Remove the scale leaves** from the plastic bag as soon as the bulblets appear on the broken basal surface. This is likely to take 6–8 weeks.

5 **Plant scale leaves** singly into 8–9cm (3–3½in) pots, or line out in a deep tray, of moist, multipurpose compost. Make sure the scale tips are visible above the compost, cover with grit, and label. Place in a warm, light area.

6 **Separate new bulblets** from the remains of the scale leaves in summer, after the bulblets' new leaves have died down. Replant the bulblets and grow on.

BULB SCOOPING & SCORING

Some bulbs, like hyacinths, form bulblets very slowly, so you need to induce their formation in order to be able to propagate them. There are two techniques by which you can use to do this: scooping and scoring.

Scooping involves removing the entire base plate with a curved cut. Use a sharpened teaspoon if possible – not only will it make a cleaner cut, cutting straight across with a knife would remove too much tissue from the base of the outer layers of the bulb. The cut surfaces will callus over, then bulblets will form. Move the scooped bulbs

into a cold frame, cold greenhouse, or sheltered site outdoors in spring. The bulblets will produce leaves and the old bulb will slowly disintegrate.

Scoring works in the same way as scooping. It produces fewer bulblets, but as these are likely to be larger, they should flower more quickly. Other bulbs like grape hyacinths, daffodils, snowdrops, and scillas can be propagated by scooping or scoring, but unless you are dealing with a variety that is very slow to increase, most of these reproduce quite quickly by natural methods.

SCOOPING BULBS

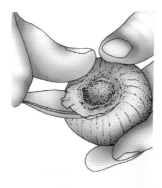
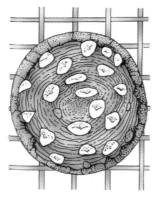

1 **Sharpen the edge** of an old teaspoon. Use it to remove the basal plate cleanly without crushing the rest of the bulb.

2 **Check the base** of every leaf scale is removed. Dust the cut surface with fungicidal powder. Set upside down on a wire rack or a small tray of dry sand.

3 **Leave in a dry**, dark place at 20°C (68°F). In 2–3 months, when bulblets appear, plant the bulb upside down, with bulblets just below the compost surface.

4 **Separate the bulblets** after lifting the remains of the old bulb at the end of the season. Replant at once. They should flower in 3–4 years' time.

SCORING BULBS

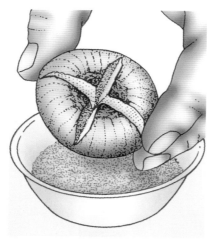
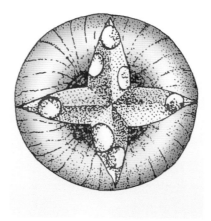

1 **Score 2 cuts** at right angles to each other across the basal plate of the bulb and about 8mm (⅜in) deep, with a sharp knife. On large bulbs, make 2 further cuts at 90-degree angles to produce an eight-pointed star.

2 **Leave the bulb** in a warm, dry area for a day or so, until the bulb opens out. Dust the cut surfaces with a fungicide, such as powdered sulphur.

3 **Place the bulb** on a wire tray. Store in a warm place, such as an airing cupboard, at 20°C (68°F) until bulblets develop, then treat as for scooped bulbs. Bulblets should reach flowering size in 2–3 years.

DIVISION

Dividing clump-forming plants is such a straightforward process that it barely merits being called a technique at all. However, timing can be important, and it is also worth knowing about ways of making the process easier and more successful. Although it does not yield as many new plants as seeds or cuttings, division is a common way to propagate many herbaceous perennials, and is also used periodically to rejuvenate plants, keeping them young, vigorous, and free flowering. Some herbaceous perennials produce offsets or runners that lend themselves to division.

Herbaceous plants

Most division is carried out on herbaceous perennials; many naturally form crowns with numerous, distinct stems that make it easy to separate the crown into sections. Often, the crown extends outwards, producing the newest shoots at the edges, and the centre becomes woody and less productive over the years. Division is the easiest method of rejuvenating such plants. As well as perennials with fleshy or fibrous crowns, shown here, you can divide those with tuberous roots, tubers, and rhizomes.

Plants with fleshy crowns

Many herbaceous perennials, such as astilbes, hostas, European primulas, and meadow rues (*Thalictrum*), develop a compact, fleshy crown that is not easy to pull apart. The best time to divide these plants is towards the end of their dormant season, when buds will begin to shoot and you can more easily select the most vigorous sections of the crown. Replant or pot up the divisions quickly to avoid the roots drying out too much (*see below*).

DIVIDING A HERBACEOUS PLANT WITH A FLESHY CROWN

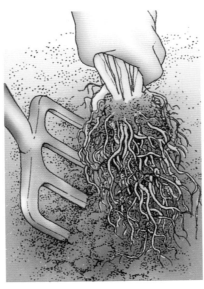

1 **Lift the plant** to be divided towards the end of its dormant season, using a garden fork. Shake off as much soil as possible.

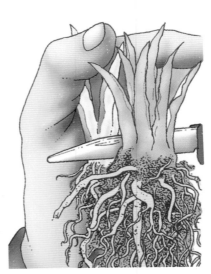

2 **Cut the crown** into pieces with a suitably sized, sharp knife. Washing it first will help you to see the roots. Make sure that each section has at least one, well-developed bud.

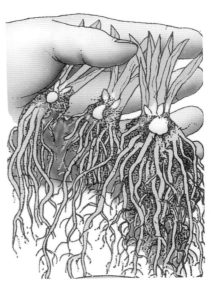

3 **Dust the cut surfaces** with fungicidal powder to reduce the risk of rotting. Replant immediately, either in the ground or in a pot of multipurpose compost.

HERBACEOUS PLANTS

Herbaceous perennials *see page 77* | **Methods of propagation** *see page 404* | **Roots, bulbs, corms & tubers** *see page 411*

DIVIDING A HERBACEOUS PLANT WITH A FIBROUS CROWN

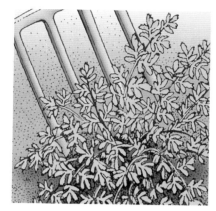

1 Dig up the plant to be divided at a time when new shoots are being produced; this depends on when it flowers.

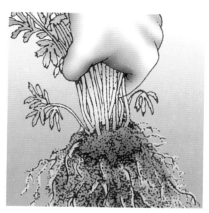

2 Shake off as much soil as possible. Wash the crown and roots in water or hose it clean to make the task easier. Remove any weeds at the same time.

3 Cut down tall stems to minimize water loss while the new divisions are being prepared; this is especially important if you are dividing the plant during summer.

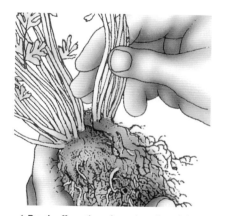

4 Break off sections from the edge of the crown, where the young shoots are generally produced, making sure that each has at least 1 good basal bud or shoot.

5 Replant new divisions without delay, at the same depth as the plant was before. Discard the woody sections from the centre of the old clump.

6 Water very thoroughly to settle the soil in around the roots, using a watering can with a rose. Keep the new plants free of weeds while they become established.

Plants with fibrous crowns

Many herbaceous perennials that have fibrous roots and relatively loose crowns, such as chrysanthemums and Michaelmas daisies, need to be divided every two or three years to maintain performance (*see above*). For most species, the best time to do this is immediately after flowering; for very late-flowering plants, it will be the following spring. If the crown is very tough, use an old carving knife or similar blade to split it up.

Plants that divide naturally

Some plants, such as alpine bellflowers (*Campanula*), are very easy to divide since their crowns separate naturally into individual plantlets each year. After flowering, or in spring if the plant flowers in autumn, lift the plant and tease apart the plantlets. Replant as soon as possible and water well. Crowns that are lifted and divided fairly frequently will produce large numbers of divisions; plants left where they are growing for a long period may only produce a few, although the divisions will be larger.

Dividing shrubs

A few shrubs naturally develop as dense clumps of stems: lift each plant in its dormant season and wash off any soil. Divide the clump into suitably sized portions; discard any older parts that have few roots. Cut back the stems fairly hard to reduce water loss when the buds break in spring, before the damaged roots have regrown. Replant the divisions to the same depth as the original plant. You can also divide shrubs that produce suckers (*see page 411*).

Offsets & runners

Offsets and runners are very similar: they are both plantlets that develop on the ends of stems arising from the parent plant. The main differences are that offsets tend to have thicker, shorter stems and may be slower than runners to develop their own roots.

If a plant produces few offsets, remove its growing tip to prompt offsets to form. Most offsets can be removed in their first year, but with some plants, such as yuccas, the offsets grow slowly and should only be separated when they are a few years old.

Offsets

These plantlets develop on the ends of sideshoots growing above or below ground (*see bottom*), on plants like houseleeks (*Sempervivum*) and New Zealand flax (*Phormium*). Most offsets initially have only minimal roots and are dependent on the parent plant. Roots normally develop towards the end of the growing season; encourage them by severing the connecting stems.

Runners

A runner is a more or less a horizontal stem that arises from the plant crown and creeps over the ground (*see below*). It will produce a plantlet at the end, although it may first develop scale leaves and roots at intervals along its length. Once a new plant establishes, the runner often dies away. This is how strawberries, *Geum reptans*, herbaceous potentillas, and some grasses reproduce.

PROPAGATING WITH RUNNERS

1 **Thin out some runners** in early summer to encourage strong growth: if new plants are required, it is best to have a few, larger plants rather than a tangled mat of smaller ones.

2 **Fill a pot** with loam-based compost and firm to within 1cm (½in) of the rim. Dig a hole beneath the plantlet; set the pot in the hole, and pin the plantlet onto the compost.

3 **Pin down as many plantlets** as you need in a star-shaped pattern around the plant. When they are fully established, sever the connecting stems and transplant.

PROPAGATING WITH OFFSETS

1 **Separate a young offset** from the parent plant, here a houseleek, by gently pulling it away, preferably in spring. Trim any broken stems from the parent plant to avoid rot.

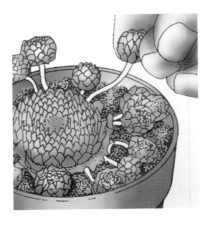

2 **Plant each offset** in a pot filled with multipurpose compost with added grit; this will ensure the compost is free-draining and will encourage good root development. Once the offset has established, you can plant it out.

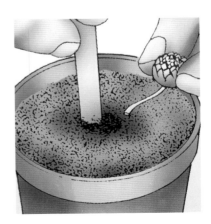

Growing under glass *see page 375* | **Propagation basics** *see page 396* | **Methods of propagation** *see page 404*

STEMS

Growing plants from short sections of stem is the most useful method of vegetative propagation, because it can be used for so many different plants. The various techniques all involve initiating, developing, and establishing a root system on a portion of stem. This may be done by encouraging the stem to produce roots before severing the new plant from the old, a technique known as layering, or you can separate the stem section from the parent plant first, to create a cutting. Layering usually only produces a small number of new plants; cuttings, on the other hand, can yield a large quantity of new plants.

Understanding cuttings

Cuttings may be taken successfully from almost any type of plant, and they are widely used to propagate climbers, conifers, herbaceous perennials, herbs, shrubs, and soft fruit, as well as many indoor plants.

Suitable cutting material

The ability of a stem to produce roots, and therefore its suitability for propagation, depends greatly on its age. New shoots from a hard-pruned plant root more easily than old stems. However, if the plant is old, even new shoots root less readily than new stems from a young plant.

Plants that can only be propagated vegetatively, such as named varieties of camellia, are often difficult to propagate. This is because all the plants in cultivation are clones and therefore all the same age. You will find it easier to root cuttings taken from a newly introduced variety than one from a plant bred 50 years ago.

PARTS OF A STEM

Apical bud

Node

Internode

Leaf

Leaf axil

Axillary bud

Different types of cutting may use different sections of stem, so it is useful to recognize the parts of a stem. At the top, or apex, is the apical bud. Below it are the leaves, each joining the stem at an angle at the axil; in each axil is an axillary bud.

The often slightly swollen area of stem that produces the leaf and bud is called the leaf joint, or node. The section of stem between two nodes is called the internode.

WAYS TO GIRDLE A STEM

When layering, you may find it difficult to encourage old stems, or the stems of old plants, to take root. One ancient technique that can be useful in such cases is girdling, where the stem is wounded deliberately – in one of a variety of ways (*see right*) – to either impede or stop the flow of nutrients to the rest of the branch. This extra bit of help should stimulate rooting if it is layered in the normal way (*see pages 426–427*). Girdling is also used in air layering (*see page 428*).

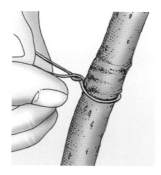

Twist copper wire tightly around the stem where it will be bent.

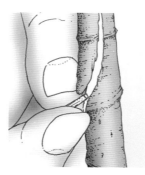

Cut at an angle into the bark. Push a matchstick into the gap.

Remove a ring of bark from around the stem 5mm (¼in) wide.

Layering

This is one of the oldest techniques used to propagate woody plants, exploiting a process that occurs naturally with some shrubs like dogwoods. The advantage of layering is that the young, new plant is kept alive by the parent until its own roots are established. For this reason,

layering can be successful with plants that are very difficult to propagate from cuttings. The technique is most often used for shrubs and climbers and is the best way to propagate desirable but difficult shrubs, such as magnolias, parrotias, or the dramatically coloured vine,

SIMPLE LAYERING

1 **Prune back some** low branches on the parent plant during winter. This will encourage the production of young, flexible, vigorous shoots that will root more readily and are more amenable to being layered.

2 **Cultivate the soil** around the plant in late winter or early spring. If needed, add grit and bulky, organic material to open up the soil for good rooting.

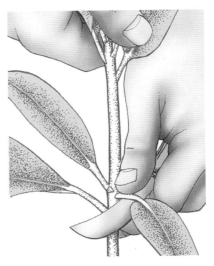

3 **Trim the leaves** and sideshoots from a young, vigorous stem along a 10–30cm (4–12in) length below the growing tip.

4 **Bring the stem** down to ground level and mark its position on the soil, 20–25cm (8–10in) behind its tip.

5 **Dig a small trench** from the marked point. Start the end of the trench with a straight side 10–15cm (4–6in) deep and slope it up towards the parent plant.

6 **Bend the stem** at right angles 20–25cm (8–10in) behind the tip. If necessary, girdle the stem to promote rooting (*see page 425*). Peg the shoot down in the trench against the straight side, using a strong wire staple.

Vitis coignetiae. Simple layering (*see below*) is also good for raising border carnations, which will root in just six weeks if pegged down in mid- or late summer.

The main drawback of layering is that it is usually practical to take only one or two layers at a time from the parent plant. Also, it is not always convenient to propagate shoots where the plant is growing.

Bending the shoot during the process induces root formation by restricting the movement of food and hormones through the tissues of the stem. With plants that are reluctant to root, you should also wound the stem by girdling it (*see page 425*). While the stem is buried, keep the soil reasonably moist, especially in dry periods. Rooting usually occurs in summer.

7 **Return the soil** to the trench, burying the stem, but leaving the tip exposed. Firm in well. Excluding light from the stem is vital to encouraging rooting, so the earlier this is done, the earlier roots will start to form.

8 **Water the stem well**, using a watering can with a coarse rose. Keep the soil moist, especially in dry weather. Rooting should occur during summer.

9 **Sever the layered stem** close to the parent plant in autumn, using clean secateurs. Leave the stem buried and undisturbed to establish independently.

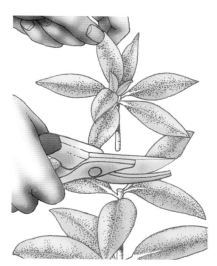

10 **Cut off the growing tip** from the rooted layer 3–4 weeks later, in order to direct the plant's resources to the roots.

11 **Lift the layer** to check whether it is well rooted. If not, replant it and leave in place for another year.

12 **Replant the well-rooted layer**, either in the open ground or in a pot of multipurpose compost. Label, and leave it to establish.

AIR LAYERING

This interesting technique is sometimes known as Chinese layering, or by its French name of marcottage. It makes it possible to layer a plant without having to bend a stem to soil level or find space for the layer to root. It is useful for plants like Japanese maples, which are difficult to root as cuttings. Carry out air layering in spring on mature growth of the previous season, or in late summer on semi-ripe shoots of the current season's growth.

AIR LAYERING

1 Trim any leaves and sideshoots from a 15–30cm (6–12in) length below the tip of the stem to be air layered. Girdle the stem (*see page 425*) to encourage food and growth hormones to build up in this region of the stem and help root formation. Treat the stem or cut surfaces with hormone rooting powder.

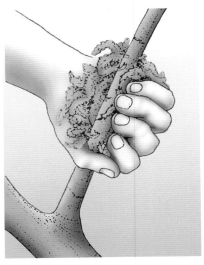

2 Soak some moss overnight so that it is thoroughly wet. Knead 2 large handfuls into a ball about 6cm (2½in) across. Split the ball in half, using your thumbs, in the same way as you would divide an orange. Place the two halves around the wounded stem and knead the moss together again so that the ball remains firm.

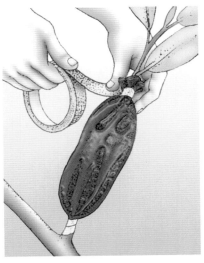

3 Secure the moss in place with a square of black plastic. Fix it to the stem with sticky insulating tape. The black plastic will retain moisture, maintain a warm environment, and exclude light from the stem.

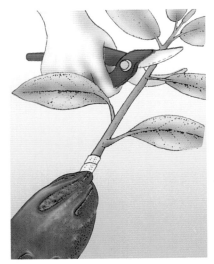

4 Prune back any new growth on the rooted layer towards the end of winter. The layered stem will usually take at least a full growing season to produce adequate roots – remove the plastic to check.

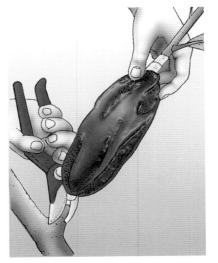

5 Cut the stem just below the point of layering, using a pair of secateurs, once it has produced a good root system. Remove the black plastic wrapping.

6 Loosen the moss and roots slightly. Then pot in loam-based, multipurpose compost and firm in gently. Place in a protected environment until more roots grow and the new plant becomes established.

LAYERING

Growing under glass *see page 375* | **Propagation basics** *see page 396* | **Methods of propagation** *see page 404*

TIP LAYERING

This specialized technique is used for blackberries and other *Rubus* species. Many of these plants tip layer themselves naturally – a process that enables wild blackberries to colonize new ground. You can harness this ability, with a little modification, to increase suitable plants. Cultivate the soil where the layer is to root, to ensure that it is opened up for good rooting. It also lessens damage to the roots when the layers are lifted.

TIP LAYERING

1 **Select a stem** arising from the plant crown in spring; it should be new and strong. As soon as the stem reaches 40–45cm (16–18in), remove the tip. Continue to remove the tips until midsummer when 6–8 sideshoots should have developed. Cultivate the soil, adding grit and bulky organic matter to the top 15cm (6in).

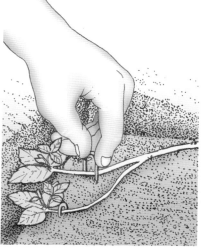

2 **Dig a sloping trench** 10cm (4in) deep where the bent stem tip touches the ground. It should be sloped towards the parent plant. Pin down the stem tip in the deepest part of the trench with a strong wire staple.

3 **Firm and water**, using a watering can fitted with a coarse rose, after you have replaced the soil, completely covering the tips of the shoot. Shoots should appear above ground level in about 3 weeks.

4 **Cut the stem** close to the parent plant in early autumn, to encourage the layer to become established as an independent plant.

5 **Cut away the** remainder of the layered stem, on the side of the parent plant, once it has dropped its leaves. Shorten some of the new topgrowth made by the rooted layer.

6 **Lift the layer** carefully to avoid damaging its fine, fibrous roots. Plant it at once in well-cultivated soil. Protect layers that cannot be replanted immediately from drying out by wrapping in damp newspaper in a plastic bag.

Stem cuttings

Taking a cutting is very simple – the difficulty lies in keeping the stem alive and healthy while encouraging it to root and develop into a new plant. Drying out and attack by fungal rots are your main enemies.

Until the cutting forms new roots, it relies on its food reserves to stay alive. Immature (softwood) cuttings have the lowest food reserves and are at greatest risk of dehydration and rot; you must encourage them to root as quickly as possible, by artificially controlling the environment. Hardwood cuttings are less prone to drying out or rotting as they have greater food reserves; they can be left to root more slowly, with less protection.

Environmental control

The rate at which a stem cutting roots depends on the temperature around it. If the entire cutting is warm, the tip grows, diverting nutrients away from new roots, so keep the base warm and the rest of the shoot cool.

Softwood cuttings benefit from bottom heat of 20°C (68°F) and cool air; keep them enclosed to maintain humidity and stop them wilting. Hardwood cuttings root well outdoors if the soil is warm enough. Protect greenwood, semi-ripe, and evergreen cuttings in a cold frame, polytunnel, or greenhouse.

WHERE TO CUT A STEM

Nodal cut   Internodal cut

You can take cuttings at several different places on the stem. A nodal cutting is severed just below a bud at a leaf joint, known as a node. Nodal cuttings are used for soft, immature stems because the tissue just below a node is harder and is more resistant to fungal rots. With an internodal cutting, you sever the stem between the nodes; this type of cutting is used mainly for more mature, woodier stems and is more economical since you can obtain more cuttings from a stem.

WHEN TO TAKE CUTTINGS

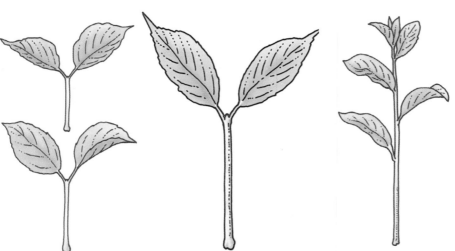
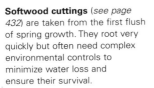

Softwood cuttings (*see page 432*) are taken from the first flush of spring growth. They root very quickly but often need complex environmental controls to minimize water loss and ensure their survival.

Greenwood cuttings (*see page 433*) are taken from the tips of leafy stems from early to midsummer. Their stems are still soft, and they need the protection of a controlled environment.

Semi-ripe cuttings (*see page 435*) are taken in late summer from stems that are growing more slowly, although still in active growth, and have started to harden. They are more resilient than softwood cuttings.

Hardwood cuttings (*see page 436*) are taken from the leafless, dormant stems of deciduous plants. They require only minimal environmental control to ensure their survival.

MAKING A LEAF-BUD CUTTING

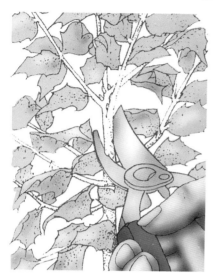

1 **Prune the parent plant** in winter to encourage new, vigorous stems. Select a new, semi-ripe stem later in the season.

2 **Cut the chosen stem**, which should have viable buds in its axils. The 4 leaves shown here are divided into leaflets.

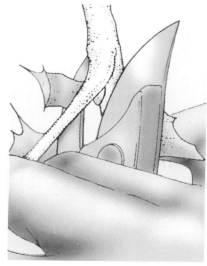

3 **Make an angled cut** just above the leaf axil bud (here, the stem is held upside down).

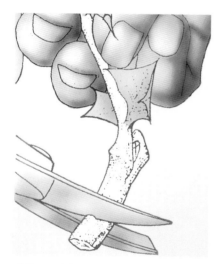

4 **Cut straight across** the stem, 3–4cm (1¼–1½in) below the top cut, to give enough stem to anchor the cutting while it produces roots.

5 **Reduce the size** of the leaf if it is large, so that the cutting is easier to handle and takes up less space. It will also reduce water loss from the cutting.

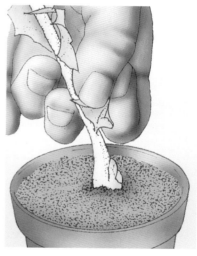

6 **Plant the cutting** in a pot of cuttings or multipurpose compost so that the bud is roughly level with the compost surface. Firm sufficiently to prevent rocking, and water in.

LEAF-BUD CUTTINGS

This type of cutting is generally taken from semi-ripe stems. Each cutting consists of a leaf, a bud in the leaf axil, and a very short piece of stem. The leaf supplies energy to support the cutting and regenerative process, the bud forms the basis of the new stem system, and the section of stem produces the roots. A large number of cuttings can be taken from a small amount of propagation material. As with other types of cutting, young shoots produce the best results so, where possible, prune the parent plant back hard beforehand to encourage new, vigorous growth. Take care to select suitable shoots with healthy, mature leaves when taking the cuttings. An immature leaf may wilt or rot or continue to grow and use up nutrients needed to produce new roots.

After preparing, place cuttings from hardy plants in a cold frame, and less hardy material in a well-lit, protected environment, such as a propagator.

SOFTWOOD CUTTINGS

Soft stem growth is produced continuously at the tips of all stems during the growing season. As it matures, this new growth gradually hardens and becomes woody. Softwood cuttings are taken in spring from the fast-growing tips, as soon as they are long enough.

Because they are taken from the youngest part of the stem while it is in active growth, softwood cuttings have the greatest capacity to form new roots relatively quickly. Unfortunately, they are also the most difficult type of

cutting to keep alive; their immature leaves dry out very easily, especially in warm conditions, and the soft stems are very vulnerable to attack from fungal rots.

Many houseplants are also propagated from softwood cuttings. They will frequently root more readily in a heated propagator, which keeps the bases of the cuttings at a temperature of 21–24°C (70–75°F). Some plants, such as busy Lizzies (*Impatiens*) and fuchsias, root so easily that they can simply be stood in a jar of water.

MAKING A SOFTWOOD CUTTING

1 **Firm the compost** to within 1cm (½in) of the rim. Do this before taking the cuttings, so they are potted up as quickly as possible.

2 **Remove a fast-growing tip** of a stem in spring. Take shoots less than 10cm (4in) long with a heel (*see page 434*).

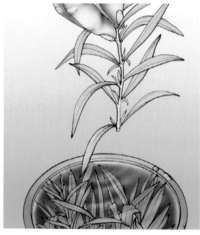

3 **Put the cuttings** at once into a plastic bag or bucket of water in shade, or store in the fridge if you cannot prepare them immediately.

4 **Shorten each cutting** to about 10cm (4in) long, cutting 3mm (⅛in) below a leaf joint with a sharp knife – or trim the tail if the cutting has a heel (*see inset*).

5 **Remove the leaves** from the lower one third of the stem. Hormone rooting powder may encourage some softwood cuttings to root, but it is not usually needed.

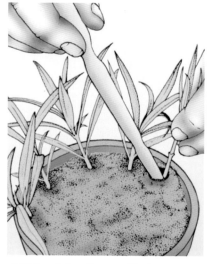

6 **Make a hole** with a pencil in the compost. Plant each cutting up to its leaves, taking care not to damage the stem base. Space the cuttings so their leaves do not touch.

PREPARING THE PARENT PLANT

If you have time to plan ahead, in winter you can prune back hard woody plants from which you want to propagate. This encourages the production of fresh, fast-growing stems in spring, providing a good supply of cuttings material with a high capacity to produce new roots.

Tips of plants taken later, in early summer, will be slower growing, more mature, and root less easily than softwood cuttings. They are referred to as greenwood cuttings and are often used to propagate herbaceous plants. The procedure is the same as for softwood cuttings.

Taking a softwood cutting

First prepare the containers so that you can plant the cuttings immediately, as it is vital to avoid any water loss from the cuttings material. Fill the container with moist, free-draining, multipurpose or cuttings compost.

Early morning is the ideal time to gather cuttings material, because the shoots will be turgid (full of water) after the cool of the night. Take fast-growing tips of stems because they will be full of growth hormones. If you cannot deal with the cuttings immediately, you can store them for approximately 24 hours by putting them in a sealed, plastic box in the salad drawer of the fridge.

After planting the cuttings, cover them to avoid loss of moisture through transpiration: put the container in a propagator or cover with a plastic bag supported on a loop of wire, and seal it around the pot with a rubber band. It is important that the cuttings root quickly, before they succumb to the vagaries of their environment, so use bottom heat if possible to encourage rooting. If the atmosphere is too warm, it will force cuttings to grow upwards, diverting energy from root production; too dry an atmosphere will cause the cuttings to wilt. They need a delicate balance of warmth, bright, indirect light, humidity, and adequate ventilation.

7 **Settle in the cuttings** by watering from above, using a can with a fine rose. Label, then place in a propagator, or cover with a plastic bag, to maintain humidity.

8 **Harden off cuttings** gradually when they have rooted, by opening the vents in the propagator, or cutting off the corners of the plastic bag.

9 **Pot the cuttings** individually in soil-based, multipurpose compost once they are hardened off.

HEEL & MALLET CUTTINGS

With some plants, it helps the cutting to survive if a small section of older, parent wood is left attached to the cutting, which helps to protect the base of the cutting from fungal rots. The technique is used with material taken from plants that may be particularly susceptible to rot, such as those with hollow stems, and for cuttings that take a long time to root. The two methods of taking such material are heel cuttings and mallet cuttings.

Heel cuttings: These can be taken as semi-ripe, greenwood or hardwood cuttings (*see below, top*). They are often used for some evergreen shrubs such as azaleas and pieris, deciduous shrubs with pithy stems like berberis and elder, and those with greenwood stems, like broom.

Mallet cuttings: These are taken as semi-ripe or hardwood cuttings (*see below, bottom*) from shrubs with hollow or pithy stems, like spiraea and deciduous berberis.

MAKING A HEEL CUTTING

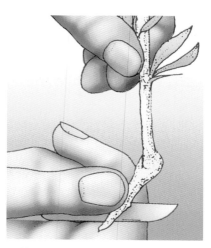

1 **Hold the base of a sideshoot** between your thumb and forefinger. Pull it down sharply so it comes away with a tail, or heel, of bark. If it does not come away easily, use a knife to cut it away with a small heel.

2 **Neaten the long tail** on the heel with a knife and remove any leaves near the base of the shoot. If the cutting is from semi-ripe or hardwood, remove the tip of the cutting. Dip the base in hormone rooting powder.

3 **Make a hole** in the soil or compost, insert the cutting, and water in. You can plant hardwood cuttings directly into open ground, semi-ripe cuttings in a cold frame, and less hardy cuttings in a propagator.

MAKING A MALLET CUTTING

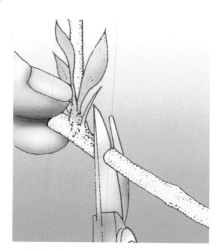

1 **Cut horizontally** with secateurs across the parent stem, just above a healthy, semi-ripe or hardwood sideshoot. Make this top cut close to the sideshoot to reduce the risk of dieback and rotting.

2 **Make a basal cut** 2cm (¾in) below the sideshoot so the cutting has a stump or 'mallet' of old stem attached. Split the mallet with a knife if it is thick. Dip the basal cut in hormone rooting powder.

3 **Make a hole** that is large enough to bury the mallet and about one third of the sideshoot. Plant semi-ripe cuttings in compost in a cold frame and hardwood cuttings in the open ground. Water in well.

STEM CUTTINGS

Growing under glass *see page 375* | **Propagation basics** *see page 396* | **Methods of propagation** *see page 404*

SEMI-RIPE CUTTINGS

In late summer, when growth slows and stems harden up, you can take semi-ripe cuttings. They are thicker and harder than softwood cuttings, so with a greater store of food, they survive more easily and can form roots even when grown on under poor light levels.

Semi-ripe cuttings do not need extra heat, but like humidity. Root them in a cold frame, a pot in an unheated greenhouse, or on a bright but cool windowsill.

Put pots in an unheated propagator or cover each with a plastic bag on a wire hoop, sealed with a rubber band.

Before taking cuttings, dig over the soil in the cold frame and add peat, or a peat substitute, to improve its water holding capacity, and grit to aid drainage. Cover with a 2–3cm (¾–1¼in) layer of fine sand. Semi-ripe cuttings root mostly in late winter and spring, but some root in mild autumns. Insulate the cold frame over winter until spring.

MAKING A SEMI-RIPE CUTTING

1 **Prune the parent plant** at the start of the winter, if possible, to encourage strong stems to grow rapidly.

2 **Cut off the** current season's growth from a main shoot, or sideshoot, in late summer. Remove the soft tip, unless it has stopped growing. Trim the cutting to 10–15cm (4–6in).

3 **Remove the leaves** from the bottom 5cm (2in) of the stem. Dip the base in rooting powder. Insert each cutting 3–4cm (1¼–1½in) deep, so its end enters the soil below the sand.

4 **Space the cuttings** 7–10cm (3–4in) apart, with leaves not touching. Close and shade the frame. Water as needed. In autumn, remove any fallen leaves. Insulate over winter.

5 **Remove the insulation** during the day once buds develop, but replace it at night if still frosty. Open the frame fully once all risk of frost has passed.

6 **Apply liquid feed** regularly to the cuttings in the frame all summer and water as needed. Lift and transplant the new plants once their leaves drop in autumn.

HARDWOOD CUTTINGS

These are taken from dormant shoots of woody plants. They are undemanding, as they have no leaves and plenty of food reserves. The best time to take them is at leaf fall. Run your hand down the stem in early autumn, as the leaves start to turn. If they come away easily, take your cuttings.

Make cuttings of an exact length. This does not work on plants with hollow or pithy stems, as the stem is prone to rotting; if the leaf nodes are reasonably close together,

cut just below a node that is 15cm (6in) or more from the stem tip. The stem at a node should be solid and more resilient. However, if the nodes are too far apart to make this practical, cut at 15cm (6in) and seal the stem by dipping it into partly molten candle wax.

Gooseberries and red currants are often grown as bushes, each with a clear, short trunk, or leg. To achieve this, take a longer hardwood cutting than usual, 25–35cm (10–14in)

MAKING A HARDWOOD CUTTING

1 **Prune the parent plant** hard during the dormant season. The following autumn at leaf fall, when the shoots are fully mature and buds firmly dormant, remove a new shoot.

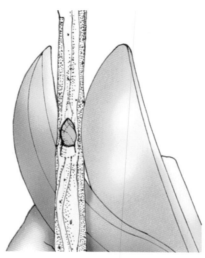

2 **Make a sloping** cut, using secateurs, just above the proposed top bud of the cutting.

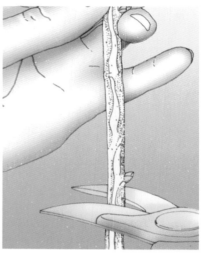

3 **Cut horizontally** across the stem, exactly 15cm (6in) below the top cut. Dip the basal cut only in hormone rooting powder.

4 **To plant cuttings,** dig the soil over, then make a trench 13cm (5in) deep with 1 vertical and 1 sloping side. Place the cuttings at the vertical edge, 10–15cm (4–6in) apart.

5 **Backfill the soil** and firm, leaving about 2.5cm (1in) of each cutting exposed. Leave in place until the following autumn. Water when needed to keep moist.

6 **Lift the cuttings,** which should have rooted and produced several stems. Transplant to their final positions.

long, and cut out all but the top three buds. Remove them by cutting shallowly into the bark beneath them with a sharp knife, ensuring no latent buds or part-buds remain. Painting the disbudded area with molten candle wax or pruning paint will help avoid desiccation. Plant each cutting with the lowest remaining bud about 5cm (2in) above the soil surface. Replant rooted cuttings once they are established with 15–20cm (6–8in) of stem exposed.

EVERGREEN CUTTINGS

Evergreen cuttings are taken from very ripe, almost hard, wood. They are not hardwood cuttings as they have leaves and need protection from excessive water loss. Wound cuttings from difficult-to-root shrubs such as daphnes, elaeagnus, and *Magnolia grandiflora* and treat with rooting powder. You can take cuttings from softer wood earlier in the season: treat them according to the condition of the stems (softwood, greenwood, or semi-ripe wood).

MAKING AN EVERGREEN CUTTING

1 **Prune the parent plant** in winter to encourage strong, young shoots that will root easily. Dig over the soil in the cold frame; add grit and peat, or peat substitute, as needed to improve drainage and water holding.

2 **Take a heel cutting** (*see page 434*) from a stem of the current season's growth in late summer or early autumn. Trim the tail of the heel and pinch out any soft growing tip on the cutting.

3 **Remove any leaves** from the bottom one third to half of the cutting stem. The cuttings will normally be 10–15cm (4–6in) long, although they will be shorter on dwarf and slow-growing shrubs.

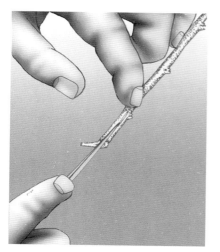

4 **Wound the cut base** of slow-growing plants with a shallow 2cm (¾in) cut. Dip the basal cut in rooting powder, so it is covered. Cut down large leaves to reduce water loss.

5 **Insert each cutting** up to its leaves in the cold frame. Ensure leaves do not overlap. Water; close the lid. Shade, water, and protect from frost as needed. Harden off in spring.

6 **Transplant the cuttings** in autumn, after you have given them all summer to grow. Take care when lifting – many evergreens produce brittle, fleshy roots.

CONIFER CUTTINGS

You can propagate many conifers from softwood, greenwood, semi-ripe, and ripewood cuttings, but spruces, firs, and pines do not grow well from cuttings and are best raised from seed. Select cuttings from young, actively growing plants that are clipped regularly and so have many strong, vigorous shoots. Take cypress, false cypress, Leyland cypress, and *Thuja* cuttings in autumn or winter, and yew and juniper cuttings in late winter, after the parent plants have been subjected to frost.

Conifer cuttings can be rooted under cover (*see below*) or in a cold frame. Lift the cuttings the following autumn, and pot up or transplant into the garden.

Prepare the soil in a cold frame by building it up to 20cm (8in) from the lid. Insert the cuttings in the soil, firm in, and water. In cold weather you will need to insulate the frame. When taking cuttings to root outdoors, take cuttings with a heel (*see page 434*). Trim the heel and remove the leaves on the lower one third of the cutting.

MAKING A CONIFER CUTTING

1 **Take cuttings** from actively growing leaders or lateral shoots (sideshoots). Avoid feathered shoots, which lack the vigour to root.

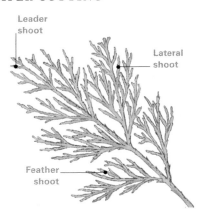

Leader shoot

Lateral shoot

Feather shoot

2 **Cut off** a suitable leader or lateral shoot, then fill a container with multipurpose compost, firmed to within 1cm (½in) of the rim. Trim the leaves from the bottom 2.5–4cm (1–1½in) of the cutting stem.

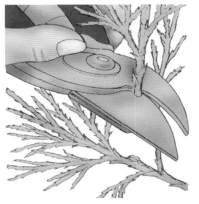

3 **Dip the basal cut** in hormone rooting powder (*see page 401*), to encourage rooting. Apply to the cut surface only; if it is dry, dip the end of the cutting in water first.

4 **Make a hole** about 2.5cm (1in) deep in the compost, using a stick or pencil. Insert the cutting and gently firm into place. If placing several cuttings in a single pot, space them 4–5cm (1½–2in) apart. Label and date.

5 **Water in the cuttings** with a fine rose. Place the pot of cuttings in a propagator to stop them from drying out. Alternatively, cover the pot with a plastic bag supported on a loop of wire; seal the bag around the pot with a rubber band.

6 **Leave the cuttings** in a warm environment to root – this should take 3–4 months. Harden off the cuttings once they have developed a good set of roots, and pot them on or plant them out the following autumn.

LEAF CUTTINGS

Growing under glass *see page 375* | **Propagation basics** *see page 396* | **Methods of propagation** *see page 404*

LEAVES

Of all the propagation techniques, leaf cuttings are perhaps the most magical. You can watch, in a few weeks, how they create one or many miniature plantlets from the cut surface of a mature leaf. A few plant species produce these plantlets naturally, including foam flower (*Tiarella cordifolia*) and hen-and-chicken fern (*Asplenium* × *lucrosum*). Some others, most of which are house plants, can be induced to do so under particular conditions. The range of plants that can be propagated from leaf cuttings is relatively small, but many of them are commonly grown and popular species.

Leaf cuttings

Leaf cuttings should be taken from leaves that have recently expanded fully to their mature sizes. If a leaf is less than full sized and immature, all its energy will first go towards developing and maturing. This will delay the production of young plantlets, and allow more time for problems such as drying out or rotting.

A newly expanded leaf will photosynthesize (manufacture energy) efficiently, so there will be food to produce the new plantlets. It will also still have a good life expectancy and will be young enough to have a high capacity to reproduce. The selected leaf should be complete, typical for the plant, and undamaged. It should also be free of pests and diseases.

Making the cuttings

The most common cause of failure in propagation of leaf cuttings is the leaf rotting before it has a chance to produce an independent plant. It is therefore crucial that all the materials – knives and secateurs, containers, composts, and leaves – are clean.

Conditions required

Most plants propagated by leaf cuttings are normally grown indoors, or in a greenhouse, so you can take leaf cuttings all year round, provided that there is a suitable leaf available. However, with lower temperatures and light levels, propagation is likely to be slower in winter.

Once separated from the parent plant, a leaf loses moisture quickly, so you need to raise the leaf cuttings in a closed environment, such as in a propagator, under a plastic sheeting tent on the greenhouse bench, or in a pot with a plastic bag over it.

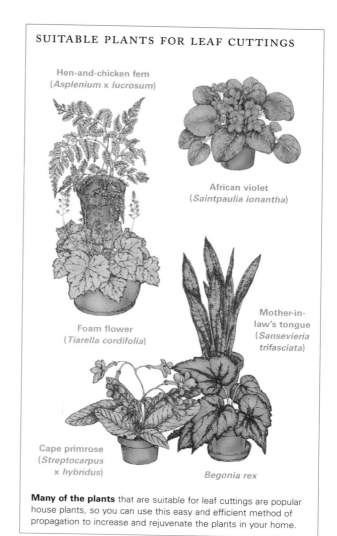

SUITABLE PLANTS FOR LEAF CUTTINGS

Hen-and-chicken fern (*Asplenium* x *lucrosum*)

African violet (*Saintpaulia ionantha*)

Foam flower (*Tiarella cordifolia*)

Mother-in-law's tongue (*Sansevieria trifasciata*)

Cape primrose (*Streptocarpus* x *hybridus*)

Begonia rex

Many of the plants that are suitable for leaf cuttings are popular house plants, so you can use this easy and efficient method of propagation to increase and rejuvenate the plants in your home.

Leaf-stem cuttings

The simplest and most reliable way to produce new plants from leaf cuttings is to use a complete leaf with its stalk. The disadvantage is that it produces only a few new plants from each leaf. Rotting and disease are the main causes of failure, so always use clean tools and containers and fresh, sterile compost. You can take a cutting at any time, if a new, fully expanded leaf is available.

To prepare a container for leaf-stem cuttings, fill it with equal parts of sifted peat, or peat substitute, and grit. This light, free-draining compost lessens the risk of rot and holds air. Inserting the cuttings at an angle (*see below*) also allows air to reach the cut surface of the stems, where the plantlets will develop, and it encourages them to root more quickly. Pot on each plantlet to form a new plant.

MAKING A LEAF STEM CUTTING

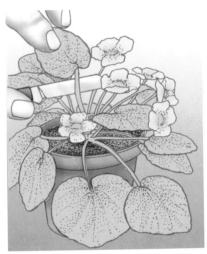

1 **Slice off an undamaged leaf** that has recently matured. Cut the leaf stalk about 5cm (2in) below the leaf blade; use a sharp knife or safety razor blade to reduce bruising.

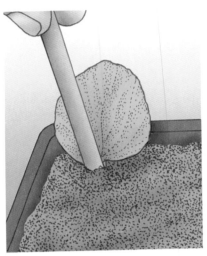

2 **Make a shallow**, sloping hole with a pencil in the compost of a prepared container and insert the cutting at a shallow angle, so that the leaf blade is almost flat on the compost.

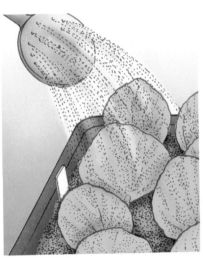

3 **Firm in gently** around the stalk, then insert the rest of the cuttings at the same angle. Label them and water, using a fine rose to avoid damaging them.

4 **Place the cuttings** in light shade in a propagator that is heated from below, ideally at about 20°C (68°F). This will create the warm, humid conditions required.

5 **Leave the cuttings** for 5–6 weeks, then apply a liquid feed once plantlets appear on each cutting. Leave them to grow on until they are large enough to handle.

6 **Pot up the plantlets** individually, once they can be separated without damage, into pots of free-draining potting compost. Once they are established, harden them off.

Growing under glass *see page 375* | Propagation basics *see page 396* | Methods of propagation *see page 404*

Midrib & lateral vein cuttings

A few species will produce plantlets from the veins of their leaf blades. Always use leaves that have recently expanded fully. You can cut them across the midrib (*see below*) or across the lateral veins (*see bottom*). Plantlets should appear after five to eight weeks, but they will not be big enough to transplant for several more weeks. Separate and pot them up once they can be handled.

The midrib cutting technique can be adapted for leaves with several main veins, such as begonias, by simply making 1cm (½in) cuts across several of the main veins with a very sharp knife or safety razor blade. Lay the leaf flat on a tray of moist compost and weigh it down so that the cut ends of the veins are in contact with the compost. Then treat the leaf as for a midrib cutting.

MAKING A MIDRIB CUTTING

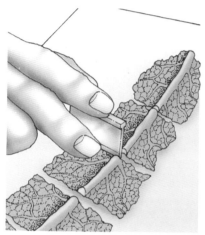

1 **Cut an undamaged leaf** from the parent plant. Lay the leaf upside down on a clean sheet of glass. Cut it into strips no wider than 5cm (2in), using a safety razor blade or scalpel.

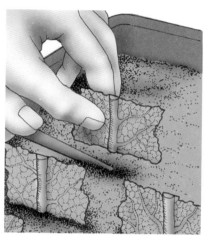

2 **Draw a shallow trench** in moist cuttings or multipurpose compost. Insert each cutting just deep enough to stay upright. Firm gently. Space the cuttings 2.5cm (1in) apart.

3 **Place the cuttings** in humid conditions at 20°C (68°F), such as in a heated propagator. Re-wet the compost when needed: stand the tray in water, then allow it to drain.

MAKING A LATERAL VEIN CUTTING

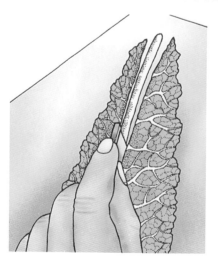

1 **Lay a suitable leaf** upside down on a clean sheet of glass. Remove the midrib with a razor blade or scalpel, so all lateral veins in the 2 halves have an exposed cut surface.

2 **Draw a shallow trench** in moist cuttings or multipurpose compost. Insert each cutting, or leaf half, vertically, with the cut surfaces facing downwards. Firm and label.

3 **Place the container** in a propagator. Plantlets should develop from the cut veins in 5–8 weeks. Separate and pot them on once they are large enough to be handled.

Monocot leaf cuttings

Monocotyledonous plants, such as snowdrops and mother-in-law's tongues (*Sansevieria*), have a series of parallel veins running the length of each leaf. Some of these plants have the capacity to produce a plantlet on the cut surface of a leaf vein, so may be propagated from leaf cuttings. The leaves of bulbous plants tend to be very soft and rot easily; when preparing cuttings, make sure that you keep the propagation environment scrupulously clean. It will also help to provide optimum conditions for plantlets to develop as quickly as possible.

Making a monocot leaf cutting

Before taking the cuttings, prepare a container, such as a standard seed tray, by filling it with multipurpose compost. Press it down lightly to within 1cm (½in) of the rim, water it, and allow it to drain. Prepare the cuttings and insert in the compost (*see below*).

Place the container in a warm (20°C/68°F), humid environment, so the cuttings do not dry out and wilt. Ensure that the cuttings are in bright but not direct sunlight, which can cause scorching. Plantlets should develop at the bases of the cuttings after four to eight weeks. Repot the young plants once they are large enough to handle easily, allow them to establish indoors, then harden them off if they are for outdoor planting.

HOOPING LEAF CUTTINGS

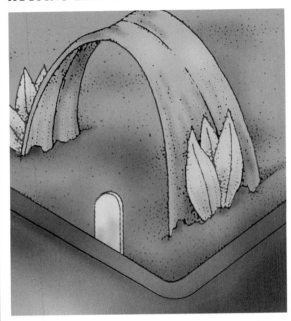

Leaf cuttings of *Heloniopsis* will regenerate from both ends. Reduce a leaf to 4–5cm (1½–2in) by cutting off the top and bottom ends. Plant the cutting in a hoop, with both ends set into the compost. Treat the cutting as other monocot leaf cuttings.

MAKING A MONOCOT LEAF CUTTING

1 **Remove a leaf** that is fully expanded and undamaged from the parent plant, here a mother-in-law's tongue.

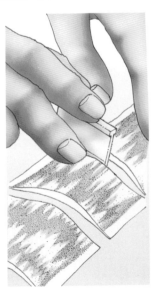

2 **Make a series of cuts** across the leaf 2.5cm (1in) apart, at right angles to the veins, using a safety razor blade or scalpel.

3 **Draw shallow trenches** with a dibber and insert the cuttings vertically, in rows 2.5cm (1in) apart. Firm in and label.

4 **Leave the cuttings** to form plantlets. Re-wet the compost when necessary by standing the tray in water.

GLOSSARY

Acid: Soil with little or no lime content, less than 7 on the pH scale.

Aerate: To expose the soil to air, either by digging or, on lawns, by puncturing the turf.

Alkaline: Soil with a high lime content, more than 7 on the pH scale.

Alpine: Plant suitable for rock garden or alpine house.

Annual: Plant that survives for only one season. Germination, growth, flowering, seeding, and death all take place in this time. *See also* Biennial, Perennial.

Apex: Growing tip of a branch or shoot. For example, apical bud refers to the bud at the tip of a branch. *See also* Axil.

Axil: Junction between a branch and a side branch or a leaf stalk that grows from it. For example, axillary bud refers to the bud at the base of a leaf stalk. *See also* Apex.

Bedding plant: Plant used for temporary display.

Biennial: Plant that lives for just two seasons. Germination and growth usually take place in the first season; flowering, seeding, and death in the second season. *See also* Annual, Perennial.

Bog garden: Garden where the soil is kept damp at all times, but is not waterlogged.

Bone meal: Slow-release fertilizer high in phosphorous and nitrogen, with some calcium. Manufactured from ground animal bones.

Brassica: Plant belonging to the cabbage family.

Bulbous plant: Underground plant organ. The term includes bulbs, tubers, corms, and rhizomes.

Bush: Term used by fruit growers to describe a short fruit tree grown with little or no stem.

Chitting: To promote the germination of seed before sowing, or the sprouting of potatoes before planting.

Chlorosis: Yellowing of leaves, often caused by mineral deficiency.

Climber: Plant that has a climbing habit; also a type of rose with this habit. *See also* Rambler.

Cloche: Glass or plastic temporary cover, which can be placed over plants where they are growing to offer frost protection.

Cold frame: Glass or plastic frame, into which plants are placed for frost protection and hardening off.

Compost: Decayed vegetable matter used as an organic mulch or soil additive. Also used to describe a potting mixture for growing container plants.

Conifer: Cone-bearing tree or shrub, such as a pine or fir.

Controlled-release fertilizer: Type of fertilizer that releases its nutrients slowly over a long period of time.

Coppice: To cut a tree or shrub back to ground level to produce new stems.

Cordon: Plant trained to a single stem, or double stem if a U-cordon.

Crop rotation: System of growing vegetable crops whereby the same crop is not grown in the same place for a number of years.

Cultivar: A combination of the words 'cultivated' and 'variety' to describe a plant variety that is derived from cultivation. *See also* Variety.

Cutting: Part of a plant removed for the purposes of propagation.

Damp down: To spray the floor and benches of a greenhouse to reduce the temperature and increase humidity in hot weather.

Defoliation: To lose or remove leaves from a plant.

Division: To split the roots of a plant into two or more pieces for the purposes of propagation or to reinvigorate an old plant.

Dormancy: A period of slowed or stalled growth during unfavourable environmental conditions, usually winter. Also refers to seeds before they germinate.

Dressing: Application of dried fertilizer to the soil. Base dressings are applied before planting; top dressings after planting.

Earthing up: To cover the base of plants with a heap or ridge of soil to prevent greening of stems or tubers.

Ericaceous: Plants that require a lime-free or acidic potting compost.

Espalier: Tree with a vertical trunk and several vertical branches trained horizontally.

F1 hybrid: Plant with very consistent characteristics, such as size, shape, vigour, and colour. They are created by crossing two pure varieties of plant by hand pollination. F2 and F3 hybrids are second and third generations respectively and show much less consistent characteristics.

Fish, blood, and bone: General-purpose fertilizer made from a mixture of animal and fish matter.

Floribunda: Type of bush rose, with flowers that grow in clusters. *See also* Hybrid Tea.

Frost pocket: Area in a garden more prone to frost than other areas.

Germination: First growth stage of a plant, as it emerges from a seed.

Graft: Where a shoot or bud is inserted onto a rootstock to create a new plant. *See also* Rootstock.

Green manure: Fast-maturing crop that is dug into the soil while still green to improve soil fertility.

Growing bag: Plastic bag containing growing media for planting fruit and vegetable crops.

Growmore: General-purpose fertilizer in granular form.

Half-standard: Tree with a short, unbranched trunk to 1m (3ft).

Harden off: To slowly adjust plants to lower temperatures outdoors before planting in the open ground.

Herb: Plant grown for its aromatic, culinary, or medicinal properties.

Herbaceous: Non-woody plant.

Hoe: Tool for weeding.

Humus: Dark substance in soil created by decay of organic matter.

Hybrid: Offspring from the cross-fertilization of two different species.

Hybrid Tea: Type of bush rose, with flowers that grow singly or in clusters of three. *See also* Floribunda.

John Innes compost: Various potting compost formulations devised by the John Innes Horticultural Institute.

Larva: Immature stage in the development of an insect.

Lateral: Sideshoot or stem growing from a larger branch.

Layering: Method of propagation where shoots are induced to root.

Lime: Chemical compound found in soil that affects pH.

Mulch: Soil covering, often but not always made of organic material.

Neutral: Soil that is neither acid nor alkaline with a pH of 7.

Peat: Low-nutrient additive of potting composts derived from bog or fenland areas.

Perennial: Plant that lives more than three seasons. Many die down over winter. *See also* Annual, Biennial, Herbaceous.

pH: Measure of the acidity or alkalinity of a soil.

Pollination: Transfer of pollen from the male to the female part of a flower, leading to fertilization.

Pot-bound: Container plant where the roots have filled all the available space, circling around the pot. *See also* Potting on.

Potting on: To move a plant from a smaller to a larger container.

Rambler: Type of rose with a rambling habit. *See also* Climber.

Rootball: Root system and enclosed soil of a contained plant.

Rootstock: Root and trunk system of a woody plant onto which a shoot or bud of another plant is grafted. See also *Graft*.

Scarify: To scrape the surface of a lawn to remove moss and thatch.

Sexual propagation: Reproduction of a plant by seed to create a new, genetically distinct plant. *See also* Vegetative propagation.

Species: Group of plants that share the same characteristics and breed freely with one another.

Specimen plant: Plant set out in a prominent position to create a focal point in a garden.

Standard: Plant grown on a tall, single, upright stem or trunk.

Subsoil: Layer of soil immediately below the topsoil. *See also* Topsoil.

Sucker: Shoot arising from the root or rootstock of a plant.

Sulphate of ammonia: Fast-acting high-nitrogen fertilizer.

Sulphate of potash: Fast-acting high-potassium fertilizer. *See also* Superphosphate.

Superphosphate: Fast-acting high-potassium fertilizer. *See also* Sulphate of potash.

Tamp: To lightly compact the soil.

Thatch: Layer of dead plant matter that collects at soil level on lawns.

Thinning: To remove seedlings, flower buds, shoots, or branches to reduce overcrowding and improve performance.

Topiary: To create an elaborate shape from a shrub by close clipping and training.

Topsoil: The top layer of soil. *See also* Subsoil.

Variety: Group of plants of the same species that form a slight variation on common species characteristics, but are not sufficiently distinct to form a separate species. Varieties may arise naturally or in cultivation. *See also* Cultivar, Species.

Vegetative propagation: To remove tissue from a parent plant and grow it on to form a new plant. The new plant will be a clone of the parent. *See also* Sexual propagation.

INDEX

Page numbers in italics refer to pages in which there are relevant illustrations. In plant entries topics of general information relating to the main entry appear first; subentries for species and cultivars always follow the general subentries.

A

Abelia × *grandiflora* 67
Acacia
    propagation 404
Acanthus
    for containers 355
    propagation 404
Acer
    for autumn 72
    for containers 357
    diseases 37, 111
    for shade 68, 69
    for winter 73
    griseum 73, *73*
    japonicum 58, *104*
        air layering 404, 428
        pruning 104
        pruning for foliage 97
    negundo 37
    palmatum 58, 69
        air layering 404, 428
        for autumn 72
        pruning 104
        pruning for foliage 97
        for shade 68, 69
Achillea
    for containers 355
    millefolium 294
    'Moonshine' 67, *67*
Achimenes
    tubercles 416
Acorus

for containers 355
    calamus 329
Adelgids 110
Aegopodium podagraria
    rhizomes 39, 412
Aeonium
    for containers 355
Aesculus
    pest resistance 109
    hippocastanum 109
    indica 109
African marigold
    for containers 353
African violet
    leaf cuttings 404, 439
Agapanthus
    for containers 85, 355
Agave
    in the greenhouse 383
    propagation 404
Ageratum
    for containers 353
Agrostis nebulosa
    for containers 353
Air layering 404, 428
Ajuga reptans 330
    for shade 69
Alchemilla
    for containers 355
    propagation 404
    mollis 355
Alders
    pruning 105
Allamanda cathartica
    in the greenhouse 386
Allium
    bulbils 419
    for containers 354
    deadheading 79
    propagation 419
    for summer 71

wildflower garden 54
    cristophii 67
    hollandicum 'Purple Sensation' 71
    schoenoprasum see Chives
Aloe
    in the greenhouse 383
Alpine strawberries 231, 232
    see also Strawberries
Alyssum
    for containers 353
Amaranthus
    for containers 353
Amaryllis
    propagation 419
Amelanchier lamarckii 70
Amphibians 27, 44, 48, 50
Anemone
    for containers 354
    propagation 404
    for shade 68
    nemorosa 84
Anethum graveolens see Dill
Angel wings
    tubers 416
Annuals
    borders 74–5
        maintenance 76
    for containers 341, 353
    growing 74–6
    half hardy, sowing under cover 75
    hardy
        sowing direct 75
        winter protection 75
    sowing
        in autumn 75
        direct 75
        in pots 75
        under cover 75
        using modules 75
    for summer 71
    for sun 67

Anthemis tinctoria
for containers 355
Antirrhinum
for containers 353
Ants 296
Aphelandra
in the greenhouse 386
Aphidoletes pupae 32
Aphids 28, 35
black bean aphid 29, 179
bulbs 86
currant blister aphid 29, 270
herbaceous perennials 81
interplanting 28
mealy cabbage aphids 162, 169, 170
predators 27
root aphids 27, 152
woolly aphid 268
Aponogeton distachyos 326
Apple & pear scab 271
Apples *223*, 243
biennial bearing 252
blossom hardiness 221
care 251–2
choosing rootstocks 243
cordons 246
espaliers 248
choosing a site 243
choosing trees 243
for containers 359
cordons 246
choosing plants 246
choosing rootstock 246
forms 247
maintaining 247
planting 246
pruning 246–7
spacing 246
supporting 246
training 246
diseases 271
dwarf pyramids 250–1
mature 251
planting 250–1
pruning 250, 251
spacing 251
supporting 250–1
training 251
espaliers 248–9
choosing plants 248

choosing rootstock 248
planting 248
pruning 248–9
spacing 248
supporting 248
training 248–9
freestanding trees 243
harvesting 251–2
maintaining 252
maypoling 252
overcrowded spur systems 248
pests 268
pruning
cordons 246–7
dwarf pyramids 250, 251
espaliers 248–9
restorative 267
pruning for fruit 244
renewal pruning 244
spur pruning 244
renovating 267
rootstock 243, 246, 248, 250, 251
training 243
wildlife garden 55
Apricots 264
aftercare 264
fans 264
harvesting 264
planting 264
pruning 264
spacing 264
storing 264
training 264
Aquatic plants *see* Water plants
Aquilegias
pests 81
Armoracia rusticana
root cuttings 412
Arrowhead 329, *329*
Artemisia
for containers 355
dracunculus see Tarragon
lactiflora 355
'Powis Castle' 67, *67*
Arum corm rot 391
Arum lilies *see Zantedeschia*
Aruncus
pests 81
Asparagus 171–3
common problems 173

conditions required 171
cultivation 171
first year 172
harvesting 172
management of mature crop
172–3
mulching 172
planting 171
site preparation 171
sowing 171
sprue 172
thinning 171
Asparagus beetle 173, 212
Aspect of garden 14
Asplenium × lucrosum
leaf cuttings 439
Aster
for autumn 72
for containers 355
disease 82
pests 81
propagation 404
wilts 82
amellus 81
'King George' 72, *72*
novae-angliae 81
novi-belgii 81
Aster wilts 82
Astilbe 330
Astrantia
for containers 355
cutting 79
major 'Claret' 71
Aubergines 205
common problems 205
cultivation 205
harvesting 205
pinching out 205
planting 205
in unheated greenhouses 379
Aubrieta
propagation 404
Aucuba
for containers 357
propagation 404
for shade 69
japonica 69
Australian stonecrop *see* New Zealand
pygmy weed
Autumn crocus *see Colchicum*

Autumn garden 72
Azalea *see Rhododendron*
Azalea gall 111
Azalea whitefly 109
Azolla
   caroliniana 328
   filiculoides 328, 331, *331*

B

Bacterial canker 272, 273
Bacterial diseases 30, 82
  symptoms 30
Ballota
  for containers 357
Bamboo
  propagation 404
Banana 66
Barriers 33, 34
  cabbage root fly mats 33
  carrot fly barrier 33, 190
  copper 32, *32*
  grease band 33
  mini cloche 33
Basal rot
  bulbs 87
  cuttings 403
Basil 209
  for containers 358
    ornamental 353
  cultivation 209
  storing 208
Baskets *see* Hanging baskets;
  Water plants
Bassia scoparia f. *trichophylla*
  for containers 353
Bats 27
  attracting 47
  bat boxes 47
Bay 209
  for containers 357
  cultivation 209
Bay sucker 210
Bean rust 214, 215
Beans
  see also Broad beans; French beans;
    Runner beans
  for containers 358
  field beans 145
  green manure 145

mineral deficiency 31
  pests 211, 214
  watering 148
Bedding plants 58
  for containers 353
  in the greenhouse 383
Bees
  attracting 47, 113
  bee tube box 47
Beetles
  attracting 48
  habitat 48
  pests
    asparagus beetle 173, 212
    flea beetle 34, 156, 192, 195, 211
    lily beetle 86
    raspberry beetle 270
    rosemary beetle 212
    viburnum beetle 109
Beetroot 193
  common problems 193
  conditions required 193
  for containers 358
  cultivation 193
  harvesting 193
  sowing 193
  thinning 193
  varieties 193
  watering 193
Begonia
  for containers 353, *353*
  frost damage 13
  in the greenhouse 386
  propagation
    leaf cuttings 439
    tubers 416
  for shade 68
  grandis subsp. *evansiana* 416
  rex 439
Bellflower *see Campanula*
Bellis
  for containers 353
  perennis 294
Berberis
  for containers 357
  heel cuttings 434
  mallet cuttings 434
  pests 110
  thunbergii 110
Berberis sawfly 110

Bergenia
  propagation 404, 417
  cordifolia, for shade 68
Betula
  for autumn 72
  diseases 111
  pruning 105
  for winter 73
  alleghaniensis 72
  utilis var. *jacquemontii* 73
Bidens
  for containers 353
Biennials 76
Bindweed *see Convolvulus*
Biological control 32, 33, 35, 204
  cucumbers 157
  nematodes *see* Nematodes
  vine weevil 36
Birch *see Betula*
Birch rust 111
Bird scarers *210*
Birds
  attracting 46, 49, 50, 55, 113
  pests 27
  predators 27
Black bamboo 73
Black bean aphid 29, 179
Black currant 226
  flowering 226
  pests 269, 270
  planting 226
  propagation 404
  pruning 226
Black currant big bud mite 269
Black death 82
Black spot 28, 30, 128
  life cycle 128
Blackberries 230
  aftercare 230
  harvesting 230
  pests 270
  planting 230
  pruning 230
  spacing 230
  tip layering 429
  training 230
Blackfly 35, 179, 181, 183
Blanching
  celery 174
  endive 153

leeks 188
Bleeding heart
    for containers 355
Blight
    box blight 112
    cane blight 272, 273
    fireblight 272, 273
    potato blight 199, 214, 215
    pythium blight 298
    quince leaf blight 272, 273
    spur blight 272, 273
    tomato blight 160–1, 214
Blossom end rot
    peppers 204
Blossom wilt 271
Blue flag 329
Bluebells *see Hyacinthoides*
Blueberries 227
    aftercare 227
    choosing a site 227
    for containers 227, 357, 359, *359*
    dwarf 227
    harvesting 227
    planting 227
    pruning 227
    Vaccinium corymbosum 227
Bog arum 329
Bog garden 50, 51, 308
    excavating 318
    making 318
    preparing 318
Bog plants 330
    astilbe 330
    bugle 330
    daylily 330
    drumstick primula 330, *330*
    ferns and grasses 330, *330*
    giant rhubarb 330
    monkey flower 330
    planting 330
    preparing 330
    primrose 330
    royal fern 330, *330*
    wildlife pond 50
Bolting 31
    onions 184
Borage 209
    conditions required 209
    for containers 358
    propagation 209

    sowing 209
Borago officinalis see Borage
Borders
    annual 74–5
    herbaceous 64, 77–80
    maintenance 76, 78–80
    mixed 64
    planning and design 64
    planting plan 74, 77
    preparation 77
    watering 15
    width 64
Bottlebrush *see Callistemon*
Box *see Buxus*
Box blight 112
Box sucker 110
Boysenberry 230
Brachyscome
    for containers 353
Bracket fungi 111
Brandling worms 24
Brassicas *210*
    caterpillars 34, 162, 164, 166, 169
    conditions required 162
    crop rotation 162
    growing 162
    pests 34, 162
    raising plants 162
    root collars 162, 169
    transplanting 162
Briza maxima
    for containers 353, 355
Broad beans 178–9
    common problems 179
    conditions required 178
    cultivation 178–9
    harvesting 179
    sowing 178
    tops 179
Broad-leaved plantain 294
Broccoli 165, 167
    common problems 167
    conditions required 167
    cultivation 167
    harvesting 167
    purple cape 167
    sowing 167
    spring-cropping 167
    sprouting 167
    transplanting 167

Broom
    heel cuttings 434
Brown rot 272, 273
Brunsfelsia paucifolia
    in the greenhouse 386
Brussels sprouts 168–9
    common problems 169
    conditions required 168
    foliar feed 169
    harvesting 168, 169
    intercropping 41
    planting out 168
    puddling in 168
    raising 168
    root collars 169
    sowing 168
    transplanting 168
    varieties 168, 169
    watering 168
Bud blast 112
Buddleja
    alternifolia
        pruning
            to encourage flowers 97
            renewal pruning 100
    davidii
        pruning 101
            to encourage flowers 96
            hard 102
Bugle 330
Bulb fibre 350
Bulbils
    propagation by 419
    weeds 39
Bulblets
    propagation by 419
Bulbs
    for autumn 72
    borders 70, *70*
    buying 28, 354
    care 85
    for containers 83, 84, 354
        compost 350
        height and planting depths 354
    deadheading 79, 85
    diseases 87, 391
    in grass 84, 85
    group planting 83
    height and planting depths 354
    hybrids 84

keeping 354
lifting 83, 85
looking after 85
in mixed borders 84
naturalizing 85
pests 86
planting 83–5
   in grass 52, 84, 85
   groups 83
   individually 83
   situation 84
propagation 419–21
   bulbils 419
   bulblets 419
scaling 420
scooping 421
scoring 421
for shade 68, 69
for spring 70
staking 85
storing 85
for summer 71
for sun 67
viral diseases 87
wildlife gardening 52
for winter 73
woodland 68, 84
Bulrush *see* Reedmace
Bur-reed 331
Busy Lizzies *see Impatiens*
Butterflies
   attracting 48
Butterfly bush *see Buddleja davidii*
Buxus
   for containers 357, *357*
   propagation 404

C

Cabbage caterpillars 211
Cabbage root fly 169, 170, 212
   fleece 162, 166
   larvae 195
   predators 27
   protection against 34
   radishes 192
Cabbage root fly mats 33
Cabbage whitefly 162, 166, 169, 211
   cycle 28
Cabbages 163–4, *163*

autumn 163, 164
Chinese 163
club root 164
common problems 164
conditions required 163
cultivation 164
fertilizer 163
harvesting 163, 164
hoeing 163
intercropping 28
lifting 164
mulching 22
ornamental, for containers 353
planting 163
planting out 164
raising 164
spring 163, 164
spring greens 163
storing 164
summer 163, 164
trimming 164
types 163
watering 148
winter 163, 164
Calabrese 165–6, *165*
   common problems 166
   conditions required 165
   cultivation 165–6
   harvesting 165
   planting out 165
   raising 165
   watering 148
Caladium
   tubers 416
Calamagrostis
   × *acutiflora* 'Karl Foerster' 67
   brachytricha, for containers 355
Calceolaria
   for containers 353
Calendula
   for containers 353
   wildlife garden 55
   English marigold 55
      winter protection 75
Calla palustris 329
Callistemon 67
   propagation 404
   as wall shrub 136
Calluna vulgaris 67
   for summer 71

Caltha palustris
   for shade 68
Camellia
   for containers 357
   in the greenhouse 380
   oedema 31
   pests 109
   renovation 107
   for shade 68, 69
   for spring 70
Campanula
   for containers 355
   propagation 404, 423
Campsis
   × *tagliabuana* 'Madame Galen' 67
   radicans, propagation 404
Canadian pondweed 327
Cane blight 272, 273
Cane spot 272, 273
Cankers 30
   bacterial 272, 273
   horse chestnut bleeding canker 112
   nectria canker 271
   parsnip canker 191
   rose canker 129
Canna
   for containers 355
   lifting 85
   propagation 404, 417
   storing 85
Cape primrose
   leaf cuttings 404, 439
Capillary matting 374
Capillary watering systems 402
Capsid bugs 35, 81
Cardiocrinum
   propagation 404
   for shade 68, 69
   giganteum 68, 69
Cardoon *71*
Carex
   for containers 355
   propagation 404
Carnations
   border, layering 427
Carrot fly 190, 191, 211
   barrier 33, 190
Carrot root fly 28
   predators 27
   protection against 34

Carrots 189–90, *189*
  Amsterdam types 189
  Autumn King types 189
  Berlicum types 189
  Chantenay types 189
  common problems 190
  conditions required 189
  for containers 358
  cultivation 189–90
  'fanged' roots 189
  harvesting 190
  Imperator types 189
  intercropping 28
  Nantes types 189, 190
  Paris Market types 189
  sowing 189–90
  trimming foliage 190
  in unheated greenhouses 379
  watering 148
Caryopteris
  for containers 357
  hard pruning 102
Catalpa 37
  bignonioides 103
    pruning 97, 103
  Aurea 103
Catch cropping 143
Caterpillars
  brassicas 34, 162, 164, 166, 169
  control 36, 152
  herbaceous perennials 81
  pea moth 212
  protection against 34
  tomatoes 160
  wildlife gardens 55
Catmint *see Nepeta*
Cauliflowers 165–6
  autumn 165
  biennial 165
  common problems 166
  conditions required 165
  cultivation 165–6
  cutting 166
  harvesting 166
  mini-cauliflowers 165
  planting out 165, 166
  raising 165
  summer 165
  watering 148, 166
Ceanothus 67

  propagation 404
  pruning
    hard 102
    renewal 100
    spring-flowering 137
  as wall shrub 136
  'Autumnal Blue' 136
  'Burkwoodii' 136
Celery 174
  blanching 174
  conditions required 174
  cultivation 174
  diseases 174
  harvesting 174
  pests 174
  sowing 174
  watering 148
Celery leaf mining fly 174
Celery leaf spot 174
Celosia
  for containers 353
Centaurea cyanus
  sowing 75
  wildflower meadow 53, 55
  wildlife garden 54
Centipedes 26, 27
  attracting 48
  habitat 48
Centranthus ruber 55, *55*
Ceratophyllum demersum 327, *327*
Ceratostigma
  for containers 357
  hard pruning 102
Cerinthe major 'Purpurascens'
  for containers 353
Chaenomeles
  for containers 357
  propagation 404
  pruning 137
  training 137
  as wall shrub 137
  × *superba* 137
    'Crimson and Gold' 70
Chafer grubs 296
Chamaecyparis
  for containers 357
  propagation 404
Chamaerops humilis 66
  for containers 357
Chamomile

  for containers 358
Chard 155
Cheiranthus
  for containers 353
Cherries 256, *256, 257*
  aftercare 257
  choosing a site 256
  conditions required 256
  diseases 272
  fans, pruning 256–7
  harvesting 257
  planting 256
  pruning 257
  spacing 256
  storing 257
  training 257
  wildlife garden 55
  morello 240
Cherry laurel
  renovation 107
Chicken fern
  leaf cuttings 439
Chicory 154
  Belgian or witloof 154
  conditions required 154
  cultivation 154
  cut-and-come again 154
  harvesting 154
  planting out 154
  radicchios 154
  sowing 154
  sugarloaf 154
Children
  garden design and 59, 61
  pools and 207
    wildlife ponds 51
Chimonanthus praecox 73
Chinese artichokes and yams
  propagation 416
Chinese cabbage 163, 164
Chinese layering *see* Air layering
Chionochloa rubra
  for containers 355
Chionodoxa
  for containers 354
Chives 209
  for containers 358
  cultivation 209
  wildlife garden 55
Chlorophytum

propagation 404
Chocolate spot 179
Choisya
   for containers 357
   ternata
      propagation 404
      Sundance ('Lich') 67
Christmas box *see Sarcococca*
Chrysanthemum
   for containers 353
   diseases 82, 391
   division 423
   in the greenhouse 383
   pests 81
   winter-flowering 383
Chrysanthemum leaf miner 388, 389
Chrysanthemum rusts 391
   chrysanthemum white rust 82
Cineraria
   for containers 353
Cistus 67
   for containers 357
   propagation 404
Citrus
   for containers 359, *359*
   in unheated greenhouses 379
   limon, propagation 404
Clay soils 16, *17*, 193
   herbs 206
   raised beds 142–3
Clematis 132, *132*
   for containers 357, *357*
   group 1 132
   group 2 132–3
   group 3 133
   initial training 132
   planting 132
   propagation 404
   pruning 132–3
      formative 133
      mature clematis 133
   wilt 112
   for winter 73
   alpina 132
   armandii 132
   cirrhosa var. *purpurascens* 'Freckles' 73
   'Constance' *132*
   'Duchess of Albany' 133
   'Étoile Violette' *132*, 133
   'H.F. Young' *132*

'Jackmanii' 133
'Nelly Moser' 132
macropetala 132
montana 112, 132
'Perle d'Azur' 133
'The President' 132
'Rouge Cardinal' 133
'Star of India' 133
texensis 133
viticella 112, 133
'William Kennet' 132
Clematis wilt 112
Cleome
   for containers 353
Clerodendron
   for containers 357
Climate 12–13
   local 12
   microclimates 14, 220
Climate change 12, 15
Climbers
   roses 67, *117*, 122, *123*
Climbers and wall plants 59, 130–7
   floppers 130
   general care 131
   in the greenhouse 383
   growing 131
   growth habit 130
   hedges 49
   natural clingers 130
   planting 66, 131
   pruning 131
      roses 122, 124
   rain shadow 131
   roses 67, 122, *123*, 124
   scramblers 130
   for sun 67
   supports 130
      free-standing 131
   training 131
   twiners 130
   wall shrubs 130, 136–7
   for winter 73
Cloches 149, 161, 186
   cucumbers 157
   hardy annuals 75
   lettuce 152
   mini cloche 33
   for propagation 398–9
   types 149, 369

using 378
Club root 170, 213
   brassicas 162, 164
   potatoes 197
Cobaea scandens
   for containers 353
Codiaeum
   in the greenhouse 386
Codling moth 268
Colchicum
   for containers 354
   autumnale 72
Cold frames 149, 369
   conifer cuttings 438
   cucumbers 157
   hardening off in unheated frames 378
   leaf-bud cuttings 431
   lettuce 152
   melons 238
   for propagation 399
   strawberries 233
   types 369
   using 378
Coleus
   propagation 404
Comfrey
   cultivating 21
   liquid feed 21
   'Bocking 14' 21
Common scab 214, 215
Compost
   bulb fibre 350
   compostable materials 24
   container and basket composts 350
   ericaceous 227, 350
   grass clippings 293
   John Innes 236, 350, 354, 401
   lawn clippings 24
   making 23–5, 401
   mixing 401
   multipurpose 350, 401
   potting compost 350, 387, 401
   for propagation 401
   rotted down 23
   soil-based 401
   soilless 401
   spent mushroom compost 21
   worm composting 23, 24
Compost bins
   home-made 23

proprietary 23
two or three bin system 23
types 23
Compost heap 23
  building-up 25
  grass clippings 293
  temperature 25
  turning 24
Conifers
  cuttings 438
  evergreen 66, 68
  hedges 49, 116
Consolida ajacis 75
Containers 340–63
  aftercare 360–3
  annuals 341, 353
  bedding plants 353
  biodegradable 400
  brick planters 348
  bulbs 83, 84, *349*, 354
    buying 354
    height and planting depths 354
    keeping 354
  clay 342–3
  climbers 356–7
  compost 350
  concrete 342, 343
  corms 354
  disposable pots 400
  drainage 350
  drip-feeders 15
  dumpy bags 347
  feeding 361
  fibreglass 343
  fleece 362
  foliage plants 356
  frost protection 362
  fruit
    blueberries 227, 357, 359, *359*
    strawberries 232, *232*, 346, 359, *359*
  grasses 355
  in the greenhouse 375–6
  growing bags 375–6
  hanging baskets *see* Hanging baskets
  herbs 358
  improvised 346–7
  larger containers 346–7
  maintenance 360–3
  metal 343

modular trays 75, 400, *400*
moving 350
perennials 355
permanent displays 341
planting 349–59
  compost 350
  drainage 350
  from pots or boxes 351
  hanging baskets 352
  potting compost 350
  preparing for 349–50
  techniques 351
  useful additives 350
planting bags 347
plastic 343
  baskets 344
potatoes 199
potting on 363
for propagation 400
  biodegradable 400
  choosing 400
  disposable pots 400
  modular trays 75, 400, *400*
  seed containers 400
protecting pots 362
raised beds 348, *348*
  brick planters 348
  frost protection 355
  kits 348
  wooden beds 348
recycled materials 343
recycling smaller containers 346
replanting 363
shrubs 356–7
sowing seed in 406–7
sprucing up displays 363
staking 361
stone 343
supports 361
terracotta 342–3, 346
  baskets 344
tidying plants 363
topiary 356
trees 356–7
  buying 88
types 341, 342–3
vegetables 358
water plants 323
watering 15, 360
wind protection 362

windowboxes 344, *344*, 345
  wooden 343
  wooden beds 348
Convallaria
  for containers 354
  majalis
    propagation 404
    for shade 69
Convolvulus
  for containers 353
  rhizomes 39, 412
  arvensis 412
Copper bands 33
Copper barriers 32, *32*
Coppicing 102
Coral spot 111–12
Coriander 209
  for containers 358
  freezing 208
  sowing 209
Coriandrum sativum see Coriander
Corkscrew rush 329
Corms
  for containers 354
Corn
  smut 214
Cornfield annuals 53
Cornflower *see Centaurea cyanus*
Cornus
  for autumn 72
  for containers 357
  deciduous 73
  hard pruning 102, 103
  propagation 404
  for winter 73
  alba 102, 103
   'Sibirica' 73
  kousa var. *chinensis* 72, *72*
  sanguinea 102
  sericea 102
Cortaderia
  propagation 404
Corylus maxima 'Purpurea'
  pruning 97, 103
Cosmos
  for containers 353, *353*, 355
  atrosanguineus 355
Cotinus 37
  coggygria
    propagation 404

pruning
    hard pruning for maximum
        foliage effect 103
    minimal 103, 104
Cotoneaster
    for containers 357
    hedges 49
    propagation 404
    pruning 104
    as wall shrub 136
    horizontalis 69
        for shade 69
Cottage garden 59
Couch grass
    rhizomes 39
Courgettes *202*
    black plastic sheet mulch 201
    common problems 202
    conditions required 200
    for containers 358, *358*
    flowers 201
    harvesting 201
    intercropping 143
    pinching out 201
    planting 201
    site 201
    situation 201
    sowing 201
    transplanting 200
    watering 148, 201
Courtyard garden 59, *64*
Cowslips
    naturalizing 85
Crab apple *see Malus*
Crassula
    propagation 404
    helmsii 328, 331, *331*
Crinodendron hookerianum
    for shade 69
Crinum × powellii 'Album' 84
Crocosmia
    for containers 355
    'Lucifer' 67, *67*
Crocus
    for containers 354
    diseases 87
    early flowering 73
    naturalized on lawns 85
    for spring 70
Crop covers 34

Crop rotation 143
    brassicas 162
Crown gall 272, 273
Crown rot 31, 175
Cucumbers 157
    biological controls 157
    cloches 157
    cold frames 157
    common problems 157
    conditions required 157
    for containers 358
    cutting 157
    fleece 149
    greenhouse 157
    growing outdoors 157
    harvesting 157
    outdoor 157
    pests 157
    planting 157
    pollination 157
    supporting 157
    in unheated greenhouses 379
Cupressus see Cypress
Curled pondweed 327, *327*
Curly waterweed 327
Currant *see* Red currants; *Ribes*; White
    currants
Currant blister aphid 29, 270
Cushion scale 109
Cuttings
    basal rot 403
    conifer 404, 438
    evergreen 404, 437
    greenwood 433
        heel cuttings 434
        when to take 430
    hardwood 404, 436–7
        disbudding 436–7
        mallet cuttings 434
        when to take 430
    heel 434
    leaf-bud 404, 431
    leaves 404
        hooping leaf cuttings 442
        lateral vein cutting 441
        leaf cuttings 439
        leaf-stem cutting 440
        midrib cutting 404, 441
        monocot 442
    mallet 434

root 404, 412–14
    care of new plants 414
    size 413
    starting 414
    trimming 413
    when to take 412
semi-ripe 404, 435
    mallet cuttings 434
    when to take 430
softwood 404
    fungal rot 432
    making 432
    preparing parent plant 433
    taking 433
    when to take 430
stem 430–8
    environmental control 430
    girdling 425
    leaf-bud cutting 431
    parts of the stem 425
    suitable cutting material 425
    when to take 430
    where to cut 430
Cycas
    for containers 357
Cyclamen
    for containers 354
    for shade 68, 69
    coum 69, *69*, 354
    hederifolium 354
Cymbidiums
    in the greenhouse 385
Cymbopogon citratus see Lemon grass
Cypress
    propagation 404, 438
Cyrtanthus
    pests 86

D

Daffodil *see Narcissus*
Dahlia
    for containers 354
    lifting 85
    pests 26, 35
    planting 84
    staking 85
    storing 85
Daikon 192
Daisies 294

Damping off 390, 403
Damselflies 51
Damsons
  renovation 108
Danae
  for containers 357
Dandelions
  taproots 39
Daphne
  for containers 357
  evergreen cuttings 404, 437
  as wall shrub 136
  for winter 73
  bholua 'Jaqueline Postill' 73
Day length 13
Daylily *see Hemerocallis*
Deadheading
  bulbs 79, 85
  herbaceous plants 79
  roses 120
  shrubs 98
Deadnettles
  for shade 68
Deer *36*
  bulbs 86
  herbaceous perennials 81
  protection against 33, 34, 36
  trees 92
Delphinium 66, 67
  deadheading 79
  diseases 82
  propagation 404
  for summer 71
Delphinium black blotch 82
Deschampsia
  for containers 355
Design *see* Design and planning
Deutzia
  renewal pruning 100, 101
Dianthus
  for containers 353, 355
Dicentra
  for containers 355
Dicksonia antarctica
  for shade 69
Die-back 37
Digging 142
  benefits 18
  double 18–19, 142
  no-dig gardening 19

single 18
techniques 18–19
time for 18
trenching 19, 142
vegetable garden 142
Digitalis 76
Dill 209
  cultivation 209
  sowing 209
  use 208
Dimorphotheca
  for containers 353
Dioscorea batatas see Chinese artichokes
  and yams
Diseases
  see also Disorders
  bacterial 30, 82
  bulbs 87, 391
  common 37, 403
  common damage 37, 38
  fruit 271–3
  fungal *see* Fungal diseases
  greenhouses 390–1
  herbaceous perennials 81, 82
  identifying 11, 29, 30, 213, 215
  lawns 297–8
  management 11
  preventative gardening 28
  propagated plants 403
  roses 118, 119, 129
  soil-borne 143
  symptoms 37, 38
  vegetables 213–14
  viral 30, 213
  woody plants 111–12
Disorders 31
  see also Diseases
  bolting 31
  crown rot 31, 175
  distorted growth 31
  frost damage 31
  identifying 31
  mineral deficiencies 31
  oedema 31
  poor fruit set 31
  potassium deficiency 31
  splitting 31
Distorted growth 31
Division 404
  cormels 418

fibrous crowns 423
fleshy crowns 422
herbaceous plants 79, 422–3
natural division 423
perennials 355
rhizomes 417
shrubs 423
tuberous roots 415
tubers 416
Docks
  taproots 39
Dogwood *see Cornus*
Double digging 18–19
Downy mildew 30, 391
  lettuce 152
  onion 187, 213
  spinach 155
Dracunculus
  for containers 354
Dragonflies 51
Drumstick primula 330, *330*
Ducks
  wildlife ponds 51
Duckweed 331
Dwarf reed 329

E
Earwigs 26, 81
Eccremocarpus
  for containers 353
  propagation 404
Echeveria
  propagation 404
Echinacea
  for autumn *72*
  for containers 355
  for summer 71
  purpurea 'White Swan' 71
Echinops
  for containers 355
  for summer 71
  ritro 71
Echinopsis
  in the greenhouse 383
Eelworms
  leaf and bud 81
  Narcissus 86
  potato cyst 199, 212
Eichhornia crassipes 328

Elaeagnus
  for containers 357
  diseases 111
  evergreen cuttings 404, 437
Elder
  dark-leaved 103
  golden 103
  hedges 49
  heel cuttings 434
  pruning
    for foliage 97, 103
    hard 97, 103
    minimal 103
  wildlife garden 54
Eleocharis acicularis 327, *327*
Elephant ears *see Bergenia cordifolia*
Elodea
  canadensis 327
  crispa 327
Elymus magellanicus
  for containers 355
Endive 153
  blanching 153
  common problems 153
  conditions required 153
  harvesting 153
  sowing 153
Epimediums
  for shade 68
Eragrostis airoides
  for containers 355
Eranthis
  for containers 354
  for shade 68, 69
  for winter 73
  hyemalis 69, 84
Erica
  for containers 357
  trimming 99
  carnea 'Springwood White' 73
Erigeron
  propagation 404
Eryngium
  for containers 355
  propagation 404
  bourgatii 67
Erysimum 76
  wildlife garden 55
Erythronium
  for containers 354

'Pagoda', for shade 69
Escallonia
  propagation 404
Eschscholzia californica 67
Eucalyptus
  pruning 98–9
Eucomis 84
Euonymus
  for autumn 72
  for containers 357
  pests 109
  pruning 104
  as wall shrub 136
  for winter 73
  alatus 72
  fortunei 'Emerald 'n' Gold' 73
Euphorbia
  characias subsp. *wulfenii* 67
  polychroma, for containers 355
Evening primrose
  wildlife garden 55
Evergreens
  conifers 68
  pruning evergreen shrubs 98–9
  for shade 68
Exotic salad leaves 156

F

Fairy moss 328
Fairy rings 297
False acacia
  propagation 404
False cyprus *see Chamaecyparis*
Family garden 59
× *Fatshedera lizei*, for containers 357
Fatsia
  for containers 357
  japonica, for shade 68
Felicia
  for containers 353
Fennel 209
  for containers 358
  cultivation 209
  use 208
Ferns
  bog plants 330, *330*
  frost protection 14
  for shade 68
  tree ferns 14

water fern 331, *331*
Fertilizers
  aquatic 336
  base dressing 20
  herbaceous plants 77
  homemade 336
  nutrient content 20
  soil improvement 10, 15, 17, 20
  topdressing 20
Festuca
  for containers 355
Field beans
  green manure 145
Field woodrush 294
Figs 258–60
  aftercare 259–60
  choosing a site 258
  conditions required 258
  for containers 359
  cultivation 258
  diseases 111
  fans 258, 259
  in the greenhouse 260
  harvesting 260
  indoor figs 260
  planting 258–9
  pruning 259, 260
  storing 260
  supports 258
  training 259
Films 149
Fireblight 272, 273
Fish
  wildlife ponds 51
Flag iris
  wildlife garden 54
Flea beetle 156, 192, 195, 211
  protection against 34
Fleabane
  propagation 404
Fleece 149
  containers 362
  in frames 378
  fruit cultivation 221
  pest control 156, 195
  pest deterrent 34
Floating pennywort 328
Flowering cherries 58
Flowering currant *see Ribes*
Flowering quince *see Chaenomeles*

Foam flower
    leaf cuttings 439
Focal points 63
Fodder radish
    green manure 145
Foeniculum vulgare see Fennel
Foliage plants 66
    for containers 356
    evergreen 73
    pruning for foliage 97
    pruning for maximum effect 103
    for shade 68
    winter garden 73
Foot & stem rot 214, 215
Forsythia
    for containers 357
    pests 35
    propagation 404
    renewal pruning 100
    × *intermedia* 70
Fountains *see* Pools
Foxes 49
Foxglove 76
Fragaria vesca subsp. *alpina see* Alpine
    strawberries
Frames *see* Cold frames
Fremontodendron
    as wall shrub 136
French beans 180, 182–3
    common problems 183
    conditions required 182
    cultivation 183
    dwarf types 182, *182*
    fleece 149
    harvesting 183
    intercropping 28
    planting out 183
    sowing 182–3
    successional sowing 182
    supporting 182
Fritillaria
    bulb scaling 420
    for containers 354
    naturalizing 85
    pests 86
    imperialis 84
    meleagris 85
Frogbit 328
Frogs 27, 48, 50, 51
Frost

altitude and 13
    damage 13, 31
        fruit 220
    hardiness 59
    pockets 14, 221
    protection 14
    spring gardens 70
Fruit
    choice of site 220–1
    conditions required 220–1
    for containers 359
    diseases 271–3
    drainage 220
    frost 221
        damage 220
        pockets 221
    mineral deficiency 31
    ornamental 59
    pests 268–70
    placing of plants 222
    planning 222
    poor fruit set 31
    rainfall 220
    for shade 68, 224
    soft fruit 224–39
    soil 221
    splitting 31
    training 222
    tree forms *see* Fruit trees
    wind 221
Fruit trees 59, 222, 240–65
    buying 28
    certified virus-free 28
    common problems 266–7
    cordons 222, 240, 246–7
    corrective pruning 108
    dwarf pyramids 250–1
    espaliers 222, 240, 248–9
    fans 222, 240
        apricots 264
        cherries 256–7
        figs 258, 259
        nectarines 262–3
        peaches 262–3
        plums 255
    forms 222
    greenhouses 379
    heeling in 242
    neglected 267
    ornamental 59

over-vigorous 267
    planting 242
        heeling in 242
    pollination 241
        fertilization 241
        groups 241
        hand pollination 241
        incompatibility groups 241
        ineffective pollinators 241
        poor 31
        structure of blossom 241
    pyramids
        dwarf pyramids 250–1
        plums 254
    renovation 108, 266, 267
    restorative pruning 267
    restricted 222
    staking 242, 266
    stunted 266–7
    suckers 411
    in unheated greenhouses 379
    wall-trained 265
Fuchsia
    for containers 357
    pests 35
    softwood cuttings 432
    for summer 71
    magellanica 71
        hard pruning 102
Fungal diseases 30, 214, 273
    endive 153
    fruit 272
    herbaceous plants 37, 82
    lawn 297, 298
    leaf spots 82, 87, 174, 213
    rhubarb 175
    rusts *see* Rusts
    symptoms 30
    tomatoes 160–1
    woody plants 37, 111
Fungus gnats (sciarid flies) 388, 389, 403
Fusarium patch 298

G

Galanthus
    for containers 354
    diseases 87
    pests 86
    planting 84

propagation 421
transplanting 83
for winter 73
Galium odoratum
  for shade 69
Garden design *see* Planning and design
Garden peas *see* Peas
Garden rooms 63
Garlic 187
  elephant 187
  growing 187
  planting 187
  rust 187
Garrya elliptica
  for shade 69
Gaura lindheimeri
  for containers 355
Gazania
  for containers 355
Gazebos 63
Geranium 355
  for containers 355
  cutting 79
  hardy, for shade 68
  pests 35
  propagation 404
  for summer 71
  'Johnson's Blue' 71
Gesneria
  propagation 404
Geum
  for containers 355
  pests 81
  reptans, propagation from runners 424
Giant hogweed 41, *41*
Giant rhubarb 330
Gingko biloba 72
Gladiolus
  for containers 354
  pests 86
  planting 84
  propagation 404
  staking 85
  storing 85
Gladiolus thrips 86
Glasshouse leafhopper 388, 389
Glasshouse red spider mite 388, 389
Glasshouse whitefly 388, 389, 403
Gloxinia

propagation 404
Golden club 326
Gomphrena
  for containers 353
Gooseberries 225
  aftercare 225
  conditions required 224
  conditions tolerated 224
  for containers 359
  diseases 111
  harvesting 225
  pests 269
  planting 224, 225
  propagation 404
  pruning 225
  for shade 68
  spacing 225
  storing 225
  training 68, 225
Gooseberry sawflies 269
Grape hyacinth *see Muscari*
Grapes 234, *237*
  growing indoors 236–7
    aftercare 237
    planting 236
    pruning 236–7
  growing outdoors 234–5
    aftercare 235
    erecting supports 234
    Guyot system of training 235
    harvesting 235
    planting 234
    pruning 234
    training 234–5
  growing season 220
Grasses
  annual meadow grass 298
  for containers 355
  pampas grass 80, 404
  prairie planting 66, 67
  propagation 424
  red fescues 298
  rye grass 277
  Agrostis species 277
  Festuca species 277
  Lolium perenne 277
Grease band 33
Green manures 41, 145
Greenfly 177
  control 35

courgettes 202
marrows 202
spinach 155
Greenhouses *381*
  annuals in 75
  base 370
  basic requirements 368
  blinds 372
  cleaning 387
  construction 370
  cool 382–4
    early strawberries 384
    fruit 384
    ornamentals 382–3
    raising plants 383
    shrubs 384
    summer bedding plants from seeds 382
    trees 384
    vegetables 384
    winter-flowering chrysanthemum 383
  cucumbers 157
  diseases 390–1
  electricity 372
  extractor fans 371
  figs 260
  foundation 370
  fruit, cool greenhouse 384
  growing in 367, 375–86
    border soil 375, 376
    containers 375–6
    growing bags 375
  hardy annuals in 75
  heating
    carbon dioxide by-product 373
    fan heaters 372, 373
    gas heaters 372, 373
    paraffin heaters 373
    solar panels 373
    sources 372–3
    surface area calculation 373
    tubular heaters 372, 373
  humidity, raising 374
  hygiene 387–91
  insulation 373
  lean-to greenhouses 377
  maintenance 387
  meeting plant needs 366–7
  melons 239

mini greenhouses 378
ornamentals
cool greenhouse 382–3
unheated greenhouse 380
pests 35, 388–9
plant supports 377
canes 377
cordon grape vines 377
galvanized wires 377
mesh 377
netting 377
permanent 377
stakes 377
string 377
tall plants 377
temporary 377
twine 377
walls 377
shading 372, 385
blinds 372
paint 372
shelter from wind 370
site 370
situation 370
strawberries 233, 379, 384
structural materials 368
temperature 373
tidying 387
tomatoes 158–60, 161
unheated greenhouse 379
types 368
unheated 379–80
annuals for spring flowering 380
hyacinth bulbs 379
ornamentals 380
tree fruit 379
vegetables 379
utilizing space *376*
vegetables
cool greenhouse 384
unheated greenhouse 379
ventilation 371
automated vents 371
chimney effect 371
extractor fans 371
louvred vents 371
methods 371
viruses 390
warm 385–6
cymbidiums 385, 386

epiphytic orchids on bark 385, 386
water butts 374
water harvesting 374
water supply 374
watering 374
capillary matting 374
timing 374
trickle irrigation 374
watering cans 374
Grey mould 30, 403
endive 153
greenhouses 391
snowdrop 87
Ground cover
perennials 41
roses 125
shade 68
weed control 41
Ground elder
rhizomes 39, 412
Growing bags
in the greenhouse 375–6
Gunnera manicata 330

H

Hair grass 327, *327*
Hakonechloa macra
for containers 355
Hamamelis 73
propagation 404
pruning 104
for winter 73
'Pallida' 73
Hanging baskets 344
compost 350
fibre 344, 345
fixing 345
liners 345
moss lining 352
planting 352
plastic 344
rise-&-fall 361
terracotta 344
watering 360
wicker 344–5
wire 344
wooden 344, 345
Hard wood cutting 396
Hardening off 395

seedlings 408
in unheated frames 378
Hawthorn
wildlife garden 54, 55
Hazels
purple, pruning 97, 103
'Heat island' 14
Heather *see Erica*
Hebe
for containers 357
propagation 404
Hedera
for containers 357
hedge 49
propagation 404
for shade 68, 69
wildlife garden 49, 54, 55
Hedgehogs 26, 27, 49
attracting 48
Hedges 113–16
bases 49
choosing 113
climbers 49
conifers 49, 116
cutting 94, 114
dead hedge 49
formal 114
informal 114
mixed selection 49
native 49, 113
planting 113
pruning 94, 114–16
coniferous 116
deciduous 115
established hedge 116
evergreen 115
formative 115, 116
renovation 116
renovation 116
spacing the plants 113
thickening at the base 114
types 114
wildlife habitat 49, 113, 114
Heeling in
fruit trees 242
roses 119
shrubs 92
trees 92
Helenium
for containers 355

propagation 404
stopping 79
Eupatorium 79
Veronicastrum 79
Helianthemum 'Wisley Primrose' 67
Helianthus 66, 75
for containers 353
annuus 67
Helichrysum petiolare
for containers 355
Heliotropium
for containers 353
Hellebore black death 82
Helleborus 73
for containers 355
diseases 82
for shade 68
for winter 73
niger 69
Heloniopsis
leaf cuttings 442
Hemerocallis 330
for containers 355
diseases 87
pests 81
propagation 404
for summer 71
lilioasphodelus 330
Hemerocallis gall midge 81
Herb wheel 208
Herbaceous perennials 77–82
bare-root 77
borders 64, 77–80
maintenance 78–80
clearing away old growth 80
container-grown 77
cutting back in autumn 80
deadheading 79
diseases 37, 82
division 79, 422–3
fibrous crowns 423
fleshy crowns 422
feeding 78
fungal diseases 37, 82
greenwood cuttings 433
mulching 78
pests 35, 81
planting 77
prairie planting 66
renovation 79

staking 78–9
stopping 79, 80
thinning 80
Herbs *151, 206, 207, 208*
clay soil 206
conditions required 206, 209
conditions tolerated 209
for containers 358
cultivation 206
drainage 206
drying 208
freezing 208
gravel 206
growing 206–8
harvesting 208
ornamental 59
propagation 206, 209
raised beds 206
site preparation 206
storing 208
for sun 67, *67*
Hesperis matronalis 55, *55*
Heuchera
for containers 355
Heucheras
for shade 68
Hibiscus
propagation 404
pruning 104
Hieracium pilosella 294
Himalayan balsam 41, *41*
Hippeastrum
pests 86
Hoeing 155, 163, 195
roses 119
weed control 39, 148
Holcus lanatus 294
Holly *see Ilex*
Honesty *see Lunaria annua*
Honey fungus 37, 175
hedge 49
roses 129
Honeydew 109, 110, 403
Honeysuckle *see Lonicera*
Hordeum jubatum
for containers 355
Hornwort 327, *327*
Horse chestnut
pruning 97
Horse chestnut bleeding canker 112

Horse chestnut leaf-mining moth 109
Horseradish
root cuttings 412
Hosta
for containers 355
cutting back in autumn 80
for shade 68, 69
'Gold Standard' *69*
sieboldiana 330
Hottonia palustris 326
House leek *see Sempervivum*
Hoverflies 26
attracting 48
habitat 48
larvae 26, 27
Hoya
propagation 404
Humus 16, 20
Hyacinth *see Hyacinthus*
Hyacinthoides
for shade 68
Hyacinthus
for containers 354
propagation 421
for spring 70, 379
in unheated greenhouses 379
Hydrangea
pests 35
renewal pruning 100, 101
macrophylla, propagation 404
paniculata 69
hard pruning 102
for shade 68, 69
petiolaris, propagation 404
Hydrocharis morsus-ranae 328
Hydrocotyle
ranunculoides 328
vulgaris 328
Hypericum
for containers 357
calycinum, propagation 404
Hypoaspis miles
biological control 403

I

Ilex
for autumn 72
for containers 357
pests 109

renovation 107
wildlife garden 55
Impatiens
  for containers 353
  for shade 68
  softwood cuttings 432
Imperata cylindrica 'Rubra'
  for containers 355
Incarvillea
  propagation 404
Indian bean tree *see Catalpa*
  bignonioides
Insects
  beneficial 26, 47, 48
  predators 26, 27, 32
Intercropping 41, 143
Interplanting
  pest prevention 28
Ipheion
  for containers 354
Iris
  bulbous, propagation 419
  for containers 354
  diseases 87
  foetidissima 79
  laevigata 329
    'Variegata' 329
  pseudacorus 329
  reticulata 354
  versicolor 329
Iris leaf spot 87
Iron deficiency 31
Isotoma
  for containers 353
Italian ryegrass
  green manure 145
Itea ilicifolia
  for shade 69
Ivy *see Hedera*

J

Japanese knotweed 41, *41*
Japanese maples *see Acer japonicum; Acer*
  palmatum
Jasmine
  for containers 357
Jerusalem artichokes
  propagation 416
Juncus

'Curly-wurly', for containers 355
  effusus f. *spiralis* 329
Juniper
  for containers 357
  propagation 404

K

Kale 170
  conditions required 170
  cultivation 170
  harvesting 170
  ornamental 170
  pests 170
  sowing 170
  Italian black kale *170*
    'Nero di Toscano' 170
  red curly kale *170*
    'Redbor' 170
  red winter kale *170*
Kalmia
  propagation 404
Kerria
  renewal pruning 100, 101
  japonica, propagation 404
Kirengeshoma palmata
  for shade 69
Knautia macedonica
  for containers 355
Knife
  choosing 397
  cutting hardwood 396
  sharpening 397
  using 397
Kniphofia 67
  for containers 355
Kohlrabi 194
  for containers 358, *358*
Kolkwitzia
  renewal pruning 100

L

Laburnum
  pruning 97
  × *watereri* 'Vosii' 70
Lacewings 26, 119
  attracting 48
  habitat 48
  larvae 27

Ladybirds
  attracting 48
  habitat 48
  larvae 119
Lady's mantle *see Alchemilla*
Lagarosiphon major 327
Lagurus
  for containers 353
Lamium
  for shade 68, 69
  maculatum 'White Nancy' 69
Large rose sawfly 128
Larkspur 75
Larval food plants 55
Lathyrus odoratus
  growing 76
  sowing 76
  training 66
Laurus
  for containers 357
  nobilis see Bay
Lavandula angustifolia 'Hidcote' 67
Lavatera
  propagation 404
Lavender
  for containers 357, *357*
  pruning 99
  sea lavender 404
  wildlife garden 55
Lawn 276–301
  access points 279
  aeration 288, 299
    machines 288
    methods 288
  aspect 278–9
  bare patches 301
  boundaries and 279
  broken edges 300
  bumps 300
  choosing the type 277
  circular *278*
  clippings
    composting 293
    removing 293
  common problems 294–8
    diseases 297–8
    over-application of feed 286
    pests 296
    weeds 293, 294–5
  converting to meadow 52, 53

crocuses naturalized on 85
curves 279, *279*
dead patches 297
diseases 297–8
drought 15
entrances 279
fairy rings 297
family garden 59
feeding 286
    application methods 286
    organic approach 286
    proprietary mixes 286
    renovation 299
flower beds in 279
fungal diseases 297, 298
fusarium patch 298
grasses
    annual meadow grass 298
    red fescues 298
    rye grass 277
    Agrostis species 277
    Festuca species 277
    Lolium perenne 277
hollows 300
levelling bumps and hollows 300
long and narrow *278*, 279
maintenance 286–93
molehills 296, *297*
mosses 294
moulds 298
mowers 291
    cylinder 291
    electric 291
    hover 291
    petrol 279, 291
    rotary 291
mowing 279, 292–3
    composting clippings 293
    correct height 292
    dew 292
    dry periods 292
    frequency of cut 292
    leaving clippings 293
    removing clippings 293
    renovation 299
    striped finish 293
    techniques 293
    timing 292–3
neglected, repairing 299–301
ophiobolus patch 297

patches
    bare 301
    dead 297
    fusarium 298
    ophiobolus 297
pests 296–7
planning 64, 278–9
planting around 279
planting in 84, 85
practical considerations 279
pythium blight 298
raised 279
red thread 298
renovation 299
repairing 299–301
    bare patches 301
    broken edges 300
    levelling bumps and hollows 300
scarifying 287, 299
    aeration process 288
    tools 287
seeds 282
    advantages 282
    disadvantages 282
shade 279
shape 64
shaping 279
site 279
site preparation 280–1
    clearing 280
    fallowing 281
    final preparation 281
    firming the soil 281
    grading 280
    herbicide 281
    levelling 280, 281
    soil preparation 280
    using a rotavator 280
slime moulds 298
snow mould 298
sowing 283
    aftercare 283
    bare patches 301
    by hand 283
    rate 283
    with a seed distributor 283
thatch 287
tools
    aerating machine 288
    edging shears 291, 293

    forks 288
    rakes 287
    scarifying 287
    trimming 291
    watering 290
topdressing 289
    applying 289, 299
    making mixes 289
    timing 289
    using a lute 289
trees and 279
    weeds 294
trimming tools 291
turf 282
    advantages 282
    disadvantages 282
turves 284–5
    aftercare 285
    checking 285
    initial checks 284
    laying 284, 285
    storing 285
watering 15, 290, 299
    equipment 290
    hose reel 290
    method 290
    run off 290
    sprinkler 290
    timing 290
weeds 293, 294–5
    chemical weedkillers 295
    creeping 294
    grasses 294
    hand weeding 295
    lichens 294–5
    liverworts 294–5
    mosses 294
    removing manually 295
    rosette-forming 294
    spot treatment 295
    trees and 294
    white clover 293, 294
wormcasts 296
Layering 404, 426–7
    air 404, 428
    girdling a stem 425, 427
    tip 429
Leaf & bud eelworm 81
Leaf mining flies 191, 193
Leaf spots 82, 213

celery 174
iris 87
Leaf-rolling sawfly 128
Leafmould 25
Leafy gall 390
Leatherjackets 29, 296
Leek rust 213
Leeks 188
  blanching 188
  common problems 188
  conditions required 188
  cultivation 188
  earthing up 188
  harvesting 188
  intercropping 143
  sowing 188
  watering 188
Lemna 331
Lemon *see Citrus*
Lemon grass 209
  sowing 209
Lesser celandine
  tubers 39
Lettuces 150–2
  common problems 152
  for containers 358
  cultivation 152
  growing 150
  harvesting 150
  intercropping 41, 143
  leafy 150
  loose-leaved *152*
  pests 152
  site 152
  soil 152
  sowing 150, 152
  thinning seedlings 152
  in unheated greenhouses 379
  watering 148, 150
  butterheads 150
  Cos 150
  crispheads 150
  Little Gem 150
  stem (celtuce) 150
Leycesteria
  hard pruning 102
Leyland cypress
  propagation 438
Lichens 294–5
Lilac

propagation 404
Lilium 354
  bulb scaling 420
  for containers 354
  diseases 87
  pests 86
Lily *see Lilium*
Lily beetle 86
Lily disease 87
Lily of the valley *see Convallaria*
Liminium
  propagation 404
Limnanthes 75
Limonium
  for containers 353
Liquid feed
  making 21
Liquidambar styraciflua 72
Liverworts 294–5
Lobelia
  for containers 353
  for summer 71
Loganberry 230
Lonicera 55
  for containers 357
  evergreen 136
  pruning 136
  training 136
  as wall shrub 136
  henryi 136
  hildebrandiana 136
  japonica 136
  periclymenum 136
Loosestrife *see Lythrum*
Lotus
  for containers 353
Love-in-a-mist
  sowing 75
Lunaria annua
  sowing 75
Lupin
  propagation 404
Lupin anthracnose 82
Luzula
  campestris 294
  nivea, for containers 355
Lythrum
  propagation 404
  salicaria 55
    wildlife garden 55

M

Magnesium deficiency 31
Magnolia
  for containers 357
  diseases 111
  propagation
    evergreen cuttings 404, 437
    layering 404, 426
  pruning 104
  grandiflora 437
  stellata 70, 357
    for spring 70
Mahonia
  pests 110
  propagation 404
  renovation 107
  for winter 73
  aquifolium, for shade 68
  × *media* 'Charity' 73
Malus
  for autumn 72
  diseases 38
  hedges 49
  for spring 70
  wildlife garden 54
  for winter 73
Mandevilla sanderi
  in the greenhouse 383
Mangetout peas 176
Manure 20
  animal 21, 143
  green 145
  roses 119
Maples *see Acer*
Maranta
  in the greenhouse 386
Marigold *see Calendula*
Marjoram 209
  for containers 358
  cultivation 209
Marrows *202*
  black plastic sheet mulch 201
  common problems 202
  conditions required 200
  for containers 358
  flowers 201
  harvesting 201
  pinching out 201
  planting 201

site 201
situation 201
sowing 201
transplanting 200
watering 201
Maypoling 252
Meadow *see* Wildflower meadow
Mealy cabbage aphids 162, 169, 170
Mealybugs 388, 389
Melianthus major
for containers 355
Melons 238, *238*
cold frame 238
growing in a greenhouse 239
planting 239
supporting the fruit 239
growing outdoors 238
protecting 238
in unheated greenhouses 379
cantaloupe 238
'Charantais' 238
Mentha spicata see Mint
Mesh 186, 195
Mesh netting 34
Mice
rodent tree guard 92
Michaelmas daisies
division 423
Michaelmas daisy mite 81
Microclimates 14, 220
Mildew
downy 30, 155, 391
lettuce 152
onion 187, 213
powdery *see* Powdery mildew
Mimulus 330
for containers 353
guttatus 330
luteus 330
Mina lobata
for containers 353
Mineral deficiencies 31
Mini cloche 33
Mint 209
for containers 358
cultivation 209
propagating 206
Mint rust 214, 215
Mirabilis
for containers 353

Miscanthus 73
for containers 355
cutting 80
for summer 71
sinensis 71
'Zebrinus' *71*
Mites
black currant big bud mite 269
glasshouse red spider mite 388, 389
Michaelmas daisy mite 81
pear blister mite 269
predatory 32
raspberry leaf & bud mite 270
spider mites 403
Modular trays 75, 400, *400*
Molehills *297*
Moles 296
Molinia
for containers 355
Monkey flower *see Mimulus*
Mooli 192
Morning glory
for containers 353
Mosses 294
sphagnum moss 345
Mother-in-law's tongue *see Sansevieria trifasciata*
Moths
attracting 48, 55
pests
codling moth 268
horse chestnut leaf-mining moth 109
pea moth 177, 212
plum moth 268–9
tortrix moths 388, 389
winter moth 270
Mouse-ear hawkweed 294
Mulberries 265
buying 265
conditions required 265
cultivation 265
harvesting 265
pruning 265
wall-trained 265
Mulching 22
applying 22
asparagus 172
bark chips 21
biodegradable mulches 22, 41

climbers 131
fruit-growing 221
herbaceous borders 78
loose mulches 40
no-dig gardening 19
sheet mulches 40–1, 143, 202
shrubs 92
temperature and 22
trees 92
water conservation 15
weed control 40, 148
Musa basjoo 66
Muscari
for containers 354
propagation 421
Mustard
green manure 145
Mycorrhizal fungi 89–90
Myosotis scorpioides 329
Myriophyllum
aquaticum 327
spicatum 327, *327*
verticillatum 327
Myrtle
for containers 357

N

Nandina
for containers 357
Narcissus
for containers 354
deadheading 79
diseases 87
naturalized on lawns 85
pests 86
planting 83
propagation 419
for shade 68
for spring 70
bulbocodium 68
Jonquil 87
Poetaz 87
Poeticus 87
Polyanthus 87
Tazetta 87
Triandus 87
Narcissus bulb flies 86
Narcissus eelworm 86
Narcissus leaf scorch 87

Narrow gardens
  planning 64
Nassella trichotoma
  for containers 355
Nasturtium *see Tropaeolum*
Native planting 59
Nectar
  wildlife plants 55
Nectarines 261–3
  aftercare 263
  choosing a site 261
  conditions required 240
  disease 272
  fans 262–3
  harvesting 261, 263
  planting 261
  pruning 261
  spacing 261
  storing 263
  thinning 261
  training 261–3
  in unheated greenhouses 379
Nectria canker 271
Nematodes 32
  slug control 33, 35
  vine weevil control 36
  Heterorhabditis megidis 296
  narcissus eelworm 86
  Phasmarhabditis hermaphrodita 33, 35
  Steinernema krauseii 36
Nemesia
  for containers 353
Nepeta
  for containers 355
  propagation 404, 417
  for summer 71
Nerine
  for containers 85
  sarniensis, in the greenhouse 383
New Zealand flax *see Phormium*
New Zealand pygmy weed 328, 331, *331*
Newts 27, 48, 50, 51
Nicotiana
  for containers 353
Nierembergia
  for containers 353
Nigella damascena 75
Nitrogen 17
  compost making 23, 24

fertilizers 20
locking–up 21
No-dig gardening 19
Nolana
  for containers 353
Nuphar 324, 326
  lutea subsp. *advena* 326
Nymphaea 50, 324
  propagation 404, 416
  alba 331
  'Aurora' 324
  'Californiana' 324
  'Gonnère' 324
  'James Brydon' 324
Nyssa sylvatica
  for autumn 72
  'Wisley Bonfire' 72

O

Oak 58
Ocimum basilicum see Basil
Oedema 31
Oil-seed rape 53
Olea europaea 67
  for containers 357, *357*
Olive *see Olea europaea*
Onion downy mildew 187, 213
Onion fly 186
Onion thrips 186
Onion white rot 186, 188, 213
Onions 184–6, *186*
  bolt-resistant 185
  bolting 184
  cloches 186
  common problems 186
  conditions required 184
  for containers 358
  cultivation 185
  diseases 186, 188, 213
  drying 186
  feeding 185
  harvesting 184, 185–6
  intercropping 28
  pests 28, 186
  planting 184
  sowing 184, 185
  spring or salad onions 185
    in unheated greenhouses 379
  storing 186

Ophiopogon planiscapus 'Nigrescens'
  for containers 355
Orchids
  epiphytic, grown on bark 385, 386
Origanum majorana see Marjoram
Ornamentals 58
  in the greenhouse 380, 382–3
  types of garden 59
Orontium aquaticum 326
Osmanthus
  for containers 357
Osmuna regalis 330, *330*
Oxalis 39

P

Pachysandra terminalis
  for shade 69
Palms
  for containers 357
  frost protection 14
  Chamaerops humilis 66
  Trachycarpus fortunei 66
Pampas grass 80, 404
Panicum
  for containers 355
Pansies
  for containers 353
Papaver
  annual 75
  propagation 404
  wildflower meadow 53
  winter protection 75
Paper-bark maple 73, *73*
Parrotias
  layering 426
Parrot's feather 327
Parsley 209
  for containers 358
  cultivation 209
  freezing 208
  propagating 206
  sowing 209
Parsnip canker 191
Parsnips 191
  common problems 191
  conditions required 191
  cultivation 191
  harvesting 191
  intercropping 143

sowing 191
watering 148
Parthenocissus
   propagation 404
Pasque flower
   root cuttings 413
Passiflora
   propagation 404
   caerulea 67
Passion flower *see Passiflora*
Pea & bean weevil 211
Pea moth 177, 212
Peach leaf curl 29, 272, 273
Peaches 261–3, *261*
   aftercare 263
   choosing a site 261
   conditions required 240
   for containers 359
   disease 272
   fans 262–3
   harvesting 261, 263
   planting 261
   pruning 261
   spacing 261
   storing 263
   thinning 261
   training 261–3
   in unheated greenhouses 379
Pear & plum rusts 271
Pear blister mite 269
Pear midge 268, 269
Pears 243
   biennial bearing 252
   care 251–2
   choosing rootstocks 243
   choosing a site 243
   choosing trees 243
   cordons 246
      choosing plants 246
      choosing rootstock 246
      forms 247
      maintaining 247
      planting 246
      pruning 246–7
      spacing 246
      supporting 246
      training 246
   diseases 271
   dwarf pyramids 250–1
      mature 251

planting 250–1
   pruning 250, 251
   spacing 251
   supporting 250–1
   training 251
   espaliers 248–9, *248*
      choosing plants 248
      choosing rootstock 248
      planting 248
      pruning 248–9
      spacing 248
      supporting 248
      training 248–9
   freestanding trees 243–4
   frost damage 220
   harvesting 251–2
   maintaining 252
   maypoling 252
   overcrowded spur systems 248
   pests 268, 269
   pruning
      cordons 246–7
      dwarf pyramids 250, 251
      espaliers 248–9
      restorative 267
   pruning for fruit 244
      renewal pruning 244
      spur pruning 244
   renovating 267
   rootstock 248, 250, 251
   training 243
Peas *176*
   conditions required 176
   for containers 358
   cultivation 177
   garden peas 176–7
   green manure 145
   growing conditions 176
   harvesting 177
   insecticides 177
   mangetout 176
   pests 177, 211
   petit-pois 176
   sowing 177
   successive sowing 176–7
   sugarsnap 176
Pelargonium
   oedema 31
   propagation 404
Pennisetum

for containers 355
Penstemon
   pests 81
   for summer 71
   'Blackbird' 71
Peony
   propagation 404
Peony wilt 82
Peperomia
   in the greenhouse 386
   oedema 31
   propagation 404
Peppers 204
   blossom end rot 204
   common problems 204
   conditions required 204
   for containers 358
   cultivation 204
   fleece 149
   harvesting 204
   lack of water 204
   pinching out 204
   planting 204
   plug plants 204
   in unheated greenhouses 379
Perennials 58, 67
   for autumn 72
   for containers 355
   division 355
   ground cover 41
   herbaceous *see* Herbaceous perennials
   late-flowering 72
   for shade 68
   short-lived 76
   for spring 70
   for summer 71
   for sun 67
   for winter 73
Periwinkle *see Vinca*
Perovskia
   for containers 357
   hard pruning 102
   'Blue Spire' 67, *67*
Persicaria
   for containers 355
Pests 11, 29
   barriers 33
   beans 211, 214
   birds 27
   brassicas 34, 162

bulbs 86
common 35–6
common damage 35, 36, 110
control
    animal predators 26, 27
    barriers 33, 34
    biological 32, 33, 35, 204
    chemical 32
    crop covers 33
    insect predators 26, 27, 32
    interplanting 28
    preventative gardening 28
    repelling devices 34
    traps 34, 157
crop covers 33
cucumbers 157
fruit 268–70
greenhouses 35, 388–9, 403
herbaceous perennials 81
identifying 29, 212
large pests 34
lawn 296–7
lettuce 152
management 11
repelling devices 34
roses 119, 128–9
sap-sucking 35
scaring devices 34
severity of infestation 110
shrubs 35, 109–10
soil-borne 143
symptoms 11, 29
vegetables 210–12
winter shelter 80
woody plants 109–10
Petroselinum crispum see Parsley
Petunia
for containers 353
frost damage 13
sowing 75
Philadelphus
propagation 404
pruning
    for foliage 97
    renewal pruning 100
for summer 71
'Belle Étoile' 71
Phlomis
for containers 357
fruticosa 67

Phlox
for containers 355
cutting back 79
propagation 404
for summer 71
paniculata 71
Phormium
for containers 355
propagation 404
    offsets 424
Phosphorus 17
fertilizers 20
Phyllostachys nigra 73
Phytophthora 37–8, 112
    infestans see Potato blight
Pickerel weed 329, *329*
Pieris
pests 110
propagation 404
Pieris lacebug 110
Pileostegia
propagation 404
Pink
for containers 355
Pistia stratiotes 328
Pittosporum
for containers 357
Planning and design
autumn garden 72
balance 62
basics 60–5
borders 64, *64*
children 59, 61
colour planning 64
computer design package 61
courtyard garden 59, *64*
crops 143
deciding what to keep 60–1
focal points 63, *64*
fruit 222
function 62–3
garden rooms 63
gazebos 63
harmony 62
intrigue 63
jungle feel *64*
lawn 64, 278–9
location 61
narrow gardens 64
path 64

planting
    balance 62
    gardens in shade 68–9
    gardens in sun 66–7
    massed 62
    sparse 62
plants
    foliage 66
    placing 66–73
    plant qualities 64
    structure 66
    style 66
    types 58–9
pools 306
practicality 62–3
rural gardens 61
screening 63
sculptures 63
shrubs 64
simplicity 62
sketch 61
small garden 62, 64
small town garden 61
spring garden 70
suburban gardens 61
summer garden 71
summerhouses 63
trees 63, 64
tricks 64
vegetable garden 143
wildlife garden 46
wildlife pond 50–1, 319
winter garden 73
Plantago major 294
Plum moth 268–9
Plumbago capensis
in the greenhouse 383
Plums 253–5
aftercare 255
choosing a site 253
choosing trees 253
diseases 271
fan 255
harvesting 255
pests 268
planting 253, 254
pollination 255
pruning 254
pyramid 254
renovation 108

spacing 254
storing 255
thinning 253
training 254–5
Poached-egg plant 75
Pollarding 102, 103
Pollen
wildlife plants 55
Pollination
fertilization 241
fruit trees 241, 255
groups 241
hand pollination 241
incompatibility groups 241
ineffective pollinators 241
poor 31
structure of blossom 241
Polyanthus
for shade 68
Polygonatum
pests 81
propagation 404
× *hybridum*, for shade 69
Polytunnels 149, 369
using 378
Pondlily *see Nuphar*
Ponds *see* Pools
Pontederia
albiflora 329
cordata 329, *329*
Pools
algae 307, 337
filters 310, 337
seasonal changes 337
autumn care 333
care 332–7
cascade *306*
cleaning 334
concrete 309
repairing 335
defences 337
designs 306
draining 334
edging 317
liner ponds 317
paving 315, 317
pre-formed ponds 315
stones 317
turf 317
electric heaters 333

emptying 334
evaporation 333
filters 310
algae and 310, 337
biological 310
function 310
mechanical 310
flat 307
floating ring 333
formal 306
fountains 312
barrel 312
choosing 312
installing 312
ornamental 312
pebble 312
positioning the pump 312
sprays 312
wall 312
freezing over 332, 333
protecting liner 333
ventilation hole 333
heaters 310
informal 306
island, building 319
lighting 311, *311*
above-water 311
floating 311
floating candles 311
permanently submerged 311
liners 309
butyl rubber 309, 335
calculating size 316
cross-section 309
edging 317
EPDM 309
excavating 317
expanding ice 333
installing 316, 317
laying 316–17
marking out 313
polythene 309
preventing cracking 333
PVC 309
repairing 335
underlining 316, 317
linking features 308
see also Bog garden
marking out 313
excavating 313

irregular shapes 313
levelling 313
liner pond 313
pre-formed pond 313
muddy water 337
nutrient content 51
oxygenators 331
perspective and 308
plants *see* Water plants
plastic herons 337
pre-formed 309
edging with paving 315
installing 314–15
laying the edging 315
marking out 313
repairs 335
underlining 314
predators 337
problems 337
algae 337
muddy water 337
protecting 337
pumps 310
submersible 310
surface 310
waterfall 310
raised 307
repairs 335
butyl liner 335
concrete pond 335
pre-formed pools 335
safeguarding children 307
seasonal care 332–3
seasonal changes 337
sight line 307
siting practicalities 307
on slopes 308
spring care 332
suiting the site 308
summer care 333
topping up 333
trees and 307
weedkillers 331
wildlife *see* Wildlife ponds
winter care 333
Poplar rusts 111
Poppy *see Papaver*
Potamogeton crispa 327, *327*
Potassium 17
deficiency 31

468

fertilizers 20
Potato blight 199, 214, 215
   see also Phytophthora
Potato cyst eelworms 199, 212
Potatoes 196–9
   buying 28
   certified virus-free 28
   chitting 197
   common problems 199
   conditions required 196
   for containers 199
   cultivation 198–9
   diseases 197, 214, 215
      blight 199, 214, 215
   earlies 149, 196, 197
   early maincrop 196
   frost damage 31
   growing under black polythene 198,
     199
   harvesting 199
   maincrop 196
   microplants 197
   'mini-tubers' 197
   pests 35, 199, 212
   planting 196, 198–9
   potted 199
   propagation 416
   'rose end' 197
   salad 196–7
   scab 197, 214, 215
   second earlies 196, 197
   seed potatoes 197
   seed tubers 197
   site 197
   soil 197–8
   tuber 416
   types 196
   watering 148
   winter crops 199
Potentilla
   for containers 357
   herbaceous, runners 424
   propagation 404
   fruticosa 357
Pots *see* Containers
Powdery mildews 38, 202, 214, 215
   cucumbers 157
   fruit 272, 273
   peas 177
   rose 129

symptoms 38
   woody plants 112
Powdery scab 214, 215
Prairie planting 66, 67
Predatory mites 32
Preventative gardening 28
Primrose *see Primula*
Primula 330
   for containers 355
   division 404, 422
   naturalizing 85
   for shade 68
   for spring 70
   bulleyana 330
   denticulata 330
   rosea 330
Propagation 394–443
   basics 394, 396–404
   bulbs 419–21
   capillary systems 402
   cloches 398–9
   cold frames 399
   compost 401
      John Innes 401
      making your own 401
      mixing 401
      multipurpose 401
      soil-based 401
      soilless 401
   containers 400
      biodegradable 400
      choosing 400
      disposable pots 400
      modular trays 75, 400, *400*
      seed containers 400
   controlling the environment 398–9
   cormels 418
   corms 418
   cutting hard wood 396
   cuttings *see* Cuttings
   diseases 403
   division *see* Division
   equipment 396–7
   from runners 233
   herbs 206, 209
   homemade plastic covers 398, 399
   hormone rooting powder 401
   layering *see* Layering
   leaf cuttings 404, 439
   methods 394

offsets 424
pests 403
plastic covers 398, 399
rhizomes 39, 417
root cuttings *see* Cuttings
rooting hormone 401
runners 424
seeds *see* Seeds; Seedlings
selecting suitable plant material 395
suckers 404
   woody shrubs 411
suitable conditions for regeneration 395
tools 396–8
tuberous roots 415
tubers 39, 416
watering 402
   capillary systems 402
   from above 402
   from below 402
   via a sand bed 402
weeds 39
windowsill propagator 399
woody shrubs with suckers 411
work bench 396
Pruning
   apple trees
      cordons 246–7
      dwarf pyramids 250, 251
      espaliers 248–9
      pruning for fruit 244
      renewal pruning 244
      restorative 267
      spur pruning 244
   apricots 264
   black currant 226
   blackberries 230
   blueberries 227
   ceanothus 100, 102, 137
   cherries 257
      fans 256–7
   clematis 132–3
   climbers and wall plants 131
      roses 122, 124
   coppicing 102
   cordons 95, 246–7
   corrective 108
   cut 94
   deciduous shrubs 100–4
   drastic 107
   espaliers 95, 134–5, 248–9

evergreen shrubs 98–9
figs 259
for foliage 97, 103
    hard pruning for maximum effect
        103
formative
    clematis 133
    climbers and wall plants 131
    hedges 115, 116
    pear trees 246–7
    shrubs 95
    trees 95
    wisteria 135
gooseberries 225
grapes, indoors 234, 236–7
hard pruning 102–3
    for maximum foliage effect 103
    for winter stems 102
heather 99
hedges 94, 114–16
honeysuckle 136
lavender 99
minimal 104
mulberries 265
nectarines 261
peaches 261
pear trees
    cordons 246–7
    dwarf pyramids 250, 251
    espaliers 248–9
    pruning for fruit 244
    renewal pruning 244
    spur pruning 244
plums 254
pollarding 102, 103
renewal pruning 244
restorative 267
reverted shoots 97
roses 121–7
shrubs 94–104, 107
spur pruning 244
tools 120
trees 94–7, 105–6, 108
wisteria 134–5
Prunus
    renovation 107
Pulsatilla vulgaris see Pasque flower
Pumpkins *202*
    common problems 202
    conditions required 200

harvesting 202
pinching out 201
planting 200
sheet mulch 202
site 201
situation 201
sowing 202
transplanting 200
watering 201
weak growth 202
Purple loosestrife *see Lythrum*
Pyracantha
    diseases 38
    hedges 49
    propagation 404
    renovation 137
    training 137
    as wall shrub 136, 137
    wildlife garden 54
Pythium blight 298

Q
Quince leaf blight 272, 273
Quinces 265
    buying 265
    conditions required 265
    cultivation 265
    diseases 272, 273
    flowering *see Chaenomeles*
    harvesting 265
    pruning 265

R
Rabbits
    bulbs 86
    herbaceous perennials 81
    lawn 297
    protection against 33, 34, 36
    tree damage 36, 92
Radicchio *see* Chicory
Radishes 192
    common problems 192
    conditions required 192
    for containers 358
    cultivation 192
    fodder radish 145
    harvesting 192
    intercropping 143

Oriental 192
    sowing 192
    in unheated greenhouses 379
Rain 13
Rain-detecting devices 15
Rainwater butt 15
Raised beds 156
    brick planters 348
    container gardening 348, *348*, 355
    frost protection 355
    herbs 206
    kits 348
    vegetable garden 142–3
    wooden beds 348
Ramblers
    roses 67, 122, 124
Ranunculus aquatils 326
Raspberries 228–9, *228*
    autumn-fruiting 228, 229
    maintaining 229
    pests 270
    planting 228
    supporting 228
Raspberry beetle 270
Raspberry leaf & bud mite 270
Rebutia
    in the greenhouse 383
Red currants 225
    aftercare 225
    conditions required 224
    conditions tolerated 224
    for containers 359
    diseases 111
    harvesting 225
    pests 29, 270
    planting 224, 225
    propagation 404
    pruning 225
    for shade 68, 224
    soil 224
    spacing 225
    storing 225
    training 68, 225
Red hot poker 67
Red thread 298
Red valerian
    wildlife garden 55
Reedmace 331, *331*
Repelling devices 34
Reverted shoots

pruning 97
Rhinanthus minor 52, 53
Rhizomes 412, 417
dividing 417
weeds 39
Rhodochiton
for containers 353
Rhododendron
for containers *356*, 357
diseases 111
in the greenhouse 380
heel cuttings 434
pests 109, 110
renovation 107
for shade 68, 69
for spring 70
ponticum see Japanese knotweed
Rhododendron leafhopper 109
Rhubarb 175
conditions required 175
cultivation 175
forcing 175
harvesting 175
planting 175
propagation 404
Rhus
for autumn 72
propagation 404
suckers 97
typhina 72
pruning 103
Ribes
propagation 404
sanguineum
'King Edward VII' *70*
renewal pruning 100
for spring 70
Ricinus
for containers 353
Robinia
propagation 404
Rock rose *see Cistus*
Rocket 156
conditions required 156
harvesting 156
sowing 156
sweet 55
watering 156
Rodgersias
propagation 417

Romneya
hard pruning 102
coulteri, root cuttings 414
Root aphids 27, 152
Root collars 162, 169
Root cuttings *see* Cuttings
Rooting hormone 401
Rose canker 129
Rosemary 67, *67*, 209
for containers 358
cultivation 209
Rosemary beetle 212
Roses 117–29
bare-root
ordering 117, 119
planting 117, 118
black spot 28, 30, 120, 128
bush
pruning 121
renovation 127
buying 117
care 119–20
climbers 67, *117*, 122, *123*
floral wall 124
pruning 119, 122, 124
summer maintenance 124
tripod-tied 124
tying in 119, 124
wall-tied 124
containerized plants 117
for containers 357
deadheading 120
diseases 118, 119, 128, 129
floral wall 124
floribunda *121*
pruning 119, 121
ground cover 125
heeling in 119
hoeing 119
hybrid tea, pruning 119, 121
manure 119
miniature, pruning 126
neglected, renovation 127
patio, pruning 119, 126
pests 119, 128–9
planting 118
bare-root plants 117, 118
propagation 404
pruning
bush 121

climbers 119, 122, 124
floribunda 119, 121
hybrid tea 119, 121
loppers 120
miniatures 126
patio 119, 126
ramblers 119, 122, 124
renovation 127
saws 120
secateurs 120
shrub 119, 124
species 125
standard 119, 126
techniques 120
tools 120
ramblers 67, 122, 124
pruning 119, 122, 124
summer maintenance 124
tying in 119, 124
Rosa filipes 'Kiftsgate' 71
renovation 127
replanting 118, 129
rootstock 119, 411
Rosa canina 129
routine care 119–20
shrub
groundcover 125
once-flowering 125
pruning 119, 125
renovation 127
repeat-flowering 125
soil preparation 118
species 125
pruning 125
standard 119, 126
pruning 119, 126
staking 126
weeping 126
suckers 119, 411
for summer *71*
in trees 124
weeping standards 126
wildlife garden 54
Rosmarinus officinalis see Rosemary
Rotavator 142
Rowans 55
Royal fern 330, *330*
Rubus
tip layering 429
cockburnianus

hard pruning 102
for shade 69
Rudbeckia
for autumn 72, *72*
for containers 353, 355
cutting back in autumn 80
propagation 404
for shade 69
fulgida var. *fulgida* 355
fulgida var. *sullivantii* 'Goldsturm' 72
Runner beans 180–1, *180*
common problems 181
conditions required 180
cultivation 181
harvesting 181
planting out 180
sowing 180, 181
supporting 180–1
Ruscus aculeatus
for shade 69
Rusts 38
bean 214, 215
brown 391
chrysanthemum 82, 391
garlic 187
leek 188, 213
mint 214, 215
pear & plum 271
roses 128
trees 111
white 391
Rye
green manure 145

S

Sage 209
for containers 358
cultivation 209
Sage leafhopper 210–11
Sagittaria 329
Saintpaulia see African violet
Salad and leaves
chicory 154
cut-and-come again 154, 156
endive 153
exotic salad leaves 156
lettuce 150–2
in unheated greenhouses 379
Salix

for containers 357
diseases 112
hard pruning 102
propagation 404
for winter 73
× *sepulcralis* var. *chrysocoma* 112
Salvia
for containers 353, 355
for summer 71
argentea 67
officinalis see Sage
× *sylvestris* 'Mainacht' 71
Sandy soils 16, *17*
Sansevieria trifasciata
leaf cuttings 439
monocot 442
Santolina
for containers 357
Sanvitalia
for containers 353
Sarcococca
for containers 357
propagation 404
for shade 69
for winter 73
confusa 69, 73
Sawfly 81
berberis 110
gooseberries 269
large rose 128
leaf-rolling 128
Saxifraga
propagation 404
Scab 38, 197
apple & pear 271
common 214, 215
potato 214, 215
powdery 214, 215
Scale insects 388, 389
Scaring devices 34
Schizostylis coccinea 'Sunrise' 72
Sciarid flies (fungus gnats) 388, 389, 403
Scilla
for containers 354
propagation 421
Sclerotinia diseases 38, 214, 215
Screening 63
Sculptures 63
Sea holly
propagation 404

Sea lavender
propagation 404
Secateurs
choosing 398
maintaining 398
types 398
using 398
Sedge *see* Carex
Sedum
for autumn 72
for containers 355
stopping 79
spectabile 'Neon' 72
Seeds
chilling 410
collecting 405
drill sowing 146
germination 407, 408
failure 409
hard coats 410
ornamental 79
preparing seedbed 144
shrubs from 410
sowing 405–10
for containers 406–7
direct 146–7
drill sowing 146
fluid 146, 147
pre-germination 146, 147
station 147
troubleshooter 409
vegetable seeds 146–7
storing 405, 410
trees from 410
Seedlings
caring for 408
collapse 409
emerging in patches 409
etiolated 409
failing to grown on 409
hardening off 395
lopsided 409
pests 35
thinning 147
transplanting 408
transplants 147
bare-root 147
growing from 147
protecting 147
watering 147

troubleshooter 409
watering 408
withering 409
Sempervivum
propagation 404, 424
Shade
bulbs 68, 69
damp 68
dry 68, 69
flowers 68, 69
foliage interest 68
fruit 68, 224
gardens in 68–9
ground cover 68
lawns 279
perennials 68, 69
plants for 69
seasonal change 68
shrubs 68, 69
structure and 68
trees 68, 69
types of 68
Shallots 187
conditions required 187
for containers 358
drying 187
growing 187
harvesting 187
planting 187
Shrubs 58
aftercare 92
for autumn 72
bare-root plants 88, 89, 92
buying 88
container-grown 88, 89
for containers 356–7
deadheading 98
deciduous, pruning 100–4
diseases 111–12
evergreens 66
groundcover 41
pruning 98–9
training 99
feeding 92
from seed 410
frost protection 14
in the greenhouse 384
hard pruning
deciduous shrubs 102–3
for maximum foliage effect 103

for winter stems 102
hedges *see* Hedges
heeling in 92
moving 93
mulching 22
pests 35, 109–10
planting 89–90
aftercare 92
bare-root plants 88, 89
container-grown 88, 89
depth 89
mycorrhizal fungi 89–90
propagation
division 423
heel cuttings 434
woody shrubs with suckers 411
pruning 94, 99
cut 94
deciduous shrubs 100–4
disease prevention 96
drastic 107
to encourage flowers 96–7
evergreen shrubs 98–9
for foliage 97, 103
hard pruning for maximum
effect 103
formative 95
hard pruning 102–3
large branches 96, 97
minimal 104
renewal pruning 100–1
renovation 107
reverted shoots 97
for shape 95
suckers 97
tools 94
types of branches 96–7
renovation 107
reverted shoots 97
rootballed 88, 92
roses *see* Roses
for shade 68, 69
for spring 70
suckers 97
for summer 71
for sun 67
training
early 94, 99
evergreen shrubs 99
weeding 92

for winter 73
Silty soils 17, *17*
Silver birch 55
Silver leaf disease 108, 272, 273
Sinningia
propagation 404
Sisyrinchium striatum
for containers 355
Skimmia
for containers 357
Slender speedwell 294
Slime moulds 298
Slugs & snails 35
bulbs 86
control 35, 155, 173
copper barriers 32
endive 153
lettuce 152
nematodes 33, 35
pellets 35, 231
predators 27
herbaceous perennials 81
potatoes 199
propagated plants and 403
spinach 155
Small garden 62
planning and design 61, 62, 64
town garden 61
wildlife garden 55
Smoke bush *see Cotinus coggygria*
Smut on corn 214
Snow mould 298
Snowdrop *see Galanthus*
Snowdrop grey mould 87
Soft scale 109
Soil
acidity 17, 21
alkalinity 17, 21
clay 16, *17*, 142, 193
drainage 13
enrichment 143
evaluating 10
fruit-growing 221
humus 16, 20
improving 10, 15, 16, 20–1
animal manure 21
bulky organic material 20–1
fertilizers *see* Fertilizers
green manures 145
liquid feed 21

manure 20
    modifying pH 21
liquid feed 21
mineral deficiency 31
nutrient content 17
pH 16
    modifying 21
    raising 21
    reducing 21
    testing 17
plant nutrients 17, 31
preparing seedbed 144
profile 16
sandy 16, *17*
silty 17, *17*
sustainable approach 15
types 16–17
vegetable garden 142–3, 144
Soil structure test 321
Solenostemon
    propagation 404
Solomon's seal *see Polygonatum*
Sorbus
    for autumn 72
    aucuparia, pruning 105
Sparganium erectum 331
Spartium
    hard pruning 102
Specific replant disorder 118, 129
Specimen trees 63
Speedwell 293, 294
Spider mites 403
    glasshouse red spider mite 388, 389
Spider plant
    propagation 404
Spiders 27
Spiked milfoil 327, *327*
Spinach 155
    chard 155
    conditions required 155
    harvesting 155
    intercropping 143
    New Zealand 155
    sowing 155
    in unheated greenhouses 379
Spinach beet 155
    conditions required 155
    harvesting 155
    hoeing 155
    sowing 155

    thinning seedlings 155
Spiraea
    mallet cuttings 434
    propagation 404
    pruning
        hard 102
        renewal 100
    'Arguta' 100
    japonica 102
Splitting 31
Spotted laurel *see Aucuba*
Spring garden 70
Spring greens 163
Spur blight 272, 273
Squashes
    common problems 202
    conditions required 201
    harvesting 201
    pinching out 201
    planting 201
    site 201
    situation 201
    sowing 201
    summer 201
        black plastic sheet mulch 201
        flowers 201
        harvesting 201
        planting 201
        sowing 201
    transplanting 200
    watering 201
    winter 202
        harvesting 202
        weak growth 202
Squirrels 36
    bulbs 86
Staking
    bulbs 85
    containers 361
    herbaceous perennials 78–9
    linking stakes 78
    metal supports 78
    natural woven supports 78
    trees 90–1
        fruit trees 242, 266
Stem cuttings 430–8
    conifer 438
    environmental control 430
    evergreen 437
    girdling 425

    greenwood 433
        heel cuttings 434
        when to take 430
    hardwood 436–7
        disbudding 436–7
        mallet cuttings 434
        when to take 430
    heel 434
    leaf-bud cutting 431
    mallet 434
    parts of the stem 425
    semi-ripe 435
        mallet cuttings 434
        when to take 430
    softwood
        fungal rot 432
        making 432
        preparing parent plant 433
        taking 433
        when to take 430
    suitable cutting material 425
    when to take 430
    where to cut 430
Sternbergia
    for containers 354
Sticky yellow trap 34, 157
Stigminia shot hole 272, 273
Stipa
    for containers 355
Stopping
    herbaceous perennials 79, 80
Storage
    bulbs 85
    cabbages 164
    fruit
        apricots 264
        cherries 257
        figs 260
        gooseberries 225
        nectarines 263
        peaches 263
        plums 255
        red currants 225
        white currants 225
    herbs 208
    onions 186
    seeds 405, 410
    turves 285
Stratiotes aliodes 328
Strawberries 231–3

aftercare 232
Alpine 231, 232
clearing up the bed 233
cold frames 233
for containers 232, *232*, 346, 359, *359*
frost damage 220
in the greenhouse 233, 379, 384
growing season 220
harvesting 232
mats 232
perpetual 231
planting 231
   in plastic 232
propagation 233, 424
protected cropping 232
protecting 231
runners 233, 424
summer-fruiting 231
watering 231
Streptocarpus
propagation 404, 439
Suburban gardens 61
Suckers 97
propagation 404, 411
roses 119
woody shrubs 411
Sugarsnap peas 176
Sulphur 21
Sumach *see Rhus*
Summer garden 71
Summerhouses 63
Sun rose *see Cistus*
Sunflower *see Helianthus*
Sunlight 13
plants for sun 67
Sustainable gardening 15
Swedes 194–5
common problems 195
conditions required 194
cultivation 195
harvesting 195
lifting 194
site 194
soil 194
sowing 195
swede shoots as greens 194
Sweet flag 329
Sweet peas *see Lathyrus odoratus*
Sweet rocket *55*
wildlife garden 55

Sweetcorn 203
conditions required 203
cultivation 203
harvesting 203
smut 214
sowing 203
supersweets 203
watering 148, 203
Syringa
propagation 404

T

Tagetes
for containers 353
'Legend Series' 118
Tamarix
renewal pruning 100
Taproots 39
Tarragon 209
for containers 358
cultivation 209
Taxus
conifer cuttings 404, 438
for containers 357
hedges 49
pests 109
renovation 107
Tayberry 230
Teasle
wildlife garden 55
Thalictrum
propagation 422
Thinning
herbaceous perennials 80
Thistle
taproots 39
Thrips
gladiolus 86
onions 186
peas 177
Thuja
propagation 438
wildlife garden 54
Thunbergia
for containers 353
Thyme 67, 209
for containers 358
cultivation 209
propagating 206

Thymus see Thyme
Tiarella cordifolia
leaf cuttings 439
Tiger worms 24
Tillea
helmsii 328
recurva 328
Tip layering 429
Tithonia
for containers 353
Toads 27, 48
Tomato blight 160–1, 214
Tomato mosaic virus 215
Tomatoes 158–61, *158, 159*
bush 158
common problems 160–1
companion planting 159, *159*
conditions required 158
for containers 358, *358*
greenhouse 158–9, 160, 161
unheated 379
growing from seeds 158
growing systems 159
indeterminate 158
mineral deficiency 31
mulching 22
outdoor 159, 160, 161
picking 160
transplanting 158
vine 158
viral diseases 161, 214
watering 148, 158, 160
Tools
craft knife 397
hedge-cutting 94, 114
knife 396, 397
lawn care 287
aerating machine 288
edging shears 291, 293
forks 288
rakes 287
scarifying 287
trimming 291
watering 290
loppers 120
propagation 396–8
pruning 94
roses 120
safety razor blade 397
scalpel 397

scarifying 287
scythe 53
secateurs 120, 398
sterilizing 37
work bench 396
Topiary
    containers 356
Tortrix moths 388, 389
Trachelospermum
    for containers 357
    pests 109
Trachycarpus see Palms
Trapa natans 328
Traps 34
    pheromone-baited trap 34
    sticky yellow trap 34, 157
Tree ferns
    frost protection 14
Tree poppy *see Romneya coulteri*
Trees 58
    aftercare 92
    for autumn 72
    bare-root plants 88, 89, 92
    buying 88
    container-grown 88, 89
    for containers 356–7
        buying 88
    coppicing 102
    diseases 111–12
    feathered, pruning 105
    feeding 92
    flowering 58
    from seeds 410
    frost protection 14
    fruit *see* Fruit trees
    grease bands 33
    in the greenhouse 384
    guards 33, 92
    hedges *see* Hedges
    heeling in 92
        fruit trees 242
        roses 119
    individual specimen 63
    knobbly spurs 108
    lawn and 279
    moving 93
    mulching 22
    pests 36, 92, 109–10
    planting 89–90
        aftercare 92

    bare-root plants 88, 89
    container-grown 88, 89
    depth 89
    mycorrhizal fungi 89–90
    staking 90–1
   pollarding 102, 103
   ponds and 307
   protection 33, 92
   pruning 94
    branch-headed 106
    coppicing 102
    corrective 108
    cut 94
    disease prevention 96
    to encourage flowers 96–7
    feathered trees 105
    for foliage 97
    formative 95
    'haircut' 108
    knobbly spurs 108
    large branches 96, 97
    pollarding 102, 103
    renovation 108
    reverted shoots 97
    for shape 95
    suckers 97
    tools 94
    types of branches 96–7
    water shoots 96, 97, 108
   renovation 108
   reverted shoots 97
   rootballed 88, 92
   roses in 124
   rusts 111
   for shade 68, 69
   for spring 70
   staking 90–1
    fruit trees 242, 266
   suckers 97
   for summer 71
   for sun 67
   training 94
    fruit trees 243
   transplants 91
   water shoots 96, 97, 108
   watering 92
   weeding 92
   wildlife garden 55
   for winter 73
Trenching 19

Trickle irrigation 374
Trifolium repens 293, 294
Trillium
    planting 84
    for shade 69
    grandiflorum 69
Trollius europaeus
    for shade 68
Tropaeolum
    for containers 353, *353*
    majus 75
Trumpet vine
    propagation 404
Tuberous roots 415
    annual 415
    dividing 415
    perennial 415
Tubers 416
    dividing 416
    tubercles 416
    weeds 39
Tulip fire 87
Tulipa
    for containers 354
    disease 87
    hybrids 70, 84, 85
    planting 83, 84
    propagation 419
    for spring 70
    for summer *70*
    viruses 30
    'China Pink' 70, *70*
    'Queen of the Night' 67
Tulips *see Tulipa*
Tunnels 149, 369
    using 378
Turnips 194–5
    common problems 195
    conditions required 194
    cultivation 195
    harvesting 195
    site 194
    soil 194
    sowing 195
    tops as spring greens 195
Typha 331, *331*
    minima 329

U

Uncinia uncinata
    for containers 355
Urban gardens 14, 59
    small town garden 61

V

Vaccinium see Blueberries
Valerian 55, *55*
Vegetable fruit 200–5
Vegetable garden *151*
    catch cropping 143
    clearing a new site 143
    cloches 149
    cold frames 149
    containers 358
    converting grassland 142
    crop rotation 143
        brassicas 162
    digging 142
    diseases 213–14
    films 149
    fleece 149
    green manures 41, 145
    in the greenhouse 384
    intercropping 28, 41, 143
    onion family 184–8
    ornamental 59, *71*
    pests 210–12
    planning crops 143
    pods & seeds 176–83
    polytunnels 149
    preparing seedbed 144
    raised beds 142–3
    roots & tubers 189–99
    salads and leaves 150–61
    soil preparation 142–3, 144
    sowing seeds 146–7
    splitting vegetables 31
    stalks & shoots 171–5
    tunnels 149
    watering 148
    weeding 148
Verbena
    for containers 353, 355
    bonariensis 67
Veronica 293
    filiformis 294

Verticillium wilt 37, 205
Vetches
    green manure 145
Viburnum
    for autumn 72
    pests 109
    pruning 104
    for winter 73
    × *bodnantense* 'Dawn' 73
    opulus 72, 109
    tinus 109
viburnum beetle 109
Vinca
    for containers 357
    for shade 68, 69
    minor 69
Vine weevil 36, 403
    biological control 36
    herbaceous perennials 81
Viola
    for containers 353
Viral diseases 30, 202
    bulbs 87
    greenhouses 390
    herbaceous perennials 82
    rhubarb 175
    symptoms 30
    tomatoes 161, 214
Virginia creeper
    propagation 404
Vitis
    'Brant' 67, 72, *72*
    coignetiae, layering 426–7
    vinifera see Grapes

W

Waldsteinia ternata
    for shade 69
Wall plants *see* Climbers and
    wall plants
Wall shrubs 130, 136–7
Wallflower *see Erysimum*
Water 13
    conservation 15
    efficient use 15
    grey 15
Water butts 374
Water chestnut 328
Water crowfoot 326

Water fern 328, 331, *331*
Water forget-me-not 329
Water garden 304–37
    canal 306
    pools *see* Pools
Water hawthorn 326
Water hyacinth 328
Water irises 329, *329*
Water lettuce 328
Water plants 320–31
    aquatic weeds 331
        bulrush 331
        bur-reed 331
        controlling 331
        duckweed 331
        native plants 331
        New Zealand pygmy weed 331,
          331
        non-native plants 331
        reedmace 331, *331*
        water fern 331, *331*
    baskets 327
        depth 322
        growing in 321
        placing the plants 322
        planting 322
        preparing 321
    bog plants 330
        astilbe 330
        bugle 330
        daylily 330
        drumstick primula 330, *330*
        ferns and grasses 330, *330*
        giant rhubarb 330
        monkey flower 330
        planting 330
        preparing 330
        primrose 330
        royal fern 330, *330*
    containers 323
    deep-water 326
        golden club 326
        pondlily 326
        water crowfoot 326
        water hawthorn 326
        water violet 326
    feeding 336
        fertilizer 336
        homemade fertilizer 336
        nutrient balance 336

testing the water 336
floating 328
  fairy moss 328
  frogbit 328
  plants to avoid 328
  water chestnut 328
  water soldier 328
hardy waterlilies 324, *325*
  bare-rooted 324
  container-grown 324
  planting depths 324
  preparing 324
  Nuphar 324, 326
  Nymphaea 324
marginal 329
  arrowhead 329, *329*
  blue flag 329
  bog arum 329
  corkscrew rush 329
  dwarf reed 329
  pickerel weed 329, *329*
  preparing 329
  removing 334
  sweet flag 329
  water forget-me-not 329
  water irises 329, *329*
  wildlife pond 50
planting basics 320
small ponds 323, *323*
soil structure test 321
submerged 50, 327
  curled pondweed 327, *327*
  hair grass 327, *327*
  hornwort 327, *327*
  plants to avoid 327
  removing 334
  spiked milfoil 327, *327*
  whorled milfoil 327
types 320
wildlife pond 50
Water shoots 96, 97, 108
Water soldier 328
Water violet 326
Watering
  automatic systems 15
  borders 15
  capillary matting 374
  capillary systems 402
  containers 15, 360
  from above 402

from below 402
greenhouses 374
hanging baskets 360
herb garden 148
hose reel 290
lawn 15, 290, 299
methods 15, 290
for propagation 402
run off 290
seedlings 408
sprinkler 15, 290
timer systems 15
trees 92
trickle irrigation 374
vegetable garden 148
via a sand bed 402
Waterlily *see Nymphaea*
Wax flower
  propagation 404
Weather 12
  frost 13
  rain 13
  wind 13
Weedkillers 39–40, 89, 148
  clearing a new site 143
  contact 39
  residual 40
  systemic 39
  wildflower meadows 53
Weeds
  annual 39
  aquatic 331
  control 10, 39–41
    chemical 39–40, 148
    digging out 19, 148
    ground cover 41
    hand-weeding 40
    hoeing 39, 148
    legislation 41
    mulches 40–1, 148
    smothering 40–1
    wildflower meadow 53
  invasive 41
  perennial 19, 39, 143, 148
  removing 39–40
  rhizomes 39
  root systems 39
  smothering 40–1
  taproots 39
  tubers 39

Weigela
  renewal pruning 100
White blister 213
White clover 293, 294
White currants 225
  aftercare 225
  conditions required 224
  conditions tolerated 224
  diseases 111
  harvesting 225
  pests 29, 270
  planting 224, 225
  propagation 404
  pruning 225
  for shade 224
  spacing 225
  storing 225
  training 225
White pine blister rust 111
Whitebeams 55
Whitefly scales, cards bearing 32
Whorled milfoil 327
Wildflower meadow *52, 53*
  adapting existing lawn 52, 53
  bulbs 85
  cornfield annuals 53
  creating from scratch 52
  maintenance 53
  mowing 53
  sowing 52–3
  weeding 53
Wildlife corridors 49
Wildlife garden 45, 59
  amphibians 27, 44, 48, 50
  planning 46
  plants 54–5
  ponds *see* Wildlife ponds
  small gardens 55
  wildflower area 52–3
Wildlife habitats 46–8
  artificial 47
  bats 47
  bees 47
  beetles 48
  birds 46, 55
  butterflies & moths 48, 55
  centipedes 48
  frogs, toads & newts 48
  hedgehogs 48
  hedges 49, 113, 114

lacewings, hoverflies & ladybirds 48
natural 47
Wildlife plants 54–5
choosing 54
fruit 55
larval food plants 55
native 55
nectar & pollen 55
non-native 55
planting 54
seeds 55
small gardens 55
trees 55
Wildlife ponds 50–1, *50*
building an island 319
children and 51
constructing 319
cross-section 50
design 50–1, 319
ducks 51
encouraging wildlife 51
filling 319
fish 51
liner 50
maintaining 51
making 319
netting 51
planting 50, 51
siting 50
underliner 319
Willow *see Salix*
Willow anthracnose 112
Willow rusts 111
Wilts 82
blossom 271
clematis 112
verticillium 37, 205
Wind
damage 13
flow 13
greenhouses and 371
Wind turbulence 221
Windbreaks 31, 370
fruit garden 221
types 13
Winter aconites *see Eranthis*
Winter jasmine
for shade 68
Winter moth 270
Wintersweet 73

Wirestem 390
Wisteria 67, 134, *134*
choosing 134
for containers 357
general care 135
neglected, renovation 135
pruning
espalier 134–5
established plants 135
formative 135
maintenance 135
renovation 135
renovation 135
brachybotrys 134
floribunda 134
frutescens 134
sinensis 67, 134
Witch hazel *see Hamamelis*
Wood decay 111
Woodland garden 68
Woolly aphid 268
Work bench 396
Worm composting 23, 24
Wormcasts 296

Y

Yarrow 294
Yellow birch *see Betula*
Yellow rattle 52, 53
Yew *see Taxus*
Yorkshire fog 294
Yucca
for containers 357

Z

Zantedeschia
for containers 355
propagation 417
Zebra plant
in the greenhouse 386
Zinnia
sowing 75

ACKNOWLEDGMENTS

Nicholas Appleby/GWI 297tl

Dave Bevan/GWI 297tc

Mark Bolton/GPL 202b, 330bl, bc

Elke Borkowski/GAP 7

Botanica/GPL 400

Jonathan Buckley/The Garden Collection 55tc, 55tr, 61 (*Design: Gay Wilson*), 69br, 72t (*Paul Picton, Old Court Nurseries*), 72bc, 72br, 73bc, 73br, 170bc, 287, 290; 306bc (*Design: Susan Sharkey*), 330t, 376 (*Design: Alison Hoghton & David Chase*).

Torie Chugg/The Garden Collection 67br, 69tc, 69bc, 132c, 132b; 353c

Nigel Cattlin/FLPA 17tl

David Cavagnaro/GPL 189

Derek Croucher/Alamy 282bl

Dennis Davis/GPL 121

Francoise De Heel/GPL 23, 65

DK Images 251

Jacqui Dracup/GWI 32, 36

Liz Eddison/The Garden Collection 50 & 325 (*Natural & Oriental Water Gardens*), 66, 69tr, 70br, 182, 208; 222, 232, 248, 306bl (*Design: Paul Dyer*), 311 & 348 (*Design: Adam Frost*), 349bl & 349br (*Whichford Pottery*), 353t, 353b, 357t (*Design: Andrew Walker*), 359tl

Christopher Gallagher/GPL 261

Michelle Garrett/The Garden Collection 55tl, 67bl, 158, 202c

John Glover/The Garden Collection 151, 256, 257

GWI 279tr

Derek Harris/The Garden Collection 69bl, 104; 323, 357br

Sunniva Harte/GPL 210bl, 237

Michael Howes/GPL 331bl

Martin Hughes-Jones/GWI 41tr

Jacqui Hurst/GPL 199, 238, 240

Willem Kolvoort/Naturepl 327br

Andrew Lawson/The Garden Collection 41tl, 41tc, 53 (*Design: Mary Keen*), 64bl (*Wollerton Old Hall, Shropshire*), 67tl, 67tc, 67tr, 69tl, 70bl, 71bc, 73bl, 123, 180; 278bl (*Design: Mary Payne*), 292, 344, 354

Mayer/LeScanff/GPL 223, 245

Clive Nichols/GPL 207

Marie O'Hara/The Garden Collection 24, 71bl, 163; 357bl

Howard Rice/GPL 117; 330br, 331bc

Gary Rogers/The Garden Collection 71br, 278br (*Design: Droege-Jung*); 356bl, 356br, 358br

Science Photo Library 327tl, 327bl

Janet Seaton/GPL 282br

Jane Sebire/The Garden Collection 149t, 210br, 358tr

JS Sira/GPL 73t, 159; 329t, 331br

Derek St Romaine/The Garden Collection 52 (*Keukenhof Holland*), 145, 156, 165, 170bl, 186, 202t, 228, 240bl, 247, 306br (*Design: John Tordoff*), 332, 359bl, 359br, 443 (*Design: Russell Grant*).

Nicola Stocken Tomkins/The Garden Collection 15, 64br, 67bc, 68, 70t (*St Michael's House*), 70bc, 71t, 72bl, 103, 127, 132t, 134, 152, 170br, 176, 206, 279; 355, 358bl, 370 (*Design: Carol Klein*).

Friedrich Strauss/GPL 20

Rita Van Den Broek/GPL 329c

Juliette Wade/GPL 220, 381

Didier Willery/GPL 329b